Learning Theory Research In Mental Retardation
Implications for Teaching

Cecil D. Mercer
University of Florida

Martha E. Snell
University of Virginia

Charles E. Merrill Publishing Company
A Bell & Howell Company

Columbus   Toronto   London   Sydney

103485

To Ann, whose love, support, and encouragement sustained the writing of this book; and to Kevin, Greg, and Ken, who exhibited patience which exceeded their understanding.

Published by
Charles E. Merrill Publishing Company
A Bell & Howell Company
Columbus, Ohio 43216

This book was set in Helvetica and Parsons.
The production editor was Jan Hall.
The cover was designed by Will Chenoweth.

International Standard Book Number: 0–675–08531–4

Library of Congress Catalog Number: 76–40777

3 4 5 6 7 8 9—81 80 79

Printed in the United States of America

Foreword

This ambitious book represents both a definite source of assistance and challenge to the teacher in special education. Presented in remarkable detail are the essential features of a number of learning theory approaches to the problem of mental retardation. The reader will find a great deal of relevant material to study. From these theories the authors have also derived a large number of suggested methods and ideas for teaching the retarded in real-life situations which prospective teachers will find stimulating.

The variety of different viewpoints and variables that are emphasized in chapters 2–8 are supplementary rather than in conflict with each other. Teachers should then decide from all of the possible applications the recommended techniques that seem feasible and most appropriate for the educational task or population at hand.

This book is exactly what the field of special education needs: the "nitty-gritty" for applying learning and motivational principles thoughtfully

and sensibly presented. Thus, the book could be useful and beneficial to all teachers—for instituting whole educational programs or for just one or two pertinent ideas. In addition, I would like to emphasize that the book has every likelihood of being useful to groups of individuals other than teachers of special education. Graduate students and other investigators in psychology or education who are involved in the study of mental retardation should discover many ideas and hypotheses that deserve research. Educators of preservice and inservice teachers can definitely include the numerous ideas and suggestions for their teacher-preparation programs.

This book attempts to close the gap between theory and practice. As one who has also tried to bridge this gap by writing and getting students involved, I am grateful for the opportunity to comment and thus be a small part of this important effort.

M. Ray Denny
Michigan State University
April 5, 1976

Preface

All professionals are charged with the responsibility of closing the gap between what is known and what is practiced in their fields. In the social sciences, much research and time are required to establish facts, and unfortunately, empirically-based techniques are few. Education will be one of the first of the social sciences required to justify its practices. Trends indicate that performance contracting, the delineation of teacher competencies, and documentation of pupil growth are implicit movements in the future of education. These trends, coupled with our professional responsibility to help students grow, behoove us to examine teaching practices.

Although special education has substantial legislative and parental support, educational practices which are identified within the framework of special education are being challenged in communities and courts of law. Fortunately, some special educators have begun to use techniques which originated from empirical findings. In addition, some special educators are now involved in exploratory and hypothesis-testing research. For example, the development of educationally oriented tests and the application of behavior modification techniques have advanced the credibility of selected special education practices.

In the last 20 years, there has been increasing interest in the learning processes of retarded individuals (Robinson & Robinson, 1976) and the number of studies on the topic has soared. Zeaman (1974) acknowledges that more than 1500 articles have been reported concerning the learning processes of mentally retarded persons. Although it is rewarding to note some of the recent accomplishments in special education, complacency is not warranted. Many facts and trends existing within this mass of literature remain dormant.

The primary purpose of this book is to generate empirically based teaching practices with retarded individuals by reviewing some of the most prominent learning theories concerning mental retardation and examining the research regarding the respective learning theories. Positions which have received substantial empirical support are highlighted and subsequent teaching strategies are featured. When feasible, commercial materials as well as informal techniques which incorporate the empirically supported position(s) are presented. In essence, it is hoped that this book will serve to close the gap between knowledge and practice in the area of teaching the mentally retarded.

A second purpose of this book is to stimulate the

advancement of applied learning theory research in mental retardation. The comprehensive reviews should serve to stimulate the researcher to formulate hypotheses and design studies which continue to advance an understanding of the learning processes of retarded individuals.

This book includes detailed descriptions of theory, research studies, and teaching implications. On occasions a reader's purpose may be to acquire broad and extensive knowledge concerning learning theory research in mental retardation and resulting implications. Other readers may not want to attend to the extensive coverage of each learning theory area but read for specific content. Readers seeking specific content should identify their objective(s) and read selectively by referring to specific chapters and headings within the chapters. To illustrate, a researcher may wish to read the detailed coverage of studies in order to gain knowledge concerning types of hypotheses studied and research procedures used to investigate these hypotheses. Similarly, a teacher or teacher educator may want to read the sections reviewing studies in order to gain information regarding specific procedures used in each study which directly relate to instructional techniques. Moreover, a researcher may read the review of studies to ascertain the relative merit of a specific study or studies in terms of practical applications. Finally, a teacher or teacher educator may wish to find classroom techniques by only reading those sections pertaining to teaching implications.

Chapter 1 presents a framework for examining learning theory research in mental retardation. Methodological problems are featured and provide the reader with an approach set for examining research in mental retardation. Chapters 2–8 each include a specific learning theory, the related literature, and resultant teaching implications. In addition, each chapter contains tables which provide a synopsis of the studies reviewed. Chapter 9 presents a concise synthesis and summary of chapters 2–8 and the theories are discussed within the context of learning, i.e., expectancy, selective attention, organizing input, memory, transfer, performance, and feedback.

In graduate programs on mental retardation this book can serve as an appropriate text in both advanced curriculum courses and learning theory courses. In competency-based teacher training programs, it can enhance the development of skill-based competencies via the teaching implications sections. Moreover, the descriptive sections of the book concerning the respective learning theories provide information for the development of knowledge acquisition competencies. General learning theory and methods courses should use the text as supplemental reading.

The completion of this book was the result of the efforts of many people; however, several individuals deserve special acknowledgement for their exceptional contributions. We are grateful to Dr. Mike Epstein (University of Northern Illinois) for helping us formulate the conceptual basis and format of the book. Appreciation goes to Dr. Dave Westling, Florida Atlantic University, for his significant contribution to Chapter 4. Thanks go to the reviewers, Professor Patricia Cegelka, University of Kentucky, and Professor Gabe Nordi, University of West Virginia, for reading and critiquing the manuscript. Their constructive criticisms made us ever mindful of the purpose of the book and their suggestions enhanced the development of the final manuscript. We are especially grateful to Tom Hutchinson for his help and support as special education editor, and to Jan Hall for her significant contribution as our production editor.

Extensive appreciation and thanks go to Ann Mercer for her extraordinary efforts in preparing the manuscript for publication. In addition to editing and typing the entire book, she spent many hours doing library work.

Cecil D. Mercer

Martha E. Snell

Contents

1

Research Variables

In all organisms, learning involves a behavioral change resulting from experience. Learning cannot be directly observed or measured but must be inferred from observable changes in *performance*. Such inferences must be cautiously made, since the performance of a learner may be due to a variety of causes inside and outside the learner. A conceptual framework is necessary to examine components of the process.

Conceptual frameworks differ within different learning theories. Some theories propose entire frameworks, while others examine constructs viewed as operating prior to and within the learning process. Such constructs of learning involve examination of *orientation to the learning task* (such as attention, memory and comprehension of task instructions, and prior reinforcement history); *mental operations during the task* (such as attention, covert strategies for information intake and rehearsal, and resultant storage and retrieval systems); and *behavioral operations during the task* (overt learning strategies, type of task response, delay of response, and visual fixation). Other theories include within their framework the effects on learning of factors outside the learner, for example, magnitude, immediacy, schedule, and type of reinforcement or punishment; effects of time, distractions during the task; transfer; and the effects of instruction and practice. Additionally, an experimental examination must include:

1. supportive set of process definitions
2. selection of experimental variables
3. identification of population
4. plausible hypothesis
5. identification and control of independent variables
6. reliable collection of data
7. interpretation of results consistent with the conceptual framework
8. ultimate replication

When the learning behavior of mentally retarded individuals is selected for examination, several problems arise. For example, what classification criteria will be used in the selection of "retarded" individuals? What independent variables need to be identified and controlled: institutionalization, etiology, degree of retardation, mental age (MA), chronological age (CA)? Does external validity allow generalization of results to other retarded individuals? These complex issues must be dealt with when deriving teaching procedures for the retarded. The following sections will discuss such issues, including problems in population sampling, the influence of experimental design, and alternative classification systems.

Problems in Population Sampling

Limitations of IQ Classification Systems

The majority of studies reviewed in this text delimit the retarded samples on the basis of a single criterion: measured intelligence. For the majority of studies the upper limits of the IQ scores of the retarded subjects were in accordance with the present definition of the American Association on Mental Deficiency (AAMD) (Grossman, 1973), i.e., significantly subaverage intellectual functioning which is equated with performance on an intelligence test measuring more than two standard deviations below the mean. However, a number of studies included samples with mean group IQs at or above 70 (borderline).

Additionally, further problems are encountered when an adaptive behavior measure is not included for subjects identified as retarded. Since the AAMD definition specifies that those persons with subaverage intelligence also have deficiencies in adaptive behavior, the inclusion of subjects with IQs measuring below 70 but lacking an estimate of adaptive behavior performance is questionable. Today all researchers are plagued with this omission because reliable measurement devices for identifying level of retardation in adaptive behavior are not available. Although a device such as the *AAMD Adaptive Behavior Scales* (Lambert, Windmiller, Cole, Figueroa, 1975; Nihira, Foster, Shellhaas, Leland, 1974) has expanded the standardization group to include percentile performance scores of noninstitutionalized groups (such as regular classrooms, and special classes for the educable mentally retarded and the trainable mentally retarded), other measures must also be used (Lambert et al., 1975). Another measure of adaptive behavior, the *Vineland Social Maturity Scale* (Doll, 1964), permits estimation of adaptive behavior level when combined with Silverstein's (1971) tables for converting ratio social quotients to deviation social quotients.

Many psychologists and diagnosticians distrust the data obtained via interview and tend to stress measured intelligence as the means to classify persons by levels of retardation (Adams, 1973). However, there are several problems with an IQ-centered approach. Such an approach does not accurately measure the culturally different person (Mercer, 1975). Mercer comments:

The IQ tests now being used by psychologists are, to a large extent, Anglocentric. They tend to measure the extent to which an individual's background is similar to that of the modal cultural configuration of American society. Because a significant amount of the variance in intelligence-test scores is related to sociocultural characteristics, we concluded that sociocultural factors must be taken into account in interpreting the meaning of any individual score. (p. 139)

She suggests that intelligence and adaptive behavior be measured by a battery of tests reflecting multiple normative frameworks. Adams, McIntosh, and Weade (1973) provide data-based support for this suggestion. They found that blacks were classified as retarded more often than whites when IQ scores determined the classification level, whereas the groups did not differ on deviation social quotient as measured by the *Vineland Social Maturity Scale*.

Others (Filler, Robinson, Smith, Vincent-Smith, Bricker, and Bricker, 1975) criticize IQ-centered systems because intelligence tests do not give the parent or teacher the information they need. Such tests do not provide instructional goals nor identify behavioral categories. Instead, IQ categories result in the circular assignment of hypothetical constructs as causes of behavior, which is a nonscientific practice which both Skinner (1953) and Bijou (1966) have cautioned.

Overlapping Classification Systems

Definitions have functional value when they specify a population which does not overlap with other populations. There must be standards for applying criteria in decisions of population boundaries. For the mentally retarded, these minimal requirements required for a functional definition are incomplete. Baumeister and Muma (1975) examined the category of psychiatric disorders for inconsistent criteria and overlapping concepts:

One need only look at the category of *psychiatric disorders* to find himself caught between overlapping constructs. That is, the same behaviors can make one either "odd" or "dumb" depending upon which choice the evaluator cares to make. (Or, which kind of facility has a bed available.) Overlapping constructs in and of themselves are not necessarily an intolerable evil, for they may afford an opportunity to appreciate an underlying organization. But overlapping concepts, based upon inconsistent criteria, may leave us in the position of calling the same thing by different names with the implication that we have differential means available for treatment. (p. 298)

Hallahan and Kauffman (1976a) hypothesize that a comparative examination of the behavioral characteristics of individuals classified as *mildly* or *educable mentally retarded* (EMR), *learning disabled* (LD), and *emotionally disturbed* (ED) would yield more similarities than differences. They note that while it is likely that more similarities than differences exist in the commonly observed behaviors (achievement, emotional-social development), the frequency with which these behaviors are exhibited *does* differ somewhat from category to category. Balthazar and Stevens (1975) also present a similar position for the behavioral overlap between the emotionally disturbed and the retarded.

Assuming the existence of these cross-categorical similarities and knowing the results of measurement inadequacies when IQ tests are applied to minority groups, it is highly probable that an excess of minority children are labeled *retarded* when *LD* or *ED* labels could be applied with as much accuracy. Rather than generating more concern about the selection of an *ED* or a *LD* label (which have nebulous definitions) to replace a *MR* label, we should question the within-group unity that is purposed by any of these labels. According to Baumeister and Muma (1975), "The consistently high variances we typically observe in our dependent measures, obtained on retarded subjects supposedly homogeneous with respect to IQ, ought to tell us that something is terribly awry with respect to the basis for constituting groups" (p. 304).

When compiling teaching curriculums and methods from research findings for groups labeled *mentally retarded,* some cautions must be heeded. The construct of mental retardation produces some classification errors when its parameters consist only of IQ cut-off points. Since this construct tends to be the most universal identification procedure for the selection of mentally retarded experimental subjects, much of the learning theory research and subsequent teaching implications rests upon this IQ definition. Moreover, one should remember that when etiologies, teaching methods, and behavioral characteristics are compared for MR, ED, and LD groups (i.e., already classified and identified by educational placement), the similarities between the retarded groups and

the ED or LD groups far outweigh the differences. When applying research-based teaching procedures to retarded populations one should also remember these two factors about similarity:

1. Individuals may be more accurately part of another classification (*ED, LD, culturally different*), and thus the research of their performance will confound the results. The practice of suggesting teaching implications for a specific population would be, then, questionable.
2. The research findings and their resultant teaching implications may have a wider range of applicability (i.e., to ED and LD populations).

Institutionalization

Many studies on learning theory have included samples from institutionalized populations. However, the results might not be generalizable to persons not in institutions. Further, those studies which reflect a group of mixed placement (institutionalized and noninstitutionalized, or individuals with mixed histories) have findings confounded by within-group differences. While recognizing the methodological inadequacies frequently present in comparative studies, Filler et al. (1975) state several conclusions which were produced from a concentrate of research comparing institutionalized and noninstitutionalized retarded persons:

(1) Intellectual functioning, as measured by standardized tests of intelligence, is negatively affected by institutionalization. (2) This detrimental effect is amplified by such variables as length of institutionalization and age of residential placement. (3) Verbal ability in particular seems adversely affected by institutionalization. (4) A great percentage of individuals who are discharged from institutions fail to remain in the community because of inadequate skills for coping with societal demands. (5) Those individuals who have been discharged and remain in the community typically exist at the lower end of the social and economic continuum. (p. 206)

Measurable "treatment" effects of institutionalization on EMR individuals are abundant in the findings of Zigler and his coworkers (see Chapter 6) on positive reaction tendencies (a desire for social reinforcement from adults) and negative reaction tendencies (a reluctance to approach adult interaction).

Thus institutionalization must be regarded as a complex independent variable in comparative research, of which control has yet to be mastered.

Perhaps its control is best accomplished by adding noninstitutionalized retarded groups or by teasing out some other variable such as length and quality of institutionalization. Equally justifiable questions may be asked regarding the "treatment" effects of other ecological settings (e.g., inner-city or rural poverty) and the type of caregiver-child interaction that exists (Lewis, 1974; White & Watts, 1973).

Etiological Variables

Do the variables of learning operate differently within homogeneous retarded groups of known etiologies? Stern (1973) estimates that in less than half the retarded population no cause can be identified; but in approximately 37% of all cases, retardation can be attributed to genetic endowment, and in about 20%, it may be traced to environmental causes. If Stern's estimates of known causes, which are larger than earlier estimates, are accurate, and if these groups can be identified, the differential influences of etiology on learning may have to be more extensively examined. For example, Down's syndrome, a chromosomal aberration, has received wide attention. Robinson and Robinson (1976) summarize the research relating to the learning characteristics of Down's syndrome children:

> Aside from overall deficits in intellectual competence, there is often evidence in Down's syndrome children of limitations in higher-level integrative abilities, such as concept formation, abstraction, and expressive language (Cornwell, 1974). Abstract and complex uses of language are particularly likely to be deficient (Lyle, 1960). Miranda and Fantz (1973) were able to demonstrate an immaturity in visual-attentional responses in affected infants as early as age eight months. Among the perceptual channels, Belmont (1971) concludes that tactile perception is particularly weak in these children, although auditory perception and auditory-vocal integration are also areas of relative weakness. Even taking into account the low mental ages of Down's syndrome children, one finds that they are particularly deficient (as a group) at abstract and perceptual processes, perhaps in part to faulty perceptual input. (pp. 85–86)

This type of research is an example of experimentation which proceeds along the comparative lines of etiological classification. Even when the research includes the delineation of specific etiologies, it is important to consider the interaction of independent variables (e.g., etiology and quality of caregiver-child interaction) before making extensive generalizations from the findings.

Influence of Experimental Design

Group Comparisons

Difficulties result when experimenters try to compare groups in which a single variable of performance has been manipulated (e.g., distribution of practice in a learning task). In retarded versus nonretarded groups, or high-functioning versus low-functioning retarded groups, these difficulties yield erroneous interpretations of the differentiated responses observed in the comparison. When the experimental tasks vary either in difficulty or reliability, the performance differences which occur are likely to be a result of the task differences rather than a discrimination between the groups of subjects. Chapman and Chapman (1975) describe the troublesome situation which results if equal-CA or equal-MA comparisons are made when the groups are given different tasks.

> The design of manipulating a variable includes all studies in which an investigation gives nonretarded and retarded subjects two tasks which differ in some way in order to draw inferences about the variable that accounts for performance differences between the groups. This popular design yields artifactual findings so readily that one must question the findings of most studies in which it has been used. The defect of the design is that psychometric characteristics of a test partially determine the mean difference in accuracy between the more able and the less able subjects. (p. 404)

Common "solutions" to this problem include: (a) matching retarded and nonretarded subjects on task performance at one point on the variable and comparing at a second point and (b) equating groups statistically. However, neither of these procedures completely solve the problem. Chapman and Chapman (1975) propose a design which requires prior matching of tasks at all levels of difficulty and manipulating two variables rather than one. The variable of interest serves as the experimental variable (e.g., distribution of practice, massed versus spaced), while the second manipulated variable serves as the control variable (e.g., association value of a task, high versus low). The hypothesis of the design concerns the amount of differential deficiency that results from the manipulation of the two variables (e.g., performance deficiency greater in response to one variable than another variable). Such a hypothesis could be stated: "The inferiority of score of retarded subjects is increased more by massing of practice than by a lowering of association values" (Chapman & Chapman, 1975, p. 408). The authors report that a brief review of studies in one journal revealed slightly more than one study per month which reflected this error in group comparison design. Most comparative studies reviewed in this book provide all groups with the same task.

Estes (1970) offers related cautions regarding the methodological considerations and difficulties in comparing learning performance in normal and retarded groups. These cautions include the MA versus CA equation, and the control of previous opportunities to learn. Estes comments upon the latter variable:

> It is not uncommon to see comparisons of performance on laboratory tasks between groups differing as radically with regard to previous opportunities to learn as institutionalized retardates and college students of similar chronological age. Under such circumstances differences in performance on the reference task must be expected to reflect some unknown mixture of effects of differences in past opportunities to learn and in the type of subject variable associated with the notion of capacity (not to speak of other determiners of performance such as motivation and specific skills in dealing with test situations). (p. 55)

Kappauf (1973) questions the traditional statistical and design procedures for comparing task performance with MA, CA, and IQ. He suggests an error-free, graphic response-surface approach to the analysis of data, an approach which produces considerably different results than those obtained from correlational analyses. Rather than using two or three groups (normal subjects and retarded subjects matched on MA and perhaps CA) and correlational or analysis of variance statistical methods, Kappauf argues that a design containing nine or more subject groups is required to map and understand the task-performance response surface. These groups would be spread out over the CA and IQ ranges and would contain larger numbers of subjects who were as homogeneous as possible in CA and IQ. While adoption of these recommendations would significantly reduce the "ease" of comparative research, they would also provide a more valid measure of the effects of MA, CA, and IQ on task performance (Winters, 1974).

All the aspects of group experimental design involved in comparative studies with retarded individuals are complicated by the problems of population definition, population overlap, institutionalization, etiological variables, mental age matching,

chronological age matching, determination of task difficulty, and matching of tasks by difficulty. In order that a design test the effect of a dependent variable on two or more groups, the independent variables arising from these problems must be controlled "so that extraneous and unwanted sources of systematic variance have minimal opportunity to operate" (Kerlinger, 1964, p. 299). Although meeting these criteria is not sufficient to yield internally and externally valid data, it is essential. The group comparison studies cited in this text have been screened by publication and author reviews. Whether or not their results are equally worthy of serious scientific attention must be answered by each reader.

Single Subject Designs

Single subject designs, which emerged from animal behavior research, comprise the primary means to evaluate operant programs. As a means of testing some hypotheses, these designs offer an alternative to group design without sacrificing the scientific quality of the results. In addition, single subject designs yield treatment to individuals, which is not possible for all subjects involved in group designs.

In comparison to case studies, internally valid single subject designs depend upon the fulfillment of four criteria:

a. Data must be recorded reliably.
b. Data must be recorded repeatedly.
c. Procedures must be described in sufficient detail to permit replication.
d. The effects of the procedures must be replicated. (Birnbrauer, Peterson & Solnick, 1974, p. 192)

Group designs and single subject designs also differ in their strategies to produce generalizable data. In group comparisons, the various treatment effects of several groups are analyzed statistically to determine how probable it is that the same results will occur again under similar conditions. Although single subject designs also test the effect of dependent variables while controlling independent variables, "the strategy is to increase confidence in a cause-and-effect relationship between treatment and improvement by replicating the procedures and effects with the subject" (Birnbrauer et al., 1974, p. 193). As such, single designs are most frequently criticized for their weaknesses in external validity. Researchers such as Birnbrauer et al. (1974), and Kazdin (1973) ask how the results obtained with one individual, however internally valid, can be generalized to others. Birnbrauer et al. comment that both types of designs involve speculation about the similarity of the experimental situation to real life situations. The key to valid generalization from single subject designs lies in an examination of the similarity of the functional relationship existing between the original subject's behavior and environment and that of the new case. Although the independent variables involved in population definition (IQ, adaptive behavior, etiology, institutional history, etc.) are still present in behavioral research employing single subject designs, their recognition is of concern only as they observably affect the functional relationship between behavior and environment.

Alternative Classification Systems

After a brief examination of some of the limitations of mental retardation classification systems (i.e., IQ and IQ-adaptive behavior definitions), one can see the need to create more useful ones. The ideal classification system for the special educator and the parent would supply behavioral information which aids progress in the development of retarded persons. Existing classification systems do not provide such aid.

Silverstein's (1970) review of intelligence tests reflects his and others' dissatisfaction with the measurement of intelligence as it presently exists. Rather than depart entirely from the intelligence concept, Silverstein (1970, 1974) suggests that the *Stanford-Binet* and the *Weschler Intelligence Test* be replaced by improved standardized tests operating in two possible frameworks: Piaget's developmental psychology and Guilford's (1967) structure of the intellect. Furthermore, Hallahan and Kauffman (1976b) suggest the substitution of traditional definitions of *mental retardation, emotional disturbance*, and *learning disabilities* with more logical groupings by behavioral deficiencies.

Hobbs (1975) proposes an ecological model as an alternative classification system. By means of a systems-analysis approach, this model enables study of the "dynamic relationship between the individual and his unique set of environmental circumstances at a particular period of time" (Hobbs, 1975, p. 113). This approach necessitates an examination which extends beyond the child's deficiencies and into his daily life settings (home, school, neighborhood) and to people in these set-

tings and their interactions with the child. Obviously the parents' involvement is of vital importance to this model. Hobbs argues that his ecological-systems approach is useful across all types and degrees of handicaps, such that "the greater the handicap, physical or other, the greater the need for intervention strategies to be based on a systems analysis of the problem" (p. 115). Restoration of the child's ecological system to productive equilibrium is the proposed goal of the model's planning and programming stages.

> In the ecological system of a handicapped or troubled child, there may be a number of points at which the system is so disrupted that something must be done. These points become the targets for intervention and might be labeled as points of *discordance*—discrepancy between the way that one individual in the system is behaving and the way that others who are important to him expect him to behave or wish he were behaving. Discordance is always defined in behavioral terms. Exactly what is person *A* doing or failing to do that is causing problems? In what setting does he do it or not do it? Specifically what does person *B* expect him to be doing instead? Behavior is discordant only if it violates the expectations of important others in one's environment; points of discordance cannot be defined unless the unmet expectations are specified. Of course, some discordance is ever present and constructive, leading to adaptation and achievement. We speak here of discordances that result in the disruption of the system, at home, in school, in the community. (Hobbs, 1975, p. 119)

Consistent with other critics of present classification systems, Hobbs demonstrated that the complex effect of a handicap on a child and the child's immediate environment is masked by simple categorical labels. Secondly, these labeling procedures do not produce relevant programmatic suggestions.

Another alternative to traditional diagnostic and classification systems is described by Filler et al. (1975) as an approach which enables classification of behavior rather than of children. Their *constructive-interactive adaptation* system allows an integration of behavioral analysis principles with a Piagetian model of development. It relies heavily on the position that the full range of biological and behavioral structures and their functions interacts with genetic determiners and environmental events encountered by the organism. This interaction position represents an eclectic approach to human growth since it fully acknowledges both biological and environmental influences.

Characteristics of the constructive-interactive adaptation position extend logically from these assumptions:

1. Interactions occur between current response repertoires (schemata) and new experiences, producing opportunities for more complex responses to develop.
2. New responses may be predicted from a child's current schemata.
3. The behavioral content of this system rests upon sequentially stepped "maps" of emerging skills.

These maps should illustrate the order as well as the interdependence of development within and across skill sequences. (See Figure 1.1, which provides a sketch of skills emerging from reflexive behaviors during the sensory-motor stage.)

4. Without reference to CA or IQ, the child's existing behavioral schemata are examined in relation to a hierarchically arranged "skill map."

First, the form of behavior being tested is shown to be a fundamental step in developmental progress. . . . Second, the test is given sequentially until the response of the child is not appropriate, at which time testing stops and instruction begins. . . .

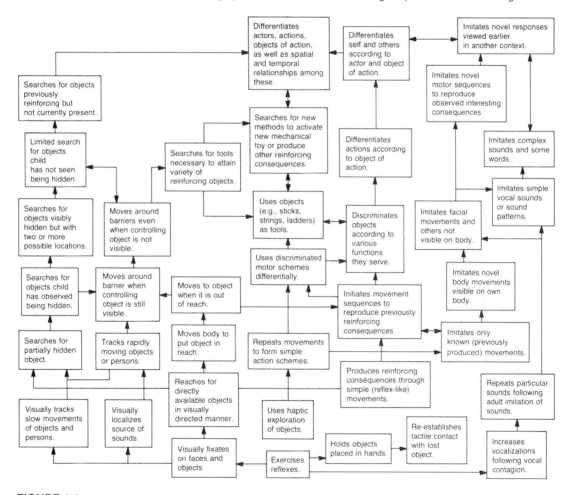

FIGURE 1.1

A hierarchy of skill sequences occurring during the sensory-motor stage.

SOURCE: Adapted from "Mental Retardation" by J. W. Filler, C. C. Robinson, R. A. Smith, L. J. Vincent-Smith, D. D. Bricker, & W. A. Bricker. In N. Hobbs (Ed.), *Issues in the Classification of Children* (Vol. 1) p. 219. San Francisco: Jossey-Bass, 1975. Copyright 1975 by Jossey-Bass. Reprinted by permission.

Third, the initial forms of instruction in an area are used to explore the parameters of the child's repertoire in that area in order to determine the reasons for his failure. (Filler et al., 1975, pp. 121–122)

More recently, research has been directed toward detailing these sequences of developing behaviors and verifying their order and presence in retarded populations (Robinson, 1974; Silverstein, Brownlee, Hubbell, & McLain, 1975; Stephens & McLaughlin, 1974; Taylor & Achenbach, 1975). Since the constructive-interactive adaptation system relies upon careful delineation of these developmental sequences, such research may stimulate its further development. This alternative classification system, which is based upon observable behaviors and easily engenders relevant instructional information, may permit new views of our present knowledge about learning processes in retarded individuals so that researchers may advance in more fruitful directions.

Baumeister and Muma (1975) also reject the IQ-bordered definition as inaccurate and unjustifiable. They suggest a substitute consistent with the constructive interactive adaptation system:

We advocate instead a theory-guided approach to the definition of human adjustment that focuses upon the developing organism and its interactions with a dynamic environment. It is not only important to identify significant personal, social, and environmental variables, but also to cast these into a hierarchical and interdependent system. We should choose our variables from the best understanding of the processes of learning, development, and socialization. In such a system there would not be "MR" but rather a complex and continually changing profile of an individual's adjustments to the constantly changing exigencies of his environment. (p. 305)

Like those systems proposed by others, Baumeister and Muma's is still in a rudimentary stage. However, it is an example of one of the innovative improvements rising from today's widespread dissatisfaction with present IQ definitions.

Conclusion

Although it is apparent that learning theory research in mental retardation is beset by problems in definition and methodology, the amount of programmatic learning research in the field is impressive. The extensive efforts of the various researchers have contributed much to our understanding. In addition, the findings are rich in teaching implications which deserve experimental application in classrooms and other therapeutic milieus. The reader's task is to be aware of research problems and at the same time to be watchful of findings with relevancy to treatment.

References

Adams, J. Adaptive behavior and measured intelligence in the classification of mental retardation. *American Journal of Mental Deficiency*, 1973, *78*, 77–81.

Adams, J., McIntosh, E. I., & Weade, B. L. Ethnic background, measured intelligence, and adaptive behavior scores in mentally retarded children. *American Journal of Mental Deficiency*, 1973, *78*, 7–14.

Balthazar, E. E., & Stevens, H. A. *The emotionally disturbed, mentally retarded: A historical and contemporary perspective*. Englewood Cliffs, N. J.: Prentice-Hall, 1975.

Baumeister, A. A., & Muma, J. R. On defining mental retardation. *The Journal of Special Education*, 1975, *9*, 293–306.

Belmont, J. M. Medical-behavioral research in retardation. In N. R. Ellis (Ed.), *International review of research in mental retardation* (Vol 5). New York: Academic Press, 1971.

Bijou, S. W. A functional analysis of retarded development. In N. R. Ellis (Ed.), *International review of research in mental retardation* (Vol. 1). New York: Academic Press, 1966.

Birnbrauer, J. S., Peterson, C. R., & Solnick, J. V. Design and interpretation of studies of single subjects. *American Journal of Mental Deficiency*, 1974, *79*, 191–203.

Chapman, L. J., & Chapman, J. P. Alternatives to the design of manipulating a variable to compare retarded and nonretarded subjects. *American Journal of Mental Deficiency*, 1975, *79*, 404–411.

Cornwell, A. C. Development of language, abstraction, and numerical concept formation in Down's syndrome children. *American Journal of Mental Deficiency*, 1974, *79*, 179–190.

Doll, E. A. *Vineland Scale of Social Maturity*. Minneapolis: American Guidance Service, 1964.

Estes, W. K. *Learning theory and mental development*. New York: Academic Press, 1970.

Filler, J. W., Robinson, C. C., Smith, R. A., Vincent-Smith, L. J., Bricker, D. D., & Bricker, W. A. Mental retardation. In N. Hobbs (Ed.), *Issues in the classification of children* (Vol. 1). San Francisco: Jossey-Bass, 1975.

Grossman, H. J. (Ed.). *Manual on terminology and classification in mental retardation*. Washington, D.C.: American Association on Mental Deficiency, 1973.

Guilford, J. P. *The nature of human intelligence*. New York: McGraw-Hill, 1967.

Hallahan, D. P., & Kauffman, J. M. *Introduction to learning disabilities: A psycho-behavioral approach*. Englewood Cliffs, N.J.: Prentice-Hall, 1976. (a)

Hallahan, D. P., & Kauffman, J. M. *Labels, categories, behaviors: ED, LD, and EMR reconsidered*. Manuscript submitted for publication, 1976. (b)

Hobbs, N. *The futures of children*. San Francisco: Jossey-Bass, 1975.

Kappauf, W. E. Studying the relationship of task performance to the variables of chronological age, mental age, and IQ. In N. R. Ellis (Ed.), *International review of research in mental retardation* (Vol. 6). New York: Academic Press, 1973.

Kazdin, A. E. Methodological and assessment considerations in evaluating programs in applied settings. *Journal of Applied Behavior Analysis*, 1973, *6*, 517–531.

Kerlinger, F. N. *Foundations of behavioral research*. New York: Holt, Rinehart & Winston, 1964.

Lambert, N., Windmiller, M., Cole, L., & Figueroa, R. *AAMD adaptive behavior scales, public school version* (Rev. ed.). Washington, D.C.: American Association on Mental Deficiency, 1975.

Lewis, M. (Ed.). *The effect of the infant on its caregiver*. New York: Wiley-Interscience, 1974.

Lyle, J. G. The effect of an institution environment upon the verbal development of imbecile children. (ii) Speech and language. *Journal of Mental Deficiency Research*, 1960, *4*, 1–13.

Mercer, J. Psychological assessment and the rights of children. In N. Hobbs (Ed.), *Issues in the classification of children* (Vol. 1). San Francisco: Jossey-Bass, 1975.

Miranda, S. B., & Fantz, R. L. Visual preferences of Down's syndrome and normal infants. *Child Development*, 1973, *44*, 555–561.

Nihira, K., Foster, R., Shellhaas, M., & Leland, H. *Adaptive behavior scales: Manual* (Rev. ed.). Washington, D.C.: American Association on Mental Deficiency, 1974.

Robinson, C. Error patterns in level 4 and level 5 object permanence training. *American Journal of Mental Deficiency*, 1974, *78*, 389–396.

Robinson, N. M., & Robinson, H. B. *The mentally retarded child* (2nd ed.). New York: McGraw-Hill, 1976.

Silverstein, A. B. The measurement of intelligence. In N. R. Ellis (Ed.). *International review of research in mental retardation* (Vol. 4). New York: Academic Press, 1970.

Silverstein, A. B. Deviation social quotients for the Vineland Social Maturity Scale. *American Journal of Mental Deficiency*, 1971, 76, 348–351.

Silverstein, A. B. Structure-of-intellect categories in Stanford-Binet performance. *American Journal of Mental Deficiency*, 1974, *78*, 762–764.

Silverstein, A. B., Brownlee, L., Hubbell, M., & McLain, R. E. Comparison of two sets of Piagetian scales with severely and profoundly retarded children. *American Journal of Mental Deficiency*, 1975, *80*, 292–297.

Skinner, B. F. *Science and human behavior*. New York: MacMillan, 1953.

Stephens, B., & McLaughlin, J. A. Two-year gains in reasoning by retarded and nonretarded persons. *American Journal of Mental Deficiency*, 1974, *79*, 116–126.

Stern, C. *Principles of human genetics* (3rd ed.). San Francisco: Freeman, 1973.

Taylor, J. J., & Achenbach, T. M. Moral and cognitive development in retarded and nonretarded children. *American Journal of Mental Deficiency*, 1975, *80*, 43–50.

White, B. L., & Watts, J. C. *Experience and environment: Major influences on the development of the young child* (Vol. 1). Englewood Cliffs, N.J.: Prentice-Hall, 1973.

Winters, J. J., Jr. Review of International Review of Research in Mental Retardation, Vol. 6, N. R. Ellis (Ed.). *American Journal of Mental Deficiency*, 1974, *78*, 765–766.

Zeaman, D. *Experimental psychology of mental retardation: Some states of the art*. Invited address to meetings of the American Psychological Association, New Orleans, August 1974.

2

Short-term Memory and Its Facilitation

Ellis's Theory

This chapter explores the research surrounding short-term memory. Presented first is a background on variables of memory. Next is a discussion of the basic Ellis experimental memory model. Following are several sections on research stemming from this model, including:

1. organization of input material
2. teaching rehearsal strategies (RS)
3. using imagery as a RS
4. developmental approach to RS
5. effects of reinforcement on short-term memory (STM)

Throughout the chapter there is an emphasis on teaching implications.

The Variables of Memory

How do humans remember? For centuries this question has intrigued and challenged investigators, teachers, and frustrated students. The complexity of the question becomes apparent when the variables of memory are systematically examined. Five broad categories of variables may be outlined: (a) those concerning the memory task, (b) those occurring during input, (c) those describing the individual learner, (d) those occurring during the recall process, and (e) the re-

sponse used to determine that memory has taken place.

Task Variables

An examination of memory task variables (see Figure 2.1) reveals at least three elements.

The first element is method of presentation. The average elementary school student spends approximately 50% of the time listening (Wilt, 1950). Not only are the auditory and visual senses tapped separately, but much information comes simultaneously to both channels. Movement (*kinesthetic*) cues become important when a person learns a motor sequence, whether it be handwriting, complex dance patterns, or orientation and direction within a building or city. A person receives incidental meaning from olfactory, gustatory, and tactual cues. Multisensory reading instruction, such as the Visual Auditory Kinesthetic Tactile approach (VAKT) (Fernald, 1943), intentionally attempts to relay information through many channels as a means of learning or memory facilitation (Hirsch, 1963).

The second element is meaningfulness of information. In diagnostic teaching, memory task information is meaningful due to prior instruction.

Memory Task	Input Process	Individual Learner	Recall Process	Remembering Response
1. mode of presentation	1. rate of presentation	1. chronological age	1. delay between input and recall	1. mode of presentation
2. meaningfulness of information	2. environmental distractions during input	2. intelligence	2. information interference between input and response	2. length of response
3. type of memory task	3. attention of learner	3. mental age $IQ \times CA \div 100$		
		4. environmental and experiential background		
		5. physical handicaps		

FIGURE 2.1
Broad categories of memory variables.

However, many test and experimental tasks are purposefully less meaningful (e.g., digit span) in an attempt to tap "pure" memory skills apart from verbal association. Examples of typical memory tasks are information presented (a) serially and (b) in a paired associate (PA) form. In a digit-span task, an example of serial presentation, the salient feature is order. In contrast, PA tasks rely upon a mental connection between the pair members. The majority of the memory tasks in daily life fall into these two general categories. For instance, finding a lost item includes serial recall and association, while connecting names to faces is a PA variation.

The type of task, a third element, is further defined by the input variable of attention (as shall be discussed next).

Input Variables

Input variables include presentation rate, distractions in the environment, and the learner's level of attention. Presentation rate affects meaningfulness and covaries with the mode of presentation. For example, when the auditory channel is used and meaning is adjusted to the MA of the individual, the average rate of listening comprehension remains between 175–185 words per minute from first grade through college levels (Taylor, Frackenpohl, & Pettee, 1960). Research in compressed speech demonstrated comprehension at 275 words per minute when certain speech sounds were eliminated using special recording equipment (Kirk, 1972). However, in reading, a more complex, visual model of presentation, comprehension rate varies from an average of 80 words per minute in the first grade to 280 words per minute in college (Taylor et al., 1960). Presentation rates for other visual information (pictures, maps, objects, etc.), as well as kinesthetic and

tactual information, also may be varied during the input process, though optimal rates remain less obvious.

Distraction during information input is minimal when the setting is quiet, well lighted, at a comfortable temperature, and without excessive visual display. Auditory distraction, referred to as *masking*, occurs when a spoken message is made less audible by the superimposition of other sounds, such as background noise and nearby conversation. Generally, as masking increases, recall of content decreases (Taylor, 1964). Strauss and Lehtinen (1947) identified visual distractions in overly stimulating classrooms as especially inhibiting to learning in brain-damaged children. However, studies have not verified this specific hypothesis (Burnett, 1962; Cruickshank, Bentzen, Ratzeburg, & Tannhauser, 1961; Rost, 1967), so that the results of excessive visual distraction during information input remain unclear.

If a learner's attention is directed towards the specific task demands, and the learner focuses on task-relevant information, the child's recall is said to be *intentional* or *central* in nature. If task-irrelevant information is attended to, *incidental* learning or recall may occur. For example, central recall occurs when one remembers directions given by a gas station attendant, whereas incidental recall includes such details as the attendant's facial characteristics, his speech, and his appearance.

Learner Variables

The individual variables of CA, intelligence, and resultant MA play prominent roles in the prediction of a person's recall. Short-term memory (STM) performance improves as a function of MA and the development of selective attention (Zeaman & House, 1963) and task-appropriate strategies for recall (Flavell, 1970; Hagen, 1972). Deprivation in a child's experiences due to institutionalization has been shown to damage cognitive development (Hagen & Huntsman, 1971; Zigler, 1966). An individual's physical limitations may also affect memory. Deficiencies in hearing and vision, as well as in movement, may reduce recall by limiting input or by hindering the child's response.

Recall Variables

When information is being processed or temporarily "held," a period of delay may occur between input and recall. Depending upon the task, the amount of delay, and the interference occurring during the delay (such as the presentation of other information), recall may be variously depressed, facilitated, or unaffected.

Response Variables

Finally, the learner's response, which often indicates whether memory has taken place, is usually verbal or motor. Recall, closely tied to the original task design, may be either a simple brief response (e.g., *yes/no* answers, imitation, or pointing) or complex and lengthy (e.g., recalling a detailed incident or playing a sonata).

To clarify further the interaction between content, process, learner characteristics, and response, two examples of school-related memory tasks follow.

Memory Task 1

A teacher uses the *DISTAR* Arithmetic I program (Engelmann & Carnine, 1970) to teach counting skills to a group of young children. Introducing one activity he says, "Listen to me count. Tell me what I counted to. One, two, three, four, five, *six*. I counted to . . .?"

The children respond in unison, "Six!"

MEMORY TASK VARIABLES. In the counting lesson:

1. The task should be presented verbally without visual stimuli.
2. Rote counting information should be relatively familiar to the learner.
3. The child must know that *counted to* means remembering the last number in the serial which the teacher presents.

INPUT PROCESS VARIABLES.

1. The task should be presented in 8 to 10 seconds.

2. Distractions will probably increase during group learning.
3. Since no hand signals are used in this activity, children should at least be listening.

INDIVIDUAL LEARNING VARIABLES. For Learner 1:

1. CA 6 years
2. IQ in normal range
3. MA 6 years
4. average middle-class background
5. vision and hearing normal

For Learner 2:

1. CA 6 years
2. IQ in mildly retarded range
3. MA 4 years
4. lower-income rural background
5. vision and hearing normal

RECALL PROCESS VARIABLES.

1. Recall was immediate.
2. If no interruptions occurred, interference would consist only of the teacher's sentence, "I counted to . . .?"

REMEMBERING RESPONSE VARIABLES.

1. The learner should say the number.
2. Less than one second is needed for the recall response.

Important questions are: Would you expect the remembering response to be different for Learner 2 in comparison to Learner 1? What might these differences be? If the following task in visual-sequential memory were presented to learners 1 and 2, what could be predicted about their probable responses? How could the teacher facilitate recall?

Memory Task 2

A teacher places six simple pictures in a row on the chalkboard tray, face away from the learner. Before showing the pictures one by one, he says, "I am going to show you some pictures. Try to remember where each picture is so you can find the one I want." The teacher shows each picture for a few seconds. Then he shows a second copy of one of the six pictures just viewed and says, "Find the picture like this one." The learner gets up from his seat and turns over the picture on the chalk tray that matches the one just viewed.

Although Task 1 also involves short-term memory, an examination of the variables in the second memory task reveals many differences in content, process, and response. For example, in Task 2: the learner must remember visual stimuli rather than auditory stimuli; short-term memory of an entire sequence is involved rather than only the last item; presentation time is longer; and the mode of response is manual rather than verbal.

Ellis's Multiprocess Memory Model

A review of Ellis's recent research (1963, 1970) aids in formulating research-based answers to questions such as those raised by the previous classroom examples. The multiprocess memory model adopted by Ellis (1970) and based upon other theoretical models (Atkinson & Shiffrin, 1965; Bower, 1967; Broadbent, 1958; Hebb, 1949; Waugh & Norman, 1965) will provide a conceptual framework for the next section. Following is the setup of the memory task, examples of the task in regard to Ellis's model, and a discussion of findings for normal and retarded learners.

Memory Task

The primary memory task employed by Ellis in his research with normal and retarded persons consisted of short-term visual memory for the position of digits shown momentarily. The nine-position memory apparatus used in these studies is illustrated in Figure 2.2. Subjects sat facing the apparatus and were shown a random series of nine digits, one exposed after the other serially from left to right. After viewing the ninth digit, the subject was shown a memory test digit called a *probe*. The subject was to press the position where the probe had been seen. Immediate feedback for correct responses was given to the learner by the sound of a doorbell chime.

Ellis referred to this task as an example of *supraspan input,* where the amount of sequential information is greater than the immediate span of attention. The learner thereby must process momentarily and "hold" the initial portion of the sequence referred to as the *primacy portion* of the supraspan (positions 1, 2, and possibly 3 in the nine-digit task). At the same time, the last portion of the sequence, or the *recency portion* (positions 9, 8, and possibly 7), is stored a few seconds without processing.

Multiprocess Memory Model

In the multiprocess memory model (illustrated in Figure 2.3) information or external stimulation is taken in by the learner through the attention (A) process. This information then goes immediately

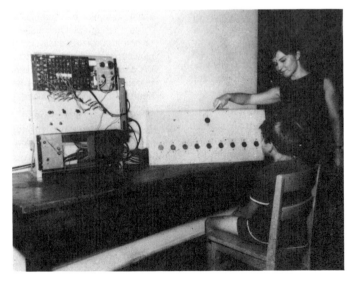

FIGURE 2.2
Nine position memory apparatus.

SOURCE: Adapted from "Memory Processes in Retardates and Normals" by N. R. Ellis. In N. R. Ellis (Ed.), *International Review of Research in Mental Retardation* (Vol. 4) p. 4. New York: Academic Press, 1970. Copyright 1970 by Academic Press. Reprinted by permission.

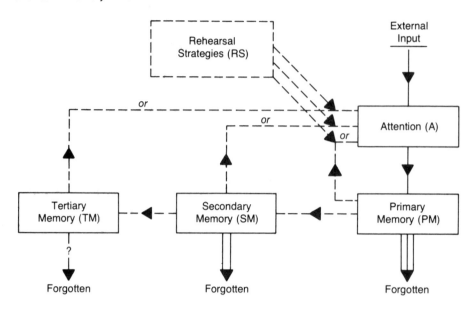

FIGURE 2.3

The multiprocess memory model.

Source: Adapted from "Memory Processes in Retardates and Normals" by N. R. Ellis. In N. R. Ellis (Ed.), *International Review of Research in Mental Retardation* (Vol. 4) p. 6. New York: Academic Press, 1970. Copyright 1970 by Academic Press. Reprinted by permission.

to the primary memory (PM), which is regarded as a limited storage system. According to Waugh and Norman (1965):

> Every verbal item that is attended to enters PM. As we have seen, the capacity of this system is sharply limited. New items displace old ones; displaced items are permanently lost. (p. 93)

It is within the PM that the recency portion of the digit-span task would be briefly and directly stored before its immediate recall. This level of memory is inefficient since it is restricted to holding momentarily only a few bits of information. Without further memory processing or with the passage of time beyond a few seconds, information stored in the PM will be lost. As illustrated in the model (Figure 2.3) by the "forgetting" arrows, not only is more information forgotten from this temporary store but also the abundance of information processed at this level of memory, even if only temporarily, is the greatest of the three levels.

The next process in the model is that of rehearsal strategies (RS). Waugh and Norman (1965) describe RS in the following way:

> We shall assume here that rehearsal simply denotes the recall of a verbal item—either immediate or de-

layed, silent or overt, deliberate or involuntary. The initial perception of a stimulus probably must also qualify as a rehearsal. Obviously a very conspicuous item or one that relates easily to what we already learned can be retained with a minimum of conscious effort. We assume that relatively homogeneous or unfamiliar material must, on the other hand, be deliberately rehearsed if it is to be retained. (p. 92)

The learner uses these rehearsal strategies when he focuses his attention upon information which is in the process of being lost from any of the three systems of memory—the primary memory (PM), the secondary memory (SM), or the tertiary memory (TM). As shown by dotted lines in Figure 2.3, RS result in the feedback looping of information through attention (A) and PM before their possible storage in SM or TM. RS are regarded as the mechanisms responsible for transferral of information from PM to SM to TM. RS thereby make retention of information by the SM and TM systems possible.

Memory Task 1. In the first example, the child answering with the number *six* knew the "counting to" rule and attended to the last, or *recency portion,* of number information given by the teacher.

This information was momentarily stored in the PM prior to its recall.

What types of RS are used? At times the particular RS may be determined by directions given preceeding the task. In this certain task the teacher's directions and the student's knowledge of the "counting to" rule would decrease the need for a RS. Instead, the learner would attend to the last number counted and process it in the PM. Since only momentary memory was required in this task, a RS was not needed.

MEMORY TASK 2. In the second example, if one of the last two pictures viewed was also probed, the attending learner would have momentarily stored this position information in his PM. Since the child was told to remember the relative position of six pictures in a series, and because the pictures were familiar, the RS used might have included transduction of visually coded information to an auditory code of labels. That is, the child may have merely labeled each picture to himself. In addition, he could have rehearsed by continuously repeating the increasing list of labels as each new picture was revealed. Since the task consisted of six items, a supraspan of information, the child probably would have needed some rehearsal strategy to store the primary and middle items (first, second, and third pictures) in SM, while the recency items may have needed only to be momentarily held in the PM.

Other RS involve basic mental classification systems. For example, if the pictures in Task 2 had included some class redundancy such as: *cow, dog, apple, hat, milk, cat,* the child may have coupled the visual input with group names: *animal, animal, food, clothing, food, animal.* With this RS, a common recall error would result in the selection of other items in the recalled class (e.g., when Position Two is probed, Position One is chosen). If item-position recall is not important, a child may use a clustering rehearsal strategy. In this strategy, items are mentally reorganized into common group membership. A list of words given to a child for memory in the order *red, seven, car, yellow, green, one, train* might be recalled as *train, car, yellow, green, red, one, seven.*

Findings

NORMAL LEARNERS. Prior research of Ellis and others (Anders, 1971; Belmont, 1966; Ellis &

Hope, 1968) supported a multiprocess memory model. Such research has uncovered that:

1. A slow presentation rate in the nine-digit serial task facilitated recall for the primary items but had no effect on recency recall.
2. When a 10-second delay occurred between the last digit presented and the probe:
   a. Primary- and middle-position recall was not affected, even if this delay was filled with another task (e.g., counting backwards by threes from a three-digit number).
   b. If the delay was filled and the presentation was fast, primary- and middle-position recall decreased, while an unfilled delay with speeded presentation facilitated recall of primary- and middle-position digits.
   c. Recency recall was unaffected whether the delay was filled or unfilled.

These results supported the idea that two memory processes were operating in short-term retention of supraspans of information. Also, it appeared, that at least for normal learners, information presented in the primary and recency positions was processed differently. As Ellis (1970) states:

> The recency and primary segments of the serial position curve (SPC) appeared to be discontinuous processes. Primacy could be influenced by rate of presentation, or when presentation rate was fast, by a delay prior to recall. It was hypothesized that rehearsal strategies was the mechanism responsible for facilitating primacy performance. Opportunity for rehearsal may be provided during (rate effect) or immediately after (delay effect) presentation. Rehearsal appeared to have no substantial effect upon recency. Instead memory for the terminal items in the series seemed transient, to decay rapidly with time (experimentally filled or unfilled). The filled delay did produce a greater decrement perhaps by preventing rehearsal or by interference. (p. 5)

RETARDED LEARNERS. Within the conceptual framework of the multiprocess memory model, Ellis (1970) conducted a series of 14 studies investigating memory processes of mentally retarded learners. Several postulates concerning the retarded learner and memory may be reaped from research of this nature.

1. Primary and secondary memories are involved when the short-term memory must hold on to information exceeding the momentary span of attention.
2. If information is to be held for longer than the momentary capacity of the primary memory, it is necessary

that active rehearsal strategies be used to process information into the secondary and tertiary memories.

3. The secondary memory, at least for institutionalized retarded learners, does not function normally.

4. The processes of primary and tertiary memories, on the other hand, are not deficient in the retarded learner but perform with efficiency similar to the memories of normal learners (Belmont, 1966).

5. Finally, Ellis (1970) proposes a conclusion that the retarded learner's deficiency in the secondary memory processes is due to a failure to use active rehearsal strategies spontaneously. This failure may be a result of inadequate language skills which minimize the retarded learner's rehearsal capacity.

The serial-position learning curve in Figure 2.4 illustrates the SM deficiency of the retarded in comparison to normals (Ellis, 1970). In this study, subjects were presented with a series of alphabet letters exposed one at a time at a rate of one per second. A probe followed immediately. When a list of three items was presented, the recall for retardates (CA 15–28; IQ 46–67) was not significantly different from college students. However, as the length of information increased beyond the capacity of the PM, the retardates' SM functioned inadequately, while normals successfully stored the first six or the primary items in SM. Storage in the retardate never went much beyond the three recency items, so that their recall was determined mainly by the PM.

Organization of Input Material

Spitz

An indirect implication of Ellis's research and the two-process memory model lies in the provision—via the organization of input material —of RS external to the retarded learner. (See Table 2.1.) If material enters the retarded learner's attention and PM in an organized state, it should more readily be processed into the SM and perhaps on into the TM, thereby facilitating later recall.

Spitz (1973) views the retarded learner's RS deficiency from a slightly different angle than Ellis. After a review of memory research, he suggests that the major difference between mildly retarded learners and normal learners of the same CA is in the retrieval of stored information. Because retardates are slow at scanning and poor in selectively organizing material at input, both retrieval and input are chaotic. Spitz emphasizes that organized input for retarded learners would facilitate easy retrieval (and that it would not allow storage into SM or TM). Unlike Ellis, Spitz states that while almost all material attended to by the retarded learner will be stored, it will not be retrievable.

MAJOR FINDINGS. The research of Spitz and his associates (Spitz, 1972; Spitz, 1973; Spitz, Goet-

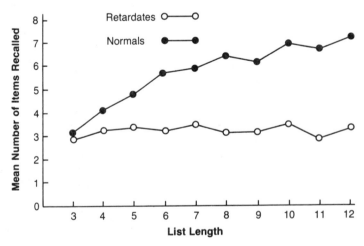

FIGURE 2.4

Total retention for retardates and normals over tasks of varying length.

SOURCE: Adapted from "Memory Processes in Retardates and Normals" by N. R. Ellis. In N. R. Ellis (Ed.), *International Review of Research in Mental Retardation* (Vol. 4) p. 19. New York: Academic Press, 1970. Copyright 1970 by Academic Press. Reprinted by permission.

tler, & Webreck, 1972; Spitz & Webreck, 1972) illustrates how material might be "pre-organized" for the retarded learner. The results of these studies will be summarized in order to relate their wealth of implications for the classroom teacher.

1. When digit-span information had 50% redundancy by repetition (3, 3, 9, 9; 3, 9, 3, 9; 3, 9, 3, 7, 7, 9; etc.), the couplet type of redundancy (3, 3, 9, 9, 7, 7) was easier for mildly retarded and equal MA normals to discover and use as a RS than was repetition redundancy (3, 9, 7, 3, 9, 7) (Spitz et al., 1972).

> The parallel relationship shows quite clearly that performance is tied to grouping strategy. It also shows that retardates do far better when the initially presented material is grouped for them, but that they do learn to recognize and utilize the redundancy, once having been given external help. (Spitz, 1973, p. 160)

In fact, Spitz and Webreck (1972) report that mildly retarded learners, when provided with a little practice and experience, discovered and utilized 50% redundancy in material without ever being given externally provided grouping!

2. In paired-associate learning the subject must learn to associate one item to another as a pair. For example, the subject might be expected to associate numbers with letters or with words (1–hate, 7–tree, 4–red, etc.) or meaningful or unmeaningful words with words (orange–ransom, clover–samlet, etc.). During recall, the subject is presented with a stimulus portion of a pair and expected to respond with the associated word or number. Paired associates may also have varying amounts of redundant pairs. Spitz (1972) showed that retarded learners, like their MA equals, were unable to discover 33% of the redundancy. Also, if all the pairs were presented simultaneously, retarded learners were overwhelmed and unable to discover a successful strategy to learn and remember the associated pairs. However, normal learners of equal age benefitted from such simultaneous presentation.

   a. Therefore, on paired-associate learning material retarded learners can use redundancy levels of 50% or greater to cluster the repetitious pairs together. Recall of a learner using redundancy in paired associates (numbers with letters) would look like this: 1–E, 1–E, 2–L, 2–L, 3–B, 3–B, while the pairs may have been presented in the following random order: 2–L, 3–B, 2–L, 1–E, 1–E, 3–B.

   b. Retarded learners do not benefit from the presentation of high information material in large amounts but rather from presentation in smaller amounts, even if the total presentation time is the same.

IMPLICATIONS FOR TEACHING. The following are some common examples of paired-associate tasks for classrooms. Presentation may be verbal, written, or pictured.

1. vocabulary words with one-word synonyms (male–boy)
2. opposites (hot–cold)
3. words and pictures of the word
4. math facts (2 + 3 = 5)
5. symbol associations of amount and number (. · . 3)
6. color words paired with color samples
7. letter-sound associations (long and soft vowels, initial consonants, etc.)
8. spelling activities ("Spell cat." "C-A-T.")

An application of Spitz's findings yields a series of rules to facilitate the memory of paired associates:

1. In groups of paired associates, make redundant at least 50% of the pairs being learned. Therefore, on ditto sheets, board words, flash cards, or taped presentation drills a teacher should repeat each paired associate at least twice or with greater frequency during instruction or memory drill. For example, a learner is presented with the following set of redundant vocabulary pairs by way of a taped playback or prerecorded Language Master (Bell & Howell, 1963) cards: elevator–escalator; manager–director; boy–male; elevator–escalator; pay–salary; girl–female; girl–female; manager–director; boy–male. Recall could be tested by having the learner listen to a delayed presentation of each pair: "girl . . . . . female." The learner would try to verbalize the associated synonym prior to its delayed presentation. To avoid representation of all the pairs simultaneously, which impedes performance, flash card presentations to self or with another learner are effective. Use of a rotating recipe or picture file, as illustrated in Figure 2.5, allows the teacher to insert paired-associate cards into the plastic pages with a given order and redundancy level which can be viewed one at a time by the learner.

   The learner may be assisted in his discovery of the redundancy and encouraged to make use of the repetition as a RS to remember more pairs. However, as Spitz's research illustrated, if the redundancy is at least 50%, the learner can discover it by himself.

2. Although less frequent than paired-associate tasks, classroom memory-span tasks also may be organized to facilitate recall by the learner. Organization can be used when an entire sequence must be recalled, as in oral spelling and counting which is echoed after a teacher, telephone number sequences, a series of directions, and perhaps a complex sequence of movements modeled by the

TABLE 2.1
Synopsis of Studies Focusing on Improving Recall in Retardates via Input Organization

STUDY	SUBJECT:IQ	MA	CA	NUMBER	DIAGNOSIS	ENVIRONMENT	TASK	METHOD OF INPUT ORGANIZATION
1. Spitz, Goettler, & Webreck (1972)	$\overline{IQ}$ = 62 (MR)*; $\overline{IQ} \geq 100$ (N)*		$\overline{CA}$ = 16 (MR); $\overline{CA}$s = 10, 13, 18, 21, 30 (5 group normal Ss)	22–44 per group MR + normals	MR Ss* had no gross physical or neurological defects; low socioeconomic class	Institutionalized (MR); regular public school and college (N)	Serial task: 6–10 digit strings were presented all at once under 2 types of redundancy conditions—repetition and couplet redundancy. Recall of entire string.	Repetition of redundancy (e.g., 5, 2, 8, 5, 2, 8) and couplet redundancy (e.g., 5, 5, 2, 2, 8, 8) with and without external emphasis; separation and underlining.
2. Spitz (1972)	$\overline{IQ}$ = 64; $\overline{IQ} \geq 100$		$\overline{CA}$ = 15.3(MR); $\overline{CA}$ = 9.16 and 14.22 (N)	144 (1/3 MR, 1/3 3rd graders, 1/3 8th graders)		MR Ss institutionalized; normals from public schools	Paired associates. PAs presented at 4 redundancy levels: 33%, 50%, 67%, & 83%. PA task consisted of letter-number pairs. In Exp. I pairs were presented singly while in Exp. II presentation was simultaneous. Recall of associated pair when given stimulus.	Paired associates. Four levels of redundancy were used so that PAs were repeated at one of four levels: 33%, 50%, 67% or 83%.

RESULTS: 1. For EMR adolescents and normals of the same MA, couplet redundancy in digit spans upon input resulted in better recall than digit-span information organized by repetition redundancy. When the latter procedures were externally emphasized by underlining and separation of groups, digit-span recall for both these groups was as good as with couplet redundancy. With only a little practice and experience, EMR adolescents discovered and used 50% redundancy in pre-organized digit-span information. NOTE: Four subexperiments were included in this study; each made MR-normal Ss comparisons.

RESULTS: 2. When paired associate (PA) information was presented at the 83% redundancy level, retarded adolescents made only 3% errors, close to the performance of 3rd to 8th graders (equal MA + CA subjects respectively). Recall errors increased greatly for retardates at lower levels of redundancy. When redundancy was reduced from 50% to 33%, it was not easily discovered or used by retardates. Retardates were better able to use redundancy in PA when material was presented sequentially rather than all at one time. NOTE: Two subexperiments were included in this study; both made MR-normal subject comparisons.

TABLE 2.1, cont.

STUDY	SUBJECT:IQ	MA	CA	NUMBER	DIAGNOSIS	ENVIRONMENT	TASK	METHOD OF INPUT ORGANIZATION
3. Spitz & Webreck (1972)	$\overline{IQ}$ = 64		$\overline{CA}$ = 15.33	70		Institutionalized	Same as Spitz, Goettler, & Webreck, 1972	Same as Spitz, Goettler, & Webreck, 1972
4. Jacobs & Foshee (1971)	*Phase 1* IQ = 68	*Phase 1* 6–0 to 9–8 $\overline{MA}$ = 7–6	*Phase 1* 10–2 to 13–9 $\overline{CA}$ = 11–1	*Phase 1* 30		EMR special class in public school	Serial task: 6 geometric shapes presented one at a time in a self-paced manner; recall of probed shape's position	von Restorff effect
	Phase 2 48 to 79 $\overline{IQ}$ = 65	*Phase 2* 4–10 to 9–4 $\overline{MA}$ = 7–0	*Phase 2* 7–2 to 14–4 $\overline{CA}$ = 11–2	*Phase 2* 20				

RESULTS: 3. EMR adolescents' performance improved considerably when material was pre-organized. External cueing of redundancy did improve initial recall performance but did not result in better long-term performance than did spontaneous discovery.

RESULTS: 4. When retardates were training on a serial task in which the von Restorff effect occurred in either the middle or primary positions of the task, later learning on the same task without the von Restorff effect was significantly improved.

$^*\overline{CA}$ = Mean chronological age
EMR = Educable mentally retarded
$\overline{IQ}$ = Mean intelligence quotient
$\overline{MA}$ = Mean mental age
MR = Mentally retarded
N = Normal
PAs = Paired associates
Ss = Subjects

19

FIGURE 2.5
Picture file for the arrangement of PA task cards with a desired order and redundancy level.

teacher. These tasks may be organized in the following ways:
a. incorporating 50% or greater redundancy into the series presentation
b. emphasizing redundant couples or repeated groups with tonal or volume cues (if spoken) and with underlining and/or spacial separation (if written)
c. using couplet redundancy rather than repetition redundancy
d. pairing underlining and spatial separation with repetition redundancy in order to facilitate its discovery

Jacobs and Foshee

The research of Jacobs and Foshee (1971) suggests another method to organize input information and overcome the retarded learner's RS deficiency. The von Restorff effect, named for its discoverer (von Restorff, 1933), describes what happens when facilitated learning of an item's serial position is due to that item's isolation against a homogeneous background. For example, in Jacobs and Foshee's study the learner had to

remember the serial position of six geometric figures seen one at a time in a self-paced, left-to-right progression. One of the six geometric figures was presented isolated against a colored background, while all others were illuminated against a white background. The isolated figure's position was probed randomly so that the other five choices were probed equally as often. The results of the study indicated that if the von Restorff effect was utilized to emphasize the primary or middle positions during a serial-learning task (see Figure 2.6), later learning of the task without the von Restorff effect would be improved for mildly retarded learners. The retarded subjects appeared to have acquired a RS which remained when the von Restorff effect was removed from the task. The researchers came to this conclusion because experimental subjects took longer to complete each task, perseverated less on one choice, and retained superior performance levels after the effect was eliminated. The von Restorff effect seemed to simplify the task for retardates whether it was fixed on one position while the designs were varied or

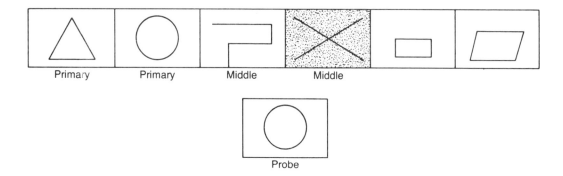

FIGURE 2.6
The von Restorff effect in the middle position of a serial learning task.

whether it was systematically varied across positions. According to Jacobs and Foshee (1971):

> Isolation by color would seem conceptually to be equivalent to the "novel" stimulus in arousal studies. By analogy, in the present experiment, the subject's attention level may be raised by the isolated item followed by a process of habituation to the subsequent black and white items. (p. 317)

IMPLICATIONS FOR TEACHING.

1. To facilitate memory of a series of six items, the teacher may emphasize one item in the beginning or middle positions. This suggestion is not to be confused with redundancy cues, since in this application the color-isolated item is not always the probed item. The color isolation of any middle or primary item provides the learner with *memory hooks* or position cues with which to break up the long sequence into memorable sections. This simple RS is illustrated in spelling word tasks.

A D D R E S S
B I C Y C L E

2. When the von Restorff effect is removed from the task, learners should be encouraged to remember the sequence in the same way by continuing to use their RS.
3. It may be possible to generalize these findings to auditory-sequential memory tasks as well. In order to facilitate memory of the entire sequence, a series of words or commands could be broken up by volume or voice variation of one word or command in the primacy or middle position. For example, in the recall of the words *ball, baby, bone, bat, bunny, blue,* "bone" should be set off by a loud, higher pitched voice.
4. Another variation of the von Restorff effect includes the use of verbal commands for attention nested within the early or middle portions of a list to be recalled:

> *ball, baby,* **now listen,** *bone, bat, bunny, blue*
> Although nested attention commands have been used (Wisenberg, 1971) to facilitate recall of the specific item they precede, the commands used here break the sequence into memorable segments.

Teaching Rehearsal Strategies

A second and more direct implication of Ellis's research includes training retarded learners to use rehearsal strategies. If the learner is able to apply RS systematically to information entering the primary memory, less information will be lost and more remembered due to its storage in the stable processes of SM and TM.

Butterfield, Wambold, and Belmont

Butterfield and his associates (Belmont & Butterfield, 1971a, 1971b; Butterfield & Belmont, 1971; Butterfield, Wambold, & Belmont, 1973) investigated the learning and retrieval processes of retardates who performed a self-paced serial memory task. In these tasks the learners pushed a button to expose letters one at a time. After the last serial item, they exposed a probe letter. Then they attempted to recall its previous position in the list.

MAJOR FINDINGS. Early studies with retarded and nonretarded adults revealed that retardates paused far less often as they paced themselves through the serial list, while normals paused increasingly longer as they went deeper into the list. As expected, normal subjects, who apparently adopted a RS spontaneously, had higher recall for primacy information.

These early studies revealed three additional findings. First, as Ellis (1970) also found, mildly retarded learners did not rehearse spontaneously. Second, they also did not appropriately sequence rehearsal and nonrehearsal learning techniques. Finally, retarded subjects were not observed to intercoordinate multiple rehearsal strategies.

To investigate methods of surmounting these difficulties, Butterfield et al. (1973) propose an active and passive memory system to replace Ellis's secondary and primary memory processes. When information in this system needs immediate recall, the passive learning process, which does not involve rehearsal, is used. However, when the learner perceives that recall will be delayed, the information is broken into chunks and rehearsed. In normal learners the combination of these two processes results in a single effective acquisition strategy. Retrieval time also covaries with the process of learning used during acquisition. That is, retrieval of actively learned (rehearsed) material takes much longer than material passively learned, with the time increasing across the serial position probed. Material learned by an active process appears to be retrieved by a serial search into the secondary store, which is discontinued upon location of the information.

Butterfield et al. (1973) taught mildly retarded adults to incorporate active and passive processing during the acquisition and retrieval of serial information. The step-by-step retrieval strategy that was taught is illustrated in Figure 2.7.

A series of three experiments demonstrated that retarded adults were capable of successfully

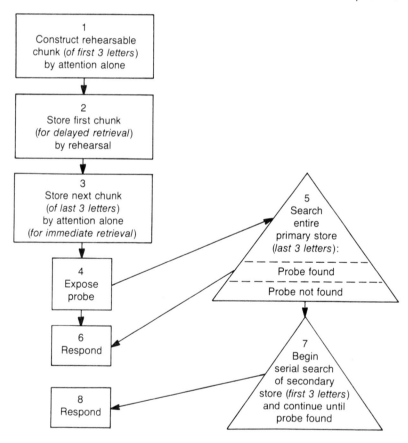

FIGURE 2.7
Sequence used in memory training of retarded adults.

SOURCE: Adapted from "On the Theory and Practice of Improving Short-term Memory" by E. C. Butterfield, C. Wambold, & J. M. Belmont. *American Journal of Mental Deficiency*, 1973, 77, 658. Copyright 1973 by The American Association on Mental Deficiency. Reprinted by permission.

employing the entire sequence of acquisition and retrieval steps pictured in Figure 2.7, thereby attaining recall comparable to normal uninstructed adults on one particular memory task. The experiments revealed, however, that accurate recall occurred only when retardates were instructed to use a retrieval strategy, which was in turn coordinated with the instructed learning strategy. Retarded adults did not assert executive control over their own cognitive processes, i.e., they lacked automatic intercoordinated selection of acquisition and retrieval strategies.

In addition, generalization and durability of the improved performance were questioned. Whenever posttraining performance retention was measured, the percent of correctly recalled items decreased. Although additional training resulted in immediate reinstatement of superior performance, it is not known if training benefits would ever be permanent. Also unanswered are other questions of generalization. Is this superior performance task-specific, i.e., tied to the specific task and strategies trained? Would improvement on a particular memory task benefit the retardate's daily need to remember and recall information? Butterfield et al. (1973) conclude that future research should not be limited to answering such specific questions but should be directed to the level of executive control, i.e., selecting, sequencing, and coordinating cognitive processes.

IMPLICATIONS FOR TEACHING. The reader of the Butterfield et al. (1973) research is not encouraged to apply directly these research findings. Although a teacher may find some classroom implications, the validity of these implications remains untested. The valuable contributions of this research to Ellis's findings include the importance of (a) teaching retarded learners retrieval strategies as well as acquisition strategies, and (b) coordinating the two to work harmoniously. While the acquisition strategy prescribes a storage pattern, the retrieval strategy prescribes a method to review stored information in an efficient manner.

Since it is doubtful that many school tasks would be identical to the six-letter serial experimental task, a teacher would not find it profitable to teach the acquisition-retrieval sequence illustrated in Figure 2.7. However, a teacher might improve a retardate's spontaneous selection and use of acquisition and retrieval strategies by assisting his progress through the following instructional steps:

1. Apply a given acquisition strategy to a simple memory task.
2. Apply a given retrieval strategy to a simple memory task and coordinate the acquisition strategy with the retrieval strategy.
3. Generalize Step 2 to other similar simple memory tasks.
4. Apply a different given acquisition strategy to a more complex memory task.
5. Apply a different given retrieval strategy to a more complex memory task and coordinate the acquisition strategy with the retrieval strategy.
6. Generalize Step 5 to other similar more complex memory tasks.
7. Select and utilize appropriate acquisition-retrieval strategies when given either type of task.
8. Continue experience with selecting and applying other acquisition-retrieval strategies.

This instructional procedure may be partially illustrated by borrowing a model of acquisition strategies from Baumeister and Kellas' (1971) review of paired-associate research with the retarded. Figure 2.8 depicts the four main features of acquisition strategy selection and usage: a strategy selector mechanism, coding operations, repetition strategies, and a feedback system. In this model, retrieval strategy selection is tied to acquisition. Although the model is based on paired-associate rather than serial-learning research, the similarities in strategy type and selection warrant its presentation. The strategy selector is analogous to Butterfield and Belmont's (1971) idea of executive control. As indicated by the arrows in Figure 2.8, retardates, in contrast to normals, do not spontaneously select a strategy other than verbalization or rote repetition of serial items. Therefore, prior to RS selection and instruction, the teacher will need to determine the meaningfulness and length of the memory task, its rate of presentation, the response necessary by the learner, as well as the learner's prior experience with acquisition and retrieval strategies. Based on this information, a rehearsal strategy could be selected and taught in a step-by-step manner similar to that of Butterfield et al. (1973).

Figure 2.8 portrays a variety of rehearsal strategies that might be selected to teach. Visual imagery strategies include the retention of concrete and meaningful verbal materials through mental pictures (e.g., sequencing the events in a story). The more primitive strategies, such as cue selection (attention to dimension of a stimulus, e.g., color) and chunking (grouping of material in

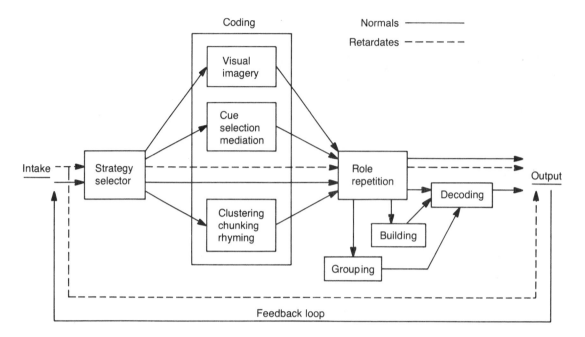

FIGURE 2.8
Model of acquisition strategies.

SOURCE: Adapted from "Process Variables in the Paired-Associate Learning of Retardates" by A. A. Baumeister & G. Kellas. In N. R. Ellis (Ed.), *International Review of Research in Mental Retardation* (Vol. 5) p. 260. New York: Academic Press, 1971. Copyright 1971 by Academic Press. Reprinted by permission.

order to remember it) tend to be reserved for material of less meaning to the learner (e.g., letter or number series). Also, when information is of supraspan length, exceeding the immediate memory span, grouping or chunking could be taught. For example, the retarded learner could be instructed to follow the policy of grouping information into three-bit units. Although it remains untested, Belmont and Butterfield (1971a) suggest that rehearsal instructions could be coordinated with the rehearsal strategy to include systematic scanning and pointing.

A teacher attempting to implement RS instruction would select a series of memory tasks which would then be coordinated with an appropriate acquisition and retrieval strategy. Next, the memory tasks and their RS would be ordered from easiest to most difficult. Ordering instruction would require evaluation of the learner's response mode (motor or verbal) as well as the teacher's mode of stimulus presentation (visual, auditory, visual-auditory). Rehearsal strategies should be not only efficient within a task but also flexible enough to be

applied to other similar tasks (Campione & Brown, in press). Similar tasks would be systematically varied across a mastered RS. The learner would gradually progress through the eight instructional steps. Thus the learner receives experience with increasingly more complex tasks and strategies and with generalization of associated strategies to similar tasks.

A sample of a few memory tasks and associated acquisition-retrieval strategies is presented in Table 2.2. Both tasks and strategies increase in complexity.

Kellas, Ashcroft, and Johnson

The research of Kellas, Ashcroft, and Johnson (1973) not only confirms Ellis's hypothesis of a rehearsal strategy deficiency in retardates but also provides more support for the hypothesis that the ability to employ strategies under conditions of induced rehearsal may be relatively unimpaired in retardates. Subjects were taught to use cumulative rehearsal—the rote repetition of increasing sets—which included naming the currently visual

TABLE 2.2

An Incomplete, Ordered Set of Memory Tasks and their Associated Acquisition-Retrieval Strategies

TASK	STRATEGIES

1. Recalling position of common concrete objects
  a. Response: arranging objects in order of presentation
  b. Response: verbalizing serial order
	Clustering, rote repetition, and grouping with group-search retrieval. Optional addition: simple visual imagery and pointing.

* * * * *	

5. Recalling serial position of digits
  a. Response: pointing to probed position
  b. Response: verbalizing serial order
	Clustering, rote repetition, and grouping with group-search retrieval. Optional addition: visual group scanning with simultaneous imaginary underlining of groups with index finger.

* * * * *	

10. Recalling story sequence
  a. Response: arranging event pictures
  b. Response: verbalizing serial order
	Visual imagery and rote repetition. Optional addition: simultaneous use of finger counting to emphasize order of events in sequence.

stimulus and then rehearsing three times in sequence all previous items plus the correct item. In the overt shadowing technique of instruction, the experimenter modeled active rehearsal of a list of pictures exposed one at a time while the subjects "shadowed" their overt rehearsal, repeating everything. The recall response consisted of naming the nine items in order. Other subjects were taught to rehearse cumulatively by silently shadowing the experimenter's overt rehearsal. Their recall performance was as good as those who rehearsed aloud. The retardates' performance, measured two weeks later, continued to demonstrate active processing of information by cumulative rehearsal.

IMPLICATIONS FOR TEACHING. Specific implications of the research of Kellas et al. (1973) may be summarized in four statements:

1. Overt shadowing not only appears to be an effective method of instruction but also allows RS usage to be monitored by a teacher.
2. Silent cumulative rehearsal, although difficult to monitor, may effectively replace rehearsing aloud and would be less disruptive in classroom situations.
3. When students are learning an active process of information storage, they should be reminded to use rehearsal. This is especially true if the student is using silent cumulative rehearsal.
4. In support of facilitating the executive control or the strategy selector of retarded students, Kellas et al. (1973) state:

> It is at least conceivable that, for retarded persons, experience in using efficient and successful strategies might promote a growth of such "planful" behavior, and with it an increase in the production of new means to process information effectively. (p. 679)

Brown et al.

Brown, Campione, Bray, and Wilcox (1973) and Brown, Campione, and Murphy (1974) trained retarded adolescents to use overt cumulative rehearsal to remember a set of four variables. Not only did the retarded subjects increase the accuracy and speed of performance, but they also demonstrated a more mature response pattern, i.e., similar to that of normal adolescents. In addition, most of the trained group demonstrated spontaneous use of the RS 6 months after original training when presented with the same task.

The task involved selection of a probed category from four pictures. For example, the following pictures were exposed for 2 seconds in sequential order: boat, bread, cat, dress. These pictures were followed by a question and a probe category picture not included in the stimulus pool, e.g., the question "What animal did you see last?" and a picture of a rabbit. Before being presented with the task, all subjects were trained to label and recall all items in each of four categories or states (food, clothing, animals, and vehicles). The number of items in each category varied from two to six. Experimental subjects were then trained in the use of overt cumulative rehearsal. This RS training consisted of simultaneously viewing all four pictures in the inspection set and shadowing or echoing the experimenter's overt cumulative labeling of the first three items (primacy positions): boat; boat–bread; boat–bread–cat. On the fourth item (recency position), the subject was told to "just try to remember."

In both studies (Brown et al., 1973; Brown et al., 1974) it was discovered that:

> Failure to keep the inspection set "alive" by rehearsal forced the nonrehearsing subjects to search the states

Using Imagery as a RS

While a group of earlier related studies (Bugelski, 1968; Bugelski, Kidd, & Segmen, 1968; Paivio, 1968; Yarmey & Bowen, 1972) demonstrated the helpfulness of employing imagery as a RS, these studies also revealed the following:

1. Instructions to use nonverbal imagery aided not only the intentional learning of normal and retarded children but also their incidental learning. That is, even under incidental learning conditions when retarded subjects did not know that imagery practice with paired associates would be followed by recall testing, their performance was improved by prior use of imagery as a RS (Yarmey & Bowen, 1972).
2. In comparison to normals, performance of educable retarded subjects was substantially improved by increasing the amount of practice and imagery processing before recall testing, and by the continued use of imagery (Yarmey & Bowen, 1972).
3. In retarded subjects, picture paired-associate learning was superior to word paired-associate learning. However, when information was presented pictorially and the retarded learner used mental imagery as a RS, initial assistance given in the decoding of nonverbal imagery codes into verbal responses may have improved recall performance (Yarmey & Bowen, 1972).
4. Normal subjects taught to use a "pegword" rhyme (*one is a bun, two is a shoe, three is a tree,* etc.) and instructed to use imagery to remember subsequent word associates for the numbers 1 through 10 did significantly better in recall than others not learning the rhyme and receiving only standard paired-associate instructions (Bugelski, 1968; Bugelski et al., 1968; Paivio, 1968).

Lebrato and Ellis

Building their investigations upon these findings, Lebrato and Ellis (1974) compared the performance of retarded and nonretarded adults using imagery mediation in paired-associate tasks. This study replicated and expanded the findings of Bugelski et al. (1968). Experimental subjects were taught to use the number-noun nursery rhyme which consisted of the following mnemonic pairs: "One is a bun, two is a shoe, three is a tree, four is a door, five is a hive, six is a stick, seven is heaven, eight is a gate, nine is wine, ten is a hen." After memorizing the rhyme thoroughly, the subjects were given a practice list of 10 number-noun pairs. They were instructed to imagine an association between the noun rhyming with a given

number and the noun to be recalled for that number. As stated by Lebrato and Ellis (1974):

> The subject is instructed to form an interacting image between the rhyming word and the word to be recalled. Thus, if the first word in the list were "nail," the subject could imagine a large nail sticking through a hamburger bun. In recall, the subject recalls bun and the image of the bun and nail. (p. 704)

MAJOR FINDINGS. A series of three studies by Lebrato and Ellis (1974) revealed the following:

1. Imagery mnemonic pretraining significantly facilitated the original learning and/or the short-term memory of mildly retarded adults.
2. Since retarded subjects seemed deficient in creating visual images of objects when given the word alone, imagery mnemonic pretraining consisted not only of verbal instructions to imagine an object but also of actual pictures. The pictures were color slides, on which each slide illustrated three items, the number, the rhyming word, and the object named by the rhyming word. Lebrato and Ellis (1974) hypothesized that "the presentation of these pictures would provide memory images which could be used in the mediation of subsequent learning and that this would further 'prime' the imaging behavior of the retarded subjects" (p. 712). According to the results, imagery mediation did occur in the experimental retarded subjects who were presented with pictures during pretraining. This conclusion is supported by a tripling in the amount of time (15 seconds versus 5 seconds) taken by experimental subjects assisted during pretraining by pictures versus control subjects who were not assisted by pictures. Therefore, the use of pictures during imagery pretraining greatly speeded later use of mnemonics to form interacting images between rhyming words and recall words.
3. To further the recall performance of retarded learners using imagery mediation, they suggest (1972):
   a. provision of additional practice during pretraining
   b. using pictures of both mnemonic rhyme objects and practice list words

IMPLICATIONS FOR TEACHING.

1. As with other imagery studies (Taylor et al., 1972; Whitely & Taylor, 1974), Lebrato and Ellis (1972) provided additional support for the classroom practice of:
   a. pretraining retarded students to use imagery as a RS in order to improve memory of associated words and/or numbers
   b. initial reliance upon instructions as well as pictures to increase the probability of later independent use of imagery
2. The use of imagery mnemonics is effective with *mildly* retarded adults. In the first of three experi-

ments (Lebrato & Ellis, 1974), the recall of *moderately* retarded subjects was not facilitated by imagery pretraining. However, because Lebrato and Ellis decided to employ a sample of less retarded subjects in later experiments, while at the same time adding the use of pictures to the pretraining procedure, it still is not known if imagery mnemonic training is effective with moderately retarded persons.

3. Different from imagery elaboration, mnemonic imagery makes use of rhyming association as well as mental picture association. Rhyming skills, therefore, are prerequisite to pretraining in mnemonic imagery. A teacher might make direct use of the rhyme Lebrato and Ellis employed to increase a child's memory for ordering events or objects. For example, to remember the steps of the "carrying" process in addition, a child might associate each successive step with the rhyming words as follows:
   a. "One is a bun." *Bun* is associated with dividing in half like a hamburger bun the two-digit number added in the one's column.
   b. "Two is a shoe" *Shoe* is associated with leaving (stepping down) the one's place digit while carrying (jumping up) the ten's place digit to the top of the next column.
   c. Etc. throughout the rhyme.

As an aid in initially remembering the production order of workshop tasks, students might be pretrained to connect the rhyme with steps in the task order. Other number rhymes could be invented which may have increased meaning when coupled with overt actions by the child.

a. "One is run." Child runs in place.
b. "Two is shoe." Child points to shoe.
c. "Three is key." Child makes key-turning motion.
d. "Four is roar." Child roars.
e. "Five is drive." Child turns imaginary steering wheel.

These mnemonic rhymes would then be associated with a sequence of words or events to be learned. Finally, if color coding is involved in an ordered task, rhymes could be created to fit the specific colors (e.g., *red is bed: green is machine*) which would then be associated with the steps in the ordered task.

Developmental Approach to RS

A look at rehearsal strategy acquisition from a developmentalist's viewpoint reveals some novel findings as well as more evidence to support the general theses already presented. Hagen (1972) employed a serial-memory task with normals and retardates in which an array of picture cards was presented for 5 seconds. Each card had two pic-

tures: a household object and an animal. The central or intentional memory task was to recall the serial locations of a probed picture, either an animal or household object. After central learning was assessed, incidental recall was measured by the child's ability to remember the associated animal-household object pairs illustrated together on a single stimulus card.

MAJOR FINDINGS. This same task was employed in a number of studies (Hagen & Huntsman, 1971; Hagen & Kingsley, 1968; Hagen & West, 1970; Kingsley & Hagen, 1969) and yielded some interesting findings.

1. In comparison to normals, retarded children were deficient in their performance on both central and incidental tasks (Hagen & Huntsman, 1971).
2. This inability to attend to central stimuli as measured by central recall was greater for institutionalized retardates than for retardates in the same IQ range but living at home (Hagen & Huntsman, 1971).
3. With pretraining in RS, retarded children improved in recall performance (Hagen & West, 1970).
4. For normal 5 year olds attempting to recall a probed position in a series of five to eight animal pictures:
   a. The induced RS of simple overt labeling *did not* facilitate overall memory performance (Hagen & Kingsley, 1968).
   b. The induced RS of cumulative repetition (e.g., *fish; fish, bear; fish, bear, dog,* did, however (although more difficult when the fourth and fifth positions were reached) result in greater primacy and overall recall than did no RS or simple labeling (Kingsley & Hagen, 1969).
5. For normal older children working with the same task:
   a. The induced RS of simple overt labeling *did* facilitate overall and recency recall in 6, 7, and 8 year olds (Hagen & Kingsley, 1968).
   b. In 10 year olds already having spontaneously acquired RS, however, overt labeling *did not* aid overall performance. Those using the RS made gains in recency which were cancelled by decreased primacy recall (Hagen & Kingsley, 1968). Hagen (1972) concludes that ongoing spontaneous rehearsal was interrupted by the induced RS.

Though not supporting the two-process short-term memory model (Waugh & Norman, 1965) adopted by Ellis (1970), Hagen (1972) discusses the development of strategy usage by synthesizing Flavell's (1970) research within the theoretical framework of Neisser's (1967) attention model.

The development of the use of strategies occurs because of two types of developmental changes, according to Flavell (1970). The *specific* changes are those which a particular mediator, such as verbal rehearsal, goes through. Labeling is not done by the young child at all. With development, overt labeling of stimulus objects in the environment becomes the normal response. When learning or remembering becomes important, strings of labels are repeated covertly. Finally, particular strategies and rules specific to the task demands at hand become perfected. The other type of developmental change is called *general*, and it involves planfulness on the part of the child. The child becomes aware that if he does some sort of activity now, he will improve his likelihood of success in the future. The rehearsal strategies will only be implemented when there is a plan in mind indicating it will be useful to do so. The child sees a purpose in his plan. (Hagen, 1972, p. 77)

IMPLICATIONS FOR TEACHING. Within this developmental context, a teacher attempting to improve short-term memory of retarded students would probably instruct specific RS as well as the more nebulous concept of "planfulness." To reach this latter objective, children could be shown the advantages of remembering particular information. For example, in teaching a multistepped art project, a teacher might show examples of finished products and say, "If you remember all the steps, your project will look nice like this one, but if you forget a step it probably will look as bad as this one." Perhaps initially the child would be expected to verbalize why he should use an induced RS. Also, reminders employed by a teacher to elicit RS usage would be gradually faded out to only intermittent questioning of the child to determine whether he is engaging in "planfulness."

In addition, Hagen's (1972) results seem to indicate that the effectiveness or ineffectiveness of a RS is related to a child's level of cognitive development or mental age. In normal children over 10 years of age, RS developed spontaneously and recall did not increase when less primitive or conflicting RS (e.g., simple overt labeling) were imposed (Hagen & Kingsley, 1968). While simple overt labeling was an effective RS for 6, 7, and 8 year olds, cumulative repetition was more effective for preschoolers (Hagen & Kingsley, 1968; Kingsley & Hagen, 1969).

Another influential variable in selective attention and resultant central recall is, as previously discussed, institutionalization. For retardates of a given MA, institutionalization appears to have depressing effects upon the selective attention for relevant stimuli and later recall (Hagen & Huntsman, 1971). By scanning Table 2.3 to corre-

late roughly RS and MA level and environmental setting with retarded students of a particular MA and environment, a teacher may be guided more logically in selecting a RS which works for a certain child. In addition, the RS selected must also be compatible with the task and the information to be remembered and recalled. It is apparent, however, that until supplemental research is performed to test the effectiveness of new and already existing rehearsal strategies with retarded groups of varying mental ages and environments, the procedure of RS selection relies primarily upon task analysis, the child's level of expressive and receptive language, and systematic trial and error.

Provision of Reinforcing Consequences

As suggested by Ellis (1970), memory in retarded learners may be indirectly influenced by the provision of incentives or reinforcing consequences for recall. Contingent reinforcement for the acquisition and later use of RS not only allows external control over motivation for remembering but also increases the probability that a child will engage in continued use of RS.

Some investigators did not use incentives for subjects attempting to learn a particular RS or the use of organized input (Brown et al., 1973; Hagen & Huntsman, 1971; Spitz, 1972; Taylor et al., 1972; Whitely & Taylor, 1973). Other studies informed subjects beforehand and gave concrete reinforcement for participation in the experiment. Depending upon the subjects, reinforcement varied. For retarded subjects, reinforcement included: 10¢ given for participation (Kellas et al., 1973); 25¢ given per session (Butterfield et al., 1973); or a prize selected by the participants before the experiment and received afterwards. For normal subjects, such things were given: college credit (Lebrato & Ellis, 1974); a toy selected beforehand and received afterwards (Yarmey & Bowen, 1972); points for attending each session with later exchange for various rewards (Brown et al., 1974); candy (Spitz et al., 1972); and candy and 15¢ (Spitz & Webreck, 1972).

A few studies reported the use of contingent reinforcement during RS training besides the praise of the experimenter. A doorbell chime was used to signal correct recall responses in the serial tasks of Butterfield et al. (1973), although it is

TABLE 2.3
Synopsis of Studies Facilitating Recall in Retardates through RS Training

STUDY	SUBJECT: IQ	MA	CA	NUMBER	DIAGNOSIS	ENVIRONMENT	TASK	METHOD OF INPUT ORGANIZATION
1. Butterfield, Wambold, & Belmont (1973)	55–80		13–21	*Exp. 1* = 24 *Exp. II* = 8		Institutionalized	Serial task: 6 letters; self-paced presentation; fixed viewing time (5 sec); recall of probed letter's position.	8 step acquisition retrieval strategy: 1. Construct primacy chunk. 2. Rehearse. 3. Construct recency chunk. 4. Expose probe. 5. Search primary store (recency). 6. Respond if probe found. 7. If not, serial search of secondary store (primacy). 8. Respond.

RESULTS: 1. Retardates did not rehearse spontaneously. Poor recall in short-term memory tasks was due to (a) improperly sequenced rehearsal (STM) techniques, (b) nonrehearsal techniques (attention alone), (c) lack of intercoordination among multiple retrieval strategies, and (d) lack of coordination between multiple retrieval strategies and acquisition strategies.

TABLE 2.3, cont.

STUDY	SUBJECT: IQ	MA	CA	NUMBER	DIAGNOSIS	ENVIRONMENT	TASK	METHOD OF INPUT ORGANIZATION
2. Kellas, Ashcroft, & Johnson (1973)	69	10	16	40	Cultural-Familial	Institutionalized	Serial task: 9 simple pictures of concrete objects; self-paced presentation and viewing time recall of entire series.	Overt and covert rehearsal with cumulative repetition. (Ex. position 4: Name digit at position and repeat positions 1, 2, 3, 4, three times; expose position 5, repeat.)
3. Brown, Campione, Bray, & Wilcox (1973)	*Exp. I* 45 to 69 $\overline{IQ}$ = 58	*Exp. I* 6 to 10 $\overline{MA}$ = 7–5	*Exp. I* 11 to 19 $\overline{CA}$ = 15–9	23		Institutionalized	*Exp. I:* Four pictures, one from each category (food, clothing, animal, vehicle). Experimenter controlled presentation with fixed viewing time (2 sec); recall of specific item exemplifying a probed category.	Overt cumulative repetition of first 3 items with attention given only to the last item.
	Exp. II $\overline{IQ} \geq 100$	$\overline{MA} \geq 15(N)$	$\overline{CA}$ = 15 (N)	58 (N)		9th grade public school	*Exp. II:* Task similar, but difficulty increased for normals.	Same

RESULTS: 2. Retardates did not rehearse spontaneously, but they could process information from secondary memory when trained to use a RS* during input. Significant recall gains resulted when retardates were instructed in RS.

Trained Ss continued to use RS after 2 week intervals. In comparison to the control groups, covert and overt rehearsers had significantly better recall accuracy and greater stimulus exposure duration.

RESULTS: 3. Retardates did not rehearse spontaneously. Retardates and normals of the same CA evidenced similar response patterns when trained to rehearse or when given no training. Both accuracy and latency of recall for RS subjects were unaffected by number of items in each category. For Ss not receiving RS training, accuracy and speed of recall declined as the number of category items increased. Significant differences resulted in recall accuracy and speed between those trained and untrained in RS.

TABLE 2.3, cont.

STUDY	SUBJECT:IQ	MA	CA	NUMBER	DIAGNOSIS	ENVIRONMENT	TASK	METHOD OF INPUT ORGANIZATION
4. Brown, Campione, & Murphy (1974)	54 to 68 $\overline{IQ}$ = 61	5.7 to 10 $\overline{MA}$ = 7.9	11 to 19 $\overline{CA}$ = 15.7	20		Institutionalized	Same as *Exp. I* in Brown et al., 1973.	Same as *Exp. I* in Brown et al., 1973.

RESULTS: 4. Eight out of 10 experimental Ss maintained RS usage (without instructions to do so) 6 months after original training terminated. Significant recall differences were maintained for RS-trained subjects.

STUDY	SUBJECT:IQ	MA	CA	NUMBER	DIAGNOSIS	ENVIRONMENT	TASK	METHOD OF INPUT ORGANIZATION
5. Taylor, Josberger, & Knowlton (1972)	$\overline{IQ}$ = 70.2		10 to 15 $\overline{CA}$ = 12.6	24	No evidence of organic impairment.	EMR public school special classes; lower-middle, urban and rural sample	Paired associates. Pairs and triplets of concrete norms read aloud to Ss at rate of 10 sec per pair. Recall was tested at same rate by giving S stimulus word with a response of the associated noun.	Imagery condition: Ss instructed to make mental pictures of objects in pair or triplet doing something together. Verbal elaboration condition: Ss instructed to make up & verbalize a sentence about the 2 or 3 nouns.

RESULTS: 5. Both imagery and verbal elaboration RS resulted in significantly greater PA recall than a simple repetition control procedure. No significant differ- ences occurred between the 2 types of elaboration.

33

TABLE 2.3, cont.

STUDY	SUBJECT:IQ	MA	CA	NUMBER	DIAGNOSIS	ENVIRONMENT	TASK	METHOD OF INPUT ORGANIZATION
6. Whitely & Taylor (1973)	$\overline{IQ}$ = 68		12.6 to 16.3 $\overline{CA}$ = 14.8	40		EMR public schools special classes; inner-city urban sample.	Paired associates same as Taylor et al., 1972.	Overt verbal elaboration: same as Taylor et al., 1972. Covert verbal elaboration: Ss trained to overtly elaborate on PA tasks were then required to covertly elaborate.

RESULTS: 6. When given brief elaboration training at an overt level, later elaboration at either overt or covert levels resulted in significantly greater PA recall than the control group, who were not permitted to overtly verbalize their elaborations during training or testing.

STUDY	SUBJECT:IQ	MA	CA	NUMBER	DIAGNOSIS	ENVIRONMENT	TASK	METHOD OF INPUT ORGANIZATION
7. Lebrato & Ellis (1974)	*Exp. I* $\overline{IQ}$ = 54 $IQ \geq 100$		$\overline{CA}$ = 18 (MR) $\overline{CA}$ = 22 (N)	24 (MR) 24 (N)		Institutionalized (MR) College students (N)	*All 3 experiments:* Paired associates: number-noun pairs presented aloud; time between presentations subject paced; recall of appropriate response word for a given number.	*Exp. I:* Mnemonic Ss learned *one–bun* rhyme with verbal instructions only in the use of an imagery mnemonic RS. *Exp. II & III:* Same as in *Exp. I* except mnemonic Ss were given RS training via pictures and verbal instructions.
	Exp. II $\overline{IQ}$ = 65 $IQ \geq 100$		$\overline{CA}$ = 25 (MR) $\overline{CA}$ = 23.4 (N)	24 (MR) 24 (N)		Institutionalized (MR) College students (N)		
	Exp. III $\overline{IQ}$ = 68 $IQ \geq 100$		$\overline{CA}$ = 18.6 (MR) $\overline{CA}$ = 20.5 (N)	24 (MR) 24 (N)		EMR public school special classes (MR); College students (N)		

RESULTS: 7. *Exp. 1:* Retardates did not profit from imagery mnemonic training. *Exp. II & III:* Imagery mnemonic training given with verbal instructions accompanied by visual aids significantly aided the learning and/or memory of retarded persons. Pictures used during training (a) resulted in imagery mediation for MR Ss; and (b) yielded later independent creation of visual images. When MR Ss used mnemonic imagery, their recall performance closely approached the recall level of normals not taught this strategy.

TABLE 2.3, cont.

STUDY	SUBJECT:IQ	MA	CA	NUMBER	DIAGNOSIS	ENVIRONMENT	TASK	METHOD OF INPUT ORGANIZATION
8. Hagen & Huntsman (1971)	*Exp. I* 46–79 (MR) 99–107 (N)	3–10 to 8–9 (MR) 4–2 to 9–0 (N)	8–9 to 11–4 (MR) 4–2 to 9–0 (N)	108	*Exp. I* Middle & lower-middle socioeconomic class	*Exp. I* 47 from EMR and TMR* special classes; 14 from private nursery school; 47 from regular classes	*Exp. I & II:* The central task consisted of recalling the position of a probed picture in a series of 3–5 cards. Cards consisted of pairs of pictures: one animal (central) one household object (incidental). Incidental task consisted of matching the animal picture which had been paired with the appropriate household object picture. The memory span task consisted of recalling the position of every animal in a series of 3–5 cards. Only animals were pictured on these stimulus cards.	*Exp. I & II:* The child's ability to verbally label all the animal stimuli was tested but no formal RS was taught nor were children requested to use a RS.
	Exp. II $\overline{\text{IQ}}$ = 77.8	$\overline{\text{MA}}$ = 7.8	*Exp. II* $\overline{\text{CA}}$ = 10.6	23	*Exp. II* Inner-city	*Exp. II* Institutionalized		

RESULTS: 8. *Exp. I:* Selective attention improved with MA and retardates performed as well as normals of equal MA. Ease in providing labels when asked was positively related to performance on central-recall tasks. Training in certain skills of labeling should increase recall for low MA retardates. *Exp. II:* The institutionalized MR Ss were less able to selectively attend to the control stimuli than either the normal Ss or the MR subjects living at home. Therefore the attention deficiency was confirmed for institutionalized retardates only. NOTE: Subjects were divided into 8 groups (normals and retardates) at 4 levels of MA and 2 levels of CA with resulting variations in IQ.

* RS = Rehearsal strategy
TMR = Trainable mentally retarded

35

unclear if this procedure extended into retention testing as well as RS training. In the serial task of geometric shapes (Jacobs & Foshee, 1971), subjects who correctly located the probe stimulus were reinforced with a red light and candy and received a penny at the end of each session for every correct response.

Implications for Teaching

Because of the frequently cited problems of motivation in retardates (Zigler, 1973), it is highly probable that RS acquisition and longevity might be increased if both the teacher and experimenter attended closely to reinforcement during RS training and usage. Not only should the schedule be manipulated so that continuous reinforcement is gradually faded into leaner schedules for long-term maintenance, but also the reinforcers themselves must be more individually determined.

Continuing along the line of Flavell's (1970) idea that children learn the value of present planfulness toward increasing the likelihood of future success, the teacher might sensitize the retarded student to the environmental reinforcers available for good memory, such as admiration by an employer for not forgetting a task, by parents for academic recall in school, and by peers for remembering names and appointments.

Summary

A review of research yields an abundance of support for the postulates produced by Ellis's findings. There is evidence to support the following:

1. the two-process theory of short-term memory
2. a predictable deficiency in the secondary memory of retardates when compared to normals of equal CA
3. Induced active rehearsal, pre-organized input, and/or pretraining in acquisition-retrieval strategies all improve the secondary memory of retardates who (a) are from institutional settings or special classrooms, (b) range in age from pre-adolescence to adulthood, and (c) have high-moderate to mild levels of retardation.

Although RS retention has been documented (Brown et al., 1974; Kellas et al., 1973), the durability of RS in retardates is still questionable. In addition, the ability for retardates to generalize RS across tasks remains unknown, i.e., it remains unclear whether or not "planfulness" can be taught to retarded persons through the practice of specific RS instruction. Finally, the use of RS in-struction and the practice of input organization (redundancy and external emphasis) as methods to facilitate retardate memory in classroom settings, although still somewhat hypothetical, are highly warranted.

References

Anders, T. R. Short-term memory for serially presented supraspan information in nonretarded and mentally retarded individuals. *American Journal of Mental Deficiency*, 1971, *75*, 571–578.

Atkinson, R. C., & Shiffrin, R. M. *Mathematical models for memory and learning* (Technical Report No. 79). Stanford, Calif.: Stanford University, Institute for Mathematical Studies in the Social Sciences, 1965.

Baumeister, A. A., & Kellas, G. Process variables in the paired-associate learning of retardates. In N. R. Ellis (Ed.), *International review of research in mental retardation* (Vol. 5). New York: Academic Press, 1971.

Belmont, J. M. Long-term memory in mental retardation. In N. R. Ellis (Ed.), *International review of research in mental retardation* (Vol. 1). New York: Academic Press, 1966.

Belmont, J. M., & Butterfield, E. C. Learning strategies as determinants of memory deficiencies. *Cognitive Psychology*, 1971, *2*, 411–420. (a)

Belmont, J. M., & Butterfield, E. C. What the development of short-term memory is. *Human Development*, 1971, *14*, 236–248. (b)

Bower, G. A. A multicomponent theory of memory trace. In K. W. Spence & J. T. Spence (Eds.), *The psychology of learning and motivation: Advances in research and theory*. New York: Academic Press, 1967.

Broadbent, D. E. *Perception and communication*. New York: Macmillan, 1958.

Brown, A. L., Campione, J. C., Bray, N. W., & Wilcox, B. L. Keeping track of changing variables: Effects of rehearsal training and rehearsal prevention in normal and retarded adolescents. *Journal of Experimental Psychology*, 1973, *101*, 123–131.

Brown, A. L., Campione, J. C., & Murphy, M. D. Keeping track of changing variables: Long-term retention of a trained rehearsal strategy by retarded adolescents. *American Journal of Mental Deficiency*, 1974, *78*, 446–453.

Bugelski, B. R. Images as mediators in one-trial paired-associate learning. II: Self-timing in successive lists. *Journal of Experimental Psychology*, 1968, *77*, 328–334.

Bugelski, B. R., Kidd, E., & Segmen, J. The image as a mediator in one-trial paired-associate learning. *Journal of Experimental Psychology*, 1968, *76*, 69–73.

Burnett, E. *Influence of classroom environment on word learning of retarded with high and low activity level.* Unpublished doctoral dissertation, George Peabody College for Teachers, 1962.

Butterfield, E. C., & Belmont, J. M. Relations of storage and retrieval strategies as short-term memory processes. *Journal of Experimental Psychology*, 1971, *89*, 319–328.

Butterfield, E. C., Wambold, C., & Belmont, J. M. On the theory and practice of improving short-term memory. *American Journal of Mental Deficiency*, 1973, *77*, 654–669.

Campione, J. C., & Brown, A. L. The effects of contextual changes and degree of component mastery on transfer in training. In H. W. Reese (Ed.), *Advances in child development and behavior* (Vol. 9). New York: Academic Press, forthcoming.

Cruickshank, W., Bentzen, F. A., Ratzeburg, R. H., & Tannhauser, M. *A teaching method for brain-injured and hyperactive children.* New York: Syracuse University Press, 1961.

Danner, F. W., & Taylor, A. M. *Pictures and relational imagery training in children's learning* (Research Report No. 29). Minneapolis, Minn.: University of Minnesota's Research, Development, and Demonstration Center in Education of Handicapped Children, December, 1971.

Ellis, N. R. The stimulus trace and behavioral inadequacy. In N. R. Ellis (Ed.), *Handbook of mental deficiency.* New York: McGraw-Hill, 1963.

Ellis, N. R. Memory processes in retardates and normals. In N. R. Ellis (Ed.), *International review of research in mental retardation* (Vol. 4). New York: Academic Press, 1970.

Ellis, N. R., & Hope, R. Memory processes and the serial position curve. *Journal of Experimental Psychology*, 1968, *77*, 613–619.

Engelmann, S., & Carnine, D. *Distar arithmetic: An instructional system.* Chicago: Science Research Associates, 1970.

Fernald, G. M. *Remedial techniques in basic school subjects.* New York: McGraw-Hill, 1943.

Flavell, J. H. Developmental studies of mediated memory. In H. W. Reese & L. P. Lipsett (Eds.), *Advances in child development and behavior* (Vol. 5). New York: Academic Press, 1970.

Hagen, J. W. Strategies for remembering. In S. Farnham-Diggory (Ed.), *Information processing in children.* New York: Academic Press, 1972.

Hagen, J. W., & Huntsman, J. Selective attention in mental retardates. *Developmental Psychology*, 1971, *5*, 151–160.

Hagen, J. W., & Kingsley, P. R. Labeling effects in short-term memory. *Child Development*, 1968, *39*, 113–121.

Hagen, J. W., & West, R. F. The effects of a pay-off matrix on selective attention. *Human Development*, 1970, *13*, 43–52.

Hebb, D. O. *The organization of behavior.* New York: Wiley, 1949.

Hirsch, E. *Training of visualizing ability by the kinesthetic method of teaching reading.* Unpublished master's thesis, University of Illinois, 1963.

Hodes, M. R. *First experiences.* New York: McGraw-Hill, 1972.

Jacobs, J. W., & Foshee, D. P. Use of the von Restorff effect to condition rehearsal in retarded children. *American Journal of Mental Deficiency*, 1971, *76*, 313–318.

Kellas, G., Ashcroft, M. H., & Johnson, N. S. Rehearsal processes in the short-term memory performance of mildly retarded adolescents. *American Journal of Mental Deficiency*, 1973, *77*, 670–679.

Kingsley, P. R., & Hagen, J. W. Induced versus spontaneous rehearsal in short-term memory in nursery school children. *Developmental Psychology*, 1969, *1*, 40–46.

Kirk, S. A. *Educating exceptional children* (2nd ed.). Boston: Houghton Mifflin, 1972.

Language master. Chicago: Bell & Howell Audio Visual Products Divison, 1963.

Lebrato, M. T., & Ellis, N. R. Imagery mediation in paired-associate learning by retarded and non-retarded subjects. *American Journal of Mental Deficiency*, 1974, *78*, 704–713.

Neisser, U. *Cognitive psychology.* New York: Appleton, 1967.

Paivio, A. Effects of imagery instructions and concreteness of memory pegs in a mnemonic system. *Proceedings of the 76th Annual Convention of the American Psychological Association*, 1968, *3*, 77–78.

Rost, K. J. Academic achievement of brain-injured children in isolation. *Exceptional Children*, 1967, *34*, 125–126.

Rowland, P. T. *Beginning to read, write, and listen.* Boston: Boston Educational Research Co., 1971.

Spitz, H. H. Effects of redundancy level and presentation method on the paired associate learning of educable retardates, third graders and eight graders. *Journal of Experimental Psychology*, 1972, *95*, 164–170.

Spitz, H. H. Consolidating facts into the schematized learning and memory system of educable retardates. In N. R. Ellis (Ed.), *International review of research in mental retardation* (Vol. 6). New York: Academic Press, 1973.

Spitz, H. H., Goettler, D. R., & Webreck, C. A. Effects of two types of redundancy on visual digit span performance of retardates and varying aged normals. *Developmental Psychology*, 1972, *6*, 92–103.

Spitz, H. H., & Webreck, C. A. Effects of spontaneous vs. externally-cued learning on the permanent storage of a schema by retardates. *American Journal of Mental Deficiency*, 1972, *77*, 163–168.

Strauss, A. A., & Lehtinen, L. *Psychopathology of the brain-injured child.* New York: Grune & Stratton, 1947.

Taylor, A. M., Josberger, M., & Knowlton, J. Q. Mental elaboration and learning in EMR children. *American Journal of Mental Deficiency*, 1972, *77*, 69–76.

Taylor, S. E. *Listening* (What Research Says to the Teacher Series No. 29). Washington, D.C.: National Education Association, 1964.

Taylor, S. E., Frackenpohl, H., & Pettee, J. L. *Grade level norms for the components of the fundamental reading skill* (Research and Information Bulletin No. 3). Huntington, N.Y.: Educational Development Laboratories, 1960.

Trace, A. S., & Hughes, A. Open Court basic readers. La Salle, Ill.: Open Court, 1963.

von Restorff. Hedwig uber die virkung von Bereichsbilduagen im Spurenfeld. *Psychologir Forschung*, 1933, *18*, 299–342. (Ideas in translation published in "Use of the von Restorff Effect to Condition Rehearsal in Retarded Children" by J. W. Jacobs and D. P. Foshee, *American Journal of Mental Deficiency*, 1971, *76*, 313–318.)

Waugh, N. C., & Norman, D. A. Primary memory. *Psychological Review*, 1965, *72*, 89–104.

Whitely, S. E., & Taylor, A. M. Covert verbalization and the continued production of effective elaborations by EMR children. *American Journal of Mental Deficiency*, 1973, *78*, 193–198.

Wilt, M. A study of teacher awareness of listening as a factor in elementary education. *Journal of Educational Research*, 1950, *43*, 626–636.

Wisenberg, S. A. Incidental and delayed retention of relevant and incidental information from a prose passage presented aurally to trainable mental retardates (Doctoral dissertation, Michigan State University, 1971). *Dissertation Abstracts International*, 1971, *32*, 263A. (University Microfilms No. 71–18, 332)

Yarmey, A. D., & Bowen, N. V. The role of imagery in incidental learning of educable retarded and normal children. *Journal of Experimental Child Psychology*, 1972, *14*, 303–312.

Zeaman, D., & House, B. J. An attentional theory of retardate discrimination learning. In N. R. Ellis (Ed.), *Handbook of mental deficiency*. New York: McGraw-Hill, 1963.

Zigler, E. Mental retardation: Current issues and approaches. In L. Hoffman & M. Hoffman (Eds.), *Review of child development research* (Vol. 2). New York: Russell Sage Foundation, 1966.

Zigler, E. The retarded child as a whole person. In D. K. Routh (Ed.), *The experimental psychology of mental retardation*. Chicago: Aldine, 1973.

3

Input Organization

Spitz's Theory

The effect of input organization on recall is now receiving considerable attention. The extensive work of Herman H. Spitz has stirred much of the interest in this topic. He advocates (1963, 1966, 1973) that compared to normals, mentally retarded individuals have more difficulty organizing input material, a lack which detrimentally effects their retrieval processes. According to Spitz (1966), poorly organized material is more difficult to retrieve than organized material. In the process of developing and empirically testing his theoretical positions, Spitz has pursued answers to many questions which are basic to our understanding of how retardates best learn. For example, preference for stimulus symmetry, clustering processes, and the effects of preorganized stimuli and redundancy on the learning of retardates are a few of the areas he and his colleagues have investigated.

This examination of the input organization theory is split into two sections. In section one Spitz's relation to gestalt theory, his views of the influence of input organization on learning, and the structure of his learning and memory system are explored. In section two the results and teaching implications of research branching from Spitz's theory are presented.

Spitz's Theory

Gestalt Roots

ORGANIZATIONAL PRINCIPLES. Although Spitz's (1963) discussions of his early work deal with the field theory framework, a close inspection of his writings reveal roots in gestalt psychology. Since the term *field theory* remains nebulous (Estes, 1970), *gestalt psychology* is a more functional term when discussing Spitz's early work. Estes (1970) summarizes the gestalt view of learning: "an individual's performance is determined largely by the way in which he perceives his environment, and that perception is in turn determined by organizational principles having to do with goodness of figure, perceptual closure, relations between figure and ground, and the like" (p. 132). Estes's statement highlights the importance that gestaltists place on organizational principles.

Marx and Hillix (1963) note that the best-known empirical statements from gestalt psychology are the principles of organization derived from the studies of visual perception. Some of the primary gestalt principles deal with the proximity, similarity, isolation, and meaning of visual stimuli. Gestaltists maintain that an organism's inherent physical processes are the source of the perception. Figures which have regularity, symmetry, and simplicity are considered "good" figures by gestaltists and are the ones more easily perceived and recalled (Koffka, 1935). Moreover, Spitz (1966) notes that self-distributing systems, such as the central nervous system (CNS) do better with organized than disorganized states. Organization in this framework is viewed as the tendency to group, to make symmetrical, and to produce harmony. Gestaltists refer to the harmonic flow of the natural systems for support of their theory. Examples include the organized ripple of water from the impact of a pebble and the emergence of a spherical shape (smallest possible surface is a sphere) from a child's bubble pipe (Spitz 1966).

CORTICAL SATIATION. Spitz's (1966) reference to the CNS as a self-distributing system underscores the importance that gestaltists placed on physiological processes. Originally developed by Kohler and Wallach (1944), the cortical satiation theory sprang from a physiological base and yielded some of the most prominent gestalt research. This theory refers to a condition characterized by the buildup of cortical inhibition consequent upon continued stimulation. A major feature of this theory is the concept of *isomorphism*, a structural and functional identity between the organism's experiences and the physiological process underlying these experiences. As Spitz (1963) notes, "This principle of psychophysical isomorphism further holds that the distribution and structure of the stimulus, and the functional interrelationship between parts and wholes, correspond to the distribution, structure, and functional interrelationship of its representation in the brain" (p. 20). As the stimulus approaches its full representation in the brain, chemical and electrical activities in the specific brain area react to formulate the representation. The development and maintenance of this representation cause the respective cells to become impermeable to other activity. Since the cells in the specific brain area are not available for processing new stimuli, the term *satiation* was used to describe the condition of isomorphism (Spitz, 1963).

PART-WHOLE RELATIONSHIP. Another major tenet of gestalt psychology involves the part-whole relationship. Marx and Hillix (1963) capture the essence of this relation: "The whole dominates the parts and constitutes the primary reality . . . the

unit most profitable to use in analysis. The whole is not the sum, or the product, or any simple function of its parts, but a field whose character depends upon all of itself" (p. 192). Thus, gestaltists view the whole as a viable component for investigation and believe the study of molecular parts is of lesser importance than the study of wholes. Parts are considered to be interdependent, but they collectively (not additively) determine the nature of the whole structure. For example, the parts of a building combine to form a building only when they are systematically arranged and connected. Nonetheless, Spitz (1966) admits that gestaltists do recognize the existence of summative distributions, but the importance of distributions is minimal; they are not part of the physical systems, i.e., central nervous system. In essence, gestaltists examine both part and whole parameters which aid understanding of the organizational agents of the whole. For example, gestalt researchers frequently manipulate various dimensions of a stimulus (e.g., length of a specific line in a stimulus field) and study the organizational influences that the manipulation has on the perception of the whole.

LEARNING. As mentioned earlier, gestaltists view the physiological processes as highly organized, self-distributing systems which process stimuli into organized patterns. Gestaltists discuss learning in terms of problem solving, which they view as involving the restructuring of the perceptual field. Thus, the more input stimuli are organized, the more the perceptual restructuring task (problem solving) is facilitated.

GESTALT THEORY AND MENTAL RETARDATION. The most conspicuous early research regarding the gestalt principles was conducted years ago by Lewin (1935) and Kounin (1941), who developed the rigidity hypothesis of mental retardation. They refer to brain areas as *psychical regions* which normally become differentiated with increasing age. Lewin and Kounin suggest that retardates' psychical regions become less differentiated than those of normals, and this reduced level of differentiation results in perservering or stereotyped behaviors. Moreover, Lewin and Kounin claim that boundaries between the retardates' psychical regions are more rigid than those of normals. In essence, they claim that retardates would have a difficult time shifting from one cognitive task to another if the switch simultaneously required a shift from one psychical region to another, e.g., switching from a verbal task to a visual sorting task.

Zigler (1962) conducted a series of investigations to examine the rigidity hypothesis. On the basis of his findings, he extensively criticizes the rigidity hypothesis. He formulated a motivation theory to account for persevering behavior. (A description of his work and its implications are more fully discussed in Chapter 6 under social learning theory.)

Spitz (1963) reviewed studies which examined gestalt principles in relation to mental retardation. In this review the concept of cortical satiation tended to yield the most meaningful research. As reported by Estes (1970):

> In a number of studies, Spitz and his associate have found support for their hypothesis that mentally retarded individuals are slower than normals in both the buildup and decay of cortical satiation as reflected in, for example, speed of locating hidden figures, rate of reversing reversible figures, and optimal intervals for successive masking in tachistoscopic perception (Spitz & Blackman, 1959; Spitz, 1959; Spitz, 1969). (p. 133)

On the basis of his review, Spitz (1963) proposed four postulates regarding mental retardation and gestalt theory. In comparison with normals, mentally retarded persons:

1. Have cortical cells which, when stimulated, take longer to respond.
2. Once stimulation has occurred, the return of their cortical cells to their normal state takes longer.
3. Have more difficulty in modifying established cortical patterns into new patterns as a result of different stimuli.
4. Have less spread of activity from stimulated cortical cells to the surrounding cortical field.

It is apparent that the early postulates generated from gestalt theory are based on physiological factors (cortical cell activity) which are difficult to research. Estes (1970) notes that the gestalt-based postulates cannot be investigated until they are detailed enough to link the cortical cell phenomena to specific behavior. In his review of 1966, Spitz reformulates some of the gestalt principles in terms compatible with learning theory and amenable to empirical investigation. This new approach resulted in the formulation of empirically testable positions and led to research pertinent to education.

Influence of Input Organization on Learning

STIMULUS AND RESPONSE SYMMETRY. Spitz (1966) began his review by positing that retardates oftentimes view the world as chaotic and poorly classified and thus are more attracted and aided by simplicity and symmetry than normals. Spitz reviewed studies (Hoats, Miller, & Spitz, 1963; House, 1964; Hyman, 1966; Spitz, 1964; Spitz & Hoats, 1961) which compared the responses (preference, recall) of normals and retardates to figures which varied in the qualities of simplicity and symmetry. The findings from these studies confirmed Spitz's position; they suggested that middle- and high-grade retardates are attracted to symmetry and that its presence can improve learning and recall.

He continued to examine the retardates' quest for these qualities by examining their response patterns. After reviewing several studies (Berenbaum & Aderman, 1964; Gerjuoy & Gerjuoy, 1964; Gerjuoy & Winters, 1965; Winters & Gerjuoy, 1966), Spitz concluded that retardates have a tendency to show perseveration and alternation response patterns.

ORGANIZATION OF INPUT. Spitz's investigations and review of the phenomenon of how retardates' organize input represent the most widely recognized areas of his work. This line of investigation was triggered when Spitz began to seek answers to questions such as, "When retardates demonstrate a learning deficiency, how much of this deficiency stems from a short-term memory (Ellis, 1970) or from a deficient ability to organize the material?" Spitz (1966) discusses his concern regarding organizational skills in the following passage:

> It is clearly possible that retardates possess the physical ability to remember as well as normals but because of a deficiency in categorizing the mass of incoming data into a few large chunks, they are simply overloaded . . . . The question is not whether or not retardates group or organize materials, but rather under what conditions, in what manner, and how efficiently they display this capacity. Retardates may include too few stimuli in a category, or too many . . . . They may form concepts more readily on a concrete or functional basis than on a higher level, abstract basis. If they do, in fact, categorize inefficiently, they must inhabit an extremely chaotic world. (p. 36)

Standard free verbal recall has been used as a convenient technique for examining grouping or clustering phenomenon. Bousfield (1953) and Tulving (1962) demonstrated that when normal adults recalled lists of words or objects, they remembered them in clusters associated with meaningful categories. Clustering increased with practice in free recall. Also, they found that the degree of clustering and amount recalled were positively correlated. These findings prompted Spitz (1966) to hypothesize that repetition is important because it provides the individual with an opportunity to group or organize the material.

Some early studies which investigated the relationship between recall and clustering to IQ showed pictures of familiar objects. In these studies little variation occurred in the recall and cluster performances of subjects who varied on IQ. Later, when verbal stimuli were introduced, it was discovered that educable retardates recalled and clustered less than normals of similar CA. When retarded and normal individuals were equated on MA, the differences in recall diminished, but the retardates continued to exhibit less clustering when the clustering performances were corrected for "categorical intrusions." Categorical intrusions occurred when a word was recalled that was not in the original list but belonged to the same meaningful categories as words which were in the list.

Spitz (1966) performed and reported on research which revealed that college students demonstrated superior recall and had higher tendencies to group and cluster than did CA-equivalent normal and retarded individuals. Based on the assumption that a causal relationship exists between recall and clustering, Spitz hypothesized that recall in retardates would be improved by using strategies which prompted them to do more clustering. Clustering was encouraged by presenting items grouped into meaningful categories and requesting recall of items by categories. Spitz discussed research which indicated that both techniques led to large increases in the recall performance of educable retarded children. These results provided further support for Spitz's position.

Next, Spitz (1966) posited that organizing does occur in paired-associate learning but it is not as obvious as the organizational strategies examined in free recall tasks. After examining studies (Cantor & Ryan, 1962; Iscoe & Semler, 1964; Jensen, 1965) concerning the interaction of meaningfulness (or difficulty) of material and IQ as predictors of performance, Spitz thought that retardates

seemed deficient in the use of mnemonic devices to facilitate recall. Based on this theory, Jensen and Rohwer's (1963a, 1963b) study produced substantial increases in retardates' rate of acquisition by instructing them to form sentences relating the stimulus and response of paired-associate items. Similarly, Spitz (1966) found that recall of digits was improved by instructions to group the digits.

In 1966 Spitz culminated his work by placing the role of input organization within the perspective of the following simplified learning paradigm:

> When a person learns an item, the process can be broken up—in an oversimplified manner—as follows:
>
> a. Arouse (person is alerted)
> b. Attend (attention is given to specific stimulus)
> c. Input (file into appropriate "hold" area)
> d. Hold (hold for permanent storage)
> e. Recall (retrieve material from temporary file if necessary)
> f. Storage (put into appropriate permanent file)
> g. Recall (retrieve material from permanent file if necessary)
>
> Retardates, and normals, may lose information anywhere along the line. Other workers have emphasized the retardate's deficit in . . . areas (a), (b), and (d). The present paper has emphasized area (c), input, and specifically the organization of the material as it enters for filing. (Spitz, 1966, pp. 52–53)

In retrospect, the placing of his theory within the learning paradigm established a framework for Spitz's forthcoming paper 7 years later. The paper, titled "Consolidating Facts into the Schematized Learning and Memory System of Educable Retardates," features an expanded learning paradigm and focuses on techniques aimed at facilitating the organizational skills of retardates.

A Schematized Learning and Memory System

Spitz (1973) uses some of the the major constructs from Atkinson and Shiffrin's (1968) memory theory to formulate an idealized memory system. The basic elements of the system are input, storage, and retrieval.

INPUT. The input stage of memory paradigm encompasses several elements. As illustrated in Figure 3.1, the input stage begins with the presentation of a stimulus (or stimuli). Once the stimulus is presented, the emphasis shifts to attention processes. Attention is complex and cannot be viewed as a simple isolated event. For example, associations regarding specific stimuli established from past experiences influence attention processes (Fisher & Zeaman, 1973). Also, numerous stimuli can simultaneously compete for attention.

A popularized view of attention is formulated by Neisser (1967). He suggests that attention includes two levels. The first level involves scanning the stimuli and the second level consists of focusing attention on a particular aspect of the material. Whereas the results of studies conducted by Spitz (1969) and Winters and Gerjuoy (1969) suggest that retardates have difficulty scanning material, the results of research conducted by Zeaman and House (1963) suggest that retarded individuals have difficulty focusing on the relevant dimensions of a stimulus.

Spitz's paradigm (1973) includes sensory registration. If one embraces Broadbent's (1958) theory of attention, sensory registration is one of the advanced stages of attending. Regardless of one's theoretical position, sensory registration involves the time that a stimulus lasts beyond the stimulus exposure. This phenomenon is referred to as the *icon* or the *poststimulus trace* and its duration is particularly dependent on the brightness and duration of the stimulus (Spitz, 1973). Spitz (1973) notes, "there appears to be no retardate deficit in the duration of the icon; in fact, it is possible that retardates have a more lasting icon which could *interfere* with rapid input of stimuli" (p. 152).

STORAGE. Storage is characterized by two levels of memory: short-term (STM) and long-term (LTM). According to Spitz (1973), digit span is one of the oldest measures of STM. Using 90% correct as criterion for digit-span recall, Spitz reviewed 12 studies from 1916 to 1973. The review includes only studies in which the exposure time per digit was approximately 1 second. The mode of presentation included auditory and visual modes, and the responses were either written or spoken. The results of the review indicated that the digit-span channel capacity for normals is six plus or minus one digit and for educable retardates it is three to four digits. These results should be tempered by the fact that the normal subjects in the studies reviewed by Spitz were older (mostly college students) than the retarded subjects ($\overline{CA} = 11.79$–15.65 years). However, Spitz examined *Wechsler Subtest* scores of 183 educable retardates at E. R. Johnstone Training and Research Center (CA = 13–19 years) and similarly concluded that their digit-span capacity was three to four (90% criterion). Spitz notes that this difference in immediate recall between normals and retardates was not great and could not be relied on to account for their respective general performance differences.

Spitz (1973) refers to LTM within a temporal framework of minutes, i.e., information recalled several minutes after presentation. Spitz notes that Wallace, Turner, and Perkins (1957), using a paired-associate task, were unable to determine the upper limit of human storage with normals. Moreover, Spitz concludes that once the material enters the system the storage capacity of educable retardates is not badly impaired.

RETRIEVAL. Free recall is a measure used to assess the last element of Spitz's paradigm—retrieval. Gerjuoy and Spitz (1966) report that the unaided free recall of retardates is poor. For example they showed that when words were presented randomly, retarded individuals recalled by the fifth trial only about 11 or 12 words, compared to 17 by college students. However, when the

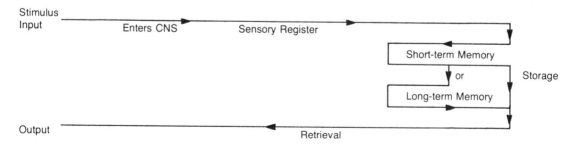

FIGURE 3.1
Simplified Memory System.

words were presented in clusters and requested by category names, the retardates recalled 17 words.

Although Spitz (1973) couches his position within a trichotomized schemata of memory, it is important to identify the primary thrust of his theory. In his discussion of retrieval processes, he highlights the essence of his position in the following passage:

> The importance of input organization for educable retardates is not in getting the material into storage; almost all of the material, apparently, will be stored. But it must be stored in a form which makes it more easily accessible . . . . In my view, a primary difference between educable retardates and normals is the speed and manner in which retardates scan and selectively organize the material for storage. Chaotic input makes for chaotic retrieval. (pp. 157–158)

Spitz (1973) continues his paper by reporting research on the effects of redundancy on the recall of educable retardates and normals. The next section of this chapter reviews these studies and others generated from Spitz's work, with an emphasis on practical teaching implications.

Input Organization Research and Teaching Implications

A brief introduction to measures and tasks commonly used in the input organization studies follows. The measures include free recall, clustering, and subjective organization. The tasks include memory-span and paired-associate tasks; all tasks involve recall in the experimental setting.

Free recall is a procedure which shows how subjects use organizational strategies. The examiner instructs the participant to recall the task items without any aids or constraints on order. Usually the free recall task has a fixed time limit, but on occasions the participant is untimed. Then a score is computed by adding up how many correct items were recalled. In addition, the order of the subject's recall is recorded from trial to trial so that the examiner can study the subject's organizational strategies.

Clustering scores represent an index of organizational processes and are included in most of the studies. Palmer (1974) reports that *clustering* is usually defined "as the occurrence of sequences of related items in recall following their random presentation in learning" (p. 454). Bousfield and

Bousfield (1966) developed a formula for computing the amount of clustering above chance. In their formula, $CL = OCL - ECL$, *CL* represents clustering above chance, *OCL* represents observed clustering, and *ECL* represents expected clustering. Thus, chance clustering is subtracted from observed clustering to produce a clustering above chance measure. The components of the formula are computed in the following manner:

$$OCL = \text{the number of occasions in any recall trial when any item is followed by another from the same category}$$

$$ECL = \frac{M_1^2 + M_2^2 + \ldots M_x^2}{n} - 1$$

In the ECL equation $M_1 + M_2 + M_x$ are the number of items recalled from the various categories, and n is the total number of items recalled. Finally, some investigators totally excluded perseveration-type responses and categorical intrusions (in which the word is not presented but is in a respective category) from the computations; other investigators did not, however, count them as correct responses but reported the frequency of their occurrence.

Herriot and Cox (1971) report that subjective organization occurs when participants impose their own organization on seemingly unrelated items. In comparing clustering to subjective organization, Herriot and Cox note that both are order measures and not item-number measures, i.e., they reflect the number of items recalled consecutively, irrespective of the total number of items recalled. Herriot and Cox state:

> In the clustering measure, the co-occurrence of items from the same category in a given recall trial is noted; in the subjective organization measure, the number of occasions when two items occurring consecutively on Trial N also occur consecutively and in the same order on Trial N + 1. In both cases, the inference of organization by subjects is possible because of the random order of items in input. (p. 702)

Subjective organization is calculated by means of a formula developed by Bousfield and Bousfield (1966). The formula is: $SO = OITR - EITR$. *SO* is subjective organization, *OITR* is observed intertrial repetitions (one item following another in recall from one trial to another), and *EITR* is expected intertrial repetitions. The components of the formula are computed in the following manner:

OITR = sum of the number of occasions when any two items occur together in the same order on successive trials

$$EITR = \frac{C(C-1)}{hk}$$

In the EITR formula, C is the number of correctly recalled items common to both trials (Trial N and Trial N + 1), h is the number of items correctly recalled on Trial N, and k is the number of items correctly recalled on Trial N + 1.

Memory-span tasks involve presenting stimuli, removing the stimuli, and instructing the participant to recall the stimuli. The reviewed studies which follow are grouped according to the type of stimuli used in the respective memory-span tasks: digit items, word items, picture items, and objects.

In addition to the memory-span tasks, paired-associate tasks were used in several of the studies. A paired-associate task involves the presentation of paired items (e.g., *3–A, 2–B, 4–C*) followed by the presentation of the stimulus portion (number) of each pair with instructions to recall the item (letter) that goes with each of the respective stimulus items. For example, the pairs *3–A, 2–B,* and *4–C* would be presented, removed, and then the *3, 2,* and *4* would be displayed and the participant would be instructed to supply the item (letter) that goes with each number. The studies in which paired-associate tasks were used are the last group of studies reviewed.

The following studies are a representative sample of the research generated by Spitz's work in recent years (1966–1975). In each section the respective studies are highlighted in a table and discussed in text.

Memory-Span Studies Using Digits

MACMILLAN'S STUDIES. MacMillan (1970a) selected 60 EMR and 60 MA-equivalent non-retarded children and compared their use of input organization on a digit-span task. He questioned whether variables not discussed by Spitz facilitated the recall scores of retarded individuals, in particular, the oral response at the time of stimulus presentation. Spitz (1966) required an oral response of his subjects at the time of the stimulus presentation and MacMillan duplicated Spitz's study but omitted the oral response requirement.

The task consisted of presenting a card with digits on it, covering the card, and instructing the

child to recall the digits. The number of digits ranged from three to nine and exposure time varied according to the number of digits, i.e., 3–4 digits—10 seconds, 5–6 digits—15 seconds, 7–8 digits—20 seconds, and 9 digits—25 seconds. One set of digits was grouped via spacing (51 24 3), whereas one set was not grouped (51243).

The retarded and nonretarded children were each divided into two groups. Children in the Order I condition were presented grouped digits first, immediately followed by the ungrouped presentation. For children in the Order II condition the digits were initially presented in an ungrouped manner, immediately followed by the grouped presentation.

The results indicated that the nonretarded children had higher recall scores than the retarded children under all conditions. For both groups the children exposed to the ungrouped digits first performed better than subjects exposed to the grouped digits first. These findings did not support Spitz's input organization hypothesis. MacMillan (1970a) notes that the oral response required at the time of presentation may be a variable which effects recall scores.

In the same year, MacMillan (1970b) investigated the effect of input organization on recall of visually presented digits by 30 primary-level and 30 intermediate-level educable retardates. Specifically, he examined whether the recall of digits could be improved for educable mentally retarded children of different ages by presenting the digits in grouped manner. Also, he attempted to ascertain whether grouping in a pretraining session would be utilized by educable retarded children in a subsequent session with digits presented ungrouped.

The task consisted of presenting a card with digits on it, asking the child to read the digits orally, and instructing the child to recall the digits immediately following their presentation. The number of digits ranged from three to nine, and exposure time varied according to the number of digits, i.e., 3–4 digits—10 seconds, 5–6 digits—15 seconds, 7–8 digits—20 seconds, and 9 digits—25 seconds. Each group of children was divided into an experimental group, an experimental-control group, and a control group. The control group children were presented the digits in an ungrouped manner in a pretraining session and in the experimental session. The children in the experimental group were presented the digits in a grouped manner, just as they had received them in their pretraining session. The children in the experimental-control group were presented the digits in a grouped manner in the pretraining session and in an ungrouped manner in the subsequent session. Digits were grouped by spacing, e.g., ungrouped—36274, grouped—36 27 4. All subjects attempted seven series of digits.

The results disclosed that older EMR children differed significantly from younger EMR children in the experimental and experimental-control conditions. These findings indicated that older (age 12) EMR children benefitted from organized input whereas younger (8–9 year old) EMR children did not. Thus Spitz's contention that input organization facilitates the recall of retarded individuals was only supported with the older children in this study. MacMillan (1970b) cautions against generalizing Spitz's hypothesis to all retarded individuals.

Two years later, MacMillan (1972) selected 30 educable retarded children and 30 MA-equivalent, nonretarded children in order to investigate the effects of verbal responses to stimuli. Specifically, he noted that previous studies regarding input organization and recall had not systematically examined such effects. He described the study as an "attempt to ascertain whether grouping alone, or grouping combined with the verbal response to the grouped digits as higher-decade numbers results in improved recall for EMR and/or nonretarded children" (p. 409).

He then assigned 10 children from each group (EMR and nonretarded) to one of three experimental conditions. The task consisted of seeing, saying, and recalling digit lists which varied in length from five to nine digits. One set of digits was spatially grouped and one set was presented with all digits equally spaced. Children in experimental Group I were presented the digits ungrouped and responded to them as single integers; Group II received the digits grouped and responded to them as single integers; and Group III received the digits grouped and responded to them as higher-decade numbers (23 instead of 2.3). Digits were exposed according to the following schedule: 5–6 digits—15 seconds; 7–8 digits—20 seconds; and 9 digits—25 seconds. Immediate recall scores were obtained across conditions and groups.

The findings revealed a trend suggesting that the retarded children improved in recall as input organization increased, while nonretarded children performed best under the least degree of experimental input organization. MacMillan (1972)

thought that spatial grouping may have interfered with the spontaneous strategies of nonretarded children and enhanced the organizational processes of the retarded children. He concludes, "The goodness of fit between the structure of the task and the subject's organizational strategy determines his recall performance" (p. 411).

HARRIS'S STUDIES. Harris (1972) selected 24 institutionalized, educable retarded adolescents, 24 nonretarded second graders, and 24 nonretarded third graders in order to investigate the effects of input and output organization on immediate, serial position recall.

Each youngster was shown slides of five 6-digit sequences and instructed to write each sequence immediately after its presentation. Each youngster performed the task under four conditions: (a) input grouping—output grouping, (b) input grouping—no output grouping, (c) no input grouping—no output grouping, and (d) no input grouping—output grouping. Input grouping was accomplished by displaying a slide of 3 digits for 3 seconds, followed by a 3-second pause and a final slide of 3 digits for 3 seconds. In the no-input grouping condition one slide with 6 digits was displayed for 9 seconds. Although total task time (9 seconds) was the same for the two input conditions, it is important to note that digit exposure time was different. Exposure time obviously favors the no-input grouping condition (9 seconds versus 6 seconds). Output grouping was accomplished by requiring the response to be written on an answer sheet which was spatially arranged to correspond to two groups of 3 digits, e.g., _ _ _ , _ _ _ . In the no-output grouping condition the response format featured equally spaced blank spaces, e.g., _ _ _ _ _ _ . Recall scores were recorded in terms of both the number of digits recalled in proper serial position and in total digits recalled.

The results showed that the serial position and total recall performances of the third graders were not affected by input organization. Input organization increased recall in the retarded and second grade group, and the second graders performed better than the retarded adolescents. Input organization had the greatest effect on the recall of the first 3 digits for the EMR and second grade group. Recall data as a function of serial position (SP) indicated that performance gains from the imposed input organization at some SPs are counterbalanced by losses at others. Under all conditions the third graders outperformed the other two groups. In the no-input grouping condition the second graders and retardates did not differ. Harris (1972) concludes:

> Since the second graders, lower than the retarded subjects in MA, exhibited equal results in the ungrouped condition but showed superior performance when sequences were grouped, an explanation other than the maturational idea proposed by MacMillan (1970) and Spitz et al. (1972) is suggested. (p. 426)

The effects of output grouping were negligible. Finally, generalization from the results of this study must be tempered because of the different digit exposure times for the two input conditions.

SPITZ, GOETTLER, AND WEBRECK'S STUDIES. In 1972, Spitz, Goettler, and Webreck conducted a series of four experiments designed to study the effects of two types of redundancy on visual digit-span performance of retardates and varying aged normals. Experiment I was designed to study the effects of both repetition and couplet redundancy on the recall of different digit lengths and to examine the relationship of the redundancy techniques to the different CA levels and mental retardation. Four groups (third graders, seventh graders, college students, and institutionalized EMRs) of 30 individuals each were presented digit-span tasks of 4, 6, and 8 digits. In addition, the college students received a span task of 10 digits. All digits were exposed for approximately 1 second. For each numerosity level the digits were presented in three ways—repetition redundancy (2, 1, 8, 2, 1, 8), couplet redundancy (2, 2, 1, 1, 8, 8), and in a nonredundant manner (random with no duplicate digits). Response patterns and recall scores were obtained.

The results indicated that the retarded and third grade groups with the 6-digit task recalled more with couplet redundancy than they did with repetition redundancy. In addition, the third graders recalled more on the 8-digit task under couplet redundancy than they did under repetition redundancy. The recall performance hierarchy revealed the following: college group > seventh graders > third graders > retardates. These differences occurred primarily on couplet and nonredundant digits at the higher numerosity levels. Although information value was similar (8 digits containing 50% redundancy = 4 nonredundant digits), the longer digits were always more difficult to recall. Redundancy in the 6- , 8- , and 10-digit lengths

consistently improved recall. Higher congruence between input organization and response patterns occurred more with the couplet redundancy than with the repetition redundancy. Spitz et al. (1972) conclude that for the lower MA groups, couplet redundancy was more easily recognized than repetition redundancy.

In a second experiment Spitz et al. (1972) concentrated on examining the effects of external cueing of repetition redundancy on the recall scores of the lower MA groups. They hypothesized that external cues of repetition redundancy would facilitate the lower MA groups' ability to recognize repetition redundancy and consequently improve their recall. They selected three groups (third graders, seventh graders, and institutionalized EMRs) of 15 individuals each and presented them with the same couplet redundancy digit and nonredundant digit tasks that were used in Experiment I. External cues were added to the repetition redundant condition. Spatial and underlining cues were used to accentuate the repetition redundancy, e.g., 218, 218.

A comparison of the recall scores of third graders and retardates in experiments I and II revealed that the external cueing of repetition redundancy in Experiment II significantly improved recall scores. The recall performance of the third graders and retardates did not significantly differ, but both groups performed less well than the seventh graders. For the lower MA groups the repetition redundancy produced higher scores than couplet redundancy. The investigators note that repetition redundancy, when recognized, resulted in higher performance than couplet redundancy. Also, they report that the results supported the position that lower MA groups (retardates and third graders) perform much better if they are shown where redundancy occurs.

Spitz et al. (1972) continued their redundancy experiments by conducting two more studies with normal adults. They hypothesized that a given number of digits of 50% redundancy was equivalent to the same units of information in half the number of nonredundant digits. From the results of a third experiment and the finding from Experiment I that longer lists (regardless of redundancy) were consistently more difficult to recall, Spitz et al. found that failure to recognize repetition redundancy adds to the processing load.

In Experiment IV, external cueing (spacing and underlining) for repetition redundancy was added to digit spans of 6, 7, 8, 12, 14, and 16 digits. The findings revealed that no differences existed between recall for 12, 14, and 16 digits with 50% repetition redundancy when compared with non-redundant digits containing the same information value. On the other hand, big differences at each numerosity level occurred between strings of digits containing 50% couplet redundancy and non-redundant lists matched for information value. Lastly, repetition redundancy produced better performances than couplet redundancy at each numerosity level.

The results from the four experiments led Spitz et al. (1972) to report that memory for digits containing repetition redundancy is superior to memory for digit strings containing couplet redundancy. Finally, Spitz et al. conclude: "As mental age increases there is an increasing capacity to discover natural organization embedded in verbal material and, in addition, to impose organization on verbal material" (p. 102).

SPITZ AND WEBRECK'S STUDIES. Spitz and Webreck (1972) examined the·effects of spontaneous and externally cued learning on the permanent storage of a schema (redundancy in digit presentations) by 70 institutionalized, educable retarded adolescents. They designed the study to investigate: (a) how readily retardates discover the presence of a schema, (b) whether external cueing aids in the discovery of a schema, and (c) the permanence of spontaneous versus externally cued schema learning.

In their task, lengths of 6, 8, and 10 digits were prepared in three different forms. The redundant, ungrouped form contained 50% redundancy with no spatial grouping, e.g., all digits had one space between them. The redundant, grouped form contained 50% redundancy with digits grouped via spacing and underlining, e.g., 691 691. The non-redundant form contained no redundancy or spatial grouping. Three trial blocks were established. Trial blocks I and II contained three strings of each length, and Trial Block III contained six strings of each length which were taken from blocks I and II.

As illustrated in Figure 3.2, four conditions were arranged with half of the children in each condition receiving trial blocks I and II and half receiving Trial Block III seven days later. In the nonredundant (NR) condition all blocks were nonredundant. In the grouped-ungrouped (GU) condition, Block I was grouped and Block II was ungrouped. In the

ungrouped-grouped (UG) condition, Block I was ungrouped and Block II was grouped. In the ungrouped-ungrouped (UU) condition, all blocks were ungrouped. Block III was ungrouped in all conditions. Stimuli were displayed via stimulus cards inserted in a loose-leaf desk calendar stand and exposure times for the 6-, 8-, and 10-digit sequences were 8, 10, and 13 seconds respectively.

The results indicated that under no condition did the recall of subjects tested 7 days later differ significantly from the recall of subjects tested 1 day later. In the nonredundant condition, improvement did not occur over the three trial blocks. Trials and numerosity were significant main effects ($p < .001$). In the UG and UU conditions, changes from trial blocks I to II, II to III, and I to III were all significant. Recall of redundant, grouped digits (G) for Trial Block I was significantly better than the recall performance on redundant, ungrouped digits (U). In the GU condition the only significant change was the increase from Trial Block II to III. Spitz and Webreck (1972) conclude that EMRs are capable of discovering and using redundancy embedded in sets of digits and that external cueing of redundancy improves performance. Also, they note that spontaneous discovery of redundancy has the same positive effect on long-term performance as does externally cued discovery of redundancy. Comparisons with studies of free recall and paired-associate learning suggest that level of constraint redundancy (obviousness and discreteness of redundant material) is a crucial factor in retardates' capacity to store a schema permanently.

SUMMARY. Table 3.1 highlights the important factors and results of each of the previous six studies. In this next discussion, observations and summaries will include the following information:

1. subject characteristics
2. recall performances
   a. EMRs versus CA-equivalent normals
   b. EMRs versus MA-equivalent normals
   c. grouped versus ungrouped presentation
3. effects of input organization
4. other relevant specific findings

The retarded participants in all six studies were characterized as *educable* (IQs ranged from 59.4 to 71.6). Except for MacMillan's (1970a, 1970b, 1972) three studies, all retarded participants were institutionalized. Also, MacMillan's retarded partic-

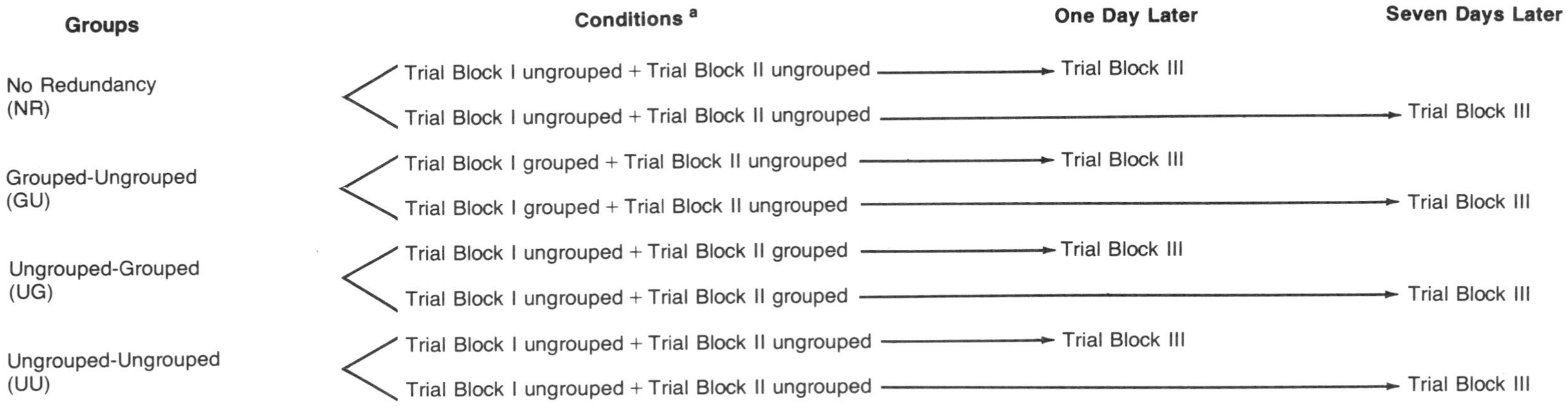

Groups	Conditions [a]	One Day Later	Seven Days Later
No Redundancy (NR)	Trial Block I ungrouped + Trial Block II ungrouped → Trial Block III	Trial Block III	
	Trial Block I ungrouped + Trial Block II ungrouped → Trial Block III		Trial Block III
Grouped-Ungrouped (GU)	Trial Block I grouped + Trial Block II ungrouped → Trial Block III	Trial Block III	
	Trial Block I grouped + Trial Block II ungrouped → Trial Block III		Trial Block III
Ungrouped-Grouped (UG)	Trial Block I ungrouped + Trial Block II grouped → Trial Block III	Trial Block III	
	Trial Block I ungrouped + Trial Block II grouped → Trial Block III		Trial Block III
Ungrouped-Ungrouped (UU)	Trial Block I ungrouped + Trial Block II ungrouped → Trial Block III	Trial Block III	
	Trial Block I ungrouped + Trial Block II ungrouped → Trial Block III		Trial Block III

NOTE: [a] In all conditions immediate recall followed the presentation of stimuli.

FIGURE 3.2
Experimental conditions of Spitz and Webreck's (1972) study.

TABLE 3.1
Summary of Memory-Span Studies Using Digits

ARTICLE	SUBJECTS	CONDITIONS AND TASKS	ANALYSIS

1. MacMillan (1970a)	1. 60 EMRs
	$\overline{IQ} = 67$
	$\overline{CA}$ approx. 11.7
	
	2. 60 normals
	$\overline{IQ}$ approx. 99
	$\overline{CA}$ approx. 8
	
	Both groups equated on MA.
		1. The task consisted of visually presenting digits on 3 x 5 in. cards and instructing the child to recall the digits after presentation. Unlike MacMillan's (1970b) other study, the S did not have to respond orally at the time of presentation.
		
		2. The Ss from each group were divided into two groups.
		  a. Order I received the stimuli in a grouped manner and then in an ungrouped manner.
		  b. Order II received the stimuli in an ungrouped manner followed by a grouped presentation.
			1. Compared recall scores of MRs and normals.
			
			2. Compared recall scores across Order I and Order II conditions.

RESULTS: Nonretarded children surpassed EMRs on recall under all conditions. For both groups, Ss exposed first to ungrouped (rather than grouped) digits remembered better. MacMillan notes that his findings are different from Spitz (1966); the fact that Spitz required verbal response to digits could possibly be an explanation.

2. MacMillan (1970b)	1. 30 primary-level EMRs
	$\overline{CA} = 8.98$
	$\overline{IQ}$ = approx. 65
	
	2. 30 intermediate-level EMRs
	$\overline{CA} = 12.79$
	$\overline{IQ}$ = approx. 66
		1. Digit-span task ranging in length from 3–9 digits.
		
		2. 10 Ss from each age group were assigned to one of 3 conditions.
		  a. Control—subjects received ungrouped digits
		  b. Experimental—subjects received grouped digits
		  c. Experimental-Control—subjects received grouped digits followed by ungrouped digits
		
		3. All Ss received some pretraining, and each digit-span card was varied in exposure according to the number of digits.
		  3–4 digits—10 sec
		  5–6 digits—15 sec
		  7–8 digits—20 sec
		  9 digits—25 sec
			1. Compared recall scores of the two groups.
			
			2. Compared recall scores across experimental conditions.

RESULTS: Older EMR children differed significantly from younger EMR children only under experimental (grouped input) and experimental-control (grouped then ungrouped) conditions. MacMillan found only support for Spitz's (1966) contention that input organization facilitates the recall of retardates with the older (12 yr old) retardates. Thus, he questions the generalizability of the hypothesis for most EMRs.

TABLE 3.1, cont.

ARTICLE	SUBJECTS	CONDITIONS AND TASKS	ANALYSIS
3. MacMillan (1972)	1. <u>30 nonretarded</u> $\overline{CA} = 8.41$ $\overline{IQ} = 98.2$ $\overline{MA} = 8.24$ 2. <u>30 EMRs</u> $\overline{CA} = 11.64$ $\overline{IQ} = 71.6$ $\overline{MA} = 8.38$	1. The task consisted of seeing, saying, and recalling digits which varied in length from 5–9 digits. One set of digits was spatially grouped and one set was presented with all digits equally spaced. 5–6 digits—15 sec 7–8 digits—20 sec 9 digits—25 sec 2. Subjects from each group were equally assigned to one of three conditions. a. Group 1—digits ungrouped; oral response to them as single integers b. Group 2—digits grouped; oral response to them as single integers c. Group 3—digits grouped; oral response to them as higher decade numbers	1. Compared recall scores between the two groups. 2. Compared the recall scores across conditions.

RESULTS: EMRs improved in recall as input organization increased, while nonretarded children performed best under the least degree of experimental input organization. MacMillan (1972) interprets the results as suggesting that spatial grouping may have interfered with the spontaneous strategies of non-retarded children and enhanced the organizational processes of the retarded children. He concludes that "the goodness of fit between the structure of the task and the subject's organizational strategy determines his recall performance" (p. 411).

ARTICLE	SUBJECTS	CONDITIONS AND TASKS	ANALYSIS
4. Harris (1972)	1. <u>24 institutionalized EMRs</u> $\overline{CA} = 16.3$ $\overline{MA} = 8.6$ $\overline{IQ} = 59.4$ 2. <u>nonretarded 2nd graders</u> $\overline{CA} = 7.7$ 3. <u>nonretarded 3rd graders</u> $\overline{CA} = 8.5$	1. The task consisted of recalling via writing 6 digits over 5 trials presented on a screen. The digits were displayed over a span of 9 sec. 2. The task was presented under 4 different conditions. Input organization consisted of spatially grouping the digits into 2 sets of 3 digits. Output organization was achieved via spacing the answer blanks to correspond to 2 groups of 3 digits, e.g., __ __ __ , __ __ __ . Conditions: No input grouping—No output grouping No input grouping—Output grouping Input grouping—No output grouping Input grouping—Output grouping	1. Compared recall scores among groups. 2. Compared recall scores across conditions. 3. The recall scores were digits recalled in the proper serial position.

RESULTS: Input organization increased recall in the EMRs and 2nd graders. Output organization did not produce a significant effect. Under all conditions the 3rd graders performed better than the 2nd graders and the EMRs. In the no input grouping condition the 2nd graders and the EMRs did not differ and both were significantly below the 3rd graders. In the input grouping condition for the 2nd graders and the EMRs. For the 2nd graders and the 2nd graders performed better than the EMRs. EMRs the input grouping had the greatest effect on the first 3 digits. According to Harris (1972), "Since the second graders, lower than the retarded subjects in MA, exhibited equal results in the ungrouped condition but showed superior performance when sequences were grouped, an explanation other than the maturational idea proposed by MacMillan (1970) and Spitz et al. (1972) is suggested" (p. 426).

TABLE 3.1, cont.

ARTICLE	SUBJECTS	CONDITIONS AND TASKS	ANALYSIS

5. Spitz, Goettler, & Webreck (1972)
Experiment I
	1. 30 3rd graders
	$\overline{CA}$ = 9.11
	$\overline{IQ}$ = 104
	
	2. 30 7th graders
	$\overline{CA}$ = 13.34
	$\overline{IQ}$ = 101
	
	3. 30 college students
	$\overline{CA}$ = 20.7
	
	4. 30 institutionalized EMRs
	$\overline{CA}$ = 15.72
	$\overline{IQ}$ = 62
		1. The task consisted of recalling digits presented visually. Each digit was displayed approximately 1 sec and digit length ranged from 4–10 digits.
		2. Two types of schematic redundancy were used.
		  a. couplet redundancy
		    e.g., 2, 2, 1, 1, 8, 8.
		  b. repetition redundancy
		    e.g., 2, 1, 8, 2, 1, 8.
		3. Recall scores were obtained; and in addition, type of response organization was recorded, e.g., did response output match input organization.
			1. Compared effects of couplet versus repetition redundancy on recall of different lengths of digits.
			2. Compared the recall performances across groups.

RESULTS: For the retarded and 3rd grade groups the two types of redundancy differentially affected recall. With 6 digits, couplet redundancy produced significantly (*p* <.001) better recall than did repetition redundancy. Also, couplet redundancy with the 3rd graders using 8 digits resulted in better recall than with repetition redundancy. Although information value was similar (8 digits containing 50% redundancy = 4 nonredundant digits), the longer digits were always more difficult to recall (*p* <.01). Redundancy in the 6- , 8- , and 10-digit lengths consistently improved recall. The recall performance hierarchy revealed that: college group > seventh graders > third graders > retardates. These differences occurred primarily on couplet and nonredundant digits at the higher numerosity levels. Higher congruence between input organization and response patterns occurred more with the couplet redundancy than with the repetition redundancy. Spitz et al. conclude that couplet redundancy was easier to recognize than repetition redundancy—especially for the lower MA groups.

ARTICLE	SUBJECTS	CONDITIONS AND TASKS	ANALYSIS
Spitz, et al. (1972) *Experiment II*	1. 30 3rd graders $\overline{CA}$ = 8.83 $\overline{IQ}$ = 107 2. 30 7th graders $\overline{CA}$ = 12.72 $\overline{IQ}$ = 102 3. 30 institutionalized EMRs $\overline{CA}$ = 15.65 $\overline{IQ}$ = 64	1. The task was identical to *Exp. I* for digits in the couplet and nonredundant conditions; however, in the repetition condition the digits were spatially separated and underlined according to the groupings, e.g., 2 19, 2 19. 2. The conditions were same as *Exp. I*.	1. Compared effects of couplet versus externally-cued repetition redundancy on recall of different lengths of digits. 2. Compared the recall scores across groups. 3. Compared the recall scores with scores from *Exp. I*.

RESULTS: A comparison of the recall scores of 3rd graders and retardates in *Exp. I* and *Exp. II* disclosed that the external cueing of repetition redundancy in *Exp. II* significantly improved recall scores. The recall performance of the 3rd graders and retardates did not significantly differ, but both groups performed significantly poorer than the 7th graders. The results revealed that for the lower MA groups the repetition redundancy produced higher scores (*p* <.05) than couplet redundancy. The authors note that repetition redundancy, when recognized, resulted in higher performance than couplet redundancy. Also, they acknowledge that the results support the position that with the lower MA group's performance is markedly improved if the group's attention is directed to the presence of redundancy.

TABLE 3.1, cont.

ARTICLE	SUBJECTS	CONDITIONS AND TASKS	ANALYSIS

6. Spitz & Webreck (1972)	70 institutionalized EMRs
	CA = 15.33 years
	IQ = 64
		1. Free recall of digits was the task used. Lengths of 6, 8, and 10 digits were prepared in 3 different forms. The redundant ungrouped form contained 50% redundancy with digits spaced and underlined, e.g., 691, 691. The nonredundant form contained no spatial grouping.
		2. Three trial blocks were set up:
		  a. Trial Block I—3 strings of each length
		  b. Trial Block II—3 strings of each length
		  c. Trial Block III—6 strings of each length taken from stimuli in I and II
		3. Four conditions were set up with half of the Ss in each condition receiving Trial Block III 1 day after presentation of Trial Block II and half receiving Trial Block III 7 days later.
		  a. NR*—all Blocks were nonredundant
		  b. GU*—Block I grouped, Block II ungrouped
		  c. UG*—Block I ungrouped, Block II grouped
		  d. UU*—Block I ungrouped, Block II ungrouped
		  Block III was ungrouped in all conditions.
		4. Recall scores were recorded.
			1. Compared recall scores in relation to redundancy, spatial grouping, and digit length.
			2. Compared storage for 1 day and 7 days.

RESULTS: In no condition did the Ss tested 7 days later differ significantly from Ss tested 1 day later. In the nonredundant condition, improvement did not occur over the three trial blocks. Trials and numerosity were significant main effects ($p < .001$). In the UG condition, changes from trial blocks I–II, II–III, and I–III were all significant. In the UU condition, changes from trial blocks I–II, II–III, and I–III were significant. In the GU condition the only significant change was the increase from trial blocks II–III. Spitz & Webreck conclude that MRs were capable of discovering and using redundancy embedded in sets of digits and that external cueing of redundancy improves performance. Also, they note that spontaneous discovery of redundancy has the same positive effect on long-term performance as externally cued discovery of redundancy. Finally, they identify the level of constraint redundancy as a crucial variable in MRs' capacity to store material permanently.

---

*GU = Grouped-ungrouped condition
NR = No redundancy condition
UG = Ungrouped-grouped condition
UU = Ungrouped-ungrouped condition

ipants were younger (CA ranged from 8 years to 11.7 years) than the retarded persons in the other studies (CA ranged from 15.3 years to 16.3 years).

The recall performance of the retarded participants was only compared with the performance of CA-equivalent normals in the two experiments conducted by Spitz, Goettler, and Webreck (1972). In both of their experiments the CA-equivalent non-retarded group had superior performance. In the six studies the recall performance of the retarded participants was compared with the recall performance of MA-equivalent, nonretarded individuals 11 times. When the digits were grouped, the retarded individuals performed more poorly than the non-retarded participants 67% of the time (4 out of 6 comparisons). When the digits were ungrouped, the retarded individuals performed more poorly than their MA-equivalent peers 80% of the time (4 out of 5 comparisons). In the one study (Harris, 1972) in which the performances did not differ, the mean MA of the nonretarded group was lower than the mean MA of the retarded group. In addition, Harris' study was the only study which required the participants to write their responses. From these studies it appears that retarded individuals recall digits more poorly than MA-equivalent normals, but that grouping does help. In one of the studies (MacMillan, 1972) in which the performances of the respective groups were similar, the participants were required to read the digits upon presentation. Grouped input plus verbal rehearsal may consistently help retarded persons to recall digits as well as MA-equivalent, nonretarded individuals.

In the six studies the recall performance of retarded participants was compared for grouped versus ungrouped presentations 10 times. In 70% of the comparisons the grouped presentations produced superior recall. Two of the comparisons which yielded no differences had younger retardates (CAs below 12 years) than the other studies (CAs above 12 years). In the Spitz & Webreck study (1972), which reported no difference in recall scores between a grouped versus an ungrouped condition, the recall scores were only obtained from the later trials. In the earlier trials differences in favor of the grouped presentation were reported. Moreover, couplet redundancy was found to be superior to repetitive redundancy unless the repetitive redundancy was externally cued. When externally cued, repetitive redundancy produced better recall than noncued couplet redundancy (Spitz et al., 1972). All studies used grouped and

then ungrouped stimuli to test the recall of normal subjects. Only half of the studies found a difference in recall when stimuli presentation differed. However, none of the studies showed significantly dissimilar patterns in subject characteristics or task variables that could account for this contrary result.

From the results of these six studies regarding the influence of input organization on recall it is reasonable to conclude that input organization consistently (80% of the time) aids the recall of retarded participants (especially if their CA is over 12 years), whereas it occasionally (50% of the time) enhances the recall of nonretarded individuals. Finally, one study (Harris, 1972) compared the effect of output organization versus no output organization with retarded and nonretarded individuals and found no differences.

Specific findings and observations reported in the six studies include:

1. Since MacMillan (1970b) found that input organization only facilitated the recall of older (age 12) EMRs, he suggests that Spitz's theory of input organization not be generalized to younger EMRs (age 9).
2. Since input organization actually produced a decrease in the performance of a young ($\overline{CA}$ = 8.41 years) group of normal children but facilitated the recall of EMRs, MacMillan (1972) suggests that input organization can be detrimental if it is not consistent with the learner's organizing strategy.
3. Spitz and Webreck (1972) report that externally cued organization and spontaneous discovery of organization did not differ in their effect on permanent memory.
4. Spitz et al. (1972) found that with lower MA levels (MA ≈ 9 years) couplet redundancy was more easily recognized than repetition redundancy.

TEACHING IMPLICATIONS. Although digit recall is important for remembering street numbers, telephone numbers, zip codes, license plate numbers, Social Security numbers, and lock combinations, it primarily represents an index for studying memory skills. Since these studies all used digit recall, direct teaching implications are difficult to ascertain unless a teacher desires to teach youngsters to remember digits. So although digit-span research probably offers specific techniques for improving memory, these techniques do not generalize to other material.

Some possible specific teaching implications might include these findings:

1. One of the major findings from the digit-span studies

was that 50% redundancy positively influenced recall. Moreover, couplet redundancy (2, 2, 4, 4, 8, 8) was more readily recognized and used than repetition redundancy (2, 4, 8, 2, 4, 8). In the classroom couplet redundancy could be used in teaching letter recognition, word recognition, numeral recognition, or addition facts by allowing each item to follow itself once. For example, work sheets or flash cards could be arranged in the following orders:

1. numerals—4, 4, 6, 6, 7, 7, 9, 9.
2. letters—A, A, B, B, C, C, D, D.
3. words—cat, cat, ball, ball, dog, dog
4. addition facts—
$$\begin{array}{cccccc} 1 & 1 & 2 & 2 & 3 & 3 \\ +1 & +1 & +2 & +2 & +3 & +3 \end{array}$$

When using couplet redundancy it would help if the learner was provided corrective feedback on the first item of each couplet so errors would not be repeated. Corrective feedback could be provided via teacher feedback, peer feedback, tape recorder, Language Master, answer key, or electric response board.

2. External cueing via underlining and spacing facilitated recall in experimental subjects. In teaching number sequences or spelling words external cueing could be used in the following ways:

   1. 376–8412—spacing and underlining phone numbers
   2. 248–61–1067—spacing and underlining Social Security numbers
   3. cat, rat, bat—underlining similar parts of different words
   4. cat tle, mus cle—spacing words by syllable and underlining

   In addition, configuration, color, and arrows are other good methods of cueing material.

3. Inherent in the redundancy technique is the principle that the repetition of items requires the learner to process less material at one time. Also, redundancy of material provides inherent drill. In the teaching of words and math facts several techniques incorporate redundancy which may foster the learning of retarded pupils. For example, the linguistically oriented reading approaches stress the introduction of words within word families, i.e., cat, rat, bat, sat, mat, pat, fat, hat. Math facts could be arranged similarly. For example:

$$\begin{array}{ccccccccc} 1 & 2 & 3 & 4 & 5 & 6 & 7 & 8 & 9 \\ +0 & +0 & +0 & +0 & +0 & +0 & +0 & +0 & +0 \end{array}$$

4. External cueing coupled with repetition redundancy provides an effective combination for improving recall. This procedure could be used in giving directions in oral or written fashion.

Write the word *cat*. Write the word *cat*.

Turn the page. Turn the page.

Draw a cat. Draw a cat.

In oral instructions cueing could be accomplished by temporal groupings and voice inflection and/or inten-

sity. In teaching a number (e.g., a lock combination) the numerals could be written as follows: 263 263.

5. Spitz's (1973) review indicates that EMR subjects were capable of recalling four or five bits of information presented sequentially for one second at a time. This finding has specific implications for giving directions to EMR adolescents. Long directions should be minimized; when they are necessary they should be given slowly and repeated.

Memory-Span Studies Using Pictures or Objects

GERJUOY, WINTERS, PULLEN, AND SPITZ'S STUDIES. Gerjuoy, Winters, Pullen, and Spitz (1969) examined the clustering and recall scores of 24 institutionalized, educable retardates and 24 MA-equivalent normals on a free recall task of visually presented stimuli. They were interested in this topic because the bulk of the clustering research prior to their study used words presented orally. They wanted to find out how clustered and random visual presentations affect clustering and recall of retardates and normals of equal MA.

Their stimulus materials consisted of 20 pictures organized into four categories: letters, numbers, colors, and geometric forms. Half of the subjects from each group were presented the 20 items in a random manner for five trials, and the remaining subjects were presented the materials in a clustered fashion for five trials. Each stimulus was exposed for 3 seconds with a 7-second interstimulus interval and 2 minutes were allowed for free recall. A recall score and a clustering (above chance) score were recorded for each trial. In addition, the investigators compared the recall and cluster scores of retardates from this study with earlier studies which used auditory stimuli with retardates.

The findings disclosed that no significant differences on recall scores resulted between MA-equivalent normals and educable retardates; however, recall significantly improved for both groups over trials. The cluster scores of the MA-equivalent normals were higher than the cluster scores of the retardates. Both groups used clustering above chance, and more clustering occurred when the material was presented in a clustered manner. Moreover, clustering improved over trials. In their visual-auditory presentation comparisons with retarded subjects only, Gerjuoy et al. (1969) discovered that randomly presented visual material was recalled better than randomly presented auditory material, but that auditory materials presented in a clustered manner were recalled better than visual materials.

Gerjuoy et al. (1969) conducted a second experiment. They selected 24 different educable retarded adolescents and 24 different MA-equivalent normals and had them perform a free recall task following a random and clustered visual presentation of 40 items, five pairs of each of the four types (same as Experiment I) of material. Thus in Experiment I the material consisted of 20 items presented one at a time, and in Experiment II the material consisted of 40 items presented in pairs (each pair was categorically related). Recall and cluster scores were obtained.

The results indicated that the MA-equivalent normals recalled more than the retardates in both random and clustered conditions. Clustered presentations improved recall, and recall improved over trials. Both groups clustered above chance expectations, but the rate of clustering increased more rapidly over trials for the normals than it did for the retardates. In both experiments the two groups recalled colors and forms better than letters and numbers. Moreover, doubling the input (40 items versus 20 items) in the clustered presentations doubled the retardates' output.

Gerjuoy and Winters's Studies. Gerjuoy and Winters (1970) used a bimodal (auditory-visual) presentation in a free recall task to examine clustering and recall scores of educable retarded adolescents. The stimuli were line drawings of words rated high in the Thorndike-Lorge (1944) tables of word frequency. The pictures were divided into two lists with five words from four categories in each list. In Session 1 the subjects were equally divided into four groups: single random (SR), single clustered (SC), group random (GR), and group clustered (GC). The SR subjects were presented each picture individually in random order. The SC subjects were presented each picture individually in a clustered order. The GR subjects were presented at the same time five pictures from different categories. The GC subjects were shown at the same time five pictures from the same category. Half of the subjects received stimuli from List I and half received List II. Two experimental sessions were planned and in Session 1 experimental conditions were primarily designed to examine recall and cluster scores after a bimodal presentation. In the task, the experimenter pronounced the

word (auditory) when the line drawing was displayed (visual). In addition, the subject was required to say the word after the experimenter said the word. Each trial consisted of 20 picture-label presentations and the subjects were given 2 minutes to recall the stimuli. The recall and cluster scores (bimodal presentation) from Session 1 were compared with similar scores from the Gerjuoy and Spitz (1966) study (unimodal presentation). Session 2 took place about 1 week later with the subjects equally divided into a single random (SR) group which received the bimodal task and an auditory random (AR) group which received the unimodal task. For the SR subjects the conditions were the same as described in Session 1 and for the AR subjects the experimenter did not say the words.

The results indicated that in Session 1 no differences in recall occurred among the conditions. However, recall was superior to the conditions in the Gerjuoy and Spitz (1966) study in which the subjects were asked to recall information (presented in an unclustered manner) in a clustered manner, for example, recall the animals words, then the food words. On the other hand, recall was inferior to the conditions in which the subjects were presented items in a clustered manner and then asked to say the items by clusters. Clustering was above chance in all conditions and clustered presentations generated more clustered recall than random conditions. Recall significantly improved over trials.

In Session 2, SR (bimodal) recall was superior to AR (auditory) recall and to the random condition in the Gerjuoy and Spitz (1966) study. The AR recall did not differ from the previous study. Clustering occurred above chance in both conditions and AR clustering was superior to the random condition in the previous study. In their discussion Gerjuoy and Winters (1970) suggest that bimodal presentations improve recall and the separate modalities affect the association between clustering and recall.

Herriot and Cox's Studies. Herriot and Cox (1971) investigated subjective organization and clustering processes in the free recall of 24 mongoloid and 24 nonmongoloid retarded children. Herriot and Cox designed their study to examine: (a) whether subjective organization (SO) and clustering occurred above chance with retarded children; (b) the relationship between clustering and SO; (c) the relationship between clustering, SO, and recall; and (d) the effect of etiological differences on SO, clustering, and recall measures.

Herriot and Cox selected three sets of six pictures from the *English Picture Vocabulary Test (EPVT)*. The items in two sets of the pictures were unrelated and the items in the third set consisted of three pairs of conceptually related items. Pretraining sessions were conducted to insure that the children could identify the pictures. In the experimental session the six items in a set were simultaneously displayed on a screen via slides. Display time was 25 seconds and recall time was 25 seconds. Recall was oral and immediately followed the stimulus presentation. Clustering was recorded in the recall of the related items and SO was recorded in the recall of the unrelated items. In addition, the rehearsal activities of the subjects, such as left to right scanning and verbalization, were observed and recorded.

The findings showed that SO and clustering occurred above chance. Clustering was related to recall, but SO was not related to recall. Clustering resulted in higher recall than did SO. For the mongoloids, rehearsal was negatively correlated to recall. In summarizing their findings, Herriot and Cox (1971) state, "It was concluded that subjective organization was the result of sequential rote recall strategies, while clustering resulted partly from hierarchical storage or retrieval strategies" (p. 710).

HOLDEN'S STUDIES. Holden (1971) investigated the effects of temporal grouping on unimodal and multimodal sequential information processing in 26 educable retarded adolescents and 26 MA-equivalent nonretarded children. Holden revealed in his 1970 study that retardates and MA-equivalent normals made more errors in a multimodal presentation than in a unimodal presentation, whereas the performance of CA-equivalent, nonretarded individuals did not change in the two different modality conditions. In this study (1971) Holden hypothesized that grouping via temporal organization (couplets) should minimize the discrepancy in the performance of retarded and MA-equivalent, nonretarded subjects in the unimodal and trimodal conditions.

The task consisted of presenting stimuli through three modalities: visual, auditory, and tactile. The visual stimuli (dots) were presented with a mini-projector, the auditory stimuli (80dB tone) were presented through headphones, and the tactile

stimuli were delivered by a hand vibrator. All stimuli were 0.05-second duration and the number of stimuli for each trial varied from 3 to 10. The stimuli were presented in two 32-trial blocks. In one block the stimuli were sequentially presented, and in the other block they were grouped into couplets via temporal spacing. For each block of 32 trials, the stimuli were presented to the same modality, alternated between two modalities, and alternated among the three modalities.

The findings were that the retarded youngsters made significantly more errors than did the MA-equivalent children, and errors increased when the rate for switching the modalities increased. The main effect of temporal grouping was not significant. However, error increments (which were obtained with ungrouped sequences) were eliminated if the modality condition included temporal grouping congruent with modality sequencing (for example, auditory two tones–pause–visual two dots–pause–tactile two pulses). This effect supports the hypothesis that congruence between temporal grouping and modality sequencing (input organization) reduces the interference effect which modality switching has for EMRs by promoting a counting strategy which equal-CA non-retarded individuals use without temporal congruence. Holden (1971) notes that these findings are in general agreement with Spitz's (1966) input organization hypothesis.

HERRIOT'S STUDIES. Herriot (1972) selected 40 severely retarded (20 mongoloid and 20 nonmongoloid) adults in order to examine the effect that the order of labeling has on subjective organization and clustering in a free recall task. Both groups, the mongoloid and the nonmongoloid, were equally divided and assigned to two experimental conditions. Two groups of 10 individuals participated in the labeling in a random order (LARA) experimental condition and the other two groups of 10 individuals participated in the labeling in same order as the previous recall (LARC) experimental condition.

In the LARA condition, slides displaying six familiar objects were presented and the subject was asked to label the items as the experimenter pointed to each object. Eight trials were conducted and the items were labeled in a different random order in each presentation phase. When the labeling was in the same order as the previous LARC condition, the slides of the six familiar objects were displayed and the subject was told to label the items in the same order as occurred on the previous trial. This was accomplished by having the experimenter point to the items in the order in which the subject recalled them on the previous trial. On the first trial random labeling occurred and an order of recall was established for the next trial.

Herriot throught that LARC would increase subjective organization more than LARA. Moreover, he predicted that the mongoloid and nonmongoloid groups would be differentially affected by the forced labeling conditions. He cited evidence that suggested that mongoloid individuals employed sequential strategies more than nonmongoloid individuals (Herriot & Cox, 1971).

SO was calculated via the formula provided by Bousfield and Bousfield (1966). The findings indicated that LARC increased SO compared to LARA. Since SO is a measure of sequential constancies, this fact was an expected result.

In a second experiment Herriot (1972) randomly assigned the same individuals to LARC and LARA conditions. Different objects were used and cluster scores were computed using Bousfield and Bousfield's (1966) formula. It was predicted that the LARA condition would produce higher clustering than the LARC condition. This predicted difference occurred only on Day 2 for the mongoloid adults and only on Day 1 for the nonmongoloid adults. Overall, LARA resulted in more clustering than LARC. The nonmongoloid adults recalled more than mongoloid adults. Herriot concludes that forced labeling had different effects on subjective organization and clustering and this finding suggests that they index different processes.

MENDE'S STUDIES. Mende (1974) selected twenty 14-year-old EMR adolescents and twenty 9-year-old EMR children in order to study the effects of age, type of stimulus, and repetition on subjective organization and recall. The task consisted of displaying 12 pictures and 12 objects and asking the participant to recall them. The name of each stimulus was spoken by the examiner as it was presented. Six trials were conducted, and subjective organization (Bousfield & Bousfield, 1966) and recall scores were recorded.

The findings indicated that 14-year-old EMRs recalled more objects and pictures and produced higher cluster scores than 9-year-old EMRs. Both age groups recalled more objects than pictures, and recall and cluster scores improved across

trials. Recall and SO scores were only related for 14-year-old EMRs for recall of objects. Mende (1974) concludes that 14-year-old EMRs were able to impose more organizational strategies on the material than 9-year-old EMRs.

PALMER'S STUDIES. Palmer (1974) selected 30 institutionalized educable retarded adults and 30 nonretarded pupils in order to examine some basic determinants of clustering. Palmer noted that a primary consideration in clustering must be given to the nature of the stimuli. In a preliminary study he selected a retarded and a MA-equivalent group in order to generate stimuli which met the following criteria: (a) the list pairs consist of highly familiar items, (b) the list pairs belong to independent categories, and (c) the list pairs have well-established indirect and direct associations for both groups. Nine object pairs were generated in the preliminary study and were used in the primary study. The object pairs were: paper–pencil, penny–nickel, knife–fork, comb–brush, cat–dog, shoes–socks, apple–banana, car–bus, and hammer–nail.

All 60 participants were shown each of 18 objects for 2 to 3 seconds. At the end of the presentations the subjects were given 90 seconds to recall the objects. Five trials were conducted. Palmer (1974) hypothesized that no difference would occur for recall or cluster scores for the two groups.

The results indicated that both groups demonstrated clustering well above chance on all five trials ($p < .001$). The normal group had higher cluster scores than the EMRs on trials 3, 4, and 5. Performance of both groups significantly improved over trials. On recall the two groups did not differ and both groups significantly improved over trials.

Using the same subjects (except for two substitutions), Palmer (1974) continued the study by collecting normative data two to four weeks after the study. Category norms were obtained by verbally presenting the participants with a category name and instructing them to list as many category members as they could in a period of 1 minute. Associate norms were obtained by presenting the participants with toys and asking for a free-associative response.

In the category-norm study, retarded and MA-matched, nonretarded individuals, when presented with names of categories, gave approximately the same number of responses. Palmer

(1974) states, "if it may be assumed that recalling category names aids in recalling corresponding category members, this finding suggests that neither group showed an advantage in the use of this aid" (p. 459). However, in the associative-norm study the nonretarded group emitted significantly more taxonomic associates than the EMR group. According to Palmer, "This suggests that the nonretarded subjects may indeed have tended to respond more readily than the retarded subjects to the presented objects with the presumably useful category retrieval cues" (p. 459). Palmer uses Jensen's theory of intelligence as a guide in his discussion of his results.

RIEGEL AND TAYLOR'S STUDIES. Riegel and Taylor (1974) selected 86 educable retarded children and 31 CA-equivalent, nonretarded second graders in order to compare the conceptual strategies used for grouping and remembering by the respective groups. Specifically, they examined sorting processes, clustering processes, and recall performances of the two groups.

Each child was administered the *Sampling Organization and Recall through Strategies Test*. The test consisted of presenting, one at a time, 20 pictures to each child. Children were asked to name the object and to place the pictures in piles so they could remember them. Each picture was from one of four categories and five pictures were in each category. When the children finished sorting the pictures, the objects were covered up and the children were instructed to name as many objects as they could. After recalling the items, they were asked their reasons for forming the piles used in sorting.

The test yielded four levels of sorting strategies. Level I, *syncretic strategies,* was characterized by a general failure to formulate relationships between items on the basis of an attribute. At this level children frequently arranged the cards by spatial contiguity. Level II, *perceptual strategies*, consisted of sorting on the basis of attributes related to color, shape, or size. Level III, *low associative strategies*, consisted of grouping the pictures according to unique associations, such as a story created about the objects. At Level IV, *superordinate and categorical strategies*, groupings were established according to a single intrinsic attribute, for example, that all the objects were furniture. In addition, the test yielded a recall score (total number correct) and a clustering score.

The findings disclosed that the nonretarded children used higher level sorting (Levels III and IV) more than the retarded children ($p < .01$). Also, the nonretarded children recalled significantly ($p < .001$) more items than the retarded children. The groups did not differ on clustering scores. Significant correlations ($p < .05$) between recall and clustering were found for both groups. The investigators conclude that EMR children did not recall items as well as CA-equivalent, nonretarded children and it is likely that their performance would be more readily comparable to that of MA-equivalent, nonretarded children. Finally, they note that the relationship between clustering and recall was not straightforward.

SUMMARY. As reflected in Table 3.2, the eight memory-span studies with pictures or objects as stimuli include considerable variation in subject characteristics and areas investigated. The variety of findings and observations will be discussed in the areas of:

1. subject characteristics
2. effects of input organization on recall
3. effects on input organization on clustering
4. effects of modality on recall and clustering
5. relationship of recall and clustering
6. subjective organization
7. effects of practice on recall and clustering
8. MR versus nonretarded subject comparisons
9. other specific relevant findings

The subjects who participated in the studies were characterized as ranging in IQ from 20 (severe) to 70 (educable). Two studies (Herriot, 1972; Herriot & Cox, 1971) included mongoloid individuals and all but two studies (Mende, 1974; Riegel & Taylor, 1974) included institutionalized retarded individuals as participants.

In the three studies (Gerjuoy & Winters, 1970; Gerjuoy et al., 1969; Holden, 1971) that included a comparison of the effects of organized versus random input on recall, a significant difference in favor of organized input was found by only Gerjuoy et al. (1969).

In the two studies (Gerjuoy & Winters, 1970; Gerjuoy et al., 1969) that compared the effects of organized versus random input, organized input produced significantly more clustering in both studies.

The influence of modality on the recall scores of EMRs was examined in several studies and numerous findings were reported. Gerjuoy and

TABLE 3.2
Summary of Memory-Span Studies Using Pictures or Objects

ARTICLE	SUBJECTS	CONDITIONS AND TASKS	ANALYSIS
1. Gerjuoy, Winters, Pullen, & Spitz (1969) *Experiment I*	1. 24 institutionalized EMRs $\underline{IQ} = 64.47$ $\overline{CA} = 15.61$ 2. 24 normal 5th graders $\underline{IQ} = 109.61$ $\overline{CA} = 10.56$ Both groups equated on MA.	1. Task consisted of recalling 20 pictures (4 categories) presented visually with 3 sec exposure for each item and 7 sec interstimulus interval. 2. Half of the Ss from each group were presented items in a random manner. 3. Half of the Ss from each group were presented items in a clustered manner. 4. Obtained recall score and expected and observed clustering scores.	1. Compared MR and normal recall scores. 2. Compared MR and normal clustering scores. 3. Examined the effects of trials on recall and clustering. 4. Compared random and clustered presentations. 5. Compared visual presentation with auditory presentations of other studies for MR Ss only.

RESULTS: The only significant difference ($p < .001$) on the recall scores was that recall increased with trials. Both groups used clustering above chance expectations. Equal MA normals clustered more than retardates ($p < .05$). More clustering occurred ($p < .01$) in the clustered input condition than in the random condition. Clustering increased over trials ($p < .001$). Presenting visual material randomly resulted in better recall than presenting auditory material randomly ($p < .001$). In the clustered presentations auditory material resulted in better recall than visual material ($p < .05$).

ARTICLE	SUBJECTS	CONDITIONS AND TASKS	ANALYSIS
Gerjuoy et al. (1969) *Experiment II*	1. 24 institutionalized EMRs $\underline{IQ} = 63.33$ $\overline{CA} = 16.25$ 2. 24 normals $\underline{IQ} = 110.29$ $\overline{CA} = 10.69$ Both groups equated on MA.	1. The task was similar to *Exp. I* except that each stimulus card contained a pair of stimuli of similar material rather than a single stimulus (40 stimuli—5 pairs of 4 categories). 2. Half of the Ss from each group received a clustered presentation, i.e., 5 pairs of each category presented consecutively. 3. Half of the Ss from each group received a random presentation, i.e., pairs were presented but not consecutively. 4. Obtained recall and cluster scores.	1. Compared MR and MA equal normals on recall and clustering. 2. Analyzed effects of clustering on recall. 3. Compared the effects of number of items on recall. 4. Examined which type of items was more easily recalled.

RESULTS: Equal MA normals recalled more ($p < .01$) than retardates. Clustered presentations improved recall ($p < .05$), which also improved ($p < .001$) over trials. Both groups clustered above chance expectations. Over trials the increase in clustering for equal MA normals was more rapid than it was for retardates ($p < .005$). The total number of items was greater with 40 items than with 20 items (*Exp. I*). For both experiments, both groups recalled over all conditions more ($p < .001$) color and form items than the letter and number items.

TABLE 3.2, cont.

ARTICLE	SUBJECTS	CONDITIONS AND TASKS	ANALYSIS

2. Gerjuoy & Winters (1970)	80 institutionalized EMRs 40 female, 40 male $\overline{IQ} = 64.89$ $\overline{CA} = 15.76$	1. The task consisted of recalling a list of 20 objects bimodally presented at a 2-sec rate. The two word lists used each had 5 words from 4 categories (5 trials).
		2. In Session 1 Ss were equally divided into 4 groups. In each condition the E* presented the picture, labelled it, and had the S repeat label.
		  a. SR*—each picture presented individually in random order
		  b. SC*—each picture presented individually in clustered order
		  c. GR*—five pictures displayed at once which were not categorized
		  d. GC*—five pictures displayed at once which were all from same category
		3. A 2nd session (1 week later) was used to compare Ss in this study with Ss in Gerjuoy & Spitz's (1966) study.
		  a. SR—same as above (40 Ss)
		  b. AR*—no pictures were used and 20 words were presented (40 Ss).
		4. Recall scores and cluster scores were obtained.
			1. Examined effects of bimodal presentations on recall and clustering.
			2. Examined relationship between recall and clustering.
			3. Examined effects of trials on recall and clustering.
			4. Compared effects of auditory presentations and visual presentations on recall and clustering (used results from earlier study).
			5. Compared bimodal presentation of this study with unimodal presentation of earlier study.

RESULTS: The experimental conditions in Session 1 did not differentially affect recall. Recall did significantly improve ($p < .001$) over trials. Recall of subjects in the structured answer condition (Ss recalled items per category) in the Gerjuoy and Spitz (1966) study was less than the combined recall scores of subjects in the 4 conditions; however, the condition of the earlier study in which items were presented in a clustered manner and the recall was requested via the same clusters produced recall scores superior to the recall scores of Session 1. Clustering above chance occurred on all 4 Session 1 conditions. More clustering occurred when stimuli were presented in a clustered manner than when presented in a random manner. In Session 2 no significant differences occurred between the retardates' recall scores in random condition of the earlier study and the AR condition of this study. The SR condition (bimodal) produced better ($p < .001$) recall than the AR condition. The SR (bimodal) condition also produced better recall scores than the random condition of the earlier study. Clustering was above chance in both SR and AR conditions which did not differ in amount of clustering. The AR condition produced significantly more clustering than the random condition in the Gerjuoy and Spitz study. Gerjuoy and Winters conclude that free recall can be improved with bimodal presentations and that the relationship between clustering and recall is modality dependent.

TABLE 3.2, cont.

ARTICLE	SUBJECTS	CONDITIONS AND TASKS	ANALYSIS
3. Herriot & Cox (1971)	1. 24 mongoloid (TMR*) $\overline{CA} = 12.8$ $\overline{MA} = 5.13$ $\overline{IQ} = 40$ 2. 24 nonmongoloid (TMR) $\overline{CA} = 12.56$ $\overline{MA} = 5.11$ $\overline{IQ} = 41$	1. 3 sets of 6 pictures of items were presented. Each set was presented simultaneously and then removed after 25 sec. The child was requested to recall orally the objects in the pictures. 25 sec were allowed for recall. 2. 2 sets of pictures appeared unrelated and the 3rd set consisted of 3 pairs of conceptually related items. All pictures were taken from the *EPVT** and were presented via slides. 3. Clustering, subjective organization, and recall scores were obtained. 4. Rehearsal scores were also obtained via observation.	1. Examined relationship between clustering and recall and between clustering and subjective organization. 2. Examined relationship between subjective organization and recall. 3. Compared the scores of the two groups.

RESULTS: The findings disclosed that clustering occurred in the categorically related items, and that subjective organization occurred with the unrelated items. Clustering and recall were significantly related, but recall and subjective organization were not. Clustering resulted in higher recall than did subjective organization. For the mongoloids, rehearsal (practice) was negatively corre-lated to recall. Herriot and Cox (1971) conclude: "(a) subjective organization was sequential in nature, while clustering was mainly hierarchical, (b) failure to internalize language leads to sequential strategies, and (c) mongoloid subjects, in particular, were retarded in internalization" (p. 702).

ARTICLE	SUBJECTS	CONDITIONS AND TASKS	ANALYSIS
4. Holden (1971)	1. 26 institutionalized EMRs $\overline{CA} = 15.2$ $\overline{IQ} = 70.0$ 2. 26 normals $\overline{CA} = 10.3$ $\overline{IQ} = 105.8$ Both groups MA and sex equated.	1. The task consisted of presenting stimuli via 3 modalities (vibrator—tactile, miniprojector—visual, earphones—auditory) and requesting the S to count the number of stimuli presented on each trial. The number of pulses ranged from 3 to 10 and all stimuli were 0.05-sec pulses. 2. The stimuli were presented in two 32 trial blocks. In one block the pulses were sequentially presented and in the other block they were grouped into couplets via temporal spacing. 3. In the 32 trial blocks the stimuli were presented to the same modality, alternated between 2 modalities, and then alternated among 3 modalities.	1. Compared the error scores of the two groups in relation to grouping and modality.

RESULTS: The EMRs made significantly more errors than did the MA-equivalent non-retarded children, and errors increased modality switching rate. The main effect of temporal grouping was not significant; however, under the modality condition in which temporal grouping was congruent with modality sequenc-ing, the error increments obtained with ungrouped sequences were elimi-nated. This effect supports the hypothesis that congruence between tem-poral grouping and modality sequencing (input organization) minimizes modality switching which EMRs find interfering by facilitating a counting strategy which equal CA nonretarded Ss use without temporal congruence.

TABLE 3.2, cont.

ARTICLE	SUBJECTS	CONDITIONS AND TASKS	ANALYSIS

5. Herriot (1972) *Experiment I*	1. 20 mongoloids $\overline{CA} = 23.29$ $\overline{MA} = 4.88$
	 2. 20 nonmongoloids $\overline{CA} = 24.08$ $\overline{MA} = 4.87$ $\overline{IQ} = 20$
		1. The children must review slides of 6 familiar objects and immediately recall the objects. Seven trials were conducted with 30 sec stimulus exposures for each trial.
		 2. 10 Ss from each of the 2 groups were assigned to one of 2 conditions:
		   a. Condition I—Upon presentation of the objects, the S randomly named the objects as the experimenter pointed to them. Following this, the S was asked to recall the objects (LARA*).
		   b. Condition II—In this condition the S had to label the items in the order in which they were just recalled on the previous trial (LARC*).
			SO* scores were obtained and compared across conditions and groups.

RESULTS: Sequential LARC increased SO compared to LARA. Since SO is a measure of sequential constancies, this was an expected result.

Herriot (1972) *Experiment II*	same as *Exp. I*	1. Pictures of objects were changed for this study. 2. Ss (regardless of etiology) were randomly assigned to LARA and LARC subgroups.	CL* scores were obtained and compared across conditions.

RESULTS: It was predicted that random order presentation would produce more clustering than presentation in the order of previous recall. This predicted difference occurred only on Day 2 for the mongoloid adults and only on Day 1 for the nonmongoloid adults.

6. Mende (1974)	1. 20 EMRs $\overline{CA} = 9$ $\overline{IQ} = 66.8$ 2. 20 EMRs $\overline{CA} = 14$ $\overline{IQ} = 67.1$	1. The task consisted of recalling pictures and objects presented visually and named by the examiner. Twelve pictures and 12 objects were used. Six trials were conducted. 2. SO scores, clustering scores, and recall scores were recorded.	1. Compared all scores between groups. 2. Examined relationship of clustering to recall.

RESULTS: The findings indicated that 14-year-old EMRs recalled more objects and pictures and produced higher cluster scores than 9-year-old EMRs. Both age groups recalled more objects than pictures and increased recall and clustering scores across trials. Recall and SO scores were only related for 14-year-old EMRs for recall of objects.

TABLE 3.2, cont.

ARTICLE	SUBJECTS	CONDITIONS AND TASKS	ANALYSIS

7. Palmer (1974)	1. 30 institutionalized EMRs
	$\overline{CA}$ = 22.3
	$\overline{IQ}$ = 65.8
	$\overline{MA}$ = 9.5
	
	2. 30 nonretarded pupils
	$\overline{CA}$ = 8.7
	$\overline{IQ}$ = 105.2
		1. Children were required to observe and name 18 objects (9 pairs) and recall them immediately. Five trials were performed. Each object was displayed 2–3 sec and 90 sec were allowed for free recall.
		2. The objects were selected on the basis of an earlier procedure used to insure that the object pairs:
		  a. comprise highly familiar members
		  b. belong to independent categories
		  c. have well-established direct and indirect associations for both retarded and MA-equal, nonretarded persons.
		3. Cluster and recall scores were recorded.
		4. Following the study normative data were collected to determine the degrees to which retarded and MA-equivalent individuals emitted associative and category responses.
			1. Compared recall and cluster scores between groups.
			2. Compared category and associative norms between groups.

RESULTS: Both groups demonstrated clustering well above chance on all 5 trials ($p < .001$). The normal group had higher cluster scores than the EMRs on trials 3, 4, and 5. Performance of both groups significantly improved over trials. On recall the two groups did not differ and both groups significantly improved over trials. In regards to the category-norm study, retarded and MA-matched nonretarded individuals, when presented names of categories, gave approximately the same number of responses. According to Palmer (1974), "if it may be assumed that recalling category names aids in recalling corresponding category members, this finding suggests that neither group showed an advantage in the use of this aid" (p. 459). However, in the associative-norm study the nonretarded group emitted significantly more taxonomic associates than the EMR group. Palmer states: "This [fact] suggests that the nonretarded subjects may indeed have tended to respond more readily than the retarded subjects to the presented objects with the presumably useful category retrieval cues" (p. 459). Finally, the results were discussed in terms of Jensen's theory of intelligence.

TABLE 3.2, cont.

ARTICLE	SUBJECTS	CONDITIONS AND TASKS	ANALYSIS

8. Riegel & Taylor (1974)	1. 86 EMRs
	$\overline{CA} = 8$
	$\overline{IQ} = 70$
	
	2. 31 nonretarded 2nd graders
	$\overline{CA} = 8$
		1. Each child was administered the *Sampling Organization and Recall through Strategies Test*. Twenty pictures were presented, one at a time, and the child named each and was told to arrange them in a way that would aid remembering them. Four levels of sorting strategies were computed:
		  a. Level I—syncretic strategies
		  b. Level II—perceptual strategies
		  c. Level III—low associative strategies
		  d. Level IV—superordinate and categorical strategies
		2. Recall scores were the total number of correct items recalled.
		3. Clustering scores were obtained by examining the responses.
			1. Compared the sorting, recall, and clustering scores of the two groups.
			2. Examined the relationship between clustering and recall.

RESULTS: The nonretarded children used higher-level sorting (levels III and IV) more than the retarded children ($p < .001$). Also, the nonretarded children recalled significantly more items than the retarded children. The groups did not differ in clustering scores. Significant correlations ($p < .05$) between recall and clustering were found for both groups. The investigators conclude that EMR children did not recall items as well as CA-equivalent nonretarded children and it is likely that their performance would be more readily comparable to that of MA-equivalent nonretarded children. Finally, Riegel and Taylor note that the relationship between clustering and recall was not straightforward.

Winters (1970) compared random bimodal (auditory-visual) and random unimodal (visual) input and reported that the bimodal input produced better recall. Gerjuoy et al. (1969) found that clustered auditory input produced higher recall scores than clustered visual input; however, they showed that when input was random, visual input generated higher recall scores than auditory input. Holden (1971) found that temporal grouping synchronized with modality switching (two items presented auditorially, then two presented visually, and then two presented tactically) generated higher recall scores than multimodality presentations without temporal groupings. Holden also found that switching input from one modality to another was not as effective in aiding recall as presenting in a single modality.

The influence of modality on the clustering scores of EMRs was examined and numerous findings were reported. Gerjuoy and Winters (1970) found that random bimodal (auditory-visual) presentations produced clustering scores similar to those generated by random unimodal (visual) presentations. Unlike the recall findings, Gerjuoy and Winters discovered that random auditory input produced more clustering than random visual input.

Recall and clustering were significantly related in the two studies (Herriot & Cox, 1971; Riegel & Taylor, 1974) in which their relationship was examined. In addition, EMRs clustered above chance in the three studies (Gerjuoy & Winters, 1970; Gerjuoy et al., 1969; Palmer, 1974) in which it was investigated.

Nine-year-old EMRs (Mende, 1974) and 12-year-old TMRs (Herriot & Cox, 1971) did not relate SO to recall. However, with 14-year-old EMRs (Mende, 1974) such a significant relationship did occur. Also, Herriot and Cox found that with TMRs, clustering had a higher relationship with recall than SO. Finally, Holden (1971) found that sequential labeling during recall resulted in higher SO scores than random labeling.

In four studies (Gerjuoy & Winters, 1970; Gerjuoy et al., 1969; Mende, 1974; Palmer, 1974) the influence of practice on the recall of EMRs was examined. Practice aided recall in 100% of these investigations. In the one study (Herriot & Cox, 1971) that examined this effect with TMR mongoloids, practice resulted in a decrease in recall scores. In three studies (Gerjuoy et al., 1969; Mende, 1974; Palmer, 1974) the influence of prac-

tice on clustering was investigated. All three found that practice aided clustering.

Comparative scores between mentally retarded and nonretarded participants were attempted in several studies. Subjects were compared on recall scores, sorting scores, and clustering scores. The comparisons are briefly outlined:

1. *Clustering*
   EMRs < MA-equivalent normals (Gerjuoy et al., 1969; Palmer, 1974)
   EMRs = CA-equivalent normals (Riegel & Taylor, 1974)
2. *Recall*
   EMRs = MA-equivalent normals (Gerjuoy et al., 1969; Palmer, 1974)
   EMRs < CA-equivalent normals (Riegel & Taylor, 1974)
3. *Sorting level*
   EMRs < CA-equivalent normals (Riegel & Taylor, 1974)

It is apparent that not enough replications in the group comparisons exist to draw definitive conclusions. The unusual finding (MR = CA-equivalent normals on clustering) by Riegel and Taylor (1974) may have resulted because: (a) the participants in both groups were young ($\overline{CA}$ = 8 years), (b) a task dissimilar to the ones in the other studies was used, and (c) clustering scores were computed in a manner that was different from the other studies.

Some specific findings from the eight studies include:

1. EMRs recalled objects better than they recalled pictures (Mende, 1974).
2. Fourteen-year-old EMRs recalled more than nine-year-old EMRs (Mende, 1974).
3. With TMRs a random order presentation generated higher clustering scores than having the subjects label each item during presentation according to the way they labeled them on the previous trial (Holden, 1971).

It is apparent that these eight studies have produced a mixture of findings with little replication and consistency. It is likely that differences in the meaningfulness and understanding of the material (for example, categories, such as *animals,* and items, such as *cats*) by the subjects has influenced some of the inconsistencies in the findings, for example, that MRs equal CA-equivalent normals on clustering. It is obvious that more memory-span studies with pictures are needed in order to test Spitz's position that EMRs lack input organizational skills which foster retrieval processes. Perhaps the primary implication of these findings is that EMRs frequently are able to use pictures to organize and retrieve information as well as their nonretarded peers.

Due to the sporadic findings of the eight memory-span studies that used pictures or objects, it is difficult to generate teaching implications sponsored by a strong empirical base. Thus, the teaching implications offered are oftentimes based on the results of a single study, and their use should be couched in a framework of tentative commitment and periodic evaluation.

TEACHING IMPLICATIONS. The following are some teaching techniques which receive support from the memory-span studies using pictures or objects.

1. Since Gerjuoy and Winters (1970) found that simultaneous auditory and visual input produced higher recall sources than unimodal (auditory or visual) presentations, it appears feasible for teachers to provide EMRs with simultaneous bimodal (auditory-visual) input. Teachers could pair the sound of the word with a picture or the word. Sometimes the teacher might not be able to provide the auditory input; other ways which do not require the teacher's presence are needed. A Language Master is an excellent device for providing simultaneous visual and auditory input. Language Master cards can be made which feature the word, a picture, and the sound of the word. A tape recorder may be used in conjunction with work sheets or flash cards to provide bimodal presentations. Also, peers may be used to provide bimodal presentations to each other.

   A logical extension of this approach is the multimodality approach which emphasizes providing input through three or four of the modalities at one time. In the multimodality approach the learner often hears the stimulus (word), traces the stimulus (which usually features a rough texture), and sees the stimulus (word). The Fernald method of teaching spelling and reading features the Visual-Auditory-Kinesthetic-Tactile (VAKT) approach and exemplifies one of the more popular multimodality techniques. Multimodality approaches may be effective for EMRs as a group, but they are not for everyone. Some youngsters seem to get "overloaded" with impinging stimuli coming via several channels simultaneously. Thus, as with most techniques, multimodality approaches need continuous monitoring to determine their effectiveness with individuals.

2. From the findings of the Gerjuoy et al. (1969) study regarding the facilitating effects of clustered auditory input on recall, it can be recommended that the teacher organize the language used in instruction. Directions need to be highly organized in order to help EMR pupils understand and remember them. For example, imagine a teacher is giving the class directions for a field trip. Rather than presenting a set of random directions, the teacher could organize the directions according to several areas, i.e., directions on the bus, directions at the zoo, directions for lunch, and directions for returning to the school. As suggested by the Gerjuoy et al. study, the teacher may want to give all the directions (material) at once and then repeat the appropriate directions at each step.

3. In Experiment II of the Gerjuoy et al. (1969) study, EMRs were able to improve their output (recall) when the stimuli were presented in a clustered manner rather than in a random manner. Unlike most of the studies in this group, Gerjuoy et al. used numbers, letters, geometric shapes, and colors as stimuli. Perhaps when stimuli are less meaningful (pictures of objects versus letters, numbers, etc.), clustered input becomes more helpful in fostering recall. These results suggest that numbers, letters, shapes, and colors should be grouped for instruction. For example letters could be grouped according to tall letters (*b, d, f, h, k, l, t*), short letters (*a, c, e, i, m, n, o, r, s, u, v, w, x, z*), and letters with a descending tail (*g, j, p, q, y*). Colors could be grouped according to hues, i.e., light hues (yellow, pink, tan) and dark hues (purple, red, brown).

4. In Experiment II of the Gerjuoy et al. (1969) study, EMRs were able to double their output (recall) when items were paired rather than being presented singly in random fashion. This finding suggests that when items are grouped into pairs the EMR pupil is able to recall more of the information than when items are presented singly. Thus teachers could present shapes, numbers, letters, and colors in pairs in order to facilitate the EMR's ability to process (remember) information. In addition, grouping the pairs according to their respective categories (color, form, etc.) would enhance the recall of EMRs.

5. Holden (1971) found that random shifting from one channel to another in sequential input can interfere with the recall of items by EMRs. Holden used nonmeaningful stimuli (dots, pulses, beeps) and the participants had to count the number of stimuli on each trial. It is unlikely that a classroom task would resemble the tasks used by Holden (nonmeaningful stimuli and intratrial modality switching). Thus, to suggest a teaching implication from Holden's study necessitates a substantial inference. With due consideration for the inferential gap, Holden's findings suggest that teachers should maintain congruence between modality switching and clustered bits of information and avoid unpatterned modality switching on a short, se-

quentially presented task. For example, congruence would be achieved by presenting two numbers via auditory channel, pausing, and then presenting two numbers via visual channel. Unpatterned switching would involve such strategies as presenting one number via one modality and, without pausing, presenting a second number via a different modality. Finally, in an earlier study Holden (1970) found no differences in the performances of EMRs in two-modality and three-modality conditions. This finding supports the position that switching modalities interferes with cognitive processing while the number of modalities used does not.

6. Herriot and Cox's (1971) study demonstrated the importance of pretraining activities with TMRs. This finding indicates that teachers should begin a memory task by reviewing (teaching) the names, labels, and directions used in the task. In addition, Herriot and Cox stress the importance of not overloading pupils when they are attempting to use subjective organization in processing material.

7. Mende (1974) found that EMRs recalled objects better than pictures. This finding indicates that objects may be used to foster memory. In the beginning of a unit of spelling, for example, objects which correspond to the words in the list may be used (paired with the respective words) to foster recall. This finding also leads to the suggestion that different sized objects (blocks) which represent numerals may foster the recall of the quantity represented by each number. Structural arithmetic (Stern, 1965) and Cuisenaire-Gattegno rods (Davidson, 1969) exemplify this strategy.

8. Riegel and Taylor (1974) showed that EMRs do not spontaneously discover and use associative relationships between items. Instead of using repetition to enhance the recall, Riegel and Taylor advocate training EMRs to discover and use relationships. This idea could be accomplished by providing EMRs with sorting activities (pictures, objects, word, etc.) and pointing out to the learner the associative relationships between items. Moreover, Palmer (1974) found that EMRs generated fewer correct items when given a category than MA-equivalent normals. Based on Palmer's finding, it appears that EMRs would benefit from training aimed at improving the number of words (items) they could generate *per* category.

9. Several of the studies revealed that practice with material improves recall and clustering. This finding suggests that EMR children be given drill or practice until proficiency is attained. Many commercial programs (e.g., *DISTAR*) which are designed to provide practice should be considered in educating EMRs.

Memory Span Studies Using Words

GERJUOY AND SPITZ'S STUDIES. Gerjuoy and Spitz (1966) selected the following subjects:

1. 20 lower-grade institutionalized educable retarded adolescents ($\overline{IQ}$ = 52.95)
2. 20 higher-grade institutionalized educable retarded adolescents ($\overline{IQ}$ = 72.05)
3. 19 nonretarded children with MAs equivalent to the higher-IQ retarded adolescents
4. 14 equal CA nonretarded adolescents
5. 20 college students

In their investigation they explored the relationship between clustering and free recall and their growth as a function of age.

Their task consisted of auditorially presenting 20 words, 5 each from four categories in a random order. On each trial 2 minutes were allowed for free recall. The retarded individuals, separately tested, were asked to say each word as it was presented and to recall orally the words after all 20 had been presented. The normals were tested in groups and were not required to say each word upon presentation; they wrote their recall responses. Clustering scores were computed (Bousfield & Bousfield, 1966) and yielded a clustering score above chance. A second clustering score (*observed maximum clustering ratio*) was developed and it measured the amount of above-chance clustering which was achieved, relative to the maximum possible clustering based on the total words recalled.

Data (recall and clustering) from the two retarded groups did not differ and it was pooled for comparisons with the other groups. On recall scores no significant differences resulted between the two lower MA groups (retarded and MA-equal normals), nor between the two higher MA groups (CA-equal normals and college students). The two higher MA groups recalled significantly more words than the two lower MA groups. The observed maximum clustering ratios disclosed that only college students and equal CA normals clustered any sizeable proportion of their maximum possible clustering. The equal MA group and the retarded adolescents clustered very little. Only on Trial 5 did the retardates significantly cluster above chance. Equal CA normals clustered significantly above chance on trials 4 and 5, while college students' clustering was significantly above chance on trials 3, 4, and 5. The investigators showed that clustering develops with an increase in MA. Finally, significant correlations between clustering and recall occurred with equal CA normals (Trial 5) and college students (trials 4 and 5).

Since clustering and recall were related for groups which consistently clustered above chance, a second experiment was conducted by Gerjuoy and Spitz (1966) to ascertain whether conditions which would increase clustering would have a positive effect on the recall of retarded individuals. The task and conditions for the 30 newly selected institutionalized retarded individuals were similar to those used in Experiment I. The participants were divided into a presented clustered (PC) group and a requested clustered (RC) group. In the PC group the words were presented in a categorized manner, and in the RC group the words were presented randomly; but recall in both PC and RC groups was requested by categories, e.g., "Say the animal words you remember."

The findings indicated that the recall scores of the PC and the RC group did not differ. When compared with the recall scores of the retarded adolescents in Experiment I, the retarded persons in Experiment II recalled significantly more. In addition, the persons in Experiment II significantly improved their recall over trials. The PC group clustered above chance on all five trials. Recall and clustering were significantly related on Trial 4.

Gerjuoy and Spitz (1966) conducted a third experiment primarily to determine whether or not the performance of retarded persons in Experiment II represented a ceiling for five trials. The retarded persons of Experiment II were equally divided and assigned to a presented-requested-clustered (PRC) group and a standard (ST) group. The 10 individuals in the ST condition heard the words in a random manner and the 10 persons in the PRC group were presented the words by the categories and were instructed to recall the words according to the categories.

The findings indicated that the PRC treatment resulted in significantly better recall than the ST presentation. The PRC condition produced superior recall when compared to the recall of the retarded individuals in the PC and RC conditions of Experiment II. Finally, the retarded participants in the ST condition did not differ in recall performance from the retarded persons in Experiment I, who were, on the average, 4 years younger.

After completing the three experiments, Gerjuoy and Spitz (1966) conclude:

1. Clustering develops and increases over trials as a function of MA.
2. Retardates appear deficient in spontaneous organization but are able to use external organization.
3. The PC method is more efficient than the RC method for improving the recall of retarded individuals. The RC method generates more categorical intrusions.

4. The PRC method is the most effective of the three methods for improving recall of retarded persons.

GALLAGHER'S STUDIES. Using a free recall task, Gallagher (1969) compared the short-term memory and subjective organization scores of 25 educable, mentally retarded adolescents and 25 nonretarded, CA-equivalent adolescents. Each individual subject was verbally presented 12 monosyllabic nouns from the Thorndike-Lorge (1944) list of the 500 most frequently occurring words and asked to recall the words in order. The same 12 words were presented (one word every 2 seconds) for 12 trials and each word appeared in a certain serial position only once over the 12 trials. Moreover, each word was preceded and followed by the same word only once. When the subject was silent for 30 seconds or indicated that no more words could be recalled, the next trial began.

Recall scores were obtained by recording the number of correct words recalled by the subject. Subjective organization scores were obtained by using Tulving's (1962) measurement method. The results of the study indicated that the subjective organization scores of the retarded and normal groups did not significantly differ. Also, the recall scores of the first six trials did not significantly differ from the recall scores of the last six trials for both groups. However, the normal group's total recall score was superior to the retarded group's. Gallagher (1969) notes that these findings support the position that retardates, when compared to CA-equivalent normals, have a short-term memory deficiency, but that the findings do not support the positions that varied repetition improves recall or that retardates have a subjective organization deficiency.

Gallagher (1969) notes that the subjective organization scores may have been influenced by several factors. First, in a study by Gerjuoy and Spitz (1966), associate clustering did not occur above chance for normal subjects younger than 14 (CA). Since the subjects in this study were not yet 14, it is possible that the normal-retardate difference did not emerge. Finally, the fast presentation rate and the varied method of presentation may have made it too difficult for subjects to organize the material.

GERJUOY AND ALVAREZ'S STUDIES. Gerjuoy and Alvarez (1969) investigated the transfer of learning in associate clustering of 60 institutionalized educable retarded adolescents and 60 equal MA normal children. As noted in Table 3.3, all subjects

TABLE 3.3

Presentation of Lists for Each Group in the Two Sessions

GROUP	SESSION 1	SESSION 2
15 EMRs	Randomized—List 1	Randomized—List 2
15 EMRs	Clustered—List 1	Randomized—List 2
15 EMRs	Randomized—List 2	Randomized—List 1
15 EMRs	Clustered—List 2	Randomized—List 1
15 Normals	Randomized—List 1	Randomized—List 2
15 Normals	Clustered—List 1	Randomized—List 2
15 Normals	Randomized—List 2	Randomized—List 1
15 Normals	Clustered—List 2	Randomized—List 1

were presented two lists of 20 familiar words (from the 1944 Thorndike-Lorge list) consisting of 5 words from each of four categories. Half of the subjects from each group were verbally presented a list of words in a randomized manner, and half received the words in clustered (categorical) manner. Session 2 occurred approximately one week later, at which time all subjects were given again their identical list of words (but in a randomized manner). In both sessions five trials were conducted on each list and 2 minutes were allowed for free recall.

They were particularly interested in examining whether or not the clustered presentation in Session 1 influenced or transferred to recall in Session 2. Recall scores were determined by recording the number of words correctly recalled. The amount of clustering above chance was determined by subtracting chance clustering from observed clustering.

The results of the study confirmed the position (Gerjuoy & Spitz, 1966) that clustered input (words presented by category) increases the retardates' recall when compared to random presentation of the same words. Likewise, when compared to a random presentation, the clustered presentation of words significantly increased the recall of MA-equivalent normals. Next, the results disclosed that recall and clustering in the second session were not influenced by participation in the first session. In addition, it was found that equal MA normals had higher recall and clustering scores than retardates, and that recall for both groups increased over trials within each session. Finally, it was found that one list was easier to learn in the first session, but in the second session both lists were learned equally as well.

In essence, the findings of this study support the positions that external organization of material facilitates recall; that MA-equal normals recall

more than retardates; and that immediate practice improves recall. However, the findings do not support the position that a clustering experience with word recall will transfer 1 week later to a similar task. It is possible that transfer did not occur because of the long interval between sessions and the lack of distributed practice with clustering in Session 1.

EVANS'S STUDIES. Evans (1970) wanted to investigate whether cognitive processes underlying reading ability affect associative clustering processes and to assess the effects of presentation mode on recall and clustering scores. He tested 60 educable retarded adolescents.

His task consisted of presenting five words (from the 1944 Thorndike-Lorge word list) from each of four categories and instructing the subject to immediately recall the 20 words. In all presentations the words were randomly arranged and displayed for 3 seconds. Each subject participated in four trials.

The subjects were divided into three groups according to presentation mode. The individuals in the auditory group received the words via tape recorder; the visual group used a slide projector; and the auditory-visual group used both. The machines were synchronized so that the auditory stimulus was presented 1 second after the onset of the slide for each word. The number of words correctly recalled was recorded, and clustering scores above chance were obtained by subtracting the number of word clusters expected from the number observed.

In order to determine the influence of reading level on clustering and recall, the subjects were divided at the median on the basis of reading grade levels. The results indicated that reading level was not significantly related to either clustering or recall. The auditory and visual presentations did not yield significantly different recall or clustering scores. The bimodal presentation had a significant facilitating effect on recall but not on clustering. Cluster and recall scores significantly improved over trials. Recall and clustering scores were significantly related in all conditions except visually.

COBB AND BARNARD'S STUDIES. Cobb and Barnard (1971) investigated the effects of implicit associative values on the free recall scores of 20 educable retarded children and 20 CA-equivalent, nonretarded children. They hypothesized that both groups would perform better as the associative strength of the words increased, and that nonretarded children would recall more words than retarded children. Moreover, they hypothesized an interaction of IQ with the varying degrees of implicit association; i.e., in relation to nonretarded children, the performance of retarded children would be better when the degree of association is higher than when the association value is lower.

The 20 children from each group participated in a pretraining session and a training session. In the pretraining session each subject was presented, via tape recorder, two word lists of six words each. Words from one list were food items and words from the other list were names of animals. At the conclusion of the pretraining session all children were able to recall (orally) all the words from the two lists.

Following the pretraining session, all children were again presented, via tape recorder, five lists of 12 words each. The lists were rated by 18 graduate students in terms of their degree of associate strength with the words used in pretraining. Words in List I consisted of the same words that were used in the pretraining session; it was regarded as the list with the strongest associative strength. The descending order of strength of the remaining four lists was: List II, List III, List IV, and List V. The presentation of the lists was counterbalanced for order. Rate of presentation was 1 word every 3 seconds.

The results indicated that CA-equivalent, nonretarded children recall more words than retarded children across all trials. The effect of the association value among the lists was significant with the mean recall for lists decreasing in order of decreasing association (see Figure 3.3, page 72). The interaction of IQ and degree of association was significant and lends support to Spitz's (1966) position that organization and meaningfulness of

stimulus lists facilitate recall. Cobb and Barnard (1971) discuss this interaction: "normal subjects make use of the cues provided by low or high meaningful stimuli, and . . . retarded subjects benefit mainly from high meaningful items" (p. 134).

BILSKY, EVANS, AND GILBERT'S STUDIES. Bilsky, Evans, and Gilbert (1972) selected 96 educable retarded adolescents in order to examine the generalization of clustering tendencies. Specifically, the investigation was designed to explore the feasibility of extending transfer effects by exposing EMR adolescents to organized word lists and then to different verbal materials. Each adolescent was asked to recall 16 words from four conceptual categories over four consecutive trials. All words were presented through earphones and simultaneously displayed on a screen. On the first two trials half of the subjects received the words organized according to categories and half received the words in a randomized manner. On the last two trials the groups were divided according to list novelty so that a third of each group received either the same list, new words from the same categories, or new words from different categories. For these last two trials all lists were randomly presented.

The results disclosed that the group who received the organized list (trials 1 and 2) displayed significantly more clustering than the group who received the randomized list. The group who received the same words improved over trials, while the two novelty groups had a decrease in performance from Trial Block 1 (trials 1 and 2) to Trial Block 2 (trials 3 and 4). The group with the same words recalled significantly more words than both the novelty groups. Bilsky et al. (1972) conclude that practice with organized lists aids clustering on later trials with the same words. In addition, they note that the ability to organize material did not transfer, i.e., practice with organized lists produced interference on later trials with new materials.

SUMMARY. Table 3.4 aids in the summarization of findings from the six studies. The findings will be summarized within the following framework:

1. Recall performances
   EMRs versus CA-equivalent normals
   EMRs versus MA-equivalent normals
2. Clustering performances
   EMRs versus CA-equivalent normals
   EMRs versus MA-equivalent normals

3. Relationship of clustering and recall
4. Effects of input organization
5. Other specific relevant findings

In the three studies (Cobb & Barnard, 1971; Gallagher, 1969; Gerjuoy & Spitz, 1966) which compared the recall performances of educable retarded individuals with CA-equivalent normals, the EMRs performed significantly poorer. These results are consistent with Spitz's (1966, 1973) find-

ings regarding recall performances of institutionalized EMRs and CA-equivalent normals. In these three studies only Gerjuoy and Spitz used institutionalized EMRs.

In the two studies (Gerjuoy & Alvarez, 1969; Gerjuoy & Spitz, 1966) which compared the recall performances of institutionalized educable retarded persons with MA-equivalent normals, the findings were dissimilar. Gerjuoy and Spitz found

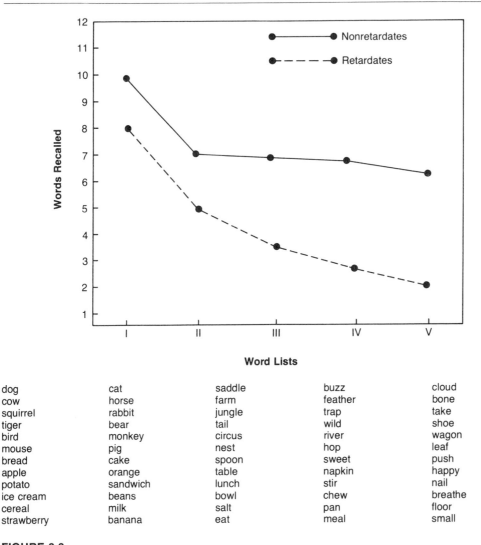

dog	cat	saddle	buzz	cloud
cow	horse	farm	feather	bone
squirrel	rabbit	jungle	trap	take
tiger	bear	tail	wild	shoe
bird	monkey	circus	river	wagon
mouse	pig	nest	hop	leaf
bread	cake	spoon	sweet	push
apple	orange	table	napkin	happy
potato	sandwich	lunch	stir	nail
ice cream	beans	bowl	chew	breathe
cereal	milk	salt	pan	floor
strawberry	banana	eat	meal	small

FIGURE 3.3

Interaction of IQ status and associative value of word lists.

Source: Adapted from "Differential Effects of Implicit Associative Values on Short-term Recall of Retarded and Nonretarded Children" by J. H. Cobb & J. W. Barnard, *American Journal of Mental Deficiency*, 1971, 76, 134. Copyright 1971 by the American Association on Mental Deficiency. Reprinted by permission.

TABLE 3.4
Summary of Memory-Span Studies Using Words

ARTICLE	SUBJECTS	CONDITIONS AND TASKS	ANALYSIS
1. Gerjuoy & Spitz (1966) *Experiment I*	1. 20 institutionalized $\overline{CA}$ = 14.52 $\overline{IQ}$ = 52.95 2. 20 institutionalized $\overline{CA}$ = 14.49 $\overline{IQ}$ = 72.05 3. 19 equal MA normals $\overline{CA}$ = 9.81 $\overline{IQ}$ = 107 4. 14 equal CA normals $\overline{CA}$ = 14.7 $\overline{IQ}$ = 117 5. 20 college students $\overline{CA}$ = 22.01	1. The task consisted of recalling 20 words presented auditorially. Two minutes were allowed for free recall on each trial. The words were from 4 categories. 2. The MRs were tested individually and oral responses were required. The normals were tested in groups and wrote their responses. 3. Clustering above chance was recorded, i.e., observed clustering minus chance clustering. Also, a second cluster score was computed (observed/maximum ratio). This score accounted for the total number of words recalled. 4. Recall scores were recorded.	1. Compared recall scores across groups. 2. Compared clustering scores across groups.

RESULTS: Since data from the 2 retarded groups did not differ in amount of recall or clustering, they were pooled for comparisons with the other groups. On recall there were no significant differences between the 2 lower MA groups, nor between the 2 higher MA groups. However, the 2 higher MA groups recalled significantly more words than the 2 lower MA groups. The equal MA normals and the retarded group clustered very little. Only on Trial 5 did the retardates significantly cluster above chance ($p < .01$). Equal CA normals clustered significantly above chance ($p < .02$) on trials 4 and 5, while college students' clustering was significantly above chance on trials 3 ($p < .06$), 4 and 5 ($p < .001$). The observed/maximum ratios revealed that only college students and equal CA normals clustered any sizeable proportion of their maximum possible clustering (trials 4 and 5 only). Significant correlations between clustering and recall occurred with equal CA normals (Trial 5) and college students (trials 4 and 5).

| Gerjuoy & Spitz (1966) *Experiment II* | 30 institutionalized retardates 15 males 15 females | 1. The task consisted of recalling 20 words presented auditorially. Stimuli were the same as in *Exp. I*.
2. The Ss were assigned to one of 2 conditions.
   a. PC*—words presented in categorized manner
   b. RC*—After the Ss had repeated each word as it was presented they were requested to recall the words via categories, e.g., clothing words, foods, etc.
3. Clustering and recall scores were recorded. | 1. Compared recall and clustering scores between conditions.
2. Computed relationship of clustering to recall.
3. Compared results to *Exp. I* data. |

RESULTS: The recall scores of the 2 groups did not differ significantly. When compared with the recall scores of retardates in *Experiment I* the retardates in this study recalled significantly more ($p < .005$). In addition, the Ss in this study significantly improved recall over trials. The PC* group clustered above chance on all 5 trials. Recall and clustering were significantly related on Trial 4.

TABLE 3.4, cont.

ARTICLE	SUBJECTS	CONDITIONS AND TASKS	ANALYSIS
Gerjuoy & Spitz (1966) *Experiment III*	20 institutionalized retardates Ss were older than Ss in *Exp. I and II*. $\overline{CA} = 18$	1. Task—same as in *Exp. II*. 2. 10 Ss were assigned to the ST* (random order) presentation and 10 received a PRC* presentation.	1. Compared recall and clustering scores between groups.

RESULTS: The PRC treatment resulted in significantly better ($p < .001$) recall than the ST condition. The PRC condition produced superior recall when compared to the recall of Ss in the PC and RC conditions of *Exp. II*. The Ss in the ST condition did not differ in recall performance from the Ss in *Exp. I*, who were on the average 4 years younger.

2. Gallagher (1969)	1. 25 EMRs $\underline{IQ}$ of 21 on *WISC* = 66.29 $\underline{IQ}$ of 4 on *Binet* = 65.75 $\overline{CA}$ = 14.1 2. 25 normals $\underline{IQ}$ = 101.2 $\overline{CA}$ = 14.3 Both groups balanced on race and sex.	1. Task—Subjects were verbally presented 12 nouns and asked to orally recall them in order remembered. Twelve trials with the presentation order different for each trial were conducted (free recall task). 2. Tulving's (1962) method of measuring organization (SO) was used.	1. Compared the recall scores of both groups. 2. Compared SO scores of both groups. 3. Compared the recall scores of the first 6 trials and the last 6 trials.

RESULTS: The normal group recalled significantly ($p < .05$) more total words correctly over the 12 trials than the EMRs. No significant differences were found between the recall scores of the first 6 trials and the last 6 trials in either group. The 2 groups did not significantly differ on SO scores. The results supported the position that EMRs have a STM deficiency when compared to CA-equivalent normals, but did not support the position that EMRs exhibit an input organization deficiency when compared to normals. Also, the findings indicate that varied repetition did not aid recall. Gallagher suggests that the speed of presentation (1 word per 2 seconds) may have been too short for subjective organization to occur. Similarly, the speed may have reduced the facilitating effects of repetition.

3. Gerjuoy & Alvarez (1969)	1. 60 institutionalized EMRs $\overline{CA}$ = 15.2 $\underline{IQ}$ = 59.4 Ss divided into 4 groups of 15 (see Table 3.3). 2. 60 MA-equivalent normals $\overline{CA}$ = 10.3 $\underline{IQ}$ = 111.3 Ss divided into 4 groups of 15 (see Table 3.3).	1. Free recall of 20 familiar words (4 categories of 5 words each) presented orally (used two different lists). 2. Recall score was obtained by adding number of words correctly recalled. 3. Clustering score was obtained by subtracting chance clustering score from observed clustering score.	1. Compared recall scores of MR and normals. 2. Compared effects of clustering in Session 1 on clustering in Session 2. 3. Examined effects of practice in each session. 4. Compared recall in relation to respective list presented. 5. Compared recall scores from clustered and randomized word presentations.

RESULTS: Equal MA normals recalled significantly more words than the EMRs. One list was easier to learn than the other, which suggests that the *Thorndike-Lorge Word Frequencies List* is outdated. Immediate practice improved recall for both groups. Recall scores with the clustered presentation were greater than the recall scores with randomized presentation. Recall scores in the second session were not affected by experience in Session 1 (no transfer).

ARTICLE	SUBJECTS	CONDITIONS AND TASKS	ANALYSIS

4. Evans (1970)	60 EMRs
	24 males, 36 females
	$\overline{CA} = 18$
	$\overline{IQ} = 66.88$
	Reading grade mean = 3.92
		1. The task consisted of presenting 5 words from each of 4 categories and asking the subject to recall the words immediately following the presentation of the 20 words. All presentations were ungrouped.
		2. The subjects were assigned to 1 of 3 conditions based on mode of presentation.
		  a. Auditory group was presented words via tape recorder.
		  b. Visual group was presented words via slide projector.
		  c. Auditory-visual group was presented words via simultaneous use of tape recorder and slide projector.
		3. All words were presented for 3 sec, and 4 trials were used. Recall time stopped 1 min after last response.
		4. Recall and cluster scores were obtained.
			1. The median reading score was obtained and Ss were divided into 2 groups according to whether they were above or below the median reading level. Then the effect of reading level on recall and cluster scores was analyzed.
			2. Recall and cluster scores from the different experimental conditions (mode of presentation) were compared.
			3. Effect of trials on recall and clustering scores was examined.

RESULTS: The combined auditory-visual condition produced significantly ($p < .01$) more correct recall responses than either the auditory or visual condition. Recall scores improved significantly ($p < .01$) over trials. Cluster scores improved ($p < .01$) over trials. Recall scores were significantly related to cluster scores in the auditory-visual condition, the auditory condition, and in the combined groups. Clustering scores were not a function of general reading ability. The modal presentation facilitated recall but not clustering.

TABLE 3.4, cont.

ARTICLE	SUBJECTS	CONDITIONS AND TASKS	ANALYSIS
5. Cobb & Barnard (1971)	1. 20 EMRs CA = 13 IQ = 57 2. 20 normals CA = 13 IQ = 114	1. The task consisted of listening via tape to 5 lists of 12 words each and recalling the words immediately after their presentation. Words were presented at the rate of 1 word every 3 sec. 2. A pretraining session and an experimental session were conducted. During pretraining the Ss were presented two lists (food, animals) of 6 words each and drilled until they could recall all 12 words. Following the pretraining all Ss were presented 5 lists of 12 words each which varied in associative strength with the words used in pretraining. The words in List 1 were the same as those used in pretraining and were regarded as having the highest associative strength. The associative strength of the remaining 4 lists was evaluated by graduate students. In descending order of associate or organizational strength they are: List II, List III, List IV, and List V. 3. Recall scores were obtained.	1. Compared recall scores between groups. 2. Compared the recall scores for each word list. 3. Examined interaction between IQ and recall.

RESULTS: Nonretarded children recalled significantly ($p < .01$) more words than retarded children. The effect of the association among lists was significant ($p < .01$), with the average recall for lists decreasing in order of decreasing association. The interaction of IQ and degree of association was significant ($p < .01$) and was interpreted as supporting Spitz's (1966) organizational hypothesis.

76

TABLE 3.4, cont.

ARTICLE	SUBJECTS	CONDITIONS AND TASKS	ANALYSIS

6. Bilsky, Evans, & Gilbert (1972)	96 EMRs
	41 males, 55 females
	$\overline{CA} = 17.2$
	$\overline{IQ} = 65.15$
	Reading grade level
	Mean 3.58
	$\overline{MA} = 10.4$
		1. Task consisted of instructing Ss to recall 16 words that had been presented at the rate of 1 word every 2 sec. The words were from 4 conceptual categories and each word was presented through the auditory (earphone) and visual (screen) modes.
		2. On the first 2 trials the Ss were equally divided with half receiving a randomized presentation and half receiving words organized via categories. On the last 2 trials all lists were randomly presented.
		3. On the last 2 trials the subjects from each condition were assigned to one of three conditions regarding list novelty:
		  a. same categories and same words
		  b. same categories and new words
		  c. new categories and new words
			1. Examined the number of words clustered above chance across conditions (list novelty, organization, and trials).
			2. Examined the number of words recalled across conditions.

RESULTS: The group presented the organized list displayed significantly ($p < .01$) more clustering than the random group. Under blocked conditions the same categories and same words group improved over trial blocks, while the 2 novelty groups had a decrease in performance from Trial Block 1 to Trial Block 2. The same category and same words group recalled significantly more words than both the other groups. The authors note that the results of the present study indicate that practice with organized lists leads to increased clustering on later trials with the same words; however, the ability to organize material did not transfer, i.e., practice with blocked lists produced interference effects on later trials with new materials.

*ST = Standard
PC = Presented clustered
PRC = Presented-requested clustered
RC = Requested clustered

no differences between the recall performance of the retarded group and the MA-equivalent normals, whereas Gerjuoy and Alvarez found that the retarded group performed poorer.

In the study (Gerjuoy & Spitz, 1966) that compared the clustering scores of institutionalized EMRs with CA-equivalent normals, the performance of the nonretarded group was superior. In the two studies (Gerjuoy & Alvarez, 1969; Gerjuoy & Spitz, 1966) which compared the clustering performances of institutionalized EMRs with MA-equivalent normals the results were mixed. Gerjuoy and Spitz found no difference between the clustering performance of the EMRs and the MA-equivalent normals, whereas Gerjuoy and Alvarez showed a superior performance for the normals.

In two studies (Evans, 1970; Gerjuoy & Spitz, 1966) the relationship between clustering and recall was examined. Gerjuoy and Spitz found a significant relationship between clustering and recall when clustering occurred above chance. Evans (1970) found a significant relationship between recall and clustering with auditory and auditory-visual presentations, but not with visual presentations.

In three studies (Cobb & Barnard, 1971; Gerjuoy & Alvarez, 1969; Gerjuoy & Spitz, 1966) the effect of input organization on recall was examined. The results of all three studies indicated that organized input improved recall. Using institutionalized EMRs, MA-equivalent normals, and CA-equivalent normals, Gerjuoy and Spitz conclude that a PC condition was better than a RC condition, and that both produced better recall than a ST presentation. They also note that the two grouping conditions (PC and RC) used together produced better recall than any other condition used alone. With institutionalized EMRs and MA-equivalent normals, Gerjuoy and Alvarez found that grouped input produced recall scores superior to those generated with random input. Cobb and Barnard found that with EMRs and CA-equivalent normals, high-association material produced higher recall scores than low-association material. The results from these studies lend support to Spitz's (1966, 1973) position that input organization facilitates recall. In addition, it is important to remember that Spitz found that with or without preclustered input, the recall of retardates tends to improve over trials.

In two studies (Bilsky et al., 1972; Gerjuoy & Spitz, 1966) the effect of input organization on clustering was investigated. Both studies found

that organized input produced clustering scores that were superior to clustering scores generated from random presentations. Some specific findings from the six studies include:

1. Equal CA low- ($\overline{IQ}$ = 52.95) and high- ($\overline{IQ}$ = 72.05) grade EMRs did not differ on recall or clustering scores of words (Gerjuoy & Spitz, 1966).
2. The recall of 18-year-old and 14-year-old EMRs did not differ for 20 words presented auditorially with 2 minute free recall (Gerjuoy & Spitz, 1966).
3. The recall scores of the first six trials were equivalent to the recall scores of the last six trials for both EMR and CA-equivalent normal children. This supports the position that varied repetition does not improve recall (Gallagher, 1969).
4. Practice with the same material aids the recall of EMR and MA-equivalent normals (Gerjuoy & Spitz, 1966).
5. Practice with clustering a group of words did not generalize to the same list one week later (Gerjuoy & Alvarez, 1969).
6. When using a random presentation, reading level did not significantly correlate with clustering or recall (Evans, 1970).
7. When using a random presentation, bimodal presentation improved recall but not clustering (Evans, 1970).
8. When using a random presentation, recall and cluster scores improved over trials (Evans, 1970).
9. Practice with organized lists failed to generalize to new word lists minutes later (Bilsky, Evans, & Gilbert, 1972).
10. Practice with the same words facilitated clustering on later trials (Bilsky et al., 1972).

TEACHING IMPLICATIONS. The six memory-span studies using words unequivocally support the position that organized input (words) fosters recall. Teaching implications primarily involve the organization of stimulus words prior to their presentation to normal and retarded students. Specific recommendations include:

1. Teachers should present new words in a categorical manner whenever possible. For example, if a word list includes animal words, food words, and directional words, they should be grouped according to their respective categories and then presented. All studies found this procedure effective for improving recall. Moreover, it is important to note that the effectiveness of this technique has been demonstrated with word lists up to 20 words and categories up to four. Also, in the studies the categories always included the same number of words. It is likely that the categorizing of words will improve recall of word lists longer than 20 words with four or more categories, but careful monitoring to achieve an optimal condition

appears warranted. Finally, the symmetry of having an equal number of words in each category may especially appeal to the retarded learner.

2. In all but one of the studies (Gallagher, 1969) practice (drill with same words) aided the recall of the words by all subjects. These findings suggest that practice and drill foster the recall of words. Due to structure and repetitive nature, programs such as the Remedial Reading Drills by Hegge, Kirk, and Kirk (1936) and *DISTAR* (Engelmann & Bruner, 1969) gain support from these findings. In order to promote and maintain motivation during practice sessions, the teacher may find it helpful to develop games, self-correcting teaching materials, recording systems (charts and graphs), and support systems (verbal praise and tokens).

3. Since Cobb and Barnard (1971) found that the recall of new words was facilitated if the words had high association with previously learned words, it seems feasible that the learning of new words would be helped if the words were from the same categories as previously learned words. For example, if recently learned words consisted of furniture items, animal items, food items, and transportation items, new words should be introduced which fit into one of these existing categories. In addition, new words should not be introduced until existing words have been mastered. Bilsky et al. (1972) found that the rapid introduction of new material may interfere with learning.

4. In order to help retarded individuals take advantage of the inherent organization of material, task instructions should explain how the assigned words may be grouped into categories. Since several of the studies (Bilsky et al., 1972; Gerjuoy & Alvarez, 1969) found that retarded individuals failed to generalize cluster skills from one list to another, it appears important to remind EMRs of clustering strategies as they go from one task to another or as they attempt the same task at different times.

5. Since Evans (1970) found a bimodal (auditory-visual) presentation to be more effective with EMRs in improving recall than a unimodal presentation, it seems likely that words would be learned more readily by retarded individuals when they are bimodally presented. This can be easily accomplished by using the Language Master and/or a tape recorder in conjunction with the stimulus words. Based on the findings reviewed, organized input presented bimodally would be an effective technique for teaching sight words.

6. Gerjuoy and Spitz (1966) discovered that the memory of EMRs was improved by requesting them to recall words according to categories. For example, after a number of words had been presented in a random fashion, the retarded individuals were asked to recall the animal words, the food words, the furniture items, etc. This requested clustered technique can be accomplished by organizing answer sheets according to the categories or by orally requesting the categorical

words, e.g., "Tell me the animal words." When using this technique a word of caution is warranted because it often increases guessing responses. Moreover, the requested clustered technique is more effective when used in conjunction with organized input (PC).

7. Cobb and Barnard (1971) found that the recall performance of EMRs approached that of CA-equivalent normals when the stimulus words were highly meaningful. Since meaningfulness is often associated with experience, it appears that the more experiences the EMR learner has with the words, the better the learning. For example, use menus for food words, pair words with appropriate picture, visit places where specific words are commonly used, pair words which go together (ball–bat, shoe–sock, ice–water). Meaningfulness could be maintained by using functional words and words that refer to concrete objects.

The implications from the memory-span studies using words have been derived from only six studies which have primarily used institutionalized EMRs. Long-term (6 months to a year) studies which focus on applying the organizational principles in educational settings are needed. Although this need is apparent, enough information is presently available to indicate that organized input aids recall. Now it seems that the following steps would represent the *optimal* conditions for fostering recall:

1. Select meaningful words.
2. Instruct the learner to notice inherent categories.
3. Present the words bimodally in an organized manner.
4. Request recall according to the categories.

Studies Using Paired-Associate Tasks

SPITZ'S STUDIES. Spitz (1972) studied the level of redundancy which separates the performance of retardates from normals. In his first experiment he selected 48 institutionalized, educable retarded adolescents, 48 nonretarded third graders, and 48 eighth graders and asked them to perform paired-associate learning tasks which varied in degree of redundancy. The eighth graders were equated on CA with the retarded children and the third graders were equated on MA. Twelve children from each group were assigned to one of the four redundancy levels: 33%— 8–C, 3–B, 7–A, 5–C, 4–A, 6–B; 50%—7–A, 4–A, 8–B, 6–B, 3–B, 5–A; 67%—6–B, 7–A, 4–A, 3–B, 5–B, 8–B; and 83%—6–B, 7–B, 4–A, 8–B, 3–B, 5–B. The stimuli for each redundancy condition were six numeral-letter pairs. Criterion was set at 2 consecutive correct trials and 30 trials were permitted to reach criterion. A trial consisted of presenting via slides each of the pairs for 3 seconds followed by the presentation of one item (numeral) from each pair with instructions to recall the item (letter) that was paired with it.

The findings revealed that errors increased as redundancy decreased. Eighth graders performed better than both the retarded youngsters and third graders; however, the latter two groups did not differ. Comparisons of each redundancy level revealed that eighth graders performed better than retardates and third graders only at the 50% redundancy level.

Spitz (1972) then selected 36 new subjects from each of the populations and assigned 12 children from each group to one of three redundancy level conditions (33%, 50%, and 67%). Since IQ data were not available on the nonretarded children, it was not possible to ascertain whether the groups were equated on MA. Spitz notes that it was likely that the characteristic comparisons of the subjects were similar to those in Experiment I. In the second experiment he used the same item pairs but changed the task so that the five pairs were presented *simultaneously* via slides. The total display time and recall time were the same as in Experiment I.

The results indicated that eighth graders performed significantly better than third graders, who, in turn, did better than the retardates. Eighth graders performed significantly better than retardates at each redundancy level; however, the third graders performed better than the retarded children only at the 33% redundancy level. In comparison with the results of Experiment I, the findings of Experiment II revealed that (a) retardates performed significantly poorer, (b) third graders exhibited no change, and (c) eighth graders did better. He notes that the results suggest that in the 33% conditions, the eighth graders exhibited greater capacity than retardates and third graders to discover and use redundancy. In discussing the results, Spitz (1972) states:

> The most significant finding is the rather catastrophic disintegration in performance by retardates who were presented high information material in complete form, and permitted free recall, compared to their relatively good performance when the same material was presented sequentially with immediate feedback. This contrasts strikingly with the improved performance of normals of equal CA under the same conditions. The normals of equal MA showed no change. (p. 169)

SPITZ AND BORYS'S STUDIES. Spitz and Borys (1974) selected 48 institutionalized EMR adoles-

cents and 48 nonretarded third and fourth graders in order to examine the effects of external emphasis and redundancy level on paired-associate learning. Six paired-associate items (6–A, 4–B, 3–C, etc.) were simultaneously displayed via a screen. Participants were asked to recall the six pairs when given the stimuli for each pair. Each six paired-associate block was presented for 18 seconds, and 18 seconds were allowed for recall. Testing terminated after 30 trial blocks if the criterion of two consecutive correct test trials had not been reached. All participants received the task with 33% and 50% redundancy.

The two groups were each equally divided and assigned to one of three experimental conditions. In the ungrouped condition the six pairs of words were randomized with the constraint that at only one point would a letter be adjacent to itself. In the grouped spatial condition the materials were displayed so that the same letters always followed each other, for example, 2–B, 8–B, 4–A, 6–A, 3–C, 9–C. In the grouped perceptual condition the material was displayed the same as in the ungrouped condition except that all pairs containing A's were enclosed in rectangles, B's in ovals, and C's in diamonds. Cluster and recall scores were recorded.

The findings disclosed that the 50% redundancy condition produced better recall performances than the 33% redundancy condition for both groups. External cueing improved the performance of the nonretarded children (especially in 50% redundancy), whereas it had little influence on the performance of the retarded group. Subjects who reached criterion used clustering by the last two trials. Clustering was highest in the spatial condition. Nonretarded subjects used clustering more than the retarded adolescents ($p < .05$). For the retarded, increased clustering did not result in increased recall performance. Spitz and Borys (1974) conclude:

> These results suggest that the third- and fourth-graders more readily recognized and utilized externally cued redundancy and, consequently, were more likely to improve their performance than were retarded adolescents. (p. 737)

Borys and Spitz (1974) selected 32 institutionalized EMR adolescents and 32 MA-equivalent, normal third graders to examine the effects of temporal grouping and redundancy level on paired-associate learning. Specifically, this study was an attempt to examine a method of presentation (other than grouping or outlining stimuli) which facilitates recognition and use of redundancy and leads to superior learning.

The task consisted of recalling six paired-associate numeral-letter items which had been displayed on a screen for 18 seconds. On 33% redundancy the items were presented in blocks of two pairs, each block being displayed for 6 seconds. On 50% redundancy the items were displayed on blocks of three pairs and each of the two blocks was presented for 9 seconds. At the conclusion of each presentation of six pairs, 18 seconds were allowed for free recall. All subjects received the paired-associate items at 33% and 50% redundancy levels. Trials were continued until a criterion of two errorless trials occurred. Thirty trials were allowed to obtain criterion.

The two groups were each divided and assigned to one of two experimental conditions: incongruent temporal (IT) and congruent temporal (CT). In the IT condition the paired-associate blocks were presented on the screen and never had the same response term for adjacent paired-associates. For example:

33% redundancy	50% redundancy
3B	7A
7A	6B
	4A
8C	
4A	3B
	5A
5C	8B
6B	

In the CT condition the blocks of paired-associates always had the same response term. For example:

33% redundancy	50% redundancy
7A	7B
2A	2B
	6B
4C	
3C	4A
	7A
6B	3A
5B	

The results indicated that there was an increase in errors as redundancy decreased. For both groups performance was superior following CT presentations, and the performance of the third graders was better than the retardates' performance in this condition. The performances of the two groups did not differ in the IT condition. They conclude that organized input improved the performance of both groups, but that the nonretarded group made greater use of the organized input. With 33% redundancy, clustering was above baseline only in the CT condition where third graders clustered more than EMRs. Most participants who reached criterion made use of clustering on the last two trials. Borys and Spitz note that these results support the position that method of presentation effects the recognition and use of redundancy.

SUMMARY. The three studies reported in the paired-associate group were all authored or coauthored by Spitz and they represent a systematic investigation of the effects of temporal grouping and redundancy level on the paired-associate learning of young retarded and nonretarded persons. Institutionalized adolescent EMRs participated in each study. As illustrated in Table 3.5, the same stimulus pairs were used in the 33% and 50% redundancy levels in each experiment. In addition, the total exposure time for the stimuli was the same for each investigation. The differences among the experiments are in the presentation and recall methods.

Spitz (1972) used the anticipation procedure which involves presenting the stimuli in a serial fashion; Spitz and Borys (1974), on the other hand, presented the stimuli in a simultaneous manner and used a combination sequential-simultaneous presentation. The simultaneous test phase was used primarily because it permitted participants to respond in any sequence, thus revealing the use of clustering. The investigators were seeking the best method for optimal learning of the material. Since the experiments were methodologically similar, Borys and Spitz (1974) statistically analyzed (analysis of variance and Tukey test) the scores across the following conditions:

1. Ungrouped (UG) (baseline)
2. Congruent blocking (G) (redundant grouping without temporal blocking)
3. Incongruent temporal (IT) (temporal blocking without redundant grouping)
4. Congruent temporal (CT) (combined redundant and temporal grouping)

TABLE 3.5
Summary of Studies Using Paired-Associate Tasks

ARTICLE	SUBJECTS	CONDITIONS AND TASKS	ANALYSIS
1. Spitz (1972) *Experiment I*	1. 48 institutionalized EMRs $\overline{CA}$ = 15.30 IQ = 64 2. 48 3rd graders $\overline{CA}$ = 9.16 IQ = 107 3. 48 8th graders $\overline{CA}$ = 14.22 IQ = 107	1. Ss were presented via slides 6 paired associates (number-letter) at each of four redundancy levels: 33%, 50%, 67%, and 83%. Each paired associate was presented individually. 2. Error scores were recorded. 3. 12 subjects from each group were assigned to 1 of the redundancy level conditions.	1. Compared the error scores of the groups. 2. Compared the error scores across redundancy levels.

RESULTS: There was a steady decrease in errors as redundancy level increased. The 8th graders performed better than both retardates ($p < .01$) and 3rd graders ($p < .05$). The scores of the retardates and 3rd graders did not significantly differ. Comparisons at each redundancy level indicated that 8th graders performed better ($p < .05$) than MRs and 3rd graders at the 50% redun- dancy level, but not at the other redundancy levels. These results suggest that it took greater redundancy to affect retardates' scores than CA-equivalent normals. Spitz notes that this may have occurred due to difficulty (due to the sequential nature of the task) in discovering the presence of redundancy. No sex differences were found.

ARTICLE	SUBJECTS	CONDITIONS AND TASKS	ANALYSIS
Spitz (1972) *Experiment II*	1. 36 institutionalized EMRs $\overline{CA}$ = 15.63 IQ = 63 2. 36 3rd graders $\overline{CA}$ = 8.55 No IQ reported. 3. 36 8th graders $\overline{CA}$ = 13.35 No IQ reported.	Same as *Exp. I*, except 83% redundancy level was omitted and 6 paired associates were presented simultaneously, then followed by recall. Overall exposure time and recall time were similar for both experiments.	1. Compared the error scores of the groups. 2. Compared results with *Exp. I*. 3. Compared the error scores across redundancy levels.

RESULTS: Eighth graders performed better ($p < .001$) than 3rd graders, who in turn performed better ($p < .01$) than retardates. Differences between retardates and 8th graders were significant at each redundancy condition ($p < .01$). Third graders performed better than the retarded Ss at the 33% level. Compared to the anticipation method (of *Exp. I*), simultaneous presentation (a) negatively affected the free recall performance of retardates (especially at low redundancy levels), (b) positively affected the performance of 8th graders, and (c) had no effect on 3rd graders.

TABLE 3.5, cont.

ARTICLE	SUBJECTS	CONDITIONS AND TASKS	ANALYSIS

2. Spitz & Borys (1974)	1. 48 institutionalized EMRs
	$\overline{CA}$ = 15.86
	$\overline{IQ}$ = 61.56
	2. 48 nonretarded 3rd and 4th graders
	$\overline{CA}$ = 8.74
	
	MAs of the two groups were considered equivalent.
		1. The task consisted of viewing the simultaneous presentation of 6 paired-associate items and immediately recalling the pairs when given the stimuli (one item of each pair). Each of the 6 paired-associate blocks was displayed for 18 sec and 18 sec was allowed for recall. Testing terminated after 30 trial blocks if the criterion of 2 consecutive correct test trials had not been reached. All Ss received the task with 33% and 50% redundancy.
		2. The 2 groups were each divided equally and assigned to 1 of 3 experimental conditions that were differentiated by level of cueing.
		  a. *Ungrouped*—The six pairs were randomized with the constraint that at only one point would a letter be adjacent to itself.
		  b. *Grouped spatial*—The materials were presented so that each letter was always adjacent to itself, e.g., 3B, 6B, 4A, 7A, 8C, 5C.
		  c. *Grouped perceptual*—The materials were presented the same as in ungrouped condition except that all pairs containing A's were enclosed in rectangles, B's in ovals, and C's in diamonds.
		3. Cluster and recall scores were obtained.
			1. Cluster and recall scores were compared across conditions and groups.
			2. The relationship between cluster and recall was examined.

RESULTS: For both groups the 50% redundancy condition produced better recall performances than the 33% redundancy condition. External cueing improved the performance of the nonretarded children (especially in 50% redundancy), whereas it had little influence on the performance of the retarded group. Ss who reached criterion used clustering by the last 2 trials. Clustering was highest in the spatial condition. Nonretarded Ss used clustering more than the retarded adolescents ($p < .05$). For the retarded, increased clustering did not result in increased performance. Spitz and Borys (1974) concluded: "These results suggest that the third- and fourth-graders more readily recognized and utilized externally cued redundancy and, consequently, were more likely to improve their performance than were retarded adolescents" (p. 737).

TABLE 3.5, cont.

ARTICLE	SUBJECTS	CONDITIONS AND TASKS	ANALYSIS

3. Borys & Spitz (1974)	1. 32 institutionalized EMRs
	$\overline{CA}$ = 16.06
	$\overline{IQ}$ = 62.22
	2. 32 3rd graders
	$\overline{CA}$ = 8.8
	MAs of the two groups were considered equivalent.
		1. The task consisted of orally recalling 6 paired associates presented via slides. Trials were continued until a criterion of 2 errorless trials was reached. Thirty trials were given to Ss who never reached criterion. All Ss received the paired-associate task at two redundancy levels—33% and 50%.
		2. The two groups of Ss were equally divided and assigned to 1 of 2 conditions.
		  a. *IT**—The 3 paired associates were simultaneously presented on the screen, never having had the same response term for any one adjacent paired associate. Each 3 pairs were presented for 9 sec; thus a trial of 6 included 18 sec of exposure time.
		  b. *CT**—The 3 paired associates simultaneously presented on the screen always had the same response term. Three paired associates (50% redundancy) were always presented for 9 sec and 2 (33% redundancy) for 6 sec. Thus display time for all trials was 18 sec.
			1. Percent error was computed and compared across groups and conditions.
			2. Clustering and recall scores were obtained and compared across groups and conditions.

RESULTS: The results indicated that there was an increase in errors as redundancy decreased. For both groups performance was superior following CT presentations and the performance of the 3rd graders was superior to the retarded adolescents in the CT condition. The performances of the groups did not differ in the IT condition. They conclude that organized input enhances the performance of both groups, but that the nonretarded group made greater use of the organized input. In 33% redundancy, clustering was above baseline only in the CT condition, where 3rd graders clustered more than EMRs. Most Ss who reached criterion made use of clustering on the last 2 trials. These results support the position that method of presentation influences the recognition and use of redundancy.

*CT = Congruent temporal
IT = Incongruent temporal

At the 33% redundancy level it was revealed that the CT condition was significantly ($p < .01$) better than either the IT, UG, or G conditions, which did not differ from each other. The retarded subjects' performance in the CT condition was superior ($p < .02$) to the UG condition at the 33% redundancy level. Thus, the retarded adolescents were helped by temporal-redundant congruency, but its effect was statistically significant only when the redundancy was low, i.e., 33%.

The results of all three studies show that as redundancy decreased, errors increased. Also, all three studies support the position that retarded persons have more difficulty than nonretarded persons in recognizing and utilizing the information-reducing properties inherent in presented material. In summarizing the studies, Borys and Spitz (1974) note:

> The most powerful form of external cueing of the presence of redundancy in paired-associate learning was the combination in which S-R pairs containing the same response terms were temporally separated from other S-R pairs containing like response terms. At optimum performance on the more highly redundancy material, retarded subjects made only 13 percent errors and nonretarded subjects of equal MA made only 6 percent errors. Improvement beyond this point is unlikely. (p. 448)

TEACHING IMPLICATIONS. Many implications for teaching from Spitz's work are reported in the Spitz section of Chapter 2 in this book. However, implications presented here are not repetitions.

Borys and Spitz (1974) found that the most effective method for facilitating the paired-associate learning of EMRs with 33% redundancy is to present all the redundancy pairs simultaneously, then present each set of redundancy pairs simultaneously. This CT procedure combines simultaneous and sequential presentations, as well as using congruence between temporal spacing and redundancy. An example of this technique using 33% redundacy can be illustrated:

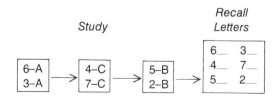

Study   *Recall Letters*

6 seconds   6 seconds   6 seconds   18 seconds

In the classroom this procedure could be used to present the sound of letters with objects in a picture. For example, the teacher would present the picture-beginning sound associations in the following way:

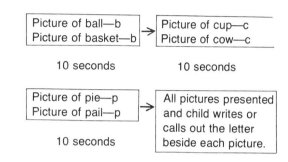

For teaching beginning multiplication facts the procedure would look like this:

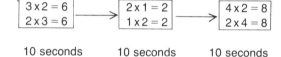

10 seconds   10 seconds   10 seconds

Present all problems and child writes the correct response beside each problem.

These procedures could be used to teach many associations (picture-words, word categories, etc.) and could be presented by using the rotating picture file displayed in Chapter 2.

When teaching EMRs it may oftentimes be helpful to use the CT procedure with 50% redundancy. For example:

| Picture of zebra—zoo |
| Picture of lion—zoo |
| Picture of elephant—zoo |

15 seconds

| Picture of potato—food |
| Picture of bread—food |
| Picture of carrot—food |

15 seconds

Present all pictures. Learner writes or says correct response for each.

Summary

The numerous findings of the various studies generated by Spitz have already been presented. The emphasis of this section is to provide a framework for examination. This chapter concludes, then, with an attempt to cluster the primary variables which characterize the studies related to Spitz's theory. The major parameters can be readily grouped according to subject variables, stimulus variables, input organization variables, output variables, and dependent measures. Table 3.6 displays all the studies with the variables organized according to the aforementioned schema.

In Table 3.6 the subject variables are reported in terms of the number of groups, CA, IQ, institutionalization, and organicity. A perusal of Table 3.6 enables the reader to compare or locate studies which included subjects with specific characteristics, e.g., MR versus CA-equivalent, nonretarded participants.

Stimulus variables are organized according to the parameters which appear important when examining or selecting input. *Channel dimension* refers to the modality in which the participant received the stimuli. An inspection of the table indicates that the stimuli used were primarily visual; however, it is noteworthy to acknowledge that several studies specifically focused on the influence of type and/or number of modalities on the recall and cluster performances of participants. The next two dimensions, *simultaneous* and *sequential presentations*, refer to the manner in which the stimuli were presented. Sequential presentations feature the presentation and removal of one stimulus at a time until all stimuli for the trial have been presented. Simultaneous presentations occur when all the stimuli for a trial are presented at once and followed by a recall period. *Time* refers to the exposure period for each item on a sequential presentation. On a simultaneous presentation *time* refers to the display time of the whole stimulus array. Items primarily consist of digits, words, and pictures. Through consulting the tables or text in each section, it is possible to ascertain information about specific item details which are not apparent in the gross categories included in Table 3.6. *Rehearsal* refers to the response that is required by the participant when an item is presented. Some investigators required the participants to say the name of the item (*verbal rehearsal*) upon presentation. In other studies no response was required at presentation. *Inherent grouping* refers to the usually obvious categories into which a group of items can readily be clustered.

Input organization refers to the ways in which input was arranged for presentation. *Redundancy* includes the repetition of the same items, for example, *2, 2, 3, 3, 6, 6*. *Spatial grouping* refers to items which are spatially arranged in a visual presentation, for example, *362 841*. *Temporal grouping* usually denotes that the items are grouped by time spacing, for example, *321–pause–864*. *Perceptual grouping* refers to items which are grouped by enclosing them in specific shape, such as all *B*s being enclosed in a rectangle. The final input organization variable, *categorical groupings*, refers to the inherent grouping of the stimulus items.

Output refers to the response that the participant must make in order to produce a dependent measure(s), for example, oral recall, written recall, or pushing a button. Most of the investigators required the participants to make an oral response. *Time* refers to the period allowed for recall of the items. *Free recall* is unstructured or noncued recall. *Recall by category* occurs when the examiner instructs the participant to recall the items by each respective category, e.g., "Say the animal words."

The *dependent measures* are recall, clustering, subjective organization, and sorting scores. Earlier in the chapter these dependent measures are discussed in detail.

As with much research in the social sciences, it is difficult to compare the results of one study to another because of the many variables which can influence experimental outcomes. Comparisons and generalizations can be more accurately made if the variables in Table 3.6 are considered. Hopefully the variables highlighted will foster closer inspection of some of the specific findings included in the studies and serve as a springboard for designing future studies and teaching techniques.

It is apparent that more research is needed regarding the varied effects of input organization on the processing of information by retarded individuals. Yet, the results of the research to date beckon practitioners to test some of the teaching strategies inherent in the investigations. It is especially important to determine the influence of input organization on learning in the classroom over a long period of time (3 to 6 months). Finally, Spitz's

TABLE 3.6
Summary of Variables of Studies Reviewed

ARTICLE	SUBJECT VARIABLES					STIMULUS VARIABLES							INPUT ORGANIZATION VARIABLES				OUTPUT VARIABLES					DEPENDENT MEASURES			
	GROUPS	CA	IQ	RESIDENTS	ORGANIC	CHANNEL	SIMULTANEOUS	SEQUENTIAL	TIME OR RATE	REHEARSAL	INHERENT GROUPING	REDUNDANCY	SPATIAL	TEMPORAL	CATEGORICAL	VERBAL	MOTOR	TIME	FREE RECALL	STRUCTURED	RECALL	CLUSTERING	SO	SORTING
Digit studies																								
1. MacMillan (1970a)	2	11.7 / 8	67 / 99			∨ ∨	× ×		10–25 / 10–25				× ×			× ×		∪ ∪	× ×		× ×			
2. MacMillan (1970b)	2	8.9 / 12.8	65 / 66			∨ ∨	× ×		10–25 / 10–25	○ ○			× ×			× ×		∪ ∪	× ×		× ×			
3. Harris (1972)	3	16.3 / 7.7 / 8.5	59 / ave / ave	×		∨ ∨ ∨	× × ×		9 sec / 9 sec / 9 sec				× × ×				× × ×	∪ ∪ ∪		× × ×	× × ×			
4. MacMillan (1972)	2	11.6 / 8.4	72 / 98			∨ ∨	× ×		10–25 / 10–25	○ ○			× ×			× ×		∪ ∪	× ×		× ×			
5. Spitz, Gerjuoy, & Winters (1972) Exp. I	4	15.7 / 9.1 / 13.3 / 20.7	62 / 104 / 101 / +ave	×		∨ ∨ ∨ ∨		× × × ×	1 sec per digit		× × × ×	× × × ×				× × × ×		∪ ∪ ∪ ∪	× × × ×		× × × ×			
Exp. II	3	15.7 / 8.8 / 12.7	64 / 107 / 102	×		∨ ∨ ∨		× × ×	1 sec per digit		× × ×	× × ×	× × ×			× × ×		∪ ∪ ∪	× × ×		× × ×			
6. Spitz & Webreck (1972)	1	15.3	64	×		∨	×		8–13			×	×			×		∪	×		×			

87

TABLE 3.6, cont.

Column groups: **SUBJECT VARIABLES** (GROUPS, CĀ, IQ̄, RESIDENTS, ORGANIC) · **STIMULUS VARIABLES** (CHANNEL, SIMULTANEOUS, SEQUENTIAL, TIME OR RATE, REHEARSAL, INHERENT GROUPING) · **INPUT ORGANIZATION VARIABLES** (REDUNDANCY, SPATIAL, TEMPORAL, CATEGORICAL) · **OUTPUT VARIABLES** (VERBAL, MOTOR, TIME, FREE RECALL, STRUCTURED) · **DEPENDENT MEASURES** (RECALL, CLUSTERING, SO, SORTING)

Picture or object studies

ARTICLE	GROUPS	CĀ	IQ̄	RESIDENTS	ORGANIC	CHANNEL	SIMULTANEOUS	SEQUENTIAL	TIME OR RATE	REHEARSAL	INHERENT GROUPING	REDUNDANCY	SPATIAL	TEMPORAL	CATEGORICAL	VERBAL	MOTOR	TIME	FREE RECALL	STRUCTURED	RECALL	CLUSTERING	SO	SORTING
1. Gerjuoy, Winters, Pullen, & Spitz (1969) *Exp. I*	2	15.6 / 10.5	64 / 110	×		V / V		× ×	3 sec / 3 sec		× ×				× ×	× ×		120 / 120			× ×	× ×		
Exp. II	2	16.2 / 10.7	63 / 110	×		V / V		× ×	3 sec / 3 sec		× ×				× ×	× ×		120 / 120			× ×	× ×		
2. Gerjuoy & Winters (1970)	1	15.7	65	×	×	VA	×	×	2 sec	O	×				×	×		U			×	×		
3. Herriot & Cox (1971)	2	12.8 / 12.6	40 / 40	× ×		V / V	× ×	× ×	25 sec / 25 sec		× ×			× ×		× ×		25 / 25			× ×	× ×	× ×	
4. Holden (1971)	2	15.2 / 10.3	70 / 106	×	×	VAT / VAT	× ×		0.05 sec / 0.05 sec							× ×		U / U			× ×			
5. Herriot (1972)	2	23.3 / 24.-	40 / 40	× ×		V / V	× ×		30 sec / 30 sec	O O						× ×		U / U	× ×	× ×			× ×	
6. Mende (1974)	2	9 / 14	67 / 67	×		VA / VA		× ×	NA / NA							× ×		U / U	× ×				× ×	
7. Palmer (1974)	2	22 / 8.7	66 / 105	×		V / V		× ×	2–3 sec / 2–3 sec	O O	× ×				× ×	× ×		90 / 90	× ×		× ×	× ×		

88

Study	N	IQ	MA		V/A		Time					Rate				
8. Riegel & Taylor (1974)	2	8	70 ave		>	X	NA	OS	X	X	X	U	X		X	X
		8			>	X	NA	OS	X	X	X	U	X		X	X
Word studies																
1. Gerjuoy & Spitz (1966) *Exp. I*	5	14.5	53	X	A	X	NA	O	X	X	X	120	X		X	X
		14.4	72	X	A	X	NA	O	X	X	X	120	X		X	X
		9.8	107		A	X	NA	O	X	X	X	120	X		X	X
		14.7	117		A	X	NA	O	X	X	X	120	X		X	X
		22	+ ave		A	X	NA	O	X	X	X	120	X		X	X
Exp. II	1	NA	MR	X	A	X	NA	O	X	X	X	120	X	X	X	X
Exp. III	1	18	MR	X	A	X	NA	O	X	X	X	120	X	X	X	X
2. Gallagher (1969)	2	14.1	66		A	X	1 @ 2 sec			X	X	U	X		X	X
		14.3	101		A	X				X	X	U	X		X	X
3. Gerjuoy & Alvarez (1969)	2	15.2	59	X	A	X	NA		X	X	X	120	X		X	X
		10.3	111		A	X	NA		X	X	X	120	X		X	X
4. Evans (1970)	1	18	67		VA	X	3 sec		X	X	X	60	X		X	X
5. Cobb & Barnard (1971)	2	13	57		A	X	1 @ 3 sec		X	X	X	U			X	X
		13	114		A	X			X	X	X	U				X
6. Bilsky, Evans, & Gilbert (1972)	1	17.2	65		VA	X	2 sec		X	X	X	U	X		X	X

89

TABLE 3.6, cont.

ARTICLE	GROUPS	CA	IQ	RESIDENTS	CHANNEL	SIMULTANEOUS	SEQUENTIAL	TIME OR RATE	INHERENT GROUPING	REDUNDANCY	SPATIAL	TEMPORAL	CATEGORICAL	VERBAL	TIME	FREE RECALL	RECALL	CLUSTERING
Paired-associate studies																		
1. Spitz (1972) Exp. I Exp. II	3 / 3	15.3, 9.1, 14.2 / 15.6, 8.5, 13.3	64, 107, 107 ave / 63, ave	X / X	> > > > > >	X X X	X X X	3 sec, 3 sec, 3 sec, 18 sec, 18 sec, 18 sec		X X X X X X				X X X X X X	U U U U U U		X X X X X X	
2. Spitz & Borys (1974)	2	15.9, 8.7	62 ave	X	> >	X X		18 sec, 18 sec	X X	X X	X X		X X	X X	18 sec	X X	X X	X X
3. Borys & Spitz (1974)	2	16, 8.8	62 ave	X	> >	X X		18 sec, 18 sec	X X	X X		X X		X X	18 sec	X X	X X	X X

*A = Auditory
NA = Not available
O = Oral
OS = Oral and sorting
U = Untimed
V = Visual
VA = Visual-auditory
VAT = Visual-auditory-tactile

90

work is extensive and certainly represents an area in which researchers and practitioners need to join forces to produce techniques which improve learning by retarded individuals.

References

Atkinson, R. C., & Shiffrin, R. M. Human memory: A proposed system and its control processes. In K. W. Spence & J. T. Spence (Eds.), *The psychology of learning and motivation: Advances in research and theory* (Vol. 2). New York: Academic Press, 1968.

Berenbaum, H. L., & Aderman, M. Comparison of binary guessing response tendencies of normal and retarded children. *American Psychologist*, 1964, *19*, 466.

Bilsky, L., Evans, R. A., & Gilbert, L. Generalization of associative clustering tendencies in mentally retarded adolescents: Effects of novel stimuli. *American Journal of Mental Deficiency*, 1972, *77*, 77–84.

Borys, S. V., & Spitz, H. H. Effects of temporal grouping and redundancy level on the paired-associate learning of retarded adolescents and nonretarded children. *American Journal of Mental Deficiency*, 1974, *79*, 443–448.

Bousfield, A. K., & Bousfield, W. A. Measurement of clustering and of sequential constancies in repeated free recall. *Psychological Reports,* 1966, *19*, 935–942.

Bousfield, W. A. The occurrence of clustering in the recall of randomly arranged associates. *Journal of Genetic Psychology*, 1953, *49*, 229–240.

Broadbent, D. E. *Perception and communication.* New York: Pergamon Press, 1958.

Cantor, G. N., & Ryan, T. J. Retention of verbal paired-associates in normals and retardates. *American Journal of Mental Deficiency*, 1962, *66*, 861–865.

Cobb, J. H., & Barnard, J. W. Differential effects of implicit associative values on short-term recall of retarded and nonretarded children. *American Journal of Mental Deficiency*, 1971, *76*, 130–135.

Davidson, J. *Using the Cuisenaire rods.* New Rochelle, N.Y.: Cuisenaire, 1969.

Ellis, N. R. Memory processes in retardates and normals. In N. R. Ellis (Ed.), *International review of research in mental retardation* (Vol. 4). New York: Academic Press, 1970.

Engelmann, S., & Bruner, E. C. *DISTAR reading I and II: An instructional system.* Chicago: Science Research Associates, 1969.

Estes, W. K. *Learning theory and mental development.* New York: Academic Press, 1970.

Evans, R. A. Use of associative clustering technique in the study of reading disability: Effects of presentation mode. *American Journal of Mental Deficiency*, 1970, *74*, 765–770.

Fisher, M. A., & Zeaman, D. An attention-retention theory of retardate discrimination learning. In N. R. Ellis (Ed.), *International review of research in mental retardation* (Vol. 6). New York: Academic Press, 1973.

Gallagher, J. R. A comparison of retarded and normals on subjective organization in short-term memory. *American Journal of Mental Deficiency*, 1969, *73*, 661–665.

Gerjuoy, H., & Gerjuoy, I. R. Choice-sequence patterns in binary-choice "learning" by retardates. *American Journal of Mental Deficiency*, 1964, *69*, 425–431.

Gerjuoy, I. R., & Alvarez, J. M. Transfer of learning in associative clustering of retardates and normals. *American Journal of Mental Deficiency*, 1969, *73*, 733–738.

Gerjuoy, I. R., & Spitz, H. H. Associative clustering in free recall: Intellectual and developmental variables. *American Journal of Mental Deficiency*, 1966, *70*, 918–927.

Gerjuoy, I. R., & Winters, J. J., Jr. Binary-choice responses of retardates, normal children, and college students to similar or dissimilar stimuli. *American Journal of Mental Deficiency*, 1965, *70*, 474–477.

Gerjuoy, I. R., & Winters, J. J., Jr. Subjective organization by EMR adolescents in free recall: Bimodal presentation. *American Journal of Mental Deficiency*, 1970, *74*, 509–516.

Gerjuoy, I. R., Winters, J. J., Jr., Pullen, M. M., & Spitz, H. H. Subjective organization by retardates and normals during free recall of visual stimuli. *American Journal of Mental Deficiency*, 1969, *73*, 791–797.

Harris, G. T. Input and output organization in short-term serial recall by retarded and nonretarded children. *American Journal of Mental Deficiency*, 1972, *76*, 423–426.

Hegge, T. G., Kirk, S. A., & Kirk, W. D. *Remedial reading drills.* Ann Arbor, Mich.: George Wahr, 1936.

Herriot, P. The effect of order of labelling on the subjective organization and clustering of severely retarded adults. *American Journal of Mental Deficiency*, 1972, *76*, 632–638.

Herriot, P., & Cox, A. M. Subjective organization and clustering in the free recall of intellectually subnormal children. *American Journal of Mental Deficiency*, 1971, *75*, 702–711.

Hoats, D. L., Miller, M. B., & Spitz, H. H. Experiments on perceptual curiosity in mental retardates and normals. *American Journal of Mental Deficiency*, 1963, *68*, 386–395.

Holden, E. A., Jr. Unimodal and multimodal sequential information processing in normals and retardates. *Journal of Experimental Psychology*, 1970, *86*, 181–185.

Holden, E. A., Jr. Effects of temporal grouping on unimodal and multimodal sequential information processing in nonretarded and retarded subjects. *American Journal of Mental Deficiency*, 1971, *76*, 181–184.

House, B. J. *Discrimination of symmetrical and asymmetrical dot patterns by retardates*. Paper presented at the meeting of the Eastern Psychological Association, Philadelphia, April 1964.

Hyman, L. M. Symmetry, numerosity and partial identity as stimulus factors in retardate discrimination learning (Doctoral dissertation, University of Connecticut, 1965. *Dissertation Abstracts, 1966, 26,* 4090A. (University Microfilms No. 66–858)

Iscoe, I., & Semler, I. J. Paired-associate learning in normal and mentally retarded children as a function of four conditions. *Journal of Comparative Physiological Psychology*, 1964, *57*, 387–392.

Jensen, A. R. Rote learning in retarded adults and normal children. *American Journal of Mental Deficiency*, 1965, *69*, 828–834.

Jensen, A. R., & Rohwer, W. D., Jr. The effect of verbal mediation on the learning and retention of paired-associates by retarded adults. *American Journal of Mental Deficiency*, 1963, *68*, 80–84. (a)

Jensen, A. R., & Rohwer, W. D., Jr. Verbal mediation in paired-associate and serial learning. *Journal of Verbal Learning and Verbal Behavior*, 1963, *1*, 346–352. (b)

Koffka, K. *Principles of Gestalt psychology*. New York: Harcourt, Brace, 1935.

Kohler, W., & Wallach, H. Figural after-effects: An investigation of visual processes. *Proceedings of the American Philosophical Society*, 1944, *88*, 269–357.

Kounin, J. Experimental studies of rigidity. II. The explanatory power of the concept of rigidity as applied to feeblemindedness. *Character and Personality*, 1941, *9*, 273–282.

Lewin, K. A. *A dynamic theory of personality*. New York: McGraw-Hill, 1935.

MacMillan, D. L. Comparison of nonretarded and EMR children's use of input organization. *American Journal of Mental Deficiency*, 1970, *74*, 762–764. (a)

MacMillan, D. L. Effect of input organization on recall of digits by EMR children. *American Journal of Mental Deficiency, 1970, 74,* 692–696. (b)

MacMillan, D. L. Facilitative effect of input organization as a function of verbal response to stimuli in EMR and nonretarded children. *American Journal of Mental Deficiency*, 1972, *76*, 408–411.

Marx, M. H., & Hillix, W. A. *Systems and theories in psychology*. New York: McGraw-Hill, 1963.

Mende, R. H. Effects of age and stimulus on recall and subjective organization of EMR children (Doctoral dissertation, University of Virginia, 1973). *Dissertation Abstracts International*, 1974, *34*, 4932–4933A. (University Microfilms No. 73–32, 450)

Neisser, U. *Cognitive psychology*. New York: Appleton, 1967.

Palmer, M. Clustering in nonretarded and retarded subjects: Some basic determinants. *American Journal of Mental Deficiency*, 1974, *78*, 454–461.

Riegel, R. H., & Taylor, A. M. Comparison of conceptual strategies for grouping and remembering employed by EMR and nonretarded children. *American Journal of Mental Deficiency*, 1974, *78*, 592–598.

Spitz, H. H. Cortical satiation as a common factor in perception and abstraction: Some postulated relationships based on the performance of atypical groups. *American Journal of Mental Deficiency*, 1959, *63*, 633–638.

Spitz, H. H. Field theory in mental deficiency. In N. R. Ellis (Ed.), *Handbook of mental deficiency: Psychological theory and research*. New York: McGraw-Hill, 1963.

Spitz, H. H. Effects on symmetry on the reproduction of dot patterns by mental retardates and equal MA normals. *American Journal of Mental Deficiency*, 1964, *69*, 101–106.

Spitz, H. H. The role of input organization in the learning and memory of mental retardates. In N. R. Ellis (Ed.), *International review of research in mental retardation* (Vol. 2). New York: Academic Press, 1966.

Spitz, H. H. Effects of stimulus information reduction on search time of retarded adolescents and normal children. *Journal of Experimental Psychology*, 1969, *82*, 482–487.

Spitz, H. H. Effects of redundancy level and presentation method on the paired-associate learning of educable retardates, third graders, and eighth graders. *Journal of Experimental Psychology*, 1972, *95*, 164–170.

Spitz, H. H. Consolidating facts into the schematized learning and memory system of educable retardates. In N. R. Ellis (Ed.), *International review of research in mental retardation* (Vol. 6). New York: Academic Press, 1973.

Spitz, H. H., & Blackman, L. S. A comparison of mental retardates and normals on visual figure aftereffects and reversible figures. *Journal of Abnormal and Social Psychology*, 1959, *58*, 105–110.

Spitz, H. H., & Borys, S. V. Effects of external emphasis and redundancy level on the paired-associate learning of retarded adolescents and nonretarded children. *American Journal of Mental Deficiency*, 1974, *78*, 734–739.

Spitz, H. H., Goettler, D. R., & Webreck, C. A. Effects of two types of redundancy on visual digit span performance of retardates and varying aged normals. *Developmental Psychology*, 1972, *6*, 92–103.

Spitz, H. H., & Hoats, D. L. *Experiments on perceptual curiosity behavior in mental retardates* (Final report, NIMH Grant M–4533). Washington, D.C.: U.S. Government Printing Office, 1961.

Spitz, H. H., & Webreck, C. A. Effects of spontaneous vs. externally-cued learning on the permanent storage of a schema by retardates. *American Journal of Mental Deficiency*, 1972, *77*, 163–168.

Stern, C. *Structural arithmetic*. Boston: Houghton Mifflin, 1965.

Thorndike, E. L., & Lorge, I. *The teacher's word book of 30,000 words*. New York: Bureau of Publications, Teachers College, Columbia University, 1944.

Tulving, E. Subjective organization in free recall of "unrelated" words. *Psychological Review*, 1962, *69*, 344–354.

Wallace, W. H., Turner, S. H., & Perkins, C. C. *Preliminary studies of human information storage* (DA Project No. 3–99–12–023). Fort Monmouth, N.J.: U.S. Army Signal Engineering Laboratories, 1957.

Winters, J. J., Jr., & Gerjuoy, I. R. Lateral preference for identical geometric forms: II. Retardates. *Perception and Psychophysics*, 1966, *1*, 104–106.

Winters, J. J., Jr., & Gerjuoy, I. R. Recognition of tachistoscopically exposed letters by normals and retardates. *Perception and Psychophysics,* 1969, 5, 21–24.

Zeaman, D., & House, B. J. The role of attention in retardate discrimination learning. In N. R. Ellis (Ed.), *Handbook of mental deficiency*. New York: McGraw-Hill, 1963.

Zigler, E. An overview of research in learning, motivation, and perception. *Exceptional Children*, 1962, *28*, 455–458.

4

Zeaman and House's Attention Theory

Researchers in psychology and education have provided many attention theories and data which offer implications for the education and training of mentally retarded persons. Reviews of much of this research are available (Alabiso, 1972; Crosby & Blatt, 1968; Denny, 1964; Fisher & Zeaman, 1973; House, Brown, & Scott, 1974; Zeaman & House, 1963). In one of these reviews Alabiso (1972) notes that over a hundred years of research on attention have led to the conclusion that attention is a multibehavioral process controlled by numerous factors. He also reports that research on attention has generally focused on attention span, focus of attention, and selectivity in the attention process, which are briefly discussed following.

Attention span research stresses the amount of time a subject attends to a standard task. Much of this experimentation has concentrated on the variability in the stimulus object, developmental levels, and specific subject characteristics.

Focusing in attention is considered by Wachtel (1967) to be analogous to the arrangement of light

Appreciation is extended to David L. Westling for his significant contribution to this chapter.

patterns in a beam of light. He considers the focus of attention to be more intense at the middle and weaker on the periphery of the perceptual field. Examination of this phenomenon has concentrated on the ability to resist distraction and continue attending to the relevant task. As Alabiso (1972) states: "Focus of attention has been more easily defined conceptually than operationally" (p. 271).

Selective attention requires the subject to attend and respond to a particular stimulus rather than other stimuli in the perceptual field. Underlying the concept of selective attention is the idea that attention is more than sensory awareness; it is a *cognitive* process which features active information processing (Hagen & Kail, 1975). Due to the extensive investigations on selective attention and subject variables, many learning theories about the mentally retarded focus on these subjects (Fisher & Zeaman, 1973; Zeaman & House, 1963).

In essence, then, research has shown that attention requires the processing of relevant stimuli (associated with reward) while simultaneously confronting irrelevant stimuli (not associated with reward). The individual must, in order to process relevant stimuli: (a) maintain a level of arousal to attend; (b) scan the stimulus field and select the relevant stimuli; (c) shift attention quickly to changing relevant stimuli; and (d) maintain attending behavior over extended spans of time.

Of these requirements, Zeaman and House (1963) and Crosby and Blatt (1968) attributed the attention problems of mentally retarded individuals primarily to *b*, the inability to sample the stimulus field and select the relevant stimulus. For example, Crosby and Blatt note that the retarded individual is often viewed as having a lower capacity for stimulus selection. They state:

> Because the information-carrying capacity of his nervous system is limited, man can respond to only part of the stimuli impinging upon him at any given time. He must, therefore, select from these stimuli, and it is this process of *stimulus selection* that constitutes *attention*. It may be useful to further conceptualize attention as two subprocesses: scanning or sampling the available stimuli (the stimulus field), and responding to those stimuli which are relevant to the on going activity or the task at hand while inhibiting response to those that are irrelevant. (pp. 67–68)

The process of selective attention is the primary focus of this chapter. Specifically, the theories originally advanced by David Zeaman and Betty House and their coworkers at the University of Connecticut and the Mansfield State Training School are described. Following the presentation of these theoretical postions, studies which are related to the theories are examined and general conclusions are drawn. Additionally, implications for the education and training of mentally retarded individuals are explored.

Zeaman and House's Attention Theory

Apparatus

Visual discrimination tasks have served as a primary vehicle for examining the attention processes of retarded individuals. These tasks usually involve simple instrumental responses and can be designed to allow comparative study of subjects who are quite varied in ability. For example, an experimenter in a simple discrimination task presents simultaneously two or three stimuli and instructs the subject to select the correct stimulus. The selection of the correct stimulus results in a reward (feedback). The correct stimulus is always distinguished by a cue [color (red), size (large),

shape (circle)] which is constant over the discrimination trials, e.g., the red object is always paired with the reward. Discrimination learning occurs when the learner *consistently* chooses the stimulus paired with the reward. For example, a square and a circle are continuously presented and a reward is always attached to the square. If the learner selects the square 10 consecutive times, the learners must be visually discriminating the form differences between a square and a circle. As noted by Robinson and Robinson (1976), the number of trials that occurs before criterion is reached serves as a measure of learning efficiency.

Zeaman and House (Zeaman, 1973; Zeaman & House, 1963) have used the discrimination learning paradigm to formulate the most widely known attention theory regarding mental retardation. In the process of developing and testing their theoretical positions, Zeaman and House used the Wisconsin General Test Apparatus (WGTA) as a device to present discrimination tasks to retarded children (see Figure 4.1). The WGTA is a desk structure with a one-way mirror screen attached perpendicular to its top. It features two trays which can be loaded from behind the desk and presented to the subject by sliding them forward under the screen until they extend onto the desk top. In a discrimination trial, each tray is loaded with a stimulus and a reward (candy) is put under the stimulus in one of the two trays. The two trays are presented to the subject, who is asked to select one of the stimuli. If the subject chooses the stimulus with the reward under it, the reward may be kept. Discrimination learning occurs when the subject consistently selects the object paired with the reward.

Framework of Study

Zeaman and House (1963) translated the visual discrimination performances of mentally retarded individuals into backward learning curves.[1] Analysis of the curves provided data which suggested that discrimination learning involved a two-stage process. During the first stage, the learning curve is somewhat horizontal and hovers around chance-level performance. Zeaman and House refer to this stage as an *attention phase*, in which the subject randomly attends to the various dimensions of the stimulus. Once the subject starts attending to the relevant dimensions of the

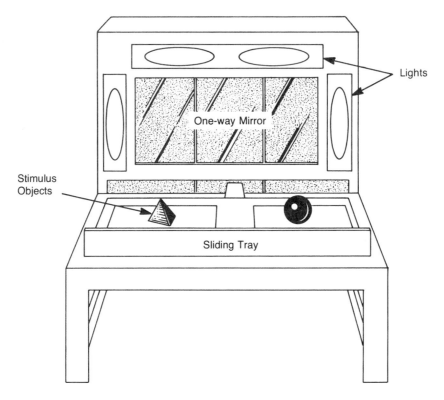

FIGURE 4.1

Discrimination learning apparatus.

stimulus, Stage 2 begins and an improvement in instrumental learning occurs. In essence, they conclude that learning curves feature two stages: (a) a flat chance-level segment and (b) a sharply rising segment.

A perusal of the curves revealed that the variance between the subjects was not the rate of improvement (once it began), but rather the number of trials necessary for improvement to start in instrumental learning. Moreover, as indicated in Figure 4.2, the data revealed that the length of the chance plateau was a function of intelligence, i.e., lower MA subjects required more trials in the attention phase (Stage 1) than higher MA subjects.

Zeaman and House (1963) defined their stimulus objects in terms of dimensions and cues within those dimensions. Within their framework a stimulus may have several dimensions (color, form, size) and respective cues (red or blue, round or square, large or small) for each of the dimensions. At least one dimension in the discrimination trials provides information concerning the correct choice. This dimension is considered relevant, whereas other dimensions which provide no information concerning the correct choice are considered irrelevant. For example, when color is the relevant dimension, form is an irrelevant dimension.

Zeaman and House (1963) also proposed a one-look observational (attention) model. In their one-look model they assumed that although the learner may be aware of all the dimensions (color, form) present on a discrimination task, the learner attends to only one immediately prior to the instrumental response. Thus they saw their one-look model within the framework of a two-response paradigm. On each discrimination trial they thought that the learner makes an observational (one-look) response and also an instrumental response.

Since retardates had longer initial chance-level curves (Stage 1—attending to the various dimensions) than higher MA subjects but similar steep slope curves (Stage 2), Zeaman and House (1963) postulated that the learning problems of

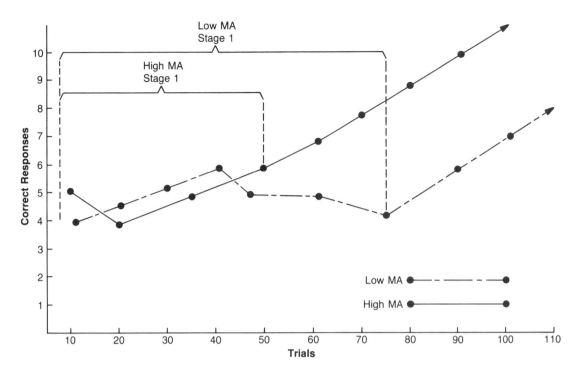

FIGURE 4.2

Learning curves in relation to mental age.

retardates are primarily a function of attention. They state:

> the *attention hypothesis* (that retardates suffer from low initial probability of observing certain relevant dimensions rather than from poor ability to learn which of two observed cues is correct) is to us a hopeful and exciting notion because it leads so quickly to a search for experimental operations that may change $Po_{(1,0)}$ [probability of observation responses to relevant stimulus dimensions] and hence accelerate discriminations of subjects who might otherwise seem to be natively and irreversibly poor discriminators. (p. 188)

In essence, Zeaman and House (1963) suggested that learning deficiencies in retarded children resulted from a deficiency in attention, not in instrumental learning. The difference between fast and slow learning, they claimed, was not the actual rate of improvement (correct responding) once it started, but the amount of time (number of trials needed) it took for correct responding above chance level to begin. Thus, according to the attention hypothesis, retarded individuals display a low probability of attending to the correct dimen-

sion rather than selecting the correct cue within the dimension.

Moreover, Zeaman and House (1963) suggested that a number of factors (aside from subject variability) could affect the probability of attending to the relevant dimension and thus shorten the initial segment of the backward learning curve. Subsequent investigators have been concerned primarily with several variables: stimulus factors, reward factors, transfer operations, oddity learning, and novelty effects.

STIMULUS FACTORS. Since the initial task in the discrimination problem appeared to be a function of attention, Zeaman and House (1963) examined stimulus factors and their relation to attention. They had subjects discriminate between stimuli which varied in forms and colors. They discovered that the number and kind of stimulus dimensions influenced considerably the flat portion of the learning curve but influenced very little the steep slope portion of the curve. In addition, they predicted that stimuli which differed along many relevant dimensions (size, brightness, and shape) would result in learning curves with fewer chance-level responses than discriminative stimuli which differed on only one subtle dimension, e.g., form. This prediction was supported when Zeaman and House discovered that the flat portion was longer for fine discrimination tasks (one dimension relevant) than it was for gross discrimination tasks (several dimensions relevant). Finally, another procedure for increasing a learner's attending to a relevant dimension is to use a dimension which the learner prefers.

REWARD FACTORS. Reward as a cue influencing attention was another factor investigated by Zeaman and House (1963). They presented evidence which suggests that anticipatory responses may precede choice and provide distinctive cue feedback. Zeaman and House relegated anticipatory mechanisms to low priority in their theoretical framework, but, later, Fisher and Zeaman (1973) considered incentive cues as a strong source that competes for attention with other stimuli.

TRANSFER OPERATIONS. In their study of stimulus dimensions, Zeaman and House (1963) examined three transfer operations: intradimensional shift, reversal, and extradimensional shift. According to attention theory, once a subject is trained to attend to the relevant dimensions of a stimulus, this attentional set can facilitate learning in certain transfer operations. For example, if a subject is trained to discriminate between red and blue triangles and then an intradimensional shift is employed which changes the colors (relevant dimension) of the triangles to green and yellow, the theory would predict that instrumental learning would occur faster than if the subject was just beginning the task. Zeaman and House found that intradimensional shifts resulted in the subjects learning the second discrimination task more quickly (shorter Stage 1 curve) than when the subjects performed the original task using the same dimension. Also, extradimensional shifts, such as changing the relevant stimulus dimension from color to shape, produced learning curves which were similar to those generated by original learning tasks. This finding is consistent with the theory since the relevant dimension was changed and correct responding involved shifting the attention to a new dimension. On the final transfer operation, reversal, a process that involves reversing the rewarded condition on the same stimulus dimension, Zeaman and House discovered that learning proceeded

more slowly than when intradimensional shifts were employed and more quickly than when extradimensional shifts were used. The attention theory would predict this finding since reversals, like intradimensional shifts, involve attending to the same stimulus dimension, while extradimensional shifts require the subject to attend to a new relevant dimension.

ODDITY LEARNING. Oddity learning is usually a more complex type of discrimination learning than simple two-choice discrimination problems. An oddity task typically involves the simultaneous presentation of three or more stimuli which are identical except for one stimulus (e.g., two red circles and one blue square). The learner is instructed to select the stimulus that is different (e.g., blue square). On oddity problems the concept of oddity must be acquired because no simple dimension can lead to problem solution. For retarded children oddity problems are often very difficult, but they perform better when taught to attend to the odd stimulus prior to beginning the specific oddity trials.

Zeaman and House (1963) found that simulus oddity, once learned, can transfer to any new situation with oddity present. Their findings were in accordance with their prediction which stated that as instrumental response approaches unity, attending to relevant stimuli is under control of the dimension (oddity) selected.

NOVELTY EFFECTS. Novelty is a discriminable aspect of stimuli which exercises some control over attention, but is also may act as a preferred aspect, thus directly influencing instrumental responses. Zeaman and House (1963) discovered that the introduction of a novel stimulus along the relevant dimension can result in sudden and unexpected learning of discriminations.

Fisher and Zeaman Attention-Retention Theory

Necessity of Expanding the Attention Theory

Much research has accrued regarding the Zeaman and House (1963) attention theory. Zeaman and House as well as many others have conducted studies with mentally retarded persons regarding theoretical aspects and predictions generated from this theory. Empirical findings have led to revisions and refinements in the original theory. Zeaman (1973) pointed out that three kinds of evidence suggested need for revision of the 1963 attention theory:

> The first kind, which we call "feedback" data, is evidence in which events that theoretically *follow* an attention response affect the likelihood of that attention response on the same trial (a backward-action-in-time paradox). The second kind of data were those showing evidence of retention loss; the third showed the facilitating effect of redundant relevant dimensions. (p. 94)

In regard to the feedback phenomenon, Zeaman (1973) realized that some mechanism must be responsible for the way cues are related to the probability of attention. As an example, he pointed out the novelty effects. Previously it had been assumed that novelty enhanced dimensional saliency. Since researchers have now learned that it is the cue that is novel and not the dimension, the question of how cue information affects selection of a dimension was not answered. In addition, studies of intradimensional and extradimensional shifts indicated that cue information was being fed back and had a bearing on the dimensional selection process. Zeaman also recognized that studies by Shepp (1962, 1964) and Denegre (1966) suggested that anticipating rewards influenced the probability of attending to a certain dimension. Therefore it was felt that a "feedback loop" needed to be added to the theoretical framework.

Since a trials-to-criterion design was used in most of the earlier studies, there was little chance to determine whether some forgetting might be occurring. However, Zeaman (1973) pointed out that a study by House and Zeaman (1963) required subjects to perform a long series of problems and some forgetting did occur. Another technique which supported the loss of retention was the delayed-response approach. Using this technique, House and Zeaman (1961) noted that after a single presentation of discriminative material there was retention loss. These bits of evidence indicated the need for including a retention (loss) component within the theory.

The third factor which Zeaman (1973) felt should be given consideration was redundancy of relevant dimensions, i.e., presenting two stimuli which differed along several dimensions (color, form, and size). In the 1963 theory they thought that the dimensions of stimuli varying along *several* relevant dimensions (toy car versus circle) were observed as *one* aggregate dimension (e.g., the shape, color, and size of the car combined to

form one aggregate dimension). Within the aforementioned one-look framework it was advanced that the learner observed the numerous dimensions as one aggregate dimension (one-look observation response) immediately prior to the instrumental response. A shortcoming of this one-look model was the omission of the possibility that several dimensions with known attention value may combine to influence attention processes, i.e., a learner may simultaneously attend to several relevant dimensions on a given trial. Thus the theory was expanded to include a multiple-look model which offered the idea that a learner may simultaneously attend to more than one dimension on each trial. The multiple-look model has generated research in which the number of relevant dimensions has been treated as the independent variable. In addition, the multiple-look model has led to the formulation of the "breadth of attention" concept, i.e., the number of dimensions to which a learner can attend simultaneously.

Components of Attention-Retention Theory

Fisher and Zeaman (1973) formulated the attention-retention theory regrading mental retardation by combining certain aspects of the Zeaman and House attention theory with the retention theory of Atkinson and Shiffrin (1969). Fisher and Zeaman noted that new data, particularly in the area of retention, necessitated an expansion of the attention theory. Figure 4.3 reveals the major components and interactions of a two-stage discrimination learning process.

In the initial stage, Dimension Selection, the Attention Selector selects one or more dimensions (color, shape, position) from the stimulus field and transforms these to respective cues. For example, attention to shape enables the individual to ascertain that squares and circles are the cues. Moreover, attention to color reveals that blue and red are cues. The next step in the process involves a choice of one of the cues in the stimulus display. This choice involves two substages. The first substage, the Cue-Significance Stage, entails scanning the memory for reward associations regarding the various cues. The second substage, Cue Selection, involves combining the cue significances to form an approach or avoidance response to the respective stimuli.

The association of the reward outcome with specific cues is stored in a tripartite memory sys-

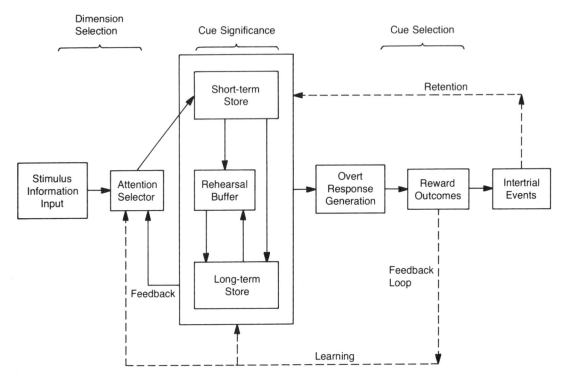

FIGURE 4.3
Diagram of attention-retention theory.

SOURCE: Adapted from "An Attention-Retention Theory of Retardate Discrimination Learning" by M. A. Fisher & D. Zeaman. In N. R. Ellis (Ed.), *The International Review of Research in Mental Retardation* (Vol. 6) p. 172. New York: Academic Press, 1973. Copyright 1973 by Academic Press. Reprinted by permission.

tem. The association of a cue with a reward outcome first enters a Short-term Store. Information entering the Short-term Store dissipates quickly as a function of time. However, this information may be entered into a Rehearsal Buffer where subjective repetition of the information may be practiced; it may go directly from the Short-term Store to the Long-term Store; or it may move from the Rehearsal Buffer to the Long-term Store.

Conflicting information may exist in the memory stores because two stimulus objects may have several cues, some of which are reward associated and others which are nonreward associated. The Response Generator considers all available cue reward information and converts it into an overt response.

The Feedback Loop enables the cue reward information to be fed back to the Attention Selector. This results in the individual remembering about the reward values of the cues and con-

sequently affects the stimulus dimension to which he elects to attend.

Fisher and Zeaman (1973) discuss some of the dynamics of the theory in the following passage:

> Two principal types of changes, or processes, are postulated by the theory: learning and retention. With respect to learning, the two inferred links in the chain (attention and cue significance) undergo changes. The terminal reward or nonreward on each trial causes acquisition or extinction, respectively, of both dimensional selection and cue-significances. (p. 173)

In relation to intelligence and mental retardation, several positions are featured in the attention-retention theory.

1. As with the original theory, Fisher and Zeaman (1973) note that learning rate does not appear related to intelligence.
2. Fisher and Zeaman note that data exist which suggest that breadth of attention is related to mental age and, hence, to retardation. Although breadth of

attention appears to be related to mental age, they caution against considering it a fixed ability.

3. As noted in the original theory, lower MA subjects require more trials before instrumental learning begins to increase. In the original theory this phenomenon was viewed as a retardate attention deficiency. However, Fisher and Zeaman acknowledge that the manipulation of stimulus characteristics can control this deficiency on discrimination tasks.

4. Fisher and Zeaman present the decay rate in Short-term Store as a fixed capacity related to intelligence. In addition, they view Buffer Size (a rehearsal region) as a process which is limited but somewhat sensitive to training techniques.

In essence, Fisher and Zeaman (1973) note that although retardates exhibit attention problems, these problems can be modified with stimulus manipulation and reward outcomes. They acknowledge that retention factors are parameters which are most likely related to capacity and thus to fixed limitations.

Studies Relating to Zeaman and His Associates

In examining the programmatic research and theoretical formulations of Zeaman and his associates, it is important to remember their experimental orientation. From a functional viewpoint the Zeaman and House (1963) attention theory continues to generate viable research and teaching implications, i.e., strategies and methods for improving the attending behavior of retarded individuals continue to emerge from the research. One of the reasons that Zeaman and his colleagues were prompted to expand the 1963 theory is because of their approach to mental retardation.[2] They are seeking to formulate a theory which traces the learning characteristics of retarded individuals to a structural problem, e.g., physiological deficiency. Since research has demonstrated that attention to relevant dimensions is easy to change in experimental settings, Zeaman (1973) was prompted to consider attention as a modifiable or control aspect of behavior rather than a structural one. This revised model proposes several new parameters of intelligence, such as (a) breadth of attention, (b) reduced buffer size resulting in restricted rehearsal, (c) short-term memory loss, and (d) a bias for retaining old information at the expense of impeding new material from being processed.

In the process of seeking structural deficiencies in mentally retarded persons, Zeaman and his colleagues continue to advance our knowledge of the learning characteristics of retarded individuals. Moreover, irrespective of the structural deficiencies discovered, the research continues to generate direct applications for training and educating retarded individuals.

In the remainder of this chapter reviews, summaries, and implications of representative research generated in the subject of attention (1968–1976) by the theories of Zeaman and his colleagues are presented. The research presented primarily includes studies in which the investigator(s) used a visual discrimination task with retarded subjects and related the study to the work of Zeaman and his coworkers. Due to the recency of the latest model, the majority of the studies directly relate to the 1963 attention theory. The research is organized and presented according to the following areas: (a) studies focusing on number of dimensions, (b) studies focusing on incentive conditions, (c) studies focusing on transfer operations, and (d) studies focusing on oddity learning.

Studies Focusing on Number of Dimensions

The number of dimensions used in stimuli of discrimination tasks may relate to either Zeaman and House's (1963) attention theory or to Fisher and Zeaman's (1973) attention-retention theory. The 1963 theory hypothesized that an increase in the number of irrelevant dimensions would decrease the learning performance of subjects on a discrimination task. In addition, this theory advanced the idea that the presentation of numerous relevant dimensions would combine to form a single aggregate relevant dimension (one-look) which, in turn, would enhance performance. Finally, Zeaman and House thought that retarded individuals would take longer to observe the relevant dimension than nonretarded children.

In Fisher and Zeaman's (1973) attention-retention theory, number of dimensions is primarily discussed within the context of breadth of attention or multiple-look observation. They feel that retarded individuals are unable to observe as many dimensions simultaneously as nonretarded children. As noted in the previous section of this chapter, this deficiency in breadth of attention is one of the parameters which the previous theory of

1963 offered as a structural deficiency, i.e., a condition not alterable.

Eight studies in which the number of dimensions was emphasized are presented in the following section. The studies are grouped according to the primary independent variables examined. The investigators in the first five studies examined the effects of varied irrelevant dimensions on discrimination learning. The next experiments focused on examining the effects of numerous relevant dimensions on discrimination learning, and the final study focused on investigating the effects of color distractors on discrimination learning.

Irrelevant Dimensions

EVANS'S STUDIES. Evans (1968) conducted a series of experiments to assess the influence of selected stimulus factors on the discrimination learning of mildly retarded adolescents. The stimulus variables included the potency of irrelevant stimulus dimensions and the number of variable irrelevant stimulus dimensions. In addition to the stimulus variables, the influence of intelligence level and sex on discrimination learning was examined. The stimuli consisted of various arrangements of eight figures presented in a filmstrip. The eight figures varied across three stimulus dimensions: form (square and circle), brightness (black and white), and size (large and small). The stimuli were:

On each trial the participants pushed a button to indicate stimulus choice. The discrimination task was established across experimental conditions by varying the relevant dimension and by varying or holding constant the type and number of irrelevant dimensions.

Experiment I was conducted to assess the effectiveness of form, size, and brightness as relevant dimensions on discrimination learning. The eight figures were arranged into mutually exclusive combinations which contained both levels of all three dimensions (brightness, size, form), e.g., dark, small square; bright, large circle. Sixty institutionalized mildly retarded adolescents were equally divided into six treatment groups which differed according to the relevant dimension (white, black, circle, square, large, small) in their respective discrimination tasks. The results indicated that brightness was significantly easier to learn than size and form. No significant differences

were found between the influence of size and form on the learning of these adolescents.

Experiment II was designed to assess the effects of the potency of variable irrelevant dimensions (VID), intelligence level, and sex on the learning of discrimination tasks. Discrimination problems in this experiment were developed with form as the relevant dimension and size (low potency) or brightness (high potency) as the irrelevant dimension. It was thought that because brightness is easily learned as a relevant dimension, it would also attract attention as an irrelevant one. Thus a more difficult relevant dimension (shape or size) would be harder to learn when paired with brightness. In one condition the irrelevant dimensions were varied (size and brightness) and in the other condition the irrelevant dimension was held constant (only size or brightness). The participants included 48 mildly retarded adolescents from special classes in a public school and 48 nonretarded students of similar CA. The subjects were assigned by sex and IQ level to one of the irrelevant dimension conditions (constant or varied irrelevant dimension). The results showed that intelligence level was significant ($p < .005$), with nonretarded participants producing fewer errors than the retarded subjects. The boys made significantly fewer errors (especially with size as irrelevant) than the girls, and irrelevant dimension potency (IDP) did not differentially affect the performance of the girls. The main effect of IDP was significant for the boys and they performed better with brightness irrelevant than with size irrelevant. Neither the boys nor the girls differed when brightness was irrelevant.

Experiment III was conducted to examine the effects of the number of variable irrelevant dimensions, intelligence, and sex on discrimination performance. Brightness was selected as the relevant dimension. Three conditions were established: (a) 1 VID—position only irrelevant dimension; (b) 2 VID—position and form varied irrelevantly; (c) 3 VID—position, form, and size varied irrelevantly. The participants consisted of 60 mildly retarded adolescents from public schools and 60 CA-equivalent nonretarded adolescents. The subjects were assigned by sex and IQ level to the three experimental conditions.

The results indicated that intelligence was significant ($p < .001$), with the performance of normals superior to the performance of retardates. The 3 VID condition produced significantly more errors than the 1 and 2 VID conditions. No significant differences existed between the performances of subjects in the 1 and 2 VID conditions. The number of irrelevant dimensions was not a significant factor with nonretarded participants but was a significant influence with the retarded participants. No significant sex differences were reported.

Evans (1968) notes that the results support Zeaman and House's (1963) position that retardates have an attention deficiency. He also acknowledges that for certain dimensions (color) the less intelligent subject may learn faster than higher MA subjects.

EVANS AND BEEDLE'S STUDIES. In another study Evans and Beedle (1970) selected 40 institutionalized retarded children ($\overline{CA}$ = 15, $\overline{IQ}$ = 55) in order to examine the role of irrelevant dimension variability. Specifically, the authors designed the study to investigate the effect of (a) irrelevant brightness variability within and between trials, (b) the distance between the size-irrelevant cues varying within trials, and (c) sex of subject.

The apparatus used to present the stimulus displays was a modified WGTA. The experimental design corresponded to a 2 x 2 x 2 design with brightness variability, distance, and sex of the subject as the three factors. In the near condition a 4½ cm square (1.755 in.) stimulus was paired with a 5 cm (1.95 in.) square stimulus, whereas in the far condition a 2½ cm (.975 in.) square stimulus was paired with a 5 cm (1.95 in.) square stimulus. Brightness was manipulated by using a black stimulus and a white stimulus (black line drawing). Four experimental conditions were established to include the appropriate variables, i.e., brightness between trials, near distancing; brightness between trials, far distancing; brightness within trials, near distancing; and brightness within trials, far distancing. A sample trial representing each condition is illustrated in Figure 4.4. Each participant completed a pretraining session before beginning the experimental sessions. In all conditions, form (circle or square) was the relevant dimension and each participant received 75 trials if he failed to reach a criterion of 10 successive correct responses prior to the completion of 75 trials.

Using number of errors as the dependent measure, Evans and Beedle (1970) found that the far condition was more difficult than the near condition. The only other statistically significant finding

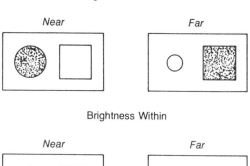

Brightness Between

FIGURE 4.4
An example of a stimulus pairing for each of the four experimental conditions.

was an interaction effect. The boys found between-trial variability more difficult than within-trial variability, whereas the performance of the girls did not differ in the two conditions. In discussing the results in terms of Zeaman and House attention theory, Evans and Beedle note:

> The absence of a significant Brightness main effect tends to support the Zeaman-House contention that dimensions which are constant within trials also compete for the subject's attention; for this position to have been contraindicated, the brightness within-trials problem should have been the more difficult. (p. 572)

CLINTON AND EVANS'S STUDIES. Clinton and Evans (1972) conducted a single alternation discrimination learning study to investigate the effects of three variables: the number of irrelevant dimensions or complexity, mental age, and initial response outcome (reward versus nonreward). In the single alternation task, position was always the relevant dimension and the position opposite the preceding position was always the correct cue.

The first independent variable (the complexity of the stimuli) was varied in order to investigate the effect of irrelevant cues within trials on the single alternation discrimination task. Also of concern was the influence of initial response outcome on subsequent performance. According to Clinton and Evans (1972), "It appears that two-choice discrimination learning performance may be facilitated when the initially presented stimulus is associated with nonreward" (p. 434). Essentially, the experimenters were investigating the hypothesis that "avoidance sets" facilitate learning better than "approach sets." Also investigated was the effect of mental age level on single alternation behavior. Clinton and Evans cite evidence which suggests that a developmental relationship exists between response pattern and MA.

In order to investigate the hypotheses, 60 mentally retarded adolescents ($\overline{CA} = 16$, $\overline{IQ} = 61$) were selected. The participants were assigned to one of six experimental conditions. The conditions consisted of:

1. low complexity level (one irrelevant dimension) with initial reinforcement
2. low complexity level (one irrelevant dimension) with initial nonreinforcement
3. intermediate complexity level (two irrelevant dimensions) with initial reinforcement
4. intermediate complexity level (two irrelevant dimensions) with initial nonreinforcement
5. high complexity level (three irrelevant dimensions) with initial reinforcement
6. high complexity level (three irrelevant dimensions) with initial nonreinforcement

In addition to analyzing the data in terms of the six experimental conditions, the investigators redivided the subjects according to high and low MA (above and below median) and analyzed the results.

In the low complexity condition, pictures with two arrows were presented with one pointing up and the other pointing down. The orientation of the arrows was the only irrelevant dimension. Intermediate complexity consisted of two irrelevant dimensions, (a) striped versus solid arrows and (b) the orientation of the arrows (up or down). The high complexity condition consisted of three irrelevant dimensions, (a) the orientation of the arrows, (b) striped versus nonstriped arrows, and (c) the size of the arrows (large or small). In all conditions, position was the relevant dimension, with the alternate of the preceding position being the correct cue. The apparatus used to present the two stimuli was the Modern Teaching Associates 400 Scholar Teaching Machine. Subjects pressed a response key to select one of the stimuli. Candy reinforced alternation responses. No reinforcement was given for nonalternation responses. In the initial reinforcement condition, the first response was rewarded; in the initial nonreinforcement condition, the first alternation response was

rewarded. Criterion was eight consecutive responses in a maximum of 50 trials.

Results of the experiment were analyzed using a three-way design: $3 \times 2 \times 2$ (complexity x MA x initial response outcome). The dependent variable was the number of errors in 50 trials (or before criterion was reached). The main effect of complexity was significant ($p < .001$), as was the complexity-reinforcement interaction ($p < .005$). The significance of complexity was primarily due to the intermediate level, which included the most errors. While there were no differences in the initial reinforcement conditions at the low and high levels of complexity, there were significantly more errors at the intermediate level of complexity. In the initial nonreinforcement condition, the effects of complexity were successively ordered from low level (least errors) to high level (most errors) of complexity. In the initial reinforcement condition, errors paralleled the main effect so that low level had the fewest, then the high level, and finally intermediate level with the most errors. This finding supported the Zeaman and House (1963) position that task difficulty is oftentimes a function of the number of irrelevant dimensions.

The main effect of MA was not significant (median MA = 10 years) but the data suggested that single alternation selection is a notable phenomenon with EMR adolescents (90% of the subjects reached criterion). In the initial reinforcement condition in which two irrelevant dimensions produced more errors than three irrelevant dimensions, the results showed the addition of an irrelevant dimension facilitated learning. In conclusion, Clinton and Evans (1972) suggest that stimulus and reinforcement components of a learning task may have interactive effects.

CLINTON'S STUDIES. In the next study Clinton (1972) investigated the effects on single alternation discrimination learning of between-trials variability (BTV) (as opposed to within-trials variability, cf. Clinton & Evans, 1972), initial response outcome (reward versus nonreward), and mental age. Sixty mentally retarded subjects were selected and assigned to 1 of 12 cells similar to the Clinton and Evans (1972) study. The only basic difference was that BTV conditions were altered instead of using varied within-trials irrelevant conditions. The experimental groups were arranged according to the following conditions: low BTV, high MA; low BTV, low MA; intermediate BTV, high

MA; intermediate BTV, low MA; high BTV, high MA; and high BTV, low MA. Two sets (12 groups in all) of these conditions existed with one set (6 groups) receiving initial response reinforcement and the other set (6 groups) not receiving initial response reinforcement.

The low BTV condition consisted of equal-size, large black arrows of different orientations. Intermediate BTV condition was the same as the low BTV condition for 50% of the pairs, while the other half consisted of pairs of smaller arrows of equal size. In the high BTV condition, 50% of the stimulus pairs were the same as in low BTV, 25% were pairs of small white arrows, and 25% were pairs of small black arrows. The apparatus used was the same as in the Clinton and Evans (1972) study. Criterion was 10 consecutive responses on a maximum of 60 trials.

The results were analyzed using a 3 x 2 x 2 factorial design (BTV x initial response outcome x MA). The dependent variable was the number of nonalternation responses (errors) in 60 trials (or before criterion). The main effect of initial response outcome was significant ($p < .05$) with initial nonreinforcement being associated with more nonalternation responses. Neither of the other main effects (MA and BTV level) was significant, nor was there any significant interaction.

In accordance with Zeaman and House (1963), higher reinforcement ratios (reinforcement on the initial response) reduced nonalternation responses (errors). Irrelevant dimensions were largely disregarded in favor of attention to the position dimension.

GRUEN AND BERG'S STUDIES. Finally, Gruen and Berg (1973) investigated the hypothesis that differences in the learning performance of all children increase as task complexity increases. *Task complexity* was defined as the number of varying irrelevant dimensions (VID) within a stimulus (Evans, 1968). In accordance with Zeaman and House (1963), it would be expected that the greater number of VIDs, the greater the deficiency in learning performance.

Thirty-six retarded subjects were selected for the study and equated on MA with 36 nonretarded subjects. Half of the retarded subjects ($\overline{CA} = 17$–4, $\overline{IQ} = 41.6$) were selected from a residential training school, while the other half ($\overline{CA} = 9$–5, $\overline{IQ} = 69.5$) were members in a special education class. Half of the subjects from each IQ group

were assigned to a 2 VID discrimination problem, while the other half were assigned to a 3 VID problem. The relevant dimension (form, color, or size) was varied across the conditions; however, each participant was assigned to only one of the relevant dimensions. The subjects were required to select from a projected image the particular form, color, or size. A penny was used to reinforce the correct selection. Responses were elicited until the subject made 10 consecutive correct responses or was given 120 trials.

With the 2 VID problem, when form was designated as the relevant dimension, color and position comprised the VIDs; size remained constant over time. When color was the relevant dimension, form and position were the VIDs; again size remained constant. Size problems, which kept form (square) constant over trials, used color and position as VIDs. The 3 VID problems were presented with the relevant and three irrelevant dimensions varied over trials and all possible settings of stimulus pairs presented in random order.

Results showed no significant differences in reaching criterion between the four types of subjects (institutionalized MR, their MA-matched normals, noninstitutionalized retardates, and their MA-matched normals). However, the main effects of dimension (form, color, size) and complexity (2 VID versus 3 VID) were significant. Significantly more trials were needed to reach the color criterion (color being the relevant dimension) than the form or size dimensions. In addition, significantly more trials were required to reach criterion on the form tasks than on the size tasks. With regard to complexity, more trials were required to reach criterion on the 3 VID problems than on the 2 VID problems.

Gruen and Berg (1973) saw no significant interactions between type of subject and complexity. This finding was inconsistent with the Zeaman and House (1963) theory; however, like Zeaman and House, they found that an increase in the number of irrelevant dimensions hindered learning.

Relevant Dimensions

ULLMAN AND ROUTH'S STUDIES. Ullman and Routh (1971) conducted a study to test the effects of several relevant dimensions on the discrimination learning of retarded subjects. It was hypothesized that increasing the number of relevant dimensions would weaken the discrimination learning deficiency of retarded subjects compared to that of normal subjects.

Ninety-six subjects were selected for the study. Forty-eight were mentally retarded special class students ($\overline{CA}$ = 11.8 years, $\overline{IQ}$ = 58.8) and 48 were nonretarded children ($\overline{CA}$ = 6.2 years, $\overline{IQ}$ = 98). Subjects were randomly assigned from each IQ level to one of four experimental groups. There were twelve subjects from each level, comprising a total of twenty-four subjects in each of the four groups.

Depending on the group the subject was in, he received the two-choice discrimination problem (via WGTA) in which both stimuli were composed of one, two, four, or eight relevant dimensions. The relevant dimensions and their respective cues were: color (red or blue), form (square or triangle), size (large or small), depth (greater or lesser), form of figures on stimulus face (circle or star), number of figures on face (one or four), size of figures on face (large or small), and direction of lines on face (horizontal or vertical). Position was varied and always irrelevant.

The task was to select the correct stimulus object. Correct choices were reinforced with candy. Each subject was given 60 trials per day for a maximum of 4 days (or 240 trials). A total of 25 consecutive correct choices in a single day was established as criterion.

Results were analyzed using a 2 x 4 x 12 design (IQ level x number of relevant dimensions x trials). The main effect of IQ was significant ($p < .05$). However, in contradiction to the hypothesized outcome, the interaction of IQ level and number of relevant dimensions was not significant. The data indicated that improvement in learning occurred over time, and that faster learning occurred with the nonretarded subjects than with the retarded participants. In addition, increasing the number of relevant dimensions improved the performances of both IQ groups.

Ullman and Routh (1971) interpreted their findings to be in support of the Zeaman and House (1963) theory because the differences between IQ groups were not in the rate of learning once learning began. The retardates performed poorer because they required more time to *begin* to discriminate correctly than normals. Also in support of the Zeaman and House theory was the finding that increasing the number of relevant dimensions aided learning. In terms of the Fisher and Zeaman

(1973) theory, the findings did not confirm a differential multiple-look ability.

ULLMAN'S STUDIES. Of the studies reviewed, perhaps the one which has the greatest bearing on the multiple-look ability (Fisher & Zeaman, 1973) was conducted by Ullman (1974). In this investigation he hypothesized similarly to Fisher and Zeaman that breadth of attention is restricted by the level of mental development. Specifically, he thought that: (a) on immediate tests retarded students would be inferior to intellectually average children of equal MA, (b) increasing the time between trials would progressively increase the deficiency of retarded children, and (c) using a correction procedure would not affect performance.

Ullman (1974) selected 100 subjects to test the hypotheses. Forty subjects ($\overline{CA}$ = 6.0, $\overline{IQ}$ = 103) were in kindergarten, 40 were EMRs ($\overline{CA}$ = 12, $\overline{IQ}$ = 64) from special education classes, and 20 were TMRs ($\overline{CA}$ = 13, $\overline{IQ}$ = 54) from trainable classes. Subjects from each IQ group were placed in either correction or noncorrection experimental groups.

A set of 32 stimulus objects, each having five relevant dimensions, was used. The dimensions and respective cues were: form (square or triangle), color (red or blue), depth (thin or thick), number of stars on face (one or four), and direction of lines on face (vertical or horizontal). In addition to the between-subjects factors of IQ level and correction versus noncorrection, there were two within-subject factors: delay (simultaneous, 0 seconds, 10 seconds, and 30 seconds) and test trials (one through five).

Ullman (1974) presented a stimulus object which contained five relevant dimensions to each subject; then a curtain was opened and 32 stimulus objects were presented. One of the objects was identical to the training stimulus. The remaining objects had a variety of cues. Many had several cues like the training stimulus, but only one contained all five of the cues presented in the training stimulus. The subject was asked to select the one which was exactly the same as the one originally presented. Twenty test trials were conducted, five tests at each of the four delay conditions (simultaneous, 0 seconds, 10 seconds, and 30 seconds). Correction or noncorrection procedures were used for the appropriate groups. The object which was selected by the subject was scored for each correct dimension and cue it contained (as on the demonstration stimulus). Search time was also recorded.

Three analyses of variance were used in the analysis of results. The first analysis of variance assessed the effects of IQ, correction, delay, test trial, and interactions in terms of the number of correct cues selected on each trial. The second analysis of variance assessed the same factors in terms of mean search time, and the third focused on dimension effects.

Ullman (1974) summarizes the major findings of the study to be: (a) TMR performance was inferior compared to EMR and average subjects; (b) increased time delay decreased TMR performance; (c) in all conditions there were no significant differences between EMRs and average children; (d) although there were no significant findings, there was a trend for feedback to improve performance; and (e) the performance of all groups suggested the ability to attend to several dimensions simultaneously. In concurrence with Fisher and Zeaman (1973), Ullman suggests that a more restricted breadth of attention and a more rapid rate of forgetting may depend on the degree of retardation. Since all the tasks used by Ullman included a memory factor (even 0 seconds delay), it is possible that memory factors accounted for some of the differences and not breadth of attention. This is especially supported by the performance of TMRs in relation to the performance of average and EMR children.

Color Distractors

KLEIN, KLEIN, OSKAMP, AND PATNODE'S STUDIES. Klein, Klein, Oskamp, and Patnode (1972) selected 10 mildly retarded children ($\overline{CA} = 8$) and 10 nonretarded children (CAs of 6 and 7) to study the influence of color distractors on a discrimination task. In following Zeaman and House's (1963) position, the investigators predicted that the retarded children would attend to the irrelevant stimuli more than the nonretarded children.

Each subject was instructed to make 40 figure discriminations. The figures consisted of four ink drawings on white cards. The subjects were presented one card on each trial and told to tell if one figure in the card was different or if all figures were the same. On some trials one of the identical figures was in red ink whereas all others were in black ink. The 40 trials consisted of the following

discrimination tasks: 10 of the cards had four identical black ink figures; 10 had four identical figures (three black and one red); 10 had three identical black figures and one different black figure; and 10 had three identical figures and one red and one different black figure. In this arrangement the red figure was never a correct response.

The results showed that the retarded children made significantly more errors ($p < .001$) on the discrimination trials than the nonretarded children. Moreover, the retarded children made significantly more errors on the color distractor cards (red ink figures) than on the nondistractor cards (all black ink figures). The performances of the nonretarded children did not differ on the color distractor and nondistractor cards. The results indicated that color is a highly prominent cue for retarded children. Also, the inappropriate attention to the irrelevant stimuli by the retarded children supports Zeaman and House's (1963) attention deficiency theory.

SUMMARY OF STUDIES. The primary characteristics of the eight studies reviewed are featured in Table 4.1. Summary information from the studies is presented within the following areas:

1. subject characteristics
2. effects of numerous irrelevant dimensions
3. effects of numerous relevant dimensions
4. experimental tasks

As noted in Table 4.1, the subjects who participated in the eight studies varied across numerous dimensions. The retarded participants ranged in age from 8 to 17 years and ranged in IQ from 41 to 73. Institutionalized retarded persons participated in three of the studies (Evans, 1968; Evans & Beedle, 1970; Gruen & Berg, 1973), whereas noninstitutionalized retarded children were in all the studies except the one by Evans and Beedle. The nonretarded children who participated in the studies ranged in age from 5–15 years. CA-equivalent nonretarded children participated in one study (Evans, 1968) and MA-equivalent nonretarded children were in four studies (Gruen & Berg, 1973; Klein et al., 1972; Ullman, 1974; Ullman & Routh, 1971).

In the five studies that examined the influence of varied irrelevant dimensions on discrimination learning, two (Evans, 1968; Gruen & Berg, 1973) compared the performances of retarded children with nonretarded children. Evans found that an

TABLE 4.1
Summary of Studies Focusing on Number of Dimensions

ARTICLE	SUBJECTS	INDEPENDENT VARIABLE	DEPENDENT VARIABLE	RESULTS
1. Evans (1968)	60 institutionalized EMRs $\overline{CA} = 17.45$ $\overline{IQ} = 64$	form, size, and brightness as relevant dimensions	number of errors prior to criterion on a two-choice discrimination task	1. Brightness was easier to learn than size or form.
Experiment I				
Experiment II	1. 48 EMRS $\overline{CA} = 14.5$ $\overline{IQ} = 73$ 2. 48 nonretarded $\overline{CA} = 14$ $\overline{IQ} = 105$	potency of variable irrelevant dimensions, IQ, sex	same as *Exp. I*	*1. Nonretarded Ss performed better ($p < .005$) than EMRs. 2. Boys made fewer errors than girls. 3. Potency of irrelevant dimension did not differentially affect girls but did affect boys.
Experiment III	1. 60 EMRs $\overline{CA} = 15$ $\overline{IQ} = 62$ 2. 60 nonretarded $\overline{CA} = 15$	number of variable irrelevant dimensions, IQ, sex	same as *Exp. I*	*1. Nonretarded performed better than EMRs. *2. The number of irrelevant dimensions was a significant factor with EMRs.
2. Evans & Beedle (1970)	40 institutionalized EMRs $\overline{CA} = 15$ $\overline{IQ} = 55$	irrelevant brightness variability within and between trials, distance between stimuli, sex	number of errors prior to criterion on a two-choice discrimination task	1. Distance between stimuli was significant (Far—more difficult). 2. Boys found between-trial variability more difficult than within-trial variability.
3. Clinton & Evans (1972)	60 EMRs $\overline{CA} = 16$ $\overline{IQ} = 61$	number of irrelevant dimensions (complexity) within trials, initial response outcome, mental age	number of errors prior to criterion on a two-choice discrimination task	*1. In the initial response nonreinforcement condition, the effects of complexity were ordered; i.e., high complexity produced more errors than low complexity. †2. In the initial response reinforcement condition more errors were produced at the intermediate level of complexity. †3. MA was not significant.
4. Clinton (1972)	60 EMRs $\overline{CA} = 15.6$ $\overline{IQ} = 67.5$	number of irrelevant dimensions between trials, initial response outcome, mental age	number of errors prior to criterion on a two-choice discrimination task	1. More errors occurred with initial response nonreinforcement. †2. MA and complexity were not significant.

TABLE 4.1, cont.

ARTICLE	SUBJECTS	INDEPENDENT VARIABLE	DEPENDENT VARIABLE	RESULTS
5. Gruen & Berg (1973)	1. 18 institutionalized TMRs $\overline{CA} = 17\text{-}4$ $\overline{IQ} = 41.6$ 2. 18 EMRs $\overline{CA} = 9\text{-}5$ $\overline{IQ} = 69.5$ 18 nonretarded equated on MA with TMRs 18 nonretarded equated on MA with EMRs	number of varied irrelevant dimensions, IQ level, institutionalization	number of errors prior to criterion or after 120 trials on a two-choice discrimination task	†1. No differences in performances occurred among the four groups. 2. Color relevant was the most difficult; form was the next most difficult; and size was the least difficult. *3. More trials were required to reach criterion when the number of irrelevant dimensions was increased from two to three.
6. Ullman & Routh (1971)	1. 48 EMRs $\overline{CA} = 11.8$ $\overline{IQ} = 58.8$ 2. 48 nonretarded $\overline{CA} = 6.2$ $\overline{IQ} = 98$	number of relevant dimensions	number of errors prior to criterion on a two-choice discrimination task	*1. An increase in the number of relevant dimensions improved the performance of both groups. *2. The nonretarded children performed better than the retarded children.
7. Ullman (1974)	1. 40 nonretarded $\overline{CA} = 6.0$ $\overline{IQ} = 103$ 2. 40 EMRs $\overline{CA} = 12$ $\overline{IQ} = 64$ 3. 20 TMRs $\overline{CA} = 13$ $\overline{IQ} = 54$	number of relevant dimensions, retention (delay time), IQ level, correction procedure	number of errors on 20 trials of a task which involved viewing a stimulus and, after its removal, selecting one like it from 32 stimuli	*1. The performance of the TMRs was the lowest of the three groups. *2. Increased delay time decreased the performance of TMRs. 3. No significant differences occurred between correction and noncorrection conditions. †4. No differences occurred between EMRs and normals.
8. Klein, Klein, Oskamp, & Patnode (1972)	1. 10 EMRs $\overline{CA} = 8$ 2. 10 nonretarded CAs of 6 & 7	color distractors	number of errors on 40 trials of a four-choice discrimination task	*1. The EMRs made more errors on the color distractor trials than on the noncolor distractor trials. *2. The EMRs made more errors than the nonretarded children. 3. The performances of the nonretarded children did not differ on the color distractor and noncolor distractor trials.

NOTE: *Supports either Zeaman and House (1963) or Fisher and Zeaman (1973).
†No support for either Zeaman and House (1963) or Fisher and Zeaman (1973).

increase in the number of variable-irrelevant dimensions decreased the performance of EMRs but not CA-equivalent, nonretarded adolescents. Also, Evans saw that CA-equivalent, nonretarded adolescents performed better on a discrimination task than did the EMRs. Gruen and Berg showed that the performances of EMRs and MA-equivalent, nonretarded children and TMRs and respective MA-equivalent, nonretarded children did not differ in any of the conditions with irrelevant dimensions varied. However, Gruen and Berg did show that an increase in number of irrelevant dimensions resulted in a decline in performance for all groups. Finally, in the studies that focused on examining the effects of number of irrelevant dimensions on discrimination learning, some specific findings were reported. They include:

1. Boys performed poorer when irrelevant dimensions were varied between trials than when they were varied within trials (Evans & Beedle, 1970).
2. Mental age was not related to performance on discrimination trials with number of irrelevant dimensions varied (Clinton, 1972; Clinton & Evans, 1972).
3. Number of irrelevant dimensions (complexity) was not significantly related to performance (Clinton, 1972).
4. When the distance between the stimuli was increased, the EMRs performed poorer (Evans & Beedle, 1970).
5. Number of irrelevant dimensions interacted with reinforcement conditions (Clinton & Evans, 1972).

In the three studies (Evans, Experiment I, 1968; Ullman, 1974; Ullman & Routh, 1971) that examined the effects of number of relevant dimensions on discrimination learning, two (Ullman, 1974; Ullman & Routh, 1971) compared the performances of retarded subjects and normals. Ullman and Routh found that MA-equivalent, nonretarded participants performed better than EMRs (supports Zeaman and House, 1963). Also, they found that increasing the number of relevant dimensions improved the performance of both IQ groups. Using a discrimination-memory task with five relevant dimensions, Ullman found no differences between the performances of EMRs and MA-equivalent normals, but he did find that TMRs did poorer than MA-equivalent, nonretarded children. Further findings from these three studies include:

1. Brightness was easier for EMRs to learn than either size or form (Evans, 1968).

2. Color was more difficult to learn than either form or size (Gruen & Berg, 1973).
3. An increase in the delay time between stimulus presentation and response hindered the performance of TMRs (Ullman, 1974).

Using color as an irrelevant dimension, Klein et al. (1972) found that EMRs were distracted by color, whereas the nonretarded children were not. In addition, they reported that nonretarded children made fewer errors than EMR children.

All investigators except two (Klein et al., 1972; Ullman, 1974) used a simple two-choice discrimination task. All stimuli included were essentially nonmeaningful or novel (e.g., arrows, dots, lines). Klein et al. used a four-choice discrimination task, and Ullman used a combination discrimination-memory task.

A perusal of the studies presented indicates that the support for the Zeaman and House (1963) and Fisher and Zeaman (1973) theories is unequivocal (11 findings are supportive and 5 are not supportive). Regardless of the support generated for the theories, the research focusing on number of dimensions provides us with numerous teaching implications.

Teaching Implications

1. Since several investigators (Clinton & Evans, 1972; Evans, 1968; Gruen & Berg, 1973) found that an increase in the number of irrelevant dimensions impeded the learning performances of retarded individuals, it is likely that teachers could enhance the learning of retarded students by reducing the number of irrelevant dimensions on a learning task. For example, the teacher should encourage students to remove all extraneous materials from their desk top while working on a specific task. In this way the student will be less inclined to attend to the many irrelevant stimuli surrounding the assigned material. In preparing teaching materials, the teacher should be careful not to include too many irrelevant stimuli, such as color, pictures, and size, unless they are relevant to solving the problem.
2. In examining the effects of variable relevant dimensions, Evans (1968) found that retarded individuals readily attended to brightness, whereas Gruen and Berg (1973) showed that retarded individuals responded well to size. In addition to these findings, Zeaman and House (1963) found that mentally retarded children tended to respond to shape more than they did to color. Hall (1971) tested the effects of dimension bias with mentally retarded children and showed that it significantly affected their performance

on discrimination tasks. Finally, Fisher and Zeaman (1973) reported that retardates learned faster when the preferred dimension is relevant. Some teaching techniques which include a consideration for dimension bias are:

a. The mentally retarded child's dimension bias may be informally tested and then featured on instructional stimuli. To test such a bias, like items may be presented which differ in size or color, and the child is asked to select the item he prefers. For example, the teacher could present a series of triangle shapes which differ in color and size, record the student's responses, and determine which dimension is most frequently selected.

b. If a dimension bias interferes with attention to relevant dimensions, a fading technique may be used to diminish the inhibitory affects of the bias. If color is the preferred dimension, it may be highlighted in initial stimulus presentations to facilitate attention and gradually be reduced during the series of stimulus presentations. For example, if a child is asked to select a word beginning with *s* from among four words, *s* words could be presented in color in initial trials and gradually faded to no color in final trials.

    initial trials: boy   ball   dog   stop (red letters)

    middle trials: bark   bell   stem (dark maroon letters) frog

    ending trials: river   cat   step   flip

c. If a child has a bias to attend to color, each of the arithmetic signs ($|+|,|-|,|\div|,|\times|$) could be paired to a color. Minus signs could always be red, plus signs blue, and so on. Gradually the color could be faded out, leaving the child responding only to the sign. $\sqsubset \triangle \bigcirc \times$

3. Evans and Beedle (1974) discovered that increasing the distance between two stimuli decreased the discrimination learning of retarded children. Thus, on initial discrimination tasks the teacher should place the stimuli to be discriminated close together.

4. Since Ullman and Routh (1971) found that an increase in the number of relevant dimensions improved the performance of retarded children on a discrimination task, it would be feasible for teachers to present tasks to retarded students which vary along several dimensions. For example, in teaching children to recognize words ending in *ing* the teacher could pair *ing* words with other words and present them as a two- or three-choice discrimination task. In order to improve the performance of the children, the *ing* words could be a different color and a different size. As the children learn to discriminate the *ing* dimension, color and size could be faded out. In another example, when a child is asked to select the letter *E* from a stimulus field including several letters, the *E* could vary along several dimensions (different

color and size) from the other letters. For example, M S E (red letter) L W

5. Larger rather than smaller stimulus differences facilitate the solution of discrimination problems (Fisher and Zeaman, 1973). This idea is implicit in the findings concerning increasing the number of relevant dimensions to foster learning. In essence, they found that attention to a dimension is a direct function of the physical difference between the cues of the respective dimension. Some teaching implications regarding cue distinctiveness and cue difference include:

a. The relevant dimensions of a stimulus need to be distinct in order to improve attention. Relevant dimensions of instructional stimuli should be highlighted. For example, if a child is to respond to a picture of a person's face and depict the mood reflected in the picture, the features of the face which cue mood (mouth, smile) should be prominent. Cue distinctiveness is also enhanced by decreasing background cues, i.e., put stimulus on plain paper. Other techniques to promote cue distinctiveness may involve:

(1) using raised letters, pictures, shapes

(2) presenting only one stimulus at a time, i.e., one letter, one number, one face, one word, one sentence

(3) using a highlight pen to draw attention to relevant dimensions; for example, highlighting the endings of words for a child not attending to word endings

(4) using arrows to denote relevant dimensions; for example, to help the child find all words beginning with *c*, the teacher could place an arrow beside all words which begin with the letter *c*

(5) using colors to denote relevant dimensions; for example, writing featured words of a story in a different color: The *cat* (red letters) ran

(6) drawing circles around selected items in an assigned reading; for example, circling specific job ads or store sales in a local newspaper

b. In instructional tasks involving visual discrimination, the cues of the relevant dimensions should differ significantly. For example, if a mentally retarded child is asked to sort stimulus cards into two piles, the two categories should be readily apparent, i.e., cards with red squares and cards with blue circles, not cards with red squares and red rectangles. Some teaching strategies which employ cue difference to elicit attention are:

(1) In the beginning stages of letter, shape, or number recognition, items which have significantly different shapes can be presented. For example, a child can more readily attend to the distinguishing differences between the letters *m* and *t* than to the letters *m* and *n*.

(2) In stimulus presentations involving more than two stimuli, the inclusion of identical stimuli aids attention to the relevant cues which distinguish between the stimuli. Brown (1970) used identical stimuli as a technique to raise the task performance of mentally retarded children. For example, if mentally retarded children are required to select the letter *E* from among five letters, their performance is increased by including several identical letters in the stimulus presentation, e.g., *D D D E C*.

6. Since Clinton and Evans (1972) found that stimulus characteristics and reinforcement arrangements on a specific learning task may have an interactive relationship, it appears that the teacher constantly needs to manipulate both reinforcement arrangements and stimulus characteristics in order to achieve optimal learning conditions. For example, it may impede learning if the teacher reinforces an arbitrary response (exploratory) on a task of moderate difficulty, yet learning may be improved if early (exploratory) responses are reinforced on a more difficult task. It appears that the only way a teacher could realistically follow these implications would be to monitor constantly the effects of reinforcement as the child changes from task to task. Thus if a plan of reinforcement increased correct responding, the teacher should continue with it; but if it did not, the teacher should alter either the reinforcement strategy or the task.

7. As mentioned previously (Evans, 1968; Gruen & Berg, 1973), a preference for a dimension influences attention processes of mentally retarded persons. Moreover, research exists which indicates that some retarded children have certain response strategies or biases. Clinton (1972) and Clinton and Evans (1972) discovered that educable retardates performed well on visual discrimination tasks which featured alternating the position of the relevant stimulus from one trial to another, i.e., relevant stimulus on left, then right, then left. Since the retardates performed the tasks so well, it was postulated that single alternation may be a phenomenon of mental retardation. Some teaching practices which consider response patterns are:

a. Informally evaluate the retarded person's response patterns on visual discrimination tasks. Note preferences for position, stimulus dimension, alternation tendencies, and perseveration tendencies. This assessment can be accomplished via 20–30 trials which require the child to select between variable numbers (two items, three items, etc.) of visual stimuli.

b. On instructional tasks which require attention to dimensions contrary to the child's preference, provide pretraining on the relevant dimensions. If a child prefers to attend to color, pretraining on form should precede an instructional task that features

form. For example, the retarded child could be trained to distinguish between the form of arithmetic symbols ($+$, $-$, $\div$, $\times$) and numbers before beginning an arithmetic task.

c. On instructional tasks which require random response patterns, provide pretraining to retarded persons who have response sets. If a retarded child tends always to select objects to the left, pretraining which includes reward for attending to stimuli in other positions should help.

d. Design the instructional task in a manner which is congruent with the retardate's response set. If a retarded child has a single alternation attention set, allow the correct responses to follow a single alternation pattern. For example, have the child select the letter *e* from each pair of stimulus letters and alternate the position of *e*.

Trial 1: *a e*
Trial 2: *e b*
Trial 3: *c e*
Trial 4: *e m*

Studies Focusing on Incentive Conditions

Fisher and Zeaman (1973) postulated that a retardate learns to attend to or avoid a stimulus dimension on the basis of reward and nonreward associated with the specific dimension. Moreover, after reviewing and conducting studies, they concluded that reinforcement and nonreinforcement affect both initial attention to the stimulus and cue selection processes throughout discrimination tasks. In short, they report: "retardates learn to associate by contiguity the reward values of the cues. . . . Learned preferences for stimulus dimensions will be generated by the differential reinforcement of attention to those dimensions yielding accurate cue-reward predictions by the subject" (p. 193).

In six studies reviewed, the following four (Harris & Tramontana, 1973; Harter, Brown, & Zigler, 1971b; Lobb, 1972; Massey & Insalaco, 1968) investigated the influence of both positive and aversive conditions on discrimination learning. These four studies are presented in chronological order. In the last two studies reviewed, one study (Harter, Brown, & Zigler, 1971a) examined the effects of social praise and task difficulty on discrimination learning, and the other study (House, 1973) examined the effect of reward ratio on discrimination learning.

Positive and Negative Conditions

MASSEY AND INSALACO'S STUDIES. Massey and Insalaco (1969) selected 40 institutionalized retarded girls (CA = 16, IQ = 32) in order to examine the effects of various combinations of punishment and reward on discrimination learning. Specifically, the investigators designed the study to see if aversive conditions could serve as a discriminative stimulus and attentuate the "attention deficiency" that retardates may exhibit on visual discrimination tasks. The stimuli consisted of a red circle and a yellow square and were projected onto two screens which were located on a 3-ft. square board. A loud speaker was centered just above the apparatus for presenting an aversive white noise (95 db for a 0.5 sec. duration). A cup for dispensing candy and a response button were located under each screen.

Four groups were established. Group I was the control group in which subjects received candy for each correct response. Group II participants received candy for a correct response and aversive noise for an incorrect response. Group III participants received the aversive noise followed by candy for a correct response and received nothing for an incorrect response. Group IV subjects received aversive noise followed by candy for a correct response and aversive noise only for an incorrect response. Criterion was established at 15 out of 20 correct responses.

An inspection of the mean number of errors indicated that Group I (control group) performed the poorest and Group II performed the best. Groups III and IV (receiving aversive noise following correct responses) made more errors than Group II but less errors than Group I. A statistical analysis disclosed no significant differences among groups II, III, and IV. However, groups II and III performed significantly better ($p < .01$ and $p < .05$ respectively) than Group I. Group IV performed significantly better at the .10 level of confidence.

Massey and Insalaco (1969) conclude that the results suggest that aversive stimulation can under certain conditions improve the acquisition of a response. Moreover, they note that this facilitation is best accomplished when it functions as a cue to an incorrect response, as in Group II.

HARTER, BROWN, AND ZIGLER'S STUDIES. Harter, Brown, and Zigler (1971b) examined discrimination learning of 51 normal children and 84 institutionalized retarded children (40 organic and 44 familials) as a function of penalty condition and

etiology. All three groups were matched on MA and the two retarded groups were matched on IQ. A modified version of the Wisconsin General Testing Apparatus (WGTA) was used to present each subject a two-choice, size-discrimination task. The organic, familial, and normal groups were each subdivided into two groups for assignment to an initial penalty + reward condition or an initial reward only condition. Subjects in the initial reward only condition received a marble after each correct response and subjects in the initial penalty + reward condition received a marble (reward) after a correct response but returned a marble (penalty) after each incorrect response. All subjects were given a maximum of 50 trials in order to reach the criterion of 9 out of 10 correct responses. Subjects in the initial reward only condition who did not reach criterion were given 50 more trials after being randomly assigned to one of two conditions: shift penalty + reward, or continuous reward only.

The organic retardates, unlike the normals and familials, did not display better learning in the initial penalty + reward condition. The normals' performance under initial penalty + reward condition significantly improved ($p < .05$) over the initial reward only condition. The familial retardates performed better ($p < .10$) under initial penalty + reward than they did under initial reward only. After the investigators examined the strategies (position and object sets) of the normals and retardates, they concluded that these findings suggest that the effect of the initial penalty + reward condition was to heighten the subjects' attention to the relevant dimensions of the task.

In reviewing the findings, Harter, Brown, and Zigler (1971) conclude that penalty conditions tended to increase attentiveness to the task in both normals and familials. Organics appeared to persist with a position response strategy rather than switch to attention to relevant stimulus dimensions. This finding supports Zeaman and House's (1963) position that the retarded have more difficulty attending to a stimulus dimension than normals of the same mental age. Although Harter et al.'s study did not primarily focus on examining the attention deficiency position of Zeaman and House, the results were applicable to interpretation within the framework of Zeaman and House's attention theory. The findings suggested that the attention deficient position purported by Zeaman and House is supported with organic retardates but not with familial retardates.

LOBB'S STUDIES. Lobb (1972) conducted a series of experiments to examine the effects of pretraining with negative cues (S −) and positive cues (S +) on the discrimination learning of retarded and MA-equivalent, nonretarded children. He saw that the results of earlier work (Riese & Lobb, 1967) suggested that nonrewarded pretraining may attenuate the discrimination learning deficiency displayed by retarded children when compared to normals of similar MA. He theorized that nonrewarded pretraining could help the retarded learners compensate for inhibition weaknesses. His study investigated this theoretical position.

In Experiment I, 60 retarded ($\overline{CA}$ = 9.3, $\overline{MA}$ = 3.5) and 60 nonretarded children ($\overline{CA}$ = 3.5, $\overline{MA}$ = 3.8) were selected and assigned to one of six experimental conditions. Prior to assignment in the respective experimental conditions, each subject participated in a screening session which consisted of 25 trials of a two-choice visual discrimination task presented via a type of WGTA. On these trials a blue cross (S +) and a red triangle (S −) covered the trays and S + always covered the candy. In the experimental conditions all six groups finished their daily sessions by receiving 10 trials of simultaneous (S + S −) discrimination tasks. The experimental trials were the same as in the screening session except S + was a yellow circle and S − was a green square for half of the subjects in each group and the cues were reversed for the remaining participants. The first trials for each experimental group were arranged in the following way:

Group I: 10 trials of choice between two identical cones without reward (10 no reward identicals NRI)
10 nonrewarded trials of choice between identical S − objects (10 S − S −)
10 regular trials (S + S −)
Group II: 2 minutes of play
10 S − S − trials
10 S + S − trials
Group III: 10 NRI trials
10 S + S+ trials (choice between two identical S + objects)
10 S + S − trials
Group IV: Play
10 S + S+ trials
10 S + S − trials

Group V: 10 NRI trials
Play
10 S + S − trials
Group VI: Play
Play
10 S + S − trials

Sessions continued until the participant chose 10 out of 10 rewarded choices in one set of S + S − trials or 9 out of 10 correct in two successive sessions. Subjects who failed to reach criterion stopped at 25 trials.

The results from Experiment I disclosed that for both IQ classes the mean number of errors on the regular discrimination tasks (S + S−) increased. Subjects in the S − S − condition made the least number of errors, followed by the S + S + and play pretraining group. Lobb (1972) notes that these results indicate that training with a relevant cue prior to discrimination tasks affects performances.

The performance of the nonretarded group was superior to that of the retarded group across all conditions. The S − S − treatment did not attenuate the gap between the performances of retarded and nonretarded participants. The effect of novelty on object choice was examined and found to be a significant factor in influencing choices on the early trials.

With some slight variations (omitted play, omitted screening, one day placed between preliminary testing and experimental trials), Lobb (1972) conducted a second experiment primarily designed to compare the effect of S − S − and S + S − pretraining on discrimination learning. The results indicated that nonretarded children ($\overline{CA}$ = 3.5, $\overline{MA}$ = 3.6) performed significantly better than the retarded children ($\overline{CA}$ = 8.8, $\overline{MA}$ = 3.7). As in Experiment I, the S − S − pretraining generated fewer errors by nonretarded participants than the S + S + training. However, unlike Experiment I, the S − S − pretraining sessions did not improve the discrimination learning performance of the retarded group more than the S + S + training. Again the effects of novelty were influential in the early trials.

Lobb (1972) designed a third experiment to investigate the respective effects of cue novelty and contingency factors on discrimination learning. The results clearly revealed that response consequences were considerably more influential on discrimination choices than cue novelty. In addition, MA-equivalent, nonretarded subjects performed better than retarded children.

In summarizing the results of the three experiments, Lobb (1972) notes that the equal-MA deficiency (up to MAs of 4.5 years) in trainable retarded children for learning simple discriminations was soundly supported. Secondly, the results disclosed that nonrewarded pretraining did not overcome the comparative disability of the retarded children. Third, the results showed that nonrewarded pretraining can greatly improve the discrimination performance of retarded children.

HARRIS AND TRAMONTANA'S STUDIES. Harris and Tramontana (1973) selected 12 borderline retarded children ($\overline{CA} = 7$–7, $\overline{IQ} = 74$) and 12 moderately retarded children ($\overline{CA} = 7$–8, $\overline{IQ} = 47$) in order to examine the influence of positive reinforcement and response cost on discrimination learning. A slide projector was used to display a two-choice visual discrimination task to each participant. The stimuli varied in color, size, form, and number of figures and cues were redundant to aid the subjects success.

Each subject participated in three reinforcement conditions: positive reinforcement, response cost, and combination positive reinforcement and response cost. In the reinforcement condition the participant received a piece of candy for each correct response. In the response cost condition a piece of candy was removed from the participant's cup each time a wrong response was made. In the combination condition the experimenter gave the subject a piece of candy for each correct response and took away a piece of candy for each incorrect response. In each condition the number of trials to criterion (10 consecutive correct responses) was recorded.

The results disclosed that the borderline retarded children reached criterion in a significantly fewer number of trials than the moderately retarded children. For all subjects, response cost was more effective than positive reinforcement. In addition, the combined reinforcement/cost condition was more effective than positive reinforcement alone. The effectiveness of the response cost condition and the combined reinforcement/cost condition did not significantly differ. When the performances of the two intelligence groups were separately analyzed, it was found that for the borderline group both response cost and the combination reinforcement/response cost condition were significantly more effective than positive reinforcement alone. Also, no significant differences

resulted between the combination condition and the response cost condition. In the moderately retarded group no significant differences were reported among the treatment conditions. Harris and Tramontana (1973) conclude that in a simple discrimination learning task, intellectual level may be an important factor to consider the determining contingency arrangements.

Social Praise

HARTER, BROWN, AND ZIGLER'S STUDIES. Harter, Brown, and Zigler (1971a) selected 38 institutionalized, mildly retarded adolescents, 37 noninstitutionalized, mildly retarded adolescents, and 33 nonretarded children in order to investigate the influence of social reinforcement and task difficulty on discrimination learning. The three groups of subjects were equivalent on MA.

An oddity problem (three pictures of birds, two of which were identical and one was different from trial to trial) and a simple three-choice discrimination task (three pictures of birds, two of which were identical and a third was always a cardinal) were presented to the children in the respective conditions. Each task was presented under either a social praise condition (marble and praise) or a standard condition (marble only). In order to examine all the stated hypotheses, 12 experimental groups were established. For each task (oddity and three-choice discrimination) the groups were: (a) nonretarded standard group, (b) nonretarded social praise group, (c) noninstitutionalized retarded standard group, (d) noninstitutionalized retarded social praise group, (e) institutionalized retarded standard group, and (f) institutionalized retarded social praise group. For both tasks criterion was set at 9 out of 10 correct responses, or a maximum of 100 trials.

The findings disclosed that the oddity problem was more difficult than the three-choice discrimination task for all three groups of subjects. The performance of the nonretarded group was better than the performances of the two retarded groups on both tasks. On the three-choice task the institutionalized retarded participants made more errors in the social condition than in the standard condition, whereas the pattern was reversed for the noninstitutionalized retarded group. There were no differences among the groups in the number of subjects who reached criterion on the three-choice task. However, more normal subjects reached criterion on the oddity task. Harter,

Brown, and Zigler (1971a) note: "praise and opportunity for social interaction led the institutionalized subjects to be more attentive to the experimenter and interfered with their attention to or interest in the task" (p. 282).

Reward Ratio

HOUSE'S STUDIES. House (1973) conducted a study to investigate the hypothesis that a longer period of learning opportunity would provide a higher reward ratio and thus strengthen instrumental learning. She suggested that "few trials per problem results in weak instrumental learning and, consequently, a low reward ratio for attention" (p. 255).

Twenty-six institutionalized mentally retarded subjects representing two levels of intelligence were selected. Sixteen subjects ($\overline{CA}$ = 12.5, $\overline{IQ}$ = 27) were in the 2–4 MA range and 10 subjects ($\overline{CA}$ = 15.2, $\overline{IQ}$ = 42) were in the 4–6 MA range. Each of the MA groups was divided into two groups which were to differ in the sequence of conditions. After extensive pretraining designed to promote attention to the relevant dimension, half of the subjects received eight daily sessions of 10-trial problems, followed by eight sessions of 3-trial problems (the 10–3 group). The other half of the subjects had the reverse sequence following their pretraining session: 3-trial problems for eight daily sessions, followed by eight sessions of 10-trial problems (the 3–10 group). Four different problems were presented in each daily session, resulting in 12 trials per session in the 3-trial condition and 40 trials per session in the 10-trial condition. Two-choice discrimination tasks were used; form was the relevant dimension and color was constant within problems but varied between problems.

Using the number of correct responses on trials 2 and 3, the results revealed that the overall percentage correct for the high MA group was 76% and the percentage correct for the low MA group was 71%. Since this was not a significant difference, the two IQ groups were combined for further analysis.

The predicted superiority on the longer problems was obtained overall; 77% correct on trials 2 and 3 in the 10-trial condition and 70% correct on trials 2 and 3 in the 3-trial condition were obtained. There were no significant differences due to MA. The 3-trial problems seemed to result in a deterioration of performance over time, whereas the per-

formance on the 10-trial problems remained high across trials. In regard to the switching procedure, House (1973) states, "It appears that extended practices on ten-trial problems may have prevented the detrimental effect of three-trial problems. However, statistical evidence for this effect was weak" (p. 259). The superior performance of the subjects on the 10-trial problems supports the viewpoint that reward ratio affects the strength of the attention response.

SUMMARY. The six studies reviewed in this section are briefly summarized in Table 4.2. Although the number of studies is small, they include a wide range of experimental variables. The characteristics and findings of the studies are summarized according to the following areas:

1. subject characteristics
2. independent variables
3. tasks

Subjects differed in many characteristics. They spanned three levels of mental retardation (IQ range of 27–74). Three studies (Harris & Tramontana, 1973; Harter, Brown, & Zigler, 1971a, 1971b) included EMRs, four studies (Harris & Tramontana, 1973; House, 1973; Lobb, 1972; Massey & Insalaco, 1969) included TMRs, and one study (House, 1973) included severely retarded (SMR) participants. Four studies (Harter, Brown, & Zigler, 1971a, 1971b; House, 1973; Massey & Insalaco, 1969) included institutionalized retarded participants. Etiology was considered in one study (Harter, Brown, & Zigler, 1971b). Finally, three studies (Harter, Brown, & Zigler, 1971a, 1971b; Lobb, 1972) included nonretarded participants and in all of these studies they were matched on MA with respective retarded subjects. In relation to subject characteristics, the findings include:

1. Although institutionalized retarded subjects were included in four studies, it was examined as a factor in only one study (Harter et al., 1971a). In that study only one finding differentiated the institutionalized group, i.e., they made more errors in a social-praise condition than in a nonsocial-praise condition. The investigators hypothesized that the institutionalized retarded participants desired social praise to such an extent that it distracted them from the task. Institutionalization was not systematically examined in any of the other studies and no pattern regarding institutionalization emerged between the studies.
2. In the one study (Lobb, 1972) that compared the performances of trainable retarded participants with MA-equivalent, nonretarded participants, the non-

retarded performed significantly better (three different comparisons). In the two studies (Harter, Brown, & Zigler, 1971a, 1971b) that compared EMRs with MA-equivalent nonretarded subjects, one comparison yielded no significant difference and the other one resulted in a higher performance by the nonretarded group.

3. Organics exhibited a position response bias, whereas familials did not (Harter, Brown, & Zigler, 1971b).
4. In the one study that compared the learning performances of EMRs with TMRs, the EMRs performed better (Harris & Tramontana, 1973).

The independent variable in four of the studies (Harris & Tramontana, 1973; Harter, Brown, & Zigler, 1971b; Lobb, 1972; Massey & Insalaco, 1969) consisted of both negative and positive consequences. Tangible reinforcers (candy and marbles) were used in all four studies. Negative conditions included removing a marble or candy or adding aversive white noise. In three of the studies (Harris & Tramontana, 1973; Harter et al., 1971b, Massey & Insalaco, 1969) the combination of reward for correct response and penalty for an incorrect response was investigated. Some selected findings in relation to the independent variables include:

1. In the five comparisons of combination reward-penalty with reward only or penalty only, the combination resulted in higher performance in three of the comparisons. In the other two comparisons that yielded no significant differences, reward only and penalty only were each compared to the combination.
2. In the one comparison of a penalty versus a positive reinforcement condition, the penalty condition yielded higher performances (Harris & Tramontana, 1973).
3. Organics were less sensitive to incentive conditions (marbles as reward) than familials in one study (Harter, Brown, & Zigler, 1971b).
4. TMRs were less sensitive to incentive conditions (candy as reward) than EMRs in one study (Harris & Tramontana, 1973).
5. In one study (Lobb, 1972) the researcher concludes that nonrewarded pretraining enhanced the discrimination learning of TMRs.
6. Social praise improved the performances of MA-equivalent, nonretarded subjects and noninstitutionalized retarded subjects; however, it impeded the performance of institutionalized retarded subjects (Harter, Brown, & Zigler, 1971a).
7. A higher reward ratio resulted in improved learning performances by TMRs and SMRs (House, 1973).

In all studies except one (Harter, Brown, & Zigler, 1971a) the tasks consisted of a two-choice discrimination task. Form was the relevant dimen-

sion in three of the studies (House, 1973; Lobb, 1972; Massey & Insalaco, 1969), whereas size was relevant in one study (Harter, Brown, & Zigler, 1971b) and one investigator (Harris & Tramontana, 1973) used a task with multiple relevant dimensions. All studies except one (Harter, Brown, & Zigler, 1971a) used relatively meaningless stimuli. Harter et al. used pictures of birds on a three-choice discrimination task.

Due to the dissimilarity in the six studies in terms of variables controlled, it is difficult to determine definitive trends. However, they do offer much support for the Zeaman and House (1963) attention theory and/or the Fisher and Zeaman (1973) attention-retention theory.

TEACHING IMPLICATIONS. The implications of operant theory are discussed in Chapter 8 and include the use of positive reinforcement, negative reinforcement, and punishment. Since reward for correct choice is inherent in most of the discrimination learning paradigms, it is not surprising to note that many of the studies reviewed focused on penalty conditions. In this section several implications are presented which appear specifically related to the six studies reviewed.

1. Since several studies (Harris & Tramontana, 1973; Harter, Brown, & Zigler, 1971b; Massey & Insalaco, 1969) found that positive reinforcement for correct responses and response cost or penalty for incorrect responses aided the learning performance of retarded individuals, it is helpful to examine some learning situations in which the application of reward and penalty is appropriate.

   a. For parents and/or teachers who have historically relied on extensive use of aversive methods (time-out or isolation), the milder form of response cost may be a good intermediary step in getting them to use a less aversive approach.
   b. Only in situations in which speed and efficiency are very important in changing a behavior (e.g., self-abuse or abuse of others) can the combination of reinforcement-response cost or response cost be justified.
   c. Response cost could be used to prepare students to function in a work or social environment in which response cost or reward-penalty are prevalent contingency arrangements (e.g., revoke driver's license for speeding, reduce insurance premiums for safe driving).

2. House (1973) reports that longer trials (10 trials versus 3 trials) result in better learning because the reward ratio is higher. This finding suggests that teachers should ensure that retarded students re-

TABLE 4.2
Summary of Studies Focusing on Incentive Conditions

ARTICLE	SUBJECTS	INDEPENDENT VARIABLE	TASK	RESULTS
1. Massey & Insalaco (1969)	40 institutionalized TMR girls $\overline{CA} = 16$ $\overline{IQ} = 32$	influence of candy reward on discrimination learning, influence of aversive (white noise) condition on discrimination learning, influence of combinations of reward and punishment	two-choice discrimination task using circles and squares	1. Performance was best when correct responses were reinforced and incorrect responses punished. 2. Aversive stimulation can function to facilitate acquisition of a response.
2. Harter, Brown, & Zigler (1971b)	1. 51 nonretarded 2. 44 institutionalized, familial-retarded 3. 40 institutionalized, organic-retarded subjects	effects of penalty conditions, effects of etiology	two-choice discrimination task with size as the relevant dimension	*1. Familials and normals learned best in the reward for correct response-penalty for incorrect response condition. 2. Incentive conditions did not differentially influence the performance of organics. *3. Organics exhibited a position response bias.
3. Lobb (1972) *Experiment I*	1. 60 nonretarded $\overline{CA} = 3.5$ $\overline{IQ} = 108$ 2. 60 retarded $\overline{CA} = 9.3$ $\overline{IQ} = 38$	effects of pretraining with negative and positive cues on discrimination learning	two-choice discrimination task with form as the relevant dimension	*1. Nonretarded subjects performed better than the retarded subjects. 2. Pretraining on a nonreward dimension did not attenuate the gap between the performances of the retarded subjects and the MA-equivalent nonretarded Ss. *3. Nonrewarded pretraining improved scores of both groups.
Experiment II	1. Nonretarded $\overline{CA} = 3.5$ $\overline{IQ} = 100$ 2. Retarded $\overline{CA} = 8.8$ $\overline{IQ} = 42$	nonrewarded pretraining, rewarded pretraining with a one day delay between pretraining and experimental session	same as *Exp. I*	*1. Nonrewarded pretraining enhanced the scores of both groups. 2. Unlike *Exp. I*, nonrewarded pretraining did not improve the performance of TMRs more than the rewarded pretraining. 3. As in *Exp. I*, cue novelty was a significant factor. *4. MA-equivalent nonretarded subjects performed better than the TMRs.

TABLE 4.2, cont.

ARTICLE	SUBJECTS	INDEPENDENT VARIABLE	DEPENDENT VARIABLE	RESULTS
Experiment III	1. Nonretarded CA = 2–4.5 2. Retarded MAs below 4.5	cue novelty, contingency factors	similar to *Exp. I*	*1. Consequences influenced discrimination learning more than cue novelty. *2. MA-equivalent nonretarded subjects performed better than the retarded Ss.
4. Harris & Tramontana (1973)	1. 12 mildly retarded CA = 7–7 IQ = 74 2. 12 TMRs CA = 7–8 IQ = 47	effects of positive reinforcement, effects of response cost, effects of combination positive reinforcement-response cost	two-choice discrimination task with redundancy of relevant cues	*1. Mildly retarded Ss performed better than the TMRs. 2. Response cost was more effective than positive reinforcement for the total group. 3. No differences resulted from the response cost and combination conditions. 4. For the TMR group no differences emerged across the conditions.
5. Harter et al. (1971a)	1. 33 nonretarded CA = 7 2. 38 institutionalized EMRs CA = 15 IQ = 60 3. 37 noninstitutionalized EMRs CA = 13 IQ = 66	effects of social reinforcement and institutionalization, effects of task difficulty	two tasks: a three-choice discrimination task and an oddity problem	*1. Oddity problem was more difficult than three-choice problem for all groups. 2. Institutionalized EMRs made more errors in social-praise condition than in standard condition. *3. The nonretarded group performed better than the two retarded groups. 4. The noninstitutionalized group performed better in the social condition than in the standard condition.
6. House (1973)	1. 16 institutionalized retarded CA = 12.5 IQ = 27 2. 16 institutionalized retarded CA = 15.2 IQ = 42	effects of reward ratio on discrimination learning	two-choice discrimination task with form as the relevant dimension	1. Learning was faster if the problem lasted longer. This effect was attributed to a higher reward ratio for the attention response during longer problems.

NOTE: *Support for either Zeaman and House (1963) or Fisher and Zeaman (1973).

ceive extensive training (on the same relevant dimension) with a high ratio of reinforcement before introducing new material.

3. Lobb (1972) found that rewarded and nonrewarded pretraining on a relevant dimension improved the learning performance of retarded subjects. Thus, teachers could improve the learning of retarded children by pointing out the relevant dimensions of stimuli before beginning the task (e.g., "Look at the color of the triangle").

4. Since Harter, Brown, and Zigler (1971a) found that social reinforcement interfered with the learning performance of institutionalized retarded individuals, it appears that the attendant or teacher should monitor the effects of praise. For example, the resident may desire social praise so much that the task becomes secondary to receiving the praise and the child focuses attention on the teacher and not the task. In these situations the teacher must be sure that only appropriate behavior is praised.

5. Harris and Tramontana (1973) found that as the level of retardation increased (became more severe) the subjects were less sensitive to the incentive conditions being used in the experiment. This finding suggests that teachers must be sure their rewards have reinforcement value for the children. As the level of retardation increases, it may be necessary for the teacher or attendant to use primary reinforcers.

IMPLICATIONS FROM FISHER AND ZEAMAN (1973).
As mentioned previously, reward for the correct choice is inherent in the discrimination learning paradigm. Fisher and Zeaman (1973) showed that attention processes are influenced by incentive conditions and cue-reward associations. This finding suggests that to increase the attention of retardates to tasks teachers should pair instructional stimuli with rewards.

1. Provide reinforcement for attention to a relevant dimension. The reinforcement should be tied specifically to attending to a specific dimension. For example, the teacher may say, "I like the way you are looking at the *red* letters" or "I like the way you are watching my hand."

2. Avoid associating punitive conditions with relevant stimuli or relevant dimensions of a stimulus. For example, "You dropped the cards and got them out of order!"

3. Reinforce successive approximations of attention to desired dimensions, saying such things as: "I like the way you are looking at the card." "Nice looking at the letters." "You did an excellent job of picking the letter *E*."

4. Play games which feature stimulus dimensions that are later used in instructional tasks; for example, play the Candyland game (Milton Bradley) which deals

with color prior to having child work with Cuisenaire rods (color).

5. Use learning centers which provide feedback to the student. For example, a learning board which lights up for a correct response can be used.

6. Strive to help students obtain positive cue-reward associations with stimuli frequently used in the classroom, i.e., letters, numbers, shapes, colors.

Studies Focusing on Transfer Operations

A number of experiments have been conducted using transfer operations of intradimensional shift, reversal, and extradimensional shift. As mentioned previously, Zeaman and House (1963) predicted that intradimensional shifts (changing a cue in same dimension) would be easier to learn than extradimensional shifts (changing an irrelevant dimension to a relevant dimension).

In this section several studies are reviewed which used one or more of the shift operations. In four studies (Lobb, 1974; Lobb & Childs, 1973; Lobb & Stogdill, 1974; Milgram & Noce, 1968) the effect of verbal labeling (overt rehearsal) by the participants on transfer operations was examined. In two studies (Bilsky & Heal, 1969; Turrisi & Shepp, 1969) novelty stimuli were used in the shift operations. In two studies (Lobb & Stogdill, 1974; Turrisi & Shepp, 1969) overtraining was examined in relation to the shift paradigm. In these studies overtraining consisted of providing the subject with continued training along the relevant dimension prior to the shift on transfer operation. Finally, a study by Switzky (1973) compared the effect of cue distinctiveness on intradimensional and extradimensional shifts. This review includes: (a) verbal rehearsal and transfer operations, (b) novel stimuli and transfer operations, and (c) cue distinctiveness and transfer operations.

Verbal Rehearsal and Transfer Operations

MILGRAM AND NOCE'S STUDIES. Milgram and Noce (1968) selected 70 institutionalized retarded adolescents ($\overline{CA} = 15.4$) and 96 MA-equivalent, nonretarded children ($\overline{CA} = 7.5$) in order to investigate the effects of verbalizing relevant and irrelevant dimensions on a discrimination task which included a reversal of the relevant dimension. They favored the position that such verbalizations would aid performance by directing attention to the dimension being reinforced constantly.

The stimuli consisted of two-dimensional squares and circles mounted in pairs on cardboard rectangles. The squares and circles varied in size and brightness (black and white). Stimuli were always paired so they differed in size, brightness, and shape.

Five experimental conditions were established and each participant was randomly assigned to one of the experimental conditions. Subjects in Group I verbalized one relevant dimension (size or brightness) during the discrimination learning trials. Group II participants verbalized one relevant and one irrelevant dimension. Group III verbalized one relevant dimension and two irrelevant dimensions. Group IV verbalized one irrelevant dimension. Group V did not verbalize during the discrimination trials. Criterion during the discrimination trials was 9 out of 10 correct responses with a maximum of 72 trials permitted. After the completion of the initial discrimination trials, reversal trials were initiated. In the reversal trials (extradimensional shift) the relevant dimension was switched from size to brighness or from brightness to size. The reversal shift trials were continued until the subject met the same success criterion employed in the initial trials.

The results disclosed that the performances of the groups were ordered as follows: Group I < Group II ($p < .05$), Group II < Group V ($p < .05$), and Group V < Group IV ($p < .05$). The performances of the retarded group and MA-equivalent nonretarded group did not significantly differ. On the reversal trials the retarded participants exhibited no significant differences among the conditions. In the reversal trials the nonretarded participants in the Group I condition peformed significantly better than the nonretarded subjects in the Group V (control) condition. No other significant differences occurred in the performances of the normals across the experimental conditions. The performances of the retarded and non-retarded groups did not differ on the reversal trials. Milgram and Noce (1968) conclude that "evidence is ample that verbalizing the relevant cue significantly improved performance over a base-line or no-verbalization condition and that verbalization of irrelevant cues interfered" (p. 173).

LOBB AND CHILDS'S STUDIES. In a similar study Lobb and Childs (1973) selected 40 mentally retarded and 40 MA-equivalent, nonretarded children in order to examine verbal control on an intradimensional shift in discrimination learning. The primary aim of the study was twofold: (a) to test the low IQ attention deficiency proposed by Zeaman and House (1963) and (b) to examine the influence of verbal labeling on discrimination learning. The low IQ attention deficiency position advanced by Zeaman and House is based on the premise that trials to criterion on a discrimination task are a function of the initial probability of observing the relevant dimension, e.g., color. They reasoned that if this probability is not comparatively low there should be no *comparative deficiency* in the rate of learning of retardates on a discrimination task. In this study the two discrimination tasks (original task and a second task involving an intradimensional shift) used the same irrelevant cues. Lobb and Childs reasoned that attention to the relevant dimension (color, black) would become established in the original discrimination task and transfer intact to the second intradimensional (color, blue) phase and greatly facilitate attainment of the new learning criterion. In summarizing, Lobb and Childs state:

> Thus, any comparative deficit of retarded groups in the rate of attaining the criterion of correct performance should be evident during original discrimination learning, but diminish or disappear after the shift to new cues, depending on the amount of appropriate learning that occurred in the first phase. (p. 183)

The subjects participated in three experimental phases. For Phase I the two groups (retarded and nonretarded) were each divided into a verbal training group and a nonverbal training group. The Wisconsin General Test Apparatus (WGTA) was used to present a two-choice discrimination task with color as the relevant dimension and form and position as the irrelevant dimensions. In the verbal condition each participant was required to say the color before selecting the stimulus. If the correct response (stimulus selection) was made, the subject received the candy in the tray and was verbally praised. If the color label was incorrect, the child was told the answer was wrong and required to say the correct color before continuing. In Phase II, half of the subjects in each condition received interpolated training and the other half were asked to draw on paper. The interpolated training consisted of extinguishing the correct color-label response used in Phase I and acquiring the correct color label (*blue*) to be used in Phase III. In Phase III all participants received the same task. Each subject was seated at the WGTA and told to find the candy. The new color cue covered the reward trays and the procedures were identical to those of the nonverbal condition in Phase I.

The results disclosed that in Phase I the rate of learning for participants in the verbal condition was superior ($p < .001$) to the rate of learning of the participants in the nonverbal condition. The performances of the retarded and MA-equivalent, nonretarded children did not differ significantly in Phase I. The results from Phase III indicated that verbalization training aided discrimination learning for both IQ groups. Moreover, positive transfer followed both initial discrimination learning and interpolated training. In Phase III the performance of the retarded participants was lower than the performance of the MA-equivalent, nonretarded children. The comparative performances of the retarded group in both phases I and III do not confirm the position advanced by Zeaman and House (1963) regarding the retardates' low probability of attention to the relevent dimension.

Lobb and Childs (1973) reasoned that it was possible that the success criterion in Phase I (eight consecutive correct verbal and removal responses) was too low to ensure that the participants established a high probability of observing the relevant dimension. They conducted a second experiment in which they extended the criterion to 15 consecutive correct responses for half of the subjects and maintained the 8 consecutive correct responses for the remaining subjects. In addition, they required half of the participants in the verbal condition to verbalize *color* in their responses, for example, by saying *red color* instead of *red*. Except for these two changes the conditions of Experiment II were similar to the conditions in Experiment I. The new subjects selected for Experiment II included 32 retarded and 32 nonretarded individuals of comparable MAs (MAs of 5 and 6).

The results indicated that the retarded participants had lower performances than the nonretarded group in phases I and III. Lobb and Childs (1973) state that "neither prolongation of the preceding criterion nor the insistence on verbalizing 'color' during Phase I influenced errors in the intradimensional shift. The equal MA deficit was quite robust under these conditions" (p. 189). These results are similar to the findings of Experiment I and, likewise, provide no support for Zeaman and House's (1963) position that retarded individuals exhibit an attention deficiency because

they have a low probability of attending to a relevant dimension.

Lobb's Studies. In another study Lobb (1974) assessed the effectiveness of overt labeling (rehearsal) on discrimination learning and intradimensional shifts. He selected 48 retarded ($\overline{CA} = 14.7$, $\overline{MA} = 5.2$, $\overline{IQ} = 43$) and 48 nonretarded subjects ($\overline{CA} = 4.7$, $\overline{MA} = 4.9$, $\overline{IQ} = 99.9$) to participate in the study. He used a modified version of the WGTA to present stimulus objects of two dimensions: form (squares and circles) and color (white, black, blue, or red).

His procedures included a verbal pretraining session, an original-learning session, and transfer learning. During verbal pretraining all subjects practiced naming all the colors on both shapes. Subjects from both groups were divided for the original learning session and one group used overt rehearsal. In the overt-rehearsal group, after every selection of an object, the experimenter said, "The candy was under the red one; point to red and say 'red for candy.' " This statement was made with the rehearsal group whether the response was correct or incorrect. Subjects in the no overt rehearsal condition remained quiet after each response. The relevant dimension was color (red, S + ; black, S −). Form and position were random and irrelevant. Criterion was eight consecutive correct responses in a maximum of 40 trials.

During the transfer-learning session, subjects from both previous groups (overt rehearsal and no overt rehearsal) were regrouped and redivided into new overt- and no overt-rehearsal groups. The same dimension (color) was relevant but new cues (blue, S + ; white, S −) were used (intradimensional shift). All subjects again received 40 trials. During the first 20 trials, either overt- or no overt-rehearsal procedures were used as in original learning. Subjects going from an overt to a no overt group were instructed to refrain from saying "Red is for candy." In the last 20 trials, no feedback was given; subjects in the transfer overt-rehearsal group were not prevented from rehearsing.

The results indicated that the main effect of rehearsal was significant ($p < .05$) with overt rehearsal reducing mean errors of both IQ groups. The main effect of IQ was not significant. In Phase II (the second 40 trials) subjects who had rehearsed in either or both phases reduced their errors during the transfer period. The main effect of trial number was also significant ($p < .001$).

Lobb (1974) concludes that overt rehearsal was effective in two ways: (a) it aided learning on the trials in which it was used and (b) its use in earlier trials had a facilitative effect on learning in later trials. Of particular interest and in support of Fisher and Zeaman's (1973) theory was the finding that 28% of the mentally retarded subjects needed continual prompting in rehearsal conditions, whereas only 6% of the nonretarded subjects needed such prompting. This was a significant difference ($p < .05$).

LOBB AND STOGDILL'S STUDIES. Lobb and Stogdill (1974) conducted a study to determine the effects of verbal feedback (and verbal rehearsal) and overtraining on discrimination learning of retarded and MA-equivalent nonretarded children. They used the intradimensional shift paradigm. They thought that if during the original learning phase the probability of observing the relevant dimension approached one, there would be no comparative deficiency in the performance of the retarded subjects after the intradimensional shift. Furthermore, they hypothesized that such a high probability could be produced by employing verbal procedures (a rehearsal strategy) and overtraining (a prolonged period of correct trials) before the intradimensional shift. Also, during the transfer phase they believed that continued verbal feedback which emphasized the consequences of selecting the positive or negative cue would differentially affect the performances of the different IQ levels.

Lobb and Stogdill selected 60 kindergartners ($\overline{CA} = 5.8$, $\overline{MA} = 6.1$, $\overline{IQ} = 101.8$) and 60 trainable mentally retarded ($\overline{CA} = 12.6$, $\overline{MA} = 5.9$, $\overline{IQ} = 50.9$) subjects to participate in the study. The mentally retarded children were noninstitutionalized special school students. The experimenters used a modified version of the WGTA and a total of eight stimuli which included both form dimensions (circle or square) and color dimensions (white, black, blue, or red).

Prior to testing all the children received verbal pretraining in which they were required to name all of the cues involved within both dimensions. The discrimination problem contained two cues from each of three dimensions: color, form, and position. Color was the relevant dimension with red (S +) and black (S −) used in the original learning phase and blue (S +) and white (S −) used in the intradimensional transfer phase.

During the first or original learning phase, the correct response consisted of three steps: (a) naming the correct cue, i.e., red; (b) naming the correct dimension, i.e., color, and (c) removing the correct cue. The original learning phase continued until the subject had selected the appropriate stimulus continuously for 8 trials or until 47 trials had occurred. Six of the original retarded subjects failed to reach criterion and were replaced with six other subjects.

After original learning, half of the subjects from each IQ group were assigned to an overtraining procedure. These subjects received 50 additional training trials using the exact same procedure as in the original learning phase. On the following day they received 50 more trials under the same conditions. Immediately following the second set of overtraining trials, these subjects were introduced to the transfer phase. The other half of the subjects who did not receive the overtraining were introduced to the transfer condition immediately following the original training period.

During the intradimensional transfer phase, a correct response consisted to two steps: (a) saying the name of the correct cue, i.e., blue; and (b) removing the correct stimulus. An incorrect trial consisted of omitting one or both of these responses. Whenever a subject (regardless of previous group membership) made a mistake during the transfer phase, the child received one of three types of feedback. These were:

Positive: "What you said is wrong. The candy is always under the blue color. Say it for me."

Negative: "What you said is wrong. The candy is never under the white color. Say it for me."

Neutral: No verbal feedback.

In the feedback conditions each subject received 40 trials during the second (intradimensional shift) phase.

The results showed that during original learning, normal subjects made significantly fewer errors ($p < .001$) than did the retarded subjects. The difference between the performances of the normal and retarded subjects in the overtraining conditions was not significant. The transfer performance of the low IQ group was significantly lower than the performance of the nonretarded group. In the transfer condition neither overtraining nor verbal feedback had a significant effect on discrimination learning. Further analysis of the transfer condition was made by blocking the trials into four 10-trial blocks. The results of this analysis indicated that performance improved across blocks (time) for all conditions even though the normal group performed significantly better ($p < .001$) than the retarded group. There were no significant differences between the IQ groups in the transfer condition after Block Two trials, a fact which suggests that learning was equivalent after numerous trials.

Lobb and Stogdill (1974) conclude that the equal MA discrimination deficiency cannot be attributed to limitations in attention to the correct dimensions as postulated by Zeaman and House (1963) since there remained a relative deficiency after overtraining. In terms of Fisher and Zeaman's (1973) theory, Lobb and Stogdill's study supports the relative deficiency of lower IQ subjects, i.e., retarded subjects exhibit a short-term memory problem. This deficiency is considered to be more of a retentional problem than one of attention, as previously postulated by Zeaman and House.

Novel Stimuli and Transfer Operations

BILSKY AND HEAL'S STUDIES. Bilsky and Heal (1969) conducted a study to investigate the effects of cue novelty and training level on the discrimination performance of retarded individuals. They hypothesized that if these variables were manipulated, attention to the relevant dimension would be improved, resulting in better performances on shift problems. Specifically, they felt that the tendency to shift attention from a formerly relevant dimension to a formerly irrelevant dimension would be aided if the new relevant dimension contained a novel cue. They also hypothesized that the "effects of novelty would be observed at low levels of training but not at high levels of training" (p. 504).

In order to test the hypotheses, 72 institutionalized moderately retarded subjects ($\overline{CA}$ = 24–10, $\overline{IQ}$ = 47.9) were initially selected. The subjects had been previously assessed for dimensional preference, and equal numbers were selected from color-preferring and form-preferring groups. Twenty-four subjects were dropped from the study because of failure to reach criterion or because of illness. Each of the 48 remaining subjects was assigned to a dimension condition in Stage II in which the relevant dimension was nonpreferred. Subjects from each of these groups (color preference and form preference) were randomly assigned to cue novelty and training level conditions.

Various color-form images were presented and the subject pressed a panel to select one of the stimuli. For a correct response a doorbell sounded and an incorrect response received a buzz. The procedure for each subject consisted of three stages. During the first stage the subjects were reassessed on dimensional preference. At this time specific color-form compounds were rewarded. After the subjects made four consecutive correct responses, they started Stage II. Stage II was a preshift training period. During this phase subjects were rewarded for selection of the appropriate cue within their nonpreferred dimension. Criterion during Stage II depended on the training-level condition to which the subjects had been assigned. Training-level conditions consisted of 4, 8, or 16 consecutive correct responses on feedback trials and no errors during the intervening nonfeedback trials (i.e., the buzzer or chime was withheld on 33% of the training trials). The subjects were introduced to special training procedures if criterion was not reached within 24 trials and were then recycled through Stage II. During Stage III all subjects received cues on their nonpreferred dimension (the relevant dimension during Stage II). However, on their preferred dimension (irrelevant in Stage II) half of the subjects received new cues and half received cues which had been presented during the first two stages. On Stage III training trials, Stage II reward contingencies were reversed. One cue from the Stage II, irrelevant (preferred) dimension was consistently paired with the new negative cue, whereas the other was paired with a new positive cue. Seven nonfeedback test trials were interspersed among the training trials of Stage III. A test trial occurred after every three consecutive correct responses. During test trials, cues were arranged so the subject had to choose between the components of the color-form compound which had been rewarded during training trials. Performance on the test trials was intended to reveal whether the subjects continued to select their nonpreferred dimension (which was relevant during Stage II) or if they shifted their attention to their preferred dimensions (which was irrelevant during Stage II).

The results indicated no significant differences between the groups during Stage I in terms of number of errors. During the first trial of Stage II, subjects made significantly fewer errors ($p < .05$) when form was the relevant dimension than when color was the relevant dimension. Overall during

Stage II the color-relevant group made more errors than the form-relevant group. Also, the analysis of overall errors on Stage II feedback trials revealed a significant difference due to training level (i.e., more training resulted in fewer errors). Results of Stage III failed to reveal significant differences of errors on feedback trials. There were, however, significant differences in extradimensional shifts on test trials. The number of extradimensional shifts was greater in the presence of novel cues than in the presence of familiar cues. There was also a significant interaction between novelty and training level. This significance primarily resulted from the performances of subjects in training levels four and eight (four consecutive correct responses, eight consecutive correct responses) because nearly all the subjects in the novelty condition made extradimensional shifts. At the 16-trial training level, both novelty and familiarity groups made approximately the same number of extradimensional shifts and reversals.

The findings indicated that cue novelty is an important influence on the subject's attention to stimulus properties. The finding that the subjects undergoing the 16-trial training condition did not exhibit the novelty effect is consistent with the overtraining effect. Bilsky and Heal (1969) conclude that the overall results of the study support the contention by Zeaman and House (1963) of the central role of attention in discrimination learning.

TURRISI AND SHEPP'S STUDIES. Turrisi and Shepp (1969) conducted three experiments to assess the effects of novelty stimuli and overtraining on discrimination reversals of mentally retarded subjects. They thought that extended training or overlearning along one relevant dimension would raise the initial probability of attending to that dimension as opposed to other irrelevant dimensions. This probability would then increase directly as more correct responses were reinforced. They hypothesized that novel stimuli introduced within the irrelevant dimension after an extended period of overtraining would have less effect on a shift within the relevant dimension.

In their first experiment (1969) there were 40 institutionalized retarded subjects ($\overline{CA} = 14.8$, $\overline{MA} = 6.7$, $\overline{IQ} = 49.0$). A modified version of the WGTA was used to present the stimuli. The stimuli consisted of a total of seven geometric shapes painted one of seven colors. Half of the subjects

were trained on form-relevant problems and the remaining subjects were trained on color-relevant problems. All subjects underwent a pretraining session in which they learned the procedure to find the candy. During the experimental session all subjects were given 30 trials per day for a maximum of 150 trials (5 days). Criterion was 9 correct in any 10 consecutive trials (Problem I). After reaching criterion, half of the subjects underwent overtraining. Subjects who underwent overtraining were labeled *OTO* and *OTN*, and those who did not were labeled *CO* and *CN*. During Problem II, the OTO group received the same stimuli as in Problem I but the reinforcement contingencies for the relevant stimuli were reversed. The OTN group had the reinforcement contingencies of the relevant stimuli shifted (similar to OTO group), but the irrelevant stimuli (dimensions) of Problem I were replaced by two different stimuli. Groups CO and CN were treated the same as Groups OTO and OTN respectively, except Problem II started on the day immediately after the subject reached Problem I criterion and there was no overtraining. Criterion for Problem II was the same as for Problem I.

The results showed no significant main effects or interactions in either the training problem or the shift problem. An analysis of results on the first trial of the reversal, however, indicated that significantly fewer subjects in the CN group than in the other three groups responded to the positive training stimulus on that trial as had been hypothesized. Again with regards to the first trial of the reversal problem, the effect of overtraining was tested by combining the data of the subjects who had received overtraining (OTO and OTN groups) and comparing the results with the combined data of the subjects who did not receive overtraining (CO and CN groups). The difference was significant ($p = .05$). From this first experiment Turrisi and Shepp (1969) conclude:

The lack of significant effects in both error scores and savings scores might suggest that neither novelty nor overtraining had an effect. On the other hand, the first-trial analysis indicates that the introduction of novel stimuli along the irrelevant dimension does in fact affect performance, although the effect on choice measures is transitory. It is important to note, however, that measures of performance on the first trial of reversal are reflecting changes in Po, which result primarily from the effects of stimulus novelty. On subsequent trials, the effects of the changed reinforcement contingency become manifest, superimposed upon, and possibly masking, any novelty effects which may obtain. Thus, weak novelty effects might be expected to occur on the first reversal trial but not over the whole course of the reversal. (p. 393)

The second experiment conducted by Turrisi and Shepp (1969) attempted again to confirm the initial hypothesis using a stronger criterion of learning in both of the problems. The subjects selected were 56 institutionalized retardates ($\overline{CA} = 19.6$, $\overline{MA} = 6.5$, $\overline{IQ} = 43$). The apparatus, stimuli, and procedures used in the second experiment were exactly the same as those in the first experiment, with the one exception that criterion for both problems of the second experiment was 25 correct responses in a session of 30 trials.

An analysis of variance on the error scores in Problem I resulted in no significant main effects or interactions. The error scores for Problem II yielded the same results. However, using saving scores (subtracting error scores of Problem II from those of Problem I) as the dependent measure revealed a significant main effect ($p < .01$) for overtraining. Overtrained subjects learned Problem II faster than Problem I, whereas the opposite was true for subjects who did not undergo overtraining. In regards to the first trial of Problem II, there was a significant ($p < .001$) tendency for both groups to perseverate on the original positive training stimulus.

The results of Experiment II support the contention that a more rigorous criterion would make a difference. In Experiment I, 55% of the subjects reverted to chance performance for two or more days during overtraining, whereas in Experiment II only 10.7% of the subjects did so—and only for one day. Also during the second experiment an overlearning-reversal effect was found. Another major difference acknowledged by the investigators was that the more rigid criterion improved attention towards the relevant dimension on the first trial of Problem II even with the presence of a novel stimulus along the irrelevant dimension.

Turrisi and Shepp (1969) suggest that perhaps the subjects were, in fact, attending to more than one dimension (as was later suggested by Fisher and Zeaman, 1973), but that the instrumental response was made to the appropriate cue within the relevant dimension. They state:

In the terms of attention theory, both the relevant and irrelevant dimensions were being attended to, but for different reasons: the relevant dimension because at-

tentional responses to it had been consistently followed by reinforced instrumental responses, the irrelevant dimension because of the introduction of novel stimuli along it. (p. 395)

A third experiment was conducted by Turrisi and Shepp (1969) using latency as the dependent variable. Their reasoning was that a strong correlation between latency and the introduction of novel stimuli along the irrelevant dimension would signify that the subjects were attending to both dimensions. Thirty-eight new subjects ($\overline{CA} = 20.7$, $\overline{MA} = 6.7$, $\overline{IQ} = 46$) were selected for the third experiment. The same stimuli and apparatus as in the first two experiments were used, and a timer was added to record response latency. The procedures were the same except that reversal conditions were presented immediately following acquisition or overtraining. This was done by giving the subject 10 trials under Problem I conditions on the first day of Problem II. They wanted to ensure that the subjects would be responding to the initial training stimulus on the first trial of the reversal. Therefore, there was no intertrial delay between the first trial of Problem II and the last trial of Problem I. On the day Problem II was to begin, subjects were required to perform correctly on 8 of the 10 Problem I trials before moving to Problem II. All subjects met this criterion.

The results showed no significant main effects or interactions for error scores in Problem I, or error scores and savings scores in Problem II. All subjects, however, responded to the original (Problem I) training stimulus on the first trial of Problem II at a significant level ($p < .001$). Mean latencies were reported for five-trial blocks, including two blocks for the last 10 Problem I trials and six blocks for the first 30 trials of Problem II. An analysis of variance on the latencies on the last 10 Problem I trials showed no differences which indicated that all subjects were performing at the same level prior to reversal. Difference scores were obtained for each subject by subtracting the latency score on the first trial of the reversal from the subject's mean latency over the last five trials of Problem I. The scores indicated changes in latency due to the introduction of the novel stimuli. The effect was significant ($p < .001$) at the first trial but not thereafter. The results indicated that those subjects given novel cues in the irrelevant dimension responded to the relevant dimension while simultaneously attending to the novel stimulus. There was no interaction between overtraining and the novel stimulus. Turrisi and Shepp (1969) conclude:

> At best, it can be stated that the introduction of novel irrelevant stimuli interrupts first-trial perseveration choice responses in reversals when Ss have received minimal amounts of training, but does not when a strong criterion or overtraining is used. (p. 400)

Cue Distinctiveness and Transfer Operations

The preceding studies (Bilsky & Heal, 1969; Turrisi & Shepp, 1969) focused on the effect of novelty cues on facilitating extradimensional shifts and interfering with intradimensional shifts. From these studies it appears that novelty can facilitate a shift of dimensions. Also, if overtraining is used, there is less of a tendency to attend to irrelevant novel cues. The last study reviewed in this section on transfer operations is concerned with cue distinctiveness and has a greater bearing on the Fisher and Zeaman (1973) theory than do the previous studies.

SWITZKY'S STUDIES. Switzky (1973) conducted a study to determine the effect of training history and the distinctiveness of cues within relevant and irrelevant dimensions on original and transfer learning. Previously Zeaman and House (1963) had postulated that retardate deficiencies in discrimination learning were due to deficiencies in attending to the relevant dimension. Therefore, if the probability of attention to a relevant dimension could be raised, the deficiency would be eliminated. In the revision of the Zeaman and House theory, Zeaman (1973) and Fisher and Zeaman (1973) suggested that the relative distinctiveness of cues within dimensions would affect the probability of attending to the dimensions. Switzky saw that in comparing the performance of subjects on intradimensional and extradimensional shifts, the extradimensional shifts might be learned faster than intradimensional shifts under certain conditions. These conditions were: (a) when the relevant cues on the extradimensional shift are much more distinctive than the irrelevant cues, (b) when cues on the relevant dimension of the intradimensional shift are much less distinctive than the cues on the irrelevant dimension, and (c) when cues on the relevant and irrelevant dimensions in the intradimensional shift are of low distinctiveness.

In order to assess the reformulated theory, Switzky (1973) selected 96 retarded subjects and divided them into two equal groups of high MA subjects ($\overline{CA} = 27.9$, $\overline{MA} = 9.6$, $\overline{IQ} = 65$) and low

MA subjects ($\overline{CA} = 26.3$, $\overline{MA} = 5.8$, $\overline{IQ} = 42.6$). A modified version of the WGTA was used to present the stimuli. Half of the subjects were trained with brightness as the relevant dimension and shape as the irrelevant dimension, while the other half had shape as the relevant dimension and brightness as the irrelevant dimension. The subjects were then randomly assigned to one of four groups: (a) brightness relevant with low distinction, shape irrelevant with high distinction; (b) brightness relevant with high distinction, shape irrelevant with low distinction; (c) shape relevant with high distinction, brightness irrelevant with low distinction; and (d) shape relevant with low distinction, brightness irrelevant with high distinction.

Thirty trials were conducted and 10 consecutive correct responses was criterion. On the second day, after 10 trials of overtraining, subjects were introduced to either an extradimensional or an intradimensional shift problem with half of the subjects from each of the four groups receiving one of the two problems. There were three intradimensional shift problems and three extradimensional shift problems. These consisted of: (a) brightness with high distinction, shape with low distinction; (b) shape with high distinction, brightness with low distinction; and (c) brightness and shape both with low distinction. Criterion was 10 consecutive responses in 60 trials.

Results were analyzed. A three-way analysis of variance, 2 x 2 x 2 (MA level x relevant dimensions x distinctiveness of relevant dimensions), was used in the analysis of original learning. The main effect of cue distinctiveness of the relevant dimension was significant ($p < .001$). When the relevant dimension was of high distinctiveness, trials to criterion were fewer than when the relevant dimension was of low distinctiveness. There was also a significant main effect ($p < .001$) due to MA with high MA subjects requiring fewer trials to criterion than low MA subjects. Results of the transfer learning were analyzed by a five-way analysis of variance: 2 (intradimensional versus extradimensional shift) x 2 (high or low distinctiveness of relevant dimension in original learning) x 3 (type of shift problem) x 2 (relevant dimensional shift–brightness or shape) x 2 (high or low MA).

Significant main effects were found for shift ($p < .001$), shift problem ($p < .001$), MA level ($p < .001$), and distinctiveness of relevant dimensions ($p < .05$) in discrimination learning. Also, there was a significant interaction among shift, MA level, and distinctiveness of relevant dimension in original learning. High MA subjects learned intradimensional shifts faster than extradimensional shifts when original learning was on dimensions of either high or low distinctiveness. Low MA subjects learned intradimensional shifts faster than extradimensional shifts only when trained on relevant dimensions of low distinctiveness, and such subjects also showed no differences in rate of learning intradimensional or extradimensional shifts when trained on relevant dimensions of high distinctiveness. In summarizing the results, Switzky (1973) states:

> (a) difference in ID and ED shift performance depended on the distinctiveness of cues on the relevant and irrelevant dimensions in acquisition and in transfer; (b) ID and ED shift performance also depended on the subject's MA level and the relative distinctiveness of the relevant dimensions in acquisition. (p. 277)

SUMMARY. The seven studies related to transfer operations are summarized in Table 4.3. Summary information for the studies includes consideration of the following variables:

1. subject variables
2. verbal labeling (rehearsal)
3. overlearning or overtraining
4. novelty
5. cue distinction

Four of the studies reviewed (Lobb, 1974; Lobb & Childs, 1973; Lobb & Stogdill, 1974; Milgram & Noce, 1968) compared retarded subjects with MA-equivalent, nonretarded subjects. Mean MAs ranged from 5–7 years. Two studies (Lobb, 1974; Milgram & Noce, 1968) reported no equal MA deficiency (mental retardation deficiency), although Lobb found that mentally retarded subjects needed more prompting for rehearsal. In Experiment I, Lobb and Childs saw no MA deficiency in original learning but found that during the transfer phase the performance of the retarded subjects was inferior to the performance of the MA-equivalent, nonretarded subjects. Lobb and Stogdill found that the performance of the retarded subjects was inferior to the performance of the MA-equivalent, nonretarded subjects in original learning and in the transfer phase, but no difference occurred in overlearning. Thus, in the seven group comparisons which featured retardates versus MA-equivalent normals, the latter performed significantly better three times. In another study Switzky (1973) compared high and low MA re-

tarded subjects and reported a superior performance by the high MA subjects.

Five studies (Bilsky & Heal, 1969; Lobb, 1974; Milgram & Noce, 1968; Switzky, 1973; Turrisi & Shepp, 1969) used institutionalized subjects. In the study by Lobb and Stogdill (1974) none of the subjects was institutionalized, and Lobb and Childs (1973) used mentally retarded subjects from both an institution and the community. None of the studies considered institutionalization as a factor and, because so few studies used noninstitutionalized retarded subjects, comparative performance between retardates in each setting are not available.

Verbal labeling effects were assessed in four studies (Lobb, 1974; Lobb & Childs, 1973; Lobb & Stogdill, 1974; Milgram & Noce, 1969), and was shown to improve the performances of subjects at different IQ levels except in one study (Lobb & Stogdill, 1974). However, high MA subjects tended to perform better and this supports the Fisher and Zeaman (1973) theory that retardates show deficiencies in rehearsal and/or feedback processes. An interesting finding made by Lobb (1974) also supporting this position is that retarded subjects needed more continued prompting to use rehearsal strategies.

The effects of overlearning (or *overtraining*) were equivocal. Lobb and Stogdill (1974) reported that during the transfer operation overlearning had no effect on mentally retarded subjects. However, Turrisi and Shepp (1969) found that overlearning helped retarded subjects ignore irrelevant, novel stimuli.

Bilsky and Heal (1969) found that novelty could improve learning extradimensional shifts. This finding suggests that the introduction of new material requiring discrimination is easier to learn if novel cues are used along the new relevant dimension (as opposed to the use of familiar cues from formerly irrelevant dimensions).

Switzky (1973) found that cue distinctiveness can facilitate learning in extradimensional shifts (sometimes making them easier to learn than intradimensional shifts). This finding is supportive of the cue feedback component (Zeaman, 1973) which predicts that attention is directed to the dimension containing the greatest difference between its constituent cues. Finally, Switzky points out that cue distinction is only one determinant of attentional response. Perceptual and experimental factors also have a bearing on attention.

TEACHING IMPLICATIONS

1. Several studies (Lobb, 1974; Lobb & Childs, 1973; Milgram & Noce, 1968) found that verbal rehearsal aided retardates in learning discrimination. This finding suggests that teachers could enhance the learning of retarded students by having them recite aloud while performing tasks. For example, the child could verbalize arithmetic problems while solving them. In addition, verbal rehearsal could be used in other tasks, such as matching pictures to words, repeating instructions, and saying directions (up, down, left, right) while moving in a specific direction.

2. Lobb (1974) showed that retarded individuals needed to be reminded to recite (rehearse) while performing discrimination tasks. This finding suggests that teachers need to monitor the activities of retarded children instructed to rehearse (verbally) and encourage them to engage in rehearsal activities.

3. Two studies (Lobb & Stogdill, 1974; Turrisi & Shepp, 1969) found that overlearning improved the discrimination learning of retarded individuals. This finding supports the position that retarded students need to review and practice material during the acqustion stage of learning. Overlearning necessitates the use of practice or drills. Since students are often reluctant to do drill activities, the teacher must devise practice activities which promote interest and motivation. This could be accomplished by developing or using games which promote specific drills. For example, games that include die allow a child to practice counting or adding. A teacher should make sure when children practice a task that they practice correctly and are not practicing incorrect responses, e.g., adding math problems wrong. To insure that children practice correct responses and maintain motivation, the teacher could develop materials which feature self-correction, such as puzzle formats, answer keys, answer windows, electrical learning board, etc. Some commercial materials (for example, *DISTAR*) stress drill.

4. Switzky (1973) found that the learning of extradimensional shifts more slowly than intradimensional shifts is not an absolute condition but may be learned as fast if the cue distinctiveness of the extradimensional stimuli is high. With low distinctive cues, intradimensional stimuli were learned faster, but with high distinctive cues no difference was noted in learning either intradimensional or extradimensional problems. This finding supports the effect of cue difference and distinctiveness on attention even in transfer conditions. The teaching implications regarding cue differences and distinctiveness are listed in this chapter under "Number of Dimensions" in the section titled "Teaching Implications."

IMPLICATIONS FROM FISHER AND ZEAMAN (1973). In their writings Fisher and Zeaman (1973) report on many studies designed to examine intradimensional (ID) and extradimensional (ED) transfer effects in discrimination learning. They note that a consensus has emerged from the research which supports the position that after training on a specific relevant dimension, retardates perform well on a task with new cues presented on the same dimension (ID). However, the retardates' performance will not be as good if the relevant dimension changes following pretraining. In other words, if shifts in cues occur within the same dimension (ID), performance is facilitated, while shifts in dimension (ED) do not enhance learning. Some teaching suggestions from these writings regarding transfer effects are:

1. In teaching letter recognition, the child must attend to many configurations. Preletter recognition instruction can include training regarding various lines and shapes. The use of intradimensional shifts to improve letter recognition may be sequenced as follows:
   a. Pretrain to select vertical lines.   [/] [o] [I]
   b. Shift task to select the vertical letter.   [a] [c] [I]
   c. Shift task to select the letter *i*.   [a] [f] [i]
   d. Pretrain on circular shapes.   [/] [\ x] [o]
   e. Shift to letter *o*.   [x] [y] [o]
   f. Shift to letters using combination, for example *b, d, p*.

2. Similar sequences focusing on concepts such as directionality can be devised to improve letter recognition. For example, recognition of the letters *b* and *d* requires left-right discriminations. Recognition of the letters *p* and *b* requires up-down discriminations.

3. Pretraining exercises, such as warm-up exercises which feature the teacher pointing out the relevant stimulus dimensions (shape, color) help students perform better.

4. In general, orientation sessions for the retarded learner to instructional stimuli tend to increase the student's attention to further stimuli.

5. When possible, abrupt changes in the relevant dimension of a stimulus from one instructional activity to another should be avoided. For example, when retarded children shift from sorting or selecting objects on the basis of color to sorting or selecting on the basis of size, they may experience difficulty attending to the relevant dimension (size) of the second task. When the changes are necessary, dimensions should be used which feature cues that are distinctly highlighted.

6. Use intradimensional shifts by training the retarded child to respond to a word configuration and then to recognize that word regardless of its size or surroundings. For example, train the child to select the word *stop* and then present the word *stop* in various milieus:

TABLE 4.3
Summary of Studies Focusing on Transfer Operations

ARTICLE	SUBJECTS	INDEPENDENT VARIABLE	TASK	RESULTS
1. Milgram & Noce (1968)	1. 70 retarded $\overline{CA} = 15.4$ $\overline{MA} = 6.9$ 2. 96 nonretarded $\overline{CA} = 7.5$ MA = not available	verbal labeling (rehearsal) of relevant and irrelevant dimensions	extradimensional shift (reversal)—from size to brightness or brightness to size	*1. Verbalizing the relevant dimension (cue) improved performance for both IQ groups. †2. The performance of the two IQ groups did not differ.
2. Lobb & Childs (1973) *Experiment I*	1. 40 retarded CA range 8–17.5 MA range 5–6 2. 40 nonretarded CA range 5–6 MA range 5–6	verbal labeling (rehearsal) of cue	intradimensional shift—from color black to color blue	*1. In the first phase rehearsal produced better performance for both IQ groups. †2. There were no IQ differences. *3. In the second phase rehearsal produced better performance, but performance of the retarded Ss was lower.
Experiment II	1. 32 retarded CA range 9–21 $\overline{MA} = 5.5$ 2. 32 nonretarded CA range 5–6 $\overline{MA} = 5.5$	verbal labeling (rehearsal) of dimension and cue	intradimensional shift with more rigorous criterion	†1. Additional rehearsal with greater criterion had no effect. *2. Retarded Ss performed poorer than the nonretarded Ss.
3. Lobb (1974)	1. 48 retarded $\overline{CA} = 14.7$ $\overline{MA} = 5.2$ $\overline{IQ} = 43$ 2. 48 nonretarded $\overline{CA} = 4.7$ $\overline{MA} = 4.9$ $\overline{IQ} = 99.9$	verbal labeling in Phase I and/or Phase II	intradimensional shift—changed cues from red to blue (S+).	*1. Rehearsal was effective. †2. No IQ differences resulted in any conditions. *3. The retarded group needed more prompting to continue rehearsal.
4. Lobb & Stogdill (1974)	1. 60 retarded $\overline{CA} = 12.6$ $\overline{MA} = 5.9$ $\overline{IQ} = 50.9$ 2. 60 nonretarded $\overline{CA} = 5.8$ $\overline{MA} = 6.1$ $\overline{IQ} = 101.8$	overtraining and positive, negative, or no rehearsal during transfer phase	intradimensional shift—changed cues from red to blue (S+)	*1. Fewer errors by nonretarded group in Phase I. *2. During overlearning the performances of the two IQ groups did not differ. †3. During the transfer operation neither overlearning nor verbal rehearsal made a difference. *4. Retarded Ss performed poorer than the nonretarded subjects.

TABLE 4.3, cont.

ARTICLE	SUBJECTS	INDEPENDENT VARIABLE	TASK	RESULTS
5. Bilsky & Heal (1969)	72 retarded $\overline{CA}$ = 24–10 $\overline{IQ}$ = 47.9	novel cue in the relevant dimension during transfer, level of training	extradimensional shift	*1. Novel cues facilitated extradimensional shifts except at the highest training level.
6. Turrisi & Shepp (1969) *Experiment I*	40 retarded $\overline{CA}$ = 14.8 $\overline{MA}$ = 6.7 $\overline{IQ}$ = 49	overtraining and novel cue in the irrelevant dimension during the transfer phase	intradimensional shift	*1. Subjects in the overtraining condition had less tendency to respond to the novel stimuli in the irrelevant dimension.
Experiment II	56 retarded $\overline{CA}$ = 19.6 $\overline{MA}$ = 6.5 $\overline{IQ}$ = 43	increased criterion in overlearning condition	same as *Exp. I*	*1. Overtraining facilitated learning in the second phase with less tendency to respond to the novel cue in the irrelevant dimension.
Experiment III	38 retarded $\overline{CA}$ = 20.7 $\overline{MA}$ = 6.7 $\overline{IQ}$ = 46	added latency as a measure to determine attendance to more than one dimension	same as *Exp. I*	*1. Latency scores were longer on first trial during rehearsal, possibly indicating attention to more than one dimension.
7. Switzky (1973)	96 retarded subjects in two groups 1. 48 high MA $\overline{CA}$ = 27.9 $\overline{MA}$ = 9.6 $\overline{IQ}$ = 65 2. 48 low MA $\overline{CA}$ = 26.3 $\overline{MA}$ = 5.8 $\overline{IQ}$ = 42.6	distinctiveness of cues in relevant and irrelevant dimensions	intradimensional shifts and extradimensional shifts	*1. Distinct relevant dimensions facilitated learning. †2. Intradimensional shifts were not always learned faster.

NOTE: *Supports either Zeaman and House (1963) or Fisher and Zeaman (1973).
†No support for either Zeaman and House (1963) or Fisher and Zeaman (1973).

a. Change its size.
b. Put it on a stop sign.
c. Present it written on the side of a car.
d. Cut it out of newspapers and books and present it on stimulus cards.
e. Present it in sentences.
f. Present it in paragraphs.

Studies Focusing on Oddity Learning

In this section five studies are reviewed which investigated the performance of retarded individuals on oddity problems. As previously stated, oddity problems include an array of stimuli (at least three) in which an odd cue is contained within a relevant dimension. House (1964) points out that oddity learning requires a three-chain response: (a) attending to the dimension carrying the oddity relationship, i.e., the vehicle dimension; (b) observing the relationship among cues in the vehicle dimension; and (c) responding instrumentally to the odd cue within the vehicle dimension.

In four of the studies reviewed (Brown, 1970; Dickerson & Girardeau, 1970; Hall, 1971; Penn, Sindberg, & Wohlhueter, 1969), the primary variable considered was MA or IQ. Other variables which were considered were response bias (Hall, 1971), the number of dimensions carrying the odd cue, the total number of stimulus objects in the array (Brown, 1970), and the effects of pretraining on oddity learning (Brown, 1970; Martin & Tyrrell, 1971).

The review is organized according to the relative complexity of the studies, starting with the less complex and proceeding to the more complex studies.

PENN, SINDBERG, AND WOHLHUETER'S STUDIES. Penn, Sindberg, and Wohlhueter (1969) investigated the oddity learning ability of severely retarded individuals by comparing the results of the retarded individuals with those of normal preschoolers whose oddity learning ability had been previously determined (Gollin & Shirk, 1966). Criterion had been reached by 42% of the preschoolers. Forty subjects were used in the study. All subjects had MA of 3 years or above and CA ranged from 7½–43 years ($\overline{CA} = 21.4$). The analysis of data (performance) was reported for MA groups of 3, 4, and 5 and above.

The stimuli used in the experiment were three colored discs which were illuminated in a black metal box. During the experiment all three discs were illuminated so that two had the same color and one had a different color. The colors red, green, and blue were used. Position (irrelevant) was varied and form (irrelevant) was constant. Candy was used as reward for selecting the odd color and subjects were tested until they reached the criterion of six successive correct responses (or until a total of 54 trials had been given).

The overall results indicated that performance increased as MA increased ($p < .001$). The difference in the performances of the MA 3 group ($\overline{MA} = 3.5$) and the MA 4 group ($\overline{MA} = 4.3$) was not significant, but the difference in the performances of the MA 4 group and the MA 5 and above group ($\overline{MA} = 7.1$) was found to be significant ($p < .02$). There were no significant differences between brain-damaged and nonbrain-damaged subjects.

In comparison with the results of the Gollin and Shirk (1966) study, the MA 4 group performed more poorly than normal 4-year-old subjects. In the Penn, Sindberg, and Wohlhueter (1969) study the mean performances for the MA 3 and MA 4 groups remained close to chance level (33%) over the 54 trials. These results supported the position of a low MA deficiency in oddity learning.

BROWN'S STUDIES. In another study investigating developmental level on oddity learning tasks, Brown (1970) compared the performances of retarded and bright children to the performances of their normal MA and CA peers. She specifically designed the study to examine the relationship of oddity learning to MA and CA. Brown selected five groups of children to participate in the study. They were: (a) Group I—normal, $\overline{IQ} = 102$; (b) Group II—bright, $\overline{IQ} = 149$; (c) Group III—CA-matched (to bright group) normal, $\overline{IQ} = 101$; (d) Group IV—retarded, $\overline{IQ} = 74$; and (e) Group V—CA-matched (to retarded group) normal, $\overline{IQ} = 105$. In addition, the normal, bright, and retarded children in groups I, II, and IV were equated on MA (approximately 6 years) by using selected subtests from the *Stanford-Binet* and the *Wechsler Preschool and Primary Scale of Intelligence*. The oddity task consisted of presenting three stimuli (two identical and one different) and instructing the participant to select the odd stimulus.

A mechanical aluminum box which featured a front display panel with three windows and a reward box under each window was used to present the stimuli. Following pretraining, the oddity sessions were initiated and two sets of pattern stimuli were used. One set consisted of black geometric forms on white background and the second set consisted of black life forms (silhouettes) on white background. A series of 36 randomly arranged trials was conducted over a 2-day period. On both days testing continued for 36 trials or until a criterion of six successive correct responses was recorded. Candy was used as a reward for each correct response.

The performance of the retarded children (Group IV) was significantly below the performances of their CA- and MA-equivalent, nonretarded peers. Also, from Day 1 to Day 2 the performance of the retarded children did not improve as much as the performances of the normal and bright children. The bright children performed significantly better ($p < .001$) than their CA-matched comparative group of normal children was well as the MA-equivalent, normal children. In discussing the results, Brown (1970) notes:

> The retarded subjects were performing poorly on the oddity task, where speed and efficiency in attaining a new problem solution were measured. Normal and bright children performed relatively well on the oddity task, reflecting their greater efficiency in learning-process tasks. (p. 146)

Furthermore, Brown (1970) discusses the poor performance of the retarded subjects in relation to an attention-deficiency position. She reasoned that if lack of attention to the relevant aspects of the stimuli contributed to the retarded children's poor performance, then techniques designed to focus attention on the relevant dimensions of the task should enhance their performance. She designed a second experiment to test this position.

In Experiment II, Brown (1970) selected three groups of retarded children who were comparable on CA, MA, and IQ with the retarded children in the first experiment. In order to foster attention to the relevant stimulus dimensions, three experimental conditions were established. In Condition I two additional windows were used in order to introduce more stimulus redundancy to the oddity problem. Thus, five forms were presented via five windows and the different form (when present) was always in one of the three middle windows. In Condition II the odd cue varied in color as well as in form, e.g., a blue triangle, a blue triangle, and a red circle (oddity choice). In Condition III, pretraining trials were provided with form as the relevant dimension. This pretraining served to make the oddity task a problem involving an intradimensional shift.

For the most part the remaining procedures were similar to those used in Experiment I.

The results indicated that the participants in Condition III required significantly more trials to reach criterion than children in conditions I and II. In a comparison of retarded groups from both experiments it was disclosed that significantly more ($p < .001$) retarded subjects reached criterion in conditions I and II of Experiment II than reached criterion in Experiment I. All conditions of Experiment II increased the number of subjects reaching criterion to a level which did not differ from the performance of the MA-equivalent, nonretarded children in Experiment I.

DICKERSON AND GIRARDEAU'S STUDIES. Dickerson and Girardeau (1970) conducted an oddity experiment to assess approach responses of mentally retarded subjects to odd stimuli under nonreward conditions. Forty-five severely retarded subjects ($\overline{CA} = 15$, $\overline{IQ} = 34$) and 45 mildly retarded subjects ($\overline{CA} = 16.5$, $\overline{IQ} = 62.3$) were selected for the study. Subjects from each level were equally divided into three groups: three-object, four-object, or five-object groups. Stimulus objects consisted of four sets of 200 identical items purchased from a department store. Each subject performed on five 10-trial oddity problems with either three, four, or five objects. No reward followed any of the choices. The odd stimulus was presented in a random fashion. A modified version of the WGTA was used. When subjects entered the room, they were seated at the apparatus and told to "pick up one of the things." Then the 50 oddity problems were presented (five 10-trial blocks).

Since there were no differences across trials, the results were collapsed and a 2 x 3 (level of retardation x number of objects) analysis of variance was performed. The data indicated that the mildly retarded subjects selected the odd stimulus significantly more ($p < .01$) than the severely retarded subjects. The main effect of number of objects and the interaction were both nonsignificant. Additional *t* tests were conducted to determine if responses were above chance level. Mildly retarded subjects selected the odd stimulus significantly above the chance level in the three-object group ($p < .05$), four-object group ($p < .01$), and five-object group ($p < .001$). For the severely retarded, responses to the odd stimulus were significantly above the chance level in the four-object group ($p < .01$) and five-object group ($p < .01$) but not in the three-object group.

HALL'S STUDIES. Hall (1971) conducted a study investigating the effects of response bias (differential responding to a set of events followed by equal consequence), attempting to determine if subjects would demonstrate greater facilitation in oddity learning if the oddity cue was contained in a biased dimension. Also, independent of response bias, MA was investigated as a variable in oddity learning.

Sixty-four subjects were selected and initially divided into high MA and low MA groups. Each of these groups were further divided into four other groups: FF, FC, CC, CF (F = form and C = color; the first letter indicates dimensional bias and the second letter represents the odd dimension). Hall (1971) used an assessment booklet with 36 plates of stimuli. Available choices included dimensions of color, form, and size. Three stimuli were presented on three translucent response keys. When the correct stimulus was selected, a buzzer sounded. All three of the stimuli were identical to one another on one dimension but differed from each other on two other dimensions. Response bias was indicated by 30 or more choices of a dimension out of 36 plates. If bias did not appear, the subject was dropped from the experiment. Of the original 129 subjects, 64 demonstrated a response bias.

After bias assessment, the subjects were tested on oddity learning. A random method of presentation was used so that the odd stimulus was presented in any one of the three positions. Subjects were directed to "guess which one is right." Sixty-four trials divided into four 16-trial blocks were conducted. Response measures were the number of correct responses and latency. Results were presented in terms of bias assessment, correct response scores and latency scores.

Of the 62 individuals in the original high MA group: (a) 43 exhibited a form bias (16 selected for study), (b) 16 exhibited a color bias, and (c) 3 exhibited no bias. Of the 57 individuals in the original low MA group: (a) 26 exhibited a form bias (16 selected for study), (b) 16 exhibited a color bias, and (c) 15 exhibited no bias. There were no significant differences between the MA groups in respect to color, form, or no bias.

A 2 x 2 x 2 x 4 (bias x odd dimension x MA x trial blocks) analysis of variance was conducted using correct number of responses as the dependent measure. The results disclosed that the oddity-learning performances of the groups

(FF and CC) whose dimension bias was relevant (odd) were superior ($p < .0009$) to the performances of the groups (FC and CF) whose nonbias dimension was relevant (odd). Bias, MA, and blocks were not significant nor were there any significant interactions.

Using the latency scores as the dependent measure, neither bias nor type of odd dimension was significant. However, the main effect of MA was significant ($p > .001$) with the high MA subjects responding faster than the low MA subjects. Also, the main effect of trial blocks was significant; latency decreased over blocks.

Overall, these results support the Zeaman and House (1963) theory since raising the probability of attending to the correct dimension (the bias dimension) increased attendance to the odd dimension. There is also some indication that a strong response bias increased with MA and that form tended to be the preferred dimension.

MARTIN AND TYRRELL'S STUDIES. Martin and Tyrrell (1971) examined the effect of object discrimination learning on subsequent oddity learning in 48 mildly retarded children ($\overline{CA} = 13-1$, $\overline{MA} = 7-9$). Specifically, they hypothesized that if a subject enters the oddity problem with a high probability (induced by object-discrimination training) of attending to the relevant dimension, the speed of oddity learning would increase.

Martin and Tyrrell assigned the participants to two experimental groups which were matched on MA and CA. Using 36 stimuli (varied on form and color) and a modified version of the WGTA, the experimenters trained half of the subjects on a color-relevant problem and half on a form-relevant problem. On each trial the subjects were presented three stimuli. The subjects in the color-relevant group received two stimuli differing in color and form and the correct choice was one of the colors. The third stimulus was always presented in the center of the array. It differed in color and form from the two end stimuli, and it was constant over trials. The center stimulus was never reinforced. Subjects in the form-relevant group underwent the same type of problem but the color was varied and irrelevant. Again, the center stimulus was held constant and never reinforced. All of the subjects were given 25 trials per day, and 20 correct responses in one daily session was criterion. A correction procedure was used so that every trial ended with the subject knowing the correct response. The maximum number of trials was 150. If a subject did not meet criterion in 150 trials, a special training procedure was used. Eleven subjects from both color and form problems underwent special training procedures. After completion of the original training, all subjects underwent two days (50 trials) of overtraining on the same problems presented in original learning.

On the day following the overlearning trials, the subjects were divided into four groups. One group received another discrimination task in which an intradimensional shift was presented. Another group received an extradimensional discrimination task. Of the remaining 24 subjects, 12 were given an oddity problem in which the odd cue was contained in a formerly relevant dimension (intradimensional shift). The last 12 subjects were presented with an oddity problem in which the odd cue was presented in a formerly irrelevant dimension (extradimensional shift).

Every trial on both types of transfer problems (oddity and discrimination) consisted of three stimuli in which the center stimulus was never reinforced. In half of the trials the center stimulus matched one of the stimuli in the cue value of the relevant dimension. In the remainder of trials it was identical to the other cue. In the following examples on a color relevant probelm, the first example would represent half of the problems and the second example would represent the other half:

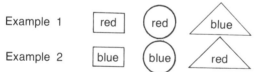

Example 1

Example 2

If these examples represented a discrimination problem, the end stimulus of one color (red or blue) would have been constantly reinforced. If these examples represented an oddity problem, the odd color (blue in first example, red in second example) would have been reinforced. In their study the specific stimuli used in the transfer problem had not been previously used in original training. All subjects were given 25 trials per day until 20 correct responses occurred in a single session or until 150 trials had been attempted.

The results of both original learning and transfer are reported in their writings. Original-learning data were analyzed by a 4 x 2 (groups x dimensions) analysis of variance. Errors to criterion was

the dependent variable. There were no significant differences between dimensions or between those groups which were to be differentiated by the transfer conditions. Results of the transfer problem were analyzed by a 2 x 2 x 6 (problem type x shift type x days) analysis of variance. The analysis indicated that object discrimination problems were learned easier than oddity problems ($p < .025$). Also, intradimensional shifts were more readily learned than extradimensional shifts ($p < .005$). There was also a significant trial effect ($p < .05$).

The results support the Zeaman and House (1963) theory regarding intradimensional and extradimensional shifts. Attention to the relevant vehicle dimension aided intradimensional shifts as compared to extradimensional oddity shifts. In addition, oddity learning was more difficult than object discrimination and this finding is consistent with Zeaman and House's theory.

SUMMARY. The primary components of the five studies focusing on oddity learning are featured in Table 4.4 The summary information is presented in the following areas:

1. subject characteristics
2. comparisons of retarded subjects with different MA levels
3. comparisons of retarded subjects with nonretarded subjects
4. specific relevant findings

The characteristics of the retarded subjects in the five studies varied considerably. The mean IQs of the retarded groups who participated in the studies ranged from 22–75. Their mean CAs ranged from 8.3–23.4 years and their mean MAs ranged from 3.5–8.5. The mean CAs of the nonretarded subjects ranged from 4.5–8.4 years. The mean MAs of the nonretarded groups ranged from 4.5–6.5 and their mean IQs ranged from 101–149. All of the five studies included retarded participants, and two studies (Brown, 1970; Penn, Sindberg, & Wohlhueter, 1969) used both retarded and nonretarded participants. Two of the studies (Dickerson & Girardeau, 1970; Penn et al., 1969) included severely retarded subjects and the remaining studies included only EMR subjects (Dickerson & Girardeau included EMR and SMR subjects). All the retarded participants except the ones in Brown's study were from institutions. Institutionalization was not specifically considered as a variable in any of the studies.

TABLE 4.4
Summary of Studies Focusing on Oddity Learning

ARTICLE	SUBJECTS	INDEPENDENT VARIABLE	TASK	RESULTS
1. Penn, Sindberg, & Wohlhueter (1969)	40 severely retarded 1. 16 MA = 3 $\overline{CA}$ = 23.4 $\overline{MA}$ = 3.5 $\overline{IQ}$ = 22 2. 17 MA = 4 $\overline{CA}$ = 21.4 $\overline{MA}$ = 4.3 $\overline{IQ}$ = 26.9 3. 6 MA = 5 + $\overline{CA}$ = 16.9 $\overline{MA}$ = 7.1 $\overline{IQ}$ = 44	MA level	three-choice oddity problem (color, odd dimension)	†1. Performance of MA = 3 group was equal to performance of MA = 4 group. *2. Performance of MA = 5 + group was superior to the performances of the lower MA groups. *3. MA = 4 group performed poorer than normal CA = 4 Ss from a previous experiment.
2. Brown (1970) *Experiment I*	16 Ss in each group 1. normal $\overline{CA}$ = 6.6, $\overline{MA}$ = 6.3, $\overline{IQ}$ = 102 2. bright $\overline{CA}$ = 4.5, $\overline{MA}$ = 6.5, $\overline{IQ}$ = 149 3. CA-matched (to bright group) normals $\overline{CA}$ = 4.6, $\overline{MA}$ = 4.5, $\overline{IQ}$ = 101 4. retarded $\overline{CA}$ = 8.4, $\overline{MA}$ = 6.5, $\overline{IQ}$ = 74 5. CA-matched (to retarded group) normals $\overline{CA}$ = 8.4, $\overline{MA}$ = 8.2, $\overline{IQ}$ = 105	MA and CA levels	three-choice oddity problem (form, odd dimension)	*1. Performance of retarded Ss was inferior to performances of CA- and MA-matched nonretarded Ss.

TABLE 4.4, cont.

ARTICLE	SUBJECTS	INDEPENDENT VARIABLE	TASK	RESULTS
Experiment II	3 groups of retardates, 16 Ss in each group comparable to retarded Ss in *Exp. I*. $\overline{CA} = 8.33$, $\overline{MA} = 6.5$, $\overline{IQ} = 75$	number of stimuli in a discrimination problem (Condition I), variation of odd stimulus across different dimensions (Condition II), pretraining to an intradimensional oddity shift (Condition III)	oddity task	*1. The intradimensional oddity shift hindered performance. *2. More Ss reached criterion in conditions I and II than in Condition III. 3. The conditions (I–III) equalized the performances of retarded Ss and matched MA normals from *Exp. I*.
3. Dickerson & Girardeau (1970)	1. 45 severely retarded $\overline{CA} = 15$, $\overline{IQ} = 34$ 2. 45 mildly retarded $\overline{CA} = 16.5$, $\overline{IQ} = 62.3$	IQ level, number of objects in stimulus array	three-, four-, or five-choice oddity task with no reward	*1. Mildly retarded Ss selected the odd stimulus more than the severely retarded Ss. 2. All Ss selected odd stimulus above chance level except severely retarded Ss in three-choice group.
4. Hall (1971)	64 mildly retarded divided into high and low MA groups 1. High MA group $\overline{CA} = 16.1$, $\overline{MA} = 8.5$ 2. Low MA group $\overline{CA} = 14.7$, $\overline{MA} = 6.5$	MA level, dimensional preference, transfer to preferred or nonpreferred dimension	three-choice oddity task on either preferred or nonpreferred dimension	†1. No differences in MA level on dimensional preference. *2. Oddity learning on preferred dimension was superior.
5. Martin & Tyrrell (1971)	48 retarded $\overline{CA} = 13–1$ $\overline{MA} = 7–9$	pretraining on relevant dimension	performance on one of four appropriate tasks: discrimination task with intradimensional shift; discrimination task with extradimensional shift; oddity task with intradimensional shift; oddity task with extradimensional shift.	1. No significant differences across groups in original learning. *2. During transfer, discrimination tasks were more easily learned than oddity tasks. *3. Intradimensional shifts were easier to learn than extradimensional shifts.

NOTE: *Supports either Zeaman and House (1963) or Fisher and Zeaman (1973).
†No support for either Zeaman and House (1963) or Fisher and Zeaman (1973).

In three studies (Dickerson & Girardeau, 1970; Hall, 1971; Penn et al., 1969) the oddity performances of retarded subjects at different MA levels were compared. Four comparisons were reported in the three studies, and the high MA retarded subjects performed better in two comparisons (Dickerson & Girardeau, 1970; Penn et al., 1969) and no differences occurred between high and low MA groups in two comparisons (Hall, 1971; Penn et al., 1969). From these comparisons it is apparent that support for the lower MA deficiency position advanced by Zeaman and House (1963) is equivocal.

In two studies (Brown, 1970; Penn et al., 1969) the oddity-learning performances of retarded participants were compared to the performances of MA-equivalent, nonretarded participants. In these studies three comparisons were reported. In two of the comparisons the MA-equivalent, nonretarded subjects performed better and in one comparison no differences occurred. Finally, in a comparison (Brown, 1970) of the oddity performances of a retarded group with a CA-equivalent, nonretarded group, the latter performed better. Three out of four of these MA versus normal comparisons support the position advanced by Zeaman and House (1963) that retarded subjects have more trouble with oddity learning than normals.

Some specific findings from the five studies focusing on oddity learning include:

1. Brown (1970) and Hall (1971) suggest that the oddity-learning problems of retarded subjects could be lessened by controlling certain variables. These are: (a) training with the odd cue within a preferred dimension, (b) increasing the number of dimensions carrying odd cues, (c) pretraining subjects on a two-choice task and then proceeding to an oddity task with an intradimensional shift, and (d) increasing the number of objects in the array.
2. Retarded subjects at different MA levels (8.5 versus 6.5) did not differ on dimension preferred (Hall, 1971).
3. Martin and Tyrrell (1971) found that for EMRs an oddity task was more difficult than a three-choice discrimination task.
4. Martin and Tyrrell (1971) also found that for EMRs extradimensional shifts were more difficult than intradimensional shifts.
5. Dickerson and Girardeau (1970) found that EMRs selected an odd stimulus (unrewarded) more than SMR subjects.

TEACHING IMPLICATIONS

1. Brown (1970) found that the use of redundancy (adding more constant stimuli) improved the oddity-learning performances of retarded individuals. Instead of instructing the learner to select the odd stimulus from among three stimuli, Brown had the learner select the odd stimulus from among five stimuli (four identical and one odd). Teachers could also enhance the recognition of a stimulus by making it odd and placing it in a stimulus array with four other identical stimuli. For example, to help a child recognize the letter *b*, the teacher could present the following task and instruct the child to select the odd stimulus (*b*):

   | b | c | c | c | c |
   | a | a | b | a | a |

   The teacher could then gradually reduce the number of identical stimuli.
2. Brown (1970) showed that varying the odd stimulus along several dimensions improved the performance of retarded learners. The implications of this finding are similar to the implications provided previously regarding cue differences and cue distinctiveness. A teacher could improve the recognition of the number 5 by having the child select it from among other stimuli which differ along several dimensions from the 5:

blue 2	red 5	blue 2
blue 4	blue 4	red 5
blue 0	red 5	blue 0
3. Hall (1971) found that retarded individuals performed oddity-learning tasks better if the dimension of the odd stimulus was their preferred dimension. For example, if an individual preferred color more than form, color as the relevant dimension in an oddity task would improve performance. A teacher could informally assess learners for their preferred dimension and then use the preferred dimension to help the student perform discrimination tasks. For example, if color is the preferred dimension, the teacher could color code certain stimuli (make *b*s red) to help the child attend to it.

The implications from the remaining findings (pretrain on relevant dimension and use intradimensional shifts rather than extradimensional shifts) in the oddity studies (Martin & Tyrrell, 1971) have been discussed in the previous sections and are not reported here.

Conclusion

In this chapter attention factors and their relation to mental retardation are recognized as parameters which have produced substantial theoretical formulations and research. Zeaman and House's (1963) attention theory is a major contribution concerning the attention processes of retarded persons on discrimination tasks. Both of these scientists have been persistent in their continuing research and sensitive to new data. Efforts to update and refine their theory culminated in the formulation of the attention-retention theory by Fisher and Zeaman (1973).

Studies generated by the Zeaman and House (1963) and Fisher and Zeaman (1973) theories may be found to include: (a) studies focusing on number of dimensions, (b) studies focusing on incentive conditions, (c) studies focusing on transfer operations, and (d) studies focusing on oddity learning. All these studies imply strategies for teaching, such as arranging stimulus characteristics and rewarding cue selection in order to improve attention processes of retarded children in educational and therapeutic settings.

Due to the recency of the Fisher and Zeaman (1973) attention-retention theory, few studies can be located which directly test some of their primary positions regarding retardate deficiencies, i.e., breadth of attention deficiency, short-term memory deficiency, and rehearsal deficiency. It is apparent that the attention-retention theory focuses more directly on retention processes than on attention processes. Memory research with retarded individuals is substantial (e.g., Ellis, 1970) and should combine with the Fisher and Zeaman formulations to enhance our knowledge in this area.

Zeaman and House (1963) must be credited with sensitizing the researcher and hopefully the practitioner to the attention parameters of the discrimination learning paradigm. In essence, it was because researchers have demonstrated that the attention factors can be altered via manipulating stimulus arrangements and consequences that Fisher and Zeaman (1973) expanded their theory. Thus, implications for improving attention to relevant dimensions are numerous. Hopefully, the attention-retention theory will, likewise, generate continuing research which enhances our understanding of mental retardation and provides the practitioner with empirically based techniques for improving retardate's chances for learning.

Notes

1. The curves are superimposed as in forward learning curves, but the shapes of the backward curves em-phasize that portion which displays the attainment of criterion (Robinson & Robinson, 1976).

2. For a review of experimental approaches in mental retardation, please refer to: Routh, D. K. Experimental approaches to the clinical psychology of mental retardation. In D. K. Routh (Ed.), *The experimental psychology of mental retardation*. Chicago: Aldine, 1973.

References

Alabiso, F. Inhibitory functions of attention in reducing hyperactive behavior. *American Journal of Mental Deficiency*, 1972, *77*, 259–282.

Atkinson, R. C., & Shiffrin, R. M. Human memory: A proposed system and its control processes. In K. W. Spence & J. T. Spence (Eds.), *The psychology of learning and motivation: Advances in research and theory* (Vol. 2). New York: Academic Press, 1969.

Bilsky, L., & Heal, L. W. Cue novelty and training level in the discrimination shift performance of retardates. *Journal of Experimental Child Psychology*, 1969, *8*, 503–511.

Brown, A. L. Subject and experimental variables in the oddity learning of normal and retarded children. *American Journal of Mental Deficiency*, 1970, *75*, 142–151.

Clinton, L. Effects of between-trials variability and initial response outcome on the alternation discrimination learning of retarded adolescents. *American Journal of Mental Deficiency*, 1972, *76*, 440–445.

Clinton, L., & Evans, R. A. Single alternation discrimination learning in retarded adolescents as a function of within-trials variability. *American Journal of Mental Deficiency*, 1972, *76*, 434–439.

Crosby, K. G., & Blatt, B. Attention and mental retardation. *Journal of Education*, 1968, *150*, 67–81.

Denegre, J. The effect on retardate discrimination learning of various stimuli associated with reward. *Journal of Experimental Child Psychology*, 1966, *3*, 74–82.

Denny, M. R. Research in learning and performance. In H. A. Stevens & R. Heber (Eds.), *Mental retardation*. Chicago: University of Chicago Press, 1964.

Dickerson, D. J., & Girardeau, F. L. Oddity preference by mental retardates. *Journal of Experimental Child Psychology*, 1970, *10*, 28–32.

Ellis, N. R. Memory processes in retardates and normals. In N. R. Ellis (Ed.), *International review of research in mental retardation* (Vol. 4). New York: Academic Press, 1970.

Evans, R. A. Some stimulus factors involved in the discrimination learning of mental retardates. *American Journal of Mental Deficiency*, 1968, *73*, 61–69.

Evans, R. A., & Beedle, R. K. Discrimination learning in mentally retarded children as a function of irrelevant dimension variability. *American Journal of Mental Deficiency,* 1970, *74,* 568–573.

Fisher, M. A., & Zeaman, D. An attention-retention theory of retardate discrimination learning. In N. R. Ellis (Ed.), *The international review of research in mental retardation* (Vol. 6). New York: Academic Press, 1973.

Gollin, E. S., & Shirk, E. J. A developmental study of oddity-problem learning in young children. *Child Development,* 1966, *37,* 213–217.

Gruen, G. E., & Berg, B. Visual discrimination learning in familial retarded and nonretarded children. *American Journal of Mental Deficiency,* 1973, *78,* 63–69.

Hagen, J. W., & Kail, R. V., Jr. The role of attention in perceptual and cognitive development. In W. M. Cruickshank & D. P. Hallahan (Eds.), *Perceptual and learning disabilities in children* (Vol. 2). *Research and theory.* Syracuse, N.Y.: Syracuse University Press, 1975.

Hall, J. E. Effect of response bias of mental retardates upon oddity learning. *American Journal of Mental Deficiency,* 1971, *75,* 579–585.

Harris, L. M., & Tramontana, J. Discrimination learning of retarded children as a function of positive reinforcement and response cost. *American Journal of Mental Deficiency,* 1973, *78,* 216–219.

Harter, S., Brown, L., & Zigler, E. Discrimination learning in retarded and nonretarded children as a function of task difficulty and social reinforcement. *American Journal of Mental Deficiency,* 1971, *76,* 275–283. (a)

Harter, S., Brown, L., & Zigler, E. The discrimination learning of normal and retarded children as a function of penalty conditions and etiology of the retarded. *Child Development,* 1971, *42,* 517–536. (b)

House, B. J. Oddity performance in retardates: I. Acquisition and transfer. *Child Development,* 1964, *35,* 635–643.

House, B. J. Problem length and multiple discrimination learning in retarded children. *American Journal of Mental Deficiency,* 1973, *78,* 255–261.

House, B. J., Brown, A. L., & Scott, M. S. Children's discrimination learning based on identity or difference. In H. W. Reese (Ed.), *Advances in child development and behavior* (Vol. 9). New York: Academic Press, 1974.

House, B. J., & Zeaman, D. Effects of practice on the delayed response of retardates. *Journal of Comparative and Physiological Psychology,* 1961, *54,* 255–260.

House, B. J., & Zeaman, D. Learning sets from minimum stimuli in retardates. *Journal of Comparative and Physiological Psychology,* 1963, *56,* 735–739.

Klein, H. A., Klein, G. A., Oskamp, L., & Patnode, C. Color distractors in discrimination with retarded and nonretarded children. *American Journal of Mental Deficiency,* 1972, *77,* 328–331.

Lobb, H. Pretraining retarded and intellectually average children for visual discrimination: Nonreward vs. reward. *American Journal of Mental Deficiency,* 1972, *77,* 59–68.

Lobb, H. Effects of verbal rehearsal on discrimination learning in moderately retarded and nursery-school children. *American Journal of Mental Deficiency,* 1974, *79,* 449–454.

Lobb, H., & Childs, R. Verbal control and intradimensional transfer of discrimination learning in mentally retarded vs. intellectually average subjects. *American Journal of Mental Deficiency,* 1973, *78,* 182–192.

Lobb, H., & Stogdill, D. Low-IQ deficit in intradimensional discrimination shift despite overtraining and verbal feedback. *American Journal of Mental Deficiency,* 1974, *79,* 455–461.

Martin, A. S., & Tyrrell, D. J. Oddity learning following object-discrimination learning in mentally retarded children. *American Journal of Mental Deficiency,* 1971, *75,* 504–509.

Massey, P. S., & Insalaco, C. Aversive stimulation as applied to discrimination learning in mentally retarded children. *American Journal of Mental Deficiency,* 1969, *74,* 269–272.

Milgram, N. A., & Noce, J. S. Relevant and irrelevant verbalization in discrimination and reversal learning by normal and retarded children. *Journal of Educational Psychology,* 1968, *59,* 169–175.

Penn, N. E., Sindberg, R. M., & Wohlhueter, M. J. The oddity concept in severely retarded children. *Child Development,* 1969, *40,* 153–161.

Riese, R. R., & Lobb, H. Discrimination learning in retarded children: Nonreward vs. reward. *American Journal of Mental Deficiency,* 1967, *71,* 536–541.

Robinson, N. M., & Robinson, H. B. *The mentally retarded child: A psychological approach* (2nd ed.). New York: McGraw-Hill, 1976.

Shepp, B. E. Some cue properties of anticipated rewards in discrimination learning of retardates. *Journal of Comparative and Physiological Psychology,* 1962, *55,* 856–859.

Shepp, B. E. Some cue properties of rewards in simultaneous object discriminations of retardates. *Child Development,* 1964, *35,* 587–592.

Switzky, H. N. Cue distinctiveness, learning, and transfer in mentally retarded persons. *American Journal of Mental Deficiency,* 1973, *78,* 277–285.

Turrisi, F. D., & Shepp, B. E. Some effects of novelty and overtraining on the reversal learning of retardates. *Journal of Experimental Child Psychology,* 1969, *8,* 389–401.

Ullman, D. G. Breadth of attention and retention in mentally retarded and intellectually average children. *American Journal of Mental Deficiency,* 1974, *78,* 640–648.

Ullman, D. G. & Routh, D. K. Discrimination learning in mentally retarded and nonretarded children as a function of the number of relevant dimensions. *American Journal of Mental Deficiency,* 1971, *76,* 176–180.

Wachtel, P. M. Conceptions of broad and narrow attention. *Psychological Bulletin,* 1967, *68,* 417–429.

Zeaman, D. One programmatic approach to retardation. In D. K. Routh (Ed.), *The experimental psychology of mental retardation*. Chicago: Aldine, 1973.

Zeaman, D., & House, B. J. The role of attention in retardate discrimination learning. In N. R. Ellis (Ed.), *Handbook of mental deficiency*. New York: McGraw-Hill, 1963.

5

Denny's Elicitation Theory and Incidental Learning of the Retarded

This chapter views Denny's Elicitation Theory in depth—its framework, terminology, and postulates. It summarizes his 1964 review and touches on his principles for creating better learning conditions for the retarded. In the second part of the chapter, research based on his theory will be presented.

The Elicitation Framework

Although Denny's Elicitation Theory (Denny & Adelman, 1955) is not widely known or understood, it does include thoughts for teaching the retarded which justify inclusion and explanation in this text. The theory represents some original variations of learning theory combined with an integration of the behavioristic theories of Hull, Guthrie, Skinner, Tolman, and Pavlov. His theory, originally based upon research in animal learning, recently has been extended to human learning and the facilitation of retardate learning. To explain learning, Denny uses a terminology system similar to that used by Skinner in operant conditioning but which corresponds to quite different definitions. This terminology results in a deceptive overlap of constructs between elicitation theory and operant

conditioning, yet the fundamental explanations of the same phenomena by both theories are highly discrepant.

According to Denny's theory, learning depends upon consistent elicitation of the to-be-learned response in close temporal contiguity with a particular stimulus situation. Thus any competing responses which could be elicited by the same or by similar stimulus situations need to be minimized or eliminated so that the learned response wins out over any competing responses. To Denny, learning occurs when a response is consistently elicited regardless of the nature of the stimulus. "The more often a response is elicited each time the stimulus is presented the more consistent the elicitation" (Denny & Adelman, 1955, p. 290). This includes elicitation by a conditioned stimulus (CS), a discriminative stimulus (S^D), or by an unconditioned stimulus (US).

Terminology

The elicitation framework uses the primary abstract concepts of stimulus (S), response (R), and response tendency (S-R) or the relationship between S and R. Following is a complete definition of each of these terms.

STIMULUS. *Stimulus* is defined according to its experimental and theoretical uses.

> When this is done, stimulus becomes quite abstract and involved. Stimulus is not a manipulable event or object or a form of physical energy, but is inferred from such events under certain conditions. These events can include electrophysiological recordings; specific movements or responses, as when kinesthesis is inferred; or the absence of an object, as when frustration elicitation is inferred from the removal of a food incentive. (Denny & Ratner, 1970, pp. 12–13)

There are three defining characteristics of stimulus which underlie the aforementioned conditions. A stimulus is anything which (a) acts through the afferent neural pathways and (b) is potentially capable of eliciting the occurrence of a response in a particular class of organisms. To further explain these characteristics, the use of *afferent* excludes direct activation of muscles but includes all neural structures in the central nervous system which are clearly *not* efferent (i.e., carrying impulses away from the brain or spinal cord) since the laws of behavior in these situations differ. *Potentially capable* means one has information that the R at some point in time has been reliably elicited in representative members of the class of organism by the "stimulus." *Elicitation* means that a R is contingent upon a S which immediately precedes that R. *Occurrence* is meant to describe in a noncircular manner the constant meaning of S which exists unchanged even if the expected R does not occur on every occasion. If S is present but does not elicit the expected R, then it is apparent that other Ss or variables are present. The implication is that "once an S, always an S, regardless of whether on a particular occasion it elicits an R or not" (Denny & Ratner, 1970, p. 13). For example, water is a stimulus to a thirsty child. The child will drink until satiated. Although the child will not approach to drink until thirsty again, water remains a stimulus. Regarding the satiation hypothesis Deny (1966) states:

> By definition, all stimuli elicit response. With continued or repeated presentation, however, all stimuli lose or partially lose the property to elicit response as a decay function of the duration or frequency of presentation. (Denny, 1966, p. 22)

RESPONSE AND RESPONSE TENDENCY. The definition of *response* centers around (a) a set of response occurrence, (b) a particular class of organisms on which the identification of the re-

sponse class is based, and (c) a recurrent aspect of the stimulus situation (Denny, 1966). If, for example, a hungry child is observed running into the dining room or kitchen, the R is classified as approach. However, it is possible that running also can be classified as an escape R if the child is leaving a place associated with punishment. In this example, the response tendency (S-R) or the ability of S (food) to elicit R (approach), is dependent upon a number of variables, such as the degree of hunger, the eliciting power of other Ss in the situation, and the strength with which approach and the cues preceding arrival to the table are conditioned by food.

INCENTIVES. Although Denny's theory is based in animal behavior research (Denny & Adelman, 1955; Denny & Dunham, 1951; Maatsch, Adelman, & Denny, 1954), further applications of the theory have been made to retarded populations (Deich, 1974; Denny, 1966; Singer, 1964). Estes (1970) uses references to animal behavior to describe the role of incentives in elicitation theory:

> The principal function of reward in a trial-and-error situation, as, for example, maze learning, is that it evokes approach to the location of the goal. Then simply through association by contiguity, approach responses become conditioned to other cues near the goal and the process works backwards over successive trials until the exposure of the animal to any portion of the pathway will initiate a sequence of movements leading to the goal. (p. 121)

When the termination of pain is used as an incentive in maze learning it is assumed that relaxation is elicited. It is further assumed that relaxation reduces competing responses that might become conditioned to stimuli in the situation. It is through a back-chaining process that both relaxation-approach and avoidance or escape responses become conditioned to situational stimuli.

Back-Chaining Learning Process

In order to clarify the postulates of elicitation theory, the following section will describe how they work in a common learning situation, illustrated in Figure 5.1. Consider a preschooler learning for the first time the rule that toys must be put away prior to snack time. The arrangement of this classroom stimulus situation is graphically illustrated in Part *A*, while Part *B* of the same figure outlines the steps needed for learning. In elicitation theory, approach to the place where the food is (rather

A. Back-Chaining Steps to Learn Approach

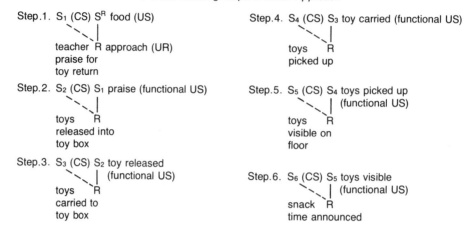

Step.1. S_1 (CS) S^R food (US)

teacher R approach (UR)
praise for
toy return

Step.2. S_2 (CS) S_1 praise (functional US)

toys   R
released into
toy box

Step.3. S_3 (CS) S_2 toy released
                   (functional US)
toys   R
carried to
toy box

Step.4. S_4 (CS) S_3 toy carried (functional US)

toys   R
picked up

Step.5. S_5 (CS) S_4 toys picked up
                   (functional US)
toys   R
visible on
floor

Step.6. S_6 (CS) S_5 toys visible
                   (functional US)
snack   R
time announced

B. The Preschool Classroom Stimulus Situation

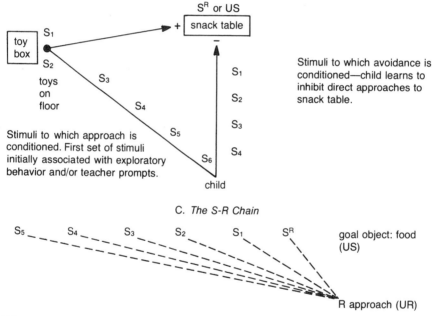

S^R or US

+ snack table

toy box

S_1
S_2
toys on floor

S_3

S_4

S_5

S_6

child

S_1
S_2
S_3
S_4

Stimuli to which avoidance is conditioned—child learns to inhibit direct approaches to snack table.

Stimuli to which approach is conditioned. First set of stimuli initially associated with exploratory behavior and/or teacher prompts.

C. The S-R Chain

S_5 S_4 S_3 S_2 S_1 S^R goal object: food
                                                          (US)

R approach (UR)

FIGURE 5.1
Conditioned approach analysis of learning to put toys away.

than eating) is identified as the unconditioned response (*UR*). The first set of unconditioned stimuli (*US*) (Part *B*, Step 1) includes the food. The tendency to approach becomes strengthened each time the child receives food at snack time, so that before the cleanup rule the child usually approaches when certain cues contiguous with the stimulus are present, including: the teacher appearing at the table with cookies and milk on a tray; the teacher saying, "Time for snack"; other children approaching the table; and internal hunger cues at 10:00 a.m.

After the rule the discriminative stimulus is changed and the child must pick up and put away one or two toys in order to get a snack. Initially the child makes only approach responses to the snack table without putting any toys away. However, this nondiscrimination of the stimulus situation means that the child does not receive reinforcement. Therefore, the absence of the incentive on the table is itself a US which elicits antagonistic responses. As illustrated in Part A, these responses of frustration-instigation are established through a process of secondary elicitation [also includes the conditioning of competing responses (R_C) during extinction] which occurs when a consistent elicitor (food) is no longer part of an established behavior sequence. These antagonistic responses consist of aggressive or tangential responses, such as moving away from the eating area, searching, and verbalizing (whining, asking, or complaining). Finally, due to these responses and initial prompts by the teacher (physical or gestural-verbal), some toys are touched, lifted from the floor, and taken to the toy box. This new response, meeting the S^D requirements, causes the snack to be set on the table and other cues to occur (e.g., teacher praise, teacher saying "Snack time," teacher holding out a cookie). The child then finds food on the table.

Next the child learns to put the toys away *before* approaching the table. In this type of learning the child begins to inhibit direct approaches to the table and learns the detour route of approaching toys, bending over, picking up toys and putting them in the toy box.

Denny and Ratner (1970) believe that "operant conditioning, or instrumental learning represents a type of discriminative learning in which the animal supplied its own discriminative stimulus" (p. 634). In this example the specific discriminative stimuli associated with getting a snack are those which occur when the child puts the scattered toys in their place. Denny and Ratner explain this point in relation to what happens when a rat learns to press a bar before approaching the food tray in a Skinner box.

> The essential ingredient for building a discriminative chain is sets of stimuli which consistently occur when the animal looks at the bar, addresses the bar, touches the bar, presses the bar, etc. For the most part these response-produced stimuli identify the appropriate behavior route to take and include the discriminative stimuli for when to approach the food tray. In sum, the discriminative stimuli involved in a rat's learning to press a bar are the kinesthetic, tactual, auditory, and visual stimuli which precede and accompany bar pressing. (p. 635)

The particular S-R chain illustrated in Part C is learned in six steps (Part B). The UR of approach which is consistently elicited by the positive reinforcer (S^R) or US of food becomes conditioned to the cues (S_1) just preceding arrival to the snack table (cues such as teacher praise for a toy's return). When this occurs, the S_1 cues serve as a functional UCS or elicitor of approach, and in turn approach is conditioned to these cues. When S_1 has good eliciting value, it seves as a functional US to S_2 (e.g., that S in close temporal contiguity with S_1) which then acts as CS. In this particular example S_2 consists of the auditory-kinesthetic-visual S involved in releasing toys into the toy box. Again after a number of trials, S_3 comes to elicit approach and serves as the functional US for conditioning S_4 (e.g., toys being picked up). As shown in Figure 5.1, this backward chaining of the approach R develops through a process of higher-order classical conditioning[1] such that S_6, the final link, comes to elicit approach R.

Figure 5.2 shows how the concepts of S^R (secondary reinforcement) and S^D (discriminative stimulus) may be equated with US and CS respectively. When a S in the chain has acquired conditioned approach value (i.e., acts as a CS) by being paired in close temporal contiguity with a US (food) or a functional US (e.g., teacher praise), it also serves as a S^D because it is associated with availability of reinforcement. When this particular CS has good eliciting value and serves as a functional US, it then acts in much the same way as a S^R.

Along with the satiation hypothesis mentioned earlier, the concept of stimulus hierarchy, though not directly named, has been implied as being important in defining response tendency. *Stimulus hierarchy* refers to the arrangement of potency of all the stimuli impinging upon an organism at any given point in time. This hierarchy is in constant flux due to the effects of S satiation, changes in level of deprivation, changes in intensity and size of a S (including magnitude of incentive), verbal instructions which produce response sets, as well as the basic associational changes of acquisition and extinction.

For the child in the example the stimulus hierarchy before snack time differs from that immediately following snack time due to the effects of S satiation and changes in the child's deprivation level. If the child did not like the food offered or if the child was not hungry, then the eliciting power of toys might surpass that of the food stimuli. Set-producing instructions given to a child (e.g., "You must put the toys in the toy box now. Then you can

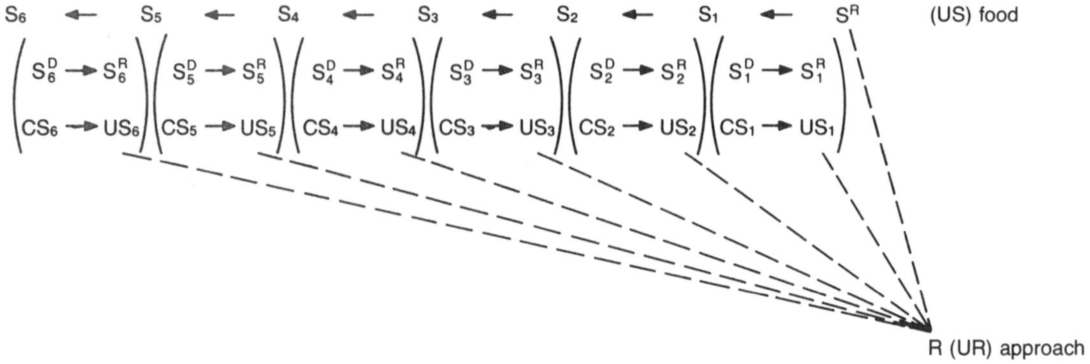

$$S_6 \;\leftarrow\; S_5 \;\leftarrow\; S_4 \;\leftarrow\; S_3 \;\leftarrow\; S_2 \;\leftarrow\; S_1 \;\leftarrow\; S^R \quad \text{(US) food}$$

$$\left(\begin{array}{c} S_6^D \to S_6^R \\ CS_6 \to US_6 \end{array}\right) \left(\begin{array}{c} S_5^D \to S_5^R \\ CS_5 \to US_5 \end{array}\right) \left(\begin{array}{c} S_4^D \to S_4^R \\ CS_4 \to US_4 \end{array}\right) \left(\begin{array}{c} S_3^D \to S_3^R \\ CS_3 \to US_3 \end{array}\right) \left(\begin{array}{c} S_2^D \to S_2^R \\ CS_2 \to US_2 \end{array}\right) \left(\begin{array}{c} S_1^D \to S_1^R \\ CS_1 \to US_1 \end{array}\right)$$

R (UR) approach

FIGURE 5.2

The parallel concepts of secondary reinforcement (S^R) equated with unconditioned stimulus (US) and discriminative stimulus (S^D) equated with conditioned stimulus (CS) in elicitation theory.

eat.") could act to affect the hierarchical S arrangement such that the toy S would move to the highest position immediately following instructions. Upon completion of the task, the food S would move into a position of higher eliciting power, and the toy S would decrease comparatively in its ability to elicit approach.

STIMULUS GENERALIZATION AND RESPONSE INHIBITION. Stimulus generalization, another primary concept in elicitation theory, is the converse of discrimination: "the transfer of response tendency from one stimulus complex to another" (Denny, 1966, p. 23). In this concept, stimuli similar to the original CS will elicit the same response even though not previously associated with that response. Therefore, the preschooler in the example may readily pick up toys before dinner at home as well as before eating at school if asked.

Because many stimulus elements rather than one typically share stimulus control, the amount of generalization is directly related to the similarity of the new situation to the original. The greater this similarity the more quickly and completely a response is generalized to a new situation and the less apt there is to be a decline in performance. However, it is possible that if stimulus control relies only upon a few relevant stimulus elements, a change in one element will result in generalization decrement, a decline in the response tendency ("Where *element* is defined as any analyzable part of a stimulus complex and *relevant* elements are those that are exclusively conditioned to the response in question") (Denny, 1971, p. 31). For example, a substitute teacher in the preschool may experience some difficulty enforcing the cleanup rule even though other controlling stimuli remain unchanged.

Another factor affecting stimulus generalization is the strength of the response tendency in the original learning situation. An inverse relationship holds true such that the stronger (weaker) the response tendency in the original learning situation the less probable (more probable) is the occurrence of stimulus generalization in altered stimulus situations.

Thus when a child incompletely discriminates the relevant cues prior to teaching, transfer is practically complete. For example, a preschooler puts toys away primarily because of a teacher's physical prompt, which is an irrelevant stimulus. This child will be just as capable of generalizing cleanup in other situations even though a few relevant stimulus items are changed, such as having a substitute teacher. However, if the surroundings take on stimulus control and are discriminated by the child, the entire complex has a strong response tendency and changes in even a few elements will stop the child from obeying the rule.

In addition to generalization decrement and forgetting, extinction is a main source of response inhibition. Denny (1966) describes the process of learning which occurs during extinction:

> The inhibition of performance which is *not* due to generalization decrement is the result of competing response tendencies being conditioned to *similar* stimulus situations. The response tendency (tendencies) pitted against the original response tendency produce singly, or in vector summation, a resultant reduced effect in the original tendency as a direct function of their relative strength and degree of incompatibility. No unhooking of responses, no *absolute*

weakening of response tendency, and no intrinsic inhibition (inhibitory drive state) are posited. The conditioning of the competing response(s) during extinction is commonly produced by secondary elicitation so that the response(s) learned during extinction is (are) usually antagonistic to the original response. (p. 25)

Learning Deficiencies of the Retarded

Denny's extension of the elicitation theory to include retardates (1966) was prompted by his 1964 review of retardate learning. This section examines the review as a background for a discussion of his principles for teaching. In his writings of 1966, he states that the retardate's learning deficiency, which appears as slow learning and poor short-term memory, has three parts: (a) short attention span, (b) inhibition deficiency, and (c) a deficiency in verbal control over motor response.

Included within attention deficiency is the inability to self-initiate learning sets in situations where instructions are not provided and the problem of being "stimulus-bound" (i.e., the child responds inconsistently to every stimulus change rather than maintaining a continuing response set). Denny states that these attentional inadequacies* result in an incidental learning deficiency.[2] Finally, the deficiencies of delayed response and lags in simple reaction time also are suggested as being attention deficiencies.

The inhibition deficiency as used by Denny (1964) includes three related characteristics in retardate learning: the tendency to continue responding during extinction, difficulty during discrimination learning, and an inability to inhibit the eliciting effects of other stimuli. The lack of verbal control over motor behavior is manifested in the following ways:

1. failure to follow verbal instructions explicitly
2. confused understanding of verbal commands (i.e., error responses which reflect misinterpreted generalization to words of similar sound rather than similar meaning)
3. a need for repetition of instructions over the duration of a task to maintain consistent responding

There is little evidence of a long-term retention deficiency for retardates and it is possible to train them to use verbal mediation (Denny, 1964). Therefore, the possibility of improved learning in the retarded appears likely in teaching situations where optimal learning conditions have been created to overcome the deficiencies previously described.

*See page 153.

The outlook for the mentally retarded is surprisingly optimistic—at least theoretically. It shall be possible to develop appropriate motivational procedures and special training techniques to overcome an appreciable portion of the retardates' difficulties, at least to the extent that they relate to the closely connected deficits in incidental learning, attention, and verbal control. These defects might be amenable to correction by (1) long-term training to attend or orient to stimuli, especially verbal stimuli, and (2) motivating the retarded children sufficiently and building in what they failed to learn incidentally during the early years, as, for example, with specially designed and programmed teaching machines. (Denny, 1964, p. 136)

Principles for Optimal Learning Conditions

Based upon his review of 1964, Denny (1966) created principles which he believed would create optimal learning conditions for the retarded. These principles, although indirectly related to elicitation theory, do not have one-to-one correspondence with the theory and are in many ways consistent with operant conditioning. The principles which follow are discussed in a descending order of importance.

1. *In early learning prevent incorrect responses and elicit as many correct responses as possible.*

   Incorrect responses may be prevented by limiting choices or blocking all response alternatives except the correct response and through the employment of "crutch cues" or prompts. Once training has established the correct response, these crutch cues and prompts are gradually faded out in adjustment with the child's error rate. Essentially the teacher using this principle is implementing an errorless discrimination procedure.

   For example, if this principle is applied to a receptive language task in which a child must learn to point when asked to a certain object in a group of objects (e.g., "Show me the spoon"), methods *a* through *c* (following) might be used to prevent error responses while methods *d* through *g* would increase the probability that the correct choice would be made.

   a. *Decrease choices*—eliminate most or all other choices from the training table (spoon alone is visible).
   b. *Physical prompts*—provide manual guidance (complete prompt) so that the child is taken through the entire correct response (place child's hand on spoon); or manually initiate (partial prompt) the beginning of the correct response chain (lift child's hand at wrist and move it a few inches in general direction of the choice).
   c. *Stop errors*—if a child moves towards an incorrect choice, intercept the movement and provide a physical prompt.

d. *Redundancy cues*—pair one or multiple dimensions (color, shape, position, or size) with the correct choice, thereby increasing the number of eliciting stimuli or the eliciting value of the CS.
   1) Color redundancy cue: place a red sheet of paper under the correct choice.
   2) Position redundancy cue: place correct choice closer to child and other choices farther away.
   3) Size: use the biggest object for correct choice.
   4) Shape: when teaching color, represent red by red paper circles, green by green triangles, blue by blue squares, etc.
e. *Match to sample cues*—includes pictoral or object representation of the correct response presented as part of the eliciting stimuli. (For example, say "This is a spoon." Hold up a spoon, and then gesture to objects on the table and say, "You show me a spoon.")
f. *Modeling or imitative prompting*—include a demonstration of the correct response as part of the eliciting stimuli. Modeling may be done by the teacher, by another child, or even by videotape and relies upon the child's ability to attend to and imitate the modeled response.
g. *Cuing a response*—include such incomplete demonstrations of the correct response as tapping a spot near the correct choice or pointing to or looking in the direction of the correct choice.

2. *Provide immediate knowledge of results.*

If the learner is informed of the correctness of the returned response, the conditioning process is facilitated. Although presence or absence of an incentive (food, toy, token, praise) is an important method of providing knowledge of results, consistent and immediately spoken words ("no," "wrong," "good, that's right,"), signals (light and bell for correct response, buzzer for incorrect response), and correction prompts following each error all serve further to specify the correct response by conditioning the presence of certain verbal control cues to the correct response. Knowledge of incorrect responses will be provided more often in later learning when prompts are faded and errors permitted. Consistently point out incorrect responses in a positive way so as not to elicit avoidance behavior. Along with knowledge of mistakes, the absence of the incentive may mediate an avoidance of the wrong response.

3. *Differential feedback.*

"The learning of the meaning of certain concepts is based on the presence of immediate feedback which is directly relevant to the meaning being learned" (Denny, 1966, p. 7). The teacher may use particular combinations of tactual, kinesthetic, visual, and auditory feedback immediately following the correct response to emphasize various characteristics of the response.

For example, when the subject is learning the concept of *behind* he actually puts a pointer *out of sight* behind the stimulus object in question. Or when he learns the concept of *through* he actually pushes the response bar through colored tissue paper, hearing, seeing, and feeling the bar tear *through* the paper. (Denny, 1966, p. 7)

This type of feedback which specifically deals with the concept being learned may not be applicable to all learning situations. Examples occurring at various stages of learning are illustrated in Figure 5.3 along with methods of eliciting correct responses (prompt column) and providing knowledge of results (consequences column).

4. *Stimulus generalization, stimulus randomization, and positive transfer.*

To promote positive transfer of the tendency to give a learned response to a new situation (one teacher, one area, one set of stimulus materials, etc.) the response must be taught in a variety of contexts which vary all the irrelevant cues but yet keep constant the relevant cues. While stimulus generalization encompasses the learning setting (teacher, command, room), stimulus randomization involves the systematic elimination of any irrelevant stimulus cues (position, object shape, size, color, orientation). Therefore, a child learning the color concept of "red" would be exposed to a wide variety of red objects which include a range of red color shades. Both processes lead to learning the specific discrimination or meaning of a concept due to the unchanging presence of the relevant cue(s) over repeated trials with simultaneous exposure to all other possible irrelevant cues. "A basic assumption of this training program is that the child must be given the clear opportunity to select the appropriate or relevant cue from a variety of irrelevant cues" (Denny, 1966, p. 8).

For example, to teach for positive transfer and for specific understanding of the concept of labeling "spoon," a child must learn to name large, brown, wooden spoons as well as silver teaspoons and colored, plastic measuring spoons (stimulus randomization of irrelevant color, size, and shape cues). In addition, the child needs to learn to name spoons at school and home, when seen on training tables and on dining tables, and when asked by a variety of people (stimulus generalization to different teachers and teaching settings).

5. *Distributed repetition and positive transfer.*

This principle concerns the concept of setting a performance criterion and training beyond its initial achievement, since it seems there is more gain in overlearning for retarded than for normals (Denny, 1966). This gain is greatest when the instruction is not massed or concentrated but spaced within teaching

Presentation of eliciting stimuli	Crutch cues	Child's response	Consequences		
			Knowledge of results	Differential feedback	Incentive
1. "What is this?" Toy car is held in view.	Partial prompt: Teacher silently mouths word.	Good approximation: "Caaa"	"Yes,	car." Teacher assists child in moving car on table.	cereal bit praise smile
2. "Snack time!" 10:30 a.m.; teacher approaches table with tray of food.	Partial cue: Teacher points to toys on floor.	Correct R: Child picks up toys and drops in box then approaches table.	"That's right,	you put away your toys!" Takes child's hand & slightly prompts toy into box.	snack praise smile
3a. "Put the ball *in* the box." Ball and 2 boxes presented (one box up and open, one upside down).		Incorrect R: Child puts ball on top of upside down box.	"Wrong, Response correction:	*in* the box." Teacher prompts child's R by placing child's hand into box.	
3b. Repeat.	Partial prompt: Teacher taps on table by open box.	Correct R: Child drops ball in open box.	"Right,	the ball is *in* the box." Teacher places child's hand in box on ball.	token praise smile

FIGURE 5.3

Stimulus-response instructional sequences illustrating methods to elicit correct responses as well as ways to provide immediate knowledge of results and differential feedback.

periods as well as across periods. Positive transfer is thereby facilitated since the distributed practice increases the probability that changes will occur in the stimulus context (stimulus generalization) while the child continues to make the same response with a reduction in the competing responses.

6. *Motivation (stimulus hierarchy)*.

Without interest for and attention to the task the child is less apt to discriminate and maintain the appropriate response, and error responses will increase. Incentives (reinforcers) are important to the motivation process for two reasons: first, they provide knowledge of results by their distinctive presence or absence; second, they serve to elicit approach responses to the learning situation. However, as Denny (1966) explains:

> A reinforcement, if one chooses to use this term, does not act back in time, per the law of effect, but occurs simultaneously with the elicitation of the response. In other words, a reinforcer is effective because it is an incentive or "bribe" not because it is a reward (the term *reward* refers more to past behavior, the term *incentive* more to future behavior). (pp. 3–4)

Motivation may also be kept high by providing enough variety in the stimulus presentation (e.g., increasing volume or wording of command) so that stimulus satiation is less likely to occur. As a result, the varying stimuli will be less apt to lose their ability to elicit the response while also affecting stimulus generalization.

7. *Sequential building*.

This principle directs the teacher to build a response sequence in easy steps upon what has already been learned. It "relates to the strategy of beginning with things which a child finds it easy to learn and building by easy steps toward more difficult goals, taking advantage of positive transfer of training whenever possible" (Estes, 1970, p. 124). Despite Denny's (1966) simple explanation of the sequential building principle, it appears to involve at least three more components:

a. familiarity with the normal developmental sequence of the behavior to be learned and its prerequisite behaviors

b. performing a task analysis of the particular behavior (especially important in regards to motor tasks such as walking and running, buttoning, and eating with a spoon) by observing its performance, specifying the small steps in a chronological order, and verifying the analysis over repeated observations

c. informally assessing the child's present level of ability on the prerequisite behaviors as well as on the sequence of steps analyzed to comprise the behavior for instruction

Research on Denny's Teaching Principles

Unfortunately there have been only a few direct applications of the teaching principles derived from elicitation theory. Of these applications most are in the form of training manuals and equipment developed primarily through intensive work with a small number of institutionalized, severely retarded children. These training procedures (Denny & Denny, 1973; Evans & Denny, 1974) and the small amount of experimental research (Evans, 1968; Sinclair, 1969; Yascolt, 1966) are difficult to evaluate in the absence of experiments which systematically compare this theoretical approach with others. However, a review of the work which has been done is paramount in furthering one's ability to comprehend and utilize Denny's principles.

The Learning Box

The teaching device previously called a *Multiple Differential Response and Feedback Apparatus* (MUDRAFA) is pictured in Figure 5.4. MUDRAFA, or more recently referred to as the *Learning Box* (Denny & Denny, 1973),[3] is a multiple choice teaching machine which presents several stimuli at the same time, allows the learner to respond differentially, and gives feedback on each response. The response handle, situated in the front middle of the two-foot-cube apparatus, can be moved in horizontal and vertical slots, as well as pushed in and pulled out towards the learner. Additional response directions can be created by rotating the panel containing the response handle slots.

All the response directions are available to provide a wide variety of responding to stimuli placed in various positions along the four slots and to prevent the presence of any particular slot (slots differ in width) from being associated with a particular position (e.g., stimulus randomization of position as an irrelevant cue). The multiple response positions allow the response handle to be moved directly above, directly below, beside, toward, away from, to the right, or to the left of a particular stimulus attached to the ends or sides of the four slots. The teacher can prevent learner errors by moving blockers across any of the four slots as illustrated in Figure 5.5. Differential feedback is provided by comments from the teacher, a light in the response handle, and incentives placed

FIGURE 5.4
The Learning Box in use with retarded student.

SOURCE: From Western Carolina Center, Morganton, North Carolina. Used by Permission.

on a shelf which is exposed immediately following a correct response.

To teach color, for example, on the Learning Box, color patches would be placed at the ends of the four slots and the child would be asked to "Go to red"—move the response handle to the red color patch. Various prompts will promote a high rate of correct responses such as holding up a sample of red and repeating directions to go to red, and by blocking all slots except the one leading to red. The position of the colors would be moved gradually over trials so as not to allow the learner to respond to position of the correct response as an eliciting cue for approach. Similarly stimulus randomization would be expanded to include rotation of the various response slots, elimination of blocked response paths, and fading of prompts.

Stimulus generalization is encouraged by using different kinds, shapes, sizes, and colors of each stimulus item as well as by practicing concepts mastered on the Learning Box in other places and situations. If the child finds generalizing concepts difficult, more sessions must be held. Denny (1966) suggests that while initial learning sessions may not last five minutes, later sessions may be lengthened to a maximum of 40–45 minutes.

However, in emphasizing the essential conditions of learner interest and attentiveness, Denny strongly recommends that sessions end before the learner becomes bored.

YASCOLT'S STUDIES. Two theses (Evans, 1968; Yascolt, 1966) tested the teaching effectiveness of the Learning Box with institutionalized retardates who functioned primarily in the severely retarded range (CA range: 5–33 years; MA range: 7 months–4 years 3 months). In Yascolt's noncomparative study eight subjects in two experimental groups worked daily with an experimenter on the Learning Box mastering simple concepts (e.g., up–down, left–right, color identification, rough–smooth, little–medium–big, etc.) and more difficult concepts (addition and subtraction of small quantities, word–picture association, word spelling, etc.). Training procedures used with the experimental subjects incorporated Denny's teaching principles and the Learning Box methods described previously (initial prompting and error prevention, knowledge of response accuracy, stimulus generalization and randomization, overlearning, etc.).

Experimental Group I received 10 weeks of training, followed by a retest, eight more weeks of

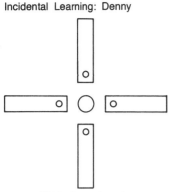

All blockers closed; handle moves in and out only.

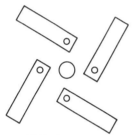

All blockers open; handle moves in all directions.

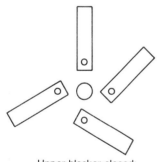

Upper blocker closed; handle will not move up.

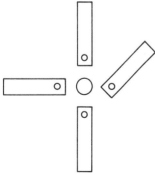

Side blocker open; handle will move to opposite side.

FIGURE 5.5
Incorrect responses are prevented by opening and closing the long wooden blockers situated on the back of the Learning Box which in turn block movement of the response handle in various directions.

SOURCE: Adapted from *Manual for the Learning Box* by M. R. Denny & R. Denny. Unpublished manuscript, Michigan State University, 1973. Used by permission.

training, a retest, five weeks with no interaction, and a final retention retest. Experimental Group II followed the same schedule with the omission of the first 10 weeks of training.

Six control subjects who were matched with both groups of experimental subjects on MA, CA, and number of known concepts on pretest received 10 or 18 weeks of control training including imitative games and interactive play with experimenter. Their knowledge for concepts was retested at the same time as the experimental subjects to whom they were matched.

Although retention was poor and slow for the first two weeks, final results revealed significant gains in the number of concepts acquired per week for both experimental groups as compared with controls. For Experimental Group I (N = 4, 10 weeks of training) a mean of 44 concepts (range: 11–79) was acquired while Experimental Group II (N = 4, 8 weeks of training) averaged 16 concepts (range: 3–34). In comparison the control group (N = 6) lost a mean of one concept (range: 5 gained to 3 lost). An examination of the learning curves revealed that experimental subjects with a higher initial number of concepts had steeper acquisition slopes than those with a low initial number of concepts, but there was no difference in retention. With the exception of one subject, concept retention averaged close to 100% five weeks after training.

EVANS'S STUDIES. In a similar study, Evans (1968) investigated the effects of modeling on Learning Box instruction in word identification, concept attainment (property concepts, such as rough–smooth and relational concepts, such as over–under), and spelling skills. His subjects were severely and profoundly retarded institutionalized retardates (CA range: 14–40; MA range: 5 months–6 years; IQ range: 10–33). Five subjects in the modeling condition were matched on MA and CA with the remaining five subjects in the nonmodeling condition. In the modeling condition where two Learning Boxes were used, the experimenter made use of match-to-sample prompts by modeling on his device the correct response to various commands (e.g., "Push the bar *over* the ball."). Subjects in this condition imitated the correct response on their Learning Box. Although modeling was based on a schedule of 100% during the first 12 trials on any concept or word, it was gradually phased out in the second 12 trials to a random 66% and finally to 33%. Whenever a subject demonstrated proficiency on the task (i.e., three consecutive correct responses without modeling prompts), modeling was discontinued. Upon demonstration of task proficiency, a free responding situation was instigated until criterion was attained or an error occurred. Errors were followed by a reinstatement of the modeling procedure. In the nonmodeling group only one subject-operated teaching box was used while the experimenter employed techniques similar to those described in Yascolt's (1966) study.

Results revealed that the effects of modeling on property concept attainment were significant as compared to learning in the nonmodeling group. All other learning data for the modeling group except for the spelling tasks were in the expected direction but nonsignificant. The spelling task, more complex than the other tasks, showed no differential effects of Modeling. Because Evans (1968) employed modeling periods of equal lengths for all tasks, he reasons that "the complex nature of compound cues in the word identification and relational concept tasks might necessitate a longer modeling period than the property concept task to provide an equal amount of facilitation" (p. 39).

SUMMARY. Both studies, though noncomparative with other methods, describe detailed procedures involving the use of the Learning Box that have demonstrated successful mastery and retention of basic verbal concepts in severely retarded institutionalized persons. Research is needed to determine the relative efficiency and effectiveness of different methods of teaching the same tasks. These methods should include the student-operated Learning Box, Learning Box modeling with modeling periods correlated to task complexity, and instruction without Learning Boxes but which incorporates Denny's (1966) teaching principles.[4] Examples of the latter instructional conditions include Ross's (1968, 1970a, 1970b) game

and number skills teaching procedure and the Reading Achievement Program (Evans & Denny, 1974).

Review of Related Research: Incidental Learning Deficiencies

The largest bulk of research related to Denny's (1964, 1966) writings on retardate learning concerns the hypothesized incidental learning deficiency. Although the results of the incidental learning research do not neatly interlock with the teaching principles derived from elicitation theory, the indirect relationship between incidental learning in the retardate and elicitation theory becomes evident after examining several statements. First, in the framework of elicitation theory, Denny and Adelman (1955) found that learning occurred only when a response was elicited in a consistent manner. By *consistent* they mean whether or not the response is elicited each time the stimulus is presented—"the more often R is elicited each time S is present, the more consistent the elicitation" (p. 290). In other words, they postulate that "the essential condition for the strengthening of one response tendency over and above another response tendency is the *consistent* elicitation of the response in question" (p. 290). According to the theory, it is this consistent response to changes in stimuli which is necessary for differential learning to occur.

Secondly, Singer (1964), whose incidental learning research will be reviewed later, makes several conclusions about the retardate's characteristic manner of responding to the changing stimuli in a learning situation:

> The retarded often responds differently to the same stimulus, and the same way to different stimuli. And if the retarded child will not respond consistently or repeatedly in an ordinary situation little incidental learning will take place. We would expect little consistent responding because the retarded is bound to the fleeting stimulus of the moment and cannot maintain an internal set. From elicitation theory it follows that the retarded child who does not respond consistently to the same stimulus in an ordinary situation fails to learn incidentally what the normal child learns incidentally. Presumably the retarded child falls behind in the first few years of learning and never catches up. That is to say, in the first years of life little directed learning takes place for most children. They are left on their own and not directly taught much of anything. But by consistent

responding to stimuli the "normal" child picks up incidentally a vast background of general data about the world which he can use to build upon when directed learning begins in kindergarten or the first grade. The retarded, however, does not incidentally acquire this information and therefore has an initial handicap from which he never seems to recover. (pp. 3–4)

With this viewpoint the incidental learning research conducted with the retarded may provide indirect support for the teaching principles derived from the elicitation theory. Thus the concept of incidental learning and research findings with retarded samples will be reviewed briefly in an effort to glean the relevant, correlative principles for teaching.

Terminology

The categories and definitions outlined by Postman (1963) in his review of the incidental learning of normals shall be discussed and used as the conceptual framework within which to understand such research with mentally retarded populations. It is thought that basic difficulties are inherent to most definitions of incidental learning because the connotations are negative, i.e., incidental learning results from "the absence of a set or intent to learn" (Postman, 1963, p. 185). In practice this means the omission of instructions which direct the learner's attention to the incidental or irrelevant features of the task or which prepare her for a test on a given type of material, designated by definition as *incidental material*.

Operationally, incidental and intentional learning are distinguished by the use of different classes of instruction stimuli—those which do and those which do not prepare the *S* for a test of retention. In practice, manipulation of the instruction stimulus is often supplemented by a postexperimental inquiry which ascertains the *S*'s response to the instructions. Incidental *S*s who anticipated a test or deliberately rehearsed the material are discarded and replaced. (Postman, 1963, pp. 185–186).

While unstable with normals, the reliability of postexperimental reports may be even more questionable or impossible with retardates. However, such a screening procedure may increase the separation of the incidental and intentional experimental conditions. Figure 5.6 illustrates the relationship of instructions, implicit set, postexperimental inquiry, and the other concepts of incidental learning.

EFFECTS OF ORIENTATION TASKS ON TYPE I INCIDENTAL LEARNING. In Type I incidental learning, the subject is shown stimulus materials but given no directions to remember particular qualities. After presentation she is given a retention test, either in recognition, transfer of information to another task, or serial or free recall.

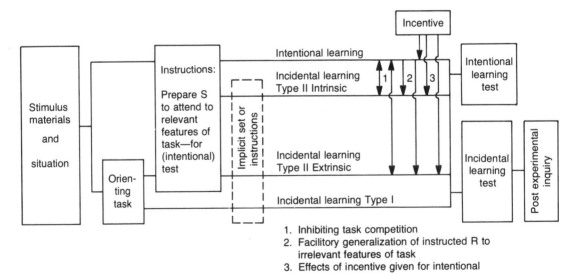

1. Inhibiting task competition
2. Facility generalization of instructed R to irrelevant features of task
3. Effects of incentive given for intentional learning on incidental learning

FIGURE 5.6
Incidental learning model based upon Postman's review of research in incidental learning.

Although no directions are given in Type I, orientation tasks preceding stimuli presentation can be given which affect incidental learning (as well as intentional learning). Such tasks may differ widely, but two criteria must be met: "(a) it must, indeed, create conditions which make it certain that the *S* perceives the incidental stimulus materials, and (b) it should minimize the development of uncontrolled sets to learn" (Postman, 1963, p. 188). Some orienting tasks may increase memory by their consistency with the instructed response, while other tasks may require responses which meet the criteria for orienting tasks but do not aid memory.

For example, imagine a particular experiment on incidental and intentional learning. The experimenter may use as an orienting task (A) the presentation of pictures of furniture and common object pairs. She might then ask the subject to respond affirmatively if the pairs have similar final sounds (*chair–bear*) and respond negatively if they have differing final sounds (*dog–table*). Or the experimenter may devise an orienting task (B) in which the subject must place quickly a disoriented series of pictures of mixed common objects (furniture, animals, food) in upright position in a stack.

In the experiment, three groups are used, one for incidental learning and two for intentional learning. As Postman (1963) notes, it is necessary to have two intentional groups in order to separate the effects and "determine the degree to which intent to learn and freedom from interference by the orienting task contribute to the advantage of the intentional learners. . . . When this design is used it is typically found that the performance of the orienting task reduces the amount learned under intentional conditions: as a consequence, the difference attributable to intent per se is correspondingly reduced." (p. 188)

One intentional group does not receive an orienting task, but such a task is given to the other groups. Before presenting a series of photos of furniture (stimuli), instructions to remember the furniture names in serial order are given to both intentional groups. The incidental group receives no instructions. After presenting the stimuli, the experimenter asks all groups to recall the furniture names in serial order.

Both the incidental and intentional learners will remember better the names of the furniture in order if they had completed Orienting Task B before stimuli presentation. While Task B involves labeling objects as the subject goes through the pile, which would aid future recall of furniture names, Task A involves a motor response, which would interfere with later serial recall.

Type II Incidental Learning. In the second type of incidental learning the subject is given a specific learning task, including directions and a set to attend to the relevant materials. However, unlike intentional learners who are also given instructions, incidental learners are exposed during practice to materials or cues not included in the learning instructions. The incidental test measures retention of these irrelevant features or unimportant materials. There are two subclasses of Type II incidental learning, intrinsic and extrinsic, which differ in the relationship existing between the relevant and irrelevant features of the total learning situation. In *Type II Intrinsic,* "the irrelevant components may be features or attributes of the materials which the *S* has been instructed to learn but which are irrelevant in the sense that their discrimination and retention are not required for the performance of the task defined by the experimenter" (Postman, 1963, p. 186). In illustration, an incidental or irrelevant component of the preceding task was furniture color, which also was a feature of the relevant component, furniture picture, thereby making the incidental task of remembering furniture color a Type II intrinsic task. With this intrinsic association between instructions to learn the relevant features of the materials and automatic exposure to the irrelevant features, no orienting task is needed, because the subject is guaranteed exposure to the incidental materials.

However, in *Type II Extrinsic*, the irrelevant features are materials or cues which have no direct association to the learning task and an orienting task is needed prior to testing for incidental learning to ensure their exposure. If in the previous example the furniture were not pictured singly on cards (as in Figure 5.7), but illustrated with an accentuating arrow in a room containing other furniture and one or more people, the incidental extrinsic features of the stimulus materials could be the people in the room. To test incidental learning the subject might be asked to associate pictures of people with names of the furniture. An orienting task could be used that required the subject to count and total the number of people in all the

Two pictures in a set of stimulus materials for a Type II intrinsic incidental learning task. Whether the piece of furniture has arms is an irrelevant (incidental) feature which is an intrinsic attribute of the relevant (intentional) feature—the particular piece of furniture (i.e., regular chair, rocking chair, bench, sofa).

Two pictures in a set of stimulus materials for a Type II extrinsic incidental learning task. Name of indicated furniture piece is the relevant (intentional) feature of the picture. Extrinsic to the furniture (i.e., its perception not required for discrimination of the relevant feature) is the irrelevant (incidental) feature of people (number and identity). An orienting task is needed to ensure exposure of the learner to the extrinsic incidental features of the stimulus materials.

FIGURE 5.7

Examples of stimulus materials for Type II intrinsic and extrinsic incidental learning tasks.

pictures thereby ensuring exposure to the irrelevant features (people) extrinsic to the relevant features (furniture piece).

Incidental Learning in the Retarded

In the conclusions of his review of retardate learning research, Denny (1964) suggests that:

Perhaps, the retarded are poor performers because they are much poorer incidental learners than normals. Perhaps they learn little in the ordinary course of events, requiring special stimulation, guidance, and motivation to learn effectively. To the reviewer's knowledge very few studies have been done specifically on incidental learning in the mentally retarded. . . . Thus with hardly a shred of direct evidence we suggest an incidental learning deficit, which in turn may be basically an attention deficit. (p. 134)

Hardman and Drew (1975), in a review of the same topic, emphasize the importance of incidental learning in school and everyday settings.

The student is surrounded by people, objects and various stimulus conditions from which he may broaden his learning background. Even though the teacher does not bring these stimuli into the formal instructional setting, their proximity makes them available and they may constitute an important body of content or skill. Any child who is unable to learn incidentally, by reason of ability or external contingencies, is seriously impaired with regard to performance potential. It would seem crucial that educators be aware of and manipulate any factors possible which would improve the child's opportunity for incidental learning. (pp. 3–4)

Since Denny's (1964) review of retardate learning, a series of studies have been carried out in the area of incidental learning with the retarded. These studies, which yield some conflicting results, unfortunately do not systematically attack the hypothesis of incidental learning deficiency. In many cases methodological difficulties occur, such as the following:

1. Mentally retarded samples are used which include large numbers of subjects functioning in the borderline intelligence range (above 70 IQ).
2. No postexperimental inquiry is done when Type II incidental learning tasks are used.
3. Intentional learning is not measured along with incidental learning.
4. If a normal MA match is included, no normal CA match is also included.
5. Researchers fail to build upon Postman's (1963) definitional foundation for incidental learning.

6. Operational definitions of incidental and intentional learning are inconsistently applied.

The following outline of important research includes 14 studies which are also summarized in Table 5.1. These studies comprise the bulk of incidental learning research done with mentally retarded populations.

CHARACTERISTICS OF INCIDENTAL LEARNING. Postman (1963) and Deese (1963) draw a number of conclusions regarding the properties of incidental learning in normal subjects.

1. As in intentional learning, conclusions about incidental learning are specific to the method of measurement (serial recall, recognition test, etc.).
2. Both Type I and Type II extrinsic incidental learning tasks must be preceded by an orienting task to ensure exposure to the irrelevant or incidental features of the materials.
3. Incentives:
   a. When no orienting task is used as in a Type II intrinsic incidental situation, the amount of incidental learning is inversely related to the strength of the incentive for performance of the intentional task. This shift in the amount of intentional and incidental learning is due to a corresponding shift in the relative frequency of differential responses from the incidental to intentional materials.
   b. However, "when responses to the materials are controlled by an orienting task, incentives do not influence either type [(incidental or intentional)] of learning" (Postman, 1963, p. 190).
4. In Type II incidental learning, the instructions have two consequences:
   a. A general class of responses, specific to the set to learn, is activated. "To the extent that such instrumental responses generalize to the irrelevant features and materials, the Type II situation is in principle more favorable to incidental learning than is the Type I situation. In the former, cue-producing responses are generalized to the irrelevant items where in the latter they must be aroused by materials alone" (Postman, 1963, p. 187).
   b. When exposure time is limited during the instructed task, responses to irrelevant features are evoked along with responses to relevant features of the materials and response competition results. In Type I no task competition occurs. Therefore the Type II situation is less conducive to incidental learning than the Type I situation. "The net difference between the two situations will depend on the extent to which the beneficial effects of a generalized set to learn are offset by the effects of task competion" (Postman, 1963, p. 187).

TABLE 5.1
Summary of Research on Incidental Learning in the Mentally Retarded

ARTICLE	MA MATCH	CA MATCH	MA-CA MATCH	ALL MR	INTENTIONAL TASK	INCIDENTAL TASK + TYPE
1. Goldstein & Kass (1961)	2 groups: MR group Gifted group MR: mod-B.L. $\overline{IQ}$ = 73 $\overline{MA}$ = 6-2 $\overline{CA}$ = 10-3 N = 42				Instructed to locate all the 2s in the picture in one min.	**Type II Intrinsic** Picture of color street scene was viewed for 1 min: 1. Naming: free recall of items in picture 2. Detailing: elaborate on each object named 3. Identification: respond to single items as having been present or not present in picture*
2. Hetherington & Banta (1962)	3 groups MR—organic MR—familial Normal MR: mild $\overline{IQ}$ = 60 $\overline{MA}$ = 5.9 $\overline{CA}$ = 9.9 N = 60				Instructed to identify object and try to remember as many of the 15 as possible. Five presented at a time followed by 3 *intentional learning* tests. 48 hr later Ss asked to recall as many objects as could (*Intent. recall*) and then to *recognize* each picture embedded in a group of 4 new pictures used for intentional.	**Type II Intrinsic** Told to name colors of 15 pictures of common objects; named object upon presentation. *Incidental learning* measured immediately by asking Ss to name as many objects as could. 48 hr later *incidental recall* measured—Ss asked to name as many objects again; then *incidental recognition* measured by asking Ss to recognize each picture embedded in a group of 4 pictures.
3. Baumeister (1963)		4 groups: MR—normal MR: mild-B.L. $\overline{IQ}$ = 73 $\overline{MA}$ = 9.1 $\overline{CA}$ = 12.5 N = 60			Replication of Hetherington and Banta's method except (1) CA match used and MA match omitted; (2) 4 groups used: MR incidental and intentional, and normal incidental and intentional	

Research continues on facing page, Results column.

*Research continues on facing page, Results column.

TABLE 5.1, cont.

RESULTS	CONCLUSIONS-IMPLICATIONS	SUPPORTIVE/NONSUPPORTIVE	PROBLEMS
No difference on incidental tasks 1 or 2 or on intentional task. Significant difference in favor of gifted on incidental Task B. Retardates gave more responses on Task B, but also gave more inaccurate responses.	1. Teachers can assume MRs have potential for incidental learning which probably is limited to the gross and obvious information while abstract information is either overlooked or insufficiently learned incidentally. 2. Complex incidental tasks are difficult for MRs as are complex intentional or directed tasks. Therefore in directed learning situations the teacher should go beyond mere label memory and into associations between objects, and their characteristics and functions, which should generalize into incidental learning skill improvement.	As incidental task becomes more complex MRs are inferior in accuracy but superior in number of responses. Only immediate incidental recall tested. Deficiency specific to complexity of tasks.	1. No etiological classification. 2. No incidental learning retention test. 3. No postexperimental inquiry. 4. B.L. Ss with IQs to 81 included.
Familial MR and normals scored significantly higher on *incidental learning* and *incidental recognition* than did organic retardates but did not differ from each other. No significant differences for any groups on *intentional learning, incidental recall, intentional recall* or *intentional recognition.* Therefore the initial *incidental learning* superiority disappeared for normals and familial MRs after 48 hr—they learned more than organics but recalled no more.	1. For children of this MA level, intentional and incidental learning processes appear to be independent—no correlations found between incidental learning and successive trials of intentional learning. Disagrees with Plenderleith and Postman (1956) who correlated these scores for college students. 2. Organic MRs demonstrate an incidental learning deficiency on certain tasks which is unrelated to their intentional learning ability. Familial retardates of the same MA do not show this deficiency.	Partially supportive of Type II deficiency as related to etiology and immediacy of incidental deficiency.	1. Methods of diagnosing etiology inexact (Hardman & Drew, 1975). 2. No postexperimental inquiry.
Normals performed significantly better on both *incidental* and *intentional* (immediate recall) *learning* tests. After 48 hr groups were equal on the *recognition* test of incidental learning while MRs retained intentional learning (*intentional recall*) better than normals.	1. "Normal children of the same CA as noninstitutionalized defectives learn more (with one presentation), both incidentally and intentionally" (p. 407). 2. This advantage was not evident on the recognition test 48 hr later. Therefore no support for a long-term memory deficiency.	Incidental learning deficiency in the mentally retarded is task specific rather than visible in all learning tasks. Supportive of an immediate incidental learning Type II and intentional learning (or short-term memory) deficiency in mild MRs.	1. No postexperimental inquiry. 2. B.L. Ss with IQs to 74 included.

159

TABLE 5.1, cont.

ARTICLE	MA MATCH	CA MATCH	MA-CA MATCH	ALL MR	INTENTIONAL TASK	INCIDENTAL TASK + TYPE
4. Singer (1964)			4 groups: MR—normal MR: mod-mild $\overline{IQ}$ = 51 $\overline{MA}_1$ = 5.7; $\overline{MA}_2$ = 9.9 $\overline{CA}_1$ = 11; $\overline{CA}_2$ = 19.3 Normals $\overline{IQ}$ = 101 $\overline{CA}_1$ = 6; $\overline{CA}_2$ = 10.5 N = 60		Instructed to remember as many names of plastic doll furniture as could. Presented for 4 sec. *Test*: 2 min immediate free recall of furniture names.	**Type I** 1. 6 tasks *active incidental*: e.g., S played with toy clock hands. Test: where was hand pointing when clock removed; color of large hand? 2. 8 tasks *passive incidental*: e.g., S watched E draw 9 circles in a row with the last circle larger than those preceding. Test: What did E do to the circle? **Type II Intrinsic** 3. *Misdirected incidental*: S named color of plastic doll furniture. *Test*: recall furniture names *Note*: tests presented only after all tasks administered to avoid giving learning set.*
5. Gardner & Brandl (1967)				3 groups: MR NI*, SR*, TI* MR: mild to B.L. $\overline{IQ}$ = 72 $\overline{MA}$ = 10.4 $\overline{CA}$ = 14.5 N = 54	Instructed to watch exposure window on drum and learn order of shapes by guessing each shape before its exposure. S continued until criterion of 1 perfect trial or 24 trials. *Measurement*: number trials to criterion and number of errors to criterion. *TI* selected prize or 50¢, which was received at criterion. *SR* intermittent praise for correct Rs and encouragement between trials.	**Type II Intrinsic** S viewed 5 colored geometric shapes at 2 sec rate on a revolving drum; each shape appeared twice per trial in a fixed order and had 2 colors associated with it. *Test*: recognition test involving matching color strips to 10 shape outlines arranged in order of presentation. *Measurement*: Number of correct matchings; ratio of number of trials in intentional task to number of correct matchings.

160

*Research continues on facing page, Results column.

TABLE 5.1, cont.

RESULTS	CONCLUSIONS-IMPLICATIONS	SUPPORTIVE/NONSUPPORTIVE	PROBLEMS

1. MRs in both age groups showed less incidental learning on the:
  a. active incidental tasks
  b. passive incidental tasks
2. No significant MA match difference on misdirected incidental task.
3. Significant CA match difference on misdirected incidental task (in agreement with Baumeister, 1963).
4. No significant difference on intentional learning between MA or CA match groups; however young MRs gave more incorrect responses than MA and matched normals and than older MRs.
	1. The ability to learn incidentally increases with age in normals as well as MRs.
	2. The incidental learning deficiency appears to be present in MRs over a wide age range (5–20 yr) and seems related to inability to respond consistently.
	3. Young and older MRs can learn well intentionally but young MRs tend to over respond and are less accurate than normals (supports notion of inhibition deficiency).
	4. Educational programs for MRs should include much directed, specifically detailed instruction. This direction should increase with task complexity. On very simple tasks MRs have some potential for incidental learning. MRs need encouragement to respond consistently.
		Supportive of incidental learning deficiency on Type I tasks in moderate MRs when compared to MA- and CA-matched normals.
		Supportive of inhibition deficiency for younger MRs.
			1. No postexperimental inquiry.

1. SR learned intentional task in fewer trials than NI and TI who did not differ on either measure. 2. Incidental learning was as good in SR as in TI and NI despite the fact that these Ss had significantly less exposure to the incidental stimuli. 3. Postexperimental inquiry results revealed that the 67% in TI reporting no implicit set (true incidental learners) showed no incidental learning beyond chance.	1. Social incentives which provide MRs with immediate knowledge or correct responses increase speed of intentional learning. 2. "Social incentive condition resulted in more efficient incidental learning" (p. 218). 3. The tangible incentive condition seems to reduce attention to irrelevant cues (decreases incidental learning) by directing learners to use the specific set and limit attention to relevant cues.	Consistent with Postman's (1963) conclusions about effect of incentive in Type II Intrinsic incidental task with normals. No normal comparison group therefore no conclusions regarding incidental learning deficiency in MRs.	1. MR sample included B.L. Ss with IQs to 85.

TABLE 5.1, cont.

ARTICLE	MA MATCH	CA MATCH	MA-CA MATCH	ALL MR	INTENTIONAL TASK	INCIDENTAL TASK + TYPE
6. Logan, Prehm, & Drew (1968)		4 groups: MR normal HAV* LAV* MR: mod-B.L. IQ = 71 MA = 11.0 CA = 16.4 N = 96			Instructions not reported but all Ss were trained to criterion or a specified number of trials either on HAV or LAV paired associates such that the first word was the S for the second word (R). *Test:* Half in each treatment group were tested in a Forward S-R manner on the paired associates. Testing was immediate recall, and recall 24 hr later.	**Type II Intrinsic** Trained to learn paired associates in S-R order. *Test:* Half in each treatment group tested in a backward R-S manner on the paired associates. Testing was immediate recall, and recall 24 hr later.*
7. Mintzes (1970)			12 groups: Institutionalized or noninstitutionalized. Intentional or incidental task. MR, young normal (MA matched), or older normal (CA matched).		S shown same series of figures but was directed to attend to the last figure in each series by E's words: "Now, watch what I'm going to do to this one." The test for intentional recall was the same as for incidental recall. The 3-min, unrelated intermediate task also preceded the test for intentional learning. It involved repeated tracing of a stencil to make a pattern.	**Type I** Similar to Singer's (1964) *passive incidental* task. S watched E draw 10 separate series of figures. In each series the end figure was drawn slightly different (e.g., 11 x's drawn and the last in the row had a circle made around it). The test was given following a 3-minute unrelated intermediary task by asking the S to recall or show what was done to one of the figures in each of the 10 series.

162

*Research continues on facing page, Results column.

RESULTS	CONCLUSIONS-IMPLICATIONS	SUPPORTIVE/NONSUPPORTIVE	PROBLEMS

1. Analysis of immediate recall data revealed no significant differences between main effects (MR vs. normal; HAV vs. LAV; forward or intentional vs. backward or incidental learning) nor any interaction effects.
2. For the 24-hr recall data only the subject classification was significant—24-hr recall, in all conditions, was better for normals than retarded Ss.
	1. "In so far as backward recall is a test of incidental learning, no support for the hypothesis that retardates exhibit an incidental learning deficit is provided by the present data" (p. 495).
	2. "When amount of original learning is taken into account through statistical control, the immediate associative recall performance of the MR, HAV or LAV and S-R or R-S, does not differ from that of normals while 24-hr recall does."
		1. Provides no support of incidental learning deficiency but weaknesses are evident in:
		  a. MR sample too much like normal
		  b. incidental task too simple
		2. The second conclusion is in direct contrast to previous investigation since no short-term memory deficiency was found (Hardman & Drew, 1975).
			1. No postexperimental inquiry.
			2. MR sample included many B.L. Ss (5 with IQs > 83).
			3. R-S is a very simple test of incidental learning.

1. Institutionalized retardates were deficient in their incidental learning skills when compared to normals (institutionalized and noninstitutionalized as well as CA- or MA-matched) while the same was not true for noninstitutionalized retardates. 2. Institutionalized retardates were also deficient in their intentional learning skills as a result of a low MA and low IQ. However, noninstitutionalized retardates were not significantly different in intentional learning from noninstitutionalized normals. 3. In general subjects receiving the intentional task performed better than did subjects receiving the incidental task.	1. Institutionalization affects retardates in their ability to learn incidentally as well as intentionally. 2. The incidental learning deficiency, a result of a low MA-low IQ, appeared when MRs were compared to CA- or MA-matched normals. Therefore, "having a low IQ is sufficient to cause the deficit on incidental learning among institutionalized retardates" (Mintzes, 1970, p. 50). 3. Intentional learning among institutionalized retardates in comparison to institutionalized normals is depressed only by the combination of lower MA and IQ (i.e., younger normals matched on MA with retardates were not significantly different from retardates). 4. The institutionalized retardate's attention must be directed to materials and information rather than assume she will learn on her own. Tasks relying upon incidental learning should be replaced by tasks involving structured intentional learning.	Supportive of the incidental learning deficiency for only institutionalized retardates who performed significantly worse than older and younger institutionalized normals on Type I tasks.	1. Institutionalized MR Ss were institutionalized for a noticeably longer period than were the other institutionalized groups. 2. Institutionalized MR Ss had a much lower mean IQ than did the noninstitutionalized retardates.

TABLE 5.1, cont.

ARTICLE	MA MATCH	CA MATCH	MA-CA MATCH	ALL MR	INTENTIONAL TASK	INCIDENTAL TASK + TYPE
8. Williams (1970)		6 groups: MR Normal Gifted Readiness and nonreadiness. MR: mod-B.L. $\overline{IQ} = 67$ $\overline{MA} = 5.8$ $\overline{CA} = 8.7$ Normal $\overline{MA} = 8$ Gifted $\overline{MA} = 13.8$ $N = 90$			Ss instructed to match numeral puzzle pieces (1–8) into formboard holes which had the matching set of dots beside it. Also on the other side of each hole and unmentioned by E were single pictures of objects viewed during readiness. Formboard was filled 3 times. Intentional learning was measured by the association between number pieces and the count of dots.	**Type II Extrinsic** *Orienting task (readiness):* Ss played with and talked about model toys which were later represented by pictures in intentional task. *Test:* Ss placed numeral pieces into a second formboard with pictures but without sets of dots by holes. Order of pictures varied from Formboard 1. Number of correct picture-numeral associations was measured.*
9. Ross (1970a)				2 groups: Experimental (Exp.) and control (C). Ss matched on MA, CA, IQ. *Number Knowledge Test* and *Game Skill Test* scores. $\overline{IQ} = 66$ $\overline{MA} = 5.1$ $\overline{CA} = 7.7$ $N = 40$	Control group Ss spent 100 min/wk over 9 mo in a traditional special class numbers instructional program. Ss also spent same amount of time as Exp. group with E in Exp. setting to control for Hawthorne effect. Ss received: 1. *directed* classroom instruction in number concepts 2. no instruction in game skills Learning in both groups measured on: 1. *Number Knowledge Test* 2. *Game Skill Test*	**Type II Extrinsic** Exp. Ss spent same amount of time with E in Exp. room in a small group game instruction program which incidentally covered the same number concepts covered in classroom control group. Ss received: 1. Incidental learning of number concepts as related to game content 2. Directed, but play-oriented, instruction of game skills and behavior (models used, active participation, knowledge of results and shaping employed, prevention of continued failure).

164

*Research continues on facing page, Results column.

TABLE 5.1, cont.

RESULTS	CONCLUSIONS-IMPLICATIONS	SUPPORTIVE/NONSUPPORTIVE	PROBLEMS

1. Interaction effect between IQ groups and readiness was significant.
  a. Effect of readiness significantly improved incidental learning in both MRs and normals to a point equal with that of gifted (in readiness condition).
  b. Readiness did not affect incidental learning among gifted; gifted incidental learning performance was higher in nonreadiness condition.
2. In nonreadiness condition gifted had significantly higher levels of incidental learning than MRs and normals.
	1. "The assumption that preparation for learning or readiness is necessary for learning to occur more rapidly if familiarization with the learning material has been established was validated for the EMR and normal subjects" (p. 119). Readiness activities of primary classrooms (looking at, feeling materials, etc.) appear to be of significant value in increasing the amount of incidental learning for EMR and normal students.
	2. However, children in gifted range may require another type of preparation for learning since readiness appears to depress their incidental learning.
		1. Provides some support for less efficient incidental learning which is remediable in mild MRs and normals: "The author's statement that incidental learning is not contingent upon intelligence is not entirely supported by the data. Incidental learning does not seem contingent upon intelligence if it is prompted" (Hardman & Drew, 1975, p. 6).	1. No postexperimental inquiry.

1. Exp. Ss improved significantly more than control Ss on *Number Knowledge Test:*
  a. specific quantitative skills (counting time, money, etc.).
  b. spontaneous quantitative vocabulary usage (number quantitative items *S* used to describe 10 pictures)
2. Exp. Ss demonstrated significant gains in general game skills over the control group by a reduction in the number of errors made during test game situations (game rules, taking turns, being a loser, handling materials, etc.). Control group scores remained unchanged.
	Methods of instruction for MRs in game skills include:
	  a. initial prevention of failure
	  b. programming of continued and consistent correct responding
	  c. provision of immediate knowledge of accuracy of response and reinforcement for correct responses
	  d. programming of overt rehearsal of correct response by Ss telling model how to correctly play games
	  e. Highly motivating games and attention-directing game materials tend to result in more effective learning of number concepts and terminology incidentally than through tradition directed (intentional) instruction.
		Indirectly opposes incidental learning deficiency (although directed instruction in classroom group is quite different than directed instruction methods used in game group), since MRs, under optimal learning conditions, were able to learn incidentally.
		No normal comparison group—therefore no direct conclusion about MR incidental learning gains.
			1. Needs another group with intentional number instruction which incorporates methods of instruction similar to Exp. group and incidentally teaches game skills so amounts of intentional and incidental learning can be compared.

165

TABLE 5.1, cont.

ARTICLE	MA MATCH	CA MATCH	MA-CA MATCH	ALL MR	INTENTIONAL TASK	INCIDENTAL TASK + TYPE
10. Ross (1970b)				3 groups: MR tangible, praise, and neutral comment. *MR:* mild-B.L. $\overline{IQ} = 69$ $\overline{MA} = 5.4$ $\overline{CA} = 7.9$ N = 36	Ss instructed to play the game and learn to follow its 10 rules under the instruction of *E. AM* also played, broke rules repeatedly allowing *E* to draw attention to rules (remain seated during AM's turn; say "Penny for the Pig," etc.). Three days training. *Conditions:* Tangible reward—*S* picked a prize which she obtained if she won more fish in game than AM; Praise—*E* made supportive comments concerning Ss performance; Neutral—*E* commented on Ss performance but not praise. *Test:* Fourth day for knowledge of rules and on 11th day for retention (no. of rules followed).	**Type II Intrinsic** Adult model (*AM*) exhibited 16 mannerisms which were paired with verbal commands. The mannerisms (e.g., hand on chin) comprised the incidental stimuli. Neither *AM* or *E* attended to the *S* if she produced any of the mannerisms. *Test:* No. of mannerisms displayed during test playing of game. *Post-Exp. Inquiry:* Asked to explain rules of game. None referred to mannerisms rules; 6 said they were "things you could do if you wanted to."*

166

*Research continues on facing page, Results column.

TABLE 5.1, cont.

RESULTS	CONCLUSIONS-IMPLICATIONS	SUPPORTIVE/NONSUPPORTIVE	PROBLEMS

1. Intentional learning varies as a function of reward.
  a. Highest scores were associated with tangible reward (learning and retention).
  b. Praise yielded higher scores than neutral comments for learning but not for retention.
2. Incidental learning varies inversely as a function of reward.
  a. Highest scores were associated with neutral comment (for learning and retention).
  b. Praise and tangible reward both yielded lower incidental learning scores than neutral comment (for learning and retention).
	1. An inverse relationship exists between motivational level and incidental learning which is "due to a restriction of perceptual range as the incentive increases and has no relationship to the amount of learning that the S is able to acquire" (p. 1157).
	  a. Task competition (incidental vs. intentional) resulted since total number of learning responses (incidental plus intentional) was not different across groups.
	  b. The use of tangibles should be carefully limited and used on an intermittent level in directed learning tasks without letting motivational level drop.
	2. The abilities to distinguish relevant from irrelevant in a learning situation and to respond consistently (selective attention components) could be improved through graded series of Type II incidental learning tasks by varying motivational supports.
		Since there were no group comparison with normals, no direct conclusions can be drawn regarding the MR incidental learning deficiency. However, the inverse relationship between incentive and incidental learning is one that also holds true to normal populations (Postman, 1963).	1. MR sample included B.L. Ss with IQs to 79.

TABLE 5.1, cont.

ARTICLE	MA MATCH	CA MATCH	MA-CA MATCH	ALL MR	INTENTIONAL TASK	INCIDENTAL TASK + TYPE
11. Hagan & Huntsman (1971) (a) Study I	8 groups: MR—normal at four MA levels MR: mod-B.L. IQ: 46; 55; 76; 78 MA: 3–10; 6–0; 6–4; 8–9 CA: 8–9; 13; 9; 11–4 Normals: CA 4–0; 5–7; 6–5; 8–6 47 normal 61 MR				Ss instructed to point to and remember the animal in a series of 6 picture cards. Each card had a picture of an animal (central–intentional stimuli) and a common household object (incidental stimuli). The outline paired drawings were slightly touching each other on the picture card. Ss were told to ignore the household object picture and remember after 2–3 practice trials the order of each animal. *Central test:* After each of 12 trials where pictures were individually exposed 2 sec each in a series, Ss were asked to locate the facedown card in the series which matched the one presented by *E.* Score was the number correct over the 12 test trials. *Memory span test:* Recalling a given series of animal-only picture cards. Span equalled point at which 50% were correctly recalled. *Labeling Readiness: S* asked to say what she called each animal; the latency between picture presentation and response was measure of *S's* availability of labels for stimuli.	**Type II Intrinsic** Ss were asked to ignore the household object pictures (incidental stimuli) as unimportant while attending to the central stimuli. *Test:* Serial recognition was measured; Ss asked to match household object pictures to the associated animal when the series of 6 animal-only cards were presented. Score was correct matches.*

168

*Research continues on facing page, Results column.

TABLE 5.1, cont.

169

RESULTS

1. No significant difference between MA-matched normal and MR group means for intentional or incidental learning scores.
2. Significant differences found for both intentional and incidental scores and for MA.
3. The trend of correlations occurring between intentional and incidental recall scores for MRs is from high to low as MA increases.
4. A positive relationship resulted between speed of labeling (labeling readiness test) and short-term memory performance (*STM Span Test*).

CONCLUSIONS-IMPLICATIONS

"The results of this study confirmed that central versus incidental task performance showed the same improvement with increasing MA as has been found with CA. However, normal and retarded children, when matched on MA, were not found to perform differently on these measures" (p. 155).

SUPPORTIVE/NONSUPPORTIVE

No support for an incidental learning deficiency or a selective attention deficiency (ability to attend to the relevant dimension of the Ss and to respond to the correct one of that dimension) in mild to moderate MRs when compared to equal MA normals.

PROBLEMS

1. MR sample included B.L. Ss with $\overline{\text{IQ}}$ in top 2 MA groups in B.L. range.
2. Third highest MA group had 10 mo $\overline{\text{MA}}$ difference between MRs and normals.

TABLE 5.1, cont.

ARTICLE	MA MATCH	CA MATCH	MA-CA MATCH	ALL MR	INTENTIONAL TASK	INCIDENTAL TASK + TYPE
12. Hagan & Huntsman (1971) (b) Study II	2 additional groups: institutionalized MR at 2 MA levels. IQ: 79; 76 MA: 7–5; 9–0 CA: 9–4; 11–9 N = 21 MR: mild-B.L.				Same task; no test of labeling readiness given.	Same task repeated.*
13. Cegelka (1972)	4 groups: MR—normal: structured (A). MR—normal: less structured (B). MR: mild-B.L. IQ = 70 MA = 7.2 CA = 10.3 *Normals:* CA = 6.9 N = 60				In groups A only Ss were instructed to replace 10 randomly colored (4 colors) forms into a formboard as quickly as possible. Two practice trials. *Test:* No test of intentional learning given.	**Type I (B Condition)** Orienting task Ss given colored shape formboard to "play" with for same period of time as A. Forms were inserted into formboard prior to presentation. **Type II Intrinsic (A Condition)** Intentional task followed by incidental test. *Test:* Both A and B tested for incidental learning of form-color association of naming associated color when each form in an identical but uncolored formboard was pointed to. Score was number of correct associations.

170

*Research continues on facing page, Results column.

TABLE 5.1, cont.

RESULTS	CONCLUSIONS-IMPLICATIONS	SUPPORTIVE/NONSUPPORTIVE	PROBLEMS
Intentional-incidental scores of institutionalized MRs differed significantly from normals and noninstitutionalized MRs. When MA groups were compared (MA 6.4 and 8.9), incidental learning was greater and intentional learning less for institutionalized MRs than for normals and noninstitutionalized MRs.	For institutionalized MRs but not for noninstitutionalized MRs the ability to attend to the relevant aspects of the task and ignore the irrelevant aspects (selective attention) is more deficient than for equal MA normals. Hagan and Huntsman argued that the task performance deficiencies were not due to institutionalization alone; not only motivational and affective variables (Zigler, 1966) but also relevant environmental and/or biological factors may have caused the 2 MR groups to differ significantly prior to institutionalization.	The attention deficiency hypothesis was confirmed for institutionalized MRs. No support for incidental learning deficiency in institutionalized mild MRs as compared to equal MA normals.	1. Institutionalized MR sample included many from B.L. range, and all were inner-city children institutionalized for behavior/delinquency problems rather than retardation alone. 2. Third highest MA group had 13-mo difference between institutionalized MR group and noninstitutionalized MR.
1. Significant difference between mean incidental scores (A and B combined) of MRs and normals, with normals performing significantly better in incidental learning. 2. No significant difference in condition A and B incidental learning scores—no interaction between conditions and IQ level.	In intentional task for groups A the instructed response (visual motor) was nonfacilitative to the incidental response (verbal-color naming) while in the orienting task for groups B, although no visual-motor responses were requested or encouraged (since formboard was presented completed), a verbal response set was also not established. MRs were less apt to self-initiate verbal sets when given visual-motor sets (A) or no set (B) than were normals, thereby decreasing the amount of incidental learning for MRs.	Supports an incidental learning deficiency in mild MRs as compared with equal MA Ss on both Type I and Type II Intrinsic when instructed response (Type II) is visual motor and the incidental response is verbal.	1. No postexperimental inquiry. 2. No measure of intentional learning in group A (normal and MR). 3. Confused use of term *orienting task*. 4. MR sample included some B.L.

TABLE 5.1, cont.

ARTICLE	MA MATCH	CA MATCH	MA-CA MATCH	ALL MR	INTENTIONAL TASK	INCIDENTAL TASK + TYPE
14. Deich (1974)	2 groups: MR normal MR: mod-mild $\overline{IQ}$ = 51 Institutionalized "organics" $\overline{MA}$ = 6.9 $\overline{CA}$ = 18.4 Institutionalized "organics" Normals: $\overline{CA}$ = 6.1 Kindergarteners N = 36				*Task O*—Ss instructed to label color of each picture in a series of 12 pictures of common objects. Four colors were used, 3 objects colored 1 of the 4 colors. Shown series 3 times for practice in different orders. *Task G*—Ss instructed to sort by shape 20 geometric forms, 5 different shapes; identical shapes had the same color (5 colors used). Sorting was done by matching one at a time to noncolored shape outlines. Sorted shape was removed after each sort. *Test:* None; some MRs eliminated for being unable to perform intentional learning task. Both intentional tasks preceded incidental tests.	**Type II Intrinsic** (O and G) *Task O*—Free recall test: 2 minutes to name as many pictures as could remember in series. *Recognition test:* Selected stimulus picture from 12 recognition sets (4 black and white pictures in each set, 1 picture from original series). *Task G*—Free recall test: asked to name the 5 colors that appeared in the different shapes. *Recognition test:* From set of 5 colored single shapes S selected color each shape originally appeared in.*

*Research continues on facing page, Results column.

TABLE 5.1, cont.

RESULTS	CONCLUSIONS-IMPLICATIONS	SUPPORTIVE/NONSUPPORTIVE	PROBLEMS
1. For Task O, normals had a higher combined incidental learning score than MRs; when compared on recognition and recall scores, the normal's significant advantage occurred in the recognition test. 2. For Task G no significant differences occurred between normal and MR groups on combined incidental learning scores (recognition and recall test scores). a. For free recall on Task G, although there was no difference in incidental learning by groups, retardates had a higher error rate.	The two tasks (G and O) differed to the extent to which incidental learning was shown. "Where incidental learning occurred unequivocally, it did so in retardates as well as in normals. Familiar objects, Task O, clearly demonstrated that retardates learned incidentally but that they were inferior to a normal peer group, significantly so when recognition was the measure" (p. 541).	Supports an incidental learning deficiency in institutionalized moderate MRs as compared with equal MA Ss on Type II Intrinsic tasks. "One may conclude that, although the conditions under which an incidental learning deficit will arise are not precisely predictable, present retardates did more poorly than their normal peers in incidental learning" (p. 542).	1. No postexperimental inquiry. 2. No intentional learning measure.

B.L. = Borderline range of intelligence (WISC = 70–85)
E = Experimenter
HAV = High association value
LAV = Low association value
Mild = Mildly retarded range of intelligence (WISC = 55–70)
Mod = Moderately retarded range of intelligence (WISC = 40–55)
N = Total number of Ss
NI = No incentive
S = Stimulus
SR = Social reward
TI = Tangible incentive

173

5. The difference between relative amounts of intentional and incidental learning "reduces to zero under conditions which appear to approximate the two extremes of the continuum of orienting tasks, i.e., when learning is either seriously hindered or substantially facilitated by the orienting task" (Postman, 1963, p. 189). Both instructions to learn and orienting tasks have indirect effects on learning in that they activate responses to the materials which may be favorable to acquisition.

6. According to Deese (1963),

   Postman's conclusion leads to the implication, supported by the analysis of many problems in human learning, including both incidental learning and short-term memory, that variables are effective in controlling the amount and rate of learning to the extent that they control the distribution and frequency of appropriate responses to the stimulus material. Therefore, as Postman asserts in his conclusion, we do not need to appeal to special principles of intent or motivation or incentive learning. Learning will take place to the extent that it is possible to induce Ss to emit the appropriate responses. There is undoubtedly an implication here for those who design programs for machine teaching. (p. 206)

Several facts about incidental learning in the retarded have also been uncovered:

1. As the complexity of the incidental learning task increases, a deficiency in learning is more apt to appear for MRs. Incidental learning deficiency in MRs is specific to the task (Baumeister, 1963; Goldstein & Kass, 1961; Singer, 1964).
2. Organic MRs demonstrate a deficiency in incidental learning (Deich, 1974; Hetherington & Banta, 1962), while familial MRs do not demonstrate such a deficiency when compared to normals (Hetherington & Banta, 1962).
3. MRs have some potential for incidental learning in these instances (Baumeister, 1963; Deich, 1974; Hagan & Huntsman, 1971; Logan, Prehm, & Drew, 1968):
   a. Simple tasks (Goldstein & Kass, 1961; Singer, 1964).
   b. Readiness tasks provided with the incidental learning materials (Ross, 1970a; Williams, 1970).
   c. Response to incidental (irrelevant) materials similar to the response to intentional (relevant) materials (Cegelka, 1972).
   d. Tangible and social incentives given for intentional learning carefully limited in order not to narrow or restrict the learner's perceptual range to the relevant cues (Gardner & Brandl, 1967; Hardman & Drew, 1975; Ross, 1970b).
   e. Initial learning prevents failure by:

1) programming continued and consistent correct incidental and intentional responding
2) providing immediate knowledge of accuracy of response and social reinforcement for correct incidental and intentional responding
3) programming opportunities for overt rehearsal of correct incidental and intentional responses with learners correcting the errors of models
3) using highly motivating game-like learning situations (Ross, 1970a; Singer, 1964)

f. Intentional educational programs directed with specifically detailed instruction which increases with task complexity and encourages consistent responding (Mintzes, 1970; Singer, 1964).
g. Directive teaching of association skills (characteristics and functions of objects, people, etc.) rather than limiting intentional instruction to memory for labels (Goldstein & Kass, 1961).
h. The teaching of MRs to remain aware of incidental cues (through prompting and cueing) in the learning environment while concentrating on a directed instructional task (Hardman & Drew, 1975).

SYNOPSIS OF RESEARCH RESULTS. With regards to a final conclusion on the existence of an incidental learning deficiency in retardates, Table 5.2 is a rough attempt to provide a comparative synopsis of the research results. In spite of the obvious need for more systematic research, it seems that now there is somewhat more evidence showing poorer incidental learning of Type I and some Type II intrinsic tasks in the mentally retarded when their learning is compared to that of normals who are MA or CA equal. Also it appears that the effect of reinforcement on the incidental and intentional learning of retardates is similar to that of normal learners.

SUPPORT FOR DENNY'S TEACHING PRINCIPLES. In addition, the studies reviewed provide some support for Denny's principles of teaching the retarded:

1. Tangible incentives act to reduce the learner's attention for irrelevant cues (thereby decreasing incidental learning) by directing learners to use specific sets and increasing the distinctiveness of the relevant cues (Gardner & Brandl, 1967; Ross, 1970b).
2. Educational programs for the retarded should include directed, structured teaching which makes use of detailed instruction that increases with task complexity and encourages consistent responding by the learner (Singer, 1964).
3. Instruction of the retarded should incorporate teaching methods which:
   a. prevent failure in early learning
   b. encourage generalization of learned responses

TABLE 5.2
Summary of Incidental Learning Deficiency Research

	TYPE I INCIDENTAL LEARNING	TYPE II EXTRINSIC INCIDENTAL LEARNING	TYPE II INTRINSIC INCIDENTAL LEARNING
MA matched (normals + MR)	Cegelka, 1972 + Singer*, 1964 +		Cegelka, 1972 + Deich*, 1974 + Goldstein & Kass, 1961 (+) Hetherington & Banta, 1962 (+) Singer*, 1964 − Hagan & Huntsman, 1971 −
CA matched (normals + MR)	Singer*, 1964 + Mintzes, 1970 (+)	Williams, 1970 (+) Ross 1970a (−)	Baumeister, 1963 − Singer*, 1964 + Logan, Prehm & Drew, 1968 −
MR only: incidental learning characteristics similar to normals			Effects of reinforcement and no incentive: a. Gardner & Brandl, 1967 + b. Ross, 1970b + Developmental decline in incidental learning for noninstitutionalized MR: a. Hagan & Huntsman, 1971 + b. Singer, 1964 −

NOTE: *MR samples primarily from moderate range of retardation (IQ 40–55); all other samples employed primarily mild MRs, borderline normals or combinations of these two groups.
+ Data support incidental learning deficiency in MR.
(+) Data are partially supportive.
− Data do not support.
(−) Data are partially nonsupportive.

175

c. facilitate correct responding by the learners
d. provide immediate knowledge of response accuracy
e. provide reinforcement for correct responses
f. allow overt rehearsal of correct responses
g. operate within highly motivating game-like situations
h. use attention-directing materials (Ross, 1970a, 1970b)

4. Readiness (familiarity with learning materials) serves to increase the saliency of learning cues and serves as a method of increasing success in initial learning (Williams, 1970).

Summary

In this chapter a detailed description of elicitation theory was presented including the basic definitions of stimulus, response, and response tendency which underlie an understanding of the theory's principles. A few classroom stimulus situations were analyzed to illustrate the back-chaining order in which learning takes place. Also the concepts of stimulus hierarchy, the satiation hypothesis, and stimulus generalization were examined.

Next, as described by Denny (1964), the learning deficiencies of the mentally retarded were outlined. This was followed by a careful delineation of a set of instructional principles, derived from elicitation theory, meant to create optimal learning conditions for the retarded. The Learning Box, Denny's teaching machine which incorporates many of the instructional principles, and its supportive research were then presented.

The final section of the chapter dealt with the incidental learning deficiency of the mentally retarded as proposed by Denny (1964). Characteristics of incidental learning in the retarded were presented. The various incidental and intentional learning paradigms were defined followed by an outline summary of recent research in incidental learning of the retarded. Finally, some conclusions were drawn regarding retardate incidental learning and the instructional principles derived from elicitation theory.

Notes

1. This learning is more complex and occurs only after a CR to the CS has been well established (first order conditioning) and it involves conditioning the same CR to a new CS by using the original CS as the US or functional US.

2. *Incidental learning* is defined as the "acquisition of knowledge about stimuli other than those relevant to a directed learning task" (Goldstein & Kass, 1961, p. 245), and as a type of learning "when the instructions do not prepare the S for a test on a given type of material" (Postman, 1963, p. 185).

3. Learning Box was adapted from a similar device used with chronic schizophrenics, the Multiple Operant Problem Solving Apparatus (MOPSA) (King, Armitage, & Tilton, 1960).

4. Pilot studies are presently underway at Western Carolina Center, Morganton, North Carolina, to investigate further uses of the Learning Box with severely-profoundly retarded residents in the acquisition of beginning receptive labeling skills (Figpen, M., Director of Education, Personal communication, June 11, 1975).

References

Baumeister, A. A. A comparison of normals and retardates with respect to incidental and intentional learning. *American Journal of Mental Deficiency*, 1963, *68*, 404–408.

Cegelka, P. T. Incidental learning in nonretarded and retarded children. *American Journal of Mental Deficiency*, 1972, *76*, 581–585.

Deese, J. Behavioral effects of instruction to learn: Comments on Professor Postman's paper. In A. W. Melton (Ed.), *Categories of human learning*. New York: Academic Press, 1963.

Deich, R. F. Incidental learning and short-range memory in normals and retardates. *Perceptual and Motor Skills*, 1974, *38*, 539–542.

Denny, M. R. Learning through stimulus satiation. *Journal of Experimental Psychology*, 1957, *54*, 62–64.

Denny, M. R. Research in learning and performance. In H. Stevens & R. Heber (Eds.), *Mental retardation: A review of research*. Chicago: University of Chicago Press, 1964.

Denny, M. R. A theoretical analysis and its application to training the mentally retarded. In N. R. Ellis (Ed.), *International review of research in mental retardation* (Vol. 2). New York: Academic Press, 1966.

Denny, M. R. A theory of experimental extinction and its relation to a general theory. In H. M. Kendler & J. T. Spence (Eds.), *Essays in Neobehaviorism: A memorial volume to Kenneth W. Spence*. New York: Appleton-Century-Crofts, 1971.

Denny, M. R. & Adelman, H. M. Elicitation theory: I. An analysis of two typical learning situations. *Psychological Review*, 1955, *62*, 290–296.

Denny, M. R., & Denny, R. *Manual for the learning box.* Unpublished manuscript, Michigan State University, 1973.

Denny, M. R., & Dunham, M. D. The effect of differential nonreinforcement of the incorrect response on the learning of the correct response in the simple T-maze. *Journal of Experimental Psychology*, 1951, *41*, 382–389.

Denny, M. R., & Ratner, S. C. *Comparative psychology: Research in animal behavior* (Rev. ed.). Homewood, Ill.: Dorsey Press, 1970.

Estes, W. K. *Learning theory and mental development.* New York: Academic Press, 1970.

Evans, S., & Denny, M. R. *Reading achievement program for the moderately and severely retarded.* Danville, Ill.: Interstate, 1974.

Evans, T. E. The effect of a modeling technique on the learning of four tasks by retardates. Master's thesis, Michigan State University, 1968.

Gardner, W. I., & Brandl, C. Reinforcement conditions and incidental learning in mentally retarded adolescents. *American Journal of Mental Deficiency*, 1967, *72*, 215–219.

Goldstein, H., & Kass, M. A. Incidental learning of educable mentally retarded and gifted children. *American Journal of Mental Deficiency*, 1961, *66*, 245–249.

Hagan, J. W., & Huntsman, N. J. Selective attention in mental retardates. *Developmental Psychology*, 1971, *5*, 151–160.

Hardman, M. L., & Drew, C. J. Incidental learning in the mentally retarded: A review. *Education and Training of the Mentally Retarded*, 1975, *10*, 3–9.

Hetherington, E. M., & Banta, T. J. Incidental and intentional learning in normal and mentally retarded children. *Journal of Comparative and Physiological Psychology*, 1962, *55*, 402–404.

King, G. E., Armitage, S. G., & Tilton, J. R. A therapeutic approach to schizophrenics of extreme pathology: An operant-interpersonal method. *Journal of Abnormal Social Psychology*, 1960, *61*, 276–286.

Logan, D. R., Prehm, H. J., & Drew, C. J. Effects of unidirectional training on bidirectional recall in retarded and nonretarded subjects. *American Journal of Mental Deficiency*, 1968, *73*, 493–495.

Maatsch, J. L., Adelman, H. M., & Denny, M. R. Effort and resistance to extinction of the bar pressing response. *Journal of Comparative and Physiological Psychology*, 1954, *47*, 47–50.

Mintzes, B. A comparison of institutionalized and noninstitutionalized mentally retarded children and intellectually normal children on incidental and intentional learning tasks (Doctoral dissertation, Michigan State University, 1970). *Dissertation Abstracts International*, 1971, *31*, 3993. (University Microfilms No. 71–02126)

Plenderleith, M., & Postman, L. Discriminative and verbal habits in incidental learning. *American Journal of Psychology*, 1956, *69*, 236–243.

Postman, L. Short-term memory and incidental learning. In A. W. Melton (Ed.), *Categories of human learning*. New York: Academic Press, 1963.

Ross, D. *Pacemaker games program for mentally retarded children*. Palo Alto: Fearon, 1968.

Ross, D. Incidental learning of number concepts in small group games. *American Journal of Mental Deficiency*, 1970, *74*, 718–724. (a)

Ross, D. The relationship between intentional learning, incidental learning, and type of reward in preschool, educable, mental retardates. *Child Development*, 1970, *41*, 1151–1158. (b)

Sinclair, J. A. Imitation learning in the severely retarded (Doctoral dissertation, Michigan State University, 1968). *Dissertation Abstracts*, 1969, *29*, 3949. (University Microfilms No. 69–05950)

Singer, R. V. Incidental and intentional learning in retarded and normal children (Doctoral dissertation, Michigan State University, 1964). *Dissertation Abstracts*, 1964, *25*, 652. (University Microfilms No. 64–7544)

Williams, E. H. Effects of readiness on incidental learning in EMR, normal, and gifted children. *American Journal of Mental Deficiency*, 1970, *75*, 117–119.

Yascolt, M. A. Analysis of a method of training the mentally retarded. Master's thesis, Michigan State University, 1966.

Zigler, E. Mental retardation: Current issues and approaches. In L. Hoffman & M. Hoffman (Eds.), *Review of child development research* (Vol. 2). New York: Russell Sage Foundation, 1966.

6

Social Learning Theory

While constructs such as attention, memory, and perception have unequivocally persisted throughout the psychological literature concerned with learning, there has been—until recently—a definite paucity of social learning theory research. The processes concerned with the areas of personality development and socialization were considered as not adaptable to the rigorous empirical standards adhered to by most cognitive-oriented learning theorists. Rotter (1954), through his formulation of a social learning theory introduces the study of social behaviors via an empirical process. He further indicates (1975) how the social learning theory attempts to deal with the complexity of human behavior without sacrificing the use of operational constructs and empirically testable hypotheses. Moreover, he notes that SLT attempts to mesh the stimulus-response or reinforcement theories with the cognitive or field theories. In a discussion of theoretical approaches to personality development, Estes (1970) recognizes the empirical emphasis of SLT when he concludes that "the one most amenable to discussion

in the same context with theories of learning and memory is that which has been termed the 'social-learning approach' " (p. 126).

Description of Social Learning Theory

Parameters of Social Learning Theory

The social learning approach, formulated by Julian Rotter in 1954, is based on the premise that a person's interaction with his meaningful environment establishes an area rich in potential for investigation. This interaction in the meaningful environment has a directional quality which is characterized by a person moving away from (avoidance behavior) or toward (approach behavior) objects. Thus goal objects and threat objects provide a basis for predicting and examining social behavior. Within the SLT context, behavior, expectancies, reinforcements, and psychological situations are recognized as four classes of variables which influence social learning. Rotter (1975) notes that a relationship between the four classes of variables exists and this relationship is expressed in the formula:

Behavior Potential =
    f(Expectancy & Reinforcement Value)

This formula represents the relationships in their most basic form and essentially states that "the potential for a behavior to occur in any specific psychological situation is a function of the expectancy that the behavior will lead to a particular reinforcement in that situation and the value of that reinforcement" (Rotter, 1975, p. 57).

EXPECTANCY. As noted in the formula, the construct of expectancy is a salient component of SLT. Specifically, Rotter states that "Expectancies in each situation are determined not only by specific experiences in that situation but also, to some varying extent, by experiences in other situations that the individual perceives as similar" (p. 57). This statement points out the relative importance of experiences in a specific situation to expectancy formulations. The relationships between specific expectancies developed through experiences in a specific situation and generalized expectancy are expressed in the formula (Rotter, 1954):

$$E_{s_1} = f(E_{s_1}^1 + \frac{GE}{N_{s_1}})$$

In this formula, s_1 represents the specific situation; N represents the previous experiences of the individual in the situation; E is expectancy; E^1 is specific expectancy; and GE denotes generalized expectancy. Thus, expectancy in a specific situation is a function of specific expectancy for that situation plus the generalized expectancy, which is divided by the experiences of the individual in the situation. Rotter (1975) acknowledges that this formula has received substantial empirical support and that it reflects the relative importance of generalized expectancy, i.e., general expectancy becomes more influential when the situation is novel or ambiguous, and it becomes less influential as the individual's experience in the situation increases. An understanding of the relative influence of generalized expectancy enables researchers and practitioners to determine more accurately the conditions which enhance or limit the predictive power of generalized expectancy.

The generalized expectancy that one wishes to use as a basis for prediction is subject to variation

regarding the breadth of situations it might include. One might choose to predict going to work on time and select a generalized expectancy developed from a person's previous job experiences that prompt arrival enhances salary increments. This generalized expectancy could be further expanded to include the notion that prompt arrival in a variety of life situations is beneficial. The breadth of the generalized expectancy is usually guided by the criterion of functionality. However, narrowly defined generalized expectancies (e.g., a child is always prompt to dinner) lead to more accurate predictions than broadly defined generalized expectancies (e.g., the child is always prompt).

Rotter (1975) notes that two types of generalized expectancies are described in SLT. One involves the expectancy for a particular type of reinforcement, such as social approval, achievement, tangible reward, or dependency. In this type of generalized expectancy the perceived similarity in a situation is governed by the nature of the reinforcement. The second type of generalized expectancy involves expectancies that generalize from other situations which featured some similar problem-solving activity but varied in reinforcement, so that problem-solving activities encountered in a variety of situations may generalize to a specific situation irrespective of the type of reward anticipated. Generalized expectancies have become one of the most popular constructs of SLT and have been widely used in research efforts, probably because "they may be thought of (a) as important personality characteristics, (b) as defining dimensions of generalization, and (c) as allowing broad predictions from limited data" (p. 59). Although expectancy is a crucial variable in predicting behavior, Rotter points out that it is only one of three major determinants of social behavior.

REINFORCEMENT VALUE. The second determinant is the value of reinforcement. In order to predict a specific behavior accurately it is essential that we know about the reinforcements available to an individual. Before a specific behavior, such as watching TV can be predicted, it is helpful to know of competing reinforcement possibilities, such as an invitation to dinner or to a movie.

PSYCHOLOGICAL SITUATION. The third major determinant of behavior is the psychological situation. Psychological situations present both reinforcement values and expectancies and, thus, influence behavior. Also, behavioral enactment in a specific situation is preceded by a selection process which involves an assessment of the alternative behaviors available to the individual and a choosing of the behavior which seems most appropriate.

QUANTITATIVE ASPECTS. The quantitative aspects of SLT involve two principal concepts, reinforcement value and expectation. These concepts provide a framework for formulating hypotheses within the SLT framework (Mercer & Payne, 1975). These hypotheses frequently express relationships between antecedent events and specific behavior, and have generated much research. For example, it has been hypothesized that because mentally retarded persons experience more failure than normal persons, they enter task situations with a lower expectancy for success than is true for normals. Figure 6.1 illustrates the process for investigating concepts and relationships which may prove important within the SLT framework. Although it is early to evaluate SLT on its predictive prowess, it is interesting to note that the *locus of control* construct alone has generated over 600 studies. As empirical content accrues, SLT will continue to validate constructs and the accuracy of behavioral predictions will increase.

Foundation Studies in SLT and Mental Retardation

In a very comprehensive review, Cromwell (1963) presents foundation studies and early concep-

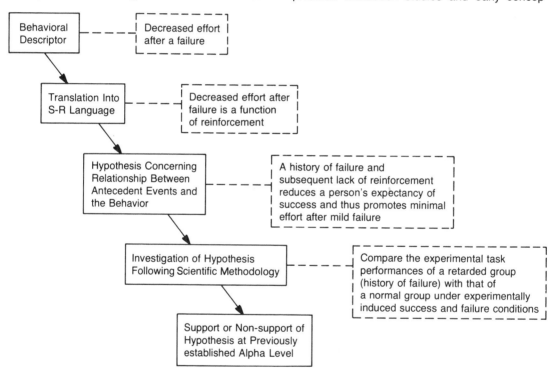

FIGURE 6.1

Procedure for investigating concepts and relationships within the social learning theory framework.

SOURCE: Adapted in part from "Learning Theories and Their Implications" by C. D. Mercer, & J. S. Payne. In J. M. Kauffman & J. S. Payne (Eds.), *Mental Retardation: Introduction and Personal Perspectives*, p. 162. Columbus, Ohio: Charles E. Merrill, 1975. Copyright 1975 by Charles E. Merrill. Reprinted by permission.

tualizations regarding SLT and mental retardation. To aid a better understanding of SLT and to establish a basis for examining further studies, selected landmark studies mentioned by Cromwell will be briefly presented.

GARDNER'S STUDIES. Gardner (1957) examined the effects of interpolated success and failure on a motor task performance of 45 retarded individuals. He divided the subjects into three groups matched on the basis of their performance on a motor task similar to the one used in the experiment. Then one group was given success on the experimental task, one group was given failure, and the last group performed the task without knowledge of performance. Gardner found that the performance of the success group exceeded the performances of the failure and control groups and that the performances of the latter groups did not differ. Later, Gardner added a fourth group and examined the effects of an interpolated experience called *partial failure*. Partial failure consisted of allowing the subjects to succeed at accomplishing 75% of the trials toward achieving a prize. The motor performance of the group experiencing partial failure was significantly below all other groups including the total failure group. Cromwell (1963) concludes that Gardner's studies demonstrated that the reactions of retarded individuals to interpolated success, failure, and partial failure experiences were sensitively revealed in motor speed measures. These studies by Gardner (1957) exemplify the early work in SLT which focused on the effects of failure (experienced or perceived) on the performance of retardates. Further, they provided a springboard for research in an area that has received considerable attention, i.e., generalized expectancy and avoidance behavior. The research concerning generalized expectancy and avoidance behavior of mentally retarded persons is based on the assumption that retarded individuals experience more failure than children with average or above intelligence and, therefore, have developed greater generalized expectancies for failure. In turn, generalized expectancies for failure foster strong tendencies in retarded individuals to avoid failure rather than strive for success. Figure 6.2, taken from Cromwell's (1963) review, highlights the retarded individual who exhibits a high generalized expectancy for failure.

HEBER'S STUDIES. Heber (1957) advanced the position that retarded individuals have a lower generalized expectancy (GE) for success when he investigated expectancy changes in normals and retarded children. He reasoned that in a novel situation only *GE* is operating as illustrated by the formula $E = f$ (*GE*) for novel situations. As experience in the novel situation accrues, E^1 (expectancy in the novel situation) becomes more influential while the influence of *GE* diminishes. With this theoretical background Heber assumed that when normal and retarded children were matched on the basis of performances on a novel task, the retarded children had the potential to show greater

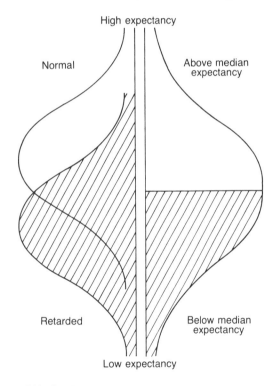

FIGURE 6.2

Illustration of expectancy levels in retarded and normal groups.

SOURCE: Adapted from "A Social Learning Approach to Mental Retardation" by R. L. Cromwell. In N. R. Ellis (Ed.), *Handbook of Mental Deficiency*, p. 49. New York: McGraw-Hill, 1963. Copyright 1963 by McGraw-Hill. Reprinted by permission.

subsequent gains because their initial matching performance was depressed due to a low *GE*. Heber postulated that retarded children would show greater increments in performance than normals in a success experience and that normals, because of their initial higher performance, would show a greater decrement in performance under failure conditions. Using a simple reaction time task, Heber compared the changes in performance of retarded and normal children under failure and success conditions. As predicted, the increment from initial to final performance under success conditions was greater for the retarded children than the increment of the normal children. The failure condition did not produce differential performances and this finding could not be explained within the domain of the constructs in use. Actually, in the failure condition both groups initially responded with an increment and then a subsequent decrement. Since Heber's findings could not be explained in terms of the success and failure conditions alone, Cromwell (1963) reasons that situations include situational cue properties as well as reinforcing properties. Heber's (1957) findings partially support the position that retarded children have a lower *GE* for success than normals.

GARDNER'S 1958 STUDIES. Gardner (1958) continued the investigations by examining the effects of experimentally induced failure on normal and retarded individuals. Sixty retarded and 60 normal children were matched on a simple card sorting task similar to the criterion task used in the experiment. After the subjects completed the preexperimental task they were assigned to an experimental group which was formulated according to failure conditions. Each group participated in a three-phase task. In the first phase all groups performed the same card sorting task under neutral conditions, i.e., no knowledge of results or no reinforcement. In the second phase some subjects performed a pencil marking task under interpolated partial failure (success on all trials except final with no prize awarded) and total failure (failure on trials) conditions. In this second phase the groups were arranged so that one group of normal children and one group of retarded children received total failure, while another group of normal and retarded children received partial failure, and

a control group of normal and retarded children performed the task without any prize or experimentally defined failure. In the third phase all subjects performed the card sorting task under neutral conditons. Change scores were obtained by comparing Phase One scores with Phase Three scores.

In accordance with Gardner's (1958) predictions, the results supported the position that the absolute magnitude of change would be greater for the normal children than for the retarded children. This prediction emerged from his assumption that the magnitude of a failure was a function of the discrepancy between expectancy level and actual failure outcome.

In addition, he predicted (and the results of his study supported the position) that normal children would more often increase their efforts after failure than retarded children. The basis for this prediction was derived from the assumption that normal children have had more opportunity than retarded children to learn that increased effort after failure may lead to success. No significant differences resulted between the normal and retarded control groups, thus indicating that when subjects did not fail there were no differences in absolute change scores or tendencies to show increased effort. Contrary to predictions, no differences resulted between the performances of total and partial failure groups. In essence, Gardner's findings support the position that a greater magnitude of failure is experienced by normal children than is experienced by retarded children as a function of expectancy and normals more often than retarded children learn to increase effort after failure.

MOSS'S STUDIES. The differential performances of retarded children under success and failure conditions provided an impetus to the study of the directional behavior of retarded persons. For example, Moss (1958) using Rotter's (1954) directionality postulate focused his attention on avoidant behavior of the retarded. Rotter purported that "approach" behavior is manifested when an individual responds primarily to goal-related environmental cues and "avoidance" behavior occurs when an individual responds primarily to cues associated with potential threat. Thus, using Rotter's postulates, the typology of two responses may be identical but differ dynamically in that one response could be a reaction to threat elements and the other could be a reaction to positive goal elements.

These concepts of directionality prompted Moss (1958) to formulate two constructs, success-striving (SS) and failure-avoiding (FA). A success-striving individual was described as one who possesses a high expectancy of success and responds to cues which lead to continued success. A failure-avoiding individual was described as one who possesses a low generalized expectancy for success and responds primarily to cues which reduce the probability of additional failure. With the establishment of the approach-avoidance (SS-FA) construct, the question of associating retarded persons with the failure-avoiding parameter emerged.

STEVENSON AND ZIGLER'S STUDIES. Stevenson and Zigler (1958) had groups of normal and retarded children press response keys under different reinforcement conditions. Two of the keys were never reinforced, but a third key was reinforced 100% for one group, 67% for another group, and 33% for the third group. Under the 33% and 67% conditions, the retarded children predominantly chose the reinforced key. Because the normals varied their responses more than the retarded children, the latter reached a higher level of correct performance. The results of this study were interpreted within the framework that normals, being success-striving, varied their behavior in order to find the 100% correct response. However, the retarded, being failure-avoiders, were content to focus on the high probability key even though it was not paying off 100% of the time.

BIALER'S STUDIES. The interest of researchers concerning the SS-FA construct helped promote the development of locus of control constructs which have continued to gain in popularity. Locus of control refers to the degree which a person perceives contingency relationships between his actions and the outcomes. When a person is characterized as having an internal locus of control, he views reinforcement as primarily the consequence of one's own actions; whereas, if a person is characterized as having an external locus of control, reinforcement is viewed as the result of outside forces, e.g., luck, fate, chance, and/or powerful others (Rotter, 1966). In the early stud-

ies, the Bialer-Cromwell Children's Locus of Control Scale (Bialer, 1960) was used to measure locus of control. Bialer reasoned that an individual could not be considered a success-striver or failure-avoider unless he perceived the outcome of an event as being due to his own ability or inability. Moreover, Bialer believed that the ability to perceive oneself as in control of events is developmental and normally matures as CA increases.

Bialer (1960) selected certain behavioral measures as indices of this developmental process. Locus of control and gratification pattern were two measures selected which correlated with MA (MA was more highly correlated with the measures than CA). As MA increased, the subjects tended to shift from an external to an internal locus of control and tended to choose delay of gratification to attain a greater reward. This relationship of MA to locus of control suggests that retarded persons develop success-failure conceptualizations and internal locus of control at a slower pace than normals.

Hopefully, this brief review of early studies as summarized in Figure 6.3 has aided an understanding of the beginnings of SLT research with retarded individuals. The constructs and ensuing hypotheses formulated in the early studies have served as a springboard for further research. Today's research with retarded persons still reflects many of these same constructs and is reviewed next in this chapter.

Although Zigler's work regarding mental retardation and motivation has not been identified as having its origins in Rotter's (1954) SLT, it parallels SLT constructs and is consistent with the research methodology used in the social learning approach. Much of Zigler's (1962, 1966, 1967) work with retarded persons has focused on three motivational variables: expectancy for failure, positive and negative reaction tendencies, and outer-directedness. Of these three variables, outer-directedness is the only dimension that has not received attention within the SLT framework. Thus, some of Zigler's work involving reaction tendencies and expectancy for failure is appropriately discussed within Rotter's SLT framework, while Zigler's work with outer-directedness needs to be viewed as a social learning phenomenon that is unique from Rotter's formulations. The review of studies in the remainder of this chapter includes implications from Zigler's research and will

Foundation Research

Early studies focused on the effect of failure and perceived failure on retardate's self-evaluation and performance. This stage was highlighted by Gardner's (1957) study and generated the basic assumption of Stage Two.

Further studies focused on examining the assumption that retardates typically experience more failure than average children and, therefore, have developed greater generalized expectancies for failure. Heber's (1957) study highlighted this stage and helped generate the basic assumption of Stage Three.

Other studies focused on the position that retardates have stronger tendencies to be failure avoiders rather than success strivers. This basic assumption led to studies which produced the following findings:
1. Retardates enter novel situations with a performance level which is depressed below their level of constitutional ability (Heber, 1957).
2. Retardates have fewer tendencies to be "moved" by failure experience than normals (Gardner, 1958).
3. Retardates have fewer tendencies than normals to increase effort following a mild failure experience (Gardner, 1958).

The development of the success-approach and failure-avoidance motivational system provided an impetus to the study of relationships between locus of control, delay of gratification, and tendency to return to interrupted versus completed tasks. In addition, studies demonstrated the developmental aspects of these variables with MA—not CA—being the crucial variable.

FIGURE 6.3
Foundation studies and constructs in social learning theory and mental retardation.

examine several topics: (a) locus of control, (b) expectancy studies and mental retardation, and (c) Zigler's motivational approach to mental retardation.

Locus of Control

Description

Prior to the review of the locus of control studies with mentally retarded persons, some elaboration regarding locus of control and its assessment is needed. As mentioned earlier, *locus of control* refers to the manner in which an individual perceives contingency relationships between his behavior and subsequent outcomes.

In a summary of research concerning locus of control, Lefcourt (1966) elaborated on the definition of the locus of control construct. He states:

As a general principle, *internal control refers to the perception of positive and/or negative events as being a consequence of one's own actions and thereby under personal control; external control refers to the perception of positive and/or negative events as being unrelated to one's own behavior in certain situations and therefore beyond personal control.* (p. 207)

A description of locus of control orientation and its development is not complete without some recognition of the degrees of external and internal orientations. People cannot be categorically dichotomized into either an external or internal orientation. The external-internal dimension must be viewed along a continuum with external at one end and internal at the other end. A person's locus of control orientation may fall on any point of the external-internal continuum. The recognition of this external-internal continuum is highlighted by Lawrence and Winschel's (1975) position that locus of control orientations might develop via a five stage process.

1. Stage I—The child attributes the events of his life, particularly failure, to forces beyond his control.
2. Stage II—Internality for success begins to emerge while externality for failure, though still evident, begins to fade.
3. Stage III—The maturing child becomes essentially internal, although this belief is principally evident in self responsibility for success.
4. Stage IV—The previous stage of development appears to be reversed as a growing awareness of responsibility and a sense of courage in the face of difficulty lead to high internality for failure coupled with a new modesty for one's successes.
5. Stage V—With the onset of genuine self reliance, the individual accepts equally the responsibility for his successes and failures. (Lawrence & Winschel, 1975, p. 487)

Measurement of Locus of Control

In order to assess an individual's external or internal orientation, several locus of control scales have been developed. The *Internal-External Locus of Control Scale* (Rotter, 1966), one of the first scales developed, is the most widely used measure in the locus of control literature. It consists of 23 question pairs presented in a forced-choice format plus 6 filler question-pairs. Scores can range from 0 (most internal) to 23 (most external). MacDonald (1973) notes that one of the limitations of the Rotter scale is that it is not suitable for use with children and retarded persons. Scales designed for school-aged children are the ones most frequently used with retarded persons. Several of these will be reviewed briefly.

1. *Bialer-Cromwell Children's Locus of Control Scale* (Bialer, 1960).
2. *Children's Picture Test of Internal-External Locus of Control* (Battle & Rotter, 1963).
3. *Intellectual Achievement Responsibility Questionnaire* (IARQ) (Crandall, Katkovsky, & Crandall, 1965).
4. *Modified Intellectual Achievement Responsibility Questionnaire* (MIARQ) (Ringelheim, Bialer, & Morrissey, 1970).
5. *Stephens-Delys Reinforcement Contingency Interview* (SDRCI) (Delys, 1971).
6. *A Locus of Control Scale for Children* (Nowicki & Strickland, 1973).

The *Bialer-Cromwell Scale* (Bialer, 1960), the first child-oriented scale, was devised for use with retardates. It evolved from adult scales and consists of 23 questions which require a *yes* or *no*

answer. The examiner reads the questions to the child and the child responds. A *yes* or *no* response may be scored as internal or external depending on the specific item. MacDonald (1973) notes that reliability coefficients obtained from nonretarded samples have been low, while reliability coefficients for retarded children have been acceptable. Gorsuch, Henighan, and Barnard (1972) report a low reliability with the *Bialer-Cromwell Scale* and indicate that it correlates with verbal ability.

The *Children's Picture Test of Internal-External Locus of Control* (Battle & Rotter, 1963) is a six-item projective test for assessing degree of internality. Like most projective tests, it is difficult to administer to large groups and data regarding its reliability are incomplete.

The IARQ (Crandall, Katkovsky, & Crandall, 1965) was developed to measure a child's beliefs about control of and responsibility for intellectual academic successes and failures. The scale is suitable for children in grades 3 through 12 and it has been widely used in studies. It has 34 forced-choice items and yields a total internality score, a responsibility for success score, and a responsibility for failure score. Lawrence and Winschel (1975) and MacDonald (1973) report that the psychometric properties of the scale are acceptable. Short forms (20 items) have been developed and are suggested for use by Crandall et al. Finally, MacDonald prefers the IARQ over the other locus of control scales for children that are currently available.

The MIARQ (Ringelheim, Bialer, & Morrissey, 1970) is essentially a shortened version of the IARQ. It contains 24 items and the authors claim that the language of the scale has been simplified to enhance its use with mentally retarded persons. MacDonald (1973) reports that the scale thus far has received limited attention.

The SDRCI (Delys, 1971) is designed for use with children from 4–10. Consisting of 40 questions, it is administered individually in a free-response structured interview. The questions are designed to elicit responses about the occurrence of some reinforcing event or cue associated with the increased probability of reinforcement, e.g., "What makes children happy?" Responses are scored in terms of whether an internal behavior is cited (e.g., "When I obey rules") or whether an external contingency is mentioned (e.g., "When Mother wakes up happy"). MacDonald (1973) reports that internal consistency and test-retest reliability of the SDRCI are acceptable, but reports about validity are inconsistent. Moreover, Mac-Donald acknowledges that a locus of control scale for use with preschoolers is needed and the SDRCI is presently the most promising candidate.

The *Nowicki and Strickland Locus of Control Scale* (Nowicki & Strickland, 1973) is a 40-item *yes-no* measure with an estimated fifth grade reading level. It is suitable for subjects ranging from third grade through college. The authors designed the scale to eliminate political and ideological items which appear on other scales and perhaps influence the scores of children from minority groups. MacDonald (1973) reports, "Information on the scale's internal consistency reliability, test-retest reliability, and convergent and discriminant validity indicates it to be the best measure of locus of control as a generalized expectancy presently available for use with children" (p. 185). Also, MacDonald notes that the authors are planning to develop alternate forms for older and preschool children.

The results of the Coleman Report (Coleman, Campbell, Hobson, McPartland, Mood, Weinfeld, & York, 1966) sparked interest in locus of control studies with children, and the continuing development of locus of control scales for children is indicative of the growing interest in this area. In regards to retarded and academically disadvantaged persons, MacDonald (1973) hypothesizes that scales designed for children may prove to be the most effective measures.

Locus of Control Studies

The internal-external (IE) construct has generated an impressive body of literature in a relatively short time. MacDonald (1973) reports that the amount of attention being given to the IE construct is phenomenal, including over 12 tests to measure IE and five literature reviews (Joe, 1971; Lefcourt, 1966, 1971; Minton, 1967; Rotter, 1966). Mac-Donald claims that its popularity is due to its wide range of generalizability and its social relevance. Most of the literature proposes that handicaps lie in the external locus of control orientations. Moreover, it has been postulated that a disproportionate number of mentally retarded persons function from an external orientation (Lawrence & Winschel, 1975). If external orientations are handicapping and the majority of mentally retarded persons are external, the study of locus of control and mental retardation should enhance our under-standing and promote the development of orientation change techniques. In one review, Lawrence and Winschel (1975) state their position about locus of control and handicapped children.

> We contend that internality in locus of control must become a conscious goal in the education of handicapped children. . . . An understanding of locus of control may constitute a modest contribution to an informed and orderly transition in special education which, at the present time, proceeds almost wholly on the level of ideology and emotion. (p. 484)

RIEDEL AND MILGRAM'S STUDIES. Riedel and Milgram (1970) compared in a general manner the performances of 49 educable retarded young adults ($\overline{CA}$ = 20.5 years) with 20 third and 19 sixth grade normal children on measures of locus of control, level of aspiration, and *n*-Achievement. These three measures represent motivational concepts that have emerged from major theoretical positions in social learning theory. Level of aspiration, which evolved from Rotter's (1954) work, involves predicting one's performance on a particular task and is often referred to as *generalized success expectancy*. *N-Achievement* basically refers to a person's need for achievement. Although Riedel and Milgram called their study an exploratory one, they cited evidence to suggest that retarded persons would score low on level of aspiration and *n*-Achievement.

Level of aspiration (LOA, abbreviation in this study) was assessed via a wooden copy of the standard LOA board described by Rotter (1942). This task involves predicting how far a ball will roll on a board and then performing the task of propelling the ball on the board. The prediction system was modified to eliminate penalties for discrepancies between performance and prediction so that predictions of performance were based on each respective trial. Prior to performing 25 experimental trials, each subject was allowed 10 practice trials. Administration of the LOA yielded four types of discrepancy scores involving performance and prediction and two shift scores (estimates of success), one following success and one following failure. Locus of control was assessed by Bialer's (1960) Locus of Control Scale (LCS) and the *Battle-Rotter Picture Test* (Battle & Rotter, 1963) which was modified to include pictures appropriate for retarded adolescents. Each picture was scored as internal, external, or neutral. *N-Achievement* was measured by A1, A9, and B6 card sets of the

Symonds Picture Story Test (similar to the *Thematic Apperception Test* [TAT]), and scoring was based on McClelland's system. In addition to the *n*-Achievement score, the cards were scored on locus of control. All tests were individually administered in two sessions spaced two weeks apart. The retarded subjects were working in an occupational training center and they received their regular hourly wage for the time spent in testing, whereas the normal children received no monetary or tangible rewards.

On the three measures of locus of control (LCS, *Battle-Rotter*, and *Symonds*) the sixth graders were significantly more internal than the third graders on the LCS and the *Battle-Rotter*. The sixth graders were more internal than the retarded adolescents on the LCS. The third graders and the retarded group did not differ on any of the locus of control measures. The sixth graders scored significantly higher on the *n*-Achievement measure than the retarded group and the third grade group. The *n*-Achievement performances of the retarded group and the third graders did not differ. On the level of aspiration task both third and sixth graders made more shifts from previous estimates of performance than the retarded group.

Although correlations among the motivation variables varied greatly, several of the correlations deserve attention. Of the locus of control measures, only the LCS and *Symonds* internal scores of the sixth graders correlated significantly. Correlations of *n*-Achievement with locus of control measures ranged from .03 to .64.

Overall, the investigators interpreted the results of their study as presenting a modest case for the developmental nature (along a cognitive, not CA, dimension) of the motivational variables examined. The sixth graders consistently scored more internal on locus of control and more realistically on level of aspiration than both the third graders and the retarded group. Since the scores of the retarded group on all three measures were more similar to the scores of the third graders than they were to the scores of the sixth graders, the investigators concluded the motivational system of the retarded group was relatively immature. Moreover, the low and inconsistent intercorrelations on the locus of control measures provided little data from which to draw conclusions and the investigators ultimately questioned the utility of the LCS measure with retarded persons. Similarly, the expected increase in internal scores and decrease

in external scores on the modified *Battle-Rotter Picture Test* were not found. Finally, the results of this study must not be generalized too liberally since the sample sizes were small and the groups received differential reinforcement.

SHIPE'S STUDIES. Shipe (1971) noted that few attempts have been made to relate locus of control to achievement in nonacademic situations. Further, she acknowledged that the relationship of locus of control and impulsivity had not been investigated. Her literature review established a strong empirical and theoretical framework for investigating the following questions: (a) Do impulsivity and locus of control relate to achievement in both academic and nonacademic realms? (b) Do they relate to ratings of personal and social adjustment? and (c) Do measures of impulsivity and locus of control correlate?

Shipe (1971) selected 46 vocational-school boys and 45 institutionalized boys to participate in the study. All subjects had IQs within the 50–85 range. The mean age for the vocational school sample was 15.9 years and the mean age for the institutionalized group was 20.6 years. The control of impulsivity was assessed for each child through individual administrations of the following tests: (a) delay of gratification test, (b) the *Porteus Mazes* (a measure of delaying capacity), and (c) the *Matching Familiar Figures Test* (MFF). Locus of control was measured for each child via individual administrations of the *Children's Locus of Control Scale* and the *Intellectual Achievement Responsibility Questionnaire*. Vocational achievement for the vocational-school group was determined by their average weekly wage. Personal and social adjustment was obtained on both groups of subjects by means of teacher and supervisor ratings on an *Adjective Checklist* and *Rating Scale*. Academic achievement was assessed via the *Information and Vocabulary Subtests* of the WISC or the WAIS.

In the vocational-school group the impulse control measures derived from the MFF and the *Porteus Mazes* correlated in the predicted direction (impulsivity related to external and reflectivity related to internal) with both of the locus of control measures. This finding suggests a degree of generality in the traits investigated. Locus of control and impulsivity measures were related to the social competence criteria. Partial correlations were found between grades in arithmetic and the MFF, the *Porteus Mazes*, the IARQ, and the *Children's Locus of Control Scale*. The locus of control measures correlated significantly with reading grades and mean achievement. Although some distinguishable trends emerged in the vocational-school data, the institutionalized group exhibited no pattern of clearly interpretable results. Finally, the five tables of correlations presented in the study identified an array of significant predictors (in the vocational-school group) for the personality construct measures of locus of control and impulsivity.

Shipe (1971) concluded that the nonintellective variables of locus of control and impulsivity are related to the behavior of mild borderline retardates who live in the community. She concluded that "the prediction of in-school achievement and, to a lesser extent, personal-social adjustment may be significantly improved by the use of such personality constructs as those investigated in the present study" (p. 21).

FOX'S STUDIES. Fox (1972) compared locus of control and self-concept measures of seventh ($N = 53$) and 11th ($N = 51$) grade mildly retarded children with 185 nonretarded seventh graders. The *Children's Locus of Control Scale* was administered as a measure of locus of control in social situations and the *Modified Intellectual Achievement Responsibility Questionnaire* (MIAR) was selected as a measure of locus of control in academic situations. Self-concept was assessed via semantic differential ratings obtained for the concepts "me," "me in school," and "me with other kids in the neighborhood."

The findings indicated that older retarded children are more external than younger retarded children, and retarded children, in general, are more external than average children who are MA or CA equal. Nonretarded and retarded subjects did not differ in their willingness to accept responsibility for academic successes, but retarded children were less willing to accept responsibility for academic failures. Retarded children tended to exhibit similar locus of control beliefs across situations more than the nonretarded. In general, locus of control beliefs were positively associated with self-concept ratings; however, acceptance of responsibility for academic failure appeared to be associated with poorer self-concept.

CHAN AND KEOGH'S STUDIES. Chan and Keogh (1974) examined the interpretation of task inter-

ruption and feelings of responsibility for failure in 30 educable mentally retarded (EMR) boys and 30 MA-equivalent, normally achieving (NA) boys. Specifically, the investigators hypothesized: (a) EMR boys would have stronger feelings of responsibility for failure than NA boys, (b) EMR boys would have stronger feelings of responsibility for failure than for success, (c) EMR boys would view task interruption as a personal failure, and (d) a significant relationship would exist between perception of interruption as failure and degree of feelings of internal control for failure.

Each subject was administered the *Intellectual Achievement Responsibility Questionnaire* (IARQ), developed by Crandall, Katkovsky, and Crandall (1965). In addition to a total score, scores were recorded for internal responsibility for successes (L +) and internal responsibility for failures (L −). Experimental task interruption was accomplished by stopping the subjects after they completed three of six block designs. Interruption was predefined by the experimenters as neutral, success, and failure. Verbal responses to task interruption were recorded and classified as *self-blaming* or *other-blaming*.

The results indicated that EMR boys were self-blaming in all interruption conditions, whereas NA boys were self-blaming in only the predefined failure condition. Compared with the NA boys, the EMR boys blamed themselves significantly more under success and control conditions. The EMR group and the NA group differed significantly in their responsibility for success (L +) and responsibility for failure (L −) scores. The NA group was higher on L + scores and lower on L − scores than the EMR group. Further, a significant relationship occurred between feelings of responsibility for failure (L − score) and interpretation of interruption (self-blaming). Chan and Keogh (1974) reported that the hypotheses of the study were confirmed and write in conclusion:

the lack of a clear relationship between interpretation and feelings regarding locus of control reported in earlier investigations (MacMillan, 1969; Mirels, 1970) may have been partly due to use of the Total L (L − + L +) as the internal responsibility measure. For EMR boys the Total L score masked a significant relationship between feelings of responsibility for failure and perception of interruption. Findings may suggest that self-blaming responses to interruption are behavioral evidence of internal feeling of responsibility for failure in EMR subjects. (p. 178)

GRUEN, OTTINGER, AND OLLENDICK'S STUDIES. Gruen, Ottinger, and Ollendick (1974) studied the effects of school-induced success and failure experiences on the probability-learning performances of retarded and nonretarded children. The authors acknowledged that previous researchers demonstrated that experimentally induced success and failure experiences effect subsequent probability-learning performances of retarded and nonretarded children. Their study was designed to determine whether these effects generated in experimental settings could be replicated in a more "life-like" school setting. According to the formulations of Stevenson and Zigler (1958), the numerous failure experiences encountered by retarded persons cause them to have low expectancies of success and a high willingness to accept low levels of success. Within a behavioral manifestation framework, retarded and/or persons with a history of failures will exhibit maximizing behavior, i.e., persistent choice of a partially reinforced stimulus.

Forty-five subjects were selected, including 15 mildly retarded children who were in regular classes and had experienced repeated failure, 15 mildly retarded children who had been exposed to a high level of success in special education classes, and 15 nonretarded children. All the children were matched on MA.

Gruen et al. (1974) hypothesized that the retarded children in the regular classes had experienced more failure than both the retarded children in the special class and the nonretarded children and thus would produce more maximizing behavior (persistent choice of partially reinforced stimulus) in a probability learning task. In addition, locus of control, need for achievement, and expectancy of success measures were obtained in an effort to determine what motivational factors might mediate the effects of success and failure.

Each child was administered the *Locus of Control Scale* devised by Miller (1965), a card sorting task (expectancy of success) devised by Diggory (1966), and three cards from the *Thematic Apperception Test* scored by Atkinson's (1958) content analysis method. Also, the *Sarason Test Anxiety Scale for Children* was administered to each child. The criterion task consisted of requiring the subject to select and push the correct knob out of three knobs available when a red light appeared. Each correct selection enabled the subject to earn a marble which could be kept and exchanged for a prize at the end of the experiment. In all groups one knob was reinforced 66% of the time and the other two knobs were never reinforced. Five subjects in each group were reinforced for a different knob, i.e., five for the left knob, five for the right knob, and five for center knob.

The results revealed that retarded children left in the regular classroom chose the "correct" stimulus (maximizing behavior) more than the MA-equivalent nonretarded group and the retarded special class group. Moreover, the regular class retarded children exhibited fewer pattern responses and fewer response shifts than did children in the other two groups. These results were interpreted as consistent with the findings of previous investigations using experimentally induced failure and success experiences. According to Gruen et al. (1974), these findings indicated that "the retarded children forced to remain in the regular classroom did, indeed, experience more failure than those enrolled in special education classes" (p. 422). Since differences in performances occurred between the MA-equivalent, retarded groups, maximizing behavior (lower expectations of success) was discussed as a feature of repeated failure and not an inherent feature of mental retardation. Also, it was acknowledged that the study showed that retarded children who experience success in special education classes have higher hopes of future success.

Of the personality measures, locus of control was the only one which differentiated the groups. Compared with the regular class retardates, the special class retarded children were significantly more internal. Scores on their need for achievement predicted both the number of correct responses made and the patterning responses made. Since only locus of control differentiated among the groups, Gruen et al. (1974) considered it the most viable parameter of those measured to account for the mediation of success-failure experiences in retarded children. No sex differences were found.

SUMMARY. In view of the recent popularity of the locus of control construct, it seems surprising that so few locus of control studies concerning retarded individuals have been reported. One could speculate that instrumentation has been a problem in studying locus of control with retarded children. However, with the development of a preschool locus of control measure (Stephens &

Delys, 1973) and the possible downward extension of *A Locus of Control Scale for Children* (Nowicki & Strickland, 1973), the problem of assessing retarded children may be ameliorated.

As shown in Table 6.1, the IQs of retarded subjects involved in these studies were all in the mild or educable range. Only one study (Chan & Keogh, 1974) involved young retarded pupils, while five studies focused on either retarded adolescents or adults. Only one study (Shipe, 1971) included institutionalized retarded subjects.

An examination of the locus of control measures used in the studies (see Table 6.1) reveals that six different instruments were used. The IARQ (Crandall et al., 1965) appeared to be the most popular (used two times) for work with young retarded subjects, while the LCS (Bialer, 1960) was used the most (three times) with adolescent and older retarded subjects.

In the studies reported in Table 6.1, internal scores were consistently related to positive parameters, while external scores were consistently viewed as handicapping. Of the five studies that compared the locus of control scores of non-retarded and retarded subjects, four found retarded subjects to be more external than non-retarded subjects. The other comparison study (Chan & Keogh, 1974) concluded that retardates had a higher expectancy of failure than normals.

Much research indicates that an external orientation is a handicapping personality variable (Lawrence & Winschel, 1975; Lefcourt, 1966; MacDonald, 1973). MacDonald (1972) expands on the handicapping nature of externality in the following passage:

> It is often truly said that one cannot change or correct his problem if he refuses to try. Externals do not try. They do not try because they do not believe that their efforts pay off. This does not mean that they do not want to change. They may want to change, but they have a negative expectancy for success. (p. 45)

It is apparent that too few studies have been reported regarding locus of control and mental retardation to draw many definitive conclusions. More research with retarded persons and external-internal orientations is warranted in order to enhance our understanding of mental retardation and foster the development of social learning techniques. To date, the consistent finding that mental retardates are external and that an external orientation tends to be handicapping challenges us to explore techniques for promoting internal orientations.

IMPLICATIONS FOR TEACHING. Although research regarding practices which promote an internal orientation is sparse, today's information suggests that locus of control orientations can be influenced (Lawrence & Winschel, 1975). Only one study (Wicker & Tyler, 1975) was found which specifically focused on promoting internality in mentally retarded children. Until there are more studies, teaching implications for retarded pupils can be developed from the available research and from our understanding of the locus of control construct. Some change techniques appear inherent in studies which have examined locus of control and mental retardation. Thus, teaching implications are presented within the framework of basic and empirically based techniques which appear feasible for promoting internality.

Some basic techniques which appear inherent in the studies reviewed are as follows:

1. Retarded individuals should be provided with many success experiences in social and academic settings. A generalized expectancy for failure appears to be directly related to external orientations, and it appears logical that continuing success experiences would decrease failure expectancies and increase success expectancies (Gruen et al., 1974). Moreover, it is important to provide these success experiences in a challenging and realistic manner. To arrange successes in a realistic setting, it would help to couple them with some opportunities for failure. Tasks should be geared at the pupil's level and altered as progress is made. In essence, the retarded child should be required to operate continuously at his independent and instructional levels while experiences at the frustrational level should be minimized. The teacher and/or parent of the retarded child should remember that they are trying to provide the child with a history of success experiences which are of such magnitude that they override the debilitating effects of continuous failures.

2. Specific behavior should be continuously paired with consistent consequences. Externals are characterized as not being able to understand the relationship of their behavior to consequences. Thus, teachers, parents, and employers of retarded persons need to be consistent in consequating behavior, i.e., provide positive reinforcement for appropriate behavior and provide negative reinforcement or punishment for inappropriate behavior. For example, apply verbal praise for being on time and administer verbal admonishment for being late. From a locus of control perspective, the object of this pairing of behavior with consistent consequences is to help the

retarded person to perceive the relationship between his actions and the positive or negative consequences which follow.

3. Immediate feedback for specific behavior should be given. This procedure would help the retarded individual to perceive the relationship between his behavior and outcomes. This technique features two salient factors: timing and specificity. The feedback, whether positive or negative, should immediately follow a specific behavior. For example, as soon as Johnny sits in his seat, the teacher says, "Johnny, thank you for sitting in your seat." The teacher's response mentions the behavior he is rewarding and follows the behavior within seconds after its occurrence.

4. Since externals tend to act less purposefully than internals, retarded individuals should be helped to work toward specific goals. In order to help retarded individuals work toward these ends, show them that their own behavior has effecting outcomes. Less mature persons would need to work on relatively short-term goals, while more mature persons could work on longer range goals.

5. Chan and Keogh (1974) found that retarded children perceived task interruption as personal failure. Teachers and parents of retardates should become sensitive to the effects of such interruption on individual children. For those children who perceive it as personal failure, tasks should be planned and scheduled in a way which minimizes task interruption. This procedure would reduce a child's failure experiences and possibly enhance a child's generalized expectancy for success.

6. Locus of control measures may be helpful in planning mainstream programs of mildly retarded pupils. According to Lawrence and Winschel (1975), an understanding of locus of control and its relationship to achievement might aid the successful placement of retardates in mainstream programs. They suggest that the retarded child's degree of internality should match the average degree of internality of the class in which he is to be placed. Moreover, they indicate that regular and special teachers of retardates need to be sensitized to locus of control orientations and consciously seek to promote internality.

7. Shipe (1971) discovered a relationship between externality and impulsivity. Impulsivity, like externality, has been frequently identified as a handicapping characteristic, whereas reflectivity, like internality, is viewed as a beneficial characteristic (Kagan, 1965). Shipe's findings that externality and impulsivity are related make it feasible to consider techniques designed to promote reflectivity as a means of influencing the development of internality. Providing children with reflective models has gained support as a technique for developing reflectivity (Yando & Kagan, 1968). Likewise, reflectivity can be developed by en-

couraging children to take their time and think about tasks before performing them. In view of the relationship between task interruption and self-blaming with retarded children (Chan & Keogh, 1974) and the impulsivity tendencies of retarded children (Shipe, 1971), time becomes a salient parameter. As such, retarded children should not consistently feel too rushed to perform tasks because of a shortage of time. This recommendation does not infer that retarded children should not learn to work within time constraints; it merely suggests that time not be inadvertently allowed to generate a history of failures and promote impulsivity.

8. Wicker and Tyler (1975) selected two groups of mildly retarded children (CA = 9–12 years) from two self-contained classes. One group served as an experimental group ($N = 13$) and the other group served as a control group ($N = 14$). All subjects were administered the *Bialer Scale* (Bialer, 1960) and the *Intellectual Achievement Responsibility Questionnaire* (Crandall, Katkovsky, & Preston, 1962) on a pre- and posttest basis. The experimental group participated in games and exercises designed to help children perceive the consequences of inappropriate social behavior. Also, everyday conflict situations were dramatized to demonstrate the relationship between pupil actions and reinforcements, as well as to show the influence of one's behavior on others. Techniques included role-playing, follow-up group discussions, and pictorial illustrations of inappropriate behavior. The control teacher continued with his regular program. On both of the locus of control measures, the experimental group achieved scores indicative of a more internal locus of control than the control group.

In many cases the techniques presented for promoting internality are not unique to a locus of control framework but simply represent good teaching methodology. For example, immediacy of feedback, pinpointing specific behavior, and providing consistent consequences are techniques which have long been identified with a behavioral approach to teaching.

In a discussion on techniques for changing orientations of disabled individuals or minority group members, MacDonald (1973) makes some salient points regarding change strategies. He states:

> It is short-sighted to focus solely on changing one's IE expectancy, however. For some people, especially for members of certain minority groups, the belief that there is little connection between effort and payoff is often realistic. For such people, an effective program for changing control orientations must produce change in the individual *and* in his immediate social surroundings. (p. 171)

TABLE 6.1

Summary of Locus of Control Studies with the Mentally Retarded

ARTICLE	SUBJECTS	INSTRUMENTATION	CONDITIONS
1. Riedel & Milgram (1970)	3 groups 1. 49 EMRs $\overline{CA}$ = 20.5, $\overline{MA}$ = 9.0 male, female, black, white 2. 20 3rd graders $\overline{CA}$ = 8.8 average ability 3. 19 6th graders $\overline{CA}$ = 11.7 average ability	LOA* Board LCS* Modified *Battle-Rotter* *N-Achievement (Symonds Picture Story Test)* *Symonds Picture for Locus of Control*	All Ss were administered all tests, and scores were compared across groups. Correlations were obtained among the measures.

RESULTS: 1. Locus of Control: 6th graders > 3rd graders and EMRs on the Battle-Rotter
6th graders > EMRs on LCS internal
3rd graders = EMRs on locus of control measures
2. *N-Achievement*: 6th graders > 3rd graders and EMRs
3rd graders = EMRs
3. LOA: 6th graders > EMRs on successful estimates
6th graders > EMRs on shifts

3rd graders > EMRs on shifts
4. Correlations: LCS r. with *Symonds* internal scores for 6th graders
N-Achievement correlations with locus of control were .03 to .64
Symonds Internal – r. with some LOA measures
5. Conclusions: Results provide modest case for developmental nature of the motivational variables examined. Also, the motivational system of the retarded group was relatively immature. No sex differences were found.

| 2. Shipe (1971) | 2 groups 1. 46 EMR vocational students $\underline{CA}$ = 15.9 $\overline{IQ}$ = 72.7 2. 45 institutionalized EMRs $\underline{CA}$ = 20.6 $\overline{IQ}$ = 64.7 | 1. Measures of Delaying Capacity a. PM* b. *Delay of Gratification Test* c. MMF* 2. Measures of Locus of Control a. LC* b. IAR* 3. Criterion Measures a. Vocational adjustment rating—wages b. *Adjective Checklist* and *Rating Scale* (personal and social adjustment) c. Academic achievement scores via information and vocabulary subtests of the WISC or WAIS | Correlations were calculated among the measures. No group comparisons were obtained because of group differences in mean CA. |

RESULTS: The measures of delaying capacity (impulsivity) were related to each other and to the two measures of locus of control. In addition the impulsivity and locus of control' measures were related to the social competence ratings. The more internal and less impulsive vocational-school youths received higher shop and academic grades. No patterns of correlations occurred in

the institutional group, but for the vocational group positive intercorrelations were found among the MFF, PM, LC, and IAR. The author concludes that impulsivity and locus of control are nonintellective variables that are related to behavioral effectiveness in the mildly retarded person who remains in the community.

| 3. Fox (1972) | 4 groups 1. 53 EMR 7th graders 2. 51 EMR 11th graders; IQs for MRs ranged from 60–85 3. 60 7th graders; IQs below 90 4. 125 7th graders; IQs above 90 | 1. LCS 2. MIAR* 3. Semantic differential ratings | Correlations were calculated among measures and groups. |

RESULTS: Retarded youths were more external than average children of same CA or MA. They also were less likely to accept responsibility for academic failure. Locus of control for retarded was more associated (race situations that it

was for normals. Locus of control scores were positively related to self-concept scores. Retarded 11th graders were more internal than retarded 7th graders and their self self evaluation, one less positive

192

TABLE 6.1, cont.

ARTICLE	SUBJECTS	INSTRUMENTATION	CONDITIONS
4. Chan & Koegh (1974)	1. 30 EMR males from special classes MA = 99.18 mo CA = 148.1 2. 30 NA* males MA = 101.9 CA = 101.0	IAR Interpretation of task interruption—scored as other-blaming or self-blaming	1. Ss performed an interruption task under success, failure, and neutral conditions. 2. Correlated interpretation of task interruption with locus of control. 3. Compared groups on all measures.

RESULTS: EMR boys were self-blaming in all conditions whereas NA boys were self-blaming in only predefined failure condition. The NA group was higher on responsibility for success (L +) and lower on responsibility for failure (L −) than the EMR group. L − scores were correlated with self-blaming. The authors conclude that self-blaming reactions to interruption are behavioral evidence of internal feelings of responsibility for failure in EMR males. These findings lend support to the position that retardates have a generalized expectance for failure.

ARTICLE	SUBJECTS	INSTRUMENTATION	CONDITIONS
5. Gruen, Ottinger, & Ollendick (1974)	3 groups 1. 15 special class EMRs IQ = 68.4 CA = 9.94 9 males, 6 females 2. 15 regular class EMRs IQ = 66.3 CA = 10.7 9 males, 6 females 3. 15 nonretarded, matched on MA with MR groups IQ = 108.4 CA = 7.78 9 males, 6 females	1. LCS (Miller, 1965) 2. A card-sorting task (Diggory, 1966) for expectancy of success 3. TAT cards for N-Achievement 4. *Sarason Test Anxiety Scale for Children* (Sarason, Davidson, Lighthall, & Waite, 1958)	1. The criterion learning task was a probability learning task requiring the S to select one of 3 knobs on each trial. One knob was always reinforced 66% of the time and the other 2 were not paired with the reward. 2. Criterion task scores for the groups were compared. 3. Scores on the personality measures were compared to each other and among groups.

RESULTS: Regular class MRs chose the "correct" stimulus more than the other two groups. They also displayed fewer pattern responses. Locus of control was the only personality measure to differentiate the groups. Special class MRs > regular class MRs on internal orientation. MA equivalent normals > regular class MRs on internal orientation. No sex differences were found. The authors conclude that the findings supported the position that repeated failure—not MR—was the variable influencing locus of control and expectancies.

MacDonald's comments certainly have implications for involving parents in intervention efforts. Although further research is warranted, our current knowledge of the locus of control construct and subsequent change techniques is sufficient enough to justify the attention of those in the helping professions.

Expectancy Studies

Introduction

As mentioned in the first part of this chapter, expectancy is a salient feature of SLT. Cromwell (1963) and Moss (1958) found that retardates tend to have generalized expectancies for failure and this expectancy for failure promotes failure avoidance rather than success-striving motivational systems. Zigler (1966) added to the theoretical development of the expectancy phenomena by finding that children approach a learning task with an expectancy for success and failure based on previous experience. Moreover, Zigler (1968) showed that an excessive number of failure experiences leads to lower levels of aspiration. Thus, the EMR child consistently sets goals which are beneath his achievement capabilities. Expectancy studies with mentally retarded persons include many tasks and variables but most focus on the expectancy of failure and/or the avoidance of failure. In order to comprehend the abundant information in this section, refer to Table 6.2.

Research

ROSEN, DIGGORY, AND WERLINSKY'S STUDIES. Rosen, Diggory, and Werlinsky (1966) examined goal-setting and expectancy of success in mildly retarded institutionalized ($\overline{IQ} = 75.4$) and noninstitutionalized ($\overline{IQ} = 75.5$) male adolescents. The two groups were matched on age and IQ and persons in each group were assigned to either a level of aspiration (LA, abbreviation used in this study) treatment or a performance prediction (PP) treatment. Before attempting a nut and bolt assembly task, subjects in both treatment conditions were asked to state an expectancy of success by responding to the question, "How sure are you that you will do 40 before you finish all your trials?" They responded by moving a wooden glider along a scale which had the word *will* at one end and *will not* at the other end. Next, individuals in the LA treatment were asked, "How many will you try to do on your next try?" Although the subjects antici-

pated 2-minute trials, the experimenter varied the timings in order to obtain a rigged performance curve. A golf tee for each completed unit was placed in a masonite board following each trial. Throughout the experiment subjects were able to check their progress by examining the masonite board.

The results indicated that institutionalized subjects set higher goals, predicted higher performance for themselves, and completed more units than subjects in the noninstitutionalized group. Another finding was that of the two conditions, the LA condition was the more motivating. For both groups, LA exceeded PP.

Rosen et al. (1966) note that the results of their study are consistent with Green and Zigler's (1962) position that residential care for retarded persons fosters more optimism and self-confidence than a nonsheltered environment. Although these findings seem in opposition to the efforts to mainstream retarded individuals, a perusal of the study calls for a discussion of several factors. First, the LAs of the noninstitutional subjects were higher than the LAs of the institutionalized subjects. If LA is related to motivation to participate in job training and/or education, then nonresidential placement would be promoting a desirable characteristic. Secondly, Rosen et al. hypothesized that realistic demands and expectations are key elements of residential environments and these elements serve to heighten optimism and self-evaluation. Skepticism regarding this hypothesis emerges when one considers that realistic standards of performance and realistic conditions of competition are not factors that are unique to residential settings. It is reasonable to believe that the inclusion of these factors in nonresidential environments would foster positive self-evaluation. Thirdly, generalization of the results of this study is restricted because: (a) the number of subjects is small, (b) the low SES level of the noninstitutionalized group may have influenced the results, and (c) institutional environments may differ markedly.

Finally, Rosen et al. (1966) did not discuss expectancy of success in relation to locus of control, but the prediction of success treatment used in their study seems related to Rotter's expectancy theory. An interpretation of the results within the locus of control construct suggests that the residential subjects were more internal than the nonresidential subjects.

KLIEBHAN'S STUDIES. Kliebhan (1967) investigated the effects of goal-setting and modeling on the job performance of mildly retarded adolescents in a workshop setting. She assigned each of the 48 retarded male workers to either an expectancy group, an imitation group, or a control group. The three groups were equaled on IQ, CA, and base rate data on the experimental task.

In the expectancy condition each subject's daily output was counted and evaluated in the worker's presence. Following the evaluation, the worker was asked how many tapes he expected to affix the next day. Prior to beginning the task on the following day, the worker was reminded of his stated expectancy. In the imitation group a confederate worker (college student) was assigned to the group to play the role of a model. The retarded workers were told to watch the model because he was a good worker and would show them how to do the task. Throughout the experiment the control group continued to receive a traditional training procedure which primarily featured verbal instructions.

All the subjects worked at the task 45 minutes a day, five days a week for five weeks. Prior to the experiment all subjects had worked on the experimental task for one week. The task consisted of affixing a variety of tape samples to unbound pages of a salesman's advertising booklet. The task involved operations which included matching by number, unwinding the correct amount of tape, pasting, and trimming. In addition to recording the number of tapes completed during the five week experimental period, workers were rated as inferior or average workers.

The results revealed that the performance of the expectancy and imitation groups was significantly better than the performance of the control group. The productions of the expectancy and imitation groups did not differ, but the trend was toward higher production in the expectancy group. The supervisors' ratings of the three groups concerning job quality yielded data which indicated that the work quality of the expectancy and imitation groups was higher than the work quality of the control group.

A hypothesis stating that work production would be higher in the expectancy group than in the imitation group was not supported. This hypothesis was based on the assumption that personal motivation (competition with self) is more effective than social motivation (competition with another).

However, this position was supported when job quality ratings were the dependent measure. Kliebhan (1967) states that the results were in the expected directions and confirms the position that techniques derived from the social learning theories of imitation and expectancy provide us with effective strategies for educating and training retarded individuals. Kliebhan concludes, "These findings strongly imply that the behavior of retarded individuals can be effectively modified by the intervention of both personal and special incentives" (p. 225).

GRUEN AND ZIGLER'S STUDIES. Gruen and Zigler (1968) examined expectancy of success and the probability learning of 60 middle-class, 60 lower-class, and 60 mildly retarded, noninstitutionalized children. Twenty subjects from each group were assigned to a success, failure, or control condition which they experienced prior to performing the criterion task. In addition, 10 subjects from each respective group were penalized for errors on the criterion task while the other 10 subjects in each group were not.

The subjects in the success and failure conditions played three simple games (Pick-a-Card, Which School, Drop-a-Marble) with the experimenter. The children in the success group were awarded nine marbles (one at a time) while they were playing each game. The children in the failure group were awarded one marble and received negative statements while they were playing each game. The subjects in the control group were only presented the criterion task. Following the failure and success experiences, the children performed a partially reinforced three-choice probability learning task which involved selecting one of three knobs. One knob was reinforced 66% of the time by the awarding of a marble (later traded for a prize), and the other two knobs were never reinforced. The 66% reinforcement schedule was randomized over the 100 trials, but at no point was a subject allowed to receive three consecutive nonreinforcements for selecting the correct knob. The subjects in the no-penalty condition received a marble for correct choices, while subjects in the penalty condition received a marble for a correct response and lost a marble for an incorrect response.

The investigators hypothesized that with failure an individual expects future failure and that this lowered expectancy of success increases maximizing behavior, i.e., continuous selection of the reinforced knob. They reasoned that the higher the expectancy for success, the more likely it is that subjects would not be content with 66% reinforcement and would seek more success via selecting other knobs. Due to the similar histories of failure experiences, it was predicted that lower-class and retarded children would exhibit more maximizing behavior than the middle-class children.

The results revealed that the lower-class normal children exhibited the most maximizing behavior and the middle-class normal children exhibited the least maximizing behavior. The maximizing performance of the retarded children fell between the other two groups. Gruen and Zigler (1968) indicated that these findings are consistent with the expectancy of failure hypothesis if one considers that lower-class normal children probably experience more failure than retarded children in special classes. No significant effects were found for preliminary conditions (success, failure, and control). However, data analysis revealed that, compared with the two other groups, preliminary conditions affected middle-class children more (failure produced more maximizing behavior). Gruen and Zigler reasoned that expectancy of failure was entrenched in the retarded and lower-class groups and that a brief experimentally induced experience had little influence on behavior. Sex of the subject did not influence criterion task performance.

MACMILLAN'S STUDIES. MacMillan (1969) used an interrupted task paradigm to examine selected motivational factors of cultural-familial and nonretarded individuals. Specifically, he selected 20 mildly retarded children with CAs ranging from 9 years–9 years 11 months and 20 mildly retarded children with MAs in the 9 years–9 years 11 months range. He compared the task performance of both retarded groups with the task performance of a group of 20 normals whose MAs and CAs were in the 9 years–9 years 11 months range. Prior to performing the experimental task, each subject was administered the *Bialer-Cromwell Children's Locus of Control Scale.*

Each person was required to manipulate nine red and white Kohs blocks to match one of six randomly presented designs on 5 x 8 inch cards. The subject was allowed to complete four designs while two were interrupted prior to completion. During an interruption sequence the subject was

told to "stop" after correctly placing the seventh block, and the partially completed design was removed. After all six designs were attempted they were simultaneously placed in front of the subject and accompanied with verbal instructions to try the design he would like to do. In addition to recording his resumption choice (RC), the subject was asked, "Why weren't two of the designs completed?" The answers were recorded and rated according to whether failure to complete the designs was the subject's fault (self-blaming) or due to externally imposed factors (other-blaming).

MacMillan (1969) found that both retarded groups had a tendency to blame themselves for not completing the task, while the proportion of normal subjects who blamed themselves was not significantly greater than those who blamed external forces. When subjects were matched on IQ and MA no differences were found regarding the assignment of blame; however, when matched on CA the retarded tended to blame themselves more than their normal peers. No relationship occurred between locus of control and the subjects' verbal explanations of why the designs were not completed. As noted previously, Chan and Keogh (1974) mention that the total score may have masked differences that might have existed between responsibility for either success or failure and verbal explanations for task interruption. Finally, a relationship between RC and blame assignment only occurred in the normal group.

He also found that typical statements by the retarded to the question regarding why the task was not completed included: "I was too slow," "I didn't work fast enough," or "I couldn't do it," while normals frequently responded with "You stopped me," or "Time ran out." These differential responses were interpreted as supporting Zigler's (1967) position that cultural-familial retarded persons have a higher expectancy for failure than do normals.

PIPER'S STUDIES. Piper (1970) examined the effect of reward value on the expectancy of an event in 24 mildly retarded male residents ($\overline{CA} = 13\text{-}7$, $\overline{IQ} = 60.3$). The subjects were divided into three groups (reward, control, and negative condition groups) of eight subjects each. In the experimental situation each subject was requested to predict whether or not 5 x 8 inch cards taken from a stack of 90 cards were blank or marked with dots. Of the 90 cards, the first 30 cards were designed to develop an expectancy for dotted cards. In the initial 30 cards, 15 were dotted and 15 were blank. The first and last cards were dotted, and the 13 other dotted cards were randomly distributed so no more than three blank cards appeared in succession. Cards 31–60 represented the extinction phase and did not include any dotted cards. The remaining 30 cards were never shown. The subjects in the reward condition received five pennies for each dotted card. The subjects in the neutral condition were asked to pause 4 seconds after a dotted card appeared, while subjects in the negative condition were required to pick a marble out of ice water after each dotted card.

The reward group predicted that dotted cards would appear more often than did either of the other two groups. Moreover, the neutral condition group predicted the occurrence of dotted cards more than the group in the negative condition. The extinction data revealed that the groups differed significantly.

The difference between the responses in the reward and the neutral conditions supports the conclusions of Cromwell and Moss (1959), i.e., a positive value paired with an event causes that event to be predicted more often by mildly retarded subjects. Piper (1970) notes:

> In addition, the present study suggests that the reverse is also true when the value is negative. The relationship between event value and expectancy was found to exist during extinction much as during acquisition. Such results do not conform to Rotter's (1954) interpretation of behavior potential. Although expectancy and reward value may be important determiners of behavior potential, a third determiner must be considered. Reward value affects expectancy. Therefore, behavior potential is the function of expectancy, reward value, and the interaction between expectancy and reward value. (p. 539).

Finally, Piper proposes that the interaction between reward value and expectancy may be unique to the mentally retarded.

SCHUSTER AND GRUEN'S STUDIES. Schuster and Gruen (1971) investigated success and failure as determinants of the performance predictions of mentally retarded and nonretarded children. The subjects were 24 mildly retarded ($\overline{IQ} = 70.04$) children, 24 MA-equivalent, nonretarded children, and 24 CA-equivalent, nonretarded children. The task consisted of defining five words displayed on a card. In each set of six cards three included five "easy" words and three contained five "difficult"

words. Subjects within each group were randomly assigned to a success first (S–F) or a failure first (F–S) experimental conditon. In the success first condition the subject was presented with the 15 easy words and praised for being correct regardless of his answer. Then the 15 difficult words were presented and the subject was told he was wrong regardless of his answer. In the F–S condition the 15 difficult words were presented and all answers were treated as incorrect. Then the easy words were presented and all answers were praised as correct. Prior to card exposure on all trials the subject was asked how many words he would be able to define.

Data analysis indicated that retarded and MA-matched controls had higher mean estimates of performance than did the nonretarded, CA-equivalent subjects. Subjects who experienced success first never lowered their predictions to the level that the failure first group exhibited. Overall the success first condition generated higher performance predictions than success after failure. Moreover, subjects in the failure first condition yielded more variable estimates than did subjects in the success first condition. The retarded children did not differ from the nonretarded children of the same MA in their mean performance predictions or in variability of performance predictions. Experimentally-induced success and failure did not differentially effect the retarded and nonretarded children.

Schuster and Gruen (1971) suggest that the similarity in the performance predictions of the two MA-equivalent groups mean that performance prediction may be a function of cognitive level and not the number of years of failure experiences. In summarizing the study the authors state:

> Finally, this study suggested that assuming a past history of failure experiences for all retarded children without examining directly pertinent life-history information is unwarranted. Programmed success experiences in special education classes, social attitudes that protect retarded persons from failure (Guskin, 1963), and, possibly, the retarded person's inability to conceptualize his role in whatever success or failure he experiences, all tend to significantly alleviate feelings of failure experienced. (p. 196)

CHANDLER AND BOROSKIN'S STUDIES. Chandler and Boroskin (1971) selected 40 retarded residents ($\overline{IQ} = 44$) in order to examine the relationship between reward value and stated expectancy. The subjects were asked to guess the color (black or yellow) of cards selected from the top of a deck of cards which contained an equal number of each color. Each subject was told that one of the colors was more highly valued than the other. Each time the valued card appeared, the subject was allowed to put white poker chips in a box to be later exchanged for a prize. In addition, each time the subject guessed the correct color a blue poker chip (exchangeable for a prize) was placed in the box.

Each subject participated in 40 trials in each of three reward conditions: (a) high reward, (b) low reward, and (c) no reward. The subjects were shown the rewards before the trials and the prizes in the high-reward and low-reward conditions were valued at five cents and one cent respectively. The no-reward condition was used to eliminate subjects with a color preference.

Results indicated that the value of the events influenced the retarded individuals' expectancy of the events. The high-reward condition generated significantly more guessing in favor of the valued color card than did the low-reward condition.

OLLENDICK, BALLA, AND ZIGLER'S STUDIES. Ollendick, Balla, and Zigler (1971) examined expectancy of success and probability learning of three groups of institutionalized retarded adolescents. They hypothesized that the retarded children have a low expectancy of success and consequently will display more maximizing behavior, i.e., persistently choose a partially reinforced stimulus in a three choice discrimination task where one stimulus is partially reinforced and the other two yield no reinforcement. The investigators based this hypothesis on the position that retarded children come to expect and settle for lower levels of success than do normal children. Ollendick et al. pointed out that greater maximizing behavior would result when a person accepted less than 100% success.

Prior to performing the criterion task, the subjects were divided into a success group, a failure group, and a control group. These three groups were equated on MA, CA, IQ, and period of institutionalization. On three different occasions the success group performed simple tasks including a block design task, a puzzle task, and a maze task. The subjects were approached in a friendly manner and praised lavishly for their work. Subjects in the failure condition were seen three times and

asked to perform difficult tasks including a block design task, a puzzle task, and a maze task. They were approached in a businesslike manner and their work was criticized extensively. The control group did not receive a preconditioning session. On the three choice visual discrimination criterion task one stimulus was reinforced 66% of the time and the other two were never reinforced.

Ollendick et al. (1971) found that the subjects in the failure condition displayed the most maximizing behavior and thus exhibited the greatest avoidance of failure of the three groups. The subjects in the success condition showed the most success striving (lose-shift strategy) of the three groups. In addition, males displayed more failure-avoiding behavior than the females. The investigators suggest that the findings of their study provide experimental support for the position that low expectancy of success is an outgrowth of failure experiences and is not an inherent factor of mental retardation per se. Since sex differences were not found in previous studies with non-institutionalized retarded subjects, it was postulated that institutionalized retarded boys experience more failure than institutionalized retarded girls. Finally, Ollendick et al. state that the results of their study supported the hypothesis that a low expectancy of success in retarded youngsters can be modified.

MACMILLAN AND KEOGH'S STUDIES. MacMillan and Keogh (1971) used an interruption task paradigm to study expectancy of failure in normal and retarded children. The investigators assumed that subjects who return to interrupted tasks (previous failure) are attempting to demonstrate competence. They hypothesized that retarded children would perceive interruption as personal failure and normals would not. Sixty mildly retarded children and 60 children in regular third grade classes were selected as subjects. Each group was subdivided into three groups (success, failure, control) and equated on MA, sex, and ethnicity.

The subjects were seen individually and asked to manipulate Kohs blocks to match designs displayed on 5 x 8 inch cards. Three designs were interrupted and three were completed. The control groups received standardized instructions and there was no comment regarding the adequacy or inadequacy of the subject's response. The success groups were told that when an interruption occurred it was because they were doing so well.

The failure groups were told that when interruption occurred it was because they were doing poorly. After the initial trials were completed, each subject was asked which design they would like to do and his repetition choice was recorded. In addition, each subject was asked why the tasks had not been completed and responses were recorded and categorized as self-blaming or other-blaming.

MacMillan and Keogh (1971) found that interruption was perceived differently by normal and retarded children. Retarded children viewed interruption as personal failure, but normals did not. Although differences in instruction did not affect the retardates' perceptions of interruption, they did influence the normals' perceptions of interruption. Normals reacted only to failure instructions by blaming themselves, whereas the retarded children blamed themselves under all conditions. The retarded and normal groups did not differ on repetition choice and MacMillan and Keogh commented on this finding by stating: "While a retarded child may respond in a fashion considered to reflect a success orientation (i.e., choose to repeat an interrupted task), he apparently continues to place responsibility for incompletion upon himself" (p. 347). Overall, the findings were interpreted as providing support for the position that retarded individuals have a high expectancy for failure.

KEOGH, CAHILL, AND MACMILLAN'S STUDIES. Keogh, Cahill, and MacMillan (1972) used the same procedures used in the MacMillan and Keogh (1971) study to compare the perception of interruption by problem learners (educationally handicapped) with the perceptions of retarded children. Using these samples, the investigators were able to test the hypothesis that failure experience, rather than IQ or MA deficiency, is a principal determinant in the development of expectancy for failure. Six block design tasks were presented under success, failure, and neutral task interruption conditions to thirty 9-year-old and thirty 12-year-old boys enrolled in public school special education programs.

Comparisons of the educationally handicapped (EH) students of average intellectual ability to mentally retarded children (from previous studies) revealed that older (12 year old) EH children were similar to the retarded children in perception of interruption. The older EH children were consistently self-blaming. The investigators noted that

such self-blaming appears to increase with prolonged school failure. It was concluded that the findings may be interpreted to support the hypothesis that persistent failure experiences produce a low expectancy for success.

LEVY'S STUDIES. Levy (1974) studied social reinforcement and knowledge of results as determinants of motor performance among EMR children. Previous research (Martens, 1971) with intellectually average subjects indicates that social reinforcement may function as supplementary evaluative feedback which may or may not be useful. Martens hypothesized that intellectually average children are optimally motivated in novel task situations and social reinforcement has little effect on performance; however, knowledge of results serves to affect performance. Based on expectancy theory generated under the auspices of social learning theory, Levy questioned whether or not one could assume that social reinforcement minimally effects the motor performance of retarded persons.

Eighty mildly retarded boys and girls were selected from special classes in a public school system. The subjects were assigned to four social reinforcement conditions (tangible, praise, reproof, and control) accompanied with knowledge or absence of results. Altogether eight groups were established: four social reinforcement incentive groups with knowledge of results and four social reinforcement incentive groups without knowledge of results.

The subjects received six blocks of five trials of a motor task using the Lafayette Photoelectric Rotary Pursuit apparatus. Each subject was required to track a moving light with a stylus. Praise, reproof, and tangible rewards (candy) were delivered on a contingency basis, and for the knowledge of results condition the subjects were furnished the number of seconds that they tracked the light on the previous trial.

The findings revealed that both social reinforcement and knowledge of results significantly influenced the motor performance (accuracy) of retarded children. Social reinforcement combined with knowledge of results affected performance to a greater degree than did social reinforcement alone. Moreover, the relative difference between the social-reinforcement conditions was greater in the knowledge-absent condition than in the knowledge-present condition. Levy (1974) interpreted this latter finding as providing some support to Marten's (1971) position that, when knowledge of performance is provided, social reinforcement may be supplementary evaluative feedback with questionable usefulness. Finally, tangible reward conditions influenced the motor performance more than the reproof or praise condition.

SUMMARY. A perusal of Table 6.2 indicates that the samples consisted mostly of mildly retarded adolescents and adults from both public school and institutional settings. Only one study (Chandler & Boroskin, 1971) involved subjects ($\overline{IQ} = 44$) below the mildly retarded range and only one study (MacMillan, 1969) selected retarded subjects ($\overline{CA} = 9.5$) below 11 years old.

The researchers used eight different criterion tasks and five of them were simple visual-motor tasks. A verbal task was used in one study (Schuster & Gruen, 1971) and two studies (Chandler & Boroskin, 1971; Piper, 1970) used tasks which simply involved predicting the occurrence of a visual stimulus (color, dots) on a card. The majority of the expectancy studies with retarded individuals stressed the use of simple motoric skills. These simple tasks enable researchers to examine the effects of independent variables without concern for penalizing retarded subjects for intellectual deficiencies which might affect performances on more complex tasks.

Since SLT implies a relationship between expectancy and reward values, it is not surprising that eight of the 11 investigators considered incentive conditions. Some of the findings, including those pertaining to incentive conditions, are presented.

1. Two studies found that the value of reward associated with an event increases a retarded person's expectancy that the event will occur (Chandler & Boroskin, 1971; Piper, 1970). In addition, Chandler and Boroskin showed that the magnitude of the reward is important, i.e., the higher the magnitude, the higher the expectancy.
2. Three studies (Gruen & Zigler, 1968; Koegh, Cahill, & MacMillan, 1972; Ollendick, Balla, & Zigler, 1971) supported the position that expectancy of failure is a function of past failure experiences, while one study (Schuster & Gruen, 1971) suggested that expectancy may be related to cognitive level. Unlike the other studies, which used simple visual-motor tasks, this one study used a verbal task. Thus differences in criterion tasks may have influenced the results.
3. In four studies (Gruen & Zigler, 1968; MacMillan, 1969; MacMillan & Keogh, 1971; Schuster & Gruen, 1971) the expectancy measures of retarded subjects in public school special education programs were compared to the expectancy measures of children in regular classes. The findings of three of the studies (Gruen & Zigler, 1968; MacMillan, 1969; MacMillan & Keogh, 1971) supported the position that mentally retarded persons tend to be higher on expectancy of failure than normals. Gruen and Zigler found this with middle-class normals but not with lower-class normals. Schuster and Gruen found that expectancy of failure for retarded and MA-equivalent, nonretarded persons was not different and, hence, suggested that expectancy is a function of individual histories and MA level and not an inherent feature of mental retardation. Also, Gruen and Zigler found no differences on an expectancy measure with retardates and MA-matched, lower-class normals.
4. Generally, retarded subjects did not demonstrate a preference for a type of incentive condition, e.g., symbolic reward, verbal praise, monetary reward. Whenever a type of reward was preferred by retarded persons, it was usually a monetary or tangible reward (Levy, 1974).
5. Striving for success as opposed to avoiding failure was examined in several studies. Levy (1974) found that EMRs uniformly increased their performances using knowledge of results. MacMillan and Keogh (1971) found no differences between normals and EMRs on a success striving measure. Overall, from these studies it appears that EMRs work towards success rather than just try to avoid failure.

The research regarding expectancy and mental retardation is characterized by diversity in methodology. It appears that more research is warranted before conclusions can be drawn with much certainty. Some parameters which need further consideration are:

1. the developmental nature of the expectancy phenomena
2. the development and testing of expectancy change techniques
3. the study of expectancy with young retarded children
4. the study of expectancy with children below the mildly retarded level
5. the consistency of expectancy orientations across situations
6. the influence of socioeconomic status on expectancy and
7. the relationship of expectancy orientation to academic achievement and adaptive behavior

Also, studies which are designed to replicate the findings of existing studies are needed to establish more clearly the trends in the literature. Research efforts as demonstrated by MacMillan, Keogh, and Zigler stress a systematic problem-solving ap-

TABLE 6.2
Summary of Expectancy Studies

ARTICLE	SUBJECTS	INSTRUMENTS AND TASKS	CONDITIONS
1. Rosen, Diggory, & Werlinsky (1966)	11 institutionalized MRs $\overline{IQ} = 74.5$ $\overline{CA} = 17.0$ all males 11 noninstitutionalized MRs $\overline{IQ} = 75.5$ $\overline{CA} = 17.1$ all males	1. *Nut and Bolt Assembly Task* (criterion task) 2. LA* via question "How many will you try to do on your next try?" 3. PP* via question "How many do you think you will do on your next try?"	1. Compared performances of institutionalized group with noninstitutionalized group. 2. Compared performances between conditions.

RESULTS: The Ss performed better ($p < .001$) under the LA conditions than they did under the PP conditions. Institutionalized Ss set higher goals, predicted higher performance for themselves, and produced more than the noninstitutionalized group. Whereas the noninstitutionalized group set higher levels of aspiration, the institutionalized group was more confident of ultimate success when predicting performance. Results were interpreted as consistent with Green and Zigler's (1962) contention that residential care is more conducive to optimism and self-confidence than is nonsheltered school and community experience. Optimism (self-esteem) may be related to the degree which a person is able to meet the demands of his social situation. Protection, encouragement, training, more realistic standards for performance and realistic completion may serve to heighten optimism and self-evaluation.

ARTICLE	SUBJECTS	INSTRUMENTS AND TASKS	CONDITIONS

2. Kliebhan (1967)	3 groups of MRs from a workshop
	1. Expectancy group
	  $N = 16$, $\overline{IQ} = 60.25$
	  $\overline{CA} = 218$ mo
	2. Imitation group
	  $N = 16$, $\overline{IQ} = 58.94$
	  $\overline{CA} = 219$ mo
	3. Control group
	  $N = 16$, $\overline{IQ} = 59.31$
	  $\overline{CA} = 212$ mo
		1. Criterion task—affixing tape to sheets for advertising booklet.
		2. Ratings of job quality.
		3. Imitation group had a model performing criterion task.
		4. Expectancy group was required to make predictions about their performance.
		5. Control group received standard instructions.
			Compared the criterion task scores and job ratings of the three groups.

RESULTS: Expectancy and modeling groups > Control group on criterion task
Modeling group = Expectancy group on criterion task
Expectancy and modeling groups > Control group on job ratings
Expectancy group > Modeling group on job ratings

The author concludes that the techniques derived from the social learning theories of imitation and expectancy are affective for training and educating MRs.

TABLE 6.2, cont.

ARTICLE	SUBJECTS	INSTRUMENTS AND TASKS	CONDITIONS
3. Gruen & Zigler (1968)	3 groups 1. 60 lower-class, normal children $\overline{CA} = 7.0$, $\overline{MA} = 6.83$, $\overline{IQ} = 98$, 30 males, 30 females 2. 60 middle-class, normal children $\overline{CA} = 6.6$, $\overline{MA} = 7.03$, $\overline{IQ} = 108$, 30 males, 30 females 3. 60 retarded children $\overline{CA} = 11.45$, $\overline{MA} = 6.9$, $\overline{IQ} = 68$, 30 males, 30 females	1. Criterion task—involved selecting correct knob from 3 knobs presented. One knob reinforced 66% of the time. The remaining knobs never reinforced. 2. Precriterion task conditions Success condition—on three games Failure condition—on three games Control condition—no games prior to criterion task 3. Criterion-task conditions Penalty condition—give and take marbles No-penalty condition—only give marbles for correct response	1. Compared performances across groups. 2. Compared performances across conditions, i.e., success, failure, control and penalty, no penalty.

RESULTS: Lower-class, normal children displayed the most maximizing responses (selection of 66% reinforced knob) while the middle-class, normal children exhibited the fewest maximizing responses. Experimentally induced failure and success did not produce significant effects. Middle-class normal children were most effected by the failure and success conditions, i.e., failure produced more maximizing behavior. The results were interpreted as supporting the position that a history of failure experiences fosters generalized lower expectancy of success.

ARTICLE	SUBJECTS	INSTRUMENTS AND TASKS	CONDITIONS
4. MacMillan (1969)	3 groups 1. 20 PR* $\overline{CA} = 9.45$, $\overline{MA} = 6.74$, $\overline{IQ} = 71.15$ 2. 20 IR* $\overline{CA} = 12.26$ $\overline{MA} = 9.01$, $\overline{IQ} = 73.10$ 3. 20 nonretarded 3rd and 4th graders, $\overline{CA} = 9.47$ $\overline{MA} = 9.41$, $\overline{IQ} = 100.85$	1. Criterion task—block design matching task with interruption. 2. LCS 3. Resumption choice of task (measure of success striving). 4. Record of verbal explanation regarding task interruption classified as self- or other-blaming. Measure of expectancy for failure.	1. Compared groups on dependent measures. 2. Correlated LCS to self- or other-blaming responses.

RESULTS: Both PR and IR groups had a tendency to blame themselves for not completing the task, while the proportion of normals who blamed themselves was not significantly greater than those who blamed external forces. On blame assignment no differences were found for subjects equated on MA or IQ, however MRs equated on CA with normals tended to blame themselves more. No relationship occurred between LCS and blame assignment. The results were interpreted as supporting Zigler's (1967) position that retarded persons generally have a higher expectancy for failure than normals.

TABLE 6.2, cont.

ARTICLE	SUBJECTS	INSTRUMENTS AND TASKS	CONDITIONS
5. Piper (1970)	3 groups 1. 8 reward group EMRs 2. 8 negative group EMRs 3. 8 neutral group EMRs For all Ss: $\overline{CA}$ = 13–7 $\overline{IQ}$ = 60.3	1. Criterion task—predicting occurrence of a dot on cards selected from a stack. 2. Task performed under reward (five cents), neutral (knowledge of results) and negative (hand in ice water) conditions.	Compared performances of the three groups in both acquisition and extinction.

RESULTS: The positive group expected the dot most often and the negative group expected the dot least often. This finding supports Cromwell and Moss's (1959) position that positive associations with an event lead to anticipation of the event by mildly retarded individuals. In addition the author suggested that behavior potential is partly a function of the interaction between reward value and expectancy.

ARTICLE	SUBJECTS	INSTRUMENTS AND TASKS	CONDITIONS
6. Schuster & Gruen (1971)	3 groups 1. 24 retarded Ss $\overline{MA}$ = 91.54 mo $\overline{CA}$ = 142.25 mo $\overline{IQ}$ = 70.04 2. 24 nonretarded Ss $\overline{MA}$ = 92.16 $\overline{CA}$ = 85.95 $\overline{IQ}$ = 103.95 3. 24 nonretarded Ss $\overline{MA}$ = 163.62 $\overline{CA}$ = 141.66 $\overline{IQ}$ = 109.75	1. Criterion task—defining words presented on cards. 2. All Ss gave performance predictions prior to each trial under experimentally induced failure-first or success-first conditions.	Compared performance predictions of the three groups.

RESULTS: Retarded and MA-matched controls had higher predictions than did the nonretarded CA-equivalent Ss. The success-first condition generated higher performance predictions than success after failure. The MR Ss did not differ from the nonretarded Ss of the same MA on estimates, performance and variability. Thus, experimentally induced failure and success did not differentially affect MRs and normals. The authors note that expectancy may be related to cognitive level—not the number of years of failure experiences.

ARTICLE	SUBJECTS	INSTRUMENTS AND TASKS	CONDITIONS
7. Chandler & Boroskin (1971)	40 institutionalized retarded Ss. $\overline{CA}$ = 16–5 $\overline{MA}$ = 7–3, $\overline{IQ}$ = 44 20 males, 20 females	1. Criterion task—guess color of card to be turned up from a deck with an equal # of black and yellow cards. 2. Ss performed the tasks under high reward (poker chips traded for five cent prize), low reward (trade chips for a one cent prize), and no reward.	Compared performances across the 3 conditions

RESULTS: The higher reward condition produced more guessing in favor of the "valued" color than did the lower reward condition. Also, high reward > no reward for guessing "valued" color. No differences were found between no-reward and low-reward conditions. Results were interpreted as supporting the contention that the value of an event increases a retarded person's expectancy that the event will occur; however, the magnitude of the reward must be considered.

TABLE 6.2, cont.

ARTICLE	SUBJECTS	INSTRUMENTS AND TASKS	CONDITIONS
8. MacMillan & Keogh (1971)	6 groups (CA & MA in mo) 1. 10 nonretarded Ss Success group $\overline{CA} = 111.9$, $\overline{MA} = 102.7$ $\overline{IQ} = 92.8$ 2. 10 nonretarded Ss Failure group $\overline{CA} = 111.3$, $\overline{MA} = 105.6$ $\overline{IQ} = 94.9$ 3. 10 nonretarded Ss Control group $\overline{CA} = 111.5$, $\overline{MA} = 102.7$ $\overline{IQ} = 92.2$ 4. 10 Mildly retarded Ss Success group $\overline{CA} = 144.8$, $\overline{MA} = 101.7$ $\overline{IQ} = 69.8$ 5. 10 mildly retarded Ss Failure group $\overline{CA} = 144.1$ $\overline{MA} = 102.9$, $\overline{IQ} = 71.0$ 6. 10 mildly retarded Ss Control group $\overline{CA} = 146.1$ $\overline{MA} = 101.1$, $\overline{IQ} = 69.2$	1. Criterion task—match block designs presented via 5 x 8 inch cards. 2. Ss were interrupted under success, failure and neutral conditions. Repetition choice (success-striving measure) was recorded as well as verbal explanation regarding interruption (self- or other-blaming). Measure of expectancy for failure.	Compared groups and conditions.

RESULTS: Retardates perceived interruption as personal failure but normals did not. The different conditions did not differentially effect the retarded Ss' perception of interruption. The normals blamed themselves only under the failure condition, whereas the MRs blamed themselves under all conditions. No differences were noted on repetition choice. Results were viewed as supporting the position that MRs have a high expectancy for failure.

ARTICLE	SUBJECTS	INSTRUMENTS AND TASKS	CONDITIONS
9. Ollendick, Balla, & Zigler (1971)	3 groups 45 institutionalized MRs MA approx. 9-0 CA approx. 14 IQ approx. 62 15 per group, success, failure, and control.	Experimental manipulation 1. Tasks—block design task, puzzle task, and maze task were used in a precondition for establishing a *success* and *failure* experience. 2. Second criterion task—3-choice probability learning task—knob selections with one stimulus rewarded 66% of the time and the other two never rewarded. An expectancy of success measure.	Compared criterion task performances (maximizing behavior) conditions. Compared strategies across groups, i.e., win-stay, lose-stay analyses.

RESULTS: The preconditions of failure and success affected the strategies used in the criterion task. Ss in the failure precondition exhibited the most maximizing behavior (greatest avoidance of failure), Ss in the success precondition showed more success or striving (lose-shift pattern). Males displayed more failure avoidance than females. The results were interpreted as supporting the hypothesis that the low expectancy of success which characterizes many MRs is an outgrowth of failure experiences and not an inherent feature of MR.

204

TABLE 6.2, cont.

ARTICLE	SUBJECTS	INSTRUMENTS AND TASKS	CONDITIONS
10. Keogh, Cahill, & MacMillan (1972)	2 groups 1. 30, 9-year-old EH* pupils with average intellectual ability. 2. 30, 12-year-old EH pupils with average intellectual ability.	1. Block design task with interruptions in success, failure, and neutral conditions. 2. Repetition choice was recorded (success-striving measure). 3. Self-blaming and other-blaming responses were recorded (expectancy of failure measure).	Compared the two groups on all measures. Also compared these groups with MRs from previous studies.

RESULTS: Blame for interruption varied with the conditions for 9 year olds, whereas 12 years olds were self-blaming in all conditions. The 12 years olds were like the EMR samples in perception of interruption. The findings suggest that self-blaming (expectancy for failure) appears to increase prolonged school failure.

11. Levy (1974)	8 groups of mildly retarded children from special classes. $\overline{MA} = 7.4$, $\overline{CA} = 11.4$. Assigned to praise, reproof, tangible and control conditions with and without feedback concerning performance.	1. Criterion task—motor tracking task using Lafayette Photoelectric Rotary Pursuit. 2. Ss performed under praise, reproof, tangible, and control conditions. 3. Ss performed either with feedback or without feedback.	8 compared performances across groups.

RESULTS: Social reinforcement and knowledge of results significantly influenced the motor performance (accuracy) of the MR Ss. Social reinforcement plus feedback was more influential than social reinforcement alone. More variation occurred in the groups where social reinforcement was absent than when it was present. Tangible rewards influenced motor performances more than the reproof or praise condition.

*PR = Primary retarded
IR = Intermediate retarded
LA = Level of aspiration
PP = Prediction of performance
EH = Educationally handicapped

205

proach to both the formulation of theories and the testing of theories. Eventually these types of efforts will enable us to function from a broader empirical foundation regarding expectancy and mental retardation.

Although more research is needed regarding expectancy orientations and mental retardation, it is possible to draw some viable implications from our present knowledge. In addition to the general findings just reviewed, many specific findings which have implications for teaching techniques are included in the next section.

IMPLICATIONS FOR TEACHING. At this point the expectancy studies are not replete with a wide selection of teaching suggestions; however, the extraction of some teaching strategies seems warranted. One of the first techniques that emerges from these studies involves the setting of goals through a mutual involvement of teacher and pupil. Rosen et al. (1966) found that the performance of retarded individuals improved by simply asking them, "How many will you try on your next try?" Also, Kliebhan (1967) found that goal-setting enabled retarded persons to function as well as another retarded group provided with a model. To use this technique, teachers, parents, or employers should work with retarded persons to select realistic goals regarding specific tasks. Also, the retarded person should be continuously reminded of the goal in a timely and appropriate manner.

A second teaching implication involves the pairing of rewards with desirable events of tasks. Several studies (Chandler & Boroskin, 1971; Piper, 1970) indicated that a value or reward associated with an event increases a retarded person's expectancy that the event will occur. Those who work with retardates should consistently pair desirable behavior (being on time, doing arithmetic, cleaning room) with rewards. Also, since the magnitude of the reward has an influence on increasing an expectancy of success orientation (Chandler & Boroskin, 1971; Ollendick et al., 1971; Piper, 1970), the reward must be reinforcing and the person must be initially prepared to provide high-valued rewards.

A third teaching implication emerges from the studies with retarded persons which show the impact of success on performance and on the development of an expectancy for success (Ollendick et al., 1971; Schuster & Gruen, 1971). It is apparent that retarded persons need to have realistic success experiences. Similar to the aforementioned locus of control studies, the expectancy studies reveal that retardates need challenging tasks (Kliebhan, 1967) within their ability range that are appropriate to their vocational, social, or academic needs. The expectancy studies reviewed supported the position that mildly retarded persons can be or are success strivers (Keogh, Cahill, & MacMillan, 1972; Levy, 1974; MacMillan & Keogh, 1971). Thus, an appropriate (challenging) task coupled with a reinforcer seems to provide the nucleus for motivating retarded persons to perform.

A fourth idea revolves around a sensitivity to individual differences regarding the interruption of a task. Several studies (MacMillan, 1969; MacMillan & Keogh, 1971) indicated that retarded persons perceived task interruption as a personal failure. Those who surround the retarded should be aware of the number of incomplete tasks that a retarded person experiences. Retarded persons should constantly receive explanations of task interruption, e.g., some tasks are not finished due to neutral factors (time allotted, equipment breakdown, task difficulty), while other interruptions are due to personal factors (attention to task, selecting the proper materials, etc.). Efforts need to be directed at correcting the personal factors and at reducing the tendency for retarded persons to blame themselves for the neutral factors. Finally, task completion could be accomplished via shorter tasks, simpler tasks, longer time periods, and setting subgoals within a task.

Since many of the expectancy studies focused on examining the influence of various incentive conditions on the performance of retarded individuals, it seems appropriate to present some of the conclusions generated by Lynch and Panda (1972) in their review article concerning the effects of social reinforcement on the retarded child. In a summary statement they note:

> (a) Social reinforcement controls behavior of retarded children in simple learning situations, (b) Feedback in the form of R–W [Right–Wrong] improves performance, and (c) Effectiveness of social reinforcement depends on the definitional structure, completeness, and contingency of occurrence. (p. 119)

They also elaborate on their review findings by noting that ambiguous, random, or indiscriminant feedback can actually depress learning and become distracting to a child engaged in a complex learning task. A teacher of the retarded should maintain a continuous balance between supportive, motivating feedback and corrective (right–wrong) feedback. The retarded child needs general encouragement in order to develop a higher expectancy of success, but corrective feedback is also needed for improved learning. It is possible to provide both types of feedback in statements such as "Good try. You sounded out every syllable except this one." In essence, the teacher needs to provide verbal support on a contingent basis and avoid too much ambiguous verbal feedback.

In addition to the implications mentioned, several others deserve recognition.

1. From Levy's (1974) study the importance of immediate feedback is recognized. Moreover, immediate feedback coupled with reinforcement appears to influence behavior more than either technique used alone.
2. The use of a combination of a model and goal setting appears to be a promising technique (Kliebhan, 1967). Specifically, the retarded person would be helped to develop a specific goal and then be provided with a model who performs the goal-oriented behavior.
3. Employers and teachers should examine individual histories before making assumptions about a retarded person's generalized expectancy. It appears that expectancy of failure is not an inherent feature of mental retardation but a product of several variables interacting (Ollendick et al., 1971; Schuster & Gruen, 1971).
4. Gruen and Zigler's (1968) study showed that punishment lowered the expectancy of success of the retarded children. This finding suggests that a teacher should limit the application of punishment for incorrect responses with retarded children. This can frequently be accomplished via reinforcing a response that is incompatible with the incorrect response, e.g., reinforce a peer for sitting in his seat while target child is out of his seat. Another way to maintain a positive approach is to wait for the target child to give a desirable response and then reinforce him.

For the most part, the teaching implications which derive from these expectancy studies with retarded persons are not unique but reflect a collection of strategies inherent in sound pedagogy. Nevertheless, the expectancy studies provide some empirical support for selected practices used in teaching. Clearly, more investigations are needed to expand our knowledge of generalized and specific expectancies and increase our effectiveness in influencing expectancies.

Zigler's Motivational Approach to Mental Retardation

Although Zigler's motivational approach to mental retardation did not originate from Rotter's (1954) social learning theory, it should be considered. As noted by MacMillan (1971), "Zigler (1966, 1967) has sensitized investigators in the field of retardation to the possibility that motivational and emotional variables depress the performance of retarded children below a level expected on the basis of their cognitive development, i.e., mental age" (p. 579). Zigler's work with motivational factors and mental retardation is extensive but the three areas which have received much attention are (a) expectancy of failure, (b) positive and negative reaction tendencies, and (c) outer-directedness.

Expectancy of Failure

As mentioned previously, expectancy orientations are an inherent part of social learning theory. (See the previous section of this chapter for expectancy studies review.) Zigler (1966) postulated that children learn to expect varying degrees of success and failure and that they approach a task with an expectancy based on past experiences. Moreover, he claimed that a common reaction to excessive amounts of failure is a lowered level of aspiration (Zigler, 1968). Since mentally retarded persons commonly experience much failure, he further hypothesized that they tend to set goals considerably beneath their performance capabilities. The expectancy studies indicate that Zigler's expectancy of failure position and a similar position by Moss (1958) have received substantial support.

Positive and Negative Reaction Tendencies

Foundation Literature

LEWIN-KOUNIN FORMULATION. The development of the positive and negative reaction theory began with Zigler's (1966) work regarding the Lewin-Kounin cognitive rigidity formulation. The Lewin-Kounin formulation maintained that retarded persons are cognitively less differentiated than normal children, i.e., they have fewer regions in the cognitive structure than normal children. In addition, it was postulated that for MR children the boundaries between psychial regions in the brain are more rigid and less permeable than the boundaries of normal children (Kounin, 1941a, 1941b). This impermeability was perceived as influencing the development of rigid behaviors, e.g., perseveration. Zigler and his colleagues used satiation-type tasks, as did Kounin, to test the rigidity hypothesis. Satiation tasks involved activities such as drawing bugs on Task 1 until the subject felt like stopping (satiation) and then Task 2 would immediately follow and involve a similar task (e.g., drawing cats) until the subject felt like stopping. According to Lewin-Kounin and Zigler's hypotheses, the normals would show more transfer from task to task, i.e., MRs would perform Task 2 longer than normals.

STEVENSON AND ZIGLER'S STUDIES. In a series of experiments Stevenson and Zigler (1957) used a reversal problem (they assumed that a reversal problem would require more than one psychial region) to test the Lewin-Kounin theory of rigidity. They found that no differences occurred between retarded and normal subjects on simple and difficult switching problems. Stevenson and Zigler rejected the rigidity hypothesis and advanced a motivational hypothesis which stated that institutionalized retarded children have been relatively deprived of adult interaction and approval and have a higher motivation to seek adult approval than do normal children.

ZIGLER, HODGDEN, AND STEVENSON'S STUDIES. Zigler, Hodgden, and Stevenson (1958), like Kounin (1941a, 1941b), used satiation and cosatiation tasks to test the motivational hypothesis. They varied the conditions of reinforcement by using the experimenter in a nonsupportive and supportive role. They found that adult support provided more of a reinforcement for the retarded sample than it did for the normal sample and they interpreted these findings as supporting the motivational hypothesis. Zigler labeled the retarded person's desire for social reinforcement the *positive reaction tendency*.

GREEN AND ZIGLER'S STUDIES. In addition, Green and Zigler (1962) conducted a study (discussed later underouter-directedness) which produced support for the positive reaction tendency hypothesis. Zigler acknowledged that the complexity of the retarded individual needs to be appreciated, and he cautioned researchers not to rely on a single motivational factor for understanding the retarded person.

ZIGLER'S STUDY. The complex nature of the retarded individual's motivational system was demonstrated when Zigler (1958) continued his work by postulating the negative reaction tendency, a formulation which appeared completely antithetical to the positive reaction tendency. Actually, the negative reaction tendency is based on the premise that some retarded persons approach adult interaction with reluctance and wariness. Zigler (1958) used the positive and negative reaction tendencies to explain why retarded subjects after satiation on Task 1 performed longer on Task 2 than they did on Task 1. In contrast, groups of normal children consistently performed longer on Task 1 than they did on Task 2. Zigler explains:

> Institutionalized feebleminded subjects begin task one with a positive-reaction tendency higher than that of normal subjects. This higher positive-reaction tendency is due to the higher motivation of feebleminded subjects to interact with an approving adult. At the same time feebleminded subjects begin task one with a negative-reaction tendency due to a wariness of adults which stems from the more frequent negative encounters that feebleminded subjects experience at the hands of adults. If task one is given under a support condition, the subject's negative-reaction tendency is reduced more during task one than is his positive-reaction tendency. (p. 91)

SHALLENBERGER AND ZIGLER'S STUDIES. Shallenberger and Zigler (1961) devised a study to examine the positive and negative reaction tendencies. The study was similar to earlier satiation studies, except that experimental games preceded the two-part satiation tasks. The games were performed under both positive and negative reinforcement conditions. All subjects performed the criterion tasks under the same conditions. As predicted, both normal and retarded groups who experienced the negative reinforcement performed longer on Task 2 than on Task 1, while the groups who received positive reinforcement performed longer on Task 1 than on Task 2. These results were interpreted as supportive of the positive and negative reaction tendencies formulation.

The aforementioned studies regarding positive and negative reaction tendencies are foundation studies and have been referred to extensively in the literature. Further studies are discussed in more detail in order to enhance our understanding of the positive and negative reaction tendencies formulations.

Further Studies

WEAVER, BALLA, AND ZIGLER'S STUDIES. Weaver, Balla, and Zigler (1971) selected three groups of 36 institutionalized retarded, noninstitutionalized retarded, and normal children of comparable MA in order to examine their social approach and avoidance tendencies. Each subject performed Placing Task I, which consisted of taking some felt forms from the experimenter and placing them on a panel. The subject was free to perform on either side of the panel and the experimenter was located on one side of the panel. A record of the subject's distance score from the experimenter was kept. Placing Task I was performed under support, punishment, and neutral conditions. These conditions were differentiated via the experimenter's facial expressions and verbalizations. A free play period followed Placing Task I in order to underscore the fact that Placing Task I and Placing Task II were separate "games." Next, Placing Task II was performed and it consisted of placing felt objects (human figures) on the panel. As with Task I, distance scores from the experimenter were recorded on Task II trials.

Weaver et al. (1971) claimed that a major facet of their study was the use of the measure which assessed how far the child situated himself from a stationary adult. They noted that previous studies had only used different time scores on satiation-type tasks. The experimental conditions (support, punishment, and neutral) were included to assess modifiability of children's approach and avoidance tendencies. On the basis of previous studies (Zigler, 1963) they predicted that a condition X game interaction would be greater for the institutionalized retarded children than for the other two groups.

The results disclosed that the institutionalized retarded children exhibited higher positive and negative reaction tendencies than did the other two groups. The institutionalized retarded children positioned themselves closer to the adult (positive reaction tendency) on both the placing and free play tasks than did the other two groups. Institutionalized retarded children whose fearfulness and wariness were reduced in the support and neutral conditions, approached the adult even more closely during Placing Task II. No condition effects were found for the noninstitutionalized retarded and normal groups. The investigators propose that the failure to find differences on the placing task performances between the noninstitutionalized retarded and normal groups may have been due to weak experimental conditions, i.e., punishment too mild. In discussing the results, Weaver et al. (1971) state, "The major contribution of the present study would appear to be the confirmation, by means of an interpersonal distance measure rather than a persistence measure, of earlier findings of the child's motivation to approach an adult and his wariness to do so" (p. 107).

GAYTON AND BASSETT'S STUDIES. In a study designed to test Zigler's (1966) theory of positive reaction tendency of retarded persons, Gayton and Bassett (1972) selected 42 retarded residents ($\overline{IQ} = 52.6$) and examined reaction tendencies and receptive language development. Each subject was administered the *Peabody Picture Vocabulary Test* (PPVT) (Dunn, 1959). Pictures that were missed which corresponded to the subjects' MAs were selected for the experimental task. In the task, subjects pointed to the correct picture when the examiner said a word. Six test cards with four pictures per card served as the experimental task stimuli. The subjects were assigned to one of three reward conditions: maximum social reinforcement, minimum social reinforcement, and nonsocial reinforcement.

In accordance with the positive reaction position, the investigators hypothesized that maximum social reinforcement would enhance task performance more than the other conditions. Half of the subjects in each reinforcement condition received reinforcement on a CFR (continuous) schedule and half received a VR–3 schedule of reinforcement. Maximum social reinforcement consisted of a pat on the back and verbal reinforcement, such as "You're doing just fine," and "That's very good." The verbal reinforcement phrases were randomly presented on a predetermined schedule. Minimum social reinforcement consisted of the experimenter saying "Good" following a correct response, while in the nonsocial reinforcement condition a bell rang after each correct response. Subjects were tested over a period of several days and each subject was terminated when he reached criterion.

The data were analyzed by inspecting two response measures, i.e., median trials to criterion and number of correct responses over trials. The subjects in the maximum reinforcement condition learned the correct responses (median trials to criterion) significantly faster than either of the other two reinforcement groups. The performances of the minimum and nonsocial reinforcement groups did not significantly differ. The schedules of reinforcement produced no differential effects. The groups did not significantly differ on the number of correct responses over trials. The investigators suggest that failure to achieve differences on the number of correct responses over trials may have been due to a ceiling effect.

Gayton and Bassett (1972) claim that the differential effects produced under the varied reinforcement conditions partially support Zigler's (1966) formulations regarding the effects of positive reaction tendency. The development of receptive vocabulary was enhanced under conditions of social reinforcement. The authors note, "The experiment showed consistently that a relationship characterized by friendly social interaction leads to more effective learning" (p. 502). The results also showed that as the amount of social reinforcement increases the beneficial effects increase. Moreover, since no differences existed in the performances of the nonsocial and minimum reinforcement groups, it appears that the magnitude of social reinforcement appears to be important.

In a second experiment Gayton and Bassett (1972) studied receptive language development of mentally retarded residents in relation to Zigler's (1966) theory of negative reaction tendency. On the basis of Zigler's theory it is feasible to predict that negative interaction prior to an event would be less effective in facilitating performance of retarded individuals than prior interaction characterized by positive or no interaction. Forty-two institutionalized retarded persons ($\overline{IQ} = 52.1$) were selected and randomly assigned to one of three treatment conditions: (a) positive prior interaction, (b) negative prior interaction, and (c) no prior interaction. Half of the subjects in each group were reinforced with maximum social reinforcement and half with minimum social reinforcement.

In the positive and negative prior-interaction groups the subjects were asked to guess (20 trials) which of two experimenter-controlled lights would come on. With the positive prior-interaction group all guesses were correct and the subjects received verbal praise, physical contact, and a candy bar. In the negative prior-interaction group all guesses were incorrect and the examiner acted in a demeaning manner. Following the prior in-

teraction conditions the subjects were required to perform the same task used in Experiment I.

The data were organized in terms of median trials to criterion and the number of correct responses per trial. The results revealed that negative prior interaction elicits a significantly poorer performance than the positive and no prior interaction when the following event involves maximum social reinforcement. Gayton and Bassett (1972) state:

> This finding suggests that the deleterious effects associated with negative prior interaction do not express themselves if the adult-child interaction is one characterized by minimum social interaction. It appears that the reluctance of the child to interact with an adult (negative reaction tendency) is not increased significantly if, following a failure experience, the adult involved with training the child does not try to quickly establish a warm, close relationship with the child (maximum social reinforcement). (pp. 506–507)

Gayton and Bassett (1972) indicate that the strength of the preceding discussion is somewhat weakened since significant results were not achieved with the number of correct responses per trial measure. As in Experiment I, the investigators discuss the possibility of a ceiling effect. Finally, they conclude that the results provided partial support for Zigler's (1966) negative reaction tendency formulation concerning retarded individuals.

SUMMARY. The small number of studies presented indicates that more research regarding Zigler's formulations of positive and negative reaction tendencies is needed before definitive conclusions can be made. Some variables that may be related to positive and negative reaction tendencies which need to be examined more systematically include: level of retardation, age of retarded subjects, criterion task difficulty, institutionalization, magnitude of reinforcement conditions, and replication studies with the distance to examiner measure used by Weaver, Balla, and Zigler (1971).

As indicated in Table 6.3, the retarded subjects used in the three studies were in the adolescent age range (CA range from 10.3–14.7 years) and were classified as mildly retarded. Only institutionalized retarded subjects performed in accordance with the positive and negative reaction tendencies position. However, only one group of noninstitutionalized subjects was used in the studies. In the one study (Weaver, Balla, & Zigler, 1971) that compared retarded subjects with MA-equivalent, normal children the institutionalized retardates performed with stronger positive and negative reaction tendencies than the normals; however, the noninstitutionalized retarded subjects responded similar to the normals. The results from these recent studies coupled with the findings from the foundation studies provide modest support for the positive and negative reaction tendencies position in adolescent institutionalized retardates.

IMPLICATIONS FOR TEACHING

1. Teachers need to employ intense social reinforcement in order to facilitate the performances of retarded students. An increase in social reinforcement with a retarded child could enhance progress in academic tasks, e.g., receptive language (Gayton & Bassett, 1972).

2. If a retarded child has experienced conditions with the teacher which make him reluctant to interact with the teacher, the teacher needs to start with minimum social reinforcement and gradually move to more intense social reinforcement. In essence, the teacher should be careful not to come on too strong with retarded students who are initially reluctant (negative reaction tendency) to engage in interaction (Gayton & Bassett, 1972).

3. Atypical high positive (overdependence) or high negative (withdrawal) reaction tendencies attentuate a child's social effectiveness and reduce the quality of his performance below his respective intellectual capacity (Weaver, Balla, & Zigler, 1971). Hence, teachers should gradually encourage highly dependent children to exhibit independent behavior in academic and social situations. For example, initially teacher could verbally encourage spelling with corrective feedback and then move to providing the child with an audio tape of the words correctly spelled, followed by an answer sheet, etc. For the children who are extremely withdrawn the teacher should introduce the task by allowing the child to work with minimal interaction. The teacher may next have the child respond to his voice on tape, then to a live peer, and then directly to the teacher. Appropriate reinforcement for either more (withdrawn children) or less (overdependent children) interaction with others would reduce atypical response tendencies and enhance the children's performance on social and academic tasks.

4. It is likely that social approval and support from the teacher enable the teacher to become a powerful reinforcer with children who exhibit positive and/or negative reaction tendencies.

Outer-directedness

Foundation Literature

From another series of investigations Zigler postulated that the repeated failures experienced by retarded individuals lead them to a style of problem solving characterized by outer-directedness. According to Zigler (1966), "the retarded child comes to distrust his own solutions to problems and therefore seeks guides to action in the immediate environment" (p. 99). Consistent with the outer-directedness position is the viewpoint that the retarded child has probably learned that a reliance on external cues is a more successful approach to problem solving than a reliance on his own cognitive resources.

ZIGLER, HODGDEN, AND STEVENSON'S STUDIES. Zigler, Hodgden, and Stevenson (1958) found that institutionalized retarded children would stop working on experimental games following a suggestion to stop from an experimenter, while normal children tended to ignore the suggestions. Green and Zigler (1962) found that noninstitutionalized retarded children had a greater tendency to terminate working on the suggestion from the experimenter than did either normals or institutionalized retarded children. These findings led Zigler et al. to postulate that institutional environments foster less failure than community environments; therefore, outer-directedness is more characteristic of noninstitutionalized retarded persons than it is of institutionalized retarded persons.

TURNURE AND ZIGLER'S STUDIES. The hypotheses generated from the Green and Zigler (1962) study were later examined in a study by Turnure and Zigler (1964). They selected MA-equivalent normal and retarded children and tested their tendency to imitate an adult and a peer following the playing of three games under either a success or a failure condition. They found that retarded children imitated more than normal children and the imitative behavior of all children increased following the failure experience. Turnure and Zigler (1964) conducted a second experiment which demonstrated that outer-directedness can be helpful. Normal and retarded subjects were required to assemble a design while the experimenter assembled a second design in full view. Normal children assembled the first design significantly faster than the retarded group, but the retarded children were significantly faster than the normals on assembling the

TABLE 6.3
Summary of Studies Regarding Positive and Negative Reaction Tendencies

ARTICLE	SUBJECTS	CONDITIONS AND TASKS	ANALYSIS

1. Weaver, Balla, & Zigler (1971)	3 groups
	1. 36 institutionalized retarded children
	$\overline{CA} = 12.9$ yr
	$\overline{MA} = 7.5$ yr
	$\overline{IQ} = 58$
	2. 36 noninstitutionalized retarded children
	$\overline{CA} = 10.3$ yr
	$\overline{MA} = 7.6$ yr
	$\overline{IQ} = 79$
	3. 36 normal children
	$\overline{CA} = 8$ yr
	$\overline{MA} = 7.7$ yr
	$\overline{IQ} = 99$
	
	All groups equated on MA and sex.
		1. The criterion tasks (tasks I and II) involved placing felt figures on a panel.
		2. The distance that the subjects placed themselves from an adult during task performances was recorded.
		3. Ss performed Placing Task I under one of 3 conditions.
		  a. support
		  b. punishment
		  c. neutral
			1. Compared group distance data.
			2. Compared distance data across conditions.

RESULTS: The institutionalized retarded children positioned themselves closer to the adult in both free play and placing task situations than did the other two groups. The institutionalized retarded children were the only group to respond differentially to the experimental conditions (support, punishment and neutral), i.e., following support and neutral experiences on Placing Task I they moved closer to the adult on Placing Task II. The social interpersonal distance measure generated data consistent with earlier studies using time persistence measures. No sex differences occurred.

2. Gayton & Bassett (1972) *Exp. I*	1 group
	42 institutionalized retarded subjects
	$\overline{CA} = 14.7$ yr
	$\overline{IQ} = 52.6$
	22 males
	20 females
		1. Criterion task involved the Ss identifying pictures from the *Peabody Picture Vocabulary Test.*
		2. Conditions consisted of:
		  a. Maximum social reinforcement group
		  b. Minimum social reinforcement group
		  c. Non-social reinforcement group
			1. Compared performances across conditions.
			2. Compared performances between schedules of reinforcement.

RESULTS: Subjects in the maximum social reinforcement condition performed significantly better than Ss in the other two conditions. The schedules of reinforcement produced no differential effects on the performances of the Ss. The authors interpret the results (effect of maximum social reinforcement) as partially supportive of Zigler's "positive reaction tendency." No differences occurred between the performances of the Ss in the minimum and nonsocial groups. This finding was interpreted as demonstrating the importance of the magnitude of the social reinforcer.

TABLE 6.3, cont.

ARTICLE	SUBJECTS	CONDITIONS AND TASKS	ANALYSIS

3. Gayton & Bassett (1972) *Exp. II*	42 institutionalized retarded subjects
	$\overline{CA} = 13.7$
	$\overline{IQ} = 52.1$
	29 males, 13 females
		1. Criterion task involved identifying pictures from the *Peabody Picture Vocabulary Test*.
		2. Three initial treatment conditions
		  a. Positive prior interaction group
		  b. Negative prior interaction group
		  c. No-prior interaction group
		3. Two later treatment conditions: half of Ss from above conditions were assigned to maximum and half of Ss to minimum reinforcement.
		  a. Maximum social reinforcement
		  b. Minimum social reinforcement
			1. Compared performances across conditions.
			2. Examined interaction between prior conditions and experimental conditions.

RESULTS: The findings indicated that negative prior interaction elicits a significantly poorer performance than the positive and no prior interaction when the following event involves maximum social reinforcement. The authors note that this finding provides some support for Zigler's "negative reaction tendency" formulation.

213

second design. Also, the retarded children glanced more often at the experimenter than did the normal children.

These early studies regarding the formulation of the outer-directedness hypothesis are cited frequently in the literature and they have provided a springboard for further articles which will now be discussed in detail.

Further Studies

SANDERS, ZIGLER, AND BUTTERFIELD'S STUDIES. Sanders, Zigler, and Butterfield (1968) examined outer-directedness in the discrimination learning of normal and mentally retarded children. They selected 100 institutionalized, moderately retarded individuals and 50 normal children of comparable MAs. The retarded subjects were classified into two equal groups: high- and low-distractible. Each subject performed a three-choice discrimination task in one of five conditions. A group of 10 high-distractible retarded subjects, a group of 10 low-distractible retarded subjects, and a group of 10 normals performed in each condition.

In the positive conditions a positive cue appeared above the correct stimulus at the beginning of every trial. In one positive condition the experimenter placed his finger above the correct stimulus and in the other positive condition a light appeared above the correct stimulus. The cues were presented as start signals to the subjects. In the negative conditions a negative cue appeared over an incorrect stimulus at the beginning of each trial. As in the positive condition the experimenter's finger and a light served as the cue signals. For subjects in the control group no cues were provided. In all conditions the criterion task involved the subject selecting which one of three blocks was located over a marble. Since the subjects in the positive conditions could reach criterion (five consecutive correct responses) without learning the discrimination task, additional trials were provided to them without cues.

The investigators used the outer-directedness hypothesis to predict that the performances of the retarded subjects would be more enhanced with positive cues and more depressed with negative cues than the respective performances of the MA-matched normals. Using the mean number of errors as a measure, Sanders et al. (1968) found that no differences occurred between high- and low-distractible retardates nor between the finger and light conditions. In the negative conditions the retarded subjects made more cued than noncued errors, while the normals did not differ in the number of cued and noncued errors. The performances by the retarded in the negative conditions confirmed the outer-directedness hypothesis. In the positive conditions the outer-directedness hypothesis was not confirmed. Upon examining the influence of etiology, Sanders et al. showed that familial retardates were less outer-directed in their problem solving than were nonfamilial retarded children. Finally, they showed that in the positive conditions some retarded subjects used the extrinsic cues to solve the discrimination problem and actually outperformed the normals.

CARLSON AND MACMILLAN'S STUDIES. Carlson and MacMillan (1970) examined the effects of countersuggestion on the probability judgments of retarded and nonretarded children. According to the outer-directedness hypothesis, mentally retarded children are more susceptible to counter-suggestions than normal children. Carlson and MacMillan selected 16 EMR children who were matched on CA (9 years) with a nonretarded group ($N = 16$) and 16 EMR children who were matched on MA with the same nonretarded group. The subjects viewed 10 trials of an experimenter who manipulated a spring device to propel a ball down a grooved board and marked the stopping place of the ball. On the observed trials the ball tended to stop in the same general area. After these observation trials each subject was asked (a) to predict how far the ball would roll, (b) to justify the prediction, (c) to respond to a countersuggestion (experimenter challenged initial prediction of subject by stating, "Isn't the ball really just as likely to stop here?"), (d) to make a second prediction, and (e) to justify the second prediction.

The findings indicated that both retarded groups changed their predictions more following the countersuggestion than the nonretarded group. The investigators concluded that the retarded children were more susceptible to countersuggestion than the nonretarded children and the results were interpreted as supporting the outer-directedness position described by Zigler.

TURNURE'S STUDIES. Turnure (1970) conducted a series of three experiments designed to examine the reactions of moderately retarded and normal children to physical and social distractors. The first study focused on studying the orienting behavior of 28 retarded children in a learning situation and comparing it with the orienting behavior of MA-equivalent, nonretarded children from an earlier study (Turnure, 1966).

The apparatus consisted of a light-proof booth which housed a projector used to present the stimuli on a panel with three windows and a one-way mirror. The distracting condition consisted of exposing the mirror, while in the control condition the mirror was covered. The task consisted of an oddity problem in which the subject had to select the odd stimulus from three stimuli presented. The odd stimulus was always on the right or left window and never in the middle. A red light came on when the correct stimulus was chosen. During the 60 trials performed by each subject, glancing data were recorded.

Analysis of the glancing data revealed that younger subjects spent more time in nontask orientation than did the older subjects. When the glancing data of the retarded subjects from this study were compared with the glancing data of MA-equivalent, nonretarded subjects from an earlier study, no differences were found. Further analysis revealed that retarded children tended to glance more than CA-equivalent normals on precriterion trials, whereas the reverse occurred for postcriterion glances. Normals tended to glance more under the distracting condition than did the retarded children. Turnure (1970) feels the findings are not supportive of the contention that retarded individuals are more distractible than normal persons. Moreover, he cautions against the wholesale comparison of retarded with CA-equivalent, nonretarded individuals on tasks of similar difficulty. He claims that task difficulty may influence nontask orienting behavior. The results of this study were not discussed in terms of the outer-directedness position, but they do have some implications concerning outer-directedness. The fact that retarded children glanced more than normals in the precriterion trials may be viewed as supportive of the outer-directedness position.

In a second investigation Turnure (1970) tested the outer-directedness position by studying the effect of adult presence on nontask orientation of moderately retarded subjects who participated in the first study. The task was identical to that of the first study except the experimenter did not go to the rear of the booth as in Study I but remained beside the subject. The experimenter could be seen in the mirror and by a slight turn of the head. Nine subjects participated in a relevant cue condi-

tion which consisted of the experimenter tilting his head toward the correct stimulus and looking at the correct stimulus displayed on a clipboard he was holding. Eight subjects participated in the irrelevant cue condition which consisted of the experimenter keeping his head on the median plane.

The results disclosed that glancing under both conditions of Study II was greater than the glancing recorded in Study I. No significant differences occurred between the number of correct responses in Study I and Study II and between the correct responses of subjects in the relevant and irrelevant conditions. Although significant differences were not obtained, the results were in the expected directions, i.e., the relevant cue condition produced more correct responses than the irrelevant cue condition. Turnure (1970) interprets the findings as supporting the hypothesis that nontask orienting by retarded individuals reflects an information-seeking strategy (outer-directedness).

In a third study Turnure (1970) selected seven new retarded subjects in order to replicate Study II. Four subjects were assigned to the relevant cue condition and three subjects were assigned to the irrelevant cue condition. Although Turnure questioned the validity of the results from this study because of the small sample, he indicates findings similar to the results of Study II.

In discussing the findings of the three studies, Turnure (1970) makes several observations. First, he cautions against generalizing the results beyond institutionalized retarded children. Secondly, he notes that the aspect of attending referred to in the studies pertained only to overt orienting responses and should not be extended to include all aspects of attending. Finally, he notes that the results suggest that the nontask orientations of retarded subjects may be interpreted as information-seeking rather than evidence of distractibility.

BALLA, STYFCO, AND ZIGLER'S STUDIES. As a part of a somewhat comprehensive study, Balla, Styfco, and Zigler (1971) examined outer-directedness in intellectually average, familial retarded, and organically retarded children. Ninety-six children within each group were divided into four mental age levels (6, 7, 8, and 10 years). Next, the mental age groups within each group of 96 children were further subdivided into three experimental groups. The final sample consisted of 36 groups, 12 from each of the three major group

classifications (intellectually average, familial retarded, and organically retarded). The task consisted of selecting a circle from among four circles
opposite in size to a circle which was cued. The
nature of the cueing distinguished the three experimental conditions and consisted of a cue
pointed out by a person, a color cue, and an external cue. In the first condition each child was told,
"There is something about the circle that I am
pointing to that will help you figure it out." The
correct response involved the subject selecting the
circle opposite in size to the one pointed to by the
experimenter. In the color cue condition each child
was told that the green circle would help and again
the correct response involved the subject selecting
from among four red circles the circle opposite in
size to the green one. In the external cue condition
a circle (either smaller or larger than all others)
was presented as a cue which offered help. When
the subject selected the correct circle, he was told
of this and praised. On incorrect responses the
subject was told he was wrong.

The effect of overreliance on an obvious but
misleading cue was examined by recording the
number of trials on which the subject chose the
circle the same size as that of the cue. Data
analysis revealed that the organically retarded
children made the most cued errors, the familial
retarded children made the next most, and the
nonretarded children made the least cued errors.
The group at MA level of 10 years (oldest group)
made fewer cued errors than either of the other
groups. The most cued errors were made in the
external condition, the next most in the color condition, and the least in the pointing condition.

It was reasoned that when unsuccessful responses were encountered, the outer-directed
subjects, because of their tendency to rely on external cues, would tend to engage in a problem-
solving strategy characterized by selecting stimuli
adjacent in size or position to the incorrect cue.
Data analysis indicated that the organically retarded children committed the most errors in size
to the cue, the familial-retarded children the next
most, and the intellectually average subjects the
fewest. The group at MA level of 6 years (youngest
group) made more of these errors than each of the
other three MA groups. The most errors next in the
size to the cue were made in the color condition,
the next most in the pointing condition, and least in
the external condition.

Balla et al. (1971) note that the results (highest
MA subjects being least outer-directed) were consistent with the developmental aspect of the
outer-directedness construct. Also, they acknowledge that the greater the outer-directedness encountered in the color rather than in the pointing
condition was consistent with other findings which
suggest that a nonhuman cue elicits more outer-
directedness than does a human cue. They further
hypothesize that the influence of human cueing
may be due to the familiarity or unfamiliarity of the
person presenting the cues. In discussing generalization and outer-directedness, the investigators
note that generalization occurred more readily in
situations similar to the original learning situation.
They reason that for specific tasks, competing
outer-directed problem-solving strategies become
extinguished in the original setting, whereas a
situation change introduces new competing cues.
In summarizing the results, Balla et al. state,
"When generalization was assessed in a situation
highly similar to that in which original learning took
place, performance was more efficient than when
generalization was assessed in a dissimilar situation. Apparently in the original learning, competing
outer-directed problem-solving strategies were extinguished, but this phenomenon was relatively
task-specific" (p. 678). Finally, Balla et al. note that
organically retarded individuals appear more
outer-directed than familial retarded children.

DROTAR'S STUDIES. Drotar (1972) modified Turnure and Zigler's (1964) design to provide a
clearer test of the outer-directedness hypothesis.
He selected 30 noninstitutionalized retarded children and 30 nonretarded children from public
schools. The subjects were equated on MA and
sex, were divided into three groups of nonretarded
children and three groups of retarded children.
The groups were distinguished by their assignment to a similar cue condition, a dissimilar cue
condition, and a no-cue condition. Subjects in the
similar cue condition performed a puzzle (Task 1)
while the experimenter sat next to the subject and
assembled a puzzle which the subject would later
assemble on Task 2. In the no-cue condition the
experimenter did not assemble a puzzle. For Task
2 the experimenter did not assemble a puzzle
under any of the conditions. Drotar reasoned that
Turnure and Zigler had only one control condition
in which the experimenter did not assemble a puz-

zle. Since the stimuli of the experimenter's puzzle were not varied, it is not clear to what degree the retarded children's improved Task 2 performance resulted from information gained from previous attention to the experimenter's assembly. Thus, Drotar added the dissimilar condition in order to test whether or not the retarded children were attending to the experimenter's assembly (gaining information) when they were glancing at the experimenter.

Basing his assumption on the outer-directedness hypothesis, Drotar (1972) predicted that the retarded children's Task 1 performance (because of attention to the experimenter's puzzle) would be below that of MA-equivalent, nonretarded children in both similar and dissimilar cue conditions. The second prediction, based on the outer-directedness hypothesis, was that retarded children in the similar cue condition would score higher than nonretarded children on Task 2.

The findings regarding Task 1 confirmed Turnure and Zigler's (1964) position (outer-directedness) that the presence of an experimenter assembling a puzzle depresses the performance of retarded children significantly below the performance of MA-equivalent, nonretarded children. The performances of the retarded and nonretarded groups did not differ in the no-cue conditions. Drotar (1972) notes that the findings generated from the glancing data were somewhat suspect because of the crude nature of the data collection. The hypothesis that outer-directed responding on Task 1 would facilitate the performance of retarded children relative to the performance of MA-equivalent, nonretarded children on Task 2 was not supported. These data suggest that the outer-directed orientation of retarded subjects is not an information-seeking strategy which is relative to task completion. Drotar notes that this finding may have been effected by ceiling effects. Also, in order to avoid unequivocal comparisons, he points out the differences between his subjects and Turnure and Zigler's subjects.

TURNURE'S STUDIES, 1973. Turnure (1973) selected 21 mildly retarded boys and 21 mildly retarded girls in order to study outer-directedness while the subjects performed an oddity learning task. Specifically, the study focused on examining the relationship between learning and glancing,

the effect of experimenter presence and absence, and the effect of having the experimenter provide or not provide task relevant cues.

The 42 subjects were randomly assigned to one of three experimental conditions with seven boys and seven girls in each condition. The three experimental conditions were: (a) no experimenter present, (b) experimenter present with relevant cues (relevant cue), and (c) experimenter present with no relevant cues (irrelevant cue).

A somewhat sophisticated booth apparatus was employed which featured a one-way vision mirror, a red light for signaling a correct response, and a Kodak Carousel 800 projector for presenting the oddity task stimuli on three screens. The correct stimulus (odd figure) was always on the left or right screen and never appeared on the center screen. Each subject performed 60 oddity trials and then, without comment, 18 reversal trials were initiated. In the first 10 reversal trials the background was switched from white to red and the correct choice became the *same* rather than the *different* stimulus in either the right or left window. In the final eight trials, four of the red-colored reversal slides were presented alternately with four black and white oddity slides.

In the no-experimenter present condition, the examiner left the subject alone prior to the first slide presentation. In the relevant cue condition, the experimenter remained beside the subject and turned his head in the direction of the correct stimulus. In the irrelevant cue condition, the experimenter did not provide any cues concerning the correct stimulus but merely lifted his head with the presentation of each slide.

Glancing data (gathered via one-way mirror box observer) revealed that greater nontask orienting occurred in the presence of an experimenter, thus confirming the hypothesis that subjects would show more nontask orienting behavior when an experimenter was present than when the experimenter was absent. Learning data yielded significant treatment effects for boys and revealed that they had higher performances in the relevant cue condition than in the irrelevant cue condition.

In addition to the duplication of these findings in the reversal trials, a significant positive correlation was obtained between learning and glancing in the relevant cue condition, and a significant negative correlation occurred between learning and glancing in the irrelevant cue condition. Further, Turnure

(1973) found that no group of subjects spent more than 6% of the time available glancing away from the task.

He concluded that mentally retarded girls appear to be less outer-directed than mentally retarded boys. Moreover, the results were interpreted as in general agreement with expectations derived from an outer-directedness hypothesis.

SUMMARY. A perusal of Table 6.4 enables us to summarize some of the salient information from the outer-directedness studies. An examination of the characteristics of the mentally retarded subjects included in these studies indicates that considerable variation existed among the subjects. For example, the mean ages of the retarded groups across the studies ranged from 8.86 years to 42.75 years. Noninstitutionalized, mildly retarded subjects were included in four studies, whereas institutionalized, moderately retarded persons were included in the three studies by Turnure (1970) and in two other studies (Balla, Styfco, & Zigler, 1971; Sanders, Zigler, & Butterfield, 1968). The mean mental ages of the retarded groups ranged from 4.8–10 years. One study (Balla, Styfco, & Zigler, 1971) included a group of organically retarded subjects. Since wide variations existed on important variables across the retarded subjects, generalizations from one study to another must be limited.

Turnure (1973) compared and found differences between retarded boys and girls on outer-directedness. All the other studies included retarded boys and girls, and it is possible that differential performance between boys and girls in these studies were masked because their respective performances were not treated separately. In spite of possible differences between retarded boys and girls on outer-directedness, in three of the four studies that compared the degree of outer-directedness of retarded individuals with MA-equivalent normals, the retarded subjects were more outer-directed.

Two studies (Carlson & MacMillan, 1970; Turnure, 1970) compared and found that retarded subjects were more outer-directed than CA-equivalent normals. Two studies (Balla, Styfco, & Zigler, 1971; Turnure, 1970) supported the contention that outer-directedness is developmental, with higher-MA persons being less outer-directed than lower-MA persons. One study (Sanders, Zigler, & Butterfield, 1968) found that retardates were more outer-directed than MA-equivalent normals under

negative cue conditions but not more outer-directed in positive conditions.

More research is needed before definitive conclusions can be drawn from the outer-directedness literature. The issue of whether or not it is a problem-solving strategy still remains unanswered. In addition, factors such as task difficulty and the characteristics of persons who represent external sources have not been systematically examined in relation to outer-directedness. Although knowledge about the outer-directedness hypothesis is limited, current evidence strongly implies that retarded individuals exhibit more nontask orientations than nonretarded subjects. Specific implications have been gleaned from the outer-directedness literature and are presented in the next section.

IMPLICATIONS FOR TEACHING. The outer-directedness studies strongly suggest that teachers constantly evaluate cues that they are providing children. It is apparent that teachers are in a position to provide social as well as task-relevant cues to sensitized retarded children. Some specific implications include:

1. Teachers should not always consider nontask orientations by retarded pupils as distractibility or a waste of time. This nontask orientation may be a problem-solving strategy and not indicative of a behavior problem or boredom. For those pupils seeking information via nontask orientations it is possible that the provision of environmental cues for enhancing task success would help, such as putting a complete alphabet over the chalkboard. Also, too many nontask orientations may be a cue to the teacher that the task is too difficult (Turnure, 1973).
2. The teacher should provide cues which facilitate success and reduce cues which hinder success. The teacher can do this by demonstrating activities, such as perceptual-motor and social tasks (table manners). Also, the teacher can organize the class so that children in close proximity are performing similar tasks. In essence, children should be afforded appropriate models whenever possible.
3. In original learning situations the environment should remain constant in order that new irrelevant competing stimuli are not continuously attracting the child's attention. When transfer of learning is desired, extraneous cues may be gradually introduced into the teaching environment (Balla, Styfco, & Zigler, 1971).
4. In a failure situation retarded children tend to become more outer-directed. Thus, if a teacher notices that a child is experiencing difficulty achieving, he should make extensive efforts to provide support and encouragement.

TABLE 6.4
Summary of Outer-Directedness Studies

ARTICLE	SUBJECTS	CONDITIONS AND TASKS	ANALYSIS
1. Sanders, Zigler, & Butterfield (1968)	2 groups 1. 100 institutionalized, retarded Ss 50—high distractible 50—low distractible 52 males and 48 females $\overline{IQ}$ approx. 45 $\overline{MA}$ approx. 6.5 $\overline{CA}$ approx. 19 2. 50 normals $\overline{IQ}$ approx. 105 $\overline{MA}$ approx. 6.5 $\overline{CA}$ approx. 6.5	1. Criterion task involved a three choice discrimination task under positive and negative cue conditions. 2. Positive condition Pointing Cue Light Cue 3. Negative condition Pointing Cue Light Cue 4. Control condition No cues provided.	1. Compared the scores between the high- and low-distractible groups. 2. Compared the performances among the retarded and normal groups. 3. Compared performances across conditions.

RESULTS: In the negative condition the retardates made more cued than noncued errors while the normals did not differ on cued and noncued errors. This finding supports the outer-directedness hypothesis. No differences occurred between the high- and low-distractible groups and between the pointing and light-cueing conditions. In the positive conditions the outer-directedness hypothesis was not supported. Actually some MRs used the extrinsic cues to learn the task and performed better than their normal counterparts. Familials were less outer-directed than the nonfamililals.

ARTICLE	SUBJECTS	CONDITIONS AND TASKS	ANALYSIS
2. Carlson & MacMillan (1970)	3 groups 1. 16 EMRs $\overline{CA} = 8.86$, $\overline{IQ} = 65.5$ $\overline{MA} = 5.79$ 2. 16 EMR $\overline{CA} = 12.88$, $\overline{IQ} = 70.37$ $\overline{MA} = 9.97$ 3. 16 nonretarded $\overline{CA} = 8.89$ $\overline{IQ} = 102.2$, $\overline{MA} = 9.05$ Equal sex distribution in all groups.	1. Criterion task involved predicting how far a spring would propel a ball after watching the experimenter perform 10 trials. 2. The conditions and tasks included: a. a first prediction b. a justification of prediction c. a countersuggestion d. a second prediction e. a justification of second prediction	1. Compared Prediction 1 with Prediction 2. 2. Compared predictions across groups.

RESULTS: Both retarded groups changed their predictions more following the counter-suggestion than the nonretarded group. The authors interpreted the findings as supportive of the outer-directedness hypothesis.

TABLE 6.4, cont.

ARTICLE	SUBJECTS	CONDITIONS AND TASKS	ANALYSIS
3. Turnure (1970) *Exp. I*	4 groups of moderately retarded residents 1. Young control group $\overline{CA} = 10.6$, $\overline{IQ} = 49.0$ $\overline{MA} = 4.8$ 2. Young mirror group $\overline{CA} = 11.6$, $\overline{IQ} = 45.4$, $\overline{MA} = 4.9$ 3. Old control group $\overline{CA} = 16.1$, $\overline{IQ} = 50.7$, $\overline{MA} = 7.7$ 4. Old mirror group $\overline{CA} = 15.4$, $\overline{IQ} = 51.3$, $\overline{MA} = 7.6$	1. Criterion task consisted of an oddity task in which subjects selected the odd stimulus from 3 stimuli. 2. In the control condition the mirror was covered and in the distracting condition it was exposed. 3. Glance data were recorded while the Ss performed the tasks.	1. Compared glance data among the groups. 2. Compared glance data from Ss in this study to glance data from another study using nonretarded Ss who were matched on MA with Ss in this study.

RESULTS: The data revealed that younger Ss spent more time in nontask orientation than did the older subjects. No differences were obtained between the nontask orientation of the retarded Ss in this study and MA-equivalent, nonretarded Ss from another study. When retardates are matched with CA-equivalent normals they tend to glance more on precriterion trials, while normals glance more on postcriterion trials. The findings were viewed as not supporting the position that MRs are more distractible than normals. Since MRs glanced more during precriterion trials, it was reasoned that this nontask orienting is related to task difficulty and was an information-seeking strategy (outer-directed).

ARTICLE	SUBJECTS	CONDITIONS AND TASKS	ANALYSIS
4. Turnure (1970) *Exp. II*	2 groups of moderately retarded from *Exp. I* 1. 9 Ss in relevant cue condition $\overline{CA} = 13-10$, $\overline{IQ} = 45$, $\overline{MA} = 6-1$ 2. 8 Ss in irrelevant cue condition $\overline{CA} = 13-5$, $\overline{IQ} = 49$, $\overline{MA} = 6-0$	1. Criterion task—same as *Exp. I*—oddity task. 2. Relevant cue condition—experimenter remained beside Ss and provided correct cues. 3. Irrelevant cue condition—experimenter remained beside the Ss and provided irrelevant cues.	1. Glance data were compared between the conditions. 2. Compared correct responses between the groups. 3. Compared glancing and task data of *Exp. I* with that of *Exp. II*.

RESULTS: Nontask orientation (glancing) was greater in both conditions of *Exp. II* than it was in *Exp. I*. No differences occurred between the number of correct responses in *Exp. I* and *Exp. II*. No differences occurred between correct responses recorded in the relevant and irrelevant conditions. Turnure interprets the findings as supporting the position that the nontask orienting by retarded individuals is an information-seeking strategy (outer-directedness).

TABLE 6.4, cont.

ARTICLE	SUBJECTS	CONDITIONS AND TASKS	ANALYSIS
5. Turnure (1970) *Exp. III*	2 groups IQ ≤ 50 1. 4 Ss in relevant cue condition 2. 3 Ss in irrelevant cue condition CA, MA, IQ not available	1. Criterion task—same oddity task used in *Exp. I* and *Exp. II.* 2. Relevant cue condition same as *Exp. I* and *Exp. II.* 3. Irrelevant cue condition same as *Exp. I* and *Exp. II.*	1. Compared glancing data between conditions. 2. Compared glancing data of *Exp. II* with *Exp. III.*

RESULTS: Due to the small sample comparisons via inferential statistics are questionable. However, the data showed patterns similar to those obtained in *Exp. I.* The relevant cue group showed greater glancing than the irrelevant cue group. Turnure tempered his generalization of the findings from the three studies because the same Ss participated in 2 studies and the 3rd study used a small N.* Overall, the results were seen as supporting the outer-directedness hypothesis.

ARTICLE	SUBJECTS	CONDITIONS AND TASKS	ANALYSIS
6. Balla, Styfco, & Zigler (1971)	3 groups 1. 96 nonretarded at 4 MA levels (6, 7, 8, 10) 2. 96 familial retarded at 4 MA levels (6, 7, 8, 10) public school (mildly retarded) 3. 96 organically retarded at 4 MA levels (6, 7, 8, 10). 86 residents, 7 nonresidents (moderately and mildly retarded).	1. Criterion task consisted of the subject selecting from 4 circles the circle opposite the cued circle. 2. Pointing cue condition. 3. Color cue condition. 4. External cue condition.	1. Compared the performances across cueing conditions. 2. Examined the selection of the circle next in size to the cued circle. 3. Compared the performances across the groups.

RESULTS: Cued errors were used the most by organically retarded children, and the least by the nonretarded. The older children made less cued errors than the other children. The most cued errors were made in the external condition and the least errors were made in the pointing cue condition. When selecting the cue next in size to the cued circle, the most errors were made by the organically retarded and the least by the nonretarded. The authors note the findings support the developmental position regarding outer-directedness. Also, the results supported the contention that nonhuman cues elicit more outer-directedness. Generalization and outer-directedness were discussed.

221

TABLE 6.4, cont.

ARTICLE	SUBJECTS	CONDITIONS AND TASKS	ANALYSIS

7. Drotar (1972)	2 groups divided in 3 subgroups each.
	1. 30 mildly retarded Ss, males and females were equally distributed.
	$\overline{CA}$ approx. 12 yr
	$\overline{MA}$ approx. 7.5 yr
	$\overline{IQ}$ approx. 64
	2. 30 nonretarded
	$\overline{CA}$ approx. 7.5 yr
	$\overline{MA}$ approx. 7.5 yr
	$\overline{IQ}$ approx. 100
		1. Criterion task involved assembling 2 puzzles.
		2. Ss were assigned to condition according to cues provided.
		  a. Similar Cue—experimenter provided cue by assembling second puzzle while S assembled 1st puzzle.
		  b. Dissimilar Cue—experimenter provided irrelevant cue by assembling different puzzle.
		  c. No-cue condition
		3. Under all conditions no experimenter cues were given while subjects performed Puzzle 2.
			1. Compared Task I performance with Task 2 performance.
			2. Compared performances between groups.

RESULTS: The findings regarding Task 1 confirmed the position that the presence of an experimenter assembling a puzzle would depress the performances of retarded children more than it would that of MA-equivalent, normal children. The performances of the MR and non-MR groups did not differ under the no-cue condition. The hypothesis that outer-directed responding on Task 1 would facilitate the performance of MRs on Task 2 was not supported. Drotar notes his findings may have been affected by ceiling effects and S differences between his study and Turnure and Zigler's (1964).

ARTICLE	SUBJECTS	CONDITIONS AND TASKS	ANALYSIS
8. Turnure (1973)	1 group subdivided into 6 groups $\overline{CA} = 8.6$ yr $\overline{MA} = 6.3$ yr $\overline{IQ} = 71.3$ 21 boys were assigned to the 3 conditions and 21 girls were assigned to the 3 conditions.	1. Criterion task—select the odd stimulus from among 3 stimuli. 2. Relevant cue condition—experimenter provided helpful cues. 3. Irrelevant cue condition—experimenter provided irrelevant cues. 4. Not in condition—experimenter left the immediate task area.	1. Compared glancing data across conditions. 2. Compared learning data across conditions. 3. Compared male performances with female performances.

RESULTS: Greater nontask orienting occurred in the presence of the experimenter than it did in the experimenter's absence (supportive of outer-directedness hypothesis). Learning data revealed significant treatment effects for boys, with performances being higher in the relevant cue condition than in the irrelevant cue condition. On reversal trials a significant positive correlation occurred between learning and glancing in the relevant cue condition and a negative relationship occurred in the irrelevant cue condition. Turnure notes the results are supportive of the outer-directedness hypothesis, and that boys appear more outer-directed than girls.

*N = Number of subjects

222

5. A behavior modification technique that seems appropriate for dealing with outer-directedness is fading. In the fading technique the teacher provides a substantial number of cues early in the program in order to enhance success. Later, the cues are gradually reduced (faded out) and the child is dependent on his own cognitive resources for the solution of problems (MacMillan, 1971).

6. The teacher can challenge the student's correct answers with the intent of teaching the child to depend on his own resources for solving problems (Carlson & MacMillan, 1970).

7. The teacher needs to be aware that his cues may promote guessing in retarded children. Also, in testing settings the environment should be arranged so that the temptation to copy from another is attenuated.

Conclusion

It is apparent that social learning theory and the research it has generated have contributed constructs and findings that improve our understanding of retarded individuals. In addition, the SLT literature is rich with educational implications which suggest methods for helping retarded individuals achieve a more fulfilling life. In a field that has a tendency to overemphasize the cognitive aspects of development, SLT represents a healthy departure because it emphasizes the social learning aspects of mental retardation.

References

Atkinson, J. E. *Motives in fantasy, action, and society.* Princeton, N.J.: Van Nostrand, 1958.

Balla, D., Styfco, S. J., & Zigler, E. Use of the opposition concept and outerdirectedness in intellectually-average, familial retarded, and organically retarded children. *American Journal of Mental Deficiency,* 1971, *75,* 663–680.

Battle, E., & Rotter, J. B. Children's feelings of personal control as related to social class and ethnic group. *Journal of Personality,* 1963, *31,* 482–490.

Bialer, I. *Conceptualization of success and failure in mentally retarded and normal children.* Ann Arbor, Mich.: University Microfilms, 1960.

Carlson, J. C., & MacMillan, D. L. Comparison of probability judgments between EMR and non-retarded children. *American Journal of Mental Deficiency,* 1970, *74,* 697–700.

Chan, K. S., & Keogh, B. K. Interpretation of task interruption and feelings of responsibility for failure. *Journal of Special Education,* 1974, *8,* 175–178.

Chandler, A., & Boroskin, A. Relationship of reward value and stated expectancy in mentally retarded patients. *American Journal of Mental Deficiency,* 1971, *75,* 761–762.

Coleman, J. S., Campbell, E. Q., Hobson, C. J., McPartland, J., Mood, A. M., Weinfeld, F. D., & York, R. L. *Equality of educational opportunity* (Superintendent of Documents, Catalog No. FS 5.238:38001). Washington, D.C.: Government Printing Office, 1966.

Crandall, V. C., Katkovsky, W., & Crandall, V. J. Children's beliefs in their own control or reinforcement in intellectual-academic achievement. *Child Development,* 1965, *36,* 91–109.

Crandall, V. J., Katkovsky, W., & Preston, A. Motivational and ability determinants of young children's intellectual achievement behaviors. *Child Development,* 1962, *33,* 643–661.

Cromwell, R. L. A social learning approach to mental retardation. In N. R. Ellis (Ed.), *Handbook of mental deficiency.* New York: McGraw-Hill, 1963.

Cromwell, R. L., & Moss, J. W. The influence of reward value on the stated expectancies of mentally retarded patients. *American Journal of Mental Deficiency,* 1959, *63,* 657–661.

Delys, P. *Rationale, method, and validity of the SDRCI IE measure for preschool children.* Paper presented at the American Psychological Association, Washington, D.C., 1971.

Diggory, J. C. *Self-evaluation: Concepts and studies.* New York: John Wiley & Sons, 1966.

Drotar, D. Outerdirectedness and the puzzle performance of nonretarded and retarded children. *American Journal of Mental Deficiency,* 1972, *77,* 230–236.

Dua, P. S. Comparison of the effects of behaviorally oriented action and psychotherapy reeducation on introversion-extraversion, emotionality, and internal-external control. *Journal of Consulting Psychology,* 1970, *17,* 567–572.

Dunn, L. M. *Peabody Picture Vocabulary Test.* Minneapolis, Minn.: American Guidance Service, 1959.

Edwards, A. L. *Edwards Personal Preference Schedule.* New York: Psychological Corp., 1957.

Estes, W. K. *Learning theory and mental development.* New York: Academic Press, 1970.

Fox, P. B. Locus of control and self concept in mildly retarded adolescents (Doctoral dissertation, University of Minnesota, 1972). *Dissertation Abstracts International,* 1972, *33,* 2807B. (University Microfilms No. 72–32287)

Gardner, W. I. *Effects of interpolated success and failure on motor task performance in mental defectives.* Paper presented at Southeastern Psychological Association meeting. Nashville, Tennessee, 1957.

Gardner, W. I. *Reactions of intellectually normal and retarded boys after experimentally induced failure: A social learning theory interpretation.* Ann Arbor, Mich.: University Microfilms, 1958.

Gayton, W. F., & Bassett, J. E. The effect of positive and negative reaction tendencies on receptive language development in mentally retarded children. *American Journal of Mental Deficiency*, 1972, *76*, 499–508.

Gorsuch, R. L., Henighan, R. R., & Barnard C. Locus of control: An example of dangers in using children's scales with children. *Child Development*, 1972, *43*, 579–590.

Green, C., & Zigler, E. Social deprivation and the performance of retarded and normal children on a satiation type task. *Child Development*, 1962, *33*, 499–508.

Gruen, G. E., Ottinger, D. R., & Ollendick, T. H. Probability learning in retarded children with differing histories of success and failure in school. *American Journal of Mental Deficiency*, 1974, *79*, 417–423.

Gruen, G., & Zigler, E. Expectancy of success and the probability learning of middle-class, lower-class, and retarded children. *Journal of Abnormal Psychology*, 1968, *73*, 343–352.

Guskin, S. Social psychologies of mental deficiency. In N. R. Ellis (Ed.), *Handbook of mental deficiency*. New York: McGraw-Hill, 1963.

Heber, R. F. *Expectancy and expectancy changes in normal and mentally retarded boys.* Ann Arbor, Mich.: University Microfilms, 1957.

Joe, V. C. Review of the internal-external control construct as a personality variable. *Psychological Reports*, 1971, *28*, 619–640.

Kagan, J. Impulsive and reflective children: Significance of conceptual tempo. In J. D. Krumboltz (Ed.), *Learning and the educational process*. Chicago: Rand McNally, 1965.

Keogh, B. K., Cahill, C. W., & MacMillan, D. L. Perception of interruption by educationally handicapped children. *American Journal of Mental Deficiency*, 1972, *77*, 107–108.

Kliebhan, J. M. Effects of goal-setting and modeling on job performance of retarded adolescents. *American Journal of Mental Deficiency*, 1967, *72*, 220–226.

Kounin, J. Experimental studies of rigidity: I. The measurement of rigidity in normal and feebleminded persons. *Character and Personality*, 1941, *9*, 251–273. (a)

Kounin, J. Exprimental studies of rigidity: II. The explanatory power of the concept of rigidity as applied to feeblemindedness. *Character and Personality*, 1941, *9*, 273–282. (b)

Lawrence, E. A., & Winschel, J. F. Locus of control: Implications for special education. *Exceptional Children*, 1975, *41*, 483–490.

Lefcourt, H. M. Internal versus external control of reinforcement: A review. *Psychological Bulletin*, 1966, *65*, 206–220.

Lefcourt, H. M. Recent developments in the study of locus of control. In B. A. Maher (Ed.), *Progress in experimental personality research* (Vol. 6). New York: Academic Press, 1972.

Levy, J. Social reinforcement and knowledge of results as determinants of motor performance among EMR children. *American Journal of Mental Deficiency*, 1974, *78*, 752–758.

Lynch, W. W., & Panda, K. C. Effects of social reinforcement on the retarded child: A review and interpretation for classroom instruction. *Education and Training of the Mentally Retarded*, 1972, *7*, 115–123.

MacDonald, A. P., Jr. Internal-external locus of control. In J. P. Robinson & P. R. Shaver (Eds.), *Measures of social psychological attitudes* (Rev. ed.). Ann Arbor, Mich.: Institute for Social Research, 1973.

MacMillan, D. L. Motivational differences: Cultural-familial retardates vs. normal subjects on expectancy for failure. *American Journal of Mental Deficiency*, 1969, *74*, 254–258.

MacMillan, D. L. The problem of motivation in the education of the mentally retarded. *Exceptional Children*, 1971, *37*, 579–586.

MacMillan, D. L., & Keogh, B. K. Normal and retarded children's expectancy for failure. *Developmental Psychology*, 1971, *4*, 343–348.

Martens, R. Internal-external control and social reinforcement effects on motor performance. *Research Quarterly*, 1971, *42*, 307–313.

Mercer, C. D., & Payne, J. S. Learning theories and their implications. In J. M. Kauffman & J. S. Payne (Eds.), *Mental retardation: Introduction and personal perspectives*. Columbus, Ohio: Charles E. Merrill, 1975.

Miller, J. O. The children's locus of evaluation and control scale. *Abstracts of Peabody Studies in Mental Retardation*, 1965, *3*, 23.

Minton, H. L. Power as a personality construct. In B. Maher (Ed.), *Progress in experimental personality research* (Vol. 4). New York: Academic Press, 1967.

Mirels, H. L. Dimensions of internal versus external control. *Journal of Consulting and Clinical Psychology*, 1970, *34*, 226–228.

Moss, J. W. *Failure-avoiding and success-striving behavior in mentally retarded and normal children.* Ann Arbor, Mich.: University Microfilms, 1958.

Nowicki, S., & Strickland, B. R. A locus of control scale for children. *Journal of Consulting and Clinical Psychology*, 1973, *40*, 148–154.

Ollendick, T., Balla, D., & Zigler, E. Expectancy of success and the probability learning of retarded children. *Journal of Abnormal Psychology*, 1971, *77*, 275–281.

Piper, T. J. Effect of reward value on the expectancy of an event in EMR subjects. *American Journal of Mental Deficiency*, 1970, *74*, 537–540.

Riedel, W. W., & Milgram, N. A. Level of aspiration, locus of control and *n*-achievement in retardates and normal children. *Psychological Reports*, 1970, *27*, 551–557.

Ringelheim, D., Bialer, I., & Morrissey, H. *The relationship among various dichotomous descriptive personality scales and achievement in the mentally retarded: A study of the relevant factors influencing academic achievement at various chronological age levels.* Final Report, Office of Education, Bureau of Research, February 1970, No. 6–2685, Grant No. OEG–0–8–062685–1762(032).

Rosen, M., Diggory, J. C., & Werlinsky, B. E. Goal-setting and expectancy of success in institutionalized and noninstitutionalized mental subnormals. *American Journal of Mental Deficiency*, 1966, *71*, 249–255.

Rotter, J. B. Level of aspiration as a method of studying personality. *Journal of Experimental Psychology*, 1942, *31*, 410–422.

Rotter, J. B. *Social learning and clinical psychology.* Englewood Cliffs, N.J.: Prentice-Hall, 1954.

Rotter, J. B. Generalized expectancies for internal versus external control of reinforcement. *Psychological Monographs*, 1966, *80*(1, Whole No. 609).

Rotter, J. B. Some problems and misconceptions related to the construct of internal versus external control of reinforcement. *Journal of Consulting and Clinical Psychology*, 1975, *43*, 56–67.

Sanders, B., Zigler, E., & Butterfield, E. C. Outer-directedness in the discrimination learning of normal and mentally retarded children. *Journal of Abnormal Psychology*, 1968, *73*, 368–375.

Sarason, S. B., Davidson, K. S., Lighthall, F. F., & Waite, R. R. A test anxiety scale for children. *Child Development*, 1958, *29*, 105–113.

Schuster, S. O., & Gruen, G. E. Success and failure as determinants of the performance predictions of mentally retarded and nonretarded children. *American Journal of Mental Deficiency*, 1971, *76*, 190–196.

Shallenberger, P., & Zigler, E. Rigidity, negative reaction tendencies and cosatiation effects in normal and feebleminded children. *Journal of Abnormal and Social Psychology*, 1961, *63*, 20–26.

Shipe, D. Impulsivity and locus of control as predictors of achievement and adjustment in mildly retarded and borderline youth. *American Journal of Mental Deficiency*, 1971, *76*, 12–22.

Stephens, M. W., & Delys, P. External control expectancies among disadvantaged children at preschool age. *Child Development*, 1973, *44*, 670–674.

Stevenson, H. W., & Zigler, E. Discrimination learning and rigidity in normal and feebleminded individuals. *Journal of Personality*, 1957, *25*, 699–711.

Stevenson, H. W., & Zigler, E. F. Probability learning in children. *Journal of Experimental Psychology*, 1958, *56*, 185–192.

Turnure, J. E. Children's reactions to distractions: A developmental approach (Doctoral dissertation, Yale University, 1966). *Dissertation Abstracts*, 1966, *27*, 321B. (University Microfilms No. 66–4940)

Turnure, J. E. Reactions to physical and social distracters by moderately retarded institutionalized children. *Journal of Special Education*, 1970, *4*, 283–294.

Turnure, J. E. Outerdirectedness in EMR boys and girls. *American Journal of Mental Deficiency*, 1973, *78*, 163–170.

Turnure, J. E., & Zigler, E. Outer-directedness in the problem solving of normal and retarded children. *Journal of Abnormal and Social Psychology*, 1964, *69*, 427–436.

Weaver, S. J., Balla, D., & Zigler, E. Social approach and avoidance tendencies of institutionalized retarded and noninstitutionalized retarded and normal children. *Journal of Experimental Research in Personality*, 1971, *5*, 98–110.

Wicker, P. L., & Tyler, J. L. Improving locus of control through direct instruction: A pilot study. *Education and Training of the Mentally Retarded*, 1975, *10*, 15–18.

Yando, R. M., & Kagan, J. The effect of teacher tempo on the child. *Child Development*, 1968, *39*, 27–34.

Zigler, E. *The effect of pre-institutional social deprivation on the performance of feebleminded children.* Unpublished doctoral dissertation, University of Texas, 1958.

Zigler, E. Social deprivation in familial and organic retardates. *Psychological Reports*, 1962, *10*, 370.

Zigler, E. Rigidity and social reinforcement effects in the performance of institutionalized and noninstitutionalized normal and retarded children. *Journal of Personality*, 1963, *31*, 258–269.

Zigler, E. Research on personality structure in the retardate. In N. R. Ellis (Ed.), *International review of research on mental retardation* (Vol. 1). New York: Academic Press, 1966.

Zigler, E. Familial mental retardation: A continuing dilemma. *Science*, 1967, *155*, 292–298.

Zigler, E. *Training the intellect versus development of the child.* Paper presented at the annual convention of the American Educational Research Association, Los Angeles, 1968.

Zigler, E., Hodgden, L., & Stevenson, H. W. The effect of support on the performance of normal and feebleminded children. *Journal of Personality*, 1958, *26*, 106–122.

7

Observational Learning

Introduction to Observational Learning

Learning by direct experience has been the focus of voluminous writings which have been generated from both laboratory and field experiences. For example, operant conditioning principles have been extensively researched and applied in educational and therapeutic settings with much success. Although learning by direct experience has dominated the literature related to learning, observational learning also represents a learning parameter that accounts for the acquisition or change of many human behaviors.

Bandura (1971) indicates that social models facilitate the transmitting of human behaviors related to sex roles, social behaviors, language, occupational endeavors, and religious and political practices. Bandura recognizes the necessity of the observational learning phenomenon:

> Natural environments are loaded with potentially lethal consequences. . . . For this reason it would be exceedingly injudicious to rely on differential reinforcement of trial-and-error performances in teaching children to swim, adolescents to drive automobiles, medical students to conduct surgical operations, or

adults to develop complex occupational and social competencies. (p. 3)

Thus, Bandura reasons that when social cues are needed to convey appropriate behaviors, observational learning becomes an indispensable aspect of learning.

Thoresen and Stuhr (1972) concur with Bandura's (1971) position on the importance of social models claiming that models convey much information and are critical to the development of both appropriate and inappropriate behavior. In addition, they acknowledge that social modeling has essentially remained undeveloped and ignored as a tool for therapeutic change. Cullinan, Kauffman, and LaFleur (1975) review the literature concerning the effectiveness of observational learning with children who exhibit deviant behaviors (conduct problems, aggression, withdrawal, hyperactivity, etc.). They report that observational learning represents a viable approach for effecting behavioral change in exceptional children, but that it essentially remains untapped as a resource, not yet systematically investigated and applied in special education settings.

The failure to examine observational learning and systematically apply its principles to special education settings chances the loss of a powerful tool for enhancing the education of exceptional children. For example, Bandura (1973) notes that even in settings where the establishment of new skills via other means is possible, the learning process can often be substantially shortened by providing appropriate models. Moreover, Thoresen and Stuhr (1972) found that modeling holds the promise of being adaptive to a wide spectrum of behaviors as well as being highly efficient.

Some researchers distinguish between *modeling* and *imitation*. The distinguishing characteristic of modeling is that it involves no conscious or deliberate attempt to match a model's behavior, whereas imitation is viewed as a conscious effort to copy a model's behavior (Hutt & Gibby, 1976). In the remainder of this chapter, *modeling* and *imitation* are not considered as separate entities but are viewed within the encompassing framework of observational learning.

Modeling and Mental Retardation

Ball (1970) acknowledges the effectiveness of modeling with mental retardates and notes that imitation training with retardates may be traced to such nineteenth century pioneers as Itard and Seguin. He points out that the work of these pioneers precluded not only general aspects of modern imitation practices but technical aspects as well. For example, Seguin's "mimical generalization" was discussed as encompassing the contemporary definition of generalized imitation and Itard's "method of insensible gradation" anticipated the Skinnerian concept of successive approximations.

Altman and Talkington (1971) write that a substantial amount of evidence exists which demonstrates the effectiveness of modeling in changing an array of behaviors. They further acknowledge that a paucity of studies exists concerning the effects of modeling with mentally retarded persons. Moreover, they note that an abundance of literature exists concerning the effectiveness of operant techniques with retarded individuals. Altman and Talkington cite several advantages that modeling affords in relation to operant techniques, and they interpret this intense interest in operant techniques and omission of modeling techniques as paradoxical. These advantages include: (a) in modeling one does not have to be as concerned with breaking tasks into small steps as is necessary in many operant programs; (b) in

modeling one does not have to determine reinforcers since reinforcement is not required for a person to learn by observation; (c) the endurance for behavior acquired or changed via observation is longer than behavior acquired or changed by operant technqiues; and (d) learning by observation generalizes more than learning by operant techniques.

Altman and Talkington (1971) further reason that the use of modeling with retardates is enhanced when one considers the popular theories which purport that mental retardates are more outer-directed (Cromwell, 1963; Turnure & Zigler, 1964) and have higher suggestibility (Zigler, 1966) than normals. It is apparent that the dependency of an outer-directed, suggestible retardate would heighten her dependency on external cues for appropriate behavior, thus improving the acquisition of modeled responses.

Altman and Talkington (1971) state that the effectiveness of modeling is enhanced when reinforcement is used in conjunction with it, i.e., reinforce the observer for modeling or the model for performing. They summarize, "to employ modeling at the expense of operant methodology could only attentuate progress in a therapeutic milieu. Consequently, its deployment is recommended in conjunction with reinforcement principles" (p. 22).

In general, the writings of Ball (1970) and Altman and Talkington (1971) acknowledge the modicum of studies concerned with modeling and mental retardation and provide a rationale for investigating observational learning with retardates. It is likely that their writings are helping to establish a research need and provide an impetus and an anticipation in the field. The remainder of this chapter reviews research articles which report on modeling with retardates, including the mildly, moderately, and severely retarded. Hopefully further work on the topic is forthcoming.

Modeling Studies with the Mildly Retarded

ROSS'S STUDIES. Ross (1970a) selected 60 retarded children (CA = 6–10 years) and had them view film-mediated models performing the following activities: (a) memory for stories, (b) formboard activity, (c) phone answering, (d) phone calling, and (e) a paired associate task. Before viewing the film, the participants of one group were introduced to a child via audiovisual exposure and were told that the child model was their friend and had sent them toys. Likewise, 20 participants in a control group were exposed to a child model via audiovisual presentations but rewards and friendship were not associated with their exposure. In the subsequent experimental setting all groups viewed a film which featured the child whom the experimental group had learned to associate with rewards. The results revealed that the association of a model with rewards facilitated the learning from audiovisual presentations in retarded children. The participants who associated reward with their model imitated all tasks except calling on the phone significantly better than the children who had no prior exposure to the model. In addition, Ross found that the classroom teachers reported that the children exhibited behavior in the classroom which resembled behaviors of the reward-attached model. Ross concludes that her study not only supported the position that nurturant models are more effective but demonstrated the efficacy of audiovisual presentations for transmitting academic behaviors to retarded individuals.

Ross (1970b) selected 40 mildly retarded children in order to investigate the incidental learning of number concepts in small-group games. The participants were divided into two groups and the experimental group received 100 minutes per week in a 9-month game program and the control group spent an equivalent amount of time in a special class number program. In addition to interspersing the number concepts in the game format, the investigator focused on developing the game skills of the children in the experimental group.

Modeling procedures were used to divert direct criticism of the children and help them develop game skills, such as waiting for turn or being a good loser. Whenever the children encountered continuous difficulty over a specific game skill, an adult model entered the game, broke the rule, and was reprimanded by the adult game leader for breaking the rule and was told to exhibit correct behavior. The children were encouraged to help the model learn how to play the game and the adult model was praised for correcting his inappropriate behavior. Ross (1970b) notes, "In the process of helping the adult model, the children engaged in overt and covert rehearsal of the game skills and watched the adult model closely" (p. 719).

On a postexperimental measure of game skills (number of errors made while playing games) the experimental group made significantly fewer errors than the control group. In addition, the experimental group scored significantly higher than the control group on the test for number knowledge.

HOLT, RICKARD, AND ELLIS'S STUDIES. Holt, Rickard, and Ellis (1972) selected 12 adolescent institutionalized retarded males and 12 adolescent institutionalized retarded females to participate in a word-modeling experiment. Modeling tapes using both male and female voices were used which recited lists of 50 words. All participants listened to both male and female tapes and were told that when a light started blinking it was the cue to say a word after the presentation of each stimulus word. The results indicated that a significant word modeling effect occurred, i.e., the participants repeated words similar to those of the model. Holt et al. report that similar word modeling effects had been found with both college and kindergarten students. There were no statistically significant effects due to sex of model, sex of the observer, or of their interaction.

In a post hoc analysis, low IQ retarded participants ($\overline{IQ} = 56$) emitted more parroting responses and the high IQ retarded participants ($\overline{IQ} = 67$) produced more concept modeling. i.e., they said a word in the same class as the modeled word rather than matching the word identically. These post hoc results were discussed in terms of: (a) the lower IQ adolescents being less able to abstract or conceptualize and (b) the lower IQ adolescents being more inclined to be characterized by the outer-directedness construct discussed by Zigler (1966). It was reasoned that retarded participants with low IQ experience more failure and are less apt to trust their own ability and thus imitate more precisely than do retarded participants with high IQ.

LITROWNIK'S STUDIES. Litrownik (1972) investigated observational learning in 24 EMR children ($\overline{CA} \simeq 12$ years) and 24 MA-equivalent normals ($\overline{CA} \simeq 7$ years) as a function of delay between observation and opportunity to perform. Both normal and retarded participants were each divided into a delay group and an immediate group and were asked to view a videotape of a youngster performing several tasks of different abilities: four discrimination, four motor, and eight verbal. Participants in the immediate group were asked to perform the observed tasks immediately after viewing, and children in the delayed group were required to wait 30 minutes. The results revealed that the retarded children imitated as many behaviors as the MA-equivalent normals imitated. Also, when a delay in performance was required, the performance of both (normal and MR) groups declined significantly. Litrownik concludes that mildly retarded children have the ability to acquire and perform behaviors via observation but need an immediate opportunity to perform the observed behaviors. Finally, Litrownik points out that both groups missed a higher percentage of verbal tasks than they did other tasks.

Ross, Ross, and Downing's Studies. Ross, Ross, and Downing (1973) selected 36 educable retarded children in order to compare the effects of intentional training and observational learning on the development of mediational strategies. Each child was pretested on ability to learn paired-associate tasks and use mediational strategies. Next, each participant was randomly assigned to one of three experimental conditions: intentional training group ($N = 12$), observational learning group ($N = 12$), and control group ($N = 12$). The participants in the intentional training condition received five hours of explicit training in formulating and using mediational links. A story and a table game format were used to teach the mediational links. In this procedure the teacher told a story of how a child remembered word pairs and then a game was played in which the participants had to remember which word went with another word (paired-associate task). In the observational learning condition the children observed a live adult model verbalize mediational strategies in order to remember pairs of words. The control group played the paired-associate word game without viewing a model or receiving direct instruction.

The results indicated that both experimental groups performed better than the control group and no difference in performance occurred between the experimental groups. These findings suggest that educable retarded children can learn to use mediational links as effectively through observational learning as through intentional training. Further support for the efficacy of observational learning in transmitting mediational skills was provided by a follow-up testing (new material used) 2 months after the experimental training. The mediational skills of both treatment groups (intentional and observational) remained equivalent to performances obtained immediately after training. These findings indicate that EMR children can learn, retain, and transfer mediational strategies learned via observation or by direct instruction.

Forehand, Robbins, and Brady's Studies. Forehand, Robbins, and Brady (1973) compared 32 noninstitutionalized educable-level retardates and 32 normals. All subjects had mental ages of 5, 6, 7, and 8 on mimical, conceptual, and total verbal imitation. The participants listened to animal words presented one at a time on a tape. After each word they were instructed to respond with the first word that came to their minds. *Total imitations* included the number of animal words emitted by the participant. *Mimical responses* were defined as word emissions which were identical to the words presented on the tape. *Conceptual imitations* were defined as the emission of a nonmimical animal noun. Each type of imitation was analyzed within a $5 \times 2 \times 2 \times 4$ (trial block x IQ x sex x MA) analysis of variance.

A significant trial block main effect for each class of imitation (indicating increasing imitation) was found. The investigators showed that both IQ and MA are significant factors in imitative performance, i.e., as IQ and MA increase, modeling increases. Among the other significant findings for separate classes of imitative responses were:

1. Total imitations: MA 5 retardates > MA 5 normals
2. Conceptual imitations: MA 7 retardates > MA 7 normals
   MA 7 retardates > MA 5 retardates
3. Mimical imitations: MA 7 normals > MA 5 normals
   MA 5 retardates > MA 5 normals
   MA 7 normals > MA 7 retardates

Forehand et al. (1973) note that support for Turnure and Zigler's (1964) "outer-directedness" hypothesis, formulated on the basis of motor imitation, was not found in this verbal task, since the retarded participants gave more total imitations than normals only at the MA 5 level.

Forehand and Calhoun's Studies. Forehand and Calhoun (1973) selected 14 participants ($\overline{CA} = 11$ years) and presented to them 30 stimulus words on a tape and asked them to respond with the first word that came to mind following each word. On the basis of the previous study, half of the participants were classified *mimical responders* and the other half *conceptual responders*. The mimical responders emitted significantly more mimical responses and fewer conceptual imitations than the conceptual responders. The results suggested that modeling responses for mentally retarded subjects are influenced by response styles.

In addition, after listening and responding to each word, each participant was instructed to name as many of his own favorite words as he could (acceptance). Then each participant was asked to recall as many of the taped model's words as he could (recall). In the acceptance condition, mimical responders named significantly more of the model's responses than conceptual responders. The two groups did not differ significantly on the number of modeled words recalled.

Gardner and Forehand's Studies. Gardner and Forehand (1974) selected 14 noninstitutionalized retarded adolescents ($\overline{CA} = 18.3$, $\overline{IQ} = 61$), 14 short-term ($\overline{M} = 3.3$ years) institutionalized retarded adolescents ($\overline{CA} = 18.3$, $\overline{IQ} = 56$), and 14 long-term ($\overline{M} = 11.2$ years) institutionalized retarded adolescents ($\overline{CA} = 20.6$, $\overline{IQ} = 57$) in order to investigate the effects of institutionalization upon word modeling responses. The groups were matched on CA, MA, and IQ. Each participant was presented a tape of 50 nouns which had no animal nouns in the first 10 words, 2 in the second 10 words, 4 in the next 10 words, 6 in the next 10 words, and 8 in the final 10 words. Prior to presentation of the tape each participant was instructed to say any word that came to mind immediately following the presentation of each word. The number of animal words emitted was the dependent measure.

The results disclosed that the two institutionalized groups did not differ on the number of words imitated, but that both groups imitated significantly more words than the noninstitutionalized group. The groups did not differ on the number of parroting and conceptual responses emitted as defined by Holt, Rickard, and Ellis (1972).

Strichart's Studies. Strichart (1974) selected 128 nonretarded boys and girls to serve as models for 128 retarded adolescents ($\overline{CA} = 16$). The participants were divided into groups depending on the competence of the model and observer and on the nurturance of the model. Nurturance was determined on the basis of the observer stating whether or not he liked the model prior to the experiment. Competence was established in preexperimental conditions with tasks similar to those used in the experiment. After viewing a model perform a task on a Vertical Aspiration Board, the retarded individuals were asked to perform the tasks. The results indicated that competent models were imitated more than were noncompetent models and noncompetent observers were more imitative than competent observers. The nurturant status of the model did not generate any effect on the modeling performances. Strichart concludes that although peer modeling is a viable tool, the competence of both the model and the observer must be considered.

Striefel and Eberl's Studies. Striefel and Eberl (1974) used a multiple-baseline design to compare the influence of live and videotaped models on the imitation of six institutionalized EMRs ($\overline{CA} = 12$ years 10 months). Each participant received one session daily 5 days a week and the number of sessions ranged from 23 to 31 sessions. In a session the child viewed either a live adult model, the same adult on videotape, or a child on videotape. The sequence of presentation of the models was arranged to control for the effects of order of presentation. Each model displayed 15 simple motor behaviors three times each ($N = 45$) over an 8-minute period. Prior to each modeled behavior the model instructed the observer to "Do this." The live adult model did not establish eye contact with the observers nor did he respond to any of the observers' behaviors.

The results disclosed that all the behaviors of the live adult model were imitated by the six participants. The adult videotaped model generated nearly 100% correct imitation from four of the observers. The videotape model of the child produced 100% correct imitation in three of the observers. The imitation behavior of two of the participants drastically decreased when either of the videotape models was used. Striefel and Eberl (1974) noted:

> Since the model did not interact with the subjects and did not reinforce correct responses, imitative control must be accounted for by other variables. In all probability, control was exerted by some combination of setting events such as: the subjects' previous history with adults, their instructions, and the consequences received when the subject responded or failed to respond to an adult's instructions. (pp. 85–86)

The three female participants tended to imitate all behaviors presented regardless of mode of presentation, whereas the imitation of the males decreased with the videotape models. Striefel and Eberl (1974) suggest that the females had received more conditioning to conform than the males.

YODER AND FOREHAND'S STUDIES. Yoder and Forehand (1974) selected 40 nonretarded and 40 retarded children and divided them into eight groups of 10 participants each. Each group was asked to perform four easy items and four difficult items on the *Leiter International Performance Scale* after participating in one of four modeling conditions. The four modeling conditions involved: (a) model only, (b) model plus low verbalizations, (c) model plus concept, and (d) no model. In Condition *B* the model performed a block matching task while making some general statements, e.g., "This block goes here." In the Concept *C* condition the model performed the task while stating a rule pertaining to the task, e.g., "The water goes with the milk. They both are liquids." The results revealed no sex differences on the criterion tasks. The performance of the retardates and the nonretardates did not differ on the easy items but the retardates did not do as well as the nonretardates on the difficult items. Participants in all the modeling conditions performed better than the participants in the Condition *D*. The individuals in *C* performed better than the individuals in the other two modeling conditions. Yoder and Forehand found that modeling and verbal cues affected retarded children and normals in the same manner, i.e., each group learned via modeling, and the effectiveness of modeling improved as verbal cues increased. Yoder and Forehand conclude that modeling and verbal cues can be used successfully with retarded and normal children to facilitate the acquisition of difficult cognitive response patterns.

CLINTON AND BOYCE'S STUDIES. Clinton and Boyce (1975a) selected 20 mildly retarded children and 20 MA-equivalent, nonretarded children in order to examine the effects of social reinforcement on the imitation of two simple motor tasks. These tasks, although not reinforced, were embedded within other imitiative behavior that was reinforced. Clinton and Boyce hypothesized that affective reinforcement ("good," "fine") would generate a higher imitation performance of embedded behavior in retarded children as compared to nonretarded children. In addition, they hypothesized that informative reinforcement ("right," "correct") would produce a higher imitation performance of embedded behavior in nonretarded children as compared to retarded children. They advanced these hypotheses primarily on the basis of differences in the social reinforcement histories of retarded and nonretarded children (Green & Zigler, 1962).

Each participant received a baseline session and an experimental session. In both sessions a marble task preceded a block task. During the baseline sessions (a demonstration and imitation of matching to sample task) no occurrences of the two motor tasks (dependent measures) were observed. In the marble task portion of the experimental session the model held the marbles in her hands and shook them three times before beginning the task. In the block task portion of the experimental session the model held two blocks in her hands and clapped them together prior to performing the block task. Half of the children from each poulation received affective reinforcement and the other half received informative reinforcement.

The results indicated that the retarded children imitated more of the simple motor tasks under the affective rather than the informative social reinforcement, while the reverse was true for the nonretarded participants. Clinton and Boyce (1975a) note that their findings support Cairns' (1970) view that at least two dimensions (affective and informative) of social reinforcement exist. Moreover, Cairns suggests that a developmental pattern exists in which children initially are more responsive to affective reinforcement and, later, at approximately 9 or 10 years, they opimally respond to informative social reinforcement. Several investigators (Zigler & Kanzer, 1962) suggest that retarded children remain optimally responsive to affective reinforcement longer than their nonretarded peers.

Clinton and Boyce (1975b) selected 20 EMRs and 20 MA-equivalent, nonretarded children in order to investigate the influence on the production of plurals of modeling procedures alone and modeling plus a statement of rule. The two groups were each randomly assigned to one of the two modeling conditions and to either affective or informative social reinforcement. They hypothesized that the lower MA participants (MA < 10 years) would imitate more under affective social reinforcement than under informative social reinforcement. Also, they predicted that more imitation would occur with the modeling plus rule condition than the modeling only condition.

Each participant received a baseline session and an experimental session. In the baseline session the experimenter presented 40 pictures of common objects one at a time and asked the child to label the picture. In the experimental phase the experimenter had 20 pictures and the child had 20 different pictures. In the model only condition the experimenter overturned a picture and labeled it with a plural. Next, the child was instructed to turn a picture over and label it. The conditions were similar in the model plus rule condition except the model overturned a picture, said "More than one," and labeled the picture with a plural. The two sets of pictures were different; thus, the subjects had to apply the rule in order to respond correctly. Reinforcement was given for every fourth correct plural response. Informative reinforcement consisted of the experimenter saying, "That's right. The words you are saying are correct." Affective reinforcement consisted of the experimenter saying, "That's good. The words you are saying are fine."

A factorial analysis of variance, 2 x 2 x 2 (population x social reinforcement type x model type), was computed with the number of plurals emitted in the experimental session as the dependent measure. The only statistically significant finding was a main effect for model type. More plural responses were obtained with the model plus rule condition than with the model only condition. It appears the same subjects (same descriptive characteristics as subjects of the Clinton and Boyce [1975a] study) differentially responded to affective and informative reinforcement in an earlier study. It is probable that in this study (1975b) these children were unable to distinguish between the two types of reinforcement, because both reinforcements referred to the words emitted with one (affective) saying, "That's good. The words you are saying are fine," and the other (informative) saying, "That's right. The words you are saying are correct." In the Clinton and Boyce (1975a) study however, affective reinforcement consisted simply of "good" or "fine" and informative reinforcement consisted of "correct" or "right." Finally, Clinton and Boyce (1975b) note that some of the children exhibited concern over labeling the pictures of singular objects with plurals.

MARTIN'S STUDIES. Martin (1975) selected two retarded children (IQs = 51 and 70) in order to examine whether verbal modeling could be effective in altering verbal behavior in other settings. A teacher or nurse modeled 12 sentences and instructed the observer to imitate each sentence immediately after it was presented. Each sentence contained one of six animal names and the subjects were praised for correct imitation. The sentences varied according to their inclusion or exclusion of size and color adjectives used to describe the animals. Preexperimental observations revealed that the two subjects rarely used size adjectives and never used color adjectives. The experiment included three phases and a multiple baseline design was used. In Phase One the model presented 12 sentences for imitation which did not include any color or size adjectives. In Phase Two size adjectives were included in the sentences for Subject I, and color adjectives were in the sentences for Subject II. In Phase Three both size and color adjectives were included in the imitation sentences for both subjects. In each phase an imitation training session and a probe session were conducted daily. In the probe sessions the subject was presented 12 animal pictures (six of animals used in training and six of different animals) and instructed to tell what each one was. The use of size and color adjectives was recorded as the dependent measure. The probe sessions were not held in the same room used for the imitation training and were conducted by an adult who did not participate in the training sessions. Subject I received approximately 30 sessions and Subject II received approximately 25 sessions.

The results indicated that during probe sessions both subjects began to exhibit color and/or size adjective responses as a function of the sentence content in their respective training sessions. Moreover, generalization to descriptions of animals not used in training occurred. Martin (1975) notes, "Reinforcing simple verbal repetition of sentences was sufficient to alter the verbal behavior of the subject in the presence of another adult, in another room, at another time of the day, and with a completely different task" (p. 208).

TALKINGTON AND HALL'S STUDIES. Talkington and Hall (1975) selected 80 EMR children ($\overline{CA}$ = 14.9 years) in order to investigate the relationship between rewarding or penalizing a model and subsequent imitation performances. The participants were equally divided into four groups. Group I observed the model perform a simple perceptual motor task in which she was provided a token for each correct response (reward group). Group II observed the model lose a token for each incorrect response (penalty group). Group III observed a model who did not receive or lose tokens but was merely informed of correct responses via a light (information only group). Group IV was a non-model control group. The participants in each group were asked to perform the task immediately after viewing the model (acquisition phase) and 30 days later (relearning phase).

The findings indicated that the reward and penalty groups consistently outperformed the other groups during both the acquisition and the relearning phases. Moreover, the information only group outperformed the control group. Talkington and Hall (1975), viewing the findings within an information available framework, suggest that the reward and penalty conditions encouraged the observers to focus on the relevant cues relative to correct and incorrect responses.

SUMMARY. The modeling literature with mildly retarded subjects demonstrates that numerous variables influence the modeling process with retardates. At the risk of oversimplifying the literature, this summary features a discussion in terms of model variables, observer variables, task variables, and miscellaneous variables.

As depicted in Table 7.1, the model variables encompassed in the 15 studies represent a wide spectrum of characteristics. Three of the studies used nonretarded peers as models and 13 of the studies used adults as models. Audiovisual presentations were featured in seven studies and live models were used in nine studies. Some of the studies examined specific characteristics of the model. For example, Ross (1970a) investigated the effects of the model being associated with the rewards prior to performing the tasks to be imitated. Holt et al. (1972) studied the sex of the model as a variable influencing observer imitation, and Talkington and Hall (1975) examined the effects of rewarding the model on imitation. These investigators also studied the effects of punishing the model for incorrect responses. Litrownik (1972) and Ross (1970b) rewarded the model as part of their experimental procedures but did not specifically examine the effects of reward on imitation. Strichart (1974) considered the effects on imitation of the model being liked (nurturance) by the observers and the effects of model competence on imitation. In three of the studies (Clinton & Boyce, 1975a, 1975b; Martin, 1975) the model praised the observer for correct imitation as part of the modeling treatment.

Specific findings concerning model variables include:

1. The association of rewards with the model facilitated imitation by retarded observers (Ross, 1970a).
2. Sex of the model who was heard on audiotape did not create significant modeling effects on EMR listeners (Holt et al., 1972).
3. The viewing of a model who was either rewarded for correct responses or punished for incorrect responses produced higher acquisition and relearning performances by EMR adolescents on a perceptual motor task than the viewing of a model who was simply given corrective feedback (Talkington & Hall, 1975).
4. The fact that the model was liked by EMRs did not produce a significant imitation effect (Strichart, 1974).
5. Retarded observers imitated competent models more than noncompetent models (Strichart, 1974).
6. Models who were not reinforced for performing and who refrained from interaction or reinforcement of EMR observers generated an imitation effect by simply saying to the observers, "Do this" (Striefel & Eberl, 1974).
7. Nonretarded peers served as effective models for retarded children (Strichart, 1974).
8. Verbalizations by models concerning the tasks they are performing improved observational learning in both normals and retardates (Clinton & Boyce, 1975b; Yoder & Forehand, 1974).

In the realm of model variables it is obvious that mildly retarded individuals learn via observation from a variety of presentations, i.e., adult, peer, and audiovisual. One study (Striefel & Eberl, 1974) compared the effectiveness of audiovisual versus live model presentations, and showed that the live model was imitated more than the audiovisual model. However, 67% of the subjects imitated both models equally. Baran (1973) and Litrownik (1972) suggest the use of audiovisual presentations as a viable modeling technique with retarded individuals. This position gains credence in view of the results from the studies using audiovisual models. All seven studies using audiovisual presentations reported a modeling effect.

As noted in Table 7.1, the observer characteristics are highlighted by ability level and certain personality characteristics. In 10 of the studies, only retarded observers were used. In the remaining five investigations, MA-equivalent normals and

TABLE 7.1
Model Variables, Observer Variables, Task Variables, and Miscellaneous Variables in Imitation Studies with Mildly Retarded Subjects

ARTICLES	MODEL VARIABLES					OBSERVER VARIABLES			TASK VARIABLES								MISC. VARIABLES
	NON-MR PEERS	ADULT	LIVE	A.V.	OTHER	LEVEL OF MR	MA EQUIVALENT	OTHER CHARACTERISTICS	GROSS MOTOR	FINE MOTOR	SIMPLE VERBAL	COMPLEX VERBAL	SOCIAL BEHAVIOR	VISUAL MATCHING	MEMORY	GENERALIZATION	
Ross (1970a)	X		X		Nurturance	IQ = 60 EMR CA = 6–10			X	X				X	X	X	Association of model & rewards. A.V. presentations.
Ross (1970b)	X	X				EMR CA = 8							X			X	Reprimand and reinforce model. Adult model in game situation. Incidental learning of number concepts.
Holt, Rickard, & Ellis (1972)	X		X		Male Female	EMR adolescents		Institutionalized. Equal number of males & females		X	X						Sex of model and observer. IQ and modeling.
Litrownik (1972)	X		X		Model reinforced	EMR $\overline{CA} \approx 12$	Normals $\overline{CA} \approx 7$		X	X				X			Modeling of normals and retarded. Delay interval and reinforcement.
Ross, Ross, & Downing (1973)	X	X				EMR $\overline{CA} \approx 9$					X				X		Verbal mediation. Modeling vs. direct instruction. Retention and transfer.
Forehand, Robbins, & Brady (1973)	X		X			EMR $\overline{MAs}$ of 5, 6, 7, & 8	Normals $\overline{MAs}$ of 5, 6, 7, & 8			X							Mimical, total and conceptual verbal imitation. MA and modeling.

TABLE 7.1, cont.

ARTICLES	MODEL VARIABLES — NON-MR PEERS	ADULT	LIVE	A.V.	OTHER	LEVEL OF MR	OBSERVER VARIABLES — MA EQUIVALENT	OTHER CHARACTERISTICS	TASK VARIABLES — GROSS MOTOR	FINE MOTOR	SIMPLE VERBAL	COMPLEX VERBAL	SOCIAL BEHAVIOR	VISUAL MATCHING	MEMORY	GENERALIZATION	MISC. VARIABLES
Forehand & Calhoun (1973)	X			X		EMR CA = 11		Mimical responders. Conceptual responders.		X							Type of responses to words presented via tape.
Gardner & Forehand (1974)	X			X		EMR CA = 19		Nonresidents. Short-term residents. Long-term residents.		X	X						Institutionalization and word modeling.
Strichart (1974)	X	X	X		Nuturance Competence	EMR CA = 16		Competence	X								Model competence. Model nurturance. Competence of observer.
Striefel & Eberl (1974)	X	X	X	X	No interaction with observers	EMR CA = 13		Residents 3 male 3 female	X								Videotaped vs. live models. No reinforcement of observer or model. Sex of observer.
Yoder & Forehand (1974)	X	X	X			EMR CA = 12	Normals CA ≈ 7	Sex						X			Model only, model plus low verbal, model plus concept, & no model. Sex of observer. Difficulty of task.

235

TABLE 7.1, cont.

ARTICLES	MODEL VARIABLES					OBSERVER VARIABLES			TASK VARIABLES								MISC. VARIABLES
	NON-MR PEERS	ADULT	LIVE	A.V.	OTHER	LEVEL OF MR	MA EQUIVALENT	OTHER CHARACTERISTICS	GROSS MOTOR	FINE MOTOR	SIMPLE VERBAL	COMPLEX VERBAL	SOCIAL BEHAVIOR	VISUAL MATCHING	MEMORY	GENERALIZATION	MISC. VARIABLES
Clinton & Boyce (1975a)	X	X			Reinforced observers	EMR CA ≈ 12	X CA = 8.0		X								Affective social reinforcement of observer. Informative social reinforcement of observer. Imitation of nonreinforced modeled behavior.
Clinton & Boyce (1975b)	X	X			Reinforced observers	EMR CA ≈ 12	X CA = 8.0				X						Affective social reinforcement of observer. Informative social reinforcement of observer. Model only and model plus rule. Rule-governed verbal imitation.
Martin (1975)	X	X			Praised observers for correct imitation	EMR CA ≈ 6 & 8	Residents				X					X	Generalization in new setting with new task. Use of size and color adjectives.
Talkington & Hall (1975)	X	X			Rewarded. penalized. Corrective feedback.	EMR CA ≈ 15	Residents			X					X		Reinforcement of model. Punishment of model.

retardates served as observers and their perfor-mances were compared. The effects of sex of the observer on imitation was examined in three studies (Holt et al., 1972; Striefel & Eberl, 1974; Yoder & Forehand, 1974). Forehand and Calhoun (1973) classified the observers as *mimical* and *conceptual responders* and compared their re-spective modeling performances. The observers in five of the studies were residents in an institu-tion; however, only one study (Gardner & Forehand, 1974) included an examination of the effects of institutionalization on imitation. In Strichart's (1974) study the competence of the observer was examined.

Some findings regarding observer variables in-clude:

1. In the five studies (see Table 7.1) that compared the modeling performances of EMR observers and MA-equivalent, nonretarded observers, four of them re-ported no significant differences. Clinton and Boyce (1975a) reported that the EMR observers produced higher imitation scores when the model provided af-fective reinforcement for imitation, whereas the non-retarded observers imitated more under informative social feedback from the model. The modeling per-formance of retarded subjects on *difficult* tasks was inferior to the modeling performance of MA-equivalent normals; however, there were no differ-ences between the modeling performances of retard-ates and MA-equivalent normals on *simple* tasks (Yoder & Forehand, 1974).
2. Holt et al. (1972) and Yoder and Forehand (1974) reported that the sex of the observer was not related to modeling performances, whereas Striefel and Eberl (1975) found a significant sex effect, i.e., re-tarded girls imitated videotaped adult and peer mod-els more than boys.
3. Holt et al. (1972) and Yoder and Forehand (1974) examined the relationship between IQ and modeling tasks. They both used verbal taks and reported that as the difficulty level of the task increased, a discrep-ancy in performance resulted between Ss of different IQ levels. When the task was difficult, high IQ Ss performed better than low IQ Ss.
4. Lower IQ retardates had a tendency to parrot verbal models and higher IQ retardates tended to exhibit concept modeling (Holt et al., 1972).
5. Retarded individuals modeled tasks presented via videotape as well as MA-equivalent normals (Litrow-nik, 1972).
6. Retarded individuals attended to a videotape presen-tation more than normals (Litrownik, 1972).
7. The retarded participants needed to perform the ob-served tasks immediately in order to facilitate reten-tion and learning (Litrownik, 1972).

8. Retarded children learned to use mediational links as effectively through observation as through inten-tional training (Ross et al., 1973).
9. Some retardates responded to word modeling by mimicry and others by conceptualization (Forehand & Calhoun, 1973).
10. In a comparison of normals and retardates at four MA levels, no consistent differences were noted in conceptual, mimical, and total imitations (Forehand, Robbins, & Brady, 1973).
11. Noncompetent retarded observers were more imita-tive than competent retarded observers (Strichart, 1974).

Although many observer variables have been considered in these studies, not enough data have been generated concerning specific observer characteristics and modeling performances to draw decisive conclusions. Not only do variables included in the studies need further consideration, but also some other variables warrant attention, such as SES, impulsivity, reflectivity, and verbal ability. Finally, it would also be interesting to find out by means of a pretest, the capacity of the observers to perform the tasks before imitation.

As illustrated in Table 7.1, the task variables covered in these studies spanned a variety of di-mensions and paralleled many tasks required in education and training programs. Since none of the studies included duplicate tasks, there were a large number of different tasks used. The tasks included gross motor, fine motor, simple verbaliza-tion, complex verbalizations, social behavior, vis-ual matching, and memory items. In addition to examining the imitation of specific experimental tasks, Ross (1970a, 1970b) and Martin (1975) studied the generalization effects of modeling. The modeled behavior generalized to other settings in all three studies. Since language is basic to suc-cess in many academic areas, it is especially en-couraging to note that in six of the studies (see Table 7.1) the EMR observers were able to learn verbal behavior via observation. Finally, an impor-tant factor regarding the task selected by the prac-titioner or researcher for imitation is the establish-ment of whether the observer knows already how to make the first response.

The miscellaneous variables included in Table 7.1 reveal that three of the studies compared the effectiveness of modeling with other training methods. In these studies (Ross, 1970b; Ross et al., 1973; Yoder & Forehand, 1974) modeling was found equal or superior. Reinforcement to the model or observer was used in seven of the studies. As noted by Altman and Talkington (1971), the combination of reinforcement and modeling is worthy of research consideration. Moreover, modeling and reinforcement each represent powerful techniques which are exclusive yet offer potential when in combination.

TEACHING IMPLICATIONS

1. Since Ross (1970a) found that EMR children imitated more behavior if the model was associated with rewards, teachers could increase their effectiveness as models by establishing themselves as reinforcing individuals. In addition, if peer models are used, the teacher could encourage the peer models to reinforce their observers by giving them verbal praise or affording them the opportunity of giving tokens or prizes. For teachers who have access to videotape equipment, Ross' study indicates that videotapes can be used to present a peer model for instruction in a number of tasks, i.e., gross motor, fine motor, visual matching, and memory for stories.

2. In a small-group setting Ross (1970b) found that by having an adult game leader reprimand the adult model for breaking game rules and praise the model for obeying the rules, children improved their playing skills, e.g., taking turns, being a good loser. Also, during the sessions the children were encouraged to help the model learn how to play correctly. These procedures could be used in classroom settings to teach social skills via games which incorporate academic skills, such as number concepts.

3. Since Holt et al. (1972) found that retarded adolescents modeled words presented by a tape recorder, tapes of selected words could be used to improve vocabulary and articulation. In addition to saying the words presented, the student could be required to select the word from a work sheet of a list of words or match a picture with the word. Moreover, the results of this study indicate that the teacher should be a good language model for her students, i.e., good articulation, correct syntax, etc.

4. In order to help some students reduce parroting of models, the teacher could present words via a tape and have the student select a word or picture that is in the same category (animal words) as the presented word. This procedure would increase word meaning and, perhaps, by giving students success with nonechoic type responses, it would reduce the tendency of some students to emit parroting responses.

5. Litrownik (1972) found that retarded and MA-equivalent, nonretarded children needed an opportunity to perform immediately after viewing the model. A 30-minute delay in opportunity to perform significantly reduced the number of behaviors that both groups could perform. This finding indicates that teachers need to encourage immediate enactment by students of behaviors observed. For example, have the child immediately recall words presented, write words written by model, color a picture, or match to sample task.

6. Litrownik (1972) found that retarded and MA-equivalent, nonretarded children modeled fewer verbal tasks than they did motor or visual discrimination tasks. This finding suggests that in order to teach verbal tasks via observation the imitation effects should be constantly monitored and it is likely that much practice should be provided.

7. Ross et al. (1973) found that verbal mediational strategies could be taught to EMR children by observation and direct instruction. Teachers could model or have aids model the use of verbal mediation for students. Types of mediation strategies to model include: (a) putting words to remember in a sentence or short story, (b) joining the new words with a conjunction, (c) pairing the new words with a rhyming word or words, and (d) rehearsing the new words by writing or saying them. Ross et al. found that EMR children tended to use the sentence strategy much more than the other strategies. Much academic content in the primary grades involves associative learning tasks, and mediational training appears to be a viable undertaking in order to facilitate the acquisition of the many academic skills that require associative learning. For example, academic tasks of an associative nature include symbol-sound relationships and the recognition of words and their meanings.

8. Ross et al. (1973) provided observational learning activities for 5 hours over a period of 5 weeks in order to teach mediational skills. This training resulted in the acquisition, retention, and transfer of the mediational skills. This finding indicates that mediational training by observation needs to be taught in short sessions over a long period of time. For example, provide a half hour of training twice a week for several months. Moreover, the sessions can be used to develop vocabulary and mediational skills simultaneously.

9. Forehand, Robbins, and Brady (1973) found that MA and IQ are significant factors in modeling performance. The primary implication of their findings is to enhance our understanding of the characteristics of EMR children in relation to MA-equivalent normals. Specifically, they found that young (MA = 5) retarded children tended to imitate more than their MA-equivalent, nonretarded peers. Overall, the modeling performances of the MA-equivalent groups were equivocal. Since modeling increases with MA, retarded children will respond more like younger nonretarded children than CA-equivalent, nonretarded children.

10. Results from Forehand and Calhoun's (1973) study suggest that retarded children who imitate by mimicking incorporate the model's words as their own. This finding suggests that these retarded children espe-

cially need appropriate social and cognitive models. Also, with mimical responders teachers may want to encourage conceptual responses in order to reduce the students' vulnerability with inappropriate social models. It is likely that such children have less confidence in their own abilities and rely on exact imitation to reduce failure. If teachers could provide them with successes and reinforce independent behavior, it may help them become more independent. A teacher could easily determine which children are mimical and conceptual responders in the following manner: (a) present 30 stimulus words (animal, food) one at a time and instruct the child to respond with the first word that comes to mind; (b) record same-word responses as mimical; and (c) record emitted words in same category (animal), yet nonmimical as conceptual responses. A teacher could also perform the acceptance and recall conditions outlined in the discussion of the Forehand and Calhoun study. Classroom norms could be established to determine which, if any, children are mimical responders.

11. The effects of institutionalization should be considered in modeling studies and in learning situations. Institutionalized mildly retarded adolescents tended to imitate more than mildly retarded noninstitutionalized adolescents (Gardner & Forehand, 1974). This finding suggests that teachers of retarded adolescents need to be aware of individual differences in the modeling inclinations of their students. It is obvious that a tendency to imitate can be constructively used to foster academic and social development; however, it may represent a need for adult approval, an external locus of control, and/or an outer-directed problem-solving style. In cases in which proneness to imitation negatively affects the growth and development of an individual, the teacher should plan environments which feature appropriate models and activities which foster the development of self-confidence. The teaching activities listed in Chapter 6 on social learning theory should be consulted.

12. Strichart's (1974) findings that competent models are imitated more than noncompetent models and that noncompetent observers imitate more than competent observers has several teaching implications. If a teacher chooses to use peer models, the best combination appears to be a competent model with a noncompetent observer (competence being related to task being modeled). These peer model-observer combinations could take three forms: (a) retarded model with retarded observer, (b) nonretarded model with retarded observer, and (c) retarded model with nonretarded observer. For the third condition it may be necessary to select a retarded person with a higher CA than her nonretarded observer or pinpoint a specific behavior in which the retarded individual is more competent

than her nonretarded peer. It is likely that the gains in self-concept of a retarded individual serving as a model for a nonretarded peer would be enormous. Children could be paired for increasing desirable behavior and/or for decreasing inappropriate behavior.

13. Striefel and Eberl (1974) found that institutionalized EMR children imitated nearly 100% of an adult's gross motor behaviors simply by being told to do so by the adult model. This finding, demonstrating the powerful influence of the adult model, should alert teachers and attendants to evaluate the usefulness or value of the behaviors they instruct residents to imitate. Moreover, it indicates the efficacy of using modeling to teach motor behaviors which are related to self-help skills, vocational skills, and social development.

14. Striefel and Eberl (1974) found that the imitation of videotaped models varied from one resident to another. This finding indicates that each child needs to be assessed in terms of her attention and imitation of videotaped models. Striefel and Eberl suggested that children be reinforced for imitating designated models in order to help maintain imitation behavior. Since many children readily imitate videotaped models, Striefel and Eberl note that the imitation of televised violence by retarded individuals should be examined. Attendants and teachers in residential settings may wish to (a) encourage residents to view less violent programs (reinforce them for viewing certain programs) or (b) offer more enticing activities when violent programs are on television.

15. Yoder and Forehand (1974) discovered that when highly meaningful verbal cues were provided by the model, EMR children were able to perform difficult tasks better than when the verbal cues were omitted. This finding suggests that teachers need to supplement demonstrations of difficult tasks with verbal cues. For example, in sorting objects, shapes, or words the teacher should state why each item goes into a particular category. Moreover, this procedure could be used when teaching phonic rules and arithmetic computational skills.

16. Clinton and Boyce (1975a) found that EMRs imitated more embedded motor behavior under affective social reinforcement than under informative social reinforcement ("right," "correct"). This finding suggests that teachers should use affective social reinforcement in order to facilitate generalized imitation by retarded students. In using this technique caution should be exercised so inappropriate behavior or incorrect responses are not reinforced.

17. Clinton and Boyce (1975b) found that the model plus the verbalization of a rule yielded higher production of rule-governed imitative verbal behavior than the model only. This finding suggests that in order to facilitate observational learning by EMR

students; teachers should compliment their modeling efforts with statements of rules or cues whenever possible. This could readily be done when teaching spelling rules, phonic rules, or math concepts and operations. In some cases tape recorders could serve as vehicles for providing the rules, e.g., have the child respond to numbered pictures, words, or math problems and then turn on the tape recorder to hear the correct response and the respective rule for each numbered item.

18. Martin (1975) was able to produce generalized verbal behavior in two retarded children via simple imitation and reinforcement procedures. His procedures warrant consideration for use in academic settings, i.e., train students to imitate specific verbal behavior and later use objects or pictures for students to describe by using the imitated behavior.

19. To facilitate the acquisition of correct modeled responses by EMRs, reward the model for correct responses and penalize the model for incorrect responses (Talkington & Hall, 1975). Since no differences in imitation occurred between the reward and penalty conditions in the study, a teacher may wish to use only the reward condition.

Modeling Studies with the Moderately Retarded

FECHTER'S STUDIES. Fechter (1971) selected 20 aggressive ("often attack residents"), institutionalized retarded subjects who were matched on age, sex, and IQ with 20 nonaggressive ("never attack residents"), institutionalized retarded subjects and had them view either an aggressive or a friendly television film of a child playing with a large, inflatable doll. The results revealed that after the presentation of the aggressive film, aggressive behavior increased in the ward setting, and after the presentation of the friendly film, aggressive behavior decreased in the ward setting. Friendly subjects were less friendly after viewing the aggressive film but were still more friendly than the aggressive subjects who viewed the aggressive film. Fechter writes that "while the specifics of a television presentation may not be modeled by the retarded subject, the mood of the show may produce a similar mood in viewers, the effect being differentially related to differences in personality" (p. 267). Fechter concludes that modeling has potential use in behavior modification programs, i.e., use the film to present new behavior and then reinforce modeled behavior.

STEWART'S STUDIES. Stewart (1972) selected four TMR children (CA = 2–7 years) who would not imitate either vocal or motor behavior. Each child was stimulated visually and auditorially to elicit echoic vocal and/or motor responses. Stimulation consisted of the teacher pairing a motor movement with a word. For example, she would raise her arm and say "Arm." Two of the children were instantly rewarded for making vocal responses, and the other two children were immediately rewarded for motor responses. The two children who were not reinforced for vocal responses displayed less vocal behavior than the two children who were rewarded for vocal behavior. Stewart concludes:

> If spontaneous echoic vocal responses are not reinforced during echoic motor training, echoic vocal behavior will be extinguished. . . . Echoic vocal and/or motor responses precede motor responses. . . . Verbal cues such as "Do this" or "Say this" are not necessary when developing echoic vocal and/or motor responses. (pp. 181–182)

STEIFEL AND PHELAN'S STUDIES. Streifel and Phelan (1972) selected six trainable retarded children (CA = 5–6 years) in order to teach them to imitate simple gross motor acts. They found that when reinforced for modeled behaviors, the retarded participants learned to imitate. Streifel and Phelan state that their study demonstrated that young trainable retarded children were able to imitate a model who reinforced them for modeling, and that their ability to imitate increased with imitation training.

TALKINGTON AND ALTMAN'S STUDIES. Talkington and Altman (1973) used a 3 x 2 x 2 (modeling condition x CA level x IQ level) factorial design for assessing the effects of aggression, affection, and no-film control condition on age and on high and low ability of retarded male students. Participants in the aggressive modeling condition viewed a 3-minute silent film depicting a child displaying aggressive behavior toward a bobo doll.* Those under the affectual modeling condition saw a 3-minute film depicting a model cuddling, holding,

---

*An inflated doll about three feet tall which has sand in the bottom. When the child hits it, it slants and returns upright.

kissing, picking up, and petting a bobo doll. Participants in the aggressive and affectual modeling conditions were placed in a room with the bobo doll following a filmed viewing. Either aggressive or affectual behaviors were taken as the dependent variable.

The effect of the modeling condition was highly significant. A significant interaction of ability level with modeling condition was found. The high IQ group (EMR) exhibited significantly more aggressive responses than the low IQ participants (TMR) under the no-film treatment condition. A significant interaction was obtained between ability level and age which indicates that the low IQ group demonstrated higher aggressive responding than the high IQ group only at the high CA level (CA = 16–21 years). A complete reversal of this response pattern at the low CA level (CA = 8–15 years) was observed with high IQ subjects demonstrating increased aggressive responding. The results using number of affectual responses as the dependent variable yielded only one significant finding concerning the modeling condition main effect. The aggressive modeling condition inhibited affectual responding to a significant degree over both the affectual model and the no-film control conditions. In interpreting the results of this study it is important to realize that the bobo doll may be a discriminative stimulus for aggression. Also, it would be helpful to know if the respective behaviors generalized or transferred to other settings.

TURNURE AND RYNDERS' STUDIES. Turnure and Rynders (1973) selected 36 institutionalized TMR children in order to compare the effects of trial and error learning, imitation learning, and manual guidance learning on a problem-solving task. Each participant was assigned to one of the three learning conditions. The task consisted of instructing the child to get some candy which was beyond her reach. A rake was nearby and in order to get the candy the participant had to use the rake to reach it. In the trial and error condition the participants were simply told, "Get the candy." In the imitation learning condition an adult model picked up the rake and got the candy, returned the rake to its place, and then instructed the participant to get the candy. In the manual guidance condition the experimenter guided each participant's hands in picking up the rake and securing the candy. Then the experimenter returned the rake to its place and asked the child to get the candy.

The results disclosed that the imitation and manual guidance conditions, while not significantly different from each other, were superior to the trial and error in terms of time of acquisition of the candy and in the number of subjects who succeeded in obtaining the candy.

LUTZKER AND SHERMAN'S STUDIES. Lutzker and Sherman (1974) used imitation and reinforcement procedures to train three retarded subjects and two nonretarded toddlers to use correct sentences. A multiple-baseline design was used for each type of sentence and two types of sentences were taught. One type involved the use of a plural noun which required the use of the verb *are* and the other type involved the use of a singular noun which required the use of the verb *is*. With the use of pictures, modeling, and token reinforcement, the subjects were taught to label single item pictures with single nouns, were taught action verbs for each picture, and finally were taught to incorporate the singular noun and the action verb into a sentence using *is*, e.g., *The boy is running*. Similar procedures were used for training the subjects to use correct noun-verb agreements in sentences with *are* in them. The dependent measure consisted of presenting probe pictures to assess whether the subjects would generate appropriate sentences with correct subject-verb agreements using *is* or *are*.

The results indicated that four of the participants produced novel, untrained sentences to probe pictures when that particular class of sentence was currently being trained. The other subject (retarded) produced appropriate singular and plural sentences to singular and plural picture probes when only *is* sentences had been taught. The retarded individuals required more training trials than the nonretarded subjects to reach criterion. Lutzker and Sherman (1974) note:

> The similarity of the results between the retarded and the normal children in the present study suggests that teaching programs based on imitation and reinforcement procedures might not only be useful in remediating language deficits but also in accelerating normal language development. (p. 459)

SUMMARY. The modeling studies with the moderately retarded or trainable retarded (TMR) are presented in Table 7.2 according to modeling variables, observer variables, task variables, and miscellaneous variables. Videotaped nonretarded peers were used as models in two of the studies

TABLE 7.2

Model Variables, Observer Variables, Task Variables, and Miscellaneous Variables in Imitation Studies with Moderately Retarded Subjects

ARTICLES	MODEL VARIABLES					OBSERVER VARIABLES			TASK VARIABLES								MISC. VARIABLES
	NON-MR PEERS	ADULT	LIVE	A.V.	OTHER	LEVEL OF MR	MA EQUIVALENT	OTHER CHARACTERISTICS	GROSS MOTOR	FINE MOTOR	SIMPLE VERBAL	COMPLEX VERBAL	SOCIAL BEHAVIOR	VISUAL MATCHING	MEMORY	GENERALIZATION	MISC. VARIABLES
Fechter (1971)	X			X	Aggressive Affectual	$\overline{IQ}=36$ TMR CA = 8–38 $\overline{CA}=11$		Aggressive. Institutionalized. Nonaggressive.					X			X	A.V. presentations
Stewart (1972)	X	X				TMR CA = 2–7		No imitation displayed prior to experiment.	X								Reinforcement of observer. Echoic responses. Expressive language.
Streifel & Phelan (1972)	X	X				TMR CA = 5–6			X								Reinforcement
Talkington & Altman (1973)	X			X	Aggressive Affectual	EMR TMR		High IQ = 50–79. Low IQ = 30–49. High CA = 16–21. Low CA = 8–15.					X				IQ and modeling. CA and modeling. Aggression and affection.
Turnure & Rynders (1973)	X	X				TMR	CA = 12	Residents		X							Compared imitation, trial & error, and manual guidance learning.
Lutzker & Sherman (1974)	X	X				TMR CAs = 32, 6 & 12	Not MA-equivalent CAs = 2½ yrs.	Residents (MR). No previous use of generative sentences.				X				X	Modeling plus token reinforcement. Generative sentences with correct subject-verb agreement.

(Fechter, 1971; Talkington & Altman, 1973), while the other four investigators used live adult models. The two studies which used the videotaped models presented aggressive and affectual behavior.

Some specific findings regarding model variables include:

1. Models of aggressive and friendly behavior presented via television affected the behavior of retardates in their natural setting, i.e., viewing aggressive behavior increased aggression and viewing friendly behavior decreased aggression (Fechter, 1971).
2. Subjects who viewed a film-mediated aggressive or affectual model imitated their respective model. The aggressive or affectual responses recorded after viewing the videotapes were significantly higher than similar responses in a no-film control group (Talkington & Altman, 1973).

As illustrated in Table 7.2, the observer variables encompass several parameters. In two studies (Lutzker & Sherman, 1974; Turnure & Rynders, 1973) nonretarded observers were included. All studies included TMR persons as observers and Talkington and Altman (1973) also included EMR observers. Institutionalized subjects participated in three of the studies (Fechter, 1971; Lutzker & Sherman, 1974; Turnure & Rynders, 1973); however, none of the investigators examined the effects of institutionalization on imitation. The observers in the study by Talkington and Altman were classified according to four factors—high CA, high IQ, low CA, and low IQ. The observers in Fechter's study were categorized as *aggressive* or *nonaggressive*. Lutzker and Sherman and Stewart (1972) pretested the participants on the behavior to be modeled.

Some specific findings regarding observer variables include:

1. Friendly (nonaggressive) participants, although less friendly after viewing the aggressive film, were still more friendly than the aggressive subjects who viewed the film (Fechter, 1971).
2. In viewing film-mediated aggressive models, a significant interaction occurred between ability level and age. Low IQ (30–49) subjects at high CA (16–21 years) exhibited more aggressive responding than high IQ (50–79) subjects at high CA (16–21 years). High IQ (50–79) subjects at low CA (8–15 years) exhibited more aggressive responding than low IQ (30–49) subjects at low CA (8–15 years) (Talkington & Altman, 1973).
3. In viewing film-mediated affectual models, no significant differences occurred as a function of ability level or age. However, the observation of an aggressive film inhibited affectual responding over both affectual and no-film modeling conditions (Talkington & Altman, 1973).
4. The observers acquired new responses in three of the studies (Lutzker & Sherman, 1974; Stewart, 1972; Streifel & Phelan, 1972); however, in all three studies imitation of the model was reinforced.

The task variables in Table 7.2 indicate that a total of five tasks were presented for imitation. In two studies (Stewart, 1972; Streifel & Phelan, 1972) gross motor tasks were used. Stewart used a simple verbal task, while Lutzker and Sherman used a complex verbal task. In two studies (Fechter, 1971; Talkington & Altman, 1973) social behaviors were used, and Turnure and Rynders (1974) used a simple problem-solving task. The generalization of imitated behavior to other settings was examined in two studies (Fechter, 1971; Lutzker & Sherman, 1974).

Some specific findings regarding task variables include:

1. Young trainable retardates were taught to imitate a gross motor task by using reinforcement in conjunction with modeling (Streifel & Phelan, 1972).
2. The imitation of aggressive behavior generalized to the ward setting (Fechter, 1971).
3. The imitation of generative sentences with correct subject-verb agreement generalized to another setting with a dissimilar task (Lutzker & Sherman, 1974).
4. Subjects with no history of using correct subject-verb agreement sentences acquired this verbal behavior via observation and reinforcement (Lutzker & Sherman, 1974).
5. Subjects with no history of verbal imitation acquired some verbal responses via observation and reinforcement (Stewart, 1972).

Most of the variables listed under miscellaneous in Table 7.2 have been mentioned in the discussions on model, observer, and task variables. The comparison of modeling with other techniques deserves some discussion within the miscellaneous category. In teaching a problem-solving task Turnure and Rynders (1973) found modeling to be as effective as manual guidance and more effective than trial and error learning. In addition, the use of audiovisual models appears effective with TMRs. In comparing these studies with the studies using EMRs, it appears that more reinforcement for imitative behavior of new responses is used. Overall, these few studies indicate that TMR individuals can learn a variety of tasks from several different model types.

1. Fechter (1971) found that the mood of a television program can affect the friendly or aggressive behavior of TMR residents, i.e., aggressive films increase aggressive behavior and friendly films increase friendly behavior. In order to increase or maintain friendly behavior a teacher may wish to decrease her students' viewing of aggressive television shows and encourage them to view shows of a friendly nature. The teacher could reward the children for viewing appropriate shows. For films shown at school the teacher could reinforce her students' modeling of appropriate behaviors. Moreover, the teacher could appoint models for each day to demonstrate friendly behavior. Then she could reinforce the models for their demonstrations and the other students for imitating the friendly behaviors.

2. For children who fail to imitate vocal or motor behavior it is important to reward echoic responses (approximations) as a beginning step toward the development of verbal and/or motor skills. Echoic responses can be stimulated by providing the child with a model who exhibits discrete vocal and/or motor behaviors (Stewart, 1972).

3. Streifel and Phelan (1973) found that young TMR children learned to imitate motor acts when the model reinforced them for imitating. A teacher could praise students for imitating motor skills that she displays. The teacher could model motor skills which are prerequisites for handwriting and selected games.

4. Talkington and Altman (1973) reported that aggressive and affectional behaviors can be evoked via observational learning. This finding suggests that the teacher needs to provide students with appropriate models at appropriate times. For example, overly aggressive students need to view friendly models. Moreover, the teacher should not plan for students to observe highly active or aggressive models immediately prior to the beginning of a sedentary task. In addition, the teacher can advise parents of the effects of aggressive and friendly models. The parents may wish to reduce the watching of violent television shows and increase their own display of friendly behaviors.

5. Turnure and Rynders (1973) found modeling to be as effective as manual guidance for teaching a simple problem-solving task and more effective than trial and error learning for teaching the task. This study supports the efficacy of teachers using manual guidance and modeling to teach some simple problem-solving tasks involving simple motoric actions, e.g., using a stick to reach an object under an object, using a ladder to reach the top of the chalkboard.

6. Based on the success that Lutzker and Sherman (1974) had in using imitation and token reinforcement to teach TMR individuals to produce generative sentences with correct subject-verb agreements, it appears that classroom teachers and speech pathologists should employ these techniques in language remediation programs. Pictures could be used to teach noun associations, then verb associations, and finally sentence associations. For example, when a picture of a dog eating is displayed, the student would initially learn to say *dog* by modeling and receiving reinforcement for saying *dog*. Next the verb *eating* would be modeled and reinforced when the picture was presented. Finally the sentence *The dog is eating* could be modeled and reinforced when the picture is displayed. Success criterion would need to be established for each learning step, e.g., five correct trials of saying the correct response without the model.

Modeling Studies with the Severely Retarded

BAER, PETERSON, AND SHERMAN'S STUDIES. Baer, Peterson, and Sherman (1967) selected three severely retarded residents (CA = 9–12 years) in order to teach them to imitate the actions of adults. Prior to the experiment none of the subjects exhibited spontaneous motor or vocal imitative behavior. The initial training sessions were designed to teach each child a series of three discriminated operants. Procedures for developing each operant consisted of: (a) a discriminative stimulus modeled by the experimenter, (b) a correct response (topographically similar to modeled behavior) by the subject, and (c) a food reinforcement after a correct response. In the beginning, intensive shaping and manual guidance were used to establish imitative responses by the subject. The continuation of imitation training included sessions of: (a) probes for generalized imitation, (b) nonreinforcement of all imitations, (c) the development of imitative chains, (d) verbal imitations, and (e) imitation of other experimenters.

The findings disclosed that with training the immediate imitation of new demonstrations greatly increased. Moreover, imitation of behaviors not trained developed and persisted without reinforcement as long as other imitative behaviors were reinforced. When reinforcement was not contingent upon imitative behavior (phase of differential reinforcement of other behavior), both the previously reinforced imitative behaviors and the never-reinforced probe imitations decreased in strength. The training procedures were effective in developing imitative chains and verbal imitations.

Finally, imitative behavior generalized to other adult experimenters.

GARCIA, BAER, AND FIRESTONE'S STUDIES. Garcia, Baer, and Firestone (1971) investigated the development of generalized imitative responding as a function of response topography in four severely retarded institutionalized children. The subjects were trained via shaping and fading to imitate motor and short vocal responses modeled by the experimenter. The development of a generalized imitative response was assessed through occasional probes which consisted of a modeled response similar to those trained but unaccompanied by reinforcement. A multiple-baseline design was used which reflected the different times in which training in each topographically distinct response type occurred.

Examination of the probe response data revealed the development of generalized imitative responding in each subject. Moreover, the generalization was restricted to probes topographically similar (response types) to those trained. The investigators conclude that generalized imitation occurred for responses which were topographically similar to responses in which the subjects received training.

KINDBERG'S STUDIES. After establishing generalized imitation with 16 severely retarded institutionalized boys, Kindberg (1971) divided them into an experimental group and a control group. Prior to the modeling task (which was presented via videotape) the participants in the experimental group were provided structured opportunities for social interaction with the peer model. The control group only saw the peer model when they viewed him on the videotape. Videotape recordings were made of each child's imitations of 40 gestures and block manipulations provided by the peer model. Both groups were given social praise for correct imitations. The first recording was immediately after the participants viewed the model. The second recording occurred 12 weeks later and immediately followed the presentation of the videotape of the model. The third recording occurred 28 weeks later and was in response to a slide presentation of the model. The final recording occurred on the same day as the slide presentation but involved a response to a presentation of regular color prints of the model.

The imitative responses were high and equivocal for both groups on the initial and the 12-week-interval recordings. The imitative responses of the experimental group to the pictures of the peer model were significantly higher than the imitative responses of the control group to the pictures. Kindberg (1971) found that social interaction and verbal ability were predictors of imitative responses to pictures of a peer model presented 28 weeks after the first videotape viewing. Finally, CA, length of institutionalization, MA, and social age were not significant predictors of modeling performance to the pictures of the peer model.

SEMMEL AND DOLLEY'S STUDIES. Semmel and Dolley (1971) examined the imitation of sentences of 40 severely retarded Down's syndrome children. The children were asked to repeat declarative, negative, passive, and negative-passive sentences that were equated for length and modeled by the experimenter. The mean percent of correct responses was significantly greater for the declarative sentences than it was for the remaining sentence types. Semmel and Dolley also examined the relationship between modeling and CA and modeling and IQ. They showed that while CA was not significantly related to modeling, a strong relationship was demonstrated between IQ and modeling. However, this finding was complicated by the relationship between CA and IQ. They conclude that the imitation of sentences by the severely retarded children was a function of the transformational complexity of the sentences.

ALTMAN, TALKINGTON, AND CLELAND'S STUDIES. Altman, Talkington, and Cleland (1972) studied the effects of verbal instructions and modeling on the gross motor performance of institutionalized severely retarded children. One group observed a model sitting in, reversing, and rocking in a Dixon chair. No verbal instructions were provided. A second group was given instructions that paralleled the model's performance but no modeling was provided. A control group received neither model exposure nor verbal instructions but engaged in "small talk" with the experimenter.

No significant differences in imitative performances were found across groups. Altman et al. (1972) note that previous investigators obtained significant imitation effects with severely retarded when modeling and verbal instructions were combined. They conclude that both conditions are necessary when imitation occurs with this population. Different results may have occurred if generalized imitation had been established with the subjects before conducting the experiment. This has been done in several modeling studies involving severely retarded subjects (Garcia, Baer, & Firestone, 1971; Johnson, 1972).

BENDER'S STUDIES. Bender (1972) examined the effectiveness of visual-imitative training to teach industrial-type psychomotor tasks to 25 severely mentally retarded male subjects. After the subjects observed an adult male perform selected industrial tasks (hammering, sanding), they were asked to imitate the acts. Using a pretest-posttest design, significant differences favoring posttest performance scores were reported. Bender concludes that visual-imitative training procedures are effective in teaching motor tasks to severely retarded individuals. Moreover, he notes that the visual-imitative approach eliminates much of the verbalization that frequently characterizes other training procedures.

BRY AND NAWAS'S STUDIES. Bry and Nawas (1972) examined the development of a generalized imitative motor behavior in two severely retarded and two profoundly retarded children as a function of extrinsic reinforcement of the observer for imitative behavior. The results of the four-phase experiment indicated that the reinforcement condition was associated with an increasing development of imitative responses. Once imitation was established, the rate of imitation was equivalent for the two children in each group. Bry and Nawas conclude that reinforcement is essential to the development of imitative behavior in retarded children who have not demonstrated previous imitative behaviors.

JEFFREY'S STUDIES. Jeffrey (1972) conducted a study designed to increase verbalizations of a retarded girl. He used operant techniques to increase the rate of correct phoneme imitation. Over a period of 15 individual sessions, the number of phonemes correctly produced increased from 16 of 39 (41%) to 37 of 39 (95%). The 95% level was maintained in a one-month follow-up.

The specific procedures used to increase verbalizations were as follows:

1. Nonattending and disruptive behaviors were eliminated by administering time-outs for inappropriate behaviors and contingent reinforcement for appropriate behaviors.

2. Specific sounds were shaped to come under imitative control.
3. A high rate of phoneme imitation was established through the use of contingent positive reinforcement.
4. Two or more sounds were chained together, e.g., my teacher.
5. Objects and pictures were associated with added imitative auditory discriminative stimuli, e.g., the therapist held a picture, vocalized a sound, and then had Judy imitate the sound.
6. Imitative discriminative stimuli were faded from step 6.
7. Single demands were established, e.g., after Judy had learned to name an object, this name was required in appropriate situations before reinforcers were dispensed. (Jeffrey, 1972, p. 36)

Some additional activities which were included to facilitate generalization and transfer were:

1. The child was taught a short list of words relevant to the classroom. It was reasoned that the need for these words in the natural environment would be great and positive consequences would result from their use.
2. Through the use of the Bell and Howell Language Master the child was able to practice a self-managed language drill.
3. Classroom peers were taught the words and were instructed to use them and reinforce the subject for using them.
4. The language training program was described to the teachers and they were encouraged to reinforce the child's verbal behavior and not respond to the child's nonverbal behavior.

JOHNSON'S STUDIES. Johnson (1972) examined the effect of imitative training on the learning of manipulative skills by severely retarded subjects. She used a matched pairs design in which four experimental subjects received preexperimental imitative training (reinforcement for imitation of experimenter), while their matched controls did not. Following the training program all eight subjects were taught manipulative skills (buttoning, cutting with scissors, etc.) which they were unable to perform on a pretest. All subjects were taught eight tasks via a live model and eight tasks via directive teaching (verbal instruction). For both methods food was presented contingent upon correct responses.

When compared with the untrained subjects, the subjects who participated in the preexperimental imitative training had a proportionately higher rate of correct responses on tasks presented by the model than on tasks presented by the directive method. Moreover, the results indicated that for all subjects the imitative teaching method produced a significantly higher rate of correct responses than did the directive teaching method. Johnson (1972) concludes that imitative teaching—rather than directive teaching—can be more effective in teaching manipulative skills to severely retarded individuals and its effectiveness is enhanced if the subjects have a previous history of imitative training.

MARTIN'S STUDIES. Martin (1972) examined the imitative behavior of three severely retarded institutionalized boys as a function of instructions to "Do this" or "Don't do this" in combination with elements of:

1. extinction
2. reinforcement
3. immediate differential reinforcement of other behavior
4. differential reinforcement of other behavior in 15 seconds
5. verbal reprimand

In the 13-phase experiment, both antecedent (instructions) and consequent events were found to exert control on imitative motor productions. Specifically, the results indicated that when instructions were incongruent with consequences (e.g., "Do this" instructions when verbal reprimand was the consequence) imitative behavior was controlled by the consequences. However, subjects did produce imitative responses in those phases in which instructions to imitate were not followed by reinforcement for imitative behavior.

SCHROEDER AND BAER'S STUDIES. Schroeder and Baer (1972) used serial and concurrent training methods for instructing two institutionalized retarded girls to imitate vocal stimuli. With the serial method, successive approximations to criterion for individual words were shaped; with the concurrent training condition imitation of three words was shaped at the same time. After criterion was reached, untrained and unreinforced probe words were inserted as a means of assessing generalized vocal imitation. The results indicated that a general increase in imitative accuracy for the probe items occurred as more training items reached criterion. Also, the increase in the accuracy of imitative probes was consistently greater for concurrent training than for serial training conditions. Hutt and Gibby (1976) indicate that Schroeder and Baer's study was especially relevant in that it "helps us to determine whether the molecular or molar approach is more effective with specified kinds of material" (p. 456).

BAER AND GUESS'S STUDIES. Using differential reinforcement and imitation, Baer and Guess (1973) taught severely retarded children to use noun suffixes when labeling stimuli exemplifying the verb form of an action. Four children (three institutionalized) were selected who exhibited no usage of noun suffixes (er, ist) on pretest measures and observations. Pictures depicting individuals engaged in various activities were used as stimuli in each of three conditions. In Condition I the experimenter displayed each training picture while simultaneously describing the action (e.g., "This man swims"). This description was immediately followed by the stimulus phrase, "He is a ___." If the observer produced a verb with the correct noun suffix (e.g., swimmer), she was immediately given verbal praise ("good") and was handed a plastic token which could later be exchanged for toys or sweets. If she responded incorrectly, the experimenter said "no," provided the correct label, and after a 10-second delay presented the stimuli again. Criterion for each word trained was five correct consecutive responses.

In Condition II the same procedures were used except that the children were reinforced for producing the ist suffix to verbs which normally take the er suffix. In Condition III the subjects were again trained to give the correct er suffix. In essence, Condition III was a replication of Condition I.

The results disclosed that in each experimental condition the number of trials that were required to reach successive criterion decreased. In conditions I and III a generative outcome was developed, i.e., as each successive verb was presented it was quickly converted into a correct noun suffix without prompting or differential reinforcement. Condition II demonstrated the experimental control of the training procedures by teaching the grammatical misuse of the ist suffix when labeling verbs.

Baer and Guess (1973) conclude:

> These results substantiate previous studies in the development of morphological grammar in retarded children, in which training a few instances or examples of a class of linguistic behavior generated other members of the class not trained directly (Baer & Guess, 1971; Guess, 1969; Guess et al., 1968; Sailor, 1971; Schumaker & Sherman, 1970). (p. 503)

GARCIA, GUESS, AND BYRNES'S STUDIES. Garcia, Guess, and Byrnes (1973) used modeling and reinforcement procedures (candy) to investigate the development of sentence usage of a severely retarded institutionalized girl. The procedure consisted of a model responding to an object in singular (Experiment I) or plural (Experiment II) form with reinforcement provided for imitation of the model. Probe trials which involved absence of verbal model and reinforcement were interspersed with training trials in assessing generalization from imitation of the model to object labeling. In a third experiment modeling alone was compared to modeling with reinforcement. Two models were provided and only imitation of one was reinforced. Results of the three experiments indicated that imitative responding was under the control of reinforcing consequences and that the syntax training (singular and plural usage) resulted in additional uses of similar syntax under conditions not specifically trained.

HOLT'S STUDIES. Holt (1973) investigated the word-modeling behavior of 36 institutionalized retarded, 36 noninstitutionalized retarded, and 36 normal children. These groups were further divided into matched MA levels. All groups were presented a taped voice of an adult male who listed 50 words which contained an increasing number of words in a critical word class (animal words). After the children were presented with a word, they were required to produce a word. Three types of responses were analyzed: (a) critical responses, i.e., child's word in the same class as that of the model; (b) parroting responses; and (c) nonparroting critical responses, i.e., child's word in same word class but not identical to or a common word associate to the model's word.

The results indicated that all groups demonstrated a word modeling effect and that more retarded than normal participants showed parroting responses. Also, parroting behavior was inversely related to MA level. There were no differences in the word imitation behavior of institutionalized and noninstitutionalized retardates. Finally, the position that concept modeling would increase across MA levels was partially supported.

TALKINGTON, HALL, AND ALTMAN'S STUDIES. Talkington, Hall, and Altman (1973) divided 75 institutionalized severely retarded subjects into three groups of 25 subjects equated on age, ability level, and preprogram communication measures of (a) response to basic commands, and (b) Verbal Language Development Scale (VLDS) scores. Group I subjects were exposed to a modeling procedure wherein three peer models were given social praise for following a basic command given by the experimenter. Group II subjects received commands and were given reinforcement for appropriate responses. Group III was an attention-control group. Postexperimental VLDS and command scores were obtained on the subjects 100 days after the preVLDS and command scores were obtained. The difference between pretest and posttest scores was significantly greater on the VLDS and command items for the modeling group (Group I) than for either the praise or control groups. Similarly, changes in Group II were significantly greater than changes in the control group.

SUMMARY. The previous fifteen studies are summarized (see Table 7.3, pp. 250–51) in terms of model variables, observer variables, task variables, and miscellaneous variables. The model variables are presented in Table 7.3 and although they include numerous parameters a pattern is readily discernable. Twelve of the 15 studies used "live" demonstrations by adult models. One study (Holt, 1973) used an adult model presented via audiotape. Kindberg (1971) used a nonretarded peer via videotape as a model and had the model interact with the observers prior to presentation of the tape. Talkington et al. (1973) used mentally retarded peers as models and praised the models for performing. In two studies (Baer & Guess, 1973; Baer et al. 1967) the observer was praised by the model for correct imitation.

Some specific findings regarding model variables include:

1. Positive social interaction with a peer model predicted imitative responses of severely retarded observers when they were presented with a picture of the model 28 weeks after original imitation (Kindberg, 1971).
2. Observation of peer models who were rewarded for performance produced greater performance scores (verbal and response to commands) by severely retarded subjects than did a reinforcement condition (Talkington et al., 1973).
3. When the model reinforced the severely retarded observer for correct imitation, imitative behavior was established and maintained. In addition, the imitative behavior generalized to nonreinforced behaviors within the same response class, e.g., adding the er suffix correctly to verbs not used in training (Baer & Guess, 1973; Baer et al., 1967).

In the domain of model variables it appears that investigations regarding the effectiveness of peer models and audiovisual presentations warrant attention. In both studies (Kindberg, 1971; Talkington et al., 1973) that used peers as models, a modeling effect was demonstrated. Similarly, in the two studies (Holt, 1973; Kindberg, 1971) that used audiovisual model presentations, a modeling effect occurred. Systematic application of modeling influences through mechanical devices and peers seems to be a means of intensifying training procedures in workshops and institutions without requiring additional adult staff. With severely retarded individuals who have no history of imitative behavior the procedure of having the model reward the observers for imitation appears to be effective.

The observer characteristics outlined in Table 7.3 indicate that the observers in most of the studies consisted of institutionalized severely retarded individuals. Holt (1973) did not report the level of retardation of his subjects, but he did include MA-equivalent normals and institutionalized and noninstitutionalized retardates. Other distinguishing characteristics considered in the studies were Down's syndrome, sex, and preexperimental history of imitation behavior.

Findings on observer variables include:

1. The verbal ability of severely retarded observers was predictive of their imitative responses when they were presented a picture of the model after a 28-week interval (Kindberg, 1971).
2. Generalized imitation for severely retarded persons occurred for responses (motor, short vocal) which were topographically similar to responses in which the participants had received training (Garcia, Baer, & Firestone, 1971).
3. With severely retarded children a strong relationship seemed to exist between IQ and modeling (Semmel & Dolley, 1971).
4. For imitation to occur with severely retarded children it is necessary to combine verbal instructions with modeling (Altman et al., 1972).
5. For severely retarded institutionalized girls, generalized vocal imitation increased as a function of number of training items completed (Schroeder & Baer, 1972).
6. Institutionalized retardates, noninstitutionalized retardates, and MA-equivalent normals all exhibited a word modeling effect. However, retarded children showed more parroting responses than normals. Also, parroting was inversely related to MA (Holt, 1973).

7. MA-equivalent, institutionalized, and noninstitutionalized retarded children did not differ on word modeling (Holt, 1973).

Observer characteristics of these studies were similar, i.e., most were institutionalized severely retarded individuals. The severely retarded observers demonstrated a modeling effect in all 15 studies, but too few studies exist to draw any definitive positions regarding such observer variables as:

1. length of institutionalization
2. sex
3. age
4. socioeconomic status
5. reflectivity
6. impulsivity
7. mode preferences

The task variables highlighted in Table 7.3 include many dimensions. Seven studies used gross motor tasks, two used fine motor tasks, six used simple verbal tasks, and four used complex verbal tasks. Moreover, five of the investigators examined whether observational learning generalized to other conditions. The tasks represented in this review spanned many dimensions and represent task component which are found in many training and educational settings. The three studies (Garcia et al., 1973; Holt, 1973; Semmel & Dolley, 1971) that examined task difficulty used verbal tasks. In all three studies severely retarded subjects imitated difficult tasks less than they did more simple tasks.

Some specific findings regarding task variables include:

1. With severely retarded individuals who had no history of imitative behavior it was necessary for the model to prompt them in order to establish the responses needed to perform the desired motor and verbal tasks (Baer et al., 1967).
2. The imitation of sentences by severely retarded children appeared to be a function of the transformational complexity of the sentences, i.e., declarative sentences were imitated more than passive sentences (Semmel & Dolley, 1971).
3. Reinforcement for imitation of correct phoneme productions enabled a severely retarded person to obtain and maintain correct phoneme productions (Jeffrey, 1972).
4. Reinforcement for imitation of correct grammer usage enabled severely retarded observers to acquire a specific grammer skill (Baer et al., 1967).

TABLE 7.3

Model Variables, Observer Variables, Task Variables, and Miscellaneous Variables in Imitation Studies with Severely Retarded Subjects

ARTICLES	MODEL VARIABLES						LEVEL OF MR	OBSERVER VARIABLES				TASK VARIABLES			MISC. VARIABLES
	NON-MR PEER	MR PEER	ADULT	LIVE	A.V.	OTHER		MA EQUIVALENT	OTHER CHARACTERISTICS	GROSS MOTOR	FINE MOTOR	SIMPLE VERBAL	COMPLEX VERBAL	GENERALIZATION	MISC. VARIABLES
Baer, Peterson, & Sherman (1967)		X	X			Model rewarded observers	Severe Profound		Institutionalized. No history preexperiment imitation.	X		X		X	Models prompted observers initially. Primary reinforcement of observers.
Garcia, Baer, & Firestone (1971)		X	X				Severe		Institutionalized	X		X		X	Used reinforcement.
Kindberg (1971)	X	X	X		X	Social interaction with observers	Severe CAs = 7–13		Institutionalized males	X					Used reinforcements. Verbal ability & modeling. Follow-up. Preexperimental imitation training.
Semmel & Dolley (1971)		X	X				Severe		Down's syndrome				X		CA, IQ, & modeling. Sentence types.
Altman, Talkington, & Cleland (1972)		X	X				Severe		Institutionalized	X					Verbal instructions versus modeling.
Bender (1972)		X	X				Severe	Males		X	X				No reinforcement.
Bry & Nawas (1972)		X	X				Severe Profound			X					Reinforcement of observer vs. no reinforcement for imitation.

TABLE 7.3, cont.

ARTICLES	NON-MR PEER	MR PEER	ADULT	LIVE	A.V.	OTHER	LEVEL OF MR	MA EQUIVALENT	OTHER CHARACTERISTICS	GROSS MOTOR	FINE MOTOR	SIMPLE VERBAL	COMPLEX VERBAL	GENERALIZATION	MISC. VARIABLES
MODEL VARIABLES							OBSERVER VARIABLES			TASK VARIABLES					MISC. VARIABLES
Jeffrey (1972)		X	X	X			Severe		Females			X			Reinforcement. Follow-up.
Johnson (1972)		X	X	X			Severe				X				Previous imitation. Reinforcement. Modeling vs. directive teaching.
Martin (1972)		X	X	X			Severe		Institutionalized males	X					Antecedent events. Consequent events.
Schroeder & Baer (1972)		X	X	X			Not available		Institutionalized females			X		X	Reinforcement. Serial training & concurrent training.
Baer & Guess (1973)		X	X	X		Reinforced imitation	Severe		Institutionalized				X	X	Reinforced observer. Taught grammer usage.
Garcia, Guess, & Bymes (1973)		X	X	X			Severe		Institutionalized females				X	X	Modeling vs. reinforcement plus modeling.
Holt (1973)		X	X		X		Not available	Normals & retarded	Institutionalized. Noninstitutionalized. Normal.			X	X		MA & modeling. Institutionalization and modeling.
Talkington, Hall, & Altman (1973)	X		X	X		Models praised	Severe		Institutionalized			X			Models with models being praised vs. praise of observer without model.

The miscellaneous variables spanned a variety of parameters (see Table 7.3). Eleven of the studies employed reinforcement in conjunction with imitation conditions. Two of the studies examined the ability level (IQ, MA) of observers and modeling performances. Two other studies included a follow-up procedure. Three of the studies compared modeling with another training procedure. Other distinguishing variables were verbal ability, CA, preexperimental imitation training, antecedent instructions, and institutionalization.

Some specific findings regarding the miscellaneous variables are:

1. Imitation rather than directive instruction was more effective in teaching manipulative skills to severely retarded individuals. Moreover, the effectiveness of imitation teaching was facilitated if the subjects had a previous history of imitative training (Johnson, 1972).
2. Both antecedent and consequent events exerted control on motor imitations by severely retarded boys (Martin, 1972).
3. When instructions preceding the model presentation were incongruent with consequences, the imitative behavior of severely retarded individuals was primarily controlled by the consequences (Martin, 1972).
4. Severely retarded boys produced imitative responses when imitative behavior was not followed by reinforcement (Martin, 1972).
5. Visual-imitative training procedures were effective in teaching industrial-type motor tasks to severely retarded persons (Bender, 1972).
6. For severely retarded institutionalized girls, concurrent training (imitation of three words at a time) produced more accurate generalized vocal imitation than serial training (one word at a time) (Schroeder & Baer, 1972).
7. Reinforcement was essential to the development of imitative behavior in severely retarded children who had not demonstrated previous imitation behaviors (Bry & Nawas, 1972).
8. With severely retarded institutionalized girls, imitative responding appeared to be predominantly under the control of reinforcing consequences and seemed to generalize to nonexperimental conditions (Garcia, Guess, & Byrnes, 1973).

Other observations that accrue from an examination of miscellaneous variables suggest several patterns. Reinforcement of the observer for correct imitative responses permeated the studies. It appears that reinforcement contributes much to the modeling performances of severely retarded individuals. Also, the modeling of severely retarded observers is enhanced by preexperimental imitative training and the supplement of modeling with verbal instructions. Generalization occurred in the five studies (Baer & Guess, 1973; Baer et al., 1967; Garcia et al., 1971; Garcia et al., 1973; Schroeder & Baer, 1972) that examined it. Imitative responses were maintained in the two studies (Jeffrey, 1972; Kindberg, 1971) that included a follow-up. In two studies (Johnson, 1972; Talkington et al., 1973) that compared modeling with other techniques (directive teaching and verbal instructions), modeling was the more effective technique; however, in another study (Altman, Talkington, & Cleland, 1972) modeling was equivocal but not superior to verbal instructions.

These studies with severely retarded individuals reveal that modeling represents an effective training technique with the severely retarded. Likewise, they reflect the recency of systematic efforts to examine modeling with the severely retarded. Although the short history of research efforts limits our understanding of the many parameters which influence observational learning, available work provides a framework and an impetus for further work.

TEACHING IMPLICATIONS

1. Baer et al. (1967) demonstrated that severely and profoundly retarded children without histories of imitative behavior could be taught via modeling and reinforcement procedures to imitate motor and vocal behaviors. The findings of Baer et al. indicate that training procedures exist which enable severely mentally retarded (SMR) children to develop self-help and work skills. These training procedures include: (a) the presentation of a stimulus (via modeling), (b) the imitation of the modeled behavior, and (c) primary and social reinforcement for correct imitation. It is important to note that in their initial sessions Baer et al. used manual guidance (prompting), shaping, and fading in order to establish imitative responses.
2. Garcia et al. (1971) found that generalized imitation occurred for responses which were topographically similar to responses in which the participants received training. This finding supports the position that if modeling tasks were analyzed and presented to SMR pupils in a sequential manner, correct imitation would be aided. The object of the task analysis would be to have a task at one level which is topographically similar to the next task to be presented. For example, tasks with topographical similarities would include holding a piece of chalk and holding a pencil, or washing a chalk board and painting a wall.
3. In Kindberg's study (1971), SMR boys responded highly imitatively to pictures of a model who had

interacted socially with them 28 weeks before. In teaching or training severely retarded boys, teachers could ensure that the observers have an opportunity to interact with the model in a positive manner before imitation is required.

4. Semmel and Dolley (1971) found that SMR children imitated declarative sentences more than they imitated negative, passive, and negative-passive sentences. The primary implication of this finding is that it enhances our understanding of the type of verbal behavior SMR children tend to imitate and, perhaps, comprehend.

5. Altman et al. (1972) found that modeling plus verbal instructions are needed for imitation to occur with SMR individuals. This findings indicates that teachers or attendants need to provide the SMR observer with as many cues (verbal and motor) as possible when demonstrating a task. With SMR observers verbal cues could consist primarily of labels (*hammer*, *bed*), directional words (*up*, *down*), and action verbs (*eat*, *walk*).

6. Bender (1972) found that visual-imitative training procedures were effective in teaching industrial type psychomotor tasks to severely retarded males. This finding has implications for teaching vocational-type skills to SMR individuals who are able to function in workshop settings or on jobs in institutions. Since the visual-imitative approach does not rely on verbal skills, it appears especially appropriate for use with individuals who have limited language skills.

7. Bry and Nawas (1972) reported that reinforcement is essential for establishing imitative behaviors in severely and/or profoundly retarded children. It has been acknowledged in several of the studies reviewed that many SMR individuals need to establish generalized imitation before learning via observation can occur. The finding of Bry and Nawas indicates that before beginning observational learning tasks teachers should use reinforcement in establishing the imitative behavior of SMR individuals who do not have a history of imitative responses.

8. Through modeling and operant techniques Jeffrey (1972) was able to increase the phoneme production of a severely retarded girl. In addition, the newly acquired verbal behavior of the girl generalized to the classroom and was maintained during the follow-up period of 30 days. The techniques that Jeffrey used are explicitly described in text and they may be helpful in developing language programs for SMR children. The various procedures used in Jeffrey's training program have received substantial support from other investigators, such as:
   a. operant training—Sloane and McAulay, 1968
   b. teaching sounds by machine — Holland and Mathews, 1963
   c. peer teaching—Surratt, Ulrich, and Hawkins, 1969

   d. selecting functional words—Risley and Wolf, 1968

9. Johnson (1972) found that imitative teaching was more effective than directive teaching in teaching manipulative skills (buttoning, cutting with scissors) to SMR individuals. Moreover, its effectiveness is enhanced if the observers have a previous history of imitative training. This finding indicates that teachers and attendants should provide SMR individuals with basic generalized imitation training before presenting tasks to be imitated, i.e., reinforce the child for copying the behaviors of a model prior to beginning specific observational learning tasks. Also, Johnson's results indicate that imitative teaching is effective for teaching self-help skills. Johnson used primary reinforcers for rewarding correct imitative behavior. With SMR children it may often be necessary or efficient to add primary reinforcers to imitative training.

10. Martin (1972) found that antecedent events (verbal instructions) and consequent events (reinforcement, reprimand) controlled the imitative behavior of SMR institutionalized boys. According to this finding, teachers need to combine observational learning with preimitation instructions and systematic consequation. Moreover, Martin reported that when instructions were incongruent with consequences the consequences controlled imitative behavior. This finding acknowledges the influence that consequences exhibit on behavior occurrence and implies that in order to maintain or develop behavior, teachers and attendants should reinforce the imitation of appropriate behavior by SMR individuals.

11. Schroeder and Baer (1972) reported that two retarded girls were able to develop a generalized vocal imitation better when the stimuli were presented concurrently (three words at a time) than when the stimuli were presented serially (one word at a time). This finding suggests that some retarded children may learn more generalized vocal behavior if several words are presented simultaneously rather than serially. Teachers or attendants could quickly determine the effectiveness of each technique with an individual by teaching a few words using each method and assessing its relative effectiveness through the use of probe words.

12. Baer and Guess (1973) demonstrated that morphological grammer (*er* suffix) can be taught to severely retarded children via imitation and differential reinforcement. The description of Baer and Guess' procedures in this chapter provides the teacher or speech clinician of severely retarded children with specific techniques for developing the correct use of the *er* suffix with appropriate verbs.

13. Garcia et al. (1973) used reinforcement and modeling to develop syntactical skills (use of singular and plural sentence forms) in a severely retarded girl.

Their finding indicates that "Within a speech training program, an initial effort to train a syntactical repertoire might begin by isolating similar instances of speech used in this study" (Garcia et al., 1973, p. 310). For example, a teacher could isolate on subject-verb agreement, use of plurals, and sentence type usage. An expected result would be the acquisition of a new syntactical skill and generalization of the training to topographically similar responses.

14. Talkington et al. (1973) reported that a modeling procedure in which the model was praised for responding to basic commands produced higher response to command scores and *Verbal Language Development Scale* scores than direct reinforcement for responses to commands. These results support the efficacy of using a model plus reinforcement of the model procedure to develop direction following skills and verbal skills. A teacher could use peers as models and reinforce the peer model for correct responses. In addition, volunteers and aides could serve as models or reinforcers. Finally, this procedure could be strengthened by reinforcing both the model and observer for correct responding. Different ratio schedules of reinforcement could be maintained by having the reinforcing person turn over a card for each correct response and reinforce the child only when a particular type of card appears. The cards could be arranged to represent the desired ratio.

Conclusion

In this chapter it is possible to ascertain two primary types of studies according to their respective purposes. One type appears to spring from a theoretical or exploratory position in order to formulate or advance a theoretical viewpoint regarding mental retardation and modeling, i.e., outer-directedness or proneness of retardates to attend to audiovisual presentations more than non-retarded individuals. These theory-based studies usually include a nonretarded comparison group. At this point too few of these studies exist to draw any definitive conclusions; however, it is noteworthy to point out that the major theoretical positions being tested advance the viewpoint that retarded individuals are more prone to modeling than their nonretarded counterparts.

The second type of study is characterized by an attempt to develop and refine techniques which improve the use of observational learning with retarded individuals, i.e., use of reinforcement, the effectiveness of audiovisual presentation, the effect of model competence, type of tasks modeled, etc. Most of the studies reviewed in this chapter focused on developing and/or refining modeling techniques and they have directly generated observational learning procedures and techniques.

It is established that most retarded individuals learn (acquire and maintain behavior) via observation or are capable of learning via observation. The theory-based studies primarily help us understand any unique characteristics that retarded individuals display in observational learning, whereas the second type of studies provide examples of specific techniques and conditions which improve our ability to design environments which maximize the observational learning of retarded persons. It is obvious that both types contribute to the betterment of services and programs for the retarded.

It is intended that conclusions presented in this review be interpreted in a manner that minimizes broad generalizations. The results are based on too few studies; more studies are needed before findings can be discussed with confidence. At the present time it is obvious that modeling represents a viable educational and therapeutic tool with retarded individuals at the mild, moderate, and severe levels. It is highly probable that much information exists in the present and forthcoming literature which could serve as a springboard for developing specific educational and therapeutic techniques with retarded persons.

References

Altman, R., & Talkington, L. W. Modeling: An alternative behavior modification approach for retardates. *Mental Retardation*, 1971, *9*(3), 20–23.

Altman, R., Talkington, L. W., & Cleland, C. C. Relative effectiveness of modeling and verbal instructions on severe retardates' gross motor performance. *Psychological Reports*, 1972, *31*, 695–698.

Baer, D. M., & Guess, D. Receptive training of adjectival inflections in mental retardates. *Journal of Applied Behavior Analysis*, 1971, *4*, 129–139.

Baer, D. M., & Guess, D. Teaching productive noun suffixes to severely retarded children. *American Journal of Mental Deficiency*, 1973, 77, 498–505.

Baer, D. M., Peterson, R. F., & Sherman, J. A. The development of imitation by reinforcing behavioral similarity to a model. *Journal of the Experimental Analysis of Behavior*, 1967, *10*, 405–416.

Ball, T. S. Training generalized imitation: Variations on an historical theme. *American Journal of Mental Deficiency*, 1970, *75*, 135–141.

Bandura, A. Analysis of modeling processes. In A. Bandura (Ed.), *Psychological modeling: Conflicting theories*. Chicago: Aldine-Atherton, 1971.

Bandura, A. *Aggression: A social learning analysis*. Englewood Cliffs, N.J.: Prentice-Hall, 1973.

Baran, S. J. TV and social learning in the institutionalized MR. *Mental Retardation*, 1973, *11*(3), 36–38.

Bender, M. An experiment using a visual method of instruction followed by imitation to teach selected industrial education psychomotor tasks to severely mentally retarded males (Doctoral dissertation, University of Maryland, 1971). *Dissertation Abstracts International*, 1972, *32*, 5004A–5005A. (University Microfilms No. 72–10, 063, 254).

Bry, P. M., & Nawas, M. Is reinforcement necessary for the development of a generalized imitation operant in severely and profoundly retarded children? *American Journal of Mental Deficiency*, 1972, *76*, 658–667.

Cairns, R. B. Meaning and attention as determinants of social reinforcer effectiveness. *Child Development*, 1970, *41*, 1041–1056.

Clinton, L., & Boyce, K. Acquisition of simple motor imitative behavior in mentally retarded and nonretarded children. *American Journal of Mental Deficiency*, 1975, *79*, 695–700. (a)

Clinton, L., & Boyce, K. D. Rule-governed imitative verbal behavior as a function of modeling procedures. *Journal of Experimental Child Psychology*, 1975, *19*, 115–121. (b)

Cromwell, R. L. A social learning approach to mental retardation. In N. R. Ellis (Ed.), *Handbook of mental deficiency*. New York: McGraw-Hill, 1963.

Cullinan, D., Kauffman, J. M., & LaFleur, N. K. Modeling: Research with implications for special education. *Journal of Special Education*, 1975, *9*, 209–221.

Fechter, J. V. Modeling and environmental generalization by mentally retarded subjects of televised aggressive or friendly behavior. *American Journal of Mental Deficiency*, 1971, *76*, 266–267.

Forehand, R., & Calhoun, K. Verbal imitation in retardates: Follow-up. *Perceptual and Motor Skills*, 1973, *36*, 74.

Forehand, R., Robbins, B., & Brady, P. Effects of IQ and mental age on verbal imitative performance of children. *The Journal of Psychology*, 1973, *84*, 353–358.

Garcia, E., Baer, D. M., & Firestone, I. The development of generalized imitation within topographically determined boundaries. *Journal of Applied Behavior Analysis*, 1971, *4*, 101–112.

Garcia, E., Guess, D., & Brynes, J. Development of syntax in a retarded girl using procedures of imitation, reinforcement and modeling. *Journal of Applied Behavior Analysis,* 1973, *6,* 299–310.

Gardner, H. L., & Forehand, R. Effects of institutionalization upon word modeling responses of retarded subjects. *American Journal of Mental Deficiency*, 1974, *78*, 759–761.

Green, C., & Zigler, E. Social deprivation and the performance of retarded and normal children on a satiation type task. *Child Development,* 1962, *33*, 499–508.

Guess, D. A functional analysis of receptive language and productive speech: Acquisition of the plural morpheme. *Journal of Applied Behavior Analysis*, 1969, *2*, 55–64.

Guess, D., Sailor, W., Rutherford, G., & Baer, D. M. An experimental analysis of linguistic development: The productive use of the plural morpheme. *Journal of Applied Behavior Analysis*, 1968, *1*, 297–306.

Holland, A. L., & Mathews, J. Application of teaching machine concepts to speech pathology and audiology. *American Speech and Hearing Association*, 1963, *5*, 474–482.

Holt, M. M. Verbal imitative behavior of normal and retarded children (Doctoral dissertation, University of Alabama, 1972). *Dissertation Abstracts International*, 1973, *33*, 4542B. (University Microfilms No. 73–8041, 91)

Holt, M. M., Rickard, H. C., & Ellis, N. R. A note on word modeling in retarded adolescents. *American Journal of Mental Deficiency*, 1972, *77*, 237–239.

Hutt, M. L., & Gibby, R. G. *The mentally retarded child: Development, education, and treatment* (3rd ed.). Boston: Allyn & Bacon, 1976.

Jeffrey, B. D. Increase and maintenance of verbal behavior in a mentally retarded child. *Mental Retardation*, 1972, *10*(2), 35–40.

Johnson, V. M. Development of an imitative repertoire for teaching manipulative skills to severe retardates (Doctoral dissertation, University of Tennessee, 1972). *Dissertation Abstracts International*, 1972, *33*, 2171A. (University Microfilms No. 72–27, 476, 70)

Kindberg, M. N. Imitation of a peer model by severely retarded institutionalized boys (Doctoral dissertation, Ohio State University, 1970). *Dissertation Abstracts International*, 1971, *31*, 5605B–5606B (University Microfilms No. 71–7494, 110)

Litrownik, A. J. Observational learning in retarded and normal children as a function of delay between observation and opportunity to perform. *Journal of Experimental Child Psychology*, 1972, *48*, 117–125.

Lutzker, J. R., & Sherman, J. A. Producing generative sentence usage by imitation and reinforcement procedures. *Journal of Applied Behavior Analysis*, 1974, *7*, 447–460.

Martin, J. A. The effect of incongruent instructions and consequences on imitation in retarded children. *Journal of Applied Behavior Analysis*, 1972, *5*, 467–475.

Martin, J. A. Generalizing the use of descriptive adjectives through modeling. *Journal of Applied Behavior Analysis*, 1975, *8*, 203–209.

Risley, T., & Wolf, M. Establishing functional speech in echolalic children. In H. N. Sloane & B. D. MacAulay (Eds.), *Operant procedures in remedial speech and language training.* New York: Houghton Mifflin, 1968.

Ross, D. Effect on learning of psychological attachment to a film model. *American Journal of Mental Deficiency,* 1970, *74,* 701–707. (a)

Ross, D. Incidental learning of number concepts in small group games. *American Journal of Mental Deficiency,* 1970, *74,* 718–724.(b)

Ross, D. M., Ross, S. A., & Downing, M. L. Intentional training vs. observational learning of mediational strategies in EMR children. *American Journal of Mental Deficiency,* 1973, *78,* 292–299.

Sailor, W. Reinforcement and generalization of productive plural allomorphs in two retarded children. *Journal of Applied Behavior Analysis,* 1971, *4,* 305–310.

Schroeder, G. L., & Baer, D. M. Effects of concurrent and serial training on generalized vocal imitation in retarded children. *Developmental Psychology,* 1972, *6,* 293–301.

Schumaker, J., & Sherman, J. A. Training generative verb usage by imitation and reinforcement procedures. *Journal of Applied Behavior Analysis,* 1970, *3,* 273–287.

Semmel, M. I., & Dolley, D. G. Comprehension and imitation of sentences by Down's syndrome children as a function of transformational complexity. *American Journal of Mental Deficiency,* 1971, *75,* 739–745.

Sloane, H. N., & MacAulay, B. D. (Eds.). *Operant procedures in remedial speech and language training.* New York: Houghton Mifflin, 1968.

Stewart, F. J. A vocal-motor program for teaching nonverbal children. *Education and Training of the Mentally Retarded,* 1972, *7,* 176–182.

Streifel, J. A., & Phelan, J. G. Use of reinforcement of behavioral similarity to establish imitative behavior in young mentally retarded children. *American Journal of Mental Deficiency,* 1972, *77,* 239–241.

Strichart, S. S. Effects of competence and nurturance on imitation of nonretarded peers by retarded adolescents. *American Journal of Mental Deficiency,* 1974, *78,* 665–673.

Striefel, S., & Eberl, D. Imitation of live and videotaped models. *Education and Training of the Mentally Retarded,* 1974, *9,* 83–88.

Surratt, R. R., Ulrich, R. E., & Hawkins, R. P. An elementary student as a behavioral engineer. *Journal of Applied Behavior Analysis,* 1969, *2,* 85–92.

Talkington, L. W., & Altman, R. Effects of film-mediated aggressive and affectual models on behavior. *American Journal of Mental Deficiency,* 1973, *77,* 420–425.

Talkington, L. W., & Hall, S. M. Relative effects of response cost and reward on model on subsequent performance of EMRs. *The Journal of Developmental Disabilities,* 1975, *1*(2), 23–27.

Talkington, L. W., Hall, S. M., & Altman, R. Use of a peer modeling procedure with severely retarded subjects on a basic communication response skill. *Training School Bulletin,* 1973, *69,* 145–149.

Thoresen, C. E., & Stuhr, D. E. *Social modeling and counseling: Theory, research and practice.* Report presented at the meeting of the American Educational Research Association, Chicago, April 1972.

Turnure, J. E., & Rynders, J. E. Effectiveness of manual guidance, modeling, and trial and error learning procedures on the acquisition of new behaviors. *Merrill-Palmer Quarterly,* 1973, *19,* 49–65.

Turnure, J., & Zigler, E. Outer-directedness in the problem solving of normal and retarded children. *Journal of Abnormal and Social Psychology,* 1964, *69,* 427–436.

Yoder, P., & Forehand, R. Effects of modeling and verbal cues upon concept acquisition of nonretarded and retarded children. *American Journal of Mental Deficiency,* 1974, *78,* 566–570.

Zigler, E. Mental retardation: Current issues and approaches. In L. Hoffman & M. Hoffman (Eds.), *Review of child development research* (Vol 2). New York: Russell Sage Foundation, 1966.

Zigler, E. F., & Kanzer, P. The effectiveness of two classes of verbal reinforcers on the performance of middle- and lower-class children. *Journal of Personality,* 1962, *30,* 157–163.

8

Operant Conditioning

B. F. Skinner's Theory

Animal and human behavior operate according to a lawful system. The science of behavior which was described more than three decades ago by Skinner (1938, 1953), and the application of these laws to the behavior of the mentally retarded comprise the thrust of this chapter.

In this system, the *cause* of behavior is an observable change in an independent (environmental) variable, while *effect* refers to an observable change in a dependent (behavioral) variable.

> The old "cause-and-effect connection" becomes a "functional relation." The new terms do not suggest *how* a cause causes its effect; they merely assert that different events tend to occur together in a certain order. . . . We are concerned, then, with the causes of human behavior. We want to know why men behave as they do. Any condition or event which can be shown to have an effect upon behavior must be taken into account. By discovering and analyzing these causes we can predict behavior; to the extent that we can manipulate them, we can control behavior. (Skinner, 1953, p. 23)

Theoretical Basis of Operant Conditioning

The operant conditioning system is not a theory in the technical sense; however, it is a system which builds upon Thorndike's concepts of response selecting and connecting under the law of effect (Estes, 1970; Hilgard & Bower, 1966; Staats & Staats, 1963). Skinner's system may be placed into a stimulus-response-association classification as can Thorndike's theory of connectionism and Hull's systematic behavior theory. However, operant conditioning differs from Thorndike's theory mainly in its emphasis on the type of learning which is under the control of its consequences, and it differs from both the theories of Thorndike and Hull "in placing less emphasis upon the inference of underlying states or processes from performance and more emphasis upon the teasing out of empirical relationships between observed behaviors and controlling variables" (Estes, 1970, p. 137).

Skinner's original formulation of behavior (*The Behavior of Organisms*, 1938) grew from a series of experiments with rats in a type of apparatus which later came to be called a *Skinner Box*. His next large work was a text (*Science and Human Behavior*, 1953) developed for use with his psychology students at Harvard. This text was preceded by another classic text (Keller and Schoenfeld's *Principles of Psychology*, 1950) which also outlined the principles of operant conditioning. Both of these latter words relied upon the results of years of Skinner Box experimentation with rats and pigeons.

In the last twelve years, operant conditioning has received extensive application with mentally retarded individuals by a variety of professionals—psychologists, teachers, speech therapists, occupational therapists, social workers—and also paraprofessionals—parents, institutional attendants and teacher aides. *Behavior modification* and *applied behavior analysis* are terms more commonly used in reference to these applications in therapeutic, residential and instructional settings. *Operant conditioning* is loosely defined as an operation whereby the probability or rate of a response is increased by the contingent presentation of a reinforcing stimulus. Behavior, which is both observable and measurable, is viewed as a product of its consequences in that its probability of occurrence, or response strength, is directly altered and maintained by the schedule or pattern with which reinforcing consequences are made available. Additionally, rather extensive repertoires of behavior may be built by the reinforcement of smaller, inexact "bits" of behavior emitted by the learner prior to conditioning or teaching or prompted by the teacher during teaching. This latter procedure, shaping, which has been a highly successful teaching strategy with mentally retarded individuals, has enabled their acquisition of complex behaviors less likely to be learned through nonsystematic instruction or trial and error.

The Skinner Box

The apparatus employed by Skinner with rats and pigeons consists of a sound-resistant, darkened box into which the animal is placed (see Figure 8.1). In the rat's box a small brass lever exists which is attached to a food pellet releasing system. When the rat pushes the lever, a pellet is automatically released. The pigeon's box has a "peck spot" or key on one wall which, when pecked, releases grain into a cup below the key. Both the bar and the pecking key are connected to a recording system involving a pen that traces the cumulative responses of the animal upon a constantly rotating drum. These records, illustrated in Figure 8.2, plot passage of time along the abscissa or horizontal axis as the drum rotates from left to right and number of responses along the ordinate or vertical axis. Each time the bar or

the key is pressed, the recording line makes a small hash mark on the graph and an upward step. Therefore, when the line shows a steep upward movement, this indicates the animal is responding rapidly. When the line remains flat, in a horizontal direction, the animal is not responding at all. The response strength can be judged from the slope of the line.

By controlling various aspects of this learning environment (e.g., handling of the animal; animal weight—maintained at 70% free-eating weight; number of reinforcements per response; stimuli, such as lights, to cue the presence of reinforcement), Skinner and others applying his techniques have been able to obtain highly consistent results in the systematic study of behavior. With the addition of electronic programming systems, even more complex response patterns have been studied with animals and humans which yield "lawful" results. It is these lawful results of operant conditioning which will be outlined in the following section.

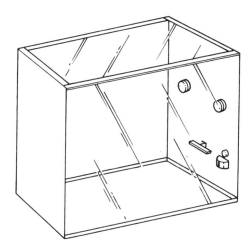

FIGURE 8.1

Skinner's apparatus for the study of operant conditioning with rats. The bar is located below the lights and to the left of the food pellet tray. Two lights above the bar may be used in discrimination training. The lights and food delivery mechanism are operated by electronic programming equipment.

SOURCE: Adapted from *Complex Human Behavior* by A. W. Staats & C. K. Staats. New York: Holt, Rinehart, & Winston, 1963, p. 43. Copyright 1963 by Holt, Rinehart, & Winston. Reprinted by permission.

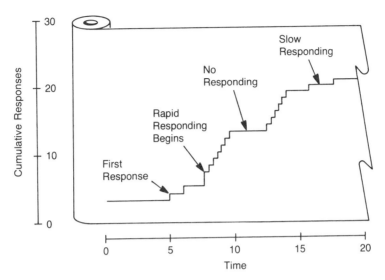

FIGURE 8.2
Example of a cumulative record.

SOURCE: Adapted from *Managing Behavior*. Part I. *Behavior Modification: The measurement of Behavior* by R. V. Hall. Lawrence, Kansas: H & H Enterprises, 1971, p. 20. Copyright 1971 by H & H Enterprises. Reprinted by permission.

A vast source of references (Bandura, 1969; Becker, Engelmann, & Thomas, 1971; Ferster & Perrott, 1968; Ferster & Skinner, 1957; Hilgard & Bower, 1975; Holland & Skinner, 1961; Honig, 1966; Skinner, 1938, 1953; Staats, 1968; Staats & Staats, 1963; Whaley & Malott, 1971) may be consulted for a more detailed explanation of operant conditioning and its applications to human behavior. In addition, many detailed reviews may be consulted which expand upon the topic of operant conditioning with retarded individuals. A partial list includes: Bijou (1966, 1968); Bijou & Baer (1966); Birnbrauer (in press); Block (1971); Gardner (1971); Krumboltz & Krumboltz (1972); MacMillan (1973); MacMillan & Forness (1973); Robinson & Robinson (1976); Spradlin & Girardeau (1966); and Weisberg (1971). Due to the massive quantity of research and writing on operant conditioning, the first portion of this chapter is limited to briefly describing the basic components of operant conditioning and sampling the related research with retarded populations.

Operant and Respondent Behavior

When Skinner proposed that two types of responses (respondent and operant) existed, he deviated significantly from the conventional S-R psychology which held as its tenet "no stimulus, no response." Although *respondents* refer to those responses elicited by known stimuli or controlled by their antecedents, such as the knee jerk reflex and pupillary constriction, the second type of response, *operant* is emitted without any corresponding dependence upon known stimuli. Operant behavior, its rate and probability of occurrence, is simply a function of its consequences. Respondents are commonly distinguished from operants in two ways. First, respondents are controlled by their eliciting stimuli or antecedents, while operants are controlled by their consequences. Secondly, respondents are unlearned, being either present at birth or through maturation, while operants are regarded as learned behavior. Because Skinner holds that stimulus conditions do not yield meaningful information about operant responses, he does not treat such responses in the conventional way, as respondents with unknown stimuli. Instead, rate of response is identified as the measure of operant response strength without necessitating reference to stimulus characteristics.

An operant may and usually does become coordinated with a prior stimulus. As with reflexes, this stimulus is *not* an elicitor of the operant; but, through learning, it becomes the occasion for the operant response to occur. Such responses, to be discussed more fully in a later section, are known as *discriminated operants*.

Conditioning, or the strengthening of behavior, occurs in two different ways which correspond to the two types of responses. In Type S (stimulus) conditioning, which is associated with respondent behavior, the conditioned stimulus (CS) (e.g., bell) is presented along with the unconditioned stimulus (US) (e.g., food) and with repeated pairings comes to elicit the response (e.g., salivation). Reinforcement is correlated with *stimuli* in Type S conditioning. The resultant "strengthening" of behavior in Type S or Pavlovian conditioning occurs when the magnitude of the response elicited by the CS is increased and when time lapses between the stimulus and response are shortened.

In his system of learning, Skinner (1938) does not give an important position to this contiguous conditioning with no operant reinforcement (Type S) and suggests that Type S may be limited to autonomic responses. Others (Hilgard & Bower, 1966) doubt and even deny whether Type S conditioning actually occurs at all.

Type R (response) conditioning, or the conditioning of operant behavior, provides the foundation for Skinner's system. In Type R, the *response* is correlated with reinforcement while the conditioned behavior is strengthened "in the sense of making a response more probable or, in actual fact, more frequent" (Skinner, 1953, p. 65).

> The experimental example which he [Skinner] originally used was lever pressing. This response may be strengthened by following it with food. It is not the *sight* of the lever which is important; it is the *pressing* of the lever. The conditioned response does not resemble the response to the reinforcing stimulus; its relationship to the reinforcing stimulus is that it causes it to appear. In operant conditioning, conditioning of Type R, reinforcement cannot follow unless the conditioned response appears; reinforcement is *contingent upon response*. (Hilgard & Bower, 1966, p. 109)

In Type R the mechanical arrangement results in a "dependence upon the posterior reinforcing stimulus" (Skinner, 1938, p. 22) such that the organism's response is instrumental in producing the reinforcement.

Skinner (1938) suggests that Type R or operant conditioning is limited to skeletal behavior while, as mentioned previously, Type S is limited to autonomic responses. Since the majority of human behaviors falls into the operant skeletal class,

Skinner's emphasis on Type R conditioning is justified. Eating, talking, reading a book, driving a car, singing, and washing dishes are emitted behaviors which demonstrate more operant than respondent characteristics.

Main Findings With Retarded Populations: Classical and Operant Conditioning

CLASSICAL CONDITIONING. Much of the research reviewed examining classical or respondent conditioning and mental retardation (Denny, 1964; Estes, 1970; Lipman, 1963; Ross, 1966; Ross & Ross, 1973) reveals agreement in the following areas:

1. Regardless of CA- or MA-matched group comparisons, there is little or no obvious difference in the acquisition rate between normals and retardates.
2. A correlation between retardate IQ and acquisition rate has not been demonstrated.
3. Although less consistency exists in the findings of extinction of classically conditioned responses, retarded individuals tend to demonstrate slower extinction rates when compared to normals of the same CA. This has been called the *inhibition deficiency* (Denny, 1964).

OPERANT CONDITIONING. The effectiveness of operant conditioning with retardates has been copiously documented (see reviews previously listed). Specific comments on examples of these applications will be made repeatedly throughout the remainder of this chapter.

Operant Reinforcement

Any stimulus which increases the probability of a response is said to be reinforcing.

> The only way to tell whether or not a given event is reinforcing to a given organism is to make a direct test. We observe the frequency of a selected response, then make an event contingent upon it and observe any change in frequency. If there is a change, we classify the event as reinforcing to the organism under the existing conditions. (Skinner, 1953, pp. 72–73)

Positive and Negative Reinforcers

Reinforcing events may be divided into two types: positive and negative (see Table 8.1). When reinforcement consists of *presenting* stimuli (i.e., adding something to a situation, e.g., food, praise for humans) and the resultant effect is an increase in

TABLE 8.1

The Effects of Various Consequences on Operant Behavior

I. CONSEQUENCE OF THE OPERANT			II. FUTURE STRENGTH OF THE OPERANT
PRESENTED	REMOVED, WITHDRAWN	WITHHELD	
Positive reinforcement occurs when a stimulus (positive reinforcer) which is added to the situation causes a strengthening in the probability of the operant.			Increase in the operant strength or the probability of the response.
	Negative reinforcement occurs when a stimulus (negative reinforcer; aversive) which is removed from the situation causes a strengthening in the probability of the operant.		Increase in the operant strength or the probability of the response.
Punishment (aversive conditioning) occurs when an aversive stimulus or a negative reinforcer is presented following an operant.	Punishment (response cost) occurs when positive reinforcers are removed following an operant.		Immediate but temporary weakening of operant strength is due to elicitation of emotional responses incompatible with the operant and also results in 1. aversive conditioning of response-produced stimuli 2. negative reinforcement of escape behavior 3. nonselective suppression of other responses
		Extinction of an operant occurs when reinforcement is *no longer* forthcoming or withheld.	Gradual but permanent weakening of operant strength.

261

the probability of the operant response, *positive reinforcement* has occurred. The stimuli presented are correspondingly referred to as *positive reinforcers* (S^{R+}). If waving a rattle results in a sound and movement interesting to an infant, the waving motion may be repeated. When pressing a bar releases a food pellet to a hungry rat, the operant behavior of bar pressing will increase. If leaving one's desk in a classroom consistently is followed by peer attention and ignored by the teacher, a youngster will spend more time out of his desk.

However, when reinforcement consists of *removing* stimuli (e.g., loud noise, cold) from a situation and the effect is also an increase in the probability of the operant response, *negative reinforcement* has occurred. If the painful assaults of a youngster stop once the victim begins yelling for assistance, cries for aid will tend to increase when the child is attacked again. When a rat, placed in a chamber with an electrified floor, presses a bar which stops the continuous shock for a period of time, the rat will quickly increase his rate of bar pressing. When the fastening of a car seat belt eliminates the buzzing signal, the fastening behavior, which results in escape from an annoying noise, will tend to increase and occur more quickly. A stimulus, such as a shock, which strengthens the response towards removal of the shock, is a negative reinforcer (S^{R-}). This function of negative reinforcers must not be confused with punishment. Although the term *negative reinforcement* is considered synonymous with aversive stimulus, the function of such negative reinforcers must not be confused with punishment. A later section will define the arrangement and effect of punishment.

Both positive and negative reinforcement always increase the *operant strength* or the probability of response. Reinforcers are defined by their effect.

> It is not correct to say that operant reinforcement "strengthens the response that precedes it." The response has already occurred and cannot be changed. What is changed is the future probability of responses in the same *class*. It is the operant as a class of behavior, rather than the response as a particular instance, which is conditioned. . . . Instead of saying a man behaves because of the consequences which *are* to follow his behavior, we simply say that he behaves because of the consequences which *have* followed similar behavior in the past. That is of course, the Law of Effect or operant conditioning. (Skinner, 1953, p. 87)

Findings with Retarded Populations

POSITIVE REINFORCERS. An enormous variety of positive and negative reinforcers has been reported, from chocolate candy to vibratory stimulation (Bailey & Meyerson, 1969) and colored motion pictures of attendants and children (Rynders & Friedlander, 1972). Since reinforcers are defined only by their effect, the determination of reinforcers for individuals with low MAs and with unusual reinforcement histories has been of concern as has been the concept of the reinforcer hierarchy (Hewett, 1968; MacMillan, 1968; Zigler, 1962). Reinforcers range along a continuum from the unlearned primary type (e.g., food) to the conditioned and generalized reinforcers (e.g., social approval, self-approval).

> The teacher (clinician) has a responsibility to lead a child along a continuum to more mature levels of performance. That is, the child must not be allowed to stagnate at a reinforcement level on the continuum below the level at which he is capable of functioning. (MacMillan, 1970, p. 6)

The following hierarchical list of reinforcers is arranged roughly in order from immature to mature:

1. primary rewards (food and water)
2. toys or trinkets
3. tokens or checks with back-up reinforcers (toys or food)
4. visual evidence of progress (graphs or letter grades)
5. social approval
6. sense of mastery—"learning for the love of it" (MacMillan, 1968, p. 71)

The results of several studies comparing the reinforcer value of tangibles to nontangible or social consequences support the idea that as severity of retardation increases, the effectiveness of less tangible reinforcers decreases (Byck, 1968; Locke, 1969). Watson, Orser, and Sanders (1968) demonstrated that the very low functioning child preferred edible to manipulable tangible reinforcers such as toys. However, the vast number of studies which have employed token economies with mildly, moderately, and severely retarded populations emphasizes that, when systematically programmed, lower functioning individuals may be led to more mature levels of reinforcement.

Due to the wide variation in reinforcement preferences of retarded children, it is essential to determine the reinforcement preference of an individual child in order to facilitate learning. The following procedures to determine reinforcers have been used with both retarded and normal individuals.

1. *Direct questioning:* Ask the verbal child what types of activities, toys, etc. he would like to earn, or with whom he would like to spend time (Tharp & Wetzel, 1969). Pictures may be used to reduce reliance on verbal communication.
2. *Indirect questioning:* Ask others who are familiar with the child (e.g., parent, peer, sibling, teacher) what objects, foods, events, or persons the child particularly likes. The child may have different reinforcers for different settings.
3. *Structured observation:* Provide the child with samples of reinforcers from a larger group (e.g., bites of different foods, sips of liquids, brief play periods with different toys) and, while allowing him to select freely from the groups, note frequency and duration of selection (Ayllon & Azrin, 1968a, 1968b).
4. *Natural observation:* Watch the child during various activities and observe the activities, toys, and people for which he appears to demonstrate a preference.

These methods are arranged in order of decreasing reliance on the child's prerequisite abilities. The structured observation or reinforcer sampling method does not depend upon the ability to recall items from memory or the use of any receptive language; however, it is time consuming. Both the second and fourth methods may be used to expand and partially verify results obtained from the direct questioning and structured observation. The final verification, however, rests in the observed effect of a consequent on the occurrence of a specific response.

Rynders and Friedlander (1972) applied a variation of the structured observation method to determine reinforcer preferences in severely and profoundly retarded institutionalized children using an automated learning device called Playtest. By pressing a specific panel surface to obtain the visual reinforcer, the children demonstrated a significant and consistent preference for viewing a colored motion picture of attendant-child caretaking interaction instead of black and white slides of the same caretaking or neutral stimuli (out-of-focus black and white projections). However, the data revealed that satiation to the reinforcer was gradually surfacing with a decrease in response duration.

Various studies and reviews provide additional suggestions for increasing the effectiveness of positive reinforcers with retardates.

1. A child's reinforcer "menu" should be periodically updated and a choice of reinforcers should be pre-

sented whenever possible to avoid a satiating effect (Bijou & Sturges, 1959; Spradlin & Girardeau, 1966).
2. The satiation problem also may be resolved by pairing and interspersing a conditioned reinforcer (e.g., reinforcer dispenser noise, lights, or buzzers) with the primary reinforcer on an increasing variable-ratio schedule. This allows the primary reinforcer to be reduced gradually and provides on a contingent basis a partial exposure to the reinforcer (e.g., child is allowed to see or hear the reinforcer) with the actual receipt provided on a ratio schedule (Bijou & Baer, 1966).
3. To promote the advancement of a child to more mature levels of reinforcement, praise and smiles (potential secondary reinforcers) should be continuously paired with primary reinforcers as well as with generalized reinforcers (e.g, tokens, check marks) (MacMillan, 1973).

NEGATIVE REINFORCERS. Negative reinforcers or aversives arranged on a similar continuum are also related to the functional maturity and reinforcement history of the child (Burchard & Barrera, 1972; MacMillan, Forness, & Trumbull, 1973). Aversives for a higher functioning child may include frowning by the teacher, withdrawal of classroom privileges, or poor grades, while for the reduction of extreme levels of self-abusive behavior electric shock at times may be appropriate (Foxx & Azrin, 1973; Lovaas & Simmons, 1969). As with positive reinforcers teachers must not resort to guessing based upon their own perception.

> The acid test of whether an aversive is high or low on the continuum, or is even aversive, is the individual child's response to it. If, indeed, behavior increases following presentation of the stimulus, it is a positive reinforcer; if behavior decreases, then it is aversive. For example, Levin and Simmons (1962) demonstrated that social praise actually functioned as an aversive stimulus for emotionally disturbed boys. (MacMillan, Forness, & Trumbull, 1973, p. 89)

As with positive reinforcers, the amount of the aversive stimuli and its scheduling in relation to the behavior are critical variables in the resultant effect on a punished behavior. These considerations are discussed in the later section on punishment.

Conditioned Reinforcement

SECONDARY REINFORCERS. Conditioned or secondary reinforcers (S^R) are stimuli not originally reinforcing that have acquired their reinforcing properties by being paired repeatedly with reinforcers. This pairing may be with primary reinforcers (S^R), ones which do not rely on conditioning (e.g., S^{R+}—food, water, sex; S^{R-}—shock, extreme cold), or with previously conditioned reinforcers.

Once a stimulus acquires reinforcing properties through conditioning, it also acquires the power to condition. To illustrate this occurrence, Skinner (1953) depicts the reinforcement of a particular pigeon behavior to grain which has been immediately preceeded by a light. After a brief period of continued reinforcement, the light acquires reinforcing power. This same process causes the initially neutral or unmeaningful consequences of smiling and applauding praise (which generally preceed the presentation of food and holding) to acquire reinforcing power for the young child.

As shall be described in a later section, conditioned reinforcers play an important role in response chaining or the combined processes of stimulus discrimination and response differentiation which are important counterparts of complex learning.

GENERALIZED REINFORCERS. Generalized Reinforcers are a class of conditioned reinforcers which have been paired with more than one primary reinforcer. Because of this multiple association, the power of a generalized reinforcer does not rely upon specific states of deprivation in order to be reinforcing, as do conditioned reinforcers. For example, food is reinforcing to a hungry organism; the light stimulus (S^{R+}) in the preceding example also relies upon a deprivation state of hunger. Therefore, a generalized reinforcer is more durable and more likely to reinforce a response.

The attention of people, a common generalized reinforcer, becomes one "because it is a necessary condition for other reinforcements from them. In general, only people who are attending to us reinforce our behavior. The attention of someone who is particularly likely to supply reinforcement—a parent, a teacher, or a loved one—is an especially generalized reinforcer and sets up especially strong attention-getting behavior" (Skinner, 1953, p. 78). Likewise, approval and affection are broad classes of generalized reinforcers whose specific form varies widely. The reinforcing power of money and tokens stems from their wide association with primary and conditioned reinforcers.

Keller and Schoenfeld (1950) summarize the important characteristics of conditioned reinforcers:

1. A stimulus that occasions or accompanies a reinforcement acquires thereby reinforcing value of its own, and may be called a conditioned, secondary, or derived reinforcement. A secondary reinforcement may be extinguished when repeatedly applied to a response for which there is no ultimate primary reinforcement.
2. A secondary reinforcement is positive when the reinforcement with which it is correlated is positive, and negative when the latter is negative.
3. Once established, a secondary reinforcement is independent and nonspecific; it will not only strengthen the same response which produced the original reinforcement, but it will also condition a new and unrelated response. Moreover, it will do so even in the presence of a different motive.
4. Through generalization, many stimuli besides the one correlated with reinforcement acquire reinforcing value—either positive or negative. (p. 260)

Findings With Retarded Populations

SOCIAL CONDITIONED REINFORCERS. Social consequences (spending time with an adult, smiles and physical contact, praise) have been effectively applied to retarded individuals to increase weight loss, classroom attentiveness, and other appropriate behaviors (Foxx, 1972; Hollis, 1965; Kazdin, 1973). However, Weisberg (1971) and others have questioned the procedures used to establish functional classes of social reinforcers with retardates and their actual effectiveness.

Cairns and Paris (1971) demonstrated that expressions of social approval ("fine," "good") given contingently for correct sorting responses were not effective in increasing the performance of young, noninstitutionalized, mildly retarded children. To the degree that these terms of social approval had an imprecise and discriminative meaning, the less apt they were to serve as social reinforcers which effected performance. Spradlin and Girardeau (1966) offer similar comments on the results of social reinforcers with lower functioning retarded individuals.

Our casual observations indicate that its effects with severely retarded children are quite unpredictable. This is not to say that social reinforcers will not work with some severely retarded children. Rather, they will work only with selected children and, even then, their effects may be limited and unpredictable. Social comments have limited value as reinforcers due to the fact that they depend so much upon the unique history of the child. If an adult's comments have, in the past, set the occasion where responses were reinforced, it is quite likely that comments by adults now will be reinforcing, at least for a while. However, if such comments have not been positively backed up or have been associated with aversive conditions, it is quite likely that they will have either no effect or an aversive effect. (pp. 267–268)

TOKEN REINFORCEMENT. Tokens, another type of generalized conditioned reinforcer, have had wide successful application to retarded populations in institutional, public school, workshop, and home settings (Kazdin & Bootzin, 1972; O'Leary & Drabman, 1971) (see Table 8.2). In a token economy, tokens are given contingent upon certain desirable behaviors (appropriate social, vocational, and academic responses) and also may be removed contingent upon certain undesirable behaviors (response cost). The tokens are redeemable for merchandise and activities such as toys, trinkets, food, clothing, free time, and academic games. Although procedures vary widely from one token economy to another, MacMillan (1973) and Kazdin and Bootzin (1972) comment on the essential stages involved in the use of token reinforcement systems with most classrooms.

1. Introduction of system to class and establishment of token values.
    a. Introduce at natural break in year.
    b. Positively specify target behaviors (Kuypers, Becker, & O'Leary, 1968).
    c. Clarify contingencies (e.g., two check marks for starting work) (Hewett, 1968).
    d. Immediately establish token values.
2. Acquisition stage.
    a. Increase socially appropriate behaviors (tokens rewarded).
    b. Increase academic and on-task behaviors (tokens rewarded).
    c. Decrease socially inappropriate behaviors (extinction, tokens removed, or time out).
    d. Give immediate and frequent token reinforcement with frequent token exchanges.
    e. Record target behaviors daily to evaluate effect.
    f. Review token rules (Kuypers, Becker, & O'Leary, 1968).
    g. Make small adjustments in token schedules (ratio and interval) (O'Leary & Becker, 1967).
    h. Make small adjustments in token exchange schedules.
3. Maintenance stage or stimulus and response generalization—"weaning" the child from extrinsic tangible reinforcers to natural consequences (Kazdin & Bootzin, 1972; MacMillan & Forness, 1970; O'Leary & Drabman, 1971).
    a. Thin token reward schedules (higher ratio of behavior to reinforcement).
    b. Thin token exchange schedule (larger interval between receipt and exchange).
    c. Always pair social reinforcers with tokens (development of conditioned reinforcers).
    d. Substitute natural activities for tangible reinforcers (Knapczyk & Livingston, 1973).
    e. Continue fading of token reinforcement schedules.
    f. Involve regular class teacher and/or parents to encourage generalization.
    g. Involve the child in selecting behaviors for reinforcement.

Operant Extinction

When reinforcement is withheld, operant extinction occurs, resulting in a weakening of operant strength (refer to Table 8.1). A response is emitted less frequently during extinction and eventually stops. For example, one might stop writing if one's letters are never answered. The eventual result of extinction is the removal of an operant from the behavioral repertoire of an organism. The following series of statements about the properties of extinction serves to expand this concept.

1. Operant extinction is much more gradual than operant conditioning. In Skinner's (1933, 1938) research even as much as a single reinforcement was enough to make rats and pigeons produce 50 or more conditioned, operant responses (bar pressing or pecking) during extinction.
2. At times during extinction the organism may engage in emotional behaviors. "The failure of a response to be reinforced leads not only to operant extinction but also to a reaction spoken of as frustration or rage" (Skinner, 1953, p. 69). Emotional responses reoccur as additional responses are unreinforced. In pigeons, this behavior may consist of wing flapping, turning away from the response key, and cooing. In adults, swearing and aggression may result, and in children, crying often occurs. Repeated exposure to extinction tends to eliminate these emotional responses.
3. The results of reinforcement can be measured by the rate of response and the total number of responses. The rate and total number should be examined during extinction to see how much the organism resists extinction before returning to baseline level response (rate prior to conditioning). In other words, "behavior during extinction is the result of the conditioning which has preceded it, and in this sense the extinction curve gives an additional measure of the effect of reinforcement" (Skinner, 1953, p. 70). A long history of reinforcement results in continued responding over a long extinction period, while extinction occurs comparatively quickly if only a few responses have been reinforced. Despite the surface implications of this latter example, the relationship between the number of responses reinforced during conditioning and the number of responses emitted during extinction

TABLE 8.2
Applications of Token Reinforcement

STUDY	NO. OF Ss	POPULATION	CA	SETTING	TOKENS CONTINGENT ON:	RESULTS
1. Ayllon & Kelly (1972)	12 30 12	TMR Normals TMR	I*	special classroom regular classroom	Correct responses on *Metropolitan Readiness Test* (token reward)	+ + +
RESULTS: Normals and TMRs showed improved scores on standardized achievement tests when reinforced for correct responses with tokens. Also a 6-week history of token reinforcement with TMRs yielded higher test scores over controls when both were tested with token reward.						
2. Baker, Stanish, & Fraser (1972)	19	TMR	P*,I	special classroom	Academic improvements in math and language (token reward)	+
RESULTS: Token reward and time out resulted in more decline in socially inappropriate and disruptive behavior than occurred for a similar group not exposed to token reward or systematic reinforcement and time out procedure.						
3. Bath & Smith (1974)	45	TMR	A*	institutional classroom	Correct responses on match-to-sample tasks (token reward, response cost)	±
RESULTS: Token economy effects were significantly disrupted when staff change occurred; tokens were given less consistently which resulted in a temporary reversal of behavior gains.						
4. Burchard & Barrera (1972)	6	EMR	A	institutional ward	Decreases in antisocial behavior (token reward, response cost, time out)	+
RESULTS: A functional relationship was demonstrated between response suppression and the magnitude of the response cost and the time out duration. Advantages of response cost over time out were discussed as well as the problems of using response cost.						
5. Dalton, Rubino, & Hislop (1973)	13	TMR	P,I	special classroom	Academic improvements in math and language (token reward)	+
RESULTS: Token reward children made and maintained 1 yr later significant arithmetic gains over groups receiving only praise. Language gains of token group, though not greater, were maintained while praise group's gains declined.						
6. Hislop, Moore, & Stanish (1973)	10	EMR TMR	P	special classroom	Relevant classroom behavior and correct academic responses (token reward)	+
RESULTS: Decreases in negative behaviors occurred under token reward-plus-praise conditions which tended to generalize to the regular class setting and were maintained when measured during 6-mo follow-up.						

TABLE 8.2, cont.

STUDY	NO. OF Ss	POPULATION	CA	SETTING	TOKENS CONTINGENT ON:	RESULTS
7. Iwata & Bailey (1974)	15	EMR	I	special classroom	Decreases in rule violations and off-task behavior (token reward, response cost)	+

RESULTS: When tokens were given for rule following and on-task behavior, or when response cost was used for rule violation and off-task behavior, arithmetic output doubled although accuracy remained unchanged. Both procedures, token reward and response cost, were equally effective in decreasing rule violations and off-task behavior (response cost consisted of being given tokens at the beginning of a period and losing them contingent on misbehavior).

STUDY	NO. OF Ss	POPULATION	CA	SETTING	TOKENS CONTINGENT ON:	RESULTS
8. Knapczyk & Livingston (1973)	13	EMR	A	special classroom	Accurate completion of reading assignments (token reward)	+

RESULTS: Accuracy in reading comprehension increased under token reward conditions and varied only slightly when students did not record their own performance and when the system was generalized to a student teacher. Educational games, given noncontingently prior to the study, were effective back-up reinforcers.

STUDY	NO. OF Ss	POPULATION	CA	SETTING	TOKENS CONTINGENT ON:	RESULTS
9. Repp, Klett, Sosebee, & Speir (1975)	7	TMR	A	institutional classroom	Correct responses on match-to-sample tasks (token reward, response cost)	+

RESULTS: No differences in correct responses were observed between those receiving token reward alone or token reward and response cost together. Response cost decreased errors but did not influence correct responding. Even nonexchangeable token reinforcement resulted in more correct responses than no tokens.

STUDY	NO. OF Ss	POPULATION	CA	SETTING	TOKENS CONTINGENT ON:	RESULTS
10. Sachs (1971)	8	EMR (plus emotionally disturbed and orthopedically handicapped)	P I	special classroom	Appropriate classroom behavior (eye contact, attention span, etc., and academic performance) (token reward)	+

RESULTS: Significant gains in IQ scores on the WISC were made by children enrolled for a year in a token reward classroom. The WISC was suggested as an evaluative device for assessing gains of MR children in token reward settings.

*CA: P = primary (5–8 yr)
I = intermediate (9–13 yr)
A = advanced (14–18 yr)
RESULTS: + appropriate behaviors increased, inappropriate behaviors decreased under token contingencies
± mixed results

(resistance to extinction) is a complex one, as will be seen in the next section on schedules of reinforcement.

4. *Extinction* is not synonomous with *forgetting*. Both the process and the effect are different. During extinction the conditioned response is repeatedly emitted without reinforcement, while true forgetting appears to be a gradual decay process over time. While the predictable effect of extinction is to remove an operant from an organism's response repertoire, the same cannot be said of forgetting. Skinner (1953) cites examples from human and animal research in which conditioned responses, unused for half the life of the organism, still were shown to have sizeable extinction curves.

Findings With Retarded Populations

In agreement with the results of extinction in both humans and animals, operant extinction in retardates is affected by the schedule of reinforcement prior to extinction. Spradlin and Girardeau (1966) review studies investigating the effects of extinction on moderately and severely retarded individuals. They conclude that:

1. When reinforcement of a response was completely withheld, the response strength was reduced.
2. In comparison to continuous schedules, intermittent reinforcement schedules produced responses with greater resistance to extinction effects (i.e., reduction of response strength was more gradual).
3. When the amount of reinforcement was varied during acquisition (e.g., one cigarette versus three, varying amounts of cigarettes versus candy), the resultant resistances to extinction revealed no significant differences.

Thor (1972) examined the effects of extinction on normal third graders matched on mental age with institutionalized and noninstitutionalized mentally retarded persons (CA ≃ 15) following both tangible reinforcement (i.e., candy given intermittently for pulling a plunger) and social reinforcement (i.e., intermittent praise by the experimenter and illumination of a light for a finger-tapping response). The results revealed significant sex differences which occurred independently of the task, the type of reinforcement, and the subject's chronological age and intelligence. In all groups boys responded more and longer than girls in the same group. This finding was in agreement with results of earlier studies. However, there were no significant differences in any of the three girls' groups on number of responses occurring during extinction. Noninstitutionalized retardates responded significantly more than normals and institutionalized retardates who tended to extinguish most quickly.

Thor's results, duplicated in Figure 8.3, illustrated the wide differences between the two groups of retarded boys. These differences were thought to result from the interaction of several explanations:

a) a cultural emphasis on task perseveration in males transmitted primarily through members of the family;
b) a comparative lack of previous social reinforcement in the institution;
c) a greater intrinsic reinforcement for males in manipulative behavior on a novel task . . . and
d) a greater cue dependency in females. (Thor, 1972, p. 105)

Consistent with Thor's (1972) findings for retarded males is the general finding that retarded individuals tend to exhibit more resistance to extinction than normals. For example, Bandura and Barub (1971) found that during extinction periods retarded individuals tended to repeat imitative responses. In a comparison of retarded and nonretarded children matched on MA, Viney, Clarke, and Lord (1973) found that moderately retarded children demonstrated greater resistance to extinction and more frustration responses in a match-to-sample game situation in which a puppet's praise (social reward) or candy (nonsocial reward) was given for correct responses. For both groups of children the loss of the social reward led to a greater number of responses during extinction than the loss of the candy reward.

Extinction alone or paired with reinforcement of desirable behaviors is frequently applied to normal and handicapped individuals as a method to weaken response strength and thereby reduce the occurrence of an undesirable behavior. Extinction alone has been successfully applied to eliminate aggressive behavior (Martin & Foxx, 1973) and self-destructive behavior in the retarded (Jones, Simmons, & Frankel, 1974; Lovaas & Simmons, 1969). However, both Gardner and Watson's (1969) review and Gardner's writings (1969) indicate that once in the repertoire of a retarded individual, undesirable behaviors are not easily removed by extinction alone or even extinction combined with reinforcement of incompatible behavior (Vukelich & Hake, 1971). Others (Baumeister & Forehand, 1973; Corte, Wolf, & Locke, 1971; Smolev, 1971) found that the combination of extinction with reinforcement of other behavior (DRO)

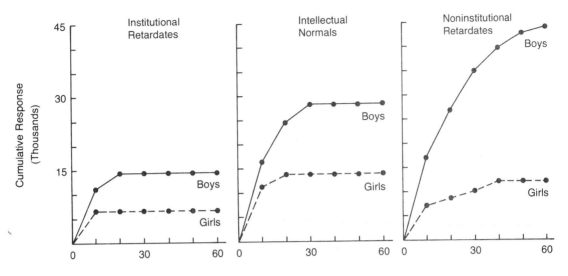

FIGURE 8.3

Cumulative responding by institutionalized and noninstitutionalized mildly retarded persons and intellectually average children (matched on MA) during extinction of social reinforcement for a tapping response.

SOURCE: Adapted from "Sex differences in extinction of operant responding by educable retarded and nonretarded children" by D. H. Thor. *American Journal of Mental Deficiency*, 1972, 77, p. 104. Copyright 1972 by *American Association on Mental Deficiency*. Reprinted by permission.

and with DRO and time out or punishment is generally regarded as a more efficient means of reducing aggressive behavior directed toward others, self-aggressive behavior, and stereotyped acts. According to Smolev (1971), "It can be seen, then, that although the extinction procedure may be effective given enough time, the danger to the child due to the high frequency of self-destructive behavior occurring during extinction must be considered. Also of concern is the apparent situational specificity of the suppression effects" (p. 296). More attention is given to this topic following the section on punishment.

Punishment

Although the arrangement of stimulus and behavior in punishment is the opposite of that in reinforcement, the effects are not the opposite. Punishment consists of two arrangements: (a) *presentation of a negative reinforcer following behavior* and (b) *removal of a positive reinforcer following a behavior* (refer to Table 8.1). The effects of punishment include a temporary reduction in the behavior following punishment but no actual reduction of response strength which, as men-

tioned earlier, can be measured by the total number of responses during extinction as well as the rate of responding at that time (Estes, 1944; Skinner, 1953).

> Extinction as operant behavior refers only to the permanent weakening that a response undergoes when it occurs and is no longer followed by reinforcement. Punishment will also suppress a response, . . . but there are differences in the effects of punishment and extinction. . . . the punishment effects are thus temporary, whereas full weakening of the response through extinction would be permanent. (Staats & Staats, 1963, p. 57)

The Effects of Punishment

The first effect of punishment is the elicitation of reflexes which generally are emotionally based (e.g., fear, anger, pain, embarrassment). This results in the second effect, the immediate reduction or elimination of a response following the contingent or noncontingent presentation of an aversive stimulus or removal of a positive reinforcer. The punishment elicits emotional responses which are incompatible with the punished response and strong enough to temporarily suppress it.

When a young child's hand is slapped (primary aversive) for attempting to touch the icing on a cake, he withdraws immediately. The pain, fear, and embarrassment resulting from being slapped are incompatible with continued expression of happy anticipation about eating a sweet glob of icing. The same suppression of response could be achieved from many children by the presentation of conditioned aversives such as a glare from an authority figure or a loud comment such as "No. Stop that!" Finally, the punishment may involved the removal of reinforcers: "OK, you can not have any cake at all!" The emotional responses elicited range from fear to anger and act in a manner incompatible with the desire to eat cake icing.

The third effect involves the conditioning of stimuli (S_1, S_2) which accompany the punished (S^{R-}) response (R). Stimuli which occur concurrently with the punished response may be related to the response or may simply be a random occurrence in that setting or at that time. This conditioning process results in the production of additional negative reinforcers $(S_1 = S_1^{R-}; S_2 = S_2^{R-})$. The very presence of these negative reinforcers will elicit the first two effects: emotional reaction and response suppression due to an elicitation of incompatible emotional behaviors. For example, when the child who has been slapped and glared at by his mother for attempting to steal icing begins to reach for the icing later, the reaching behavior may generate *response-produced, conditioned aversive stimuli* sufficient to stop reaching. The emotional reaction (i.e., fear of punishment) results from the presence of these conditioned aversives and is incompatible with the formerly punished behavior. Therefore, the child's own emotional reaction may serve the same effect as the mother's threatening glare—to modify an emotional predisposition to behave in a certain way.

Consider the rat who formerly was reinforced for pressing a bar and is then shocked for the same behavior. As the rat moves closer to the bar, conditioned aversive stimuli $(S_1^{R-}$ and $S_2^{R-})$ which were *formerly* conditioned positive stimuli (e.g., sight of lever, getting into position to press bar) increase with proximity of the bar and approach behavior. In this situation any behavior which decreases or eliminates these conditioned aversive stimuli is reinforced by the process of negative reinforcement. This reinforced behavior consists of "doing something else" to avoid future punishment and may include an action (e.g., running away) or doing nothing (e.g., standing still). A cyclical effect then takes place.

If punishment is repeatedly avoided, the conditioned negative reinforcer undergoes extinction. Incompatible behavior is then less and less strongly reinforced, and the punished behavior eventually emerges. When punishment occurs, the aversive stimuli are reconditioned, and the behavior of doing something else is then reinforced. If punishment is discontinued, the behavior may emerge in full strength. (Skinner, 1953, p. 189)

Additional side effects often result in punishment situations. The aroused emotional state which accompanies punishment may be produced in any or all of the following consequences:

1. The punisher himself may become a conditioned aversive interfering with any concurrent role of being a positive reinforcer.
2. The nonselective suppression of other responses may occur in addition to the one punished.
3. The elicitation of self-protective or counter-aggressive responses may occur.

Finally, the response suppression effects vary with the schedule of punishment. Although the rate of responding is not as completely depressed with intermittent punishment as with continuous punishment, the effects of punishment endure longer when punishment is intermittently applied rather than continuously applied every time the response occurs. Hilgard and Bower (1966) summarize Estes' (1944) reasoning for this phenomenon: Since avoidance responses (e.g., rat stands still or runs away from bar which, when pressed, resulted in shock) are negatively reinforced by an elimination of the aversive, then, consistent with reinforcement scheduling effects, "withdrawal responses are conditioned more strongly through intermittent reinforcement than through ordinary continuous reinforcement" (p. 137).

Alternatives to Punishment

Because punishment alone cannot eliminate a response from an individual's repertoire and results in numerous objectionable side effects, its use can be avoided by selecting other ways to weaken an operant. These alternatives to punishment include:

1. Changing the antecedent circumstances (e.g., removing the opportunity for the operant to occur; communicating and enforcing rules describing the limits for performance of the behavior).
2. Waiting for behaviors which are a function of developmental age to disappear with the passage of time.

3. Weakening conditioned responses by the process of forgetting or the passage of time while avoiding situations which are associated with the behavior.
4. Extinguishing the behavior.
5. Conditioning incompatible behaviors through positive reinforcement.

Each of the first three techniques is increased in effectiveness if combined with the simultaneous use of the last two. That is, whenever the operant occurs with the first three alternatives, it is ignored and incompatible behaviors are reinforced. However, Skinner (1953) states that extinction, even though it is time consuming, is the most effective alternative to punishment. It does not result in objectionable side effects but acts to eliminate an operant from an individual's repertoire. When positive reinforcement of incompatible or alternative responses is combined with extinction, the suppression of the undesirable operant is facilitated by: (a) conditioning "alternatives to the goal" or substitute operants, and (b) increasing the strength of an operant which, when performed, prevents the emission of the undesirable operant.

Effective Use of Punishment

In their extensive review of the effects of punishment on behavior, Azrin and Holz (1966) summarize the procedures one should use to maximize the effectiveness of punishment if purposefully used as a means to eliminate behavior.

(1) The punishing stimulus should be arranged in such a manner that no unauthorized escape is possible. (2) The punishing stimulus should be as intense as possible. (3) The frequency of punishment should be as high as possible. (4) Ideally the punishing stimulus should be given for every response. (5) The punishing stimulus should not be increased gradually but introduced at maximum intensity. (6) Extended periods of punishment should be avoided, especially where low intensities of punishment are concerned, since the recovery effect may thereby occur. Where mild intensities of punishment are used, it is best to use them for only a brief period time. (7) Great care should be taken to see that the delivery of the punishing stimulus is not differentially associated with the delivery of the reinforcement. Otherwise the punishing stimulus may acquire conditioned reinforcing properties. (8) The delivery of the punishing stimulus should be made a signal or discriminative stimulus that a period of extinction is in progress. (9) The degree of motivation to emit the punished response should be reduced. (10) The frequency of positive reinforcement for the punished response should similarly be reduced. (11) An alternative response should be available which will not be punished but which will produce the same or greater reinforcement as the punished response. For example, punishment of criminal behavior can be expected to be more effective if non-criminal behavior which will result in the same advantages as the criminal behavior is available. (12) If no alternative response is available, the subject should have access to a different situation in which he obtains the same reinforcement without being punished. (13) If it is not possible to deliver the punishing stimulus itself after a response, then an effective method of punishment is still available. A conditioned stimulus may be associated with the aversive stimulus, and this conditioned stimulus may be delivered following a response to achieve conditioned punishment. (14) A reduction of positive reinforcement may be used as punishment when the use of physical punishment is not possible for practical, legal, or moral reasons. Punishment by withdrawal of positive reinforcement may be accomplished in such situations by arranging a period of reduced reinforcement frequency (time-out) or by arranging a decrease of conditioned reinforcement (response cost). Both methods require that the subject have a high level of reinforcement to begin with; otherwise no withdrawal of reinforcement is possible. If nonphysical punishment is to be used, it appears desirable to provide the subject with a substantial history of reinforcement in order to provide the opportunity for withdrawing the reinforcement as punishment for the undesired responses. (pp. 426–427)

Applications to Retarded Populations

Two reviews (Gardner, 1969; Weisberg, 1971) on the effects of punishment with the retarded and another review (MacMillan, Forness, & Trumbull, 1973) of its effects on normal and handicapped children yield a series of conclusions concerning the use of punishment to suppress behavior (durability and generalization of suppression, etc.) and its resultant side effects. A summary of these conclusions is outlined next, along with the correlated findings from 12 recent punishment studies abstracted in Table 8.3.

1. Response contingent punishment (e.g., shock, physical restraint, conditioned aversives, time out from primary or secondary reinforcement) has been reported to reduce unwanted behavior in retarded children and adults.
   a. Punishment seems to be most effective with single isolated behaviors (e.g, self-abusive) occurring at a steady rate and intensity which do not involve interaction with other individuals (Gardner, 1969).
   b. A variety of aversive procedures have been investigated which have varying suppressive results:

TABLE 8.3
Punishment Studies with Retarded Populations

STUDY	LEVEL OF RETARDATION	RESPONSE PUNISHED	PUNISHMENT PROCEDURE
1. Azrin & Wesolowski (1974)	Severe/Profound	Stealing	Overcorrection and simple correction of stealing.

RESULTS: Overcorrection procedures were compared to simple correction as methods to reduce stealing among 34 residents in a ward setting. Simple correction consisted of returning the stolen items while overcorrection required not only return but giving an additional item to the victim. Thefts under simple correction occurred at a rate of 20 per day; for days 1, 2, 3, and 4 through 16 following theft overcorrection, thefts decreased by 50%, 75%, 90%, 100% respectively. Overcorrection required staff guidance and took an average of 106 ± 7 sec to carry out in comparison to simple correction at 7 ± 2 sec.

STUDY	LEVEL OF RETARDATION	RESPONSE PUNISHED	PUNISHMENT PROCEDURE
2. Clark, Rowbury, Baer, & Baer (1973)	Moderate	Chokes and arm-wraps, other attacks toward people; attacks toward materials	Time out (3 min).

RESULTS: When 5-min time outs were made contingent upon every choking and aggressive hugging behavior toward others for an 8-year-old child, these behaviors rapidly decreased to zero. When the contingency was extended to other attacks toward people and materials (e.g., tearing, breaking, and throwing things), these behaviors also declined to zero. A change-over delay contingency for time outs was used which required the child to remain quiet at least the last 15 sec before release. During the 2nd phase of the study the same child was exposed to 4 conditions with 3 using a different schedule of intermittent time out (VR–4, VR–8, VR–3) and the last condition applying DPH or differential punishment of high rates of behavior for total disruptive behavior (i.e., the number of 10-sec intervals per hr containing one or more categories of disruptive behavior). Under VR–4, for example, every 4th interval of disruptive behavior, on the average, was followed by time out. DPH consisted of giving a time out for any disruptive behavior that occurred within 10 min of the last recorded disruptive behavior. The behavior was reduced most under VR–3 followed by DPH, VR–4, then VR–8. These results suggested that some schedules of intermittent time out are as effective as FR–1 or continuous time out which would allow less removal from the learning setting while still obtaining a large suppression in disruptive behavior.

STUDY	LEVEL OF RETARDATION	RESPONSE PUNISHED	PUNISHMENT PROCEDURE
3. Corte, Wolf, & Locke (1971)	Profound	Self-abuse (pulling own hair, slapping and scratching face, banging head, and biting fingers)	Shock. Additional procedures: differential reinforcement of other behavior (DRO), elimination of social consequences.

RESULTS: The self-abusive behaviors of 4 adolescents were treated with 3 procedures: elimination of all social consequences (1 hr noncontingent isolation periods), DRO or reinforcement of nonself-abusive behaviors with food, and electric shock. With 2 subjects elimination of social consequences did not reduce the behaviors, while DRO was effective with 1 of the 2 subjects but only under conditions of food deprivation. With all 4, response contingent shock resulted in the elimination of self-abusive behaviors. The reduction of the punished behavior was shocked in a variety of settings.

TABLE 8.3, cont.

STUDY	LEVEL OF RETARDATION	RESPONSE PUNISHED	PUNISHMENT PROCEDURE
4. Foxx & Azrin (1973)	Severe/Profound	Self-stimulatory behaviors (mouthing objects and hands, clapping hands, weaving head)	Overcorrection; physical aversives; distasteful solution placed on the hands. Additional procedures: differential reinforcement of other behavior (DRO), noncontingent reinforcement.

RESULTS: In the 1st study of 2 studies the self-stimulatory behaviors of 2 young girls were followed by 4 or 5 separately applied consequences. The effects of overcorrection (last procedure) in both cases reduced mouthing to zero while other procedures were differentially less effective; noncontingent reinforcement was less effective followed by DRO and physical punishment. The 2nd study showed that overcorrection immediately reduced other self-stimulatory behaviors to zero in both autistic and retarded children (N = 4). This reduction was maintained by verbal reprimand followed intermittently by overcorrection (See Figure 8.4).

STUDY	LEVEL OF RETARDATION	RESPONSE PUNISHED	PUNISHMENT PROCEDURE
5. Lahey, McNees, & McNees (1973)	Borderline	Use of an obscene word and facial twitching	Instructed repetition of obscene word, time out.

RESULTS: The behavior of swearing in combination with facial twitching was reduced in half by a mild aversive treatment called instructed repetition (i.e., child had to repeat the obscene word for 15 min in a setting isolated from the class) for a 12 days. Then time out was made contingent on saying the obscene word (i.e., one min in small room) which resulted in a reduction close to zero. A reversal to baseline which resulted in a significant increase was followed by reduction to zero with reimplementation of time out. Instructed repetition, which had been viewed as being less effective than time out, did result in a rapid decline in the behavior.

STUDY	LEVEL OF RETARDATION	RESPONSE PUNISHED	PUNISHMENT PROCEDURE
6. Paluck & Esser (1971)	Moderate to profound	Aggressive acts in ward "territories"	Verbal aversives ("No!"), extinction.

RESULTS: Three groups of 7 young boys were observed for a 3-wk period on an institutional ward to determine their territory preferences (spending noticeably more time on one location than others) during which all groups were verbally reprimanded for any aggressive behavior. Group I continued in a verbal punishment treatment for 2 more wk, while in Group II all reprimands were discontinued for aggressive behavior occurring in the subject's territory. Punishment had a significant effect across groups on the number of aggressive acts per group daily. In Group I the aggressive behavior decreased, while in Group II it increased during the 2nd wk, and in Group III it remained the same as that observed during the 1st wk. The authors concluded that territorial behavior was not only quickly determined and consistent over time but more resistant to verbal punishment procedures than other behaviors.

STUDY	LEVEL OF RETARDATION	RESPONSE PUNISHED	PUNISHMENT PROCEDURE
7. Pendergrass (1972)	Severe	Banging objects and string twirling were punished while biting hands and jerking his own body were not.	Time out, verbal aversives. Additional procedures: observation of the other child receiving contingent time out.

RESULTS: One of two undesirable behaviors in 2 young boys was punished with time out (2 min in time out room). During other conditions the child, though not exposed to time out, did witness the time out contingency for the 2nd child. For one child the behavior which was punished by time out decreased while the rate of the unpunished behavior was unaffected. However, in the second child both the punished and unpunished behaviors were suppressed during time out treatment. Besides eye contact there was a decrease in other social behaviors measured (touching others, speaking, and responding) during time out treatment. For both subjects punishment had systematic effects on a number of other nonpunished behaviors. Some aggressive behavior was displayed toward experimenters during the time out condition.

273

TABLE 8.3, cont.

STUDY	LEVEL OF RETARDATION	RESPONSE PUNISHED	PUNISHMENT PROCEDURE
8. Salzberg & Napolitan (1974)	Profound	Playing with doors and staring out windows	Physical restraint in chair.

RESULTS: During 20-min sessions an adolescent boy was physically restrained by the teacher in a chair with his head positioned forward (2 min) contingent on the misbehaviors. This treatment was alternated with withdrawal of punishment during which the child could engage in any behaviors. With session timing discontinued during restraint both inappropriate behaviors were reduced from baseline levels of 90% to 15%, 10%, and finally close to 0% during the last restraint period. The authors concluded that short periods of contingent physical restraint resulted in neutral and effective punishment which could be most useful in the reduction of self-abusive behavior.

STUDY	LEVEL OF RETARDATION	RESPONSE PUNISHED	PUNISHMENT PROCEDURE
9. Tanner & Zeiler (1975)	Autistic	Slapping own face and approximations of behavior (during later sessions)	Aromatic ammonia. Additional procedures: negative reinforcement.

RESULTS: During 5-min treatment sessions a young woman's restraints and protective helmet were removed while the crushing of an ammonia capsule under her nose was made contingent on face slapping. Removal of the ammonia was contingent on cessation of slapping. Behavior immediately declined from baseline rate of 30 per session to zero, returned to 42 per session during 2nd baseline and back to zero during reintroduction of punishment. Suppression of behavior was substantially reduced outside experimental sessions as well as when ward staff applied same procedures. Authors described this procedure as an effective substitute for shock.

STUDY	LEVEL OF RETARDATION	RESPONSE PUNISHED	PUNISHMENT PROCEDURE
10. Vukelich & Hake (1971)	Profound	Aggressive attacks on others (choking and grabbing others)	Time out (restraint in chair). Additional procedures: increased amounts of reinforcement for all nonaggressive behaviors.

RESULTS: Gradual changes were made in positive reinforcement and the amount of unrestrained time provided to a dangerously aggressive young woman who had to be restrained most of the day. Following time out alone, food and extra attention (smiles, hugs, hand holding, laughs, praise, playing ball) were provided upon release from time out whenever no aggressive responses or undesirable behavior (pulling objects from the table) occurred. Only choking responses were punished with time out while grabbing and other undesirable behavior resulted in withdrawal of attention, stopping of the response (removing her grabbing hands), and prompting of appropriate behavior. Reinforcement was finally made contingent on incompatible behavior which appeared capable of producing staff attention (laughing, playing ball). During the 4th phase grabbing and choking resulted in time out while sessions were increased to 15 hr per day. Social attention was provided for incompatible responses and food was discontinued. During the next phase extra attention was discontinued while time outs continued. Choking and grabbing declined greatly in the 2nd and 3rd phases while unrestrained time increased from 30 min per day to 14 hr. Because of a slight increase in grabs and chokes in the 4th phase, a 5th phase was implemented in which extra attention (3 min) in an attempt to reduce the conditions for extinction induced aggression (Phase IV). Also to reduce attention during time out, the time out chair was partitioned. This resulted in the reduction of choking to zero and grabbing to near zero levels.

STUDY	LEVEL OF RETARDATION	RESPONSE PUNISHED	PUNISHMENT PROCEDURE
11. White, Nielsen, & Johnson (1972)	Moderate and severe	Aggression, self-destruction, tantrums, and running away	Time out.

RESULTS: Twenty young & adolescent residents were divided into 3 groups which received 3 time out durations (1, 15, 30 min) in different orders for target behaviors over 2-wk periods. Time out consisted of placement in small rooms on ward. Averaged results revealed that 15-min time outs were most effective in behavior reduction (37%) followed closely by 30 min (34%), while 1-min time outs resulted in an average *increase* in deviant behaviors (12%). However, 1 min time outs were as successful as 15- and 30-min time outs when the 1-min duration was used first. The short time out produced increases in target behaviors only when scheduled *following* 15- and 30-min time outs. Sequence effects were observed for individuals in each group.

274

1) Overcorrection has yielded rapid suppression of stealing, self-stimulatory behavior, and toileting accidents (Azrin & Foxx, 1971; Azrin & Wesolowski, 1974; Foxx & Azrin, 1973). (See Figure 8.4.) There are two basic types of overcorrection. Restitution includes restoring various aspects of a situation to a condition improved over the condition existing prior to the occurrence of the deviant behavior. For example, Azrin and Wescolowski (1974) required retarded individuals caught stealing to return the stolen item *and* provide a new item in addition. Overcorrection also can be the *positive practice* or the performance of extremely correct forms of behavior contingent upon deviant behavior. For example, Foxx and Azrin (1973) required the performance of highly "correct" forms of self-stimulatory behavior as punishment for stereotype behavior.

2) Stimuli aversive to the smell and taste senses [e.g., distasteful solution on hand of a "mouther" (Foxx & Azrin, 1973); aromatic ammonia (Tanner & Zeiler, 1975)].

3) The effectiveness of time out from positive reinforcement may stem from one of two sources:

   a) "the *removal* of the possibility of positive reinforcement for the negative behavior or of the child receiving *any* positive reinforcers for *any* behavior for a period of time or

   b) the suppressing effects of the *presentation* of conditioned aversive stimuli" (Gardner, 1969, p. 94).

Time out was found to be:

   a) faster in suppressing swearing behavior than was the response contingent aversive condition of repeating a swear word for 15 minutes (Lahey, McNees, & McNees, 1973)

   b) effective in suppressing two targeted self-stimulatory behaviors when time out was contingent on one and not the other (Pendergrass, 1972)

   c) as effective whether the duration was 15 minutes or 30 minutes, or when only one minute in length but *not* preceded by time outs of longer durations (White, Nielsen, & Johnson, 1972)

4) Response cost or the removal of earned tokens or points contingent upon a behavior has been applied successfully to reduce disruptive classroom behavior. (Refer to application section on conditioned reinforcers and token reinforcement.)

5) Contingent periods of physical restraint (Salzberg & Napolitan, 1974; O'Brien, Azrin, & Bugle, 1972).

Overcorrection

Head Weaving

Hand Clapping

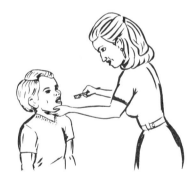

Mouthing

FIGURE 8.4

An illustration of overcorrection procedures used by Foxx and Azrin (1973) to reduce the self-stimulatory behaviors. When overcorrective functional movement training was contingently applied to head weaving and hand clapping, both self-stimulatory behaviors were eliminated. Additionally, when an overcorrective oral hygiene procedure (oral cleansing with an antiseptic) was applied to hand and object mouthing, mouthing was eliminated.

SOURCE: Adapted from "The Elimination of Autistic Self-stimulatory Behavior by Overcorrection" By R. M. Foxx & N. H. Azrin. *Journal of Applied Behavior Analysis,* 1973, *6,* p. 12. Reprinted by permission. Copyright 1973 by the Society for the Experimental Analysis of Behavior, Inc.

6) Contingent shock—Shock reduced self-abusive behaviors more quickly and thoroughly than DRO or isolation from social consequences; however, response suppression was situation specific (Corte, Wolf, & Locke, 1971).

2. The suppressive effects of punishment have been nontemporary "when used in a broader program of behavior instatement and acceleration of prosocial responses" (Gardner, 1969, p. 97).

a. Generalization of the effects of shock to other settings was facilitated when shock was made contingent upon the behavior in a variety of settings (Corte, Wolf, & Locke, 1971; Weisberg, 1971). Similar results occurred when the aversive was aromatic ammonia (Tanner & Zeiler, 1975).

b. The lack of generalization of the effects of shock to other related but unshocked responses (response specificity) may be a weakness of shock punishment (Weisberg, 1971).

c. "There does appear to be some suggestion that for the severely/profoundly retarded a relationship does exist between intensity of punishment and behavior suppression effect" (Gardner, 1969, p. 98).

d. While smaller ratio schedules of punishment are more effective than larger schedules in decreasing the rate of inappropriate responses, intermittent schedules of punishment can effectively maintain acceptable low rates of inappropriate behavior (Clark, Rowbury, Baer, & Baer, 1973).

e. When the recovery of a response suppressed by punishment occurs, reinstatement of punishment procedures results in the same suppression but at a faster rate. "These findings suggest that with continued punishment training the shock stimulus assumes discriminative properties, informing the subject of what not to do as well as what class of behaviors are desirable" (Weisberg, 1971, p. 125). These recovery effects were also observed during reversal designs using overcorrection (Foxx & Azrin, 1973), time out (Lahey, McNees, & McNees, 1973), physical restraint (Salzberg & Napolitan, 1974), and aromatic ammonia (Tanner & Zeiler, 1975).

3. Increases in emotional responses, behavior rigidity, and disruption of social behavior do not appear to be a predictable side effect of appropriately applied punishment with severely and profoundly retarded populations. However, Gardner (1969) cautions that the converse must not be assumed, i.e., that the side effects will be desirable or neutral. Since these related outcomes appear to be highly influenced by an individual's reinforcement history, and since a large fraction of punishment studies involve institutionalized populations, a conclusion regarding the negative side effects of noninstitutionalized retarded populations is premature.

4. The characteristics of appropriately applied punishment should include the following:

a. Especially with the unsocialized severely-profoundly retarded population, response contingent punishment should be used in combination with systematic reinforcement of appropriate alternate behaviors which will replace the inappropriate behaviors (e.g., punishing self-stimulating behavior while reinforcing appropriate use of toys) (Gardner, 1969).

b. According to MacMillan, Forness, and Trumbull (1973):

1) A prior positive relationship with the recipient renders punishment more effective.

2) Punishment, if it must be used, should be early in the sequence of misbehavior and consistently applied.

3) ∧ relatively intense aversive at the onset may be more effective than having to gradually escalate the intensity, but at the same time one must guard against "punishment overkill."

4) Whenever possible, punishment should be paired with cognitive structure, i.e., specification of the behavior being punished.

5) Punishment is more effective if an alternative is available to the punished behavior and if incompatible behavior is positively reinforced.

6) The same aversive should not be used over and over, e.g., the wording of a reprimand should be changed.

7) Soft reprimands, i.e., reprimands directly only at the recipient, are probably more effective. (p. 95)

Shaping and Maintaining Operant Behavior

In situations which require a change in response rate, the concept of reinforcement schedules is of particular importance. Additionally, when more than a change of response rate is necessitated, the complimentary processes of stimulus discrimination and response differentiation serve to describe the development of complex forms of behavior. That is, "in operant conditioning, reinforcement may be made contingent upon on either a) the properties of accompanying stimuli (when the result is a discrimination), or b) the properties of the response (when the result is a differentiation)" (Hilgard & Bower, 1966, p. 126).

Schedules of Reinforcement

The arrangement or timetable of reinforcement is an important factor in determining response strength. Most behavior in natural settings is not on a regular and uniform schedule but rather one that is intermittent in nature. When contingencies for reinforcement require participation of others, which is usually the case in the natural environment, the predictability of reinforcement is especially uncertain. However, the characteristics of response acquisition, emission, and extinction vary in specifically different and lawful ways according to the reinforcing contingencies operating on the environment.

Skinner (1953) differentiated between two general categories of reinforcement schedules: that which is determined by some system outside the individual and that which is actually controlled by the response itself.

> An example of the first is a schedule of reinforcement which is determined by a clock—as when we reinforce a pigeon every five minutes, allowing all intervening responses to go unreinforced. An example of the second is a schedule in which a response is reinforced after a certain number of responses have been emitted—as when we reinforce every fiftieth response the pigeon makes. (p. 100)

Reinforcement may be contingent on an interval schedule (i.e., contingent on the passage of time between responses) or a ratio schedule (i.e., contingent on the number of responses which have been emitted) (see Table 8.4). However, the actual number of specific reinforcement schedules is not countable since numerous variations may be made on themes of ratio reinforcement, interval reinforcement, and mixed schedules (Ferster & Skinner, 1957).

INTERVAL REINFORCEMENT. When reinforcement is made contingent upon time, the interval units may be standard, fixed units (e.g., every 3 minutes, every 24 hours), or variable units (i.e., randomly varied in length averaged around a midpoint between zero and some specified length). In *fixed interval* (FI) schedules, reinforcement occurs following the first response after the completion of each interval. In both fixed and variable interval schedules there may be a slight additional interval before reinforcement occurs, depending upon the delay that occurs from the end of the interval to the completion of the first response following the interval. However, a logical pattern of behavior results from FI schedules which includes a decrease in responding just following reinforcement, with a gradual increase in responding towards the end of the interval.

This again shows how the contingencies of reinforcement shape the organism's behavior. Immediately following a reinforcement there is a zero probability of a response being followed by a reinforcer, and a response in the presence of these stimuli conditions is weakened by this extinction. However, later, when the taste of the food, and so on, has disappeared and several responses have been made, there is a much higher probability that the response will be reinforced. (Staats & Staats, 1963, p. 63)

We cannot explain this response pattern by saying that the animal "knows" when the reinforcer will be given. The scalloped response pattern that is characteristic of FI schedules (see Figure 8.5, p. 279) results when the schedule-produced stimuli are discriminated by the organism.

A common nonexperimental example of FI schedules occurs when a person is expecting a letter. As the approximate time for mail delivery approaches, he keeps checking his mailbox, while immediately following the actual delivery and receipt (or nonreceipt!) of mail the probability of the checking behavior is zero. Another common example of an FI schedule is the paycheck, which is made available on a biweekly or monthly basis roughly approximating a fixed interval schedule of reinforcement for two or four weeks of work.

Reinforcement in *variable interval* (VI) schedules occurs after the first response following an average interval which varies from zero to a set maximum. With this arrangement a response on a VI–5 minute schedule may be reinforced for the first response following time intervals of 2, 7, 10, 1, 9, 5, 3, and 3 minutes. The scalloping or minor hesitations following FI reinforcement are eliminated with this schedule and more stable and uniform response rates are produced. Additionally, when responses learned under VI and FI schedules are compared during extinction, a difference in resultant operant strength is revealed (i.e., the rate of response and the total number of responses occurring). The variable schedule produces a response highly resistant to extinction while the fixed schedule does not (see Figure 8.6, p. 280).

RATIO REINFORCEMENT. The frequency of reinforcement in ratio schedules, for both the *fixed ratio* (FR) and *variable ratio* (VR) types, is controlled by the number of responses emitted. When FR schedules are employed, a reinforcement occurs and is repeated after a specified number of responses (e.g., every single, seventh, one hun-

TABLE 8.4

Schedules of Reinforcement

	FIXED	INTERVAL
RATIO	*Fixed-Ratio Schedules (FR)* Reinforcement is made contingent upon the emission of a set, fixed number of responses, such that the last emitted response of the fixed number is reinforced.	*Variable-Ratio Schedules (VR)* Reinforcement is made contingent upon the emission of an average number of responses varying randomly from trial to trial to between 2 arbitrary extremes and around a specified mean value, such that the last emitted response of randomly average number is reinforced.
INTERVAL	*Fixed-Interval Schedules (FI)* Reinforcement is made contingent upon the passage of a standard, fixed unit of time (sec, min, day) such that the first response emitted *following* the fixed interval is reinforced.	*Variable-Interval Schedules (VI)* Reinforcement is made contingent upon the passage of an average unit of time which randomly varies from trial to trial from zero to a predetermined maximum, such that the first response that is emitted following each randomly average interval is reinforced.

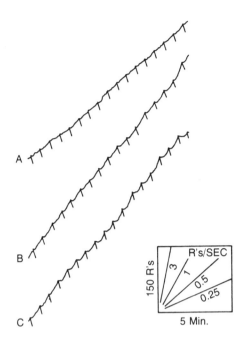

FIGURE 8.5

The FI–schedule performance of a pigeon formerly on a continuous reinforcement schedule for three sessions (A, B, and C). FI–1 schedule included reinforcement given for the first response occurring at the end of every minute. "In record C, the fourth session following crf, the interval segments are consistently scalloped; the terminal rate reaches 1.5 to 1.7 responses per second, and the period of pausing and acceleration extends over half of the interval. The all-over rate of responding remains about the same" (Ferster & Skinner, 1957, p. 142).

NOTE: Rate of responding may be read from the small set of coordinates in the box which illustrate the rate of representative slopes.

SOURCE: Adapted from *Schedules of Reinforcement* by C. B. Ferster & B. F. Skinner. New York: Appleton-Century-Crofts, 1957, p. 143. Copyright 1957 by Appleton-Century-Crofts. Reprinted by permission.

dredth). The characteristics of FR schedules are reliant upon the ratio employed. Starting a learner (animal or human) with a high FR schedule may mean that reinforcement is never given because the response may extinguish before it is reinforced. However, gradually advancing or fading the ratio will allow the production of a rapid response rate for a comparatively small amount of

reinforcement (see Figure 8.7, p. 281). For example, if a continuous FR–1 schedule is replaced in a gradual fashion by schedules of FR–2, FR–4, FR–8, FR–12, FR–15, etc., the response rate can be maintained and increased because the response following FR–1 already was being produced at a high rate.

> Under a ratio schedule the more rapidly the animal presses the bar, the more immediately it is reinforced. Therefore, it would be expected, according to the principle of operant conditioning, that rapid responding would be strengthened to a greater extent than slow responding. And that is what fixed-ratio schedules produce. (Staats & Staats, 1963, p. 61)

As with FI schedules, a response pause may develop following reinforcement when longer fixed ratios are used. This pattern includes a burst of responding just before reinforcement. This activity is then followed by a slow period of responding (or no responding for very high schedules) just after reinforcement.

If a *variable ratio* schedule is adopted (i.e., one that employs a range of ratios around the mean value), this pause is eliminated.

> Because the probability of reinforcement at any moment remains approximately constant, a uniform rate of responding ensues; because this probability is increased with rapid responding, the rate tends to be high. A pigeon may respond as rapidly as five times per second and keep up this rate for many hours. (This rate corresponds to that of the ticking of a watch). (Hilgard & Bower, 1966, p. 117)

VR schedules produce response rates more stable than FR schedules, but both schedules act to reinforce rapid responding. Additionally, behavior produced by aperiodic or VR schedules is more resistant to extinction than behavior strengthened by periodic or fixed-ratio schedules (see Figure 8.8, p. 281).

Findings With Retarded Populations

In *The Technology of Teaching*, Skinner (1968) advises teachers on the delicate balancing of reinforcement schedules to response frequency and strength.

> The student will be less dependent on immediate and consistent reinforcement if he is brought under the control of intermittent reinforcement. If the proportion of responses reinforced (on a fixed or variable ratio schedule) is steadily reduced, a stage may be reached

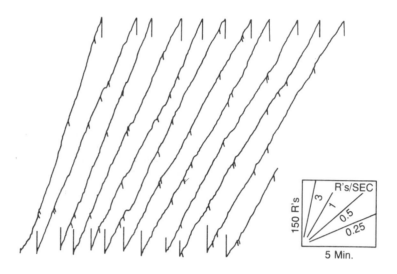

FIGURE 8.6

Performance of a pigeon after 45 hours on a VI-3 schedule which consisted of intervals as follows: 300, 30, 280, 120, 360, 300, 0, 240, 220, 180, 10, 280, 100, and 60. "The bird maintains a constant over-all rate throughout the session, with marked local changes, and shows the same tendency to respond at a higher rate immediately after the reinforcement" (p. 333).

SOURCE: Adapted from *Schedules of Reinforcement* by C. B. Ferster, & B. F. Skinner. New York: Appleton-Century-Crofts, 1957, p. 334. Copyright 1957 by Appleton-Century-Crofts. Reprinted by permission.

at which behavior is maintained indefinitely by an astonishingly small number of reinforcements. The teacher's assignment is to make relatively infrequent reinforcements effective. One technique is to "stretch the ratio"—that is, to increase the number of responses per reinforcement as rapidly as the behavior of the student permits. (p. 159)

In general, Skinner's (1968) advice holds true for teachers of retarded individuals as well as for teachers of normal children. Following is a summary of earlier studies and reviews of reinforcement schedule research (Bijou & Baer, 1966; Spradlin & Girardeau, 1966; Weisberg, 1971) concerning the performance of retarded individuals.

FIXED SCHEDULES. According to Weisberg, (1971), "In general better initial and long lasting control is achieved with fixed ratio and variable ratio schedules than with fixed interval and variable interval ones" (p. 132). Spradlin, Girardeau, and Corte (1965) found that under FR schedules retarded individuals demonstrated high response rates with pauses in responding limited primarily to times preceding and following reinforcement. Generally, once the individual began to respond he did not hesitate until the ratio was completed.

Under FR and VR schedules, responding does not appear to suffer in terms of increased delays between responses until either the ratio of reinforcement to responses is too high or the subject's motivation level is too low (a variable confounded with past and immediate reinforcement schedule) (Weisberg, 1971). If the individual's baseline response strength is low, the ratio schedule initially employed also should be low or continuous. Gradually the number of responses required to obtain reinforcement is increased, thereby strengthening the response (increasing the resistance to extinction) and avoiding extinction of the response before the first reinforcement is given. Such gradual schedule "thinning" has yielded good response rates in retarded individuals under schedules as high as FR–128 (Ellis, 1962) and FR–1024 (Ellis, Barnett, & Pryer, 1960).

Baumeister and Hawkins (1966) investigated resistance to extinction in severely retarded children as a function of VR schedules. Consistent with the results of past studies, resistance to extinction was found to be inversely related to the percentage of reinforced trials during acquisition. That is, the higher the number of reinforced trials

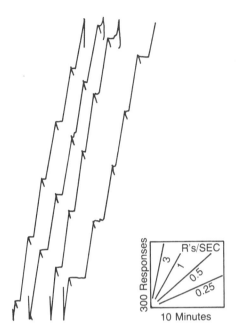

strate an increased resistance to extinction. Additionally, all FR schedules greater than FR–1 (continuous) produce behaviors more durable during extinction than do continuous schedules (MacMillan, 1973).

INTERVAL SCHEDULES. The reviews of Weisburg (1971) and Spradlin and Girardeau (1966) describe two response patterns which emerge in retarded individuals as a result of FI schedules: (a) low response rate with pauses following reinforcement, and (b) higher, smooth response rates with an absence of pauses following reinforce-

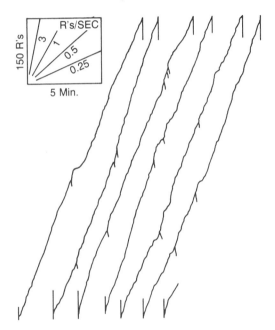

FIGURE 8.7

Final performance of a pigeon on a FR-200 schedule following 4000 reinforcements on fixed ratios varying from 50 to 180. "The bird pauses after each reinforcement for a period varying from a few seconds to more than a minute; the rate then shifts (usually abruptly) to 3.5 to 4 responses per second, which is maintained (though possibly with a slight decline) until reinforcement" (p. 51).

SOURCE: Adapted from *Schedules of Reinforcement* by C. B. Ferster & B. F. Skinner. New York: Appleton-Century-Crofts, 1957, p. 52. Copyright 1957 by Appleton-Century-Crofts. Reprinted by permission.

during acquisition of a knob-pulling response (i.e., the lower the ratio schedules), the lower the number of responses during extinction. Additionally, when a buzzer was sounded immediately after the extinction criterion had been met (i.e., no responses for a 30-second period), the same inverse relationship held between the number of resultant knob-pulls following extraneous stimulation (disinhibition) and reinforcement schedule during acquisition: the higher the number of reinforced trials, the lower the number of responses occurring after the buzzer. When behaviors maintained on VR schedules are compared with those on FR schedules, the former behaviors demon-

FIGURE 8.8

Performance of a pigeon on a VR–360 schedule. Note that the bird shows a higher rate of response immediately following reinforcement (as indicated by the oblique pip to the right of the record). "The short period of a high rate of responding immediately following the reinforcement is followed either by an abrupt shift to a lower rate which is maintained until the next reinforcement, by a pause and acceleration to that rate, or by a pause and an abrupt shift to the lower rate of responding" (p. 393).

SOURCE: Adapted from *Schedules of Reinforcement* by C. B. Ferster & B. F. Skinner. New York: Appleton-Century-Crofts, 1957, p. 393. Copyright 1957 by Appleton-Century-Crofts. Reprinted by permission.

ment. At least three factors operating separately and in combination appear to influence the occurrence of these response patterns:

1. Instructions given to the individual regarding the response upon which reinforcement is made contingent. When VI schedules were preceded by definitive instructions (e.g., "Pull the knob to get pennies") or ambiguous reinforcement (continuous reinforcement for three to eight responses), high response rates were produced with little or no temporal discrimination and high resistance to extinction (Headrick, 1963).
2. The individual's history of reinforcement schedules preceding the FI schedule. If a low FR schedule was followed by a low FI schedule, which was then faded to a higher FI schedule, the high response rate developed initially was more likely to be maintained (Headrick, 1963).
3. Response cost in FI responding. Responses emitted between reinforcement were penalized by point or token removal (Weiner, 1962).

   a. High rate–no pause behavior with a history of ratio schedules continued when FI schedules were introduced. The behavior was not noticeably disrupted by FI response cost.
   b. A history of differential reinforcement of low rates of responding (DRL) resulted in the development of a low rate response pattern with postreinforcement pauses. Response cost increased the probability that this response pattern developed.
   c. When the individual's history reflected both DRL and ratio schedules, the resultant response pattern (a low rate–pause pattern) that developed during VI schedules was a product of DRL.

An interesting point made by MacMillan (1973) may be noted here regarding what appears to be FI schedules. In classroom situations, consequences are often applied erroneously at the completion of time interval rather than contingent upon a response occurring at the termination of the interval.

> In most examples for the school, consequences are presented at the end of the time period but not after the child responds. For example, a six-week grading period is somewhat like the FI schedule in that six weeks of time must pass and then the grade (potential reinforcer) is presented and is contingent on the behavior during that six-week period. (MacMillan, 1973, p. 102)

This phenomenon is probably closer to a high ratio schedule (many responses before a grade is awarded) than a VI schedule. However, in cases where "new" responses precede the reinforce-

ment of "old" responses (e.g., grades given after study has begun in new coursework), what actually exists is an extreme reinforcement delay with the effects further complicated by adventitious reinforcement of intervening behavior. When applying the results of FI schedule research, care should be taken to identify or create actual FI situations.

Unlike the interest that surrounds the FI schedule with retarded individuals, the VI schedule has not received much experimental attention. Because of the desirability of obtaining constant response rates, neither the VR or the VI schedule has been as popular as the ratio schedule in work with retardates (Weisberg, 1971).

Stimulus Discrimination

When a child first learns to label objects, people, and actions, many errors are present. Learning to use a label in the presence of the appropriate referent is a stimulus discrimination task. For example, if a child has learned to say the word *Daddy*, the word's production in the presence of his father will be met with praise, hugs, and smiles of approval, while its production in the presence of inanimate objects or other men will not be reinforced. Eventually the response of *Daddy* is likely to occur when the child's own father is present and not at other times. Likewise, when a pigeon receives food for pecking only in the presence of a light, he comes to peck when the light is on and not peck when the light is off. Learning in both examples proceeds through a process called *discrimination*.

This discrimination learning process involves different stimuli and a constant response operating within two three-term contingencies:

1. A stimulus (S^D, discriminative stimulus) that is the occasion upon which a response is followed by reinforcement: $$\begin{bmatrix} S^D \\ R \end{bmatrix} \quad\underline{\hspace{1cm}}\quad S^{R+}$$
2. A stimulus ($S^\triangle$) that is the occasion upon which a response is not followed by reinforcement: $$\begin{bmatrix} S^\triangle \\ R \end{bmatrix}$$

Initially, before discrimination occurs, the situation consists of a variation of intermittent reinforcement because the response should be reinforced only part of the time. Also, in the first stages of learning, responses which are emitted in the presence of the positive stimulus are available to be emitted in the presence of the negative stimulus, which is the principle of *inductive conditioning or generalization*. As soon as the response is emitted in the presence of the negative stimulus, however, extinction occurs which also affects the availability of the response for emission in the presence of the positive stimulus (principle of *inductive extinction*). Both induction principles concern the basic fact that "whatever happens to one operant affects the other to some extent" (Hilgard & Bower, 1966, p. 125). In discrimination learning there are *two* operants with the same form of response. For example in the previous illustration of a child's first words, S^D is the actual father present and $S^\triangle$ is another man present. In the pigeon illustration, S^D is the light on and $S^\triangle$ is the light off. These operants are both selectively reinforced and extinguished which eventually results in: (a) an increase in the number of responses recurring in the presence of the positive stimulus (positive half of discrimination), and (b) a decrease in the number of responses available for emission in the presence of the negative stimulus (negative half of discrimination). Once discrimination has occurred:

1. Intermittent reinforcement is replaced by continuous reinforcement; therefore, "the resistance to extinction that is built up at this stage is not that of interval reinforcement; but that of ordinary every-trial reinforcement" (Hilgard & Bower, 1966, p. 125).
2. "The positive stimulus which acts as the occasion for the response and for the reinforcement becomes itself a secondary reinforcing agent" (Hilgard & Bower, 1966, p. 126)
3. "When a discrimination has been established, we may alter the probability of a response instantly by presenting or removing the discriminative stimulus" (Skinner, 1953, p. 108).

Findings With Retarded Populations

In traditional discrimination learning studies a response is strengthened through positive reinforcement during periods when the S^D (e.g., blue light, high frequency tone) is present and is weakened through extinction during presentation of the $S^\triangle$. Both stimuli are not presented simultaneously. Spradlin and Girardeau (1966) review some early discrimination studies of this type. They identify significant differences in discrimination learning with increasing severity of retardation. That is, for the severely and profoundly retarded the usual discrimination procedure may not yield a discriminated response. This lack of discrimination tends to increase if the S^D is dependent upon a time schedule and independent of the behavior because superstitious chains of responses occurring during the $S^\triangle$ near the end of the interval are accidently reinforced. Two procedures were described to remediate this difficulty and facilitate discrimination learning by retarded individuals. First, if the individual was required to make a response during the $S^\triangle$ to obtain the S^D *and* a different response to receive reinforcement, superstitious chaining would not develop. A second procedure included making the S^D contingent on no responding for a fixed period of time during the $S^\triangle$.

Bijou and Orlando (1961) applied a variation of this latter procedure with moderately and severely retarded individuals which resulted in rapid acquisition of a multiple-schedule discrimination. The specific discrimination involved the response of pushing a lever in the presence of a red light, S^D, which was reinforced with candy, while in the presence of $S^\triangle$, a blue light, no responses were reinforced (see Figure 8.9, p. 284).

The technique involved manipulation of the relative lengths and distribution of S^D and $S^\triangle$ periods, and considerable care to the specific steps in the initial shaping and strengthening of the response. Basically it consisted of a DRL contingency between response during $S^\triangle$ and the presentation of the next S^D period. That is, during $S^\triangle$ not only were all responses extinguished, but in addition any response served to delay the next presentation of S^D for a certain number of seconds. Hence, the $S^\triangle$ extinction schedule remained in effect until the response was extinguished sufficiently to produce an interresponse interval, or pause, exceeding a certain time limit. Then S^D was represented, and responding during the S^D period was reinforced. With the next presentation of $S^\triangle$, the pattern was repeated. As S's behavior began to shape to the reinforcement contingencies, the length of pauses during $S^\triangle$ required for presentation of the S^D increased according to objective criteria, and the length of S^D periods was also increased (Initial S^D periods terminated with the first response, which was always reinforced. Subsequently, S^D periods were lengthened to half-minute, minute, and two-minute intervals, with FR, VR, FI, or VI schedules of reinforcement, which were also increased as the discrimination stablized). (Bijou & Baer, 1966, p. 766).

Redd (1969) conducted a discrimination study similar to the study of Bijou and Orlando (1961) in that various schedules of reinforcement were discriminated by retarded individuals; however,

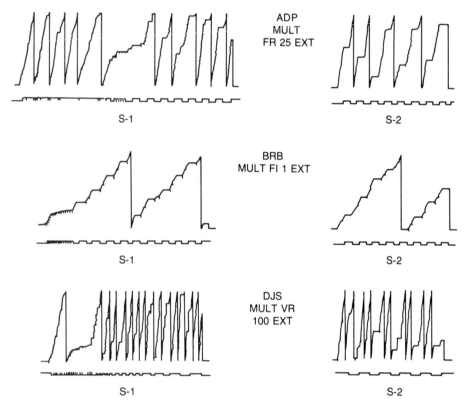

FIGURE 8.9

The cumulative response curves of three subjects who have developed multiple-schedule discrimination. By the second session each of the three subjects demonstrated fairly stable discriminations. Presentation of the reinforcement is represented by blips in the cumulative curve, while S^D presentations appear on the timeline as offsets of depressions.

SOURCE: Adapted from Operant Methods in Child Behavior and Development by S. W. Bijou & D. M. Baer. In W. K. Honig (Ed.), *Operant behavior: Areas of research and application.* New York: Appleton-Century-Crofts, 1966, p. 767. Copyright 1966 by Appleton-Century-Crofts. Reprinted by permission. Also in Rapid Development of Multiple-Schedule Performances with Retarded Children by S. W. Bijou & R. Orlando. *Journal of the Experimental Analysis of Behavior,* 1961, *4*, p. 15.

adults served as the discriminative stimuli rather than lights, an experimental situation more closely approximating reality. In the study two severely retarded boys exhibiting low levels of cooperative play were placed separately in a playroom as members of a five-boy play group. In a predetermined sequence three adults entered the room for 5-minute periods. Adult I presented reinforcers (candy and praise) on a mixed schedule of contingent reinforcement for cooperative play of a target child with another child and noncontingent reinforcement. After a 2-minute baseline Adult II entered the room and dispensed reinforcers contin-

gent on cooperative play (FI 45 seconds). Finally, Adult III distributed reinforcers on a noncontingent schedule without regard to the child's behavior. The four buffer children in the group received candy and praise noncontingently from all adults.

The number of reinforcers distributed to the target child across adults was controlled over sessions. Figure 8.10 contrasts for one subject the first session and the 14th session when stimulus control criterion was met. That is, stimulus discrimination had occurred when the child: (a) emitted cooperative play responses within 45 seconds following entrance of the contingent adult, (b) dis-

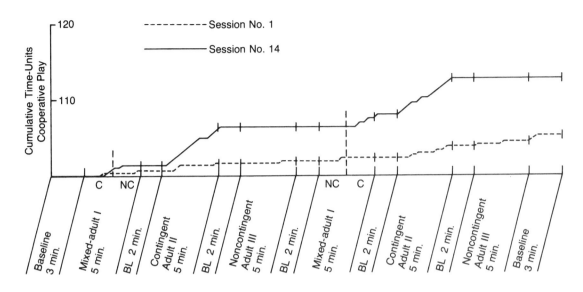

FIGURE 8.10

Two cumulative records of cooperative play responses are shown for a severely retarded boy exposed to three adults providing reinforcement under various schedules (contingent on cooperative play, noncontingent, mixed schedules of contingent and noncontingent reinforcement). As contrasted with the first session, the 14th session illustrates attainment of the stimulus control criteria by the subject.

NOTE: BL = Baseline
       C = Contingent
       NC = Noncontingent

SOURCE: Adapted from Effects of Mixed Reinforcement Contingencies on Adults' Control of Children's Behavior by W. H. Redd. *Journal of Applied Behavior Analysis,* 1969, *2,* p. 253. Copyright 1969 by the Society for the Experimental Analysis of Behavior. Reprinted by permission.

continued performance of the target response 45 seconds after the contingent adult's departure, and (c) demonstrated both (a) and (b) for three consecutive sessions. For both subjects presence of the mixed adult showed no consistent effect—it was not discriminative because it had not been paired with contingent reinforcement on a consistent basis.

> The results of this experiment suggest that children react to adults in a manner consistent with how these adults have reinforced their behavior in the past. The entrance of the contingent adult controlled the cooperative play behavior of the two target children whereas the noncontingent adult had no effect. The presence of the mixed adult, while not meeting the stimulus control criterion, did disrupt baseline behavior and result in high steady terminal rates of cooperative play. (Redd, 1969, p. 254)

Operant audiometry represents a functional application of the more traditional stimulus discrimination paradigm for the purpose of assessing the hearing of nonverbal, uncooperative, and/or lower functioning individuals (Bricker, D. & Bricker, 1969; Bricker, W. & Bricker, 1969; Freeman, Leibowitz, & Linseman, 1974). The procedure generally includes a clearly audible sound with or without an accompanying light (S^D) while periods of no sound (or light) are designated as the $S^\triangle$. The child's response may be button or lever pushing which results in automatic dispensing of candy during S^D or, with informal applications, dropping a block into a container during S^D periods. Freeman et al. suggested that the individual be taught both an S^D response and a different $S^\triangle$ response (e.g., S^D—touch one toy when light is on; $S^\triangle$—touch a second toy when light is off) in order to differentiate between instances of nonresponding and failure to perceive the stimulus. Additionally, they recommended that the task (touching a toy) be taught in a visual modality and sound be faded in to allow the trainer to discriminate between possible types of response errors (e.g., whether the child is unable to learn a two-choice discrimination task versus being unable to perceive the S^D itself).

During a gradual shaping process accompanied by response primes the child's response levels are increased during the S^D and decreased during the $S^\triangle$. At the same time extra stimuli (lights, hand-held vibrator) are faded out and the reinforcement schedule is thinned (e.g., FR–1 to FR–7 over six training steps) (Bricker, Bricker, & Larsen, 1968). As soon as this point of discrimination is reached and the child is wearing headphones, audiometric assessment may begin with reinforcement given for responses preceded by a sound. Operant audiometry has allowed accurate assessment of hearing children unable to respond meaningfully in the usual audiometric procedure.

Because the range of discrimination studies with retarded populations is so extensive, only one additional type of discrimination training procedure, errorless discrimination, will be discussed. Two- or multi-choice simultaneous discrimination procedures are covered in more detail in Chapter 4.

When discrimination training includes the errorless transfer of stimulus control, learning becomes a process of error elimination.

> In discrimination learning, the analogue of response shaping is stimulus shaping. The teacher starts by reinforcing a stimulus-response relation that the learner already has or can acquire easily, and gradually changes the stimuli until he arrives at the restricted stimulus-response relation he wants to teach. (Sidman & Stoddard, 1967. p. 3)

Originally studied by Terrace (1963) as a procedure to shift the stimulus control of a pigeon's responses, fading or stimulus shaping in combination with reinforcement has been demonstrated to produce far fewer errors in retarded individuals than the same reinforcement techniques without stimulus shaping. Sidman and Stoddard (1966, 1967) compared the effectiveness of these two procedures for teaching a circle-elipse form discrimination in two groups of institutionalized adolescents who functioned in the severe-profound ranges of retardation. Both groups were taught to sit before a nine-key matrix, press a key, and locate the candy which was released when the key was depressed. Upon pressing the correct key the lighted keys became dark and a chime sounded. Following this, both groups were exposed to the circle-ellipse discrimination task.

Figure 8.11 illustrates the training stimuli involved in the programmed or stimulus shaping group. The first series of steps which involved background fading were designed to transfer stimulus control from bright keys versus dark keys to keys with form versus keys with no form. During the ellipse-fading portion of the program the sequence of training stimuli transferred discriminative stimulus control from form versus no form to circle versus ellipse, which was the criterion discrimination. The test group, no stimulus shaping program, was exposed to a series of circle-ellipse slides on the matrix. Whenever the circle key was

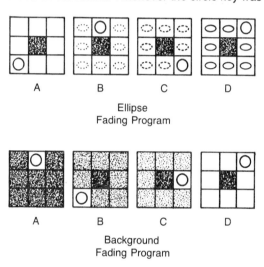

Ellipse
Fading Program

Background
Fading Program

FIGURE 8.11

Background fading program: A few sample steps in the background fading program. The discrimination task increases gradually in difficulty as it progresses from A to D. As the dark keys are slowly increased in brightness, they become more like the correct choice (bright key with circle). Ellipse fading program: A few sample steps in the ellipse fading program. Again the discrimination increases in difficulty from A to D. Ellipses appear gradually and are faded to dark outlines similar to the circle.

NOTE: Dots are used to indicate that a figure is being faded in or out. For example, in Background Program the seven blank blocks are gradually filled with ovals going from A to D. In Ellipse Fading Program the dark blocks are faded to a blank condition.

SOURCE: Adapted from The Effectiveness of Fading in Programming a Simultaneous Form Discrimination for Retarded Children by M. Sidman & L. T. Stoddard. *Journal of the Experimental Analysis of Behavior*, 1967, *10*, p. 6. Copyright 1967 by the Society for the Experimental Analysis of Behavior. Reprinted by permission.

depressed reinforcement occurred. Without the program one of the nine subjects learned the discrimination, while 7 of 10 subjects learned it with the fading program. An analysis of the responses made by the test group children unable to learn the circle-ellipse discrimination revealed that once an error response pattern had been reinforced (e.g., adventitiously reinforced sequences, such as pushing each of the outside eight keys in a circle) the child tended to return to its use upon reaching a difficult part of the program. While children in the program group made similar types of errors, they did not fall back upon the error patterns as alternatives to correct choices. According to Sidman and Stoddard (1967), "The appearance of error patterns, then, must be attributed primarily to the relative ineffectiveness of extinction as a teaching technique. This conclusion supports the practical sanction against allowing children to make errors in a teaching situation" (p. 14).

Dorry and Zeaman (1973, 1975) demonstrated the effectiveness of a simple fading procedure in reading instruction. Fading involved the shifting of stimulus control in such a way that the child learned to make the same response in the presence of several different stimuli. Children were taught to read picture-word cards by labeling the picture. Over a series of five steps the picture was gradually eliminated, thereby shifting stimulus control to the printed stimuli.

Since the learning processes of stimulus discrimination and response differentiation are usually in simultaneous operation during applied conditioning studies, the reader is referred to the summaries of applied research with retarded individuals in token reinforcement programs (Table 8.2), punishment (Table 8.3), self-care skills (Table 8.5), gross motor behavior (Table 8.6), language acquisition (Table 8.7), functional academics (Table 8.8), vocational skills (Table 8.9), and social skills (Table 8.10).

Response Differentiation: Shaping

Response differentiation occurs when reinforcement is made contingent upon certain properties of a response. Skinner (1953) distinguishes between reinforcement of responses for the purpose of producing an entirely new behavior versus modifying various aspects of an existing behavior.

> In the first case, we are interested in how behavior is acquired; in the second, in how it is refined. It is the difference between "knowing how to do something"

and "doing it well." The latter is the field of *skill*. The contingency which improves skill is the differential reinforcement of responses possessing special properties. (p. 95)

When differential reinforcement or shaping is employed to develop complex forms of behavior, Skinner's (1953) distinction between differential reinforcement for producing a complete new unit of behavior versus mere skill improvement is less clear. However, regardless of the point at which skill acquisition becomes skill refinement, a series of events occurs in response differentiation which leads to significant changes in the intensity, duration, or topography of behaviors.

1. The response must be emitted before it can be reinforced.
2. The reinforcement must immediately follow the response so as not to sacrifice the precision of the differential effect.
3. Only the successive approximations occurring in a response class presently in the organism's repertoire which lead to a target behavior not presently in the repertoire are reinforced. According to White (1971)

> As successively more precise classes of behavior are reinforced, the less exact classes, which were formerly reinforced, are placed on extinction. At this point shaping yields increased response variability such that better approximations are more likely to be emitted while less exact classes of behavior are extinguished.

Although the complimentary processes of stimulus discrimination and response differentiation have been separately defined and detailed, in everyday life these processes are more often intertwined rather than separately observed. The inadvertent shaping of temper tantrums by parents described by Staats and Staats (1963) provides an undersirable but succinct example of this common combination of conditioning processes.

> The parents continually raised the level of crying that was necessary to procure reinforcement and eventually shaped up temper tantrums. Such a process would take place over an extended period of time, during which the process of discrimination would also be occurring. Reinforcement by the parents of the child's crying behavior will strengthen the tendency of the child to cry in the presence of similar stimuli, such as other adults. When the parents strengthen extreme cases of crying, this behavior will also generalize to similar adults. However if the child cries in the presence of these adults and is not reinforced, a discrimination will occur, the child will come to have temper tantrums in the presence of the parents, but not other people.

TABLE 8.5
Summaries of Studies on Self-Care Skills

STUDY	LEVEL OF RETARDATION	ABSTRACT
1. Abramson & Wunderlich (1972)	Severe	Nine institutionalized boys learned to brush their teeth by systematic application of discrimination training, response priming by modeling, and shaping procedures.
2. Azrin & Armstrong (1973)	Profound	Two methods of eating instruction were compared with 22 adults in an institutional setting. Control procedures made use of hourly "mini-meals" (regular meals divided into small portions) which included manual priming, systematic fading of primes, shaping, verbal-tactual reinforcer, error prevention and correction, isolated training and positive practice. Intensive mini-meal training procedures resulted in all residents trained in 12 days with a decline in errors during follow-up. Control procedures after 18 days resulted in only 36% of the subjects achieving criterion.
3. Azrin & Foxx (1971)	Profound	An intensive toilet training method was used to train 9 institutionalized adults which employed an automatic buzzing apparatus to signal elimination, shaping of response chains, artificially increasing urination, cleanliness training, as well as specific procedures for handling accidents and maintenance procedures. The training resulted in a significant decrease in daily accidents (i.e., by 80% during the 12 days following training).
4. Ball, Seric, & Payne (1971)	Severe	Six institutionalized boys were trained in dressing/undressing skills for 90 days. Procedures included teaching response chains by shaping, response priming and fading of primes, reinforcement with bites of meals, and one to two 15-min sessions per day. The immediate gains in undressing skills were extinguished since ward routine did not encourage use of verbal cues to evoke undressing. Implications of 4 years of follow-up data are discussed.
5. Barton, Guess, Garcia, & Baer (1970)	Severe	Time out procedures and removal of food tray for 15 sec were used to reduce undesirable mealtime behaviors of stealing food, using fingers inappropriately, messy use of utensils, and stuffing food.
6. Groves & Carroccio (1971)	Severe/Profound	Sixty institutionalized females from 13–59 yr old learned to use a spoon during eating. Methods included instruction in small groups, shaping, prompting, fading, and termination of eating whenever the maximum number of eating with hand responses had been exceeded.
7. Horner & Keilitz (1975)	Mild to moderate	The task of toothbrushing was analyzed into 15 steps which were then used as the sequence of instruction for 8 institutionalized boys. Three increasing levels of response priming were successively applied as needed and then faded (verbal instruction, demonstration and instruction guidance and instruction). As subjects performed more of the steps without help, less response priming was needed on remaining steps. Tokens and praise or praise alone were used as reinforcers.

Table 8.5 cont.

STUDY	LEVEL OF RETARDATION	ABSTRACT
8. Mahoney, Van Wagenen, & Meyerson (1971)	Moderate to profound	Five children were toilet trained by first shaping response chains (approach toilet, pants down, etc.) in response to an auditory signal triggered by the trainer. Next, elimination training was taught during which children drank increased amounts of liquids, wore pants with a urinary sensing device which automatically provided an auditory signal, and were prompted as needed to use the toilet. Finally, the auditory signal was faded out. Criterion was reached after 29 hr of training.
9. Martin, Kehoe, Bird, Jensen, & Darbyshire (1971)	Severe	Eleven girls and young women were taught to dress themselves via reinforcement (praise and food) of correct responses and punishment (10-sec time outs and "No") of errors. Subjects were taught to put on sweaters, socks, underpants, etc., and to tie knots and bows. Attention span training was necessary for some.
10. O'Brien, Bugle, & Azrin (1972)	Profound	A young girl was taught to eat with a spoon by means of shaping a response chain in a backward order. Prior to this instruction, following 6 meals of baseline, the child was mildly punished with an interruption-extinction procedure whenever she tried to eat with her hands (i.e., child's hands were stopped before she could eat and emptied of food). No correct spoon responses occurred in either of these phases or in the 2nd baseline. Manual guidance was used to shape spoon use, followed by manual guidance and interruption-extinction for eating with hands. A reversal to baseline, then to interruption-extinction, and back to baseline revealed that interruption-extinction was necessary to maintain the spoon response.
11. O'Brien & Azrin (1972)	Severe	Six institutionalized adults were taught appropriate mealtime behaviors (use of utensils, napkins, butter transport and spreading; reduction of spill, drooling large bites, etc.) by a combination of verbal instruction, imitative prompts, and manual guidance. A maintenance program was implemented which consisted of praise, warnings, and 30-sec food removal. Follow-up measurement revealed 0% of eating errors for the trained group with 55% of the total eating responses for untrained subjects being error responses. In a 2nd study, 6 residents were trained by ward staff using the same procedures, while 6 were untrained. Maintenance was implemented following training. The eating errors of trained residents remained under 10% for 3 mo in comparison to untrained with an error rate of 75%.
12. Song & Gandhi (1974)	Profound	Four institutionalized children were taught to use a spoon to feed themselves by aides employing a 7-step backward chaining technique. Aides worked from behind the child. Lumpy, sticky food was used to reduce spilling. Milk, juice, and dessert were used as reinforcers. Food tray "time outs" and hand restraint were used to punish inappropriate eating behavior. Posttrain measures 5 to 34 wk later revealed that 3 of the 4 children had maintained appropriate eating behavior 90% of the time with only general supervision.

NOTE: The reader is referred to Osarchuk (1973) and Rentfrow and Rentfrow (1969) for reviews of toilet training retarded persons.

289

TABLE 8.6
Summaries of Studies on Gross Motor Behavior

STUDY	LEVEL OF RETARDATION	ABSTRACT
1. Angney (1974)	Moderate	Twenty-month-old child was taught to walk by a shaping procedure. Edible reinforcers were given initially for taking steps without aid from one chair to another. The walking distance required for reinforcement was gradually increased. Total teaching time was 3 hr.
2. Horner (1971)	Moderate	A 5-year-old child handicapped with *spinal bifida* learned to walk using crutches by means of shaping and fading of physical prompts. After the use of parallel bars was established a 10-step successive approximation sequence was used to establish use of crutches.
3. Michealis & Etzel (1967)	Moderate	A 31-month-old child was taught to walk, get up from a sitting position, and climb stairs. The procedure included shaping the 3 target behaviors from formerly existing undesirable behaviors (scooting and pulling up with support).
4. O'Brien, Azrin, & Bugle (1972)	Profound	Four profoundly retarded children were taught to walk by means of a restraint-for-crawling method (child held from behind so no forward movement was possible) and a priming-of-walking method (child raised to a standing position and allowed to walk in direction initiated by crawling).
5. Peterson & McIntosh (1973)	Mild to severe	Five retarded children were taught to approach, mount, and pedal a tricycle. An "automatic exercycle" which delivered cereal reinforcers first on FR schedules then FI schedules was used during initial training to build prerequisite level of strength. All training transferred to regular tricycles.

Response Differentiation: Findings With Retarded Populations

A perusal of the summaries of applied behavior research with retarded individuals (see tables 8.2, 8.3, and 8.5–8.10) illustrates the reliance of learning upon response shaping and the complimentary process of stimulus discrimination or stimulus shaping. In particular, research evidences repeated use of response priming as a means to evoke the response emission which is prerequisite to the shaping process. Additionally, successful response differentiation has been found to depend upon the identification of successive approximations leading to the targeted behavior. A classic example of these shaping characteristics with retarded individuals is evident in the work of Baer, Peterson, and Sherman (1965). In attempting to teach motor imitation to several severely retarded individuals, they found that repeated presentations of a model and a request to imitate ("Do this") resulted in no spontaneous imitation. There was no evidence that imitative responses were being emitted and shaping could not proceed. Therefore, a combination of response priming and shaping was employed to evoke an approximation of the imitated response which was then immediately reinforced. As the children began to emit those approximations more on their own, response primes were eliminated while shaping of successive approximations was continued. As new models were presented, responses were primed initially with concurrent shaping. During the process of the experiment a complex response class of generalized imitation was developed resulting in immediate imitations of untrained models and chains of imitative responses.

Task analysis, or the process to identify successive approximations leading to a more complex behavior, has been identified as a needed step in applied behavior analysis with retarded individuals (Azrin & Armstrong, 1973; Azrin & Foxx, 1971; Bricker, W., 1972; Crosson, 1969; Gold, 1972; Horner & Keilitz, 1975; O'Brien & Azrin, 1972). Horner and Keilitz (1975) observed videotapes of normal and retarded individuals to identify the steps in the chain of toothbrushing. Various levels of skill development in the retarded individuals were observed (those with poor, sufficient, and excellent toothbrushing skills) to further delineate approximate responses. Gold (1975), Smith, Smith, and Haring (1975), and Williams (1975)

detailed various methods of task analysis: method-content-process, modified latticing, vertical skill listing, and simple latticing. These procedures of "task slicing" have become particularly important in the shaping of behavioral repertoires in severely and profoundly retarded individuals in whom additional handicaps often complicate the learning process (Brown, Williams, & Crowner, 1974; Gold, 1972; Haring & Gentry, 1976).

Extinction is a process which necessarily operates in conjunction with shaping, i.e., early approximations are extinguished while the successive reinforced approximations increase in strength. If retarded individuals exhibit more resistance to extinction and if sex appears to be variable in this resistance (Thor, 1972), it is possible that retarded individuals, males in particular, will demonstrate a slower rate of response differentiation than normals due to an increased resistance to extinction. This hypothesis needs further attention.

The Development of "Superstitious Behaviors"

The important effect of "one-trial learning" or single reinforcements is well illustrated by the shaping process. While differential reinforcement leads predictably to produce new behavior, the phenomenon of "superstitious behavior" is the result of periodic delivery of reinforcers independent of the subject's behavior (response-independent schedule). Therefore, when an adventitious rather than an intentional contingency exists between the response and the presentation of a reinforcer, the behavior that develops is labeled *superstitious*. Both animals and humans are susceptible to noncontingent reinforcement. Skinner (1953) described the accumulated effect of several noncontingent reinforcements on the pigeon's behavior.

> Suppose we give a pigeon a small amount of food every fifteen seconds regardless of what it is doing. When food is first given, the pigeon will be behaving in some way—if only standing still—and conditioning will take place. It is then more probable that the same behavior will be in progress when food is given again. Eventually a given bit of behavior reaches a frequency at which it is often reinforced. It then becomes a permanent part of the repertoire of the bird, even though the food has been given by clock which is unrelated to the bird's behavior. The topography of the behavior may continue to drift with further reinforcements, since slight modification in the form of response may coincide with the receipt of food. (p. 85)

TABLE 8.7

Summaries of Studies on Language Acquisition of Early Language Skills

STUDY	LEVEL OF RETARDATION	ABSTRACT
6. Ausman & Gaddy (1974)	Severe	A 17-year-old girl demonstrating frequent echolalic behavior was taught to verbalize to questions appropriately 100% of the time with 31 of 32 responses in 75 days of training. Training consisted of an imitative prompt and fading procedure (Risley & Wolf, 1967)
7. Baer & Guess (1973)	Severe	Four adolescents were taught to use productive noun suffixes to label pictured stimuli exemplifying the verb form of an action or activity by converting verbs (e.g., *farms, waits*) to nouns by adding the *er* morpheme (e.g., *farmer, waiter*). Training procedures included shaping and imitative prompts, such as pointing to a picture and saying "This man farms. He is a . . ." so that the answer is modeled after a 10-sec delay. Approval and tokens were used to reinforce the subjects. A reversal procedure used to demonstrate experimental control resulted in temporary grammatical misuse of the *ist* morpheme in place of the *er* morpheme. A return to experimental conditions resulted in the generative reoccurrence of the correct noun-suffix response.
8. Bricker, D. (1972)	Severe	Twenty-six institutionalized adolescents with severely limited language skills were divided into experimental and control groups. The experimental group was a sequence of imitative-sign, sign-word, and sign-object training on the development of labels as discriminative stimuli for choice between objects. Training procedure included shaping, response prompting as needed, and fading of prompts. Probes involving a 2-choice discrimination test for all objects taught were given between training stages and before and after the study. The control group received only probe tests and no training. A reliable difference was found to favor the experimental group, which suggested that imitative sign training served to facilitate word-object association.
9. Frisch & Shumaker (1974)	Moderate, severe, and autistic	Three children were trained to discriminate 3 types of positional verbal requests to place objects "next to," "under", and "on top of" other objects by means of shaping and prompt-fade procedures. Training stages included instruction of one class of requests to criterion level of performance. Probes for generalization of the requests to untrained items were alternated with training. Results not only revealed that the children learned to follow prepositional instructions through reinforcement and shaping techniques but also showed that "as the children learned to respond to prepositional requests of one category, or learned a discrimination between categories, their responses to untrained requests of those categories became increasingly correct" (p. 619).
10. Garcia (1974)	Profound	Two "nonverbal" subjects were taught to make a chain of productive responses when shown pictures. Their responses were preceded by experimenter-provided SDs such that conversational units were formed; for example: Picture shown to subject. S: "What is that?" E: "This is a _____; what do you see?" S: "It's a _____." E: "Do you want the _____?" S: "Yes, I do." Three persons other than the trainer measured the use of each sentence in 3 settings different than the one in which training took place. In these settings 2 types of generalization sessions were used; general and intermix. In general sessions 10 new pictures were displayed and noncontingent reinforcement was given. In the intermix session 10 untrained pictures and 1 trained picture were displayed with intermittent reinforcement only provided for correct responses to the trained picture. Although both subjects did learn the 3-sentence conversational repertoire, little generalization to new trainers and settings occurred. The author concludes that speech training should include training by more than 1 individual in more than 1 setting.

Table 8.7 cont.

STUDY	LEVEL OF RETARDATION	ABSTRACT
11. Garcia, Guess & Byrnes (1973)	Severe	A 10-year-old girl who had motor and verbal imitation skills and little speech beyond single word labels was trained by reinforcement procedures to imitate a model's single declarative sentences, for example, "That is one hat." Probes, which were randomly intermixed with training trials, consisted of asking the child directly (e.g., "What do you see?") when a trained or new object was presented without a preceding response from the model. This "item in sentences" condition was followed by an "item alone" condition (i.e., model answered question with label only) and then the sentence condition was reinstated. Experimenters used a similar procedure to train plural items in a sentence, for example, "These are two hats." In *Exp. I* experimental imitation remained high while single sentence and single word labeling, and plural sentence and plural word labeling were brought under experimental control. Probe results revealed that control extended to labeling of items not preceded by a model and also never trained. In another experiment, 2 models were used with each modeling 1 of 2 forms (singular or plural declarative sentences) when a single object was presented. After both models responded the child was asked, "What do you see?" Contingent consequences were provided first for singular sentence imitation, then for plural sentence imitation, and then singular sentence again. Results showed that the child imitated the probe items using the same modeled sentence form that was reinforced during training trials.
12. Guess & Baer (1973)	Severe	Four "subjects" were taught generative pluralization rules concurrently in both the receptive and productive modalities of language" (p. 311). During receptive training, reinforcement was provided first for pointing responses made to objects labeled in the singular (when 1 exemplar and a pair of exemplars were available), then to the set of objects labeled in the plural, and finally to requests for singular and plural object sets which the subject was taught in a mixed order. Productive plural training followed a similar 3-stage training sequence. Plural endings (s and es words) and training baselines (receptive and productive) were alternated among 4 subjects so that all combinations were possible. The results revealed that an internally generative plural rule would generalize *within* 2 modalities (receptive-productive) but not *across* modalities when the rule was trained both receptively and productively using separate plural forms (s and es). That is, each subject learned the s or es plural ending in either the receptive or expressive modality and generalized the response to untrained instances in that modality, but generalization occurred only for 1 subject from the training modality to its nonreinforced modality with the same plural ending.
13. Lutzker & Sherman (1974)	Moderate (3) and normal (2)	Three institutionalized retarded persons (CAs of 6, 12, and 32) and 2 normal preschoolers (CAs = 2½) were taught to use descriptive sentences with correct subject-verb agreement in the presence of pictures depicting an activity, for example, "Girl(s) is (are) riding." Singular and plural subject-verb agreement sentences were taught. Imitative primes were used along with reinforcement procedures as the instructional methods. Multiple baselines measuring acquisition of each type of sentence were used for each subject and subjects were taught sentences in varying orders (e.g., S_1—*is* then are to criterion; S_2—*are* then *is* to criterion). Generalization probe pictures were presented following attainment of criterion to test responses to untrained pictures of the trained type (trained singular followed by probe with singular pictures) and to pictures involving the untrained type. During the probes, 4 subjects produced novel untrained sentences to generalization pictures when the particular type of sentence was currently being trained. However, only 1 subject produced correct sentences to both stimulus picture types (singular and plural) when only singular sentences had been taught. Retarded subjects tended to perform in a manner comparable to normals but needed more training to display the generative forms.

NOTE: The reader may refer to additional studies in the conditioning of:
1. Early language skills: Jeffrey (1972); MacCubrey (1971); Sailor (1971); Stremel (1972); Tawney (1974); Twardosz and Baer (1973).
2. More advanced language behaviors: Glass and Goldgraber (1974); Keilitz, Tucker, and Horner (1973); Locke and Gates (1971); Locke and Strayer (1971); Whitman, Burish, and Collins (1972).
3. Imitative skills: Bricker and Bricker (1972); By and Nawas (1972); Streifel and Phelan (1972).
Also Garcia and DeHaven (1974) provide an extensive review of the use of operant techniques to train language.

293

TABLE 8.8
Summaries of Studies on Functional Academic Skills

*Coin Discrimination and Counting Behavior**

STUDY	LEVEL OF RETARDATION	ABSTRACT
1. Bellamy & Buttars (1975)	Mild/moderate	Students were taught to count coins of varying amounts under a dollar and to use these skills in counting amounts indicated by price tags. Modeling and priming were used to correct errors; praise and points served as reinforcement.
2. Wunderlich (1972)	Mild/moderate	Programmed instruction was used to teach coin discrimination. Tasks increased in difficulty from match to sample to coin equivalences. The 8 subjects appeared to advance through most programs with few errors except for some difficulties in size discrimination between the nickel and quarter. Candy reinforcers were perhaps inappropriate for the age of the subjects (9–13).
Reading† 3. Dorry & Zeaman (1973)	Moderate to severe	Two groups of 9 adolescents were exposed to 1 list of 8 words under the conditions of fading or nonfading of picture cues. The fading procedure consisted of 4 exposures to the stimulus word and its picture while the picture was gradually faded from full contrast to barely visible. The word remained fully visible over the 4 trials. The nonfading procedure consisted of viewing the source word-picture slide 4 times. In each condition the child was noted by a "no" from the experimenter. After training, both groups were tested for their ability to read all 8 words without picture cues. Then both groups were trained on another 8-word list under the nonfading condition. The fading group learned significantly more words under both fading and nonfading training conditions, which was interpreted as evidence of a learning strategy transfer.
4. Dorry & Zeaman (1975)	Moderate to severe	Thirty-six adolescents were divided into 4 treatment groups: mixed, control, faded, and standard. The stimulus flash slides used in training the two 8-word lists varied across conditions. In the standard condition every slide showed the word (w) and a pictured representation (p); in the faded condition the first slide showed both w and p followed by 5 slides which faded out the picture to a barely visible level; in the control condition the 6 training trials for each word were alternated: p, w, p, w, p, w; and in the mixed condition the training trials' aspects of fading were involved: w-p, w, w-p, w, w-p, w. Training on each list proceeded as in Dorry and Zeaman's (1973) study and was followed by an immediate test on the words and two retention tests. The order of the study was as follows: train List 1, test on 1, train List 2, test on 2, retest on 1, retest on 2. Results revealed significant differences between conditions and immediate and delayed tests on each list. Those in the faded condition learned the most (mean of 5 words on immediate, 4.5 on delayed). The mixed condition was next highest (4.5 words; 3 words), followed by standard (2.5; 1.5) and control (1; .5).

NOTE: *The reader is referred to a series of studies applying operant principles to the instruction of math skills in slow learning and underachieving students: Curtiss and Lovitt (1968); Esveldt and Lovitt (1970); Ferritor, Buckholdt, Hamblin, and Smith (1972); Husazi and Husazi (1972); Kirby and Shields (1972); and to a related research: Hallahan and Kauffman (1976); Kauffman (1975).

†The reader is referred to additional studies (Brown, Huppler, Pierce, York, & Sontag, 1974; Rydberg, 1971) and to reviews of related research (Hallahan & Kauffman, 1976; Kauffman, 1975).

TABLE 8.9

Summaries of Studies on Vocational Skills

VOCATIONAL BEHAVIOR STUDY	LEVEL OF RETARDATION	ABSTRACT
1. Bateman (1975)	Severe	Ten adolescents working on an assembly task were systematically exposed to a token system and less preferred work. This opportunity resulted in a significant increase in the amount of time spent on less preferred activities. Also, when reinforcement schedule was slowly decreased (less time on preferred task), time spent on unpreferred task increased.
2. Crosson (1969)	Severe	Seven adults were taught two workshop tasks (drill press and an assembly task) which had first been task analyzed. Clients were taught the chains of responses by a process involving modeling, shaping, and stimulus discrimination training. All reached criterion in less than 3 hr. Retention tests at 2 mo revealed that of the 5 subjects who were tested, 99% of the discriminations were in tact and only 1 trial was needed to regain criterion. At 12 mo about 95% of the discriminations were in tact and 3 trials were needed to regain criterion.
3. Gold (1972)	Moderate Severe	Sixty-four retarded adults enrolled in sheltered workshops learned to assemble a complex 15-piece brake. The use of color-form cues in comparison to form cues was shown to facilitate number of trials to criterion. Overlearning training (20 trials beyond learning) did not affect transfer to a new task. Task analysis procedures and redundancy cues resulted in successful discrimination and retention of a complex assembly task.
4. Karen, Eisner, & Endres (1975)	Severe	Ten adolescents working on a nursery can task were systematically exposed to a token system and partitions to block the rest of the workshop from view. In general, work production increased and average error decreased with tokens, while average visual inattention and verbal prompts tended to decrease independently of the tokens.
5. Schroeder (1972)	Mild to severe	Eleven adults in an automated sheltered workshop with a token economy were placed on various reinforcement schedules while records were kept on their work rate. The first study showed that if amount of token reinforcement was held constant "work rates were positively related to reinforcement rates on FR schedules" (p. 431). Study II, which investigated the relationship between amount of torque needed to complete a work unit and frequency of ratio reinforcement, revealed that "work rates were positively related to reinforcement rates when required response force was high and negatively related to reinforcement rates when required response force was low" (p. 431). A third study showed that if reinforcement frequency was held constant, amount of reinforcement and work rate had an inverse relationship.

295

TABLE 8.10
Summaries of Studies to Modify Socially Undesirable and Desirable Behavior

REDUCTION OF UNDESIRABLE BEHAVIOR

STUDY	LEVEL OF RETARDATION	NO. OF Ss	BEHAVIOR REDUCED	CONSEQUENCE CONTINGENT ON DESIRABLE BEHAVIOR
1. Ausman, Ball, & Alexander (1974)	Severe	1	Pica; eating nonedible items	DRO with food. Consequence contingent on undesirable behavior: 15 min in time out helmet.
RESULTS: Pica eliminated in experimental setting and through generalization training. This control was extended to outdoor and ward settings.				
2. Edelson & Sprague (1974)	Mild	16	In-seat movement and out-of-seat behavior in a classroom setting	Mechanized stabilimetric seat cushions which were attached to blinker lights; pennies.
RESULTS: In-seat movement was brought under experimental control; however, there was little resistance to extinction.				
3. Flavell (1973)	Severe/Profound	3	Stereotype: repetitive movement of any part of the body	Positive reinforcement of toy play.
RESULTS: Stereotypes were reduced when toy play was reinforced.				
4. Foxx (1972)	Mild	1	Excessive eating	Social reinforcement and weekly trip to canteen contingent on loss of 1½ lbs.
RESULTS: Weight of subject dropped from 264 to 160 lbs.				
5. Greene & Pratt (1972)	Mild	65	Rudeness, talking out of turn, insulting others, obscenities, refusal to follow directions	Reward period of 30 min. Consequence contingent on undesirable behavior: one min lost from 30 min reward period for *all* in class and peer disapproval.
RESULTS: For all classes having a mean greater than 5 misbehaviors per student per day the misbehaviors were reduced with the punishment contingency.				
6. Lutzker (1974)	Profound	1	Self-exposure	DRO
RESULTS: Self-exposure was brought under experimental control and reduced to zero.				
7. Marks & Ball (1974)	Severe	1	Purposeful falling from a stool and a bed	Food, cake, praise and touch; rug (conditioned reinforcer).
RESULTS: Child was trained to remain on small rug which was then placed on a stool and bed; purposeful falling decreased near zero.				

Table 8.10 cont.

REDUCTION OF UNDESIRABLE BEHAVIOR

STUDY	LEVEL OF RETARDATION	NO. OF Ss	BEHAVIOR REDUCED	CONSEQUENCE CONTINGENT ON DESIRABLE BEHAVIOR
8. Martin, McDonald, & Omichinski (1971)	Profound	4	Slopping food, yelling at meals, playing with eating utensils	Social approval. Consequence contingent on undesirable behavior: time out for slopping.
RESULTS: Slopping was lower under time out than praise for nonslopping; most mis-behaviors maintained at low rate.				
9. Repp, Deitz, & Speir (1974)	Severe	3	Stereotypic behaviors (rocking, hand-waving, and lip-flapping)	DRO with hugs and praise. Consequence contingent on undesirable behavior: "No!"
RESULTS: Stereotypic behaviors reduced to zero in all 3 subjects.				
10. Weisberg, Passman, & Russell (1973)	Severe/Profound	2	Stereotypic behaviors of hand-flicking, hand-staring, swaying, etc.	Reinforcement given for following imitative commands (for behaviors incompatible with stereotypic behavior) and for following "Do not do this" commands (E modeled stereotypic behavior).
RESULTS: Stereotypic behaviors reduced to less than 10%.				

INCREASING DESIRABLE BEHAVIORS

STUDY	LEVEL OF RETARDATION	NO. OF Ss	BEHAVIOR REDUCED	CONSEQUENCE CONTINGENT ON DESIRABLE BEHAVIOR
11. Morris & Dolker (1974)	Severe	6	Cooperative play; rolling a ball to another child or experimenter and back	Candy and praise.
RESULTS: When experimenter-child dyads and dyads consisting of highly social children and low social children were used, ball rolling increased under the contingency and remained high during test trials.				
12. Nelson, Gibson, & Cutting (1973)	Mild	1	Smiling, use of grammatically correct questions, and speaking about appropriate topics	Social reinforcement.
RESULTS: Child was exposed to videotaped models and instructions to smile, ask appropriate questions, etc. All 3 target behaviors increased.				
13. Stokes, Baer, & Jackson (1974)	Profound	4	Waving (to greet another)	Candy, potato chips, smile or a pat, "Hello _____."
RESULTS: Subjects taught to wave and were then reinforced for all greeting waves. Waving to probe staff increased to 100%.				

TABLE 8.11
Description of Response Chains in Toothbrushing

1. *Pick up and hold the toothbrush*. The student should turn on the water and pick up the toothbrush by the handle.
2. *Wet the toothbrush*. The student should continue to hold the toothbrush, placing the bristles under the water for at least 5 sec. Then the student should turn off the running water and lay the toothbrush down.
3. *Remove the cap from the toothpaste*. The student should place the tube of toothpaste in his least preferred hand, unscrew the cap with the thumb and index finger of his preferred hand, and set the cap on the sink.
4. *Apply the toothpaste to the brush*. The student should pick up the toothbrush by the handle, hold the back part of the bristles against the opening of the toothpaste tube, squeeze the tube, move the tube toward the front bristles as toothpaste flows out on top of the bristles, and lay the toothbrush on the sink with the bristles up.
5. *Replace the cap on the toothpaste*. The student should pick up the toothpaste cap with the thumb and index finger of the preferred hand, screw the cap on the toothpaste tube, which is held in the least preferred hand, lay the tube of toothpaste down, and with the preferred hand pick up the toothbrush by the handle.
6. *Brush the outside surfaces of the teeth*. The student should brush the outside surfaces of the upper and lower teeth on both sides and in the center of the mouth, using either an up and down or back and forth motion, for at least 30 sec.
7. *Brush the biting surfaces of the teeth*. The student should brush the biting surfaces of the upper and lower teeth on both sides and in the center of the mouth, using a back and forth motion, for at least 30 sec.
8. *Brush the inside surfaces of the teeth*. The student should brush the inside surfaces of the upper and lower teeth on both sides and in the center of the mouth, using a back and forth motion, for at least 30 sec.
9. *Fill the cup with water*. The student should lay the toothbrush down, pick up the cup, place it under the faucet, turn on the water, fill the cup, and turn off the water.
10. *Rinse the mouth*. The student should spit out any excess toothpaste foam, take a sip of water, hold it in the mouth, swish it around in the mouth, and spit it out. If any toothpaste foam remains, the rinse should be repeated.
11. *Wipe the mouth*. The student should pull a tissue from the container (or pick up a hand towel) and dry his mouth.
12. *Rinse the toothbrush*. The student should pick up the toothbrush by the handle, turn on the water, and place the bristles under the running water until the bristles are free of toothpaste (any toothpaste not removed by the water may be dislodged by drawing the fingers across the bristles), turn off the water, and lay the toothbrush down.
13. *Rinse the sink*. The student should turn on the water, rub around the inside of the sink with the hand to wash any residue of toothpaste or toothpaste foam down the drain, then turn off the water.
14. *Put the equipment away*. The student should put the toothpaste and toothbrush in the proper storage place. (If a glass and hand towel are used, these should be placed in the proper place.)
15. *Discard the disposables*. Any used paper cups and tissues should be placed in a waste receptacle.

SOURCE: Adapted from "Training Mentally Retarded Adolescents to Brush Their Teeth" by R. D. Horner & I. Keilitz. *Journal of Applied Behavior Analysis*. 1975, *8*, p. 303. Copyright 1975 by the Society for the Experimental Analysis of Behavior. Reprinted by permission.

ing of response chains have also applied feedback on error responses occurring during the acquisition of eating (Azrin & Armstrong, 1973), dressing (Martin, Kehoe, Bird, Jensen, & Darbyshire, 1971), and walking chains (O'Brien, Azrin, & Bugle, 1972).

Deviant behaviors as well as adaptive behaviors may be learned as response chains. Zlutnick,

Mayville, and Moffat (1975) conceptualized seizures as the final link in a behavioral chain. With the assistance of parents they identified the pre-seizure behaviors (e.g., lowered activity levels or vacant staring followed by sudden flexion of arms and legs) of five children (three retarded, one emotionally disturbed, and one with learning problems) ranging in age from 4–17 years old. Following

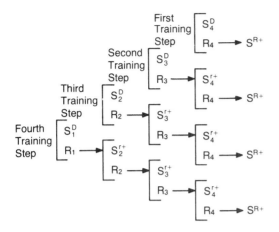

FIGURE 8.13

Reverse chaining: In each of the successive steps in the chaining of this hypothetical four component chain, the step actually being trained is indicated by the darker lettering and lines. Subsequent components, already learned by the subject, are indicated by light lettering and lines. In Step One the fourth and last component in the chain is trained first. The stimulus in the presence of which it will produce the primary reinforcer (S_4^D and S^{R+} respectively) is presented and that response trained until a specified criterion is obtained. The stimulus for the third component is then presented (S_3^D) and the third response is trained (R_3). Notice, however, that the completion of R_3 does *not* produce the primary reinforcer (S^{R+}), but rather the stimulus associated with the fourth component (S_4). Note also that S_4 has been re-labeled a conditioned reinforcer (S^{r+}) instead of a discriminative stimulus (S^D). Although S_4 will still retain its discriminative ability and "cue" the subject to emit the fourth response (which will result in the primary reinforcer), it has also gained secondary reinforcing ability via its association with the primary reinforcer during the first step. The "reinforcer" for learning the third component of the chain, therefore, is the opportunity to emit the fourth component and thereby receive the primary reinforcer. In the third training step the stimulus associated with the third component is relabeled a conditioned reinforcer and the reinforcement for learning that component is the opportunity to complete the chain. In the fourth and last step the same conditions apply.

SOURCE: Adapted from *A Glossary of Behavioral Terminology* by O. R. White. Champaign, Ill.: Research Press, 1971, p. 19. Copyright 1971 by Research Press. Reprinted by permission.

baseline conditions, an aversive consequence was used to interrupt the chain whenever the preseizure behaviors were observed. The interruption procedure consisted of grabbing the child, shouting "No!" and shaking him vigorously once. In four of the five cases some level of control was demonstrated and seizures were reduced or eliminated.

Response Priming

Skinner (1968) described response priming as the solution to the "problem of the first instance." That is, behavior must occur before it can be shaped and it is often inefficient to simply wait for this occurrence. Primes are stimuli which precede or accompany the response and act to elicit or evoke a response which is then reinforced. Priming alone does not result in learning: "learning does not occur because behavior has been primed; it occurs because behavior, primed or not is reinforced" (Skinner, 1968, p. 212). These priming stimuli may take any of the following forms:

1. Physically forcing the behavior to occur (e.g., holding the child's hand around a pencil and making the lead move to form letters).
2. Presenting stimuli which elicit (e.g., shock to elicit leg flexion) or evoke the response (e.g., waving a toy to evoke a baby's attending response).
3. Presenting models for imitation.
   a. Reinforcement of movement duplications:
      The teacher can use the imitative repertoire resulting from such contingencies, but he usually extends it, reinforcing a student when his behavior resembles that of a model, often the teacher himself. Parents set up an imitative repertoire when they teach a baby to wave or to clap hands and they later use it for purposes of instruction. (Skinner, 1968, p. 208)
   b. Reinforcement of product duplication (e.g., vocal imitation or copying a sketch in which the model's behavior may be only partially viewed or not viewed at all but the effects of the behavior are imitated).
4. Presenting preestablished, nonduplicative repertoires "in which neither the responses nor their products resemble controlling stimuli" (Skinner, 1968, p. 210). In this strategy, for example, a teacher may instruct a student verbally to behave in a specified way and then reinforces him for doing so.

In many cases primes need to be subtly faded or vanished to permit the behavior to come under the control of other stimuli (e.g., showing a child how to reproduce certain letters, instructing a child to look before crossing the street). Generally, this transfer of stimulus control does not occur in a single trial. In fact, if primes are abruptly omitted the learner resorts to guessing and errors will increase.

> In traditional face-to-face teaching we solve this problem by using only as much of a prime as is needed to evoke a response. In teaching a child to ask for or name an object, for example, a parent begins with a full prime: the name of the object is pronounced and the child echoes it. Later, the parent may supply only part of a prime: he may whisper or murmur the name or pronounce only the initial sound. These fragments would not suffice to evoke the response if other variables had not acquired some degree of control. A fragment of a prime has the special effect to which the term "prompt" has been applied. . . . The stimulus encourages a prompt appearance of behavior which already exists in some strength. To reduce the extent of a prompt is to "vanish" it. (Skinner, 1968, p. 214)

Therefore, when a priming or prompting stimulus (S_1^D) controlling the response is gradually changed to another stimulus (S_{10}^D), fading is said to have occurred. This subtle process may include the gradual substitution of the primes by various levels of prompts. Eventually, the artifically imposed stimuli $(S_1^D - S_9^D)$ are successively faded, thereby placing the behavior under the control of stimuli (S_{10}^D) which existed in the natural environment prior to the introduction of priming.

Applications to Retarded Populations

Response priming in the forms of physical guidance, modeling, and verbal instructions is a commonly used practice to evoke responses to be shaped in the mentally retarded such as imitation (Baer et al., 1965; Streifel & Phelan, 1972), simple self-care skills (Nelson, Cone, & Hanson, 1975; O'Brien & Azrin, 1972), complex discrimination tasks (Gold, 1972; Touchette, 1971), as well as a variety of academic tasks (Dorry & Zeaman, 1975). Horner and Keilitz's (1975) study, discussed in more detail in a previous section, included the use of a series of three primes $(S_1^D - S_3^D)$ to evoke correct responses which were successively faded until stimulus control (S_4^D) was under a simple request ("Brush your teeth") and situational stimuli (toothbrush, sink, etc.): S_1^D—equipment present, physical guidance and instruction; S_2^D—equipment present, demonstration and verbal instruction; S_3^D—equipment present, verbal instruction; S_4^D—equipment present, no help provided.

Nelson et al. (1975) compared modeling and physical guidance as priming strategies to teach correct utensil usage, such as eating, cutting, and spreading grips, as well as appropriate use of utensils with various foods. Physical guidance procedures were found to be superior to modeling for a number of reasons:

1. In comparison with the visual and auditory modeling condition in which the subject only observed the correct responses, more cues as to correct response were given in the physical guidance condition in which the subject evoked the correct response. Physical information included tactile, kinesthetic, proprioceptive, visual, and auditory guidance.
2. Consistent imitation of the model's responses was not prevalent.
3. The trainer's physical contact and proximity in the physical guidance condition may have been reinforcing to some subjects (which in some cases may have *delayed* their performance).

In a study designed to reduce the child's eating with his hands and teach spoon usage, O'Brien, Bugle and Azrin (1972) found that manual guidance alone was not sufficient to eliminate incorrect eating responses. Therefore, an interruption-extinction procedure was added to the manual guidance technique during which incorrect responses were stopped, hands emptied and cleaned, and the child's food removed briefly. With this combination (priming correct responses and mildly punishing incorrect responses) correct eating behavior was obtained. The behavior was maintained after the primes were faded by retaining the interruption-extinction procedure for incorrect responses (see Figure 8.14).

Two studies (Striefel & Wetherby, 1973; Whitman, Zakaras, & Chardos, 1971) demonstrated the successful use of priming instruction-following behavior with a combination of positive reinforcement and fading of physical guidance. Three lower functioning children were trained to follow commands such as "Sit down," "Pick up the cup," "Push the car," and "Raise your hand." Although some generalization was demonstrated to untrained behaviors in one study (Whitman et al., 1971), none was demonstrated in the Striefel and Wetherby study. This lack of generalization may have been due to a lower baseline level of receptive language as well as to the order of training which did not include single concept instruction (e.g., "Throw"), followed by generalization of the concept across instructions (e.g., "Throw ball," "Throw block").

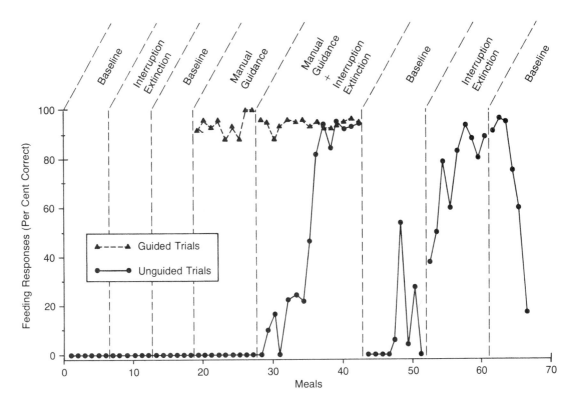

FIGURE 8.14

The percentage of correct feeding responses (using spoon rather than hands) for a 6-year-old profoundly retarded child during the five small training meals provided within a 6-hour period each day. Manual guidance procedures consisted of assisting the child through as much as the spoon-feeding response as needed. Interruption extinction was used to stop the child from completing an eating-with-hand response. The child's hands were stopped, emptied and cleaned, and the food was removed briefly.

SOURCE: Adapted from "Training and Maintaining a Retarded Child's Proper Eating" by F. O'Brien, C. Bugle, & N. H. Azrin. *Journal of Applied Behavior Analysis,* 1972, *5,* p. 70. Copyright by the Society for the Experimental Analysis of Behavior. Reprinted by permission.

Applied Behavior Analysis: Implications for Teaching

In his book, *The Technology of Teaching,* Skinner (1968) defined *teaching* as "the arrangement of contingencies of reinforcement under which students learn" (p. 64). His comments continue:

> They learn without teaching in their natural environments, but teachers arrange special contingencies which expediate learning, hastening the appearance of behavior which would otherwise be acquired slowly or making sure of the appearance of behavior which might otherwise never occur. (pp. 64–65)

Skinner's words have particular value for teachers of retarded individuals. Mildly retarded students often have experienced so much failure by the middle and secondary school levels that externally supplied reinforcement and programming for the achievement of schoolwork success become essential teaching strategies. With the lower functioning retarded the realization of normal developmental milestones are so gradual it becomes mandatory to analyze and shape the sequences of transitional behaviors between the milestones.

As a compliment to this view of teaching, Bijou (1966) suggests that the concept of mental retardation *not* be viewed as an internally caused symptom but rather as definable stimulus-response relationships between observable variables (social, physical, biological) and individuals with limited repertoires of behavior. Retardation therefore is a result of unplanned or poorly planned contingencies. Teaching techniques for individuals exhibiting retarded behavior would be consistent with applied behavior analysis.

There are three basic components of *applied behavioral analysis* which precede this effective arrangement of contingencies to expedite the shaping of new behavior. These include: (a) the direct observation of the individual's behavior, (b) continuous measurement of that behavior, and (c) systematic environmental changes consistent with the relevant principles of behavior. Such an outline is deceptive by its simplicity, but the procedural steps within each component are complex. Since it is beyond the scope of this chapter to detail the procedures of applied behavior analysis and behavior modification, the reader is referred to a partial list of resources available on this topic: Bijou and Ribes-Inesta, 1972; Browning and Stover, 1971; Cartwright and Cartwright, 1974; Cooper, 1974; Gardner, 1968; Hall, 1971; Hall, Hawkins, and Axelrod, 1975; Hallahan and Kauffman, 1976; Haring and Phillips, 1972; Haring and Schiefelbusch, 1976; Kauffman, 1975; Keller and Ribes-Inesta, 1974; Neisworth and Smith, 1973; Reith and Hall, 1974; Worell and Nelson, 1974.

Direct Observation of the Behavior

The direct observation or measurement of the individual's behavior proceeds through a sequence of steps:

1. Clearly describe the targeted behavior in observable terms.
2. Identify the parameters of the behavior which will be observed, such as continuous duration or frequency in a period of time, sampled duration and frequency.
3. Specify the conditions for observation which will yield accurate measurement of the target behavior such as measurement of time, place, and length of observation.
4. Select a corresponding procedure for measurement.
5. Specify the means to record ongoing behavioral data which may include the construction of a data recording form.
6. Without changing the situational variables (antecedent and consequent to the behavior) observe for the purpose of collecting baseline data.
7. Compute inter-observer reliability by comparing data independently and concurrently collected in the same manner on the same behavior by another individual. If agreement is better than 80%, continue into the next

component, but if it is less than 80% return to the first step.
8. Repeat baseline measurement procedure over several days until a stable baseline estimate is obtained. During this component of the applied behavior analysis an accurate baseline measurement or series of preintervention measurements is obtained.

Actual procedures for behavioral measurement generally are of two main classes: direct observation of behavior and the measurement of products resulting from the behavior (Cooper, 1974; Hall, 1971; Hall, Hawkins, & Axelrod, 1975; Kauffman, 1975). Direct measurement procedures include a wide range of specific types: continuous, event or frequency, duration, interval, and time sampling. The selection of measurement procedure is influenced by a variety of factors. For example, when measurement occurs in a classroom setting, the student-teacher ratio may determine which procedure can be used since some are more time consuming than others. At times the assistance of an aide or student may be employed to facilitate the measurement process. If the behavior is visible (e.g., hitting others) and not of low frequency, a noncontinuous method such as time sampling or interval recording may be most easily applied. Resolution of behavior measurement problems is a necessary, though time-consuming, initial step in applied behavior analysis. Therefore, it is during this first component "in an analysis of behavior that the independent (environmental) variables and the dependent (behavioral) variables are carefully defined and their relationship is established" (Haring & Phillips, 1972, p. 40).

Continuous Measurement

During the remainder of the behavior analysis "new independent variables are introduced under carefully controlled conditions, and their effect on the dependent variables is determined on the basis of changes in the rate of response" (Haring & Phillips, 1972, p. 40). In this process the second and third components are implemented concurrently so that measurement occurs during every environmental change and during any reversals to baseline conditions made for the purpose of demonstrating experimental control. Additionally, experimental control may be demonstrated with other single subject designs such as multiple baselines (i.e., for different individuals, different behaviors in the same individual, or the same behavior in different settings) and changing criterion design (Baer, Wolf, & Risley, 1968; Bijou, Peterson, Harris, Allen, & Johnson, 1969; Browning & Stover, 1971; Cooper, 1974; Kauffman, 1975).

Relevant Principles of Behavior

Underpinning any applied behavior analysis are the relevant principles of behavior—an understanding which allows the successful arrangement of contingencies to modify a target behavior in a predictable direction. A brief summary of these previously described principles follows.

1. *A behavior must be emitted before it can be modified by changes in environmental conditions.*

   For retarded populations a "limited repertoire of behavior" is a frequent occurrence (Bijou, 1966). Response primes of various types (modeling, manual guidance, verbal direction cues) have served to resolve this "problem of the first occurrence." Fading of response primes is a gradual process which must occur so that the response comes under the control of the relevant stimuli.

2. *A behavior may be strengthened through immediate and carefully scheduled reinforcement.*

   Ratio schedules and fixed interval schedules have had the most frequent application to retarded individuals. As with populations of normal individuals, a low or continuous schedule is needed initially to increase a low baseline response strength. As response strength increases, gradual schedule "thinning" should take place. This procedure not only increases the resistance of a response during extinction but also facilitates the maintenance of a response.

3. *The procedure of fading—the gradual withdrawal of "artificially imposed" stimulus support—must be applied following acquisition of a behavior.*

   Since traditional discrimination learning procedures may not result in discriminated responses or may yield slower rates of learning with retarded individuals, stimuli introduced early in learning to aid attention, to help the discrimination of stimulus (errorless discrimination programs), and to prime a low frequency or nonexistent behavior must be withdrawn. This fading process is carried out in a gradual manner to decrease the probability of response extinction and the development of error response patterns which are incompatible to the development of appropriate stimulus control.

4. *Contingent reinforcement rather than punishment should be regarded as the primary means for modifying behavior in predictable ways.*

   Although for the most part this principle is true with normal as well as retarded individuals, some evidence to the contrary exists for institutionalized retarded persons. In a number of studies, punishment alone or in combination with reinforcement of other behaviors has been demonstrated as being the more effective means to eliminate such undesirable behaviors as self-destruction, aggression towards others, and stereotypes when compared to positive reinforcement and extinction. Often the individuals involved in these studies have histories of institutionalization, demonstrate minimal repertoires of appropriate behavior, and are functioning in the severe and profound ranges of retardation with or without an overlay of disturbances in emotional behavior.

5. *Response differentiation is facilitated when shaping proceeds through a sequence of small, graduated gains to the eventual achievement of a more complex behavioral repertoire.*

   The wide application of task analysis procedures in successful operant conditioning studies with retarded populations supports the notion that shaping proceeds sequentially through small steps.

6. *Continuous measurement of the target behavior serves to regulate the pace and direction of learning* (e.g., fading reinforcement schedules, introducing and fading response primes or changes in the controlling stimuli, and the elimination and addition of independent variables consequent and antecedent to the behavior).

Summary

The system of operant conditioning has been described in a necessarily condensed manner. The basic components described included: operant versus respondent behavior, operant reinforcement, conditioned reinforcement, operant extinction, punishment, schedules of reinforcement, stimulus discrimination, response differentiation, noncontingent reinforcement, response chaining, and response priming. The immense volume of research relating these components to retarded populations was sampled for the purpose of identifying the legitimate applications of operant conditioning with this group. Finally, the methodology involved in applied behavior analysis was outlined.

References

Abramson, E. E., & Wunderlich, R. A. Dental hygiene training for retardates: An application of behavioral technique. *Mental Retardation*, 1972, *10*(3), 6–8.

Angney, A. *Establishing walking responses in a twenty-month old child by a parent trained in behavioral analysis*, 1970. (ERIC Document Reproduction Service No. ED 102 784)

Ausman, J., Ball, T. S., & Alexander, D. Behavior therapy of pica with a profoundly retarded adolescent. *Mental Retardation*, 1974, *12*(6), 16–18.

Ausman, J. O., & Gaddy, M. R. Reinforcement training for echolalia: Developing a repertoire of appropriate verbal responses in an echolalic girl. *Mental Retardation*, 1974, *12*(1), 20–21.

Ayllon, T., & Azrin, N. H. Reinforcer sampling: A technique for increasing the behavior of mental patients. *Journal of Applied Behavior Analysis*, 1968, *1*, 13–20. (a)

Ayllon, T., & Azrin, N. H. *The token economy: A motivational system for therapy and rehabilitation*. New York: Appleton-Century-Crofts, 1968. (b)

Ayllon, T., & Kelly, K. Effects of reinforcement on standardized test performance. *Journal of Applied Behavior Analysis*, 1972, *5*, 477–484.

Azrin, N. H., & Armstrong, P. M. The "mini-meal"—A method for teaching eating skills to the profoundly retarded. *Mental Retardation*, 1973, *11*(1), 9–13.

Azrin, N. H., & Foxx, R. M. A rapid method of toilet training the institutionalized retarded. *Journal of Applied Behavior Analysis*, 1971, *4*, 89–99.

Azrin, N. H., & Holz, W. C. Punishment. In W. K. Honig (Ed.), *Operant behavior: Areas of research and application*. New York: Appleton-Century-Crofts, 1966.

Azrin, N. H., & Wesolowski, M. D. Theft reversal: An overcorrection procedure for eliminating stealing by retarded persons. *Journal of Applied Behavior Analysis*, 1974, *7*, 577–581.

Baer, D. M., & Guess, D. Teaching productive noun suffixes to severely retarded children. *American Journal of Mental Deficiency*, 1973, *77*, 498–505.

Baer, D. M., Peterson, R. F., & Sherman, J. A. *Building an imitative repertoire by programming similarity between child and model as discriminative for reinforcement*. Paper presented at the biennial meeting of the Society for Research in Child Development, Minneapolis, Minn., March 1965.

Baer, D. M., Wolf, M. M., & Risley, T. R. Some current dimensions of applied behavior analysis. *Journal of Applied Behavior Analysis*, 1968, *1*, 91–97.

Bailey, J., & Meyerson, L. Vibration as a reinforcer with a profoundly retarded child. *Journal of Applied Behavior Analysis*, 1969, *2*, 135–137.

Baker, J. G., Stanish, B., & Fraser, B. Comparative effects of a token economy in nursery school. *Mental Retardation*, 1972, *10*(4), 16–19.

Ball, T. S., Seric, K., & Payne, L. E. Long-term retention of self-help skill training in the profoundly retarded. *American Journal of Mental Deficiency*, 1971, *76*, 378–382.

Bandura, A. *Principles of behavior modification*. New York: Holt, Rinehart, & Winston, 1969.

Bandura, A., & Barub, P. G. Conditions governing nonreinforced imitation. *Developmental Psychology*, 1971, *5*, 244–255.

Barton, E. S., Guess, D., Garcia, E., & Baer, D. M. Improvement of retardates' mealtime behaviors by timeout procedures using multiple baseline techniques. *Journal of Applied Behavior Analysis*, 1970, *3*, 77–84.

Bateman, S. Application of Premack's generalization on reinforcement to modify occupational behavior in two severely retarded individuals. *American Journal of Mental Deficiency*, 1975, *79*, 604–610.

Bath, K. E., & Smith, S. A. An effective token economy program for MR adults. *Mental Retardation*, 1974, *12*(4), 41–45.

Baumeister, A. A., & Forehand, R. Stereotyped acts. In N. R. Ellis (Ed.), *International review of research in mental retardation* (Vol. 6). New York: Academic Press, 1973.

Baumeister, A. A., & Hawkins, W. F. Extinction and disinhibition as a function of reinforcement schedule with severely retarded children. *Journal of Experimental Child Psychology*, 1966, *3*, 343–347.

Becker, W. C., Engelmann, S., & Thomas, D. R. *Teaching: A course in applied psychology*. Chicago: Science Research Associates, 1971.

Bellamy, T., & Buttars, K. L. Teaching trainable level retarded students to count money: Toward personal independence through academic instruction. *Education and Training of the Mentally Retarded*, 1975, *10*, 18–26.

Bijou, S. W. A functional analysis of retarded development. In N. R. Ellis (Ed.), *International review of research in mental retardation* (Vol. 1). New York: Academic Press, 1966.

Bijou, S. W. Behavior modification in the retarded: Application of operant conditioning principles. *Pediatric Clinics of North America*, 1968, *15*, 969–987.

Bijou, S. W., & Baer, D. M. Operant methods in child behavior and development. In W. K. Honig (Ed.), *Operant behavior: Areas of research and application*. New York: Appleton-Century-Crofts, 1966.

Bijou, S. W., & Orlando, R. Rapid development of multiple-schedule performances with retarded children. *Journal of the Experimental Analysis of Behavior*, 1961, *4*, 7–16.

Bijou, S. W., Peterson, R. F., Harris, F. R., Allen, K. E., & Johnson, M. S. Methodology for experimental studies of young children in natural setting. *Psychological Record*, 1969, *19*, 177–210.

Bijou, S. W., & Ribes-Inesta, E. (Eds.) *Behavior modification, issues, and extensions*. New York: Academic Press, 1972.

Bijou, S. W., & Sturges, P. T. Positive reinforcers for experimental studies with children—consumables and manipulatables. *Child Development*, 1958, *30*, 151–170.

Birnbrauer, J. S. Mental retardation. In H. Leitenberg (Ed.), *Handbook of behavior modification*. New York: Appleton-Century-Crofts, forthcoming.

Block, J. D. Operant conditioning. In J. Wortis (Ed.), *Mental retardation* (Vol. 3). New York: Grune & Stratton, 1971.

Bricker, D. D. Imitative sign training as a facilitator of word-object association with low-functioning children. *American Journal of Mental Deficiency*, 1972, *76*, 509–516.

Bricker, D. D., & Bricker, W. A. A programmed approach to operant audiometry for low-functioning children. *Journal of Speech and Hearing Disorders*, 1969, *34*, 312–320.

Bricker, D. D., Bricker, W. A., & Larsen, L. A. *Operant audiometry manual for difficult-to-test children*. Nashville, Tenn.: Institute on Mental Retardation and Intellectual Development, 1968.

Bricker, W. A. A systematic approach to language training. In R. L. Schiefelbusch (Ed.), *Language of the mentally retarded*. Baltimore: University Park Press, 1972.

Bricker, W. A., & Bricker, D. D. Four operant procedures for establishing auditory stimulus control with low-functioning children. *American Journal of Mental Deficiency*, 1969, *73*, 981–987.

Bricker, W. A., & Bricker, D. D. Assessment and modification of verbal imitation with low-functioning retarded children. *Journal of Speech and Hearing Research*, 1972, *15*, 690–698.

Brown, L., Huppler, B., Pierce, L., York, B., & Sontag, E. Teaching trainable-level students to *read* unconjugated action verbs. *Journal of Special Education*, 1974, *8*, 51–56.

Brown, L., Williams, W., & Crowner, T. *A collection of papers and programs related to public school services for severely handicapped students* (Vol. 4). Unpublished manuscript, University of Wisconsin, 1974.

Browning, R. M., & Stover, D. O. *Behavior modification in child treatment*. Chicago: Aldine-Atherton, 1971.

Bry, P. M., & Nawas, M. M. Is reinforcement necessary for the development of a generalized imitation operant in severely and profoundly retarded children? *American Journal of Mental Deficiency*, 1972, *76*, 658–667.

Burchard, J. D., & Barrera, F. An analysis of timeout and response cost in a programmed environment. *Journal of Applied Behavior Analysis*, 1972, *5*, 271–282.

Byck, M. Cognitive differences among diagnostic groups of retardates. *American Journal of Mental Deficiency*, 1968, *73*, 97–101.

Cairns, R. B., & Paris, S. G. Informational determinants of social reinforcement effectiveness among retarded children. *American Journal of Mental Deficiency*, 1971, *76*, 363–369.

Calhoun, K. S., & Matherne, P. The effects of varying schedules of time-out on aggressive behavior of a retarded girl. *Journal of Behavior Therapy and Experimental Psychiatry*, 1975, *6*, 139–143.

Cartwright, C. A., & Cartwright, G. P. *Developing observational skills*. New York: McGraw-Hill, 1974.

Cautela, F. R., & Baron, M. G. Multifaceted behavior therapy of self-injurious behavior. *Journal of Behavior Therapy and Experimental Psychiatry*, 1973, *4*, 125–131.

Clark, H. B., Rowbury, T., Baer, A. M., & Baer, D. M. Timeout as a punishing stimulus in continuous and intermittent schedules. *Journal of Applied Behavior Analysis*, 1973, *6*, 443–455.

Cooper, J. O. *Measurement and analysis of behavioral techniques*. Columbus, Ohio: Charles E. Merrill, 1974.

Corte, H. E., Wolf, M. M., & Locke, B. J. A comparison of procedures for eliminating self-injurious behavior of retarded adolescents. *Journal of Applied Behavior Analysis*, 1971, *4*, 201–213.

Crosson, J. E. A technique for programming sheltered workshop environments for training severely retarded workers. *American Journal of Mental Deficiency*, 1969, *73*, 814–818.

Curtiss, K. A., & Lovitt, T. C. Effects of manipulating an antecedent event on mathematics response rate. *Journal of Applied Behavior Analysis*, 1968, *1*, 329–333.

Dalton, A. J., Rubino, C. A., & Hislop, M. W. Some effects of token rewards on school achievement of children with Down's syndrome. *Journal of Applied Behavior Analysis*, 1973, *6*, 251–259.

Denny, M. R. Research in learning and performance. In H. A. Stevens & R. Heber (Eds.), *Mental retardation*. Chicago: University of Chicago, 1964.

Dorry, G. W., & Zeaman, D. The use of a fading technique in paired-associate teaching of a reading vocabulary with retardates. *Mental Retardation*, 1973, *11*(6), 3–6.

Dorry, G. W., & Zeaman, D. Teaching a simple reading vocabulary to retarded children: Effectiveness of fading and nonfading procedures. *American Journal of Mental Deficiency*, 1975, *79*, 711–716.

Edelson, R. I., & Sprague, R. L. Conditioning of activity level in a classroom with institutionalized retarded boys. *American Journal of Mental Deficiency*, 1974, *78*, 384–388.

Ellis, N. R. Amount of reward and operant behavior in mental defectives. *American Journal of Mental Deficiency*, 1962, *66*, 595–599.

Ellis, N. R., Barnett, C. D., & Pryer, M. W. Operant behavior in mental defectives: Exploratory studies. *Journal of Experimental Analysis of Behavior*, 1960, *3*, 63–69.

Estes, W. K. An experimental study of punishment. *Psychological Monographs*, 1944, *54* (263).

Estes, W. K. *Learning theory and mental development*. New York: Academic Press, 1970.

Esveldt, K. A., & Lovitt, T. C. The relative effects on math performance of single- versus multiple-ratio schedules: A case study. *Journal of Applied Behavior Analysis*, 1970, *3*, 261–270.

Ferritor, D. E., Buckholdt, D., Hamblin, R. L., & Smith, L. The noneffects of contingent reinforcement for attending behavior on work accomplished. *Journal of Applied Behavior Analysis*, 1972, *5*, 7–17.

Ferster, C. B., & Perrott, M. C. *Behavior principles*. New York: New Century, 1968.

Ferster, C. B., & Skinner, B. F. *Schedules of reinforcement*. New York: Appleton-Century-Crofts, 1957.

Flavell, J. E. Reduction of stereotypes by reinforcement of toy play. *Mental Retardation*, 1973, *11*(4), 21–23.

Foxx, R. M. Social reinforcement of weight reduction: A case report on an obese retarded adolescent. *Mental Retardation*, 1972, *10*(4), 21–23.

Foxx, R. M., & Azrin, N. H. Restitution: A method of eliminating aggressive-disruptive behavior of retarded and brain damaged patients. *Behavior Research and Therapy*, 1972, *10*, 15–27.

Foxx, R. M., & Azrin, N. H. The elimination of autistic self-stimulatory behavior by overcorrection. *Journal of Applied Behavior Analysis*, 1973, *6*, 1–14.

Freeman, B. J., Leibowitz, J. M., & Linseman, M. A. A study of an operant procedure: Testing auditory deficits. *Mental Retardation*, 1974, *12*(2), 14–17.

Frisch, S. A., & Schumaker, J. B. Training generalized receptive prepositions in retarded children. *Journal of Applied Behavior Analysis*, 1974, *7*, 611–621.

Garcia, E. The training and generalization of a conversational speech form in nonverbal retardates. *Journal of Applied Behavior Analysis*, 1974, *7*, 137–149.

Garcia, E. E., & DeHaven, E. D. Use of operant techniques in the establishment and generalization of language: Review and analysis. *American Journal of Mental Deficiency*, 1974, *79*, 169–178.

Garcia, E., Guess, D., & Byrnes, J. Development of syntax in a retarded girl using procedures of imitation, reinforcement, and modelling. *Journal of Applied Behavior Analysis*, 1973, *6*, 299–310.

Gardner, J. M. Behavior modification research in mental retardation: Search for an adequate paradigm. *American Journal of Mental Deficiency*, 1968, *73*, 844–851.

Gardner, J. M., & Watson, L. S., Jr. Behavior modification of the mentally retarded: An annotated bibliography. *Mental Retardation Abstracts*, 1969, *62*, 181–193.

Gardner, W. I. The use of punishment procedures with the severely retarded: A review. *American Journal of Mental Deficiency*, 1969, *74*, 86–103.

Gardner, W. I. *Behavior modification in mental retardation*. Chicago: Aldine/Atherton, 1971.

Glass, R. M., & Goldgraber, J. Enhancing group discussion skills of educable children: A case study. *Exceptional Children*, 1974, *40*, 289–291.

Gold, M. W. Stimulus factors in skill training of the retarded on a complex assembly task: Acquisition, transfer, and retention. *American Journal of Mental Deficiency*, 1972, *76*, 517–526.

Gold, M. W. *Task analysis: A statement and an example using acquisition and production of a complex assembly task by the retarded blind*. Unpublished manuscript, University of Illinois at Urbana-Champaign, 1975.

Greene, R. J., & Pratt, J. J. A group contingency for individual misbehaviors in the classroom. *Mental Retardation*, 1972, *10*(3), 33–35.

Groves, I. D., & Carroccio, D. F. A self-feeding program for the severely and profoundly retarded. *Mental Retardation*, 1971, *9*(3), 10–12.

Guess, D., & Baer, D. M. An analysis of individual differences in generalization between receptive and productive language in retarded children. *Journal of Applied Behavior Analysis*, 1973, *6*, 311–329.

Hall, R. V. *Managing behavior*. Part I. *Behavior modification: The measurement of behavior*. Lawrence, Kansas: H & H Enterprises, 1971.

Hall, R. V., Hawkins, R. P., & Axelrod, S. Measuring and recording student behavior: A behavior analysis approach. In R. A. Weinberg & F. H. Wood (Eds.), *Observation of pupils and teachers in mainstream and special education settings: Alternate strategies*. Minneapolis, Minn.: Leadership Training Institute, University of Minnesota, 1975.

Hallahan, D. P., & Kauffman, J. M. *Introduction to learning disabilities: A psycho-behavioral approach*. Englewood Cliffs, N.J.: Prentice-Hall, 1976.

Haring, N. G., & Gentry, N. D. Direct and individualized instructional procedures. In N. G. Haring & R. L. Schiefelbusch (Eds.), *Teaching special children*. New York: McGraw-Hill, 1976.

Haring, N. G., & Phillips, E. L. *Analysis and modification of classroom behavior*. Englewood Cliffs, N.J.: Prentice-Hall, 1972.

Haring, N. G., & Schiefelbusch, R. L. (Eds.) *Teaching special children*. New York: McGraw-Hill, 1976.

Headrick, M. W. Effects of instructions and initial reinforcement on fixed interval behavior in retardates. *American Journal of Mental Deficiency*, 1963, *68*, 425–432.

Hewett, F. M. *The emotionally disturbed child in the classroom*. Boston: Allyn & Bacon, 1968.

Hilgard, E. R., & Bower, G. H. *Theories of learning* (3rd ed.). New York: Appleton-Century-Crofts, 1966.

Hilgard, E. R., & Bower, G. H. *Theories of learning* (4th ed.). Englewood Cliffs, N.J.: Prentice-Hall, 1975.

Hislop, M. W., Moore, C., & Stanish, B. Remedial classroom programming: Long-term transfer effects from a token economy system. *Mental Retardation*, 1973, *11*(2), 18–20.

Holland, J. G., & Skinner, B. F. *The analysis of behavior: A program for self-instruction*. New York: McGraw-Hill, 1961.

Hollis, J. H. Effects of reinforcement shifts on bent wire performance of severely retarded children. *American Journal of Mental Deficiency*, 1965, *69*, 531–535.

Hollis, J. H. "Superstition": The effects of independent and contingent events on free operant responses in retarded children. *American Journal of Mental Deficiency*, 1973, *77*, 585–596.

Honig, W. K. (Ed.). *Operant behavior: Areas of research and application*. New York: Appleton-Century-Crofts, 1966.

Horner, R. D. Establishing use of crutches by a mentally retarded *spina bifida* child. *Journal of Applied Behavior Analysis*, 1971, *4*, 183–189.

Horner, R. D., & Keilitz, I. Training mentally retarded adolescents to brush their teeth. *Journal of Applied Behavior Analysis*, 1975, *8*, 301–319.

Husazi, J. E., & Husazi, S. E. Effects of teacher attention on digit-reversal behavior in an elementary school child. *Journal of Applied Behavior Analysis*, 1972, *5*, 157–162.

Iwata, B. A., & Bailey, J. S. Reward *versus* cost token systems: An analysis of the effects on students and teacher. *Journal of Applied Behavior Analysis*, 1974, *7*, 567–576.

Jeffrey, B. D. Increase and maintenance of verbal behavior of a mentally retarded child. *Mental Retardation*, 1972, *10*(2), 35–40.

Jones, F. H., Simmons, J. Q., & Frankel, F. An extinction procedure for eliminating self-destructive behavior in a 9-year-old autistic girl. *Journal of Autism and Childhood Schizophrenia*, 1974, *4*, 241–249.

Karen, R. L., Eisner, M., & Endres, R. W. Behavior modification in a sheltered workshop for severely retarded students. *American Journal of Mental Deficiency*, 1975, *79*, 338–347.

Kauffman, J. M. Behavior modification. In W. M. Cruickshank & D. P. Hallahan (Eds.), *Perceptual and learning disabilities in children* (Vol. 2). *Research and theory*. Syracuse: Syracuse University Press, 1975.

Kazdin, A. E. The effect of vicarious reinforcement on attentive behavior in the classroom. *Journal of Applied Behavior Analysis*, 1973, *6*, 71–78.

Kazdin, A. E., & Bootzin, R. R. The token economy: An evaluative review. *Journal of Applied Behavior Analysis*, 1972, *5*, 343–372.

Keilitz, I., Tucker, D. J., & Horner, R. D. Increasing mentally retarded adolescents' verbalizations about current events. *Journal of Applied Behavior Analysis*, 1973, *6*, 621–630.

Keller, F. S., & Ribes-Inesta, E. (Eds.) *Behavior modification: Applications to education*. New York: Academic Press, 1974.

Keller, F. S., & Schoenfeld, W. N. *Principles of psychology*. New York: Appleton-Century-Crofts, 1950.

Kirby, F. D., & Shields, F. Modification of arithmetic response rate and attending behavior in a seventh-grade student. *Journal of Applied Behavior Analysis*, 1972, *5*, 79–84.

Knapczyk, D. R., & Livingston, G. Self-recording and student teacher supervision: Variables within a token economy structure. *Journal of Applied Behavior Analysis*, 1973, *6*, 481–486.

Krumboltz, J. D., & Krumboltz, H. B. *Changing children's behavior*. Englewood Cliffs, N.J.: Prentice-Hall, 1972.

Kuypers, D. S., Becker, W. C., & O'Leary, K. D. How to make a token system fail. *Exceptional Children*, 1968, *35*, 101–108.

Lahey, B. B., McNees, M. P., & McNees, M. C. Control of an obscene "verbal tic" through timeout in an elementary school classroom. *Journal of Applied Behavior Analysis*, 1973, *6*, 101–104.

Levin, G. R., & Simmons, J. J. Response to praise by emotionally disturbed boys. *Psychological Reports*, 1962, *11*, 10.

Lipman, R. S. Learning: Verbal, perceptual motor, and classical conditioning. In N. R. Ellis (Ed.), *Handbook of mental deficiency: Psychological theory and research*. New York: McGraw-Hill, 1963.

Locke, B. J. Verbal conditioning with the retarded: Reinforcer, sex of subject, and stimulus pacing. *American Journal of Mental Deficiency*, 1969, *75*, 616–620.

Locke, B. J., & Gates, J. J. Verbal conditioning with retarded subjects: Experimental control of vocal duration in dyadic assemblies. *American Journal of Mental Deficiency*, 1971, *76*, 53–59.

Locke, B. J., & Strayer, D. W. Experimental modification of vocalization rate among retarded participants in three-person conversations. *American Journal of Mental Deficiency*, 1971, *76*, 101–109.

Lovaas, O. I., & Simmons, J. Q. Manipulation of self-destruction in three retarded children. *Journal of Applied Behavior Analysis*, 1969, *2*, 143–157.

Lutzker, J. R. Social reinforcement control of exhibitionism in a profoundly retarded adult. *Mental Retardation*, 1974, *12*(5), 46–47.

Lutzker, J. R., & Sherman, J. A. Producing generative sentence usage by imitation and reinforcement procedures. *Journal of Applied Behavior Analysis*, 1974, *7*, 447–460.

MacCubrey, J. Verbal operant conditioning with young institutionalized Down's syndrome children. *American Journal of Mental Deficiency*, 1971, *75*, 696–701.

MacMillan, D. L. *Behavior modification: A teacher strategy to control behavior*. Report of the Proceedings of the Forty-fourth Meeting of the Convention of American Instructors of the Deaf, Berkeley, California, 1968.

MacMillan, D. L. *Ground rules for behavior modification*. Paper presented at the Annual Meeting of the American Association on Mental Deficiency, Washington, D.C., May 1970.

MacMillan, D. L. *Behavior modification in education*. New York: MacMillan, 1973.

MacMillan, D. L., & Forness, S. R. Behavior modification: Limitations and liabilities. *Exceptional Children*, 1970, *37*, 291–297.

MacMillan, D. L., & Forness, S. R. Behavior modification: Savior or savant? In R. K. Eyman, C. E. Meyers, & G. Tarjan (Eds.), *Socio-behavioral studies in mental retardation*. Washington, D.C.: American Association on Mental Deficiency, 1973.

MacMillan, D. L., Forness, S. R., & Trumbull, B. M. The role of punishment in the classroom. *Exceptional Children*, 1973, *40*, 85–96.

Mahoney, K., Van Wagenen, R. K., & Meyerson, L. Toilet training of normal and retarded children. *Journal of Applied Behavior Analysis,* 1971, *4,* 173–181.

Marks, R., & Ball, T. S. Hazardous voluntary falling: A treatment approach. *Mental Retardation,* 1974, *12*(5), 36–39.

Martin, G. L., Kehoe, B., Bird, E., Jensen, V., & Darbyshire, M. Operant conditioning in dressing behavior of severely retarded girls. *Mental Retardation,* 1971, *9*(3), 27–30.

Martin, G. L., McDonald, S., & Omichinski, M. An operant analysis of response interactions during meals with severely retarded girls. *American Journal of Mental Deficiency,* 1971, *76,* 68–75.

Martin, J. A., & Iagulli, D. M. Elimination of middle-of-the-night tantrums in a blind, retarded child. *Behavior Therapy,* 1974, *5,* 420–422.

Martin, P. L., & Foxx, R. M. Victim control of the aggression of an institutionalized retardate. *Journal of Behavior Therapy and Experimental Psychiatry,* 1973, *4,* 161–165.

Merbaum, M. The modification of self-destructive behavior by a mother-therapist using aversive stimulation. *Behavior Therapy,* 1973, *4,* 442–447.

Michealis, M. L., & Etzel, B. C. *A case study illustrating an experimental design for evaluating the effects of shaping gross motor coordination in a 31 month old child* (Report No. VIID, Head Start Evaluation and Research Center, University of Kansas). Lawrence, Kansas: Department of Human Development, 1967.

Morris, R. J., & Dolker, M. Developing cooperative play in socially withdrawn retarded children. *Mental Retardation,* 1974, *12*(6), 24–27.

Neisworth, J. T., & Smith, R. M. *Modifying retarded behavior.* Boston: Houghton Mifflin, 1973.

Nelson, G. L., Cone, J. E., & Hanson, C. R. Training correct utensil use in retarded children: Modeling vs. physical guidance. *American Journal of Mental Deficiency,* 1975, *80,* 114–122.

Nelson, R., Gibson, F., Jr., & Cutting, D. S. Video taped modeling: The development of three appropriate social responses in a mildly retarded child. *Mental Retardation,* 1973, *11*(6), 24–28.

O'Brien, F., & Azrin, N. H. Developing proper mealtime behaviors of the institutionalized retarded. *Journal of Applied Behavior Analysis,* 1972, *5,* 389–399.

O'Brien, F., Azrin, N. H., & Bugle, C. Training profoundly retarded children to stop crawling. *Journal of Applied Behavior Analysis,* 1972, *5,* 131–137.

O'Brien, F., Bugle, C., & Azrin, N. H. Training and maintaining a retarded child's proper eating. *Journal of Applied Behavior Analysis,* 1972, *5,* 67–72.

O'Leary, K. D., & Becker, W. Behavior modification of an adjustment class: A token reinforcement program. *Exceptional Children,* 1967, *33,* 637–642.

O'Leary, K. D., & Drabman, R. Token reinforcement programs in the classroom: A review. *Psychological Bulletin,* 1971, *75,* 379–398.

Osarchuk, M. Operant methods of toilet-behavior training of the severely and profoundly retarded: A review. *Journal of Special Education,* 1973, *7,* 423–437.

Paluck, R. J., & Esser, A. H. Controlled experimental modification of aggressive behavior in territories of severely retarded boys. *American Journal of Mental Deficiency,* 1971, *76,* 23–29.

Pendergrass, V. E. Timeout from positive reinforcement following persistent, high-rate behavior in retardates. *Journal of Applied Behavior Analysis,* 1972, *5,* 85–91.

Peterson, R. A., & McIntosh, E. I. Teaching tricycle riding. *Mental Retardation,* 1973, *11*(5), 32–34.

Prochaska, J., Smith, N., Marzilli, R., Colby, J., & Donovan, W. Remote-control aversive stimulation in the treatment of head-banging in a retarded child. *Journal of Behavior Therapy and Experimental Psychiatry,* 1974, *5,* 285–289.

Redd, W. H. Effects of mixed reinforcement contingencies on adults' control of children's behavior. *Journal of Applied Behavior Analysis,* 1969, *2,* 249–254.

Rentfrow, R. K., & Rentfrow, D. K. Studies related to toilet training of the mentally retarded. *American Journal of Occupational Therapy,* 1969, *23,* 425–430.

Repp, A. C., Deitz, S. M., & Speir, N. C. Reducing stereotypic responding by the differential reinforcement of other behavior. *American Journal of Mental Deficiency,* 1974, *79,* 279–284.

Repp, A. C., Klett, S. Z., Sosebee, L. H., & Speir, N. C. Differential effects of four token conditions on rate and choice of responding in a matching-to-sample task. *American Journal of Mental Deficiency,* 1975, *80,* 51–56.

Rieth, H., Jr., & Hall, R. V. (Eds.) *Responsive teaching model readings in applied behavior analysis.* Lawrence, Kansas: H & H Enterprises, 1974.

Risley, T., & Wolf, M. Established speech in echolalic children. *Behavioral Research and Therapy,* 1967, *5,* 73–88.

Robinson, N. M., & Robinson, H. B. *The mentally retarded child* (2nd ed.). New York: McGraw-Hill, 1976.

Ross, L. E. Classical conditioning and discrimination learning research with the mentally retarded. In N. R. Ellis (Ed.), *International review of research in mental retardation* (Vol. 1). New York: Academic Press, 1966.

Ross, L. E., & Ross, S. M. Classical conditioning and intellectual defect. In D. K. Routh (Ed.), *The experimental psychology of mental retardation.* Chicago: Aldine, 1973.

Rydberg, S. Beginning reading discrimination taught at IQ 35 by conditioning. *Perceptual and Motor Skills,* 1971, *32,* 163–166.

Rynders, J. E., & Friedlander, B. Z. Preferences in institutionalized severely retarded children for selected visual stimulus material presented as operant reinforcement. *American Journal of Mental Deficiency,* 1972, *76,* 568–573.

Sachs, D. A. WISC changes as an evaluative procedure within a token economy. *American Journal of Mental Deficiency*, 1971, *76*, 230–234.

Sailor, W. Reinforcement and generalization of productive plural allomorphs in two retarded children. *Journal of Applied Behavior Analysis*, 1971, *4*, 305–310.

Salzberg, B., & Napolitan, J. Holding a retarded boy at a table for two minutes to reduce inappropriate object contact. *American Journal of Mental Deficiency*, 1974, *78*, 748–451.

Schroeder, S. R. Parametric effects of reinforcement frequency, amount of reinforcement, and required response force on sheltered workshop behavior. *Journal of Applied Behavior Analysis*, 1972, *5*, 431–441.

Sidman, M., & Stoddard, L. T. Programming perception and learning for retarded children. In N. R. Ellis (Ed.), *International review of research in mental retardation* (Vol. 2). New York: Academic Press, 1966.

Sidman, M., & Stoddard, L. T. The effectiveness of fading in programming a simultaneous form discrimination for retarded children. *Journal of the Experimental Analysis of Behavior,* 1967, *10*, 3–15.

Skinner, B. F. "Resistance to extinction" in the process of conditioning. *Journal of Genetic Psychology*, 1933, *9*, 420–429.

Skinner, B. F. *The behavior of organisms: An experimental analysis*. New York: Appleton-Century-Crofts, 1938.

Skinner, B. F. *Science and human behavior*. New York: MacMillan, 1953.

Skinner, B. F. *The technology of teaching*. New York: Appleton, 1968. ·

Smith, D. D., Smith, J. O., & Haring, N. G. *The modified lattice system: An approach to the analysis and sequence of instructional objectives*. Unpublished manuscript, University of Washington, 1975.

Smolev, S. R. Use of operant techniques for the modification of self-injurious behavior. *American Journal of Mental Deficiency*, 1971, *76*, 295–305.

Song, A. Y., & Gandhi, R. An analysis of behavior during the acquisition and maintenance phases of self-spoon feeding skills of profound retardates. *Mental Retardation*, 1974, *12*(1), 25–28.

Spradlin, J. E., & Girardeau, F. L. The behavior of moderately and severely retarded persons. In N. R. Ellis (Ed.), *International review of research in mental retardation* (Vol. 1). New York: Academic Press, 1966.

Spradlin, J. E., Girardeau, F. L., & Corte, E. Fixed ratio and fixed interval behavior of severely and profoundly retarded subjects. *Journal of Experimental Child Psychology*, 1965, *2*, 340–353.

Staats, A. *Learning, language and cognition*. New York: Holt, Rinehart & Winston, 1968.

Staats, A. W., & Staats, C. K. *Complex human behavior*. New York: Holt, Rinehart & Winston, 1963.

Stokes, T. F., Baer, D. M., & Jackson, R. L. Programming the generalization of a greeting response in four retarded children. *Journal of Applied Behavior Analysis*, 1974, *7*, 599–610.

Streifel, J. A., & Phelan, J. G. Use of reinforcement of behavioral similarity to establish imitative behavior in young mentally retarded children. *American Journal of Mental Deficiency*, 1972, *77*, 239–241.

Stremel, K. Language training: A program for retarded children. *Mental Retardation*, 1972, *10*(2), 47–49.

Striefel, S., & Wetherby, B. Instruction-following behavior of a retarded child and its controlling stimuli. *Journal of Applied Behavior Analysis*, 1973, *6*, 663–670.

Talkington, L. W. Response-chain learning of mentally retarded adolescents under four conditions of reinforcement. *American Journal of Mental Deficiency*, 1971, *76*, 337–340.

Tanner, B. A., & Zeiler, M. Punishment of self-injurious behavior using aromatic ammonia as the aversive stimulus. *Journal of Applied Behavior Analysis*, 1975, *8*, 53–57.

Tawney, J. W. Acceleration of vocal behavior in developmentally retarded children. *Education and Training of the Mentally Retarded*, 1974, *9*(1), 22–27.

Terrace, H. S. Discrimination learning with and without "errors." *Journal of Experimental Analysis of Behavior*, 1963, *6*, 1–27.

Tharp, R. G., & Wetzel, R. J. *Behavior modification in the natural environment*. New York: Academic Press, 1969.

Thor, D. H. Sex differences in extinction of operant responding by educable retarded and nonretarded children. *American Journal of Mental Deficiency*, 1972, *77*, 100–106.

Touchette, P. E. Transfer of stimulus control: Measuring the moment of transfer. *Journal of the Experimental Analysis of Behavior*, 1971, *15*, 347–354.

Twardosz, S., & Baer, D. M. Training two severely retarded adolescents to ask questions. *Journal of Applied Behavior Analysis*, 1973, *6*, 655–661.

Viney, L. L., Clarke, A. M., & Lord, J. Resistance to extinction and frustration in retarded and nonretarded children. *American Journal of Mental Deficiency*, 1973, *78*, 308–315.

Vukelich, R., & Hake, D. F. Reduction of dangerously aggressive behavior in a severely retarded resident through a combination of positive reinforcement procedures. *Journal of Applied Behavior Analysis*, 1971, *4*, 215–225.

Watson, L. S., Jr., Orser, R., & Sanders, C. Reinforcement preferences of severely mentally retarded children in a generalized reinforcement context. *American Journal of Mental Deficiency*, 1968, *72*, 748–756.

Webster, D. R., & Azrin, N. H. Required relaxation: A method of inhibiting agitative-disruptive behavior of retardates. *Behavior Research and Therapy*, 1973, *11*, 67–78.

Weiner, H. Some effects of response cost upon human operant behavior. *Journal of the Experimental Analysis of Behavior*, 1962, *5*, 201–208.

Weisberg, P. Operant procedures with the retardate. In N. R. Ellis (Ed.), *International review of research in mental retardation* (Vol. 5). New York: Academic Press, 1971.

Weisberg, P., Passman, R. H., & Russell, J. E. Development of verbal control over bizarre gestures of retardates through imitative and nonimitative reinforcement procedures. *Journal of Applied Behavior Analysis*, 1973, *6*, 487–495.

Whaley, D. L., & Malott, R. W. *Elementary principles of behavior*. New York: Appleton-Century-Crofts, 1971.

White, G. D., Nielsen, G., & Johnson, S. M. Timeout duration and the suppression of deviant behavior in children. *Journal of Applied Behavior Analysis*, 1972, *5*, 111–120.

White, O. R. *A glossary of behavioral terminology*. Champaign, Ill.: Research Press, 1971.

Whitman, T. L., Burish, T., & Collins, C. Development of inter personal language responses in two moderately retarded children. *Mental Retardation,* 1972, *10*(5), 40–45.

Whitman, T. L., Zakaras, M., & Chardos, S. Effects of reinforcement and guidance procedures on instruction-following behavior of severely retarded children. *Journal of Applied Behavior Analysis*, 1971, *4,* 823.

Williams, W. *Procedures of task analysis as related to developing instructional programs for the severely handicapped*. Unpublished manuscript, University of Texas, 1975.

Worell, J., & Nelson, C. M. *Managing instructional problems: A case study workbook*. New York: McGraw-Hill, 1974.

Wunderlich, R. A. Programmed instruction: Teaching coinage to retarded children. *Mental Retardation*, 1972, *10*(5), 21–23.

Young, J. A., & Wincze, J. P. The effects of the reinforcement of compatible and incompatible alternative behaviors on the self-injurious and related behaviors of a profoundly retarded female adult. *Behavior Therapy*, 1974, *5*, 614–623.

Zigler, E. Rigidity in the feebleminded. In E. P. Trapp & P. Himelstein (Eds.), *Readings on the exceptional child*. New York: Appleton-Century-Crofts, 1962.

Zlutnick, S., Mayville, W. J., & Moffat, S. Modification of seizure disorders: The interruption of behavioral chains. *Journal of Applied Behavior Analysis*, 1975, *8*, 1–12.

9

Learning Theory Research and Mental Retardation: Perspective

Slowness and inefficiency in the acquisition of knowledge and skills (learning) are primary factors which are consistently used to describe mentally retarded individuals. Since many researchers and theorists equate learning with intelligence, it is not surprising that learning theory research regarding mental retardation has been a voluminous and productive area. For example, Zeaman (1974) notes that between 1954 and 1974 approximately 1500 studies of learning processes with retarded individuals were conducted.

The impetus for this proliferation of studies must be credited to such intellectual giants of the 19th century as Pavlov, Guthrie, Kohler, Tolman, and Skinner, who constructed comprehensive learning theories (Robinson & Robinson, 1976). Using these early comprehensive theories, researchers in mental retardation have followed a theory development pattern characterized by a shift in emphasis from global to specific. In essence, this means that since 1950 the formulation of theories and research in mental retardation have shifted from a global perspective of learning to the examination of specific parameters in the learning paradigm. In addition to this global to specific shift, there has been a change from emphasizing simpler forms of learning to emphasizing more complex theories of learning. This emphasis on specific factors within complex learning paradigms has evolved because many investigators are trying to delineate the specific areas which account for the differences in the quanitative and to a lesser extent the qualitative learning of retarded and nonretarded individuals.

For the most part the learning research presented in chapters 2 through 8 reflects the concentration of delineating specific learning characteristics of retarded individuals via testing hypotheses originating from complex learning paradigms. Since much of the research and many of the theories are highly specific, it is necessary to combine the information from the research in order to develop an overall approach to learning that is essential for educating the retarded child in a realistic setting. A consideration of the following highlights of chapters 2–8 provides the reader with a condensed overview of the respective research and teaching implications.

Overview of Chapters Two through Eight

In Chapter 2, Ellis's multiprocess memory model (Ellis, 1970) was presented. His theory advances the position that retarded individuals tend to have a deficiency in short-term memory and that this deficiency springs primarily from failure to use rehearsal strategies or from employing inadequate rehearsal strategies. The research reviewed was generally supportive of Ellis' position. The teaching implications generated from the research on the multimemory process model are numerous. Specifically, the implications discussed primarily focused on the use of verbal and imagery rehearsal activities. Verbal rehearsal usually consists of encouraging the learner to label either silently or overtly while performing the task. Imagery rehearsal usually consists of encouraging the child (or via pretraining) to associate the stimuli of the task with a picture, event, or object in order to facilitate recall. A final rehearsal strategy simply consists of encouraging or reminding the child to use rehearsal. Some other specific teaching implications discussed include (a) organizing the stimuli at input, (b) using the von Restorff effect to facilitate recall, and (c) reinforcement for recall.

In Chapter 3, Spitz's input organization theory (1973) was presented. His theory postulates that mentally retarded individuals have more difficulty than nonretarded individuals in organizing input material and that this disorganization at input detrimentally effects retrieval processes. The research reviewed was organized according to the nature of the stimuli used (digits, pictures, objects, words, and paired-associate stimuli) in the respective studies. In general, the research was supportive of Spitz's position that retarded individuals exhibit an input organization deficiency. The results from the studies using pictures and/or objects provided less definitive support than the studies from the other areas. Teaching implications generated from the research were numerous but the primary implication consisted of grouping material at input rather than presenting it in some random fashion. Several specific implications on ways to group material were discussed and they included: (a) the use of external cueing (spacing), (b) the use of simultaneous stimulus presentations rather than serial presentations, and (c) the use of redundancy. All of these techniques were presented as techniques to help the retarded to recall information.

In Chapter 4 the attention theory of Zeaman and House (1963) and the attention-retention theory of Fisher and Zeaman (1973) were presented. In their attention theory, Zeaman and House ad-

vanced the position that in discrimination learning tasks retarded individuals have difficulty selecting and attending to the relevant dimensions of a stimulus. In essence, they attributed the retardate's learning difficulties to his inability to attend to the relevant dimensions. Later, Fisher and Zeaman added the retention factor to the original attention paradigm. Due to the recency of the Fisher and Zeaman theory, most of the research to date has focused on the original attention theory. The research was presented in terms of number of relevant dimensions, incentive conditions, transfer operations, and oddity learning.

Many teaching implications have evolved as a result of the work of Zeaman and his colleagues. Most of the teaching implications discussed focused on ways of arranging stimuli in order to facilitate attention to the relevant dimensions. Some of the specific teaching implications included in Chapter 4 were: (a) reducing the number of irrelevant dimensions, (b) including the learner's dimension bias in planning tasks, (c) increasing the number of relevant dimensions, (d) reinforcing attention to relevant dimensions, and (e) making relevant cues distinctive.

Chapter 5 focused on Denny's work concerning elicitation theory and incidental learning. In elicitation theory it was noted that learning depends upon consistent elicitation of the to-be-learned response in close temporal contiguity with a particular stimulus situation. The presentation of elicitation theory began by defining specific terms (stimulus, response, and response tendency) as they related to the theory. In addition, the concepts of stimulus hierarchy, the satiation hypothesis, and stimulus generalization were discussed. Elicitation theory was primarily established with animal studies and has not directly generated much work with retarded individuals. Thus, a position concerning the learning characteristics of retarded individuals has not yet evolved from the elicitation theory. However, the combination of elicitation theory and Denny's reviews of learning research has resulted in a composite work by Denny (1966) which has direct application for teaching retarded individuals. For example, Denny delineated a set of seven instructional principles for the retarded which were designed to foster optimal learning. These instructional principles include

1. In early learning, prevent incorrect responses and elicit as many correct responses as posible.
2. Provide immediate knowledge of results.

3. Provide differential feedback.
4. In order to enhance stimulus generalization, stimulus randomization, and positive transfer, teach the response in a variety of contexts varying all the irrelevant cues and keeping constant the relevant cues.
5. Provide distributed repetition.
6. Enhance motivation by using reinforcers.
7. Build a response sequence in easy steps and upon what the child has already learned.

The few studies that have been conducted to evaluate Denny's instructional principles were reviewed. These studies were characterized by the use of the Learning Box and resulted in promising findings regarding the teaching of basic verbal concepts to severely retarded residents. Finally, it was pointed out that systematic research with retarded individuals needs to be conducted before empirically based learning characteristics of retardates and teaching principles can be delineated.

The final section of Chapter 5 dealt with incidental learning and the retarded. In a review of retardate learning research, Denny (1964) suggests that retarded individuals are poorer incidental learners than normals. Furthermore, Denny indicates that the retardates' incidental learning deficiency is basically an attention deficiency. Studies of incidental learning with retarded subjects were presented and the results were summarized. It was noted that the data from the few studies available (Table 5.2) are mildly supportive of the idea that retardates have incidental learning deficiencies. Moreover, supportive findings for Denny's teaching principles were derived and listed from the studies on incidental learning.

In Chapter 6, social learning theory (SLT) as it applies to mental retardation was presented. Rotter's (1975) formula, Behavior Potential $= f$ (Expectancy & Reinforcement Value), was featured as a foundation of SLT. Social learning theory research generated with retarded subjects was organized and presented in three primary areas: locus of control, expectancy, and Zigler's motivational approach. In the locus of control section it was noted that retarded individuals tend to exhibit external rather than internal locus of control orientations. An external locus of control is characterized by the perception that events are unrelated to one's own behaviors in specific situations and therefore beyond personal control. The research with retarded individuals indicated that an external locus of control orientation tends to be a handicapping personality factor. The teaching implications from the locus of control research primarily featured

1. Provide retarded children with realistic successes.
2. Continuously pair specific behaviors with consistent consequences.
3. Provide retarded individuals with specific goals.
4. Reinforce statements which reflect an internal locus of control and challenge externally oriented statements.

In the expectancy section it was noted that many retarded individuals bring a history of failure to a learning situation and these past failure experiences tend to cause the retarded individual to enter a learning situation with a high expectancy of failure. The teaching implications from the expectancy studies were highlighted by the following techniques:

1. Set realistic goals with retarded individuals.
2. Consistently pair reward with desirable events or tasks.
3. Avoid ambiguous feedback with retarded individuals.

In the section on Zigler's motivational approach, research on positive and negative reaction tendencies and outer-directedness was featured. Zigler (1958) explains the positive and negative reaction tendencies in the following passage:

Institutionalized feebleminded subjects begin task one with a positive-reaction tendency higher than that of normal subjects. This higher positive-reaction tendency is due to the higher motivation of feebleminded subjects to interact with an approving adult. At the same time feebleminded subjects begin task one with a negative-reaction tendency due to a wariness of adults which stems from the more frequent negative encounters that feebleminded subjects experience at the hands of adults. If task one is given under a support condition, the subject's negative-reaction tendency is reduced more during task one than is his positive-reaction tendency. (p. 91)

Implications from this area of research included

1. Use intense social reinforcement with retarded children.
2. Gradually encourage highly dependent children (positive reaction tendency) to exhibit independent behavior.
3. Withdrawn children (negative reaction tendency) should be encouraged to participate and make appropriate overt responses.

Concerning outer-directedness, Zigler (1966) postulates that the repeated failures experienced by retarded persons lead them to a style of problem solving characterized by outer-directness.

Specifically, the retarded child learns to distrust her own solutions and therefore seeks guides to action from the immediate environment. The teaching implications derived from the outer-directedness literature focused on encouraging teachers to evaluate the cues that they provide retarded children. Teachers are in a position to provide social as well as task-relevant cues to sensitized retarded children. In addition, the outer-directedness position suggests that modeling is a technique that should be systematically used with retarded children.

In the review of the research on social learning theory, one factor repeatedly emerged as having a debilitating effect on the saluatory development of retarded individuals—failure. Many of the problems that characterize the retarded in the SLT research spring from the retarded individual's repeated failure experiences. The obvious implication (whether preventive or corrective) of this finding is to provide the retarded individual with a history of realistic success experiences.

In Chapter 7 observational learning was presented. To date, no programmatic research has been reported regarding modeling and mental retardation. However, from the modeling literature with retarded subjects two types of research emerged. One group of studies originated from a theoretical viewpoint. For example, from an outer-directedness theoretical viewpoint one can advance the position that the dependency of an outer-directed retardate would increase her dependency on external cues for appropriate behavior and would thus make her more prone to learn via observation than the individual who is not outer-directed. The second type of research was characterized by attempts to develop and refine techniques which improve the use of modeling with retarded individuals.

The modeling literature was organized and reviewed according to the level of retardation of the observers used in the studies, i.e., mild, moderate, and severe. The literature clearly established that retarded individuals at all levels learn through observation. In fact, in all the studies that compared performance via modeling to performance via other instructional techniques, modeling produced either higher or equivocal performance scores.

The results were primarily summarized in terms of observer variables, model variables, and task variables. Teaching implications were presented within the framework of each of the variable areas.

Some selected teaching implications for retarded children from the modeling literature included

1. Reward the model for the behavior to be imitated.
2. Reward observers for correct imitation.
3. To increase the effectiveness of the model, establish the model as competent.
4. Punish the model for undesirable behavior.
5. Have the model verbalize the behavior she is performing.
6. Use audiovisual models as well as live models to facilitate the learning of mild, moderate, and/or severely retarded individuals.
7. With severely retarded individuals, use reinforcement, preexperimental training, and verbal instructions to consistently enhance modeling performances.

Skinner's operant conditioning was presented in Chapter 8, featuring reviews of research and selected articles which focused on the examination of behavioral principles with retarded subjects. The position that behavior is primarily controlled by its consequences was featured as a foundation principle in operant conditioning. The description of specific components included operant behavior, respondent behavior, operant reinforcement, conditioned reinforcement, operant extinction, punishment, schedules of reinforcement, stimulus discrimination, response differentiation, noncontingent reinforcement, response chaining, and response priming. Generally the research found that retarded individuals performed according to the principles of behavior described by Skinner. However, one specific finding regarding the behavior of retarded subjects had to do with extinction, i.e., in several studies a longer period of time was needed to extinguish the behavior of retarded individuals than was needed to extinguish the behavior of nonretarded persons.

Applied behavioral analysis was offered as a framework for using operant technology in learning situations. It was highlighted by three basic components: (a) the direct observation of the individual's behavior, (b) continuous measurement of that behavior, and (c) systematic environmental changes consistent with the relevant principles of behavior. Relevant principles of behavior included

1. A behavior must be emitted before it can be modified by changes in environmental conditions.
2. A behavior may be strengthened through immediate and carefully scheduled reinforcement.
3. The procedure of fading—the gradual withdrawal of "artifically imposed" stimulus support—must be applied following acquisition of a behavior.

4. Contingent reinforcement rather than punishment should be regarded as the primary means for modifying behavior in predictable ways.

5. Response differentiation is facilitated when shaping proceeds through a sequence of graduated gains to the eventual achievement of a more complex behavioral repertoire.

6. Continuous measurement of the target behavior serves to regulate the pace and direction of learning.

The amount of literature and research on the application of behavioral principles with retarded populations is enormous. The pervasive impact of behavioral technology is reflected in the numerous behavior modification programs being implemented with retarded persons at all levels of severity. Dunn (1973) aptly recognizes this trend, stating,

> There is little doubt that the body of knowledge on the topic has grown to the point where it could revolutionize the teaching of the more retarded. Already the area of teacher training is focusing heavily on teaching behavior-modification techniques. Hopefully, the application of these procedures, in the last quarter of the twentieth century, will replace the generally unsuccessful traditional efforts of the past in teaching the moderately retarded. (p. 102)

Experimental Approaches in Mental Retardation

In order to enhance one's understanding of research in mental retardation, it is helpful to examine the experimental approaches. Such examination should provide the practitioner with a framework for seeking answers to questions concerning etiology, assessment, prevention, and treatment. Moreover, it should provide the researcher with a theoretical base and enhance the design and contribution of future experimentation. Routh (1973) found three approaches which differ primarily in their narrowness of focus. These approaches are (a) general experimental, (b) developmental, and (c) deficiency.

General Experimental Approach

The general experimental approach is on the nurture end of the nature-nurture continuum. In this approach the behavior of retarded individuals is viewed as being regulated by the same laws as is the behavior of other human beings. Moreover, new principles and/or positions are not developed to account for the behavior of retarded persons.

Within the general experimental framework the primary cause of mental retardation is due to inadequate environmental conditions. Using Gewirtz's (1968) work, Routh (1973) very aptly describes the general experimental viewpoint on etiology of mental retardation:

> Gewirtz regards the infant as having initially only certain "foundation" behaviors, such as orienting, reaching, clinging, vocalizing, and smiling. Environmental stimuli have the power to evoke these responses and to reinforce them. Since much of the important environment is human, the infant's responses also have an eliciting, signalling, and reinforcing function in relation to environmental events. If the child's caretaker is "sensitive" in providing an abundant contingent stimulation of the child's responses, the child will begin to acquire behaviors that are socially valued or "intelligent." If not, there is the possibility that even some of the adaptive responses the child has may undergo habituation or extinction. (pp. 326–327)

As described by Routh (1973) in the general experimental framework, mental retardation is best assessed via (a) direct observation of behaviors in natural environments, (b) determination of "capacity" following intensive training, and (c) experimental variation to assess particular psychological processes (e.g., present same stimuli under varying conditions). Since this viewpoint stresses the influence of environmental events on cognitive and social growth, mental retardation may be prevented by arranging learning experiences which generate responses expected of the individual by society. In this approach the remediation and/or treatment of the retarded child features operant conditioning. Of the theories reviewed in this book, Skinner's operant conditioning (Chapter 8) and Denny's elicitation theory (first part of Chapter 5) could be classified within the general experimental approach.

Developmental Approach

In the developmental approach the retarded child is thought to have cognitive characteristics which are similar to younger, nonretarded children. In addition, the developmentalist believes that additional principles are needed to account for the behavior of retarded individuals. According to Routh (1973), the developmentalist views retardation as the result of " 'normal' polygenic hereditary variations rather than of variations in experience or of subclinical organic damage" (p. 328). In assessment of mental retardation the developmentalist recommends the use of tests which measure cognitive processes, e.g., *Stanford-Binet*. Within this framework prevention of retardation could be accomplished by following the eugenic principles developed by such advocates of the polygenic theory of intelligence as Galton and Burt.

The developmentalist plans treatment programs by providing the child with tasks appropriate for her developmental level. Developmentalists claim that retarded individuals are continuously given tasks to perform that exceed their respective level. The consistent failure experienced by retarded persons oftentimes results in an expectancy of failure orientation. This condition is not viewed as an inherent aspect of mental retardation but as a secondary condition due to repeated failure. The treatment and preventive programs of the general experimentalist and the developmentalist do not markedly differ. Both endorse beginning tasks at a level commensurate with the retarded child's ability. However, the difference in orientation to treatment may lie in specific task selection and timing. A developmentalist is oftentimes guided by MA in determining what tasks are appropriate for a retarded child. New tasks may not be introduced because the child's MA level suggests she is not ready for the new task. On the other hand, a behaviorist (general experimentalist) would introduce new tasks on the basis of the child's measured progress and would not generally consider MA as

a factor influencing the introduction of new tasks. The different viewpoints of the developmentalist and the general experimentalist (behaviorist) are illustrated in Figure 9.1. The behaviorist views development as continuous, whereas the developmentalist views cognitive growth in stages characterized by a step-type pattern. Within the developmental framework the organism reaches a readiness for certain tasks at each stage or plateau. Certain tasks correspond to each stage (usually determined by MA level) and tasks that correspond to a higher stage are not generally given to a child who has not reached that respective developmental stage. The developmentalist claims that the retarded child and the nonretarded child progress through the same stages but the retarded child progresses at a slower rate. When groups are equated on MA, the developmentalist sees no cognitive difference between them.

An unfortunate omission of this book is the work of Jean Piaget, a renowned developmentalist. Robinson and Robinson (1976) may be consulted for a description of Piaget's theory and its relationship to mental retardation. Of the theories and research reviewed in this book, the work of Zigler (Chapter 6) falls within the domain of the developmental viewpoint. However, it is important to note that Zigler only holds the developmental viewpoint for familial retarded persons. Zigler's work (and some SLT research) lends credence to the

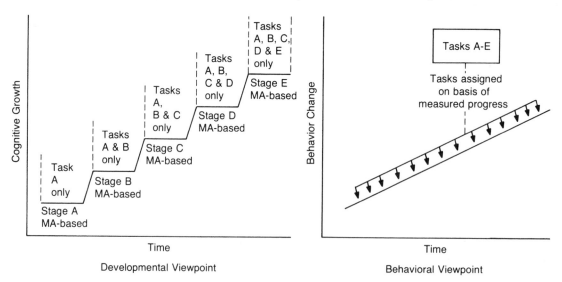

FIGURE 9.1

The developmental and behavioral viewpoints of learning progress.

developmental viewpoint because he demonstrated that retardates do not perform as well as MA-matched normals partly because of social and motivational factors.

Deficiency Approach

The deficiency approach stresses the neuro-psychological factors. According to Routh (1973), the most salient aspect of the deficiency approach concerning the familial retardate "is his history of exposure to biological environmental risks during gestation, birth, and early infancy, risks ranging from malnutrition and lack of proper obstetrical care to subclinical lead poisoning" (p. 333). In the deficiency approach the researcher attempts to identify the nature of the deficient process, e.g., attention, memory, and/or language. Then the theorist strives to relate her findings to a cognitive model or to a biological model (e.g., localized damage in central nervous system). Next the deficiency becomes a *defect* if it characterizes the retarded individuals as compared to the non-retarded individuals. In assessing mental retardation from a biological viewpoint, the deficiency approach emphasizes the use of tests which suggest brain damage. From a psychological viewpoint the deficiency approach emphasizes the use of tests which assess in the areas of the hypothesized deficiency, e.g., breadth of attention, rehearsal skills, and subjective organization.

Teaching implications must often be derived indirectly from the deficiency-oriented research. The use of devices and techniques (e.g., organizing input) which serve a prosthetic function often emerge from the deficiency approach. The majority of the theories reviewed in this book are appropriately classified as deficiency approaches to mental retardation. They are: Ellis' multimemory process model (Chapter 2), Spitz's input organization theory (Chapter 3), Zeaman and House's attention theory (Chapter 4), Fisher and Zeaman's attention retention theory (Chapter 4), and Denny's incidental learning theory (last part of Chapter 5). Although each of these theories has stressed the deficiency viewpoint of mental retardation, it is important to recognize the wealth of practical teaching implications that has emerged from the deficiency-oriented research. In summary, the theorists and corresponding experimental approaches are outlined in Table 9.1

General Learning Paradigm

Much of the learning theory research in mental retardation focuses on highly specific components of the learning paradigm. *Although many of the theorists focus on a specific aspect of learning, they generally acknowledge that their specific area of interest (e.g., selective attention) operates within a broad learning framework which includes such other processes as memory processes, response processes, and reinforcement processes.* In order to use the specific contributions of the respective learning theory research in mental retardation, it is helpful to maintain a perspective of the total learning paradigm. By maintaining an awareness of the total learning process, a researcher and/or a practitioner can avoid isolating on a specific component to the extent that the significant influences of other factors are ignored. In addition, through examining the various components of the total learning process, the practitioner is able to combine the specific findings from each of the respective theories and generate optimal learning environments. In this section a general learning paradigm is presented and each theory reviewed in the book is discussed in terms of the paradigm.

Components in Ross's *Model of the Learning Process*

Ross (1976) patterned a learning paradigm from Gagne's (1974) work to formulate a learning model which features the processes of learning. Ross' model provides a framework for examining the learning theory research in mental retardation (see Table 9.2).

EXPECTANCY. In Ross's (1976) model, expectancy is the initial component in the learning process. In general, it refers to the approach set which a learner brings to a learning situation. It is thought that an individual develops the expectancy through previous experience with contingency arrangements. For example, if a child receives a piece of candy or verbal praise for writing her spelling words, she comes to expect that if the words are written, some desirable event will follow. In the results Ross equates motivation with expectancy (process) and notes that expectancy serves as an incentive which motivates the learner to approach and continue with the learning task. From this viewpoint expectancy is not an isolated

TABLE 9.1
Approaches to Mental Retardation

EXPERIMENTAL APPROACH	ETIOLOGY	ASSESSMENT	INTERVENTION	PROPONENTS
General experimental approach	Inadequate environment	1. Direct observation—reliance on criterion tasks. 2. Teach, then test to determine "capacity." 3. Use experimental variation to test in an area.	Operant conditioning Applied behavior analysis	1. Skinner (Chapter 8) 2. Denny (elicitation theory—Chapter 5)
Developmental approach	Polygenic heredity	1. IQ tests. 2. Developmental tasks (Piaget).	Systematic exposure to tasks appropriate to developmental level.	1. Zigler (Chapter 6) 2. Piaget (not reviewed) 3. SLT (Chapter 6)
Deficiency approach	Lesions in CNS	1. Neuropsychological tests. 2. Tests in deficiency areas, e.g., attention, memory.	Delineation of devices and techniques which serve a prosthetic function, e.g., reduce irrelevant dimensions of a stimulus.	1. Ellis (Chapter 2) 2. Spitz (Chapter 3) 3. Zeaman and House (Chapter 4) 4. Fisher and Zeaman (Chapter 4) 5. Denny (incidental learning—Chapter 5)

TABLE 9.2

Components of the Learning Process and Respective Theories and Implications

LEARNING COMPONENTS	PROPONENTS	MAJOR IMPLICATION
Expectancy	Social Learning Theory	Provide continuous success.
↓		
Selective Attention	Zeaman and House Fisher and Zeaman Denny (Incidental)	Make cues of task stimuli distinctive.
↓		
Organizing Input for Storage	Spitz	Organize or group input. Pair material with meaningful event or object.
↓		
Memory and Recall	Ellis	Use verbal rehearsal.
↓		
Transfer		Train in a variety of settings. Use modeling.
↓		
Performance	Dependent measure of all the research Skinner	Develop appropriate tasks.
↓		
Feedback	Skinner	Provide systematic consequation.

phenomenon which only occurs at the beginning of the task but is an enduring component which permeates the entire learning process.

Of the theories reviewed in chapters 2 through 8, social learning theory (Chapter 6) is the only one which deals specifically with the expectancy component of the learning process. Locus of control, expectancy of success, expectancy of failure, positive reaction tendencies, negative reaction tendencies, and outer-directedness are all areas which include the expectancy phenomenon. In addition, expectancy is a major component in Rotter's (1975) formula: Behavior Potential = f(Expectancy & Reinforcement Value).

SELECTIVE ATTENTION. The next component in the learning process involves attending to the relevant stimuli of a learning task. Attention is a highly complex process which has received much emphasis in the learning literature; however, for the purposes of this section, *selective attention* is simply identified as scanning the stimulus field, locating the relevant dimensions, and attending to them.

The attention theory of Zeaman and House (1963) (Chapter 4) focuses on the selective attention component of the learning process. To date, Zeaman and House's work represents the most

systematic and comprehensive research in mental retardation regarding selective attention. In addition, the attention-retention theory of Fisher and Zeaman (1973) emphasizes selective attention. However, in the Fisher and Zeaman theory retention factors receive a primary emphasis. Since Denny (1966) (Chapter 5) attributes the incidental learning problems of retarded individuals to attention deficiencies, his theory may be identified as stressing the selective attention component of the learning process.

ORGANIZING INPUT FOR STORAGE. In this component of the learning process, information is coded for storage. Verbal labeling and visual imagery are commonly recognized as two processes used for coding information for storage. The events at this level are primarily considered internal, and inferences only can be drawn about them from observable responses.

Spitz's theory of input organization (Chapter 3) primarily focuses on the coding of information for storage component in the learning process. Spitz organized input in various ways (e.g., spatial cueing, redundancy, grouping) and examined its effect on recall.

MEMORY AND RECALL. The memory component of the learning process has received substantial attention in the learning theory research in mental retardation. Many researchers differentiate short-term (STM) and long-term memory processes and relate the learning problems of retarded learners primarily to STM problems (Ellis, 1970). The determination of specific memory problems is difficult because of the interrelated nature of the learning process (for example, in addition to memory problems, motivation, attention, and/or coding problems could result in poor recall). Moreover, memory problems must be inferred from observable responses (recall).

Ellis' multimemory process model (Chapter 2) primarily focuses on the memory component of the learning process. Ellis (1970) claims that retarded individuals have a short-term memory deficiency which primarily results from inadequate rehearsal strategies.

TRANSFER. Transfer is a very important component of the learning process. In transfer, the knowledge acquired in one setting is useful or generalizable to numerous settings. If a child learns to recognize a word on a flash card but cannot recognize the word in a sentence or in a book, then transfer has not occurred. None of the theories reviewed in chapters 2–8 featured transfer as a major factor. However, transfer was examined the most in the observational learning research.

PERFORMANCE. Performance is germane to all the theories because it is the only observable indicator available which enables us to determine if learning has occurred. However, lack of performance is not necessarily an indication that learning has not occurred. For example, a student may learn a task and not perform because of motivation.

Skinner's operant conditioning theory (Chapter 8) features responding (performance) as a major component. Within the operant framework the measurement and recording of responses have evolved into an elaborate technology.

FEEDBACK. *Feedback* refers to the information provided to learners concerning their specific responses. It usually occurs immediately following the response and is frequently characterized as informative (right or wrong), positive ("good"), or negative ("poor").

The position that behavior is controlled by its consequences is a major feature of Skinner's work. Schedules of reinforcement, positive rein-

forcement, negative reinforcement, and punishment are some of the areas examined within operant conditioning which include the feedback component of learning. Also, since reinforcement history is considered a major factor in the development of motivation (expectancy), it is an essential factor in the social learning theory.

Observational learning (Chapter 7) is a global theory of learning and encompasses each of the components in the learning process. However, much of the research in modeling stressed reinforcement and transfer.

Denny's elicitation theory (Chapter 5) does not readily stress any *one* of the components of the learning process. It features the importance of stimuli in eliciting responses, and from this framework elicitation theory primarily focuses on attention and performance.

Summary

In the first part of this chapter an overview, general findings, and selected implications are presented for the following theories: (a) Ellis' multiprocess memory model, (b) Spitz's input organization theory, (c) Zeaman, House, and Fisher's attention-retention theories, (d) Denny's elicitation theory and incidental learning, (e) social learning theory, (f) observational learning, and (g) Skinner's operant conditioning. Next, each of the theories is discussed in terms of experimental approaches in mental retardation. The general experimental approach, the developmental approach, and the deficiency approach are highlighted in this section of the chapter. In the final section of the chapter the contributions of each respective theory are presented within the framework of a general learning paradigm. This paradigm features the following processes: (a) expectancy, (b) selective attention, (c) input organization, (d) memory, (e) transfer, (f) performance, and (g) feedback.

References

Denny, M. R. Research in learning and performance. In H. Stevens & R. Heber (Eds.), *Mental retardation: A review of research*. Chicago: University of Chicago Press, 1964.

Denny, M. R. A theoretical analysis and its application to training the mentally retarded. In N. R. Ellis (Ed.), *International review of research in mental retardation* (Vol. 2). New York: Academic Press, 1966.

Dunn, L. M. Children with moderate and severe general learning disabilities. In L. M. Dunn (Ed.), *Exceptional children in the schools: Special education in transition* (2nd ed.). New York: Holt, Rinehart, & Winston, 1973.

Ellis, N. R. Memory processes in retardates and normals. In N. R. Ellis (Ed.), *International review of research in mental retardation* (Vol. 4). New York: Academic Press, 1970.

Fisher, M. A., & Zeaman, D. An attention-retention theory of retardate discrimination learning. In N. R. Ellis (Ed.), *The international review of research in mental retardation* (Vol. 6). New York: Academic Press, 1973.

Gagné, R. M. *Essentials of learning for instruction*. Hinsdale, Ill.: Dryden, 1974.

Gewirtz, J. L. The role of stimulation in models for child development. In L. L. Dittman (Ed.), *Early child care*. New York: Atherton, 1968.

Robinson, N. M., & Robinson, H. B. *The mentally retarded child: A psychological approach* (2nd ed.). New York: McGraw-Hill, 1976.

Ross, A. O. *Psychological aspects of learning disabilities & reading disorders*. New York: McGraw-Hill, 1976.

Rotter, J. B. Some problems and misconceptions related to the construct of internal versus external control of reinforcement. *Journal of Consulting and Clinical Psychology*, 1975, *43*, 56–67.

Routh, D. K. Experimental approaches to the clinical psychology of mental retardation. In D. K. Routh (Ed.), *The experimental psychology of mental retardation*. Chicago: Aldine, 1973.

Spitz, H. H. Consolidating facts into the schematized learning and memory system of educable retardates. In N. R. Ellis (Ed.), *International review of research in mental retardation* (Vol. 6). New York: Academic Press, 1973.

Zeaman, D. *Experimental psychology of mental retardation: Some states of the art*. Invited address to meetings of the American Psychological Association, New Orleans, August 1974.

Zeaman, D., & House, B. J. The role of attention in retardate discrimination learning. In N. R. Ellis (Ed.), *Handbook of mental deficiency*. New York: McGraw-Hill, 1963.

Zigler, E. The effect of pre-institutional social deprivation on the performance of feebleminded children. Doctoral dissertation, University of Texas, 1958.

Zigler, E. Research on personality structure in the retardate. In N. R. Ellis (Ed.), *International review of research on mental retardation* (Vol. 1). New York: Academic Press, 1966.

Conclusion

In this book much effort has been expended in determining the relevance and usefulness of learning theory research in mental retardation. To practitioners, we hope the detailed explanation of the studies provides the information that is needed to understand and apply the numerous teaching implications. In addition, we hope the research and the teaching implications generated from it enable the practitioner to operate from a broader empirical base. To researchers, we hope the detailed description of the theories and studies provides information which enhances the relevance and quality of forthcoming work. To students, we hope the book provides an impetus for the continuous examination of research for the purposes of improving both teaching and research. Finally, to retarded children we hope the extensive findings of learning theory research are continuously translated into classroom activities which foster their optimal development socially and cognitively.

NAME INDEX

SUBJECT INDEX